GLOBAL CIVIL SOCIETY 2006/7

Mary Kaldor, Martin Albrow, Helmut Anheier, Marlies Glasius, editors-in-chief

Fiona Holland, managing editor

⑨SAGE Publications

London • Thousand Oaks • New Delhi

© Centre for the Study of Global Governance, London School of Economics and Political Science, and Center for Civil Society, University of California, Los Angeles

First published 2007

SAGE Publications Ltd
1 Oliver's Yard
55 City Road
London EC1Y 1SP

SAGE Publications Inc.
2455 Teller Road
Thousand Oaks, California 91320

SAGE Publications India Pvt Ltd
B-42, Panchsheel Enclave
Post Box 4109
New Delhi 110 017

British Library Cataloguing in Publication data

A catalogue record for this book is available from the British Library

ISBN-10: 1-4129-3435-4   ISBN-13: 978-1-4129-3435-0
ISBN -10: 1-4129-3436-2 (pbk)   ISBN-13: 978-1-4129-3436-7 (pbk)

Typeset by People, Design Consultants
Printed in Great Britain by Cromwell Press, Trowbridge, Wilts
Printed on paper from sustainable resources
Front cover image: Behind the Saheb-ol Zaman Mosque, Shi'a Muslims drop messages and post wishes to the Imam Mahdi into mailboxes on top of the holy well of Jamkaran, in Qom, Iran. Some pilgrims believe this tenth century figure, the 12th or hidden Imam, will rise from the well signalling a new age. Jeroen Oerlemans/Panos

ACKNOWLEDGEMENTS

The production of the Yearbook depends on the support, advice and contributions of numerous individuals and organisations. We endeavour to acknowledge them all in these pages. The final publication of course remains the responsibility of the editors.

Editorial Committee

Martin Albrow, Helmut Anheier, Olaf Corry, Marlies Glasius, David Held, Fiona Holland (managing editor), Jude Howell, Armine Ishkanian, Mary Kaldor, Hagai Katz (data and maps editor), Mathias Koenig-Archibugi, Denisa Kostovicova, Ebenezer Obadare, Frances Pinter, Geoffrey Pleyers, Iavor Rangelov, Yahia Said, Hakan Seckinelgin, Sabine Selchow, Sally Stares, Jill Timms (chronology).

Consultations

Conference on Violence and Civility, 23-25 September 2005, Cairo, Egypt

In conjunction with Cairo University's Center for Political Research and Studies; supported by the UK Government's Global Opportunities Fund, Engaging with the Islamic World programme.

Ahmed Mohamed Abdalla, Hatoon Ajwad Al-Fassi, Azrae Al-Rifai, Ridwan Al-Sayyed, Omayma A Bakr, Chloe Davies, Hent De Vries, Ali Hilal Dessouki, Ian Douglas, Mohamed El-Sayed Said, Mostafa Elwy, Heba Raouf Ezzat, Mient Jan Faber, Abdul Halim Fadlallah, Seif Abdel Fattah, Tarek A Ghanem, Marlies Glasius, Basyouni Ibrahim Hamada, Hisham Hamami, Fiona Holland, Mark Juergensmeyer, Mary Kaldor, Wael Khalil, Denisa Kostovicova, Ali Leela, Azra Lowther, Rawan Maayeh, Naheed Mehta, Nadia Mostafa, Chantal Mouffe, Bashir Nafi, Lucy Nusseibeh, Jennifer Otoadese, Jenny Pearce, Dawud Price, Diaa Rashwan, Charles Reed, Haider Saeed, Yahia Said, Hakan Seckinelgin, Ayman Abdel Wahab, Sayyed Yasseen, Ahmed Zayed.

Seminar on Economic and Social Rights, 24-26 February 2005, Bellagio Study and Conference Centre, Italy

In conjunction with the Rockefeller Foundation.

Victor Abramovich, Marjolein Brouwer, Danwood Mzikenge Chirwa, Eitan Felner, Cees Flinterman, Marlies Glasius, Fiona Holland, Scott Jerbi, Rolf Kunnemann, Ezra Mbogori, Njoki Njoroge Njehu, Jean du Plessis, Ignacio Saiz, Genoveva Tisheva, Brigit Toebes, Aye Aye Win.

Other input

Guest boxes: Haled Al-Hashimi, Ridwan Al-Sayyed, Melinda Brouwer, Carolin Goerzig, Gavin Hayman, EJ Milne, Chantal Mouffe, Lucy Nusseibeh, Jean du Plessis, Geoffrey Pleyers, Anna Stavrianakis.

Chronology correspondents

Mustapha Kamel Al-Sayyid, Marcelo Batalha, Baris Gencer Baykan, Nick Buxton, Giuseppe Caruso, Hyo-Je Cho, Bernard Dreano, Louise Fraser, Iuliana Gavril, Nihad Gohar, Vicky Holland, Jeffrey Juris, Silke Lechner, Otilia Mihai, Selma Muhic, Alejandro Natal, Katarina Sehm Patomaki, Mario Pianto, Asthriesslav Rocuts, Ineke Roose, Thomas Ruddy, Kate Townsend, Caroline Watt.

Research and editorial assistance

Philippa Atkinson, Sam Bartlett (data programme, human rights violations), Rachel Bishop (proof reader), Chris Dance (indexer), Chloe Davies, Eman Ebed, Michael James (copy editor), Marcus Lam, Tahirih Lyon, Sabine Selchow, Sally Stares (data programme), Jill Timms (chronology), Hila Yogev (data programme).

Others who provided assistance or support

Anne-France Borgeaud Pierazzi (IMD), Daria Caliguire (ESCR-net), Howard Davies, Judith Higgin, Michael Oliver, Amartya Sen, Aysa September (GlobeScan Inc.), Gus Stewart, Jess Winterstein.

Design and production

People, Design Consultants; Christine Bone, Andrew Harrison, Jules Davison and Anne Wiggins. Panos Pictures: David Arnott, Adrian Evans, Teresa Wolowiec, Zoe Slotover.

Administrative support

Jocelyn Guihama, Jennifer Otoadese, Joanna Stone, Gordon Wright.

Financial support

We gratefully acknowledge the financial support of the following individuals and organisations:

Aventis Foundation
Robert Bosch Foundation
Compagnia di San Paolo
Victor Phillip Dahdaleh
Ford Foundation
LSE
Charles Stewart Mott Foundation
Rockefeller Foundation
UCLA School of Public Affairs
UK Government's Global Opportunities Fund, Engaging with the Islamic World programme

CONTENTS

Boxes

Figures

Tables

Records
Data Programme

CONTRIBUTORS

Helmut Anheier is Professor of Public Policy and Social Welfare at the University of California, Los Angeles (UCLA), and Director of the Center for Civil Society, and the Center for Globalization and Policy Research at UCLA. He is also a Centennial Professor at the Centre for the Study of Global Governance, London School of Economics and Political Science (LSE). His work has focused on civil society, the non-profit sector, organisational studies and policy analysis, and comparative methodology. He is a founding editor of *The Journal of Civil Society* and author of over 250 publications in several languages. His present research examines the emergence of new organisational forms in global civil society, the role of foundations, and methodological aspects of social science research on globalisation.

Patrick Bond is Research Professor at the University of KwaZulu-Natal School of Development Studies in Durban, where he directs the Centre for Civil Society. He has also taught at York University, Toronto, the University of the Witwatersrand, Johannesburg, and Johns Hopkins School of Public Health, Baltimore. His recent books include *Looting Africa: The Economics of Exploitation* (Zed Books and UKZN Press 2006); *Talk Left, Walk Right: South Africa's Frustrated Global Reforms* (UKZN Press 2006); *Trouble in the Air: Global Warming and the Privatised Atmosphere*, co-edited with Rehana Dada (CCS and the Transnational Institute 2005); *Elite Transition: From Apartheid to Neoliberalism in South Africa* (UKZN Press 2005); and *Fanon's Warning: A Civil Society Reader on the New Partnership for Africa's Development* (Africa World Press and CCS 2005).

Fadia Daibes-Murad specialises in water law and policy with specific emphasis on international water conflicts and resolutions. She is a Research Associate with the UNESCO Centre for Water Law, Policy and Science, Dundee, Scotland, and a Lecturer and Trainer of water law and policy at Birzeit University in the Occupied Palestinian Territory. She is a policy and strategic consultant for many international organisations. Her book, *A New Legal Framework for Managing the World's Shared Groundwaters - A Case-study from the Middle East* (International Water Association 2005), won the 2005 Edberg Prize for Environment in Sweden. She also edited *Water in Palestine: Problems, Politics Prospects* (PASSIA 2003).

Willemijn Dicke is Assistant Professor at the Faculty of Technology Policy and Management of Delft University of Technology in the Netherlands, and head of the research program Public Values within the Next Generation Infrastructures Foundation. In 2001 she published *Bridges and Watersheds: a Narrative Analysis of Water Management in The Netherlands, England and Wales* (Aksant), in which she explored the relation between globalisation and the public-private divide in water management. Her present interests include global public goods and the safeguarding of public values in a privatised context.

Heba Raouf Ezzat teaches political theory at the Department of Political Science, Cairo University. She is coordinator of the Civil Society Program at the Center for Political Research and Studies(CPRS) at Cairo University; and editor of the 'Arabic Version' of the *Global Civil Society Yearbook*, which will be published by CPRS in conjunction with LSE's Centre for the Study of Global Governance. She has published two books in Arabic on women, politics and morality in Islam, and contributed chapters on women, secularism, democracy and human rights, from an Islamic perspective, to a wide variety of English language publications. She is a member of the C-100 initiative by the World Economic Forum for Islamic-Western understanding.

Marlies Glasius is Lecturer in Global Politics at the LSE. She is the author of *The International Criminal Court: A Global Civil Society Achievement* (Routledge 2005) and *Foreign Policy on Human Rights: Its Influence on Indonesia under Soeharto* (Intersentia 1999). She was managing editor of the Global Civil Society Yearbook 2000-2003. She co-edited *Exploring Civil Society: Political and Cultural Contexts*, with David Lewis and Hakan Seckinelgin (Routledge 2004), and *A Human Security Doctrine for Europe: Project, Principles, Practicalities*, with Mary Kaldor (Routledge 2005). Her present interests include global civil society, economic and social rights, and human security.

David Goldblatt is a writer. His most recent book is *The Ball is Round: A Global History of Football* (Penguin 2006).

Mark Juergensmeyer is Professor of Sociology and Global Studies and Affiliate Professor of Religious Studies at the University of California, Santa Barbara, where he also serves as Director of the Orfalea Center for Global and International Studies. He is author or editor of 20 books including *Religion in Global Civil Society* (Oxford 2005), *The Oxford Handbook of Global Religions* (Oxford 2006), and *Terror in the Mind of God: The Global Rise of Religious Violence* (California 2003), for which he received the Grawemeyer Award in Religion and the Silver Medal of Spain's Queen Sofia Center for the Study of Violence. He is currently revising his presentation of the Stafford Little Lectures at Princeton for a book on religion and war to be published by Princeton University Press.

Mary Kaldor is Professor of Global Governance at LSE and Co-Director of the Centre for the Study of Global Governance, LSE. She has written widely on security issues and on democracy and civil society. Her recent books include *Global Civil Society: An Answer to War* (Polity Press 2003) and *New and Old Wars: Organised Violence in a Global Era* (1999). Most recently she co-edited *A Human Security Doctrine for Europe: Project, Principles, Practicalities*, with Marlies Glasius, (Routledge 2005). Mary was a founder member of European Nuclear Disarmament (END), and founder and Co-Chair on the Helsinki Citizen's Assembly. She is Convenor of the Study Group on European Security Capabilities established at the request of Javier Solana.

Hagai Katz is Lecturer at the Department of Business Administration at the School of Management at Ben Gurion University of the Negev in Beersheba, Israel, a Senior Researcher at the Israeli Center for Third-sector Research, and a Research Associate at the UCLA Center for Civil Society. He has published extensively on the non-profit sector in Israel and on global civil society. Hagai is editor of the Yearbook's Data Programme.

Sanjeev Khagram is Associate Professor of Public Affairs and International Studies, and Faculty Director of the Marc Lindenberg Center for Humanitarian Action, International Development, and Global Citizenship at the University of Washington. Most recently he was Acting Dean of the Desmond Tutu Peace Centre, and between 1998-2000 Senior Policy Advisor at the World Commission on Dams. He also co-directs Global Action Networks-Net, the Transnational Studies Initiative, and the International Advocacy NGO Initiative. He has published widely including *Restructuring World Politics* (University of Minnesota Press 2002), and *Dams and Development* (Cornell University Press 2004). Khagram has worked extensively with multilateral agencies, governments, corporations, civil society organisations, professional associations and universities, all over the world.

Denisa Kostovicova is Lecturer in the Government Department/Development Studies Institute and a Research Associate at the Centre for the Study of Global Governance, LSE. Her present research interests include nationalism and democratisation in the global age, post-conflict reconstruction and security, and European integration of the Western Balkans. She has also studied the role of education in identity formation and ethnic reconciliation in Serbia and Kosovo. Her publications include *Kosovo: The Politics of Identity and Space* (Routledge 2006), and 'Old and new insecurity in the Balkans: Learning from the EU's involvement in Macedonia' in *A Human Security Doctrine for Europe: Principles, Precepts, Practicalities*, edited by Kaldor and Glasius, (Routledge 2005). She also co-edited a special issue of *Ethnopolitics*, 'Transnationalism in the Balkans', with Vesna Bojicic-Dzelilovic.

Marcus Lam is a PhD student in the Department of Social Welfare at the UCLA School of Public Affairs and a graduate research assistant at the UCLA Center for Civil Society.

Alessandro Palmieri has worked in over 35 countries on several multi-purpose projects involving dams, hydropower, rural and urban water supply, and natural hazard management. He joined the World Bank in January 1997 after 22 years in the consulting engineering industry and is currently Lead Dams Specialist. He is co-author of two books on dam safety and reservoir sustainability, as well as several publications on water resources development. Alessandro currently represents the World Bank in the Steering Committee of UNEP's Dams and Development Project.

Jenny Pearce is Professor of Latin American Politics and Director of the International Centre for Participation Studies in the Department of Peace Studies, University of Bradford. Her work has focused on social change and social activism in Latin America and more recently in Bradford, the north of England. She is interested theoretically and empirically in exploring the conditions for a society to live without violence.

Yahia Said is a Research Fellow at the Centre for the Study of Global Governance, LSE. Yahia specialises in issues of economic transition and security in post-authoritarian and post-conflict societies. His publications include 'The New Anti-Capitalist Movement: Money and Global Civil Society', co-authored with Meghnad Desai, in *Global Civil Society 2001* (Oxford University Press 2001), 'Oil and Activism' in *Global Civil Society 2004/5* (Sage 2005), Regime Change in Iraq, co-authored with Mary Kaldor (CSGG 2003), and *New and Old Oil Wars* (Pluto Press, forthcoming), co-edited with Mary Kaldor.

Jill Timms is a Research Assistant at the Centre for the Study of Global Governance, LSE. She coordinates the Chronology of the Global Civil Society Yearbook and is completing her doctorate research on corporate social responsibility at the Department of Sociology, LSE. Her research interests include corporate citizenship, anti-corporate groups, labour activism and social forums. Her publications include 'Trade Union Internationalism and a Global Civil Society in the Making', co-authored with Peter Waterman, in *Global Civil Society 2004/5* (Sage 2005) and 'The Role of Social Forums in Global Civil Society: Radical Beacon or Strategic Infrastructure', co-authored with Marlies Glasius, in *Global Civil Society 2005/6* (Sage 2006).

Carlos B Vainer is Senior Professor at the Institute of Urban and Regional Planning and Research of the Federal University of Rio de Janeiro (IPPUR/UFRJ) and coordinates research at the Laboratory State, Labour, Territory and Nature (Estado, Trabalho, Território e Natureza). He also coordinates the Program of Research and Cooperation on Social Movements in the South: Brazil, South Africa, India and Thailand, which engages researchers and activists in a South-South dialogue. For 19 years, he has advised the Brazilian Movement of People Affected by Dams, is a member of the International Committee on Dams, Rivers and People, and the Forum of UNEP's Dams and Development Project. He has published widely on urban and regional planning models and theory, local and regional development, internal and international migration, environmental policies and conflicts, multilateral agencies and international aid, the impacts and social conflicts of large hydroelectric plants, and social movements and globalisation.

Zoë Wilson is a post-doctoral scholar at the Centre for Civil Society at the University of KwaZulu-Natal, South Africa, and a member of the Pollution Research Group at the University. Current projects concern the politics of alternative, appropriate and sustainable water and sanitation options. In affiliation with Newcastle University, Zoë leads a team of student researchers in mapping 'second order water scarcity' in South Africa. Other projects include studies into the effects of water infrastructure collapse in weak states. Zoë's first book, *The United Nations and Democracy in Africa: labyrinths of legitimacy is forthcoming* (Routledge 2006).

Patricia Wouters is Director of the Dundee UNESCO Centre for Water Law, Policy and Science, an expert in international water law and former practising lawyer in Canada. She was recruited to Dundee in 1996 to establish the water law postgraduate programme - the first of its kind in the world. Patricia has published extensively and is editor of two book series on water law and policy. A founding member of the UNESCO HELP programme and the Universities Partnership for Transboundary Waters, she also serves on the Foresight Advisory Committee for SUEZ Lyonnaise des Eaux, and was recently named a Fellow of the International Water Resources Association. Currently, Patricia is completing two books on international water law and implementing the 'Water Law, Water Leaders' programme, which aims to develop a new generation of local water leaders around the world.

VIOLENCE AND THE POSSIBILITY OF GLOBAL CIVILITY
Martin Albrow and Helmut Anheier

Only climate change has come to equal violence recently as a threat to the continued existence of human society. In each case it is the advance of technology that has brought us to stare this prospect in the face. The existence of nuclear weaponry raises the risks in great power confrontations to the point where they include the end of life as we know it on this planet.

Nearly half a century ago, Arnold Toynbee (1961: 278) wrote about technology: 'Used for destructive purposes, it has now also opened up the unprecedented prospect of our being able soon to wipe mankind and perhaps all other extant forms of life off the face of the earth.' Now the proliferation of nuclear weapons beyond the great powers, and their possible use by autocratic regimes, failed states and terror groups, brings a catastrophic culmination to the escalation of violence ever closer.

In the Global Civil Society Yearbook series (Kaldor and Muro 2002; Glasius and Kaldor 2002; Kaldor, Anheier and Glasius 2003) and elsewhere, Mary Kaldor (1999) has pointed to the contrast between old wars and new wars, between wars of nation states and violent conflicts conducted across boundaries or within failed states by non-state actors. Escalating violence in the new wars poses immense challenges to states and their established military. To none are these challenges greater than to the United States, which has responded to the destruction of the World Trade Center in New York City and the attack on the Pentagon in Washington, DC, on 11 September 2001 by declaring the 'war on terror'.

However, in such a war the casualties are not just buildings destroyed and people maimed and killed. The debate that rages among activists and policy analysts in many countries today is about the balance between security and liberty, and its implications for the very future of transnational civil society. Central to this debate is the complex role of civil society in the 'war on terror', the events it triggered, and the developments it spawned. George Soros (2006), billionaire financier and philanthropist, is one of many

social commentators who have written in scathing terms about the 'war on terror' as a misplaced metaphor. It envisages a war on an abstraction, which intrinsically can never be 'won', and places the United States and large parts of the international community it seeks to dominate or influence on a permanent war footing.

Civil society cannot evade issues of war and violence. While the first editions of the Yearbook reflect the intellectual heritage of what Mary Kaldor, in a 2000 Speaker Series at the London School of Economics, called the 'Spirit of 1989' in reference to the peaceful revolutions in central and eastern Europe, later editions show more emphasis on the 'dark side' of civil society, including acts of violence, and a growing concern about civil society shortcomings and failures (see Glasius and Kaldor 2002; Kaldor and Muro 2003; Anderson and Rieff 2004).

It is more than merely ironical, and perhaps also deeply tragic, that the development of the modern understandings of civil society has alternated with periods of violence. Adam Ferguson's early optimism about the state of European institutions that set them apart from the 'savage and uncivilised world' beyond was followed two generations later by Hegel's efforts to save the idea of civil society in the face of revolutionary terror at the heart of that self-described 'civilisation'. Moreover, we should recall that the recovery of the idea of civil society in eastern Europe at the time of perestroika occurred at a time when many were aware that one false step could have plunged the area into bloody conflict.

In Hegel's account, there was a virtual trade-off between the civil order the nation state preserved and its freedom to wage war. However, warfare between states is a greater threat to civil society than violence by non-state actors, because it is during war between states that civil liberties are suspended, when citizens are conscripted into armies, freedom of expression is restricted, privacy is invaded and the right to employment gives way to direction of labour. In times of war, civil society is virtually suspended and this becomes a severe test of the entrenchment of democracy and liberty in the mores and habitus of a society. This is why Soros (2006) is right to point to the dangers of the 'war on terror'.

When one looks back, it now seems clear how much the Introduction of *Global Civil Society 2001* was in the spirit of Ferguson's optimism when it said that 'we might want to preserve the connotation of non-violent interaction based on equal rights while we disavow the Euro-centric assumption of savage vs. civilised people' (Anheier, Glasius and Kaldor 2001: 12). Six years later, in a world soaked in images portraying and even celebrating death and destruction, carnage and brutality, we can be more emphatic. The development of the idea of civil society is entwined with the experience of conflict and the management of violence.

In this Introduction, we try to come to terms with the 'apparent ironical alternation' of civil society and violence – a task that requires us to adopt both a long-term and a theoretical perspective. Civil society in the time of old wars acknowledged a state monopoly on the means of violence as the price for securing periods of peace in which it could thrive. There is no partner global state with which civil society can make the same deal today, and global civil society has grown strong riding on the back of the very processes of globalisation that have provided fertile soil for the new wars.

New means of communication and travel, diasporas, global media events, the international arms trade, the exposure of local communities to global markets, and the worldwide mobilisation of protest are all forces that weaken the protection of civil society by the armed nation state; and global civil society is often viewed by the state as a source of disorder rather than of civility and good citizenship.

Whatever arguments there are about their moral equivalence, the restrictions on foreign-based non-governmental organisations in Putin's Russia point in the same direction as detention without trial in Blair's Britain or Bush's America. Equally, civil society is wooed by the state as a partner in mitigating conflict, enhancing solidarity and creating security. In this global age (Albrow 1996) state, culture and economy are de-linked and de-centred, crossing national boundaries, rivalling each other in their claims on individuals. Civil society is an arena of contested and competing values, a source of legitimacy with

potential for political mobilisation, impossible to ignore for states that find their military power inadequate for achieving peace and security when the sources of instability are not rooted in inter-state rivalries.

In the new field of forces in a globalising world, global civil society has achieved a degree of autonomy that was always implicit in the rights to free speech and association that the eighteenth-century proponents of civil society advocated. The advocates of those freedoms acknowledged the need for the state to defend them, but in their political economy they saw their scope extending beyond boundaries to underpin worldwide markets. Reacting to the consequences of free trade, it was free association across countries that led to the international labour movement. The universalism of those ideas from earlier centuries, plus the longstanding cosmopolitanism of academic and cultural elites, allied with the communication possibilities of our time, has helped shape today's global civil society.

Free association and free speech inherently tend to that intensification of conflict between values, which in Max Weber's (1919/1948) pessimistic world view was the mark of rationalised modernity. For him the armoury of the nation-state was the irrational bearer and arbiter of these conflicts. The potential for collective self-destruction today could induce an even bleaker mood save that this very prospect forces global civil society to look beyond states for non-violent ways of resolving conflicts.

However, we cannot take the relative autonomy that global civil society has achieved for granted. On the one hand, wooed by states, its goals can be subverted to reinforce the tendencies it aims to resist. On the other hand, its independence from the nation state can make it a scapegoat for failures in times of war. Courted by groups opposed to governments it can find itself in very non-civil company. Asserting civil liberties against authoritarian regimes it can find itself allied with resistance movements that see violence as a legitimate last resort. Therefore, engagement with issues of conflict and violence is not marginal to civil society but defining for its future. There are two main reasons for this. First, if civil liberty is no longer simply a concession granted in peacetime by the sovereign state, global civil society has to come to a fuller realisation of the values and principles on which it is based, and to develop its own solutions to conflicts that will prevent them escalating into violence that destroys victims and perpetrators alike. Second, contemporary developments in civil society require an emphatic assertion that its autonomy is justified by commitment to principles of tolerance and the non-violent resolution of conflicts. Its contribution to the realisation of these principles is independent of anything states might or might not do. We base this assertion not simply in faith in the core ideas of civil society, but also in the light of a long social scientific tradition of theory and research into conflict resolution and management.

Civil society is the beneficiary of institutional arrangements developed within state frameworks in the modern period. Those have been the outcome, in large part, of historic accommodations between parties to conflicts where a common interest in resolving differences has outweighed even long-standing mutual antipathies. The capital–labour settlement in Western democracies is a prime example, and that was significantly informed by a tradition of thought represented above all by Georg Simmel (1983), Lewis Coser (1956) and Ralf Dahrendorf (1994), which treated conflict as a social relation that, managed effectively, could have positive outcomes for the broader social configuration in which it was embedded.

Conflicts are culturally and socially embedded, even if the issues are about resources such as territory or oil (for water, see Willemijn Dicke et al. in Chapter 5 of this volume) or other economic interests like capital-labour disputes. They are typically related to tensions between values and interests, arising particularly during accelerated economic and social change. The current impact of globalisation is an obvious case in point. Tensions can result in the 'creative conflicts' that sociologists such as Dahrendorf (1994) have written about, and the 'creative destruction' of existing models and practices that economists such as Schumpeter (1942/1962) and others identified.

Indeed, the dynamism of civil society is related to such 'creative' handling of conflicts. Harnessing them through adequate institutions and ways of conflict regulation in an era of globalisation is a key challenge not just for public policy makers. The civil society that claims freedom for itself must also take on responsibilities, to help identify potential conflicts, manage existing ones, and contribute to non-violent ways and means of conflict resolution. This Introduction aims to encourage all those who take on those heavy responsibilities.

Civil society and violence in historical perspective

We want to emphasize the mutually defining nature of violence and civility in social life which renders our 'apparent ironic alternation' possible. Even in its absence, violence always threatens to occupy the space that civility vacates. Thomas Hobbes viewed violence as primordial. Life in his state of nature was 'nasty, brutish and short', peace being secured in civil society. Modern experience has taught us to be less confident. We know that the simplest societies can manage conflict, while conversely the potential for violence is ever-present in the most modern societies. If the legitimate monopoly on acts of violence asserted by a governing agency gives rise to a civil sphere of life, that monopoly has never extended to all violence, as Jenny Pearce shows in her account of the gendering of violence in private and public spaces in Chapter 2 of this volume. Legitimate violence has not been confined to modern state agencies. The right to bear arms and to use them in self-defence is fervently asserted in both strong and weak states, in the United States as much as in Afghanistan.

Civil society has historically developed in conjunction with the centralisation of power and the development of specialised military institutions. Great empires, such as the Chinese, Roman and Ottoman, achieved at various times a pacification based on specialised military organisation. The significance of the origins of Western ideas of citizenship and legal institutions in the expansion of the Roman empire from a city state is evident in the shared etymology of the terms: city, citizenship, civil, civility and civilisation.

We owe to Norbert Elias (2000) the disclosure of the intimate connections between modern Western notions of civility in interpersonal relations and public behaviour in the growth of centralised states in Europe in the fifteenth and sixteenth centuries. He pointed to the standards of behaviour required in the princely courts that regulated and removed the resort to violence in interpersonal conflict and that stemmed from the ruler's claim to monopolise the means of violence. Many princes ruled effectively over no more than city states, and Max Weber (1914/1978: 1239) drew attention to the revolutionary effect of medieval cities in dissolving feudal bonds and creating the free association of citizens. 'Stadtluft macht frei', was the old adage, 'city air makes free', a principle understood by black people fleeing their masters in nineteenth-century United States as much as by medieval serfs escaping their lords.

Civility and free association, a non-violent space of discourse and behaviour, became a potent combination when guaranteed by increasingly powerful national states anxious to align themselves with the rising bourgeois classes of early modern Europe. The growth of this space resulted in the 'civil society' of the eighteenth century, an intimate blend of political and economic institutions, that demonstrated, however, a capacity for mobilisation and self-defence when it came into conflict with an older aristocratic, feudal order.

The resulting violence of the American and French Revolutions, fought in the name of freedom and democracy, has left a permanent reminder of the potential of civil society to adopt a quite different posture if its existence is threatened. Later, both the Second World War and the Cold War demonstrated that deep commitment to ideals fortifies and strengthens solidarity in times of conflict, even to the point of abandoning those ideals where the society's existence is endangered. Armed conflict always puts civil society in jeopardy; it is suspended in time of war, lost if the war is lost, and regained in peace only through resolute advocacy and clear-minded reconstruction.

The last three centuries have experienced the evolution of civil society through alternating periods of peace and war, while the transformation of technology and economy present it with a quite different set of challenges from those it faced in the revolutionary period of Western history. But the idea of global civil society is just as much borne by, and a response to, globalisation as eighteenth century civil society was inextricably linked with the rise of capitalism. Violence could not be ignored then, and neither can we fail to respond to the popular and political currents following the events of 9/11 and their aftermath.

We need to ask how globality makes a difference; and specifically, if civil society requires a state order to guarantee the peaceful conditions of its continued existence, when national states are relatively less able to exercise control, can global civil society thrive without a global equivalent to the state, whatever it may be called? Global civil society may often resist the forces of economic globalisation but at the same time it draws strength from increased opportunities for transnational mobilisation and organising. In the absence of a global state does it have the capacity to fill the resulting void?

Indeed, intimate, even symbiotic, relations between civil society, war and conflict, long established in a frame of nation-state competition, as Mary Kaldor, Denisa Kostovicova and Yahia Said explore in Chapter 4, emphasize how global civil society becomes an even more active and responsible player in armed conflict situations where nation states are no longer sole protagonists.

What is at stake is the degree of autonomy and control global civil society can secure in promoting non-violent conditions of life. The configurations of state, economy and society in our global age are new and continually evolving. We are increasingly aware of the limited effectiveness of military intervention and the growing importance of soft power. For this reason we need to examine the scope that civil society has for expanding its influence and mitigating violence.

Conflict, institutions and globalisation

While wars might be fought in the name of free society, such is their intrusion into rights that, when won, democracy has to struggle to re-emerge in the aftermath. Even so, the struggle can be won, as the settlement after the Second World War showed, involving as it did the greatest advance in human freedom in history, with the establishment of the United Nations and the proclamation of the Universal Declaration of Human Rights, while the development of international institutions has proceeded with no significant check ever since, until perhaps – and we can't yet be sure – the present time.

This international system, aided by and part of the Cold War, helped introduce a system of conflict management. To be sure, power continued to play a crucial role, closely linked to resource availability and legitimacy, as well as to the potential of inflicting violence and the deployment of military means. Conflicts, be they violent or not, are a clash of power, a pushing and pulling, giving and taking. In this balancing process of powers confronting each other, the capabilities of those involved vary and may shift. In other words, conflicts are dynamic and rarely static.

With the end of the Cold War and a weakened system of international governance, many conflicts were 'freed up' and became re-energised, and new ones engendered.

Sociologists such as Dahrendorf (1994) remind us that conflicts are manifest tensions that arise from perceived disagreements, as opposed to latent tensions where parties may be largely unaware of the level of threat and power capabilities. Once conflicts are manifest, the conditions for communicating, mobilising and organising are critical for their process and outcome. It is precisely the wider availability of information technology such as the Internet, combined with a steep decline in communication costs, which facilitates the transformation of latent into manifest conflicts. Political entrepreneurs, activists and ideologues of many kinds find access to the means of mobilisation easier than in the past. At the same time, the capacity to keep movements in check and violent-free has not kept pace.

The mismatch between the potential for mobilisation and the capacity for controlling it stands in marked contrast to the period after the Second World War and the Cold War. This period emphasized containment, control and predictability of inter-state conflicts, including domestic ones. By doing so, it also provided the reference point for national civil societies.The transnational conflicts of the early twenty-first century are different, as Kaldor (1999) points out, and require new institutional responses in conflict management. What institutions come to mind in this respect? Again, the sociology of conflict helps in suggesting answers.

While modern societies are conflict-prone they tend to seek ways and means of managing, that is, institutionalising conflicts (panels, hearings, political parties, social movements, judiciary, and so on) rather than seeking settlement through power domination alone (Dahrendorf 1994), including violence. Such institutionalised conflicts are seen as creative conflicts that reduce the amount of tensions that could otherwise build up along major societal cleavage structures. Such tensions could threaten the social fabric of societies, while managed conflicts contribute to social stability and 'tamed' social change. Could we think of global civil society as a means of institutionalising conflicts and preventing them from becoming violent?

However, over-institutionalisation of conflicts can create inertia and stifle social change and innovation, whereas under-institutionalisation can lead to conflicts spreading into other fields and generating unintended consequences. Moreover, deep-seated core conflicts (for example, labour versus capital, value conflicts, ethnic conflicts) have the tendency to amass complicating factors around them that in the end can make some of them intractable. Such basic insights into the sociology of conflict are useful because they allow us to probe deeper into the alternating relationship between violence and civil society.

Institutions that mitigate violence within states are strengthened by the state's successful assertion of a monopoly of the means of legitimate violence. But the international system of sovereign states has also developed mechanisms to reduce the likelihood of war. Alliances, security pacts and a framework of law for the settlement of disputes, in addition to an American hegemony in conventional armed forces, have reduced the incidence and likelihood of international disputes culminating in war. Civil society has flourished for a long period without interruption from a major war.

At the same time, a new challenge has arisen and threatens state institutions and hence also civil society. In part it arises from, and is assisted by, the same set of globalising forces that favour the rise of civil society, and this affinity is sufficient for many to discredit the 'civilising power' of civil society altogether. Terror groups operate across borders employing the new means of communication, transportation, media and messaging, including smart weapons. They appeal to values that are beyond the nation state and at the same time exploit the freedoms of movement, association and speech that the democratic state serves to protect. They attack non-military targets and the civilian population. Indeed, they are an even greater challenge to civil society than they are to the state.

Let us summarise the reasons for that emphatic statement, first taking a brief overview of that challenge. In summary, these are the main issues:

- Cross-border terror provokes state reactions against non-state actors elsewhere and undermines international law.
- Non-state terror groups negate civil society and state institutions where they enjoy support.

- Terror groups employ and therefore damage civil society's access to global media, and hence undermine the mobilisation capacity civil society could have.
- Cross-border terror promotes reactionary xenophobia and repressive state action.

Thus, the danger cross-border terror poses to global civil society is the prospect of either a reversion to an international system of repressive states or the expansion of a global imperial state. At best, cross-border terror is a temporary diversion of civil society's attention and energies that could be allocated to peaceful conflict settlement and resolution, and, of course, to pressing issues like the environment, economic development, access to health care and education; at worst, cross-border terror depletes the enabling political, legal and social environment that global civil society requires for its sustainability.

It may well be too early to pass judgement on outcomes. At present, global civil society's response is in the balance, and the medium to long-term outcome will depend on how it manages to resolve the following issues:

- What are the limits of global civil society's intervention in national state–civil society relations?
- Can global civil society intervene effectively in areas where global terror groups are active?
- Can global civil society accommodate cross-border value conflicts?
- Are the causes terror groups espouse invalidated by their use of terror?
- Does global civil society now require the development of global state institutions to meet the threat of cross-border terror?

The severity and far-reaching implications of these unresolved issues suggest global civil society may indeed have reached a critical juncture. Global civil society actors can no longer avoid taking a position on violence for just causes, but if they are to assert themselves in the name of civil society they can hardly avoid contributing to the creation of institutions globally that are equivalent to those that sustain civil society within states. Global governance is then not an optional interest for civil society – its very future, globally and nationally, depends on it. Indeed, global civil society has to engage in profound self-

examination, the importance of which extends beyond itself and to the international community at large. The global conditions for its own continued existence may even be those for the survival of humankind.

The institutionalisation of conflict as understood in the past has been associated with the growth of rules of engagement and mediating agencies that channel and divert antagonisms before they reach violent confrontation, rather than remove them. Within nation states conflict management has relied both on the state's guarantee backed by legitimate use of force and the parties' perceived self-interest in observing the rules. In the international arena national self-interest is a more important factor given that hegemonic force can only acquire fitful legitimacy on a case-by-case basis. Nationally and internationally the nation state has been the key actor.

To be sure, in the past, the internationalism of the labour movement was recognised as a fundamental threat by the capitalist class, but this was a conflict replicated in each country, and each national solution contributed to a reduction of the threat of class warfare across boundaries, especially when during the Cold War the Soviet Union subverted labour internationalism for its own interest. Globalisation has come to challenge that model radically since 1989.

Globalisation processes penetrate and change the 'causal chemistry' and 'fabric' of existing conflicts, as well as emerging and re-emerging ones. By involving more frequent movements of objects, meanings and people across transnational space, they lead to a greater exposure of different audiences to each other, and to more frequent and intense contact between world views. Such contacts may challenge or reinforce long-held cultural assumptions about the world, identity and meaning, and they may also increase the frequency of 'meshing' and depths of interpenetration, including acceptance and rejection as well as patterns of innovation and diffusion. Whatever the outcome, such contacts also contribute to greater conflict potential (see Anheier and Isar 2007).

By implication, they also change the capacity of institutions, including civil society, to deal with conflicts. What the Danish cartoon crisis and other such developments point to is the importance of value systems and world views in conflicts and conflict management.

The Danish cartoon controversy has been one of the

defining events of the year for global civil society (see Box I.1). It has been at the confluence of three critical points of controversy for any global order: the relations between the national and the global, between the public and the private, and between the right to free expression and the right to respect. State and civil society actors have been involved in a turmoil that shows how the failure to define their relations in a global frame threatens the national existence of the civil sphere.

The publication of 12 cartoons depicting the Prophet Muhammed in *Jyllands Posten* on 30 September 2005, and media coverage of the subsequent series of events it initiated, became effectively a running commentary on conflicts in global society today. The parties to those events have also been willing to raise the temperature, to escalate the conflict, taking supporters and opponents with them.

The culture editor of the Danish newspaper who took the decision to publish has described his own motives (Rose 2006). Flemming Rose hoped to generate a debate 'to test the limits of self-censorship by calling on cartoonists to challenge a Muslim taboo', claiming that the subsequent establishment of a 'network of moderate Muslims' committed to the Danish constitution, and the call by the right-wing People's Party to its members to distinguish moderate Muslims from Sharia law proponents, vindicated his decision. But, while he claimed positive consequences for Denmark and Europe, the 'tragic demonstrations' in the Middle East and Asia were certainly negative.

Rose invokes Karl Popper's declaration that we cannot tolerate the intolerant and argues that giving incidental offence should not restrict freedom of expression. In other words, he claims an intentional and principled act in defence of European values, while not anticipating reaction in the rest of the world. Rose knew then he would offend many Muslims in Denmark, but asks us to accept he was naive about reaction in the rest of the world. But if the problem for him was the lack of integration into Danish society of an immigrant population, surely the counterpart of that had to be the likelihood of reaction from those with whom they sustained close bonds, namely, Muslims elsewhere. General experience is that communities and governments retain a strong interest in diaspora citizens. Moreover, in adopting a

role as defender of European, not simply Danish, values Rose contributes to the civilisational debate that preoccupies public intellectuals globally.

Rose's decision to commission and publish the cartoons was followed by decisions to republish in some form by editors in many countries, Muslim and non-Muslim. None of them could claim to be doing this unwittingly, because they were aware of protests, demonstrations and riots that were widely publicised and spread to more than 50 countries, including Iran, Indonesia, India, and Thailand. On 20 October 2005 ambassadors from ten Islamic countries complained about the cartoons to the Danish prime minister.

In Western countries Muslims sought to put their views within the public frame of protest. In Britain the Muslim Association of Britain called a rally in Trafalgar Square, London, on 11 February 2006. Spokesperson Anas Altikriti had three messages: to Britain that they were seeking to bridge the gap between Islam and the West; to Europe that Islamophobic caricatures are unacceptable; and to Muslims that 'a large number of people are on the side of reconciliation' (Muslim Association of Britain 2006). Altikriti was more clear than Rose that relations between Islam and the West were at stake. The rapid escalation of conflict over the cartoons up to a declaration of a civilisational clash illustrates the failure of both states and global civil society either to create institutions to manage cross-border cultural conflicts of this scale or to address the causes of conflict. The historical experience of the Western nation state with class conflicts was that state provision of security and welfare, coupled with a rise in prosperity for all classes, was necessary to reduce the deprivation and grievance that could breed violent social upheaval. Co-optation into the system is not enough without delivery of goods that the system has hitherto failed to provide.

Globalisation processes, being pervasive and therefore often equated with our world as a whole, have become the target for those seeking to redress the imbalances and injustices in that system. Institutionalisation, equated with absorption into a global system, is then often seen as a cause for the inability of the system to change. It was resistance to this process by the anti-globalisation movement that captured global media attention when its demonstrations brought the Seattle meetings of the World Trade Organization (WTO), in December 1999, to a premature end.

Box I.1: The cartoon controversy: from local test to global crisis

On 30 September 2005 *Jyllands-Posten*, a daily newspaper in Denmark, published an article titled 'Muhammad's face' accompanied by 12 cartoons depicting the Prophet Muhammad, an act prohibited by Islamic law in avoidance of idolatry. The cartoons also associated Islam with terrorism; one cartoon depicted Mohammed's turban in the shape of a bomb. By publishing the cartoons the paper sought to test the limits of self-censorship in the Danish media. In the past it had had difficulty finding illustrators willing to depict the Prophet out of fear of offending local Muslims (*Jyllands-Posten* 2006).

Immediately after publication, aside from a group of Danish Muslims who protested outside the offices of *Jyllands-Posten*, little notice was taken of the cartoons. But by early October many ambassadors representing Muslim countries in Copenhagen had received petitions from Danish Muslim organisations expressing anger over the cartoons. Eleven of these ambassadors wrote to Angers Fogh Rasmussen, the Danish Prime Minister, requesting a meeting to discuss the 'demeaning' caricatures and what they called an 'on-going smearing campaign in Danish public circles and media against Islam and Muslims'. They also asked the Prime Minister to take 'all those responsible to task', referring to the editors of *Jyllands-Posten* (Letter to Prime Minister, Rasmussen 2005). In his response, the Prime Minister turned down the request for a meeting, reaffirmed Danish society's respect for freedom of expression and suggested 'offended parties' bring their case to Danish courts (Rasmussen 2005).

Angered by the Prime Minister's refusal to meet, a delegation of Danish imams travelled throughout the Middle East for the next two months with the aim of gathering support for a protest against the drawings and for pressing the Danish government to condemn the cartoons (Schofield 2006). They took with them a 43-page dossier that included the original 12 cartoons published in *Jyllands-Posten* and other offensive and perverse images never published by the paper. The imams said the images were hate mail from fellow Danes, but this has never been confirmed (Spiegel Online 2006).

By targeting prominent Muslim scholars, politicians and muftis (experts in Islamic law), the delegation, in combination with the power of mass communication, globalised the cartoons. The contents of the portfolio spread across the Middle East and soon protestors began to gather outside the Danish and Norwegian embassies (Norway's *Magazinete* had published the cartoons in early January) to show their anger over the disrespect, abuse and 'demonisation' of Islam, which they felt the publication of the cartoons represented (BBC News 2006b). Protestors burned flags, chanted anti-Danish and anti-Norwegian slogans, and demanded an apology from *Jyllands-Posten* and the Danish government.

Initially, both *Jyllands-Posten* and the Danish Prime Minister refused to give an official apology, citing the right to freedom of speech and of the press, respectively. But massive protests by offended Muslims from Qatar to Palestine, combined with a Saudi-initiated region-wide boycott of Danish goods, persuaded the newspaper to change its mind. On 30 January *Jyllands-Posten* posted an apology on its website in English, Arabic and Danish for having 'indisputably offended many Muslims', but not for the publication of the cartoons themselves because this was in accordance with Danish law (Juste 2006). The next day, *Magazinete* apologised as well. The Danish Prime Minister welcomed the move, but he did not follow suit, continuing to uphold the freedom of Denmark's press.

Meanwhile, more European newspapers (in Spain, France, Germany, Poland, Finland, Portugal, Sweden, Italy, and others) decided to republish some or all of the cartoons in solidarity with *Jyllands-Posten* and *Magazinete* and in defence of freedom of speech. Many Muslims saw republication as provocation, and as a result the protests amplified in number, geographic scope and target – from Denmark and Norway to Europe and the 'West' more generally.

In total, more than 1 million Muslims protested in more than 30 countries on every continent. While the majority of protests passed peacefully, some were violent, involving demonstrators affiliated with extremist or militant Islamic organisations, who threw rocks, clashed with police, and burned vehicles, restaurants, banks and embassies. In Nigeria, a nation nearly equally divided between Muslims and Christians and no stranger to sectarian violence, the cartoons sparked brutal inter-religious killings (*Agence France Presse 2006*). Many protestors chanted violent slogans such as 'Death to Denmark' (Bilefsky 2006) and 'Hang those who insulted the prophet' (*Daily Times 2006*). More ominously, in Sudan, demonstrators shouted 'Strike, Strike Bin Laden' (scotsman.com 2006), and in London, '9/11, we want more' (Hawkins 2006). Osama bin Laden, leader of Al-Qaeda, produced a video tape aired by Al-Jazeera, urging his followers to murder those who published the cartoons (Bansal 2006).

On the diplomatic front, the violent reaction was widely condemned by government leaders and those representing multilateral bodies such as the Organization of Islamic Countries (OIC), the United Nations and the European Union. In the same breath that they denounced the cartoons, many mainstream Muslim community leaders distanced themselves from the rioters (BBC News 2006a). However some leaders and analysts, most notably Condoleezza Rice, US Secretary of State, suspected that in those states led or influenced by Islamic extremist groups, governments (or opposition factions within them) indirectly or directly encouraged anti-'Western' violence in an attempt to profit from their citizens' ire over cartoons for their own political gain (Asia-Pacific News 2006). This is thought to be the case with the violent protests in Syria, a police state where little activity takes place in public without the sanction of the government (TMCnet News 2006). Similarly, in Lebanon, half of those arrested were found to be either Palestinian or Syrian nationals (Bilefsky 2006). Other Muslim leaders, such as those gathered at a summit of the OIC in early February, blamed the violent reaction to the cartoons on Muslims' disapproval of the US-led 'war on terror'.

Apart from the human costs, the cartoon controversy caused considerable political fallout. At least four cabinet-level ministers resigned (Karen 2006), many editors were fired, at least five were arrested, and newspapers in at least five different countries were shut down entirely (Wikipedia URL). Diplomatic relations between many nations worsened, or were cut off altogether. Many ambassadors to Denmark were recalled, over a dozen Scandinavian embassies were closed, Danish citizens were evacuated from their residences and travels in the Middle East and parts of Africa and Asia, fatwas were issued and bomb threats made against the editors and offices of *Jyllands-Posten*. The boycott of Danish products in the Middle East cost Danish exporters an estimated US$30 million (Janardhan 2006). Worse yet, the cartoons served to agitate extremist Islamic organisations that employ terrorism and other forms of violence. Denmark's Prime Minister declared that the cartoon controversy represented Denmark's 'biggest foreign policy challenge since the Second World War' (Guardian Unlimited 2006).

That the publication of 12 cartoons by a small Danish newspaper can trigger a conflict of such global reach and intensity is revealing of the degree to which contemporary society has become truly 'globalised'. The initiation and prolongation of this conflict relied on global communication in order to propagate the cartoons, the subsequent apologies, and media images of protestors with their various placards and banners. It also made possible the website activism, email and text-messaging capacity that united protestors.

This box is based on the author's MSc dissertation 'The Cartoon Controversy: Prelude to a Clash of Civilizations?'

Melinda Brouwer is a postgraduate student in Global Politics at the London School of Economics

This was the backlash by identities and interests challenged by globalisation that Richard Falk (1993: 48) predicted and which UNRISD (1995) reported as 'states of disarray', including violence as a consequence. The UN offered a forum to civil society in its global conferences but Falk envisaged also a statist backlash against civil society (1999:102–3), perhaps best exemplified in the growing American disdain for the UN.

A recursive process of state co-optation accompanied by successive waves of anti-institutionalism within civil society continues unabated. Anti-globalisation was succeeded by the positive programmes of the World Social Forums with commitment to non-violence (see Glasius and Timms 2006). Geoffrey Pleyers shows (Box I.2) how resistance to being institutionalised in civil society has led others to adopt the 'alter-global' quest for a 'new culture of politics', escaping the oxymoron of 'organising worldwide to defeat globalization'. Backlash against global civil society comes then from two opposite corners: from states and from those seeking radical alternatives to institutionalisation.

There is no safe haven for NGOs, working for or against states. In Afghanistan in 2005 the UN's World Food Programme Afghanistan (2005) reported it was working through 196 local and international NGOs while facing major security problems. An organisation such as CARE, with 12,000 staff worldwide collaborating with state agencies in conflict zones, lost one worker, Margaret Hassan, to murder in Iraq in 2004; had another, Clementina Cantoni, kidnapped in Afghanistan in May 2005; and had its Kabul offices demolished in a riot on 29 May 2006. Being for or against state solutions cannot protect civil society organisations nor absolve them from adopting their own explicit policies and procedures for dealing with violence and its justifications, as Heba Raouf Ezzat and Mary Kaldor show in Chapter 1.

Toward global civility

In fact it is the multiplicity of globalisation processes, their contradictory tendencies and unregulated development that makes the world of today so dangerous (see Berger 1998). The intensity and frequency of encounters between adherents of different values and world views result from the freedom that states have in part given, in part been forced to relinquish, to individuals and business in an enormous expansion of markets and development of technology. The scope for free association worldwide by non-state actors needs now to be accompanied by a similar growth of worldwide civility. A climate of tolerance and preparedness to settle disputes peacefully can no longer be seen as the responsibility of state agencies alone, any more than good behaviour and mutual respect within states can be produced by law.

If we see states still as the main agencies through which resources may be redistributed to reduce poverty, civil society must recognise the consequences of the limits of military power in reducing conflict and accept that it has to play a major role in generating the everyday rules for global civility. If the will is there, the new means of communication make this a feasible objective. We conclude by reviewing some of a number of possible growth points for a new global civility, inadequate to be sure, but still enough to suggest that global civil society contains the potential for creating a less violent future.

Forums

The events of the cartoon controversy are actor-led and sometimes deliberately focused on highlighting areas of flux and ambiguity seeking resolution. As such, these events are open invitations to civil society agents to provide leads to the future and constructive interventions. Where are these happening? Can the World Social Forums and similar events provide a model?

Pressurised debates

The cartoon controversy is one example of developing political discourses under pressure from events where the place of civil society is negotiated. So too has been the growing debate over Russian legislation curbing civil society on grounds of foreign interference. The WTO has been under constant pressure from the debate generated at Gleneagles for a deal on trade to contribute to the global relief of poverty.

Media standards and events

The media nationally everywhere exercise discretion on matters of public morals and taste, but the standards for these are culturally specific. Equally there are zones within national culture where different standards apply. Can we have global definitions of civility, perhaps as an understanding to agree to disagree civilly on contested issues that might otherwise become more threatening to all involved? What are the new structures of offence against public morals in a globalised world? And are there non-national zonings of taste? Can the Internet and blogs provide more 'globalised' global conversations? Kaldor (1999: 126) introduced the term 'spectacle wars'. The Make Poverty History campaign and demonstration prior to the G8 Gleneagles meeting in July 2005 was 'spectacle civil society'. So, too, was the globally viewed football World Cup in June 2006, validating national rivalries through a competition that serves also as a focal point for the thousands of NGOs worldwide engaged in using football for social development (see Chapter 7 by David Goldblatt).

Discursive relations

Should the West, Russia, China, India and Islam enter into discursive relations explicitly seeking new principles of coexistence, for example, re-zoning declared areas of decency, regionalising public–private divides, finding minimum entitlements? Are these matters solely for bilateral civilisational negotiations? Is civil society the arena where the new principles with emerge, or will it descend into violence transcending states? Amartya Sen (2006) argues that the politics of global confrontation should be wrested from civilisational partitioning of the world in favour of recognising the choices open to persons in their multiple identities. Civil society is the arena where such identities could be negotiated.

Reform of global governance

National civil society thrives within established democratic law-abiding states that recognise human rights. Rights require legitimate use of force if they are to be asserted against opposition, and this is what the state supplies. Do global civil society groups require equivalent rights-based global governance? And where are the enforcing agents? Global governance problems persist, and global civil society must make its contribution to conflict management – how can it be made more effective when there is no global state. UN reform will be a major aspect dealing with growing global governance problems, of course. However, the current reform process leaves much to be desired, and remains too focused on the nation-state (see Falk 2005). Moreover, UN forays into improved UN–civil society relations, while yielding proposals of considerable potential, are in danger of becoming just that (Cardoso 2003).

Organising for peace and conflict resolution

There is a long history of civil society groups devoted to the peaceful resolution of conflicts and to principles of non-violence, raising awareness, promoting community security and community integration. But there are also groups opposed on issues of capital punishment and treatment of prisoners, for and against the rights of individuals to bear arms, to experiment on animals, to have abortions. Among these there are advocates of direct action, up to the point of justifying killing innocent civilians. Staged encounters between these groups could establish pragmatic conditions for non-violent outcomes. But global civil society might also activate democratic principles to out-argue and out-vote advocates of violence in its ranks, call for stops on the arms trade and for the reduction of nuclear weaponry. It can demonstrate the relative insignificance of civilisational divides when humankind has to measure up to global challenges. Ezzat and Kaldor, in Chapter 1 of this volume, show the affinities between Islamic and Western intellectual debates on the legitimacy of violence and their relevance for conflict resolution under global conditions. They point to new possibilities in building worldwide networks like Citizens Against Terror (URL). Civility has to be the ultimate weapon in the rhetorical armoury of global civil society, but also demonstrated in its effects.

Box I.2:   Under fire: NGOs in the alter-global movement

Civil society, I hate this term! Civil society is what we no longer are!... A lot of NGOs are now active within the UN and that hasn't changed anything. Those who want things to change are here in Porto Alegre and not in the UN...We can no longer be patient and friendly with everyone like civil society people do.

Naomi Klein, World Social Forum 2002

At the World Social Forum (WSF) in Porto Alegre, 2002, Naomi Klein expressed a widespread feeling among many in the alter-global movement (also known as the 'global social justice movement'). Later in the same workshop, the main organiser of the Genoa Social Forum coalition said that he 'totally shared Naomi Klein's position towards civil society'. During the 2004 WSF in Mumbai, an experienced French activist complained in similar terms: 'In developing countries, civil society means corruption and incompetence.'

Of course, many WSF activists don't share this conception and consider themselves part of civil society. Rather than civil society as a whole, criticism tends to be directed towards NGOs – which many actors, scholars and international institutions have identified as representing 'global civil society', to the exclusion of other components. Indeed, there is a wind of revolt blowing against NGOs in many parts of the global social justice movement. In 2000, Bernard Cassen defined ATTAC (originally, the Association for the Taxation of Financial Transactions for the Aid of Citizens) as 'a French international-oriented NGO'. His intention was to present the association in a progressive and positive way but the result was much criticism. 'To identify it as an NGO means that he wants it to become an international institution!', said one activist from ATTAC-France, (interviewed in 2000). Once perceived as a positive force, NGOs are currently under heavy fire from much of the global social justice movement.

African civil society elites complain about their dependency on Northern NGO funding and hence policies. African local actors complain that they have been instrumentalised by NGOs: 'Some NGOs use us all the time to hold money and contracts but never listen to us', said a grassroots activist during the Weekend Workshop on World Social Forums, Durban, 22 July 2006. They accuse 'NGOs and professional militants' of 'travelling all around the world following the forums' wake, getting far away from what happens locally' (Catalan activist, WSF 2003, personal interview). Young activists complain that NGOs preach democracy while sometimes practising an internal dictatorship: Libertarian activists invite all activists to 'abandon ESF, ATTAC and other NGOs and rather prepare revolution and social change in your neighbourhood' (Indymedia URL). Since the first WSF, the 'network of social movements and activists' aims to balance the 'growing weight of NGOs in the WSF' (Brazilian activist, WSF 2002, personal communication). Even leaders of small NGOs, without any social base, express their 'fear that the movement could be submerged by NGOs that may share similar preoccupations but are not directly linked with social struggles' (a member of the WSF International interviewed in 2003). Hence, a Mexican NGO leader involved in an alter-global coalition explained the 'necessity to rethink the concept of civil society starting from the social movements because social movements claim their sovereignty independent of political parties and NGOs' (interviewed in Mexico City, 2003).

Peasant activists are among the most strident critics. At the 2006 Bamako Polycentric WSF, Paul Nicholson, a leader of Via Campesina, argued that peasants 'no longer want NGOs to speak in our name about agricultural policy. We want to build our own movement, our own international network and to speak for ourselves' (lecture at the peasant space, personal notes).

Nevertheless, NGOs have played an important role in the alter-global movement. They brought new ideas, a new ways of getting involved in social and political issues, and a new repertory of action – including counter-summits. They helped finance WSF events and travel costs for Africans activists. Moreover, NGOs and alter-global actors share much in common, including their pragmatic conception of social change, ways of influencing policy makers by lobbying and expertise, and their contribution to the emergence of an international public sphere and a 'global civil society'.

A brief analysis of the complex and tense relations between NGOs and the new alter-global actors throws some light on the matter. Disappointment with NGOs is one reason for the foundation of the alter-globalisation movement, but NGOs also played a role in its creation. Therefore the relationship between these actors remains complex: on one hand, the alter-global movement has been constructed with, after and against NGOs, and trade unions; on the other hand, NGOs stand before, aside and within the alter-global movement. This is related to two major processes: the taming of new social movements and an emerging distinctive culture of politics. According to Mary Kaldor (2003; see also Kriesi 1996), NGOs result from an advanced taming process of new social movements. Many aspects of the criticisms of alter-global actors address this taming process, in particular four dimensions:

1. The taming process encourages the integration of some NGOs within international institutions and projects, which leads to criticism they have been co-opted.

2. Many activists denounce NGOs' lack of radicalism. Meanwhile some NGOs are fearful of the radicalism of the alter-global movement, an association they fear could undermine their credibility and their relations with policy makers.

3. As Kaldor explains, many NGOs no longer provide a space for debate. The production of ideas is no longer central for many of these organisations, which have become service providers or institutionalised agents. The alter-global movement aims to fill this empty space and create new 'open spaces' for public debates (Sen and Keraghel 2004).

4. Activists criticise the institutionalisation process, which they see as a specific problem of NGOs. However, they fail to acknowledge that this trend has begun in their own movement, and especially in the World Social Forum. As a radical Catholic priest explained at a 2002 WSF workshop, 'We have to avoid to start as a group of people that seek to change the world and to end being an institution like the Vatican'.

However, institutionalisation and the taming process that often characterise the evolution of social movements are not the only cause of tense relations between NGOs and alter-global activists. The alter-global new culture of politics contrasts with the dominant ideas and activities of some NGOs and humanitarian actors:

1. In contrast with the 'apolitical' commitment and conceptions of NGOs and humanitarian agencies, the alter-global movement embodies a renewed interest in political participation and debate.

2. A central divergence concerns the position on the state. NGOs are partially born from a reaction against a state-centred development model and a suspicion of political actors. In this way, they partly share some values and perspectives with neo-liberalism (for example, less institutionalised, smaller, more efficient, less 'political' development actors and projects). Conversely, alter-global actors aim to strengthen elected political actors who are seen as lacking power against economic actors.

3. The specialisation of civil society is a key element for its efficiency (Wahl 1997). But it also encourages a move away from original purpose and broader perspectives. The specialisation of NGOs on particular issues has sometimes led to their transformation into service providers or single-issue lobbyists of international institutions. The alter-global movement provides a space to debate broader issues and global perspectives, reintegrating a political dimension in social changes.

The lack of input and participation by the members of many NGOs, think tanks, and professional organisations in the decision-making and structure of their organisations is much criticised by other actors in the alter-global movement. It contrasts with the high level of concern about internal democracy among many alter-global activists who value open discussion and active participation.

However, such criticism of NGOs should not detract from their fundamental contribution to the alter-globalisation movement. Moreover, cooperation between NGOs and other alter-global actors provides an opportunity: NGOs' organisation, efficiency and expertise have often proved essential to the success of the alter-global movement. On the other hand, the dynamism and constructive criticism of alter-global actors may help NGOs to recognise the constraints of their organisational structure, tactics and strategies.

The quotations from activists reproduced here derive from field research by the author at meetings and lectures of the global social justice movement between 1999 and 2006.

Geoffrey Pleyers, Centre d'Analyse et d'Intervention Sociologiques, Paris, and FNRS Researcher at the University of Louvain

Agence France Presse (2006) 'Libyan Cartoons Death Toll Rises to 11', 18 February. http://www.findarticles.com/p/articles/mi_kmafp/is_200602/ai_n16071664 (consulted 6 August 2006).

Albrow, M (1996) The Global Age: State and Society beyond Modernity. Cambridge: Polity Press.

Anderson, K and Rieff, D (2005) 'Global Civil Society: A Sceptical View', in H Anheier, M Glasius and M Kaldor (eds), Global Civil Society 2004/5. London: Sage.

Anheier, H, Glasius, M and Kaldor, M (2001) 'Introducing Global Civil Society', in H Anheier, M Glasius and M Kaldor (eds), Global Civil Society 2001. Oxford: Oxford University Press.

– and Isar, Y R (eds) (2007) Culture and Globalization: Tensions and Conflict. London: Sage.

Asia-Pacific News (2006) 'Iranian VP Rejects US Accusations Of Inflaming Muslim Anger', 9 February. http://news.monstersandcritics.com/asiapacific/article_1096 126.php/Iranian_VP_rejects_US_accusations_of_inflaming_ Muslim_anger (consulted 6 August 2006).

Bansal, S (2006) 'Bin Laden Wants Prophet Mohammad Cartoon Offenders Killed', 24 April 2006. All Headline News. http://www.allheadlinenews.com/articles/7003300858 (consulted 29 July 2006).

BBC News (2006a) 'Four Die in Afghan Riot', 8 February. http://news.bbc.co.uk/1/hi/world/south_asia/4692172.stm (consulted 6 August 2006).

– (2006b) 'Islam–West Divide "Grows Deeper"', 10 February. http://news.bbc.co.uk/1/hi/world/asia-pacific/4699716.stm (consulted 21 July, 2006)/

Berger, P (ed) (1998) The Limits of Social Cohesion: Conflict and Mediation in Pluralist Societies. A Report of the Bertelsmann Foundation to the Club of Rome. Boulder, CO: Westview Press.

Bilefsky, D (2006) 'Leaders Seek To Calm Muslim Fury', International Herald Tribune, 7 February.

Cardoso, F H (2003) 'Civil Society and Global Governance'. Contextual paper prepared for the Level Panel on UN-Civil Society. United Nations. http://www.un.org/reform/pdfs/cardosopaper13june.htm (consulted 4 August 2006).

Citizens Against Terror (URL) http://citizensagainstterror.net/6 (accessed 24 July 2006).

Coser, L (1956) The Functions of Social Conflict. New York: Free Press.

Dahrendorf, R (1994) Der moderne soziale Konflikt. Essay zur Politik der Freiheit. Munich: DTV.

Daily Times (2006) 'Children Rally Against Cartoons', 1 March. http://www.dailytimes.com.pk/default.asp?page=2006\03\01\ story_1-3-2006_pg1_5 (consulted 21 July 2006).

Elias, N (2000) The Civilizing Process: Sociogenetic and Psychogenetic Investigation. Oxford: Blackwell.

Falk, Richard (1993) 'The Making of Global Citizenship', in J Brecher, J Brown and J Cutler (eds), Global Visions: Beyond the New World Order. Boston: South End Press.

– (1999) Predatory Globalization: A Critique. Cambridge: Polity Press.

– (2006) 'Reforming the United Nations: Global Civil Society Perspectives and Initiatives', in M Glasius, M Kaldor and H Anheier (eds), Global Civil Society 2005/6. London: Sage.

Glasius, M and Kaldor, M (2002) 'The State of Global Civil Society: Before and After September 11', in M Glasius, M Kaldor and H Anheier (eds), Global Civil Society 2002. Oxford: Oxford University Press.

– and Timms, J (2006) 'The Role of Social Forums in Global Civil Society: Radical Beacon or Strategic Infrastructure?', in M Glasius, M. Kaldor and H. Anheier (eds), Global Civil Society 2005/6. London: Sage.

Guardian Unlimited (2006) 'Two Killed In Pakistan Cartoon Protests', 14 February. http://www.guardian.co.uk/cartoonprotests/story/0,,1709661, 00.html (consulted 6 August 2006).

Hawkins, Ross (2006) 'Prayer Mats Lined the Pavement', BBC News, 11 February. http://news.bbc.co.uk/1/hi/england/london/4705342.stm (consulted 6 August 2006).

Indymedia (URL) http://paris.indymedia.org (consulted 25 October 2003).

Janardhan, M (2006) 'UAE: Boycotts of Danish Goods Make $30 Million Statement', IPS-Inter Press Service, 20 February.

Juste, C (2006) 'Honourable Fellow Citizens of the Muslim World', Jyllands-Posten, 30 January. http://www.jp.dk/meninger/ncartikel:aid=3527646 (consulted 6 August 2006).

Jyllands-Posten (2006) 'The Story Behind the Drawings', 8 February. http://www.jp.dk/udland/artikel:aid=3544932:fid=11328/ (consulted 21 July 2006).

Kaldor, M (1999) Old Wars, New Wars. Palo Alto, CA: Stanford University Press.

– (2003) Global Civil Society: An Answer to War. Cambridge: Polity Press.

– Anheier, H and Glasius, M (2003) 'Global Civil Society in an Era of Regressive Globalisation', in M. Kaldor, H Anheier, and M Glasius (eds), Global Civil Society 2003. Oxford: Oxford University Press.

– and Muro, D (2003) 'Religious and Nationalist Militant Groups', in M Kaldor, H Anheier and M Glasius (eds), Global Civil Society 2003. Oxford: Oxford University Press.

Karen, M (2006) 'Swedish Foreign Minister Latest Victim of Political Fallout from Prophet Cartoons', Associated Press Worldstream, 21 March.

Kriesi, H (1996) 'The Organizational Structure of New Social Movements in a Political Context', in Doug McAdam, J McCarty and M Zald (eds), Comparative Perspectives on Social Movements. Cambridge, MA: Cambridge University Press.

Kuppusamy, B (2006) 'Malaysia: Anger at U.S. "War on Terror" Feeds Cartoon Frenzy', IPS-Inter Press Service, 12 February.

Letter to Prime Minister Rasmussen (2005) 12 October. http://www.filtrat.dk/grafik/Letterfromambassadors.pdf (consulted 28 July 2006).

Muslim Association of Britain (2006) 'Britain to unite against Islamophobia after cartoons'. 11 February. http://www.mabonline.info/english/modules.php?name=New s&file=article&sid=656 (consulted 10 July 2006).

Rasmussen, Anders Fogh (2005) Letter to Ambassadors of 11 Muslim Countries, 21 October. http://gfxmaster.tv2.dk/ images/Nyhederne/Pdf/side3.pdf (consulted 29 July 2006).

Rose, Flemming (2006) 'Why I Published those Cartoons',
    Washington Post, 19 February.
Schofield, M (2006) 'Protests Express Frustration with the
    West, Cleric Says'. Knight Ridder, 7 February. *The Mercury
    News*.
    http://www.mercurynews.com/mld/mercurynews/news/worl
    d/13815044.htm (consulted 6 August 2006).
Schumpeter, J (1942/1962) *Capitalism, Socialism and
    Democracy*. New York: HarperPerennial.
scotsman.com (2006) 'Plea to Bin Laden to Retaliate', 3
    February.
    http://news.scotsman.com/latest.cfm?id=177952006
    (consulted 6 August 2006).
Sen, A (2006) *Identity and Violence*. London: Allen Lane.
 – and Keraghel, C (2004) 'Explorations in Open Space: The
    World Social Forum and Cultures of Politics', *International
    Social Science Journal*, 56: 483–93.
Simmel, G (1983) Soziologie. Untersuchungen über die Formen
    der Vergesellschaftung. Berlin: Duncker and Humblot.
Soros, George (2006) *The Age of Fallibility: The Consequences
    of the War on Terror*. London: Weidenfeld and Nicolson.
Spiegel Online (2006) 'Alienated Danish Muslims Sought Help
    from Arabs', 1 February.
    http://service.spiegel.de/cache/international/0,1518,398624,0
    0.html (consulted 28 July, 2006).
TMCnet News (2006) 'Mutual Incomprehension, Mutual
    Outrage', 10 February. http://www.tmcnet.com/usubmit/-
    mutual-incomprehension-mutual-outrage-
    /2006/02/10/1361629.htm (consulted 6 August 2006).
Toynbee, A (1961) *A Study of History. Vol XII: Reconsiderations*.
    London: Oxford University Press.
UNRISD (United Nations Research Institute for Social
    Development) (1995) *States of Disarray: The Social Effects of
    Globalization*. Geneva: UNRISD.
Wahl, P (1997) 'Mythos und Realität der internationalen
    Zivilgesellschaft. Zu der Perspektiv einer globalen
    Vernetzung von Nicht-Regierungs-Organisationnen', in E
    Altvater et al. (eds), Vernetzt und verstrickt. Bochum:
    Westphalisches Dampfboot.
Weber, Max (1914/1978) *Economy and Society, Vol. 2*. Berkeley:
    University of California Press.
 – (1919/1948) 'Science as a Vocation', in H H Gerth and C W
    Mills (eds), *From Max Weber*. London: Routledge and Kegan
    Paul.
Wikipedia (URL) 'List of Newspapers that Reprinted Jyllands-
    Posten's Muhammad Cartoons.'
    http://en.wikipedia.org/w/index.php?title=List_of_newspaper
    s_that_reprinted_JyllandsPosten%27s_Muhammad_cartoon
    s&action=history (consulted 31 July 2006).
World Food Programme Afghanistan (2005). *Annual Report*.
    Kabul: WFP Country Office.

CHAPTER 1

'NOT EVEN A TREE': DELEGITIMISING VIOLENCE AND THE PROSPECTS FOR PRE-EMPTIVE CIVILITY

Heba Raouf Ezzat and Mary Kaldor

Do not mutilate; do not kill little children or old men or women; do not cut off the heads of palm trees or burn them; do not cut down the fruit trees; do not slaughter a sheep or a cow or a camel except for food, and if you pass by the monasteries of believers who devoted themselves to worship... leave them to what they chose to do.

Abu Bakr, the First Caliph

Pan Islamism is dormant – yet we have to reckon with the possibility that the sleeper may awake if ever the cosmopolitan proletariat of the 'Westernized' world revolts against Western domination and cries out for anti-Western leadership...If the present situation of mankind were to precipitate a 'race war', Islam might be moved to play her historic role once again...Look at history in terms of civilizations, and not in terms of states, and think of states as rather subordinate and ephemeral political phenomena in the lives of the civilizations in whose bosoms they appear and disappear.

Arnold Toynbee, Civilization on Trial

It is symbolic of this all-pervading unpredictability, which we encounter the moment we enter the realm of violence, that those engaged in the perfection of the means of destruction have finally brought about a level of technical development where the aim, namely warfare, is on the point of disappearing altogether.

Hannah Arendt, Reflections on Violence

Introduction

On 12 July 2006 Hizbollah militants crossed the border into Israel and ambushed a group of Israeli soldiers; eight were killed and two were taken hostage. Israel responded by imposing an air and sea blockade of Lebanon. In the following days, hundreds of civilians, including children, were killed by air strikes; Lebanese civilian infrastructure was destroyed; and hundreds of thousands of 'non-combatants' were displaced. Hizbollah retaliated against Israeli targets and also killed civilians. For Israel, this attack by Hizbollah is defined as an act of aggression and the Lebanese government is held responsible; civilian casualties are regrettable but are 'collateral damage' – the Israeli government claims to be destroying the 'infrastructure of terror'. In fact, Human Rights Watch (2006a) has suggested the pattern of attacks indicate deliberate targeting of civilians; the Israelis seem to regard everyone as a potential combatant. For Hizbollah, attacks on Israeli civilians are considered a way to attack the state of Israel (see Human Rights Watch 2006b). For a full month, both sides were engaged in what they saw as war.

But Hizbollah is an autonomous non-state actor. It is true that many people in Lebanon recognise the militias of Hizbollah as legitimate defence forces, given the weakness of the Lebanese armed forces. It is also the case that the Lebanese government has been requested by the UN Security Council to disarm Hizbollah. But, even before the Israeli attacks, this would have been difficult to achieve except through a long drawn-out process involving the full political integration of the Shi'a population of Lebanon, the establishment of effective security forces, and robust security guarantees from the international community in relation to Israeli military threats. Any attempt to disarm Hizbollah forcefully could lead to renewed civil war. (It was, after all, extremely difficult for the British government to disarm the IRA in Northern Ireland – how much more difficult to disarm Hizbollah?) Suppose a similar attack had been carried out by Palestinian citizens of Israel: would Israel have bombed itself? The attacks by Hizbollah were a crime, a violation of human rights, but they should not be treated as an act of aggression by a foreign state. These kinds of attack have actually been going on for several years, and there have been many deals for the exchange of prisoners and hostages, often arranged by European mediators over the years.

Those who justify Israel's response do so within a discourse of war, in which Hizbollah's attacks are treated as foreign aggression. In fact, even within the discourse of war, the response can be criticised on grounds of disproportionality, although the Israelis can argue that this is a case of 'military necessity'; indeed, international lawyers have asserted that the attacks violate the principle of proportionality in international humanitarian law (the 'laws of war'). But no justification of Israel's response is possible within the discourse of human rights; such attacks are completely unacceptable by the standards of human rights. And this exposes the shortcomings of the language of war in today's world: the human rights regime (human rights law underpinned by global norms) is increasingly coming into conflict with the rules that govern what is called 'war'. In a global era, when the lives of individual human beings are considered to have equal value whatever their nationality or religion, violent actions such as that carried out by Hizbollah should be dealt with through recourse to international law, which addresses individual responsibility for crimes, not by launching a war against a whole population.

There is a striking parallel with the arguments used to justify terror and the 'war on terror'. The Bush administration defined the attacks of 9/11 as an act of aggression. The 'war on terror' is thus defined as a war of self-defence. Because terrorists do not fight by the rules, because they can attack anywhere and everywhere using every conceivable technique, because they are not swayed by deterrence, 'the only way to deal with the terrorist network is to take the battle to them. That is in fact what we are doing. That is in effect self-defense of a preemptive nature' (US Defence Secretary Donald Rumsfeld, quoted in Crawford 2003: 12). Moreover, because the terrorists began the war, they are responsible 'for every single casualty'. The terrorists also justify their actions in terms of self-defence. They are defending Muslims against occupation whether in Palestine, Iraq,

Afghanistan or Chechnya. Because they do not have access to sophisticated weapons and because they do not have the capacity to defend themselves against American, Israeli or Russian attacks, they also have to take the battle to the enemy. The technique of suicide bombing against civilian targets is the only way that this kind of pre-emptive defence can be carried out, they assert. Thus, one of the British suicide bombers, in a video recording made before 7 July 2005, described himself as a 'soldier'.

Yet, just as the attacks by Hizbollah and by Israel make ordinary people throughout the Middle East less, not more, secure, so the terror and the 'war on terror' do not seem to be succeeding in defending American or Muslim citizens. On the contrary, each act of 'pre-emptive self-defence' provides the justification for further acts of terror. More violence is unleashed in a vicious circle, and nobody on either side seems to care about how to re-establish peace. So how can citizens in conflict areas protect themselves? Are there ever cases when the use of violence can be justified? (see Box 1.1) And in an age when a 'clash of civilisations' between Islam and the West is propagated, what can we learn from both Western and Islamic traditions about the complex relationship between violence, civil society and legitimacy? How relevant are these traditions in a global era?

Our central argument is that war, meaning violence between socially organised groups, normally states, has become morally unjustifiable in the context of the changes we tend to group together under the label of globalisation. These changes include the growing consciousness of humanity as a single global community, the unacceptable destructiveness of war, increased interconnectedness in all fields, the importance of human rights, both as norms and as laws, and above all, new forms of overlapping political authority, often described as global governance, that involves states, international institutions, as well as civil society and, indeed, networks of individuals. There may be cases where the use of force is justifiable to protect individuals against violent crime or human rights violations, but only within a new ethical framework that could underpin the new forms of overlapping political authority. And even in those cases it is necessary to define the limitations of the use of force, the relevant authorisation, and the acceptable justifications. Global civil society seems to

The state's monopoly over 'legitimate' violence is questioned by global civil society Teun Voten/Panos Pictures

us to be the main medium through which such an ethical framework can be developed and sustained.

In developing this argument, we start with some general methodological considerations and we then explore the ways in which Western and Islamic scholars have traditionally approached the issues of war and peace, violence and civility. We have focused on these traditions both because of our own backgrounds and because of the global centrality of the widely debated notion of a clash between the West and Islam. However, we are aware of the need for a fuller investigation of other traditions to develop a complex comparative approach, as well as a global overlapping consensus within global civil society on these questions. In particular, it is important to build on the Gandhian tradition of non-violence (An-Na'im 2002). In the final section, we propose ways of re-conceptualising civility in a global era, building on both Western and Islamic traditions.

Framing the debate:
some methodological considerations

There are important methodological and philosophical issues at stake when thinking about the concepts of

war and peace, violence and civility. These require extensive elaboration beyond what can be done in this chapter. However, we can at least outline some of the directions of thinking that might be fruitful to develop.

The *first* issue is the pressing need to assess the historical legacy of the monopoly of the nation state over the use of 'legitimate' violence. This was supposed to be a 'civilising' process, which would curb violence (civil war and violent crime) within the borders of the nation state. Aggressive and destructive instincts are tamed by restriction and order, and this is what 'civilisation' as a historical and sociological process attempted to achieve (Elias 2000; Freud 1961). But it gave rise to new forms of external violence on a scale and of a degree of cruelty that are almost too horrific to grasp – two world wars and the modern practice of genocide. If the nation state with its monopoly over 'legitimate' violence was capable of placing its subjects under a permanent cloud of threatened violence, from either real or invented enemies, or from its own apparatus, can we then continue to consider this monopoly 'civilising'? Should it not instead be considered a new form of barbarity? (Keane 1996: 35–44; 1998: 124–7; Albrow 1996: 56–64; Zerzan 2005).

There is a powerful case for questioning the state's monopoly of 'legitimate' violence, not so that non-state actors can use violence freely to pursue their goals, but so that the use of force by the state itself can be placed under greater constraints. The strengthening of international law and prohibitions on war during the last half century has paralleled the emergence of global civil society. The rule of law, as Arendt pointed out, depends on legitimacy, and that legitimacy is manufactured by civil society. Whereas international law was previously largely based on a balance of power between states, today a global public opinion involving citizens' groups, global media and individuals is helping to revise the notion of legitimacy as a phenomenon restricted to the national level. Measures such as the establishment of an International Criminal Court, which hold decision makers accountable for policies that result in genocide, mass destruction of cities and their heritage, and massive casualties and death among civilians, are important steps towards holding states accountable, legally as well as morally; and such measures are often the consequence of civic ideas, campaigns and pressures (Glasius 2005). In other words, the question is not only how to challenge the nation state's monopoly of 'legitimate' violence, because this could increase the risk of privatised violence, but also how new agents, such as civil society entities and networks, can monitor the state's use of this power and take over the 'civilising' role at this crucial moment of human history, and how they can deliberate in a democratic manner about the best strategies to achieve this goal. To put it another way, can such agents live up to the promise of 'civilisation', which the nation state has failed to fulfil historically?

The *second* issue has to do with language. The very notion of violence and the various categories used to describe violence are ambiguous. A distinction is drawn between war (legitimate) and terrorism (illegitimate). The word 'terrorism' is used to describe any opposition group that uses force to challenge any established authority, be it an authoritarian nation state apparatus in the Third World or forces of occupation such as the Israeli army in the Palestinian Occupied Territory or the Russian army in Chechnya. But it is not used to describe the terrifying consequences of air strikes that kill hundreds of civilians. There are, of course, many different and contradictory definitions of terrorism, and this is why

it is so easy for all sides to exploit the term for rhetorical purposes (Tuman 2003: 1–29). We need to explore not only the language describing violence, but also the ways in which language itself is violent, violating and volatile in many contexts (Lecercle 1990).

Habermas has drawn attention to the important role that language plays in masking political interests with apparently sophisticated concepts such as the 'clash of civilisations'. Violence, he indicates, can be the result of distortion in communication and the misuse of concepts, such as war, to describe military acts against terrorism. He argues that the rhetorical use of such terms makes it difficult to retain any definite meaning. It also obscures structural forms of violence that are embedded in the modern condition and that are rarely addressed. These structural forms of violence make communication within the public sphere and across public spheres in inter-cultural relations extremely difficult, blocking any fruitful dialogue that might contribute to the construction of a common language. Indeed, Carl Schmitt's (1932/1990) definition of politics as self-assertion against the Other has actually gained more currency, resulting only in more violence (see Box 1.2). Hence violence can be seen as a form (or a manifestation) of distorted communication. As a result, Habermas sees language, and communicative and practical legal and political arrangements that foster a notion of shared humanity, as essential to achieving peace (Habermas 2003: 35–43, 63–9).

The ideas of Habermas can help us reconstruct the concept of terrorism by linking it to the threats it poses to democracy. Democracy is the means and end of individual and social emancipation, and it is the context that allows citizens to make public use of their reason, and reach autonomy of judgement and freedom, concepts that Habermas draws from the Kantian tradition. Terrorism is a threat not only to order and legitimacy but also to the emerging cosmopolitan public sphere, which is becoming increasingly vulnerable with the processes of globalisation. Terrorism exploits this vulnerability to target civilians and perform terrorist acts, using the human body as a weapon if necessary (Habermas 2003: 51–7). The language of the 'war on terror' reinforces the vulnerability of the cosmopolitan public sphere; it magnifies fear and squeezes the space for free speech and the public use of reason. It thus ends up serving the cause of the terrorist.

Box 1.1: Violence and force in civil society

The assumption that violence will succeed where all else, including non-violent strategies, has failed, often leads people to use violence as a misguided 'last resort'. But this confidence is misplaced and not borne out by history: violence only generates more destruction, feeding into an uncontrollable cycle.

Violence and force are not the same thing. Non-violence is sometimes described as a 'force more powerful' because, as examples from Russia, India, Poland, the Philippines and Chile show, non-violence is the force represented by the governed, whose consent is crucial for the maintenance of power by those ostensibly in control over them.

Strategic non-violent action (or force) does not involve threats or physical harm to individuals or societies. Not only is it legitimate for civil society to use force, but this is part of its role, particularly in order to promote justice, resist oppression and prevent exploitation. Strikes, civil disobedience and massive demonstrations are forms of force that do not involve violence, but that seek or attempt to achieve a particular course of action. The main component of a non-violent strategy is the removal or shifting of the pillars of power that maintain an unjust situation. I would argue that force is one of the key tools of civil society, and its use is legitimate. However, justifications for the use of violence are contestable.

The porosity of the term 'civil society' poses both problems and solutions to the issue of whether it is ever legitimate for non-state actors to use violence. The distinction between civil society actors, state actors and religious resistance movements is blurred. Is civil society a 'normative moral order'? (Chandhoke 2002: 36). Is the 'civility' of civil society 'determined by its commitment to abstain from the use of force'? (Ezzat 2005: 44). Are civil society actors 'the keepers of a moral conscience that applies across borders'? (Chandhoke 2002: 41). Or are they simply 'those dimensions of social life which cannot be confounded with or swallowed up in, the state'? (Taylor 1990: 95).

Can we leave all questions of violence, military intervention and military security to the state, on the basis that it is contradictory to link civil society and violence? Do civil society actors become delegitimised by using violence? Perhaps the answer to this question depends on the end uses of violence: is the use of violence legitimate when it is not part of the values of the organisation, for example in collective self-defence against a terror threat, but illegitimate if it is a central methodology of resistance?

When it comes to state violence or uncaring governments, does not their hostility demand a violent reaction by civil society in order to end oppression? Civil society could be seen to have an obligation to redress such injustice by the use of violence; conversely it could be seen as a role model for citizens' movements, standing up against the use of violence on principle. If violence is legitimate in certain cases, then where should the limits be, and who should define and monitor them?

If civil society merely fills the space between the state and the market, and its goals are social and political rather than moral, perhaps violent resistance groups should not be considered part of civil society, making their use of violence irrelevant to this discussion. However, their use of violence can never be irrelevant because violence inevitably causes harm, and goes against social and political aims. If two opposing groups use violent strategies to further their respective causes, what is to prevent them continuing to use violence in future? They are part of a cycle of violence that does not only cause casualties but creates a culture of fear, intimidation and manipulation. Violence reduces people's choices and denies much of what civil society is struggling to achieve, whether in terms of poverty reduction, social welfare, maintenance of human rights, or recognition of minority rights.

If civil society is about 'men and women making the transition from subject to citizen', then the use of violence is contradictory because brutality maintains people in a state of dependence, insecurity and fear. By contrast, non-violence ends dependence and empowers people. Non-violent action, which is based on respect for oneself and others, and on agency, requires working collaboratively, and helping people to deal with their fears so that they have the courage to act non-violently. In this way it develops a sense of security, as well as the ability to act on behalf of the collective rather than the individual.

There remains the issue of values and their application: are the values of global civil society too narrow if civility is linked to secular rationalism and excludes religious groups? Or, if global civil society is inclusive, are its values too broad? In the spirit of democracy, is civil society obliged to include that which goes against its values – and thereby risk self-destruction? Perhaps there is a way to heal the body politic with a holistic approach – a process of detoxification that helps organisations which use violence to address their grievances in a different way. We need to transform violence.

It is not only a question of defining limits and proscribing some organisations from civil society on the grounds that they use violence. We are interconnected, and increasingly so, by the general erosion of borders. Global civil society contains violent and peaceful elements, and it essential to acknowledge this and also that violence remains an inherent possibility for all of us. In any conflict, a major dynamic is the projection of negative characteristics onto adversaries, and the retreat into fantasies of perfection and righteousness. Is it better to exclude violent groups to keep civil society 'pure' or to acknowledge them as members of civil society with a different set of values?

Would global civil society be able to prevent a major threat of terror through the use of violence? Should activists try to eliminate the threat themselves or collaborate with state mechanisms? But what if there was insufficient time? For example, should a civil society group use violence against someone it discovered was about to launch a terrorist attack? Would it be possible to prevent abuses of this use of violence? There is a danger of setting precedents and loosening criteria. For example, legitimising for self-defence, even in extreme cases of provocation, raises questions of how self-defence is defined, what burden of proof is required, and who determines these issues.

One solution may be to acknowledge that there are situations when violence can be excused, although its use should never be legitimised. Refraining from violence, and its legitimisation, prevents the unleashing of further destruction.

Violence is not only anathema to the values of civil society, it undermines much of what civil society represents. Therefore the use of violence delegitimises civil society, by making it uncivil and denying its values and its goals. However, it is essential to include organisations that advocate violence for just political ends within civil society – so that they can be encouraged to move way from using violence. While the violent actions of civil society organisations are illegitimate, the actors themselves are not. They may use force, but do so illegitimately and without the approval of other actors. Through education and a culture of non-violence and peace, they can and must be encouraged to use different tools to reach their goals.

Lucy Nusseibeh, Director, Middle East Non-Violence and Democracy (MEND)

The *third* issue has to do with the cultural dimension of violence and terrorism. There is a tendency, especially in the West, to adopt a spaceless and timeless conception of culture, that is linked either to individual identity or to the belief system – mainly religion. Islam is often characterised as a religion that is prone to radicalisation and political instrumentalism, yet extremism and fundamentalism can be found in all religions and cultures, as well as secular ideologies like socialism or neo-liberalism (Juergensmeyer 2000; Eck 2005: 21–47; Piscatori et al. 2004).

Since the early 1990s the notion of a 'clash of civilisations' has become an increasingly dominant paradigm (Huntington 1993; Lewis 1990; 1993). This concept provides an implicit underpinning to both terror and the 'war on terror'. After 9/11, the space for more nuanced interpretations of culture was squeezed. Indeed, some neo-conservatives made deliberate efforts to silence critical voices, especially on university campuses (Kramer 2001; and see Campus Watch URL). Scholars that convey a more complex interpretation of the nature of Islam, revise historical assumptions about relations between Islam and Christianity and the West, encourage reconciliation, or even devise innovative and constructive concepts such as 'Islamo-Christian civilization' (Bulliet 2004), which would facilitate multicultural and cosmopolitan debates in order to build an overlapping global concept of civility, have been marginalised in the polarising rhetoric of the 'war on terror'. The questioning that is essential for understanding is seen as unpatriotic. Very little has been written about the Muslim contribution to the formation of the moral and ethical foundations of the international system (Waltz 2002). Ideas and hypotheses that advocate exclusion and conflict are more likely to attract media coverage because they are more controversial, and therefore newsworthy.

Modernity laid claim to exclusive rights over the course of history – the history of the rise of the West. In the global era, superpower hegemony has not only over-militarised the management of international relations but has also laid claim to a single definition of civility that denies the plurality of many cultures (Sen 2006). This is why the control of violence on a transnational basis can be conceived only as part of a far-reaching cultural transformation in which the duties and rights of citizenship are redefined in cosmopolitan terms.

The *fourth* issue concerns the actual context of violence. Indeed, any attempt to locate the cultural dimension in a specific context is usually dismissed as 'justifying' violence. But efforts to explain are not the same as justification. Much has been written about the modernist urban nature of violence in late capitalism, and this should be integrated into contemporary analyses of political violence. There is a general tendency to link poverty with extremism: poverty creates vulnerable people who may be easy recruits for terrorists. Yet this assumption overlooks the fact that a substantial number of the members of Al-Qaeda come from rich families, including Bin Laden and Al-Zawahri.

Recent literature has noted that the wars in our era are mainly conducted in cosmopolitan spaces. Martin Shaw asserts that modern warfare targets cities, and has used historical evidence to show the existence of a link between 'urbicide' and 'genocide' (Shaw 2004: 145–53). In the global cities of the North as well as the urban conglomerates overwhelming many poorer countries, rapid migration has created a new population, consisting to a significant extent of people who have fled violence and poverty in their own countries, and who remain attached to their homelands and ill at ease with the politics and society of their new habitat. The tendency for social violence in cities is compounded by the fact that scenes of violence form part of the visual sphere of urban life, whether these are represented in the media or other forms of entertainment.

Urban life has been romanticised ever since the early stages of the Enlightenment and modernity. Today, terms like 'multiculturalism' and 'hybrid identities' are used to describe the global character of cities (Al-Sayyad 2001: 1–18). Yet hybridity does not necessarily mean tolerance and can contain the seeds of ethnic and religious antagonism as much as more positive, syncretic practices. Moreover, hybridity is not only about mixing cultures from different geographical spaces; it is also about mixing cultures over different time periods (Albrow 1996: 10–11). Thus, marginalised religious doctrines from earlier ages that have long been abandoned by the majority of adherents are resurrected and incorporated into contemporary conflicts. Urban informality is celebrated by many as a sphere in which ideas and values are created, and as an opportunity to design

Multicultural cities may produce antagonism and alienation as much as more positive, syncretic practices °Justin Jin/Panos Pictures

and choose individual, self-fulfilling identities. Thus urban informality allows freedom from dominant cultural norms but it can also produce violent and alienated dogmas (Al-Sayyad 2004: 7–30).

War and peace in Islamic and Western traditions

In her classic essay 'Reflections on Violence', Hannah Arendt (1969) argues that power and violence are opposites. Power depends on legitimacy and all governments need legitimacy. Normally legitimacy is based on a rule of law and some sort of consent. 'Power springs up whenever people get together and act in concert but it derives its legitimacy from the initial getting together rather than from any action that may follow.' In other words, power derives from a sort of social contract. Even tyrants need some sort of consent, argues Arendt (1969), because they need the army and police to obey them. Reigns of terror, like Nazi Germany or Stalinist Russia, can only succeed through permanently atomising all form of opposition ('an outrageously pale academic word for the horror it implies') and destroying any possible nascent form of power. 'Violence can destroy power', says Arendt, 'but it is utterly incapable of creating it.'

This notion that power and violence are opposites

echoes similar distinctions that are to be found in both classical Islamic thought and in the ideas of the European Enlightenment. Classical Islamic thought distinguished between the realm of Islam *dar al-Islam* and the realm of war *dar al-harb*. The realm of Islam was a community characterised by a political authority, whose authority derived from the rule of law *Shari'a* and a social contract *Bay'a*. Islam was a system of values contained in the *Qu'ran* and the *Hadith* (the sayings and practises of Prophet Mohammed) and interpreted by scholars *Ulama*. It was based on a notion of human reason, later taken up in Enlightenment thought, which was derived from individual knowledge or awareness of God's will that is imprinted on human consciousness. Within the realm of Islam, the use of force was condemned because violence causes instability, challenges the legacy of the elected authority and results in chaos and civil war (*Bagh'ii, Fitnah*). The towering Shafi'i jurist, Abu al-Hasan al-Mawardi (d. 450/1058), includes among the definitions of the realm of Islam (*dar al-Islam*) not only legal conditions but also human and socio-political security dimensions; thus he defined the realm of Islam as any land in which a Muslim enjoys security and is able to protect himself, even if he is unable to promote the religion (Jackson

Box 1.2: Towards an agonistic multipolar world order

In *The Return of the Political* (1993) and in *The Democratic Paradox* (2000) I have proposed to distinguish between 'the political' and 'politics': the political refers to the dimension of antagonism which is inherent in all human societies, while politics refers to the ensemble of practices, discourses and institutions aiming at establishing a certain order and organising human coexistence, in conditions which are always potentially conflictual because they are affected by the dimension of 'the political'. I have argued that it is only when we acknowledge this dimension of the political and understand that politics consists in domesticating hostility and trying to defuse the potential antagonism that exists in social relations that one can pose the fundamental question for democratic politics. This question is not how to arrive at a consensus without exclusion, which is indeed an impossibility. Politics aims at the creation of unity in a context of conflict and diversity; it is always concerned with the creation of a 'we' by the determination of a 'them'. The novelty of democratic politics is not the overcoming of the we–them distinction but the different way in which it is established. The crucial issue is to establish it in a way which is compatible with pluralism. This presupposes that the 'them' are no longer seen as 'enemies' to be destroyed but as 'adversaries' against whose hegemony we are going to struggle but whose right to defend their ideas we will never question. I use the term 'agonism' to designate the relation among adversaries to distinguish it from 'antagonism', which is the relation among enemies. Following this distinction we could then say that the aim of democratic politics is to transform antagonism into agonism.

My aim so far has been to bring to the fore the consequences of the dominant post-political approach for the workings of democratic politics. In my view, the incapacity of liberalism to acknowledge the political in its antagonistic dimension constitutes a very serious obstacle to grasping the task of democratic politics and the necessity of providing an agonistic public sphere where passions could be mobilised towards democratic objectives and where antagonisms could find an agonistic outlet. The absence of an adversarial form of confrontation leads either to apathy and disaffection with the democratic system or to the emergence of collective identities which are not conducive to a democratic form of negotiation.

Can this agonistic model be useful in the field of international politics? Are there lessons to be learned from recent international events about the consequences of not acknowledging the dimension of the political? How can we make sense of September 11 and the multiplication of terrorist attacks within the agonistic framework? What could a properly political approach tell us about the antagonisms which have emerged in recent years? Those are the questions that I want to examine, and I take my bearings from Carl Schmitt, in whose work we can find many insights that help us to grasp the causes of our present predicament. For instance, Schmitt was concerned about the possible consequences of the establishment of a unipolar world order. After the Second World War, he devoted many of his reflections to the decline of the political in its modern form and the loss by the state of its monopoly of the political. This was linked, in his view, to the dissolution of the 'Jus Publicum Europaeum', the inter-state European law which for three centuries had made possible what he calls, in *Der Nomos der Erde* (1974), 'eine Hegung des Krieges' ('limitation of war'). He was worried about the consequences of this loss of monopoly because he feared that the decline of the state was creating the conditions for an 'international civil war'. How could one envisage an alternative to international civil war? What kind of order could replace the Jus Publicum Europaeum? Those questions were at the centre of Schmitt's preoccupations in several writings of the 1950s and early 1960s, where he discussed the possibility of a new 'Nomos of the Earth'. In an article from 1952 he examined how the dualism created by the Cold War and the polarisation between capitalism and communism could evolve, and imagined several possible scenarios. He rejected the idea that such a dualism was only the prelude to a final unification of the world, resulting from the victory of one of the antagonists, which would have managed to impose its system and its ideology worldwide. According to him, the more promising evolution would be the opening of a dynamics of pluralisation whose outcome could be the establishment of a new global order based on the existence of several autonomous regional blocs. This would provide the conditions for an equilibrium of forces among various large spaces, instituting among them a new system of international law. Such an equilibrium would present similarities with the old Jus Publicum Europaeum, except that in this case it would be truly global and not only Europocentric.

Schmitt did not believe that the existing dualism could last and he considered that, by establishing a 'true pluralism', only a multipolar world order could provide the institutions necessary to manage conflicts and avoid the negative consequences resulting from the pseudo-universalism arising from the generalisation of one single system. He was, however, very aware that such a pseudo-universalim was a much more likely outcome that the pluralism he advocated. And unfortunately his fears have been confirmed since the collapse of communism.

Since September 11 Schmitt's reflections on the status of a 'post-statist politics' have become more relevant than ever, and I believe that they can help us grasp the nature of the new forms of terrorism. As Jean-François Kervégan (2002) has suggested, they allow us to approach the issue of global terrorism in a very different way from the one currently accepted, that is, as the work of isolated groups of fanatics. Following Schmitt, the emergence of global terrorism can be seen as the product of a new configuration of the political which is characteristic of the type of world order being implemented around the hegemony of a single hyper-power.

I submit that Schmitt's insights about the dangers of a unipolar world order are really important for envisaging the challenge with which we are confronted today. There is no doubt a correlation between the now unchallenged power of the United States and the proliferation of terrorist groups. Of course, in no way do I want to pretend that this is the only explanation. Terrorism has always existed, and it reflects a multiplicity of factors. But it is undeniable that it tends to flourish in circumstances in which there are no legitimate political channels for the expression of grievances. It is therefore no coincidence that, since the end of the Cold War, with the imposition of a neo-liberal model of globalisation under the dominance of the United States, we have witnessed a significant increase in terrorist attacks. Even liberal theorists like Richard Falk and Andrew Strauss – who argue in favour of a cosmopolitan order – have acknowledged the link between terrorism and the present world order when they say:

With the possibility of direct and formalised participation in the international system foreclosed, frustrated individuals and groups (especially when their own governments are viewed as illegitimate and hostile) have been turning to various modes of civic resistance, both peaceful and violent. Global terrorism is at the violent end of this spectrum of transnational protest, and its apparent agenda may be mainly driven by religious, ideological and regional goals rather than by resistance directly linked to globalisation. But its extremist alienation is partly, at the very least, an indirect result of globalising impacts that may be transmuted in the political unconscious of those so afflicted into grievances associated with cultural injustices. (2003: 206)

The situation we are currently facing in the international arena is in many respects similar to the one in domestic politics which, as I have argued, explains the increasing success of right-wing populist parties: the absence of a real pluralism entails the impossibility of conflicts around the hegemonic order to find legitimate forms of expression. What is at stake in both cases is the negation of the dimension of the political and the belief that the aim of politics – be it at the national or the international level – is to establish consensus on one single model, thereby foreclosing the possibility of legitimate dissent. No wonder that, when conflicts explode, they take antagonistic forms, putting into question the very basis of the existing order.

Under such an approach, it is the lack of political channels for challenging the hegemony of the neo-liberal model of globalisation that is at the root of the proliferation of discourses and practices which, like recent forms of global terrorism, manifest a radical negation of the established order. This should warn us against the dangers arising from the delusions of the universalist globalist discourse which postulates that human progress requires the establishment of world unity based on the implementation of the Western model. Against the illusion of the universalist humanitarians to the effect that antagonisms could be eliminated by a unification of the world that would be achieved transcending the political, conflict and negativity, it is worth listening to Schmitt when he reminds us that 'The political world is a pluriverse, not a universe' (1976: 53).

Chantal Mouffe, Professor of Political Theory, Centre for the Study of Democracy, University of Westminster

DELEGITIMISING VIOLENCE

2002: 37). This is one of the definitions used by contemporary scholars to explain why Muslims in the West should be loyal to the nation states in which they live, even if those countries are not Muslim majority countries. The realm of war referred to an arena of irrationality and ignorance where there was no single political authority, and tribal conflict was endemic; and it was vis-à-vis foreign political enemies that war was permitted under certain circumstances.

This distinction between the realm of Islam and the realm of war was paralleled by the distinction between civil society and the state of nature in Enlightenment thought. Civil society, like the realm of Islam, was a political community with a single political authority, based on a rule of law and a social contract. Indeed, the Arabic term for civil society, *Almujtamaa Almadani*, derives both from the word for city and from Medina, the city where Mohammed first established his Islamic society/city state. The state of nature was an arena without any political authority, where man was more or less prone to violence, depending on the assumptions about human nature of different Enlightenment thinkers. For a pessimist like Hobbes, it was 'war of all against all' but for Locke violence arose when there was no way of arbitrating differences of interpretation of the law of nature (understood as God's will imprinted on human consciousness).

It is sometimes argued that civil society is different from this concept of Islamic society because it is a secular notion that can apply to all human beings. But Islam was also a universal creed that claimed global relevance to any human community; hence we find the *Qu'ran* addressing 'mankind' in many verses with ideas related to human nature and principles calling for inter-cultural and inter-religious dialogue and coexistence. In practice, however, both were bounded concepts. Civil society was bounded by territory and Islamic society was bounded by belief and by territory, even if it adopted some measures of religious pluralism. Within these communities, there was a presumption of non-violence, a notion of peace with justice, and this was contrasted with the external world of violence. In both systems of thought, war against the external world was generally justified, although there were thinkers with different ideas, as discussed below.

For Ibn Khaldun, the fourteenth century historian, the only legitimate wars were *Jihad* and wars to suppress internal rebellions. The word *Jihad* is often referred to as the Islamic doctrine of holy war, yet in the *Qur'an* it is used to describe the struggle for the ultimate virtues of Islam, in the sense of testimony, as in Christian ethics; and the word used to describe military affairs is *Qital*, which was governed by strict laws of war. Thus, *Jihad* is not necessarily a violent act; on the contrary it is first and foremost a peaceful endeavour and struggle. Indeed, *Jihad* was not understood by the majority of scholars as a military term, and there were very few voices that made the case for war against an enemy for the mere reason of their disbelief (*Kufr*). The majority, including prominent scholars and established *Ulama* over centuries, such as Imam Abu Hanifa, Imam Malik, Muhammad Al-Hassan Al-Shaybani, Imam Al-Awzaii, Muhammad Ibn Rushd, Ibn Taymiyyah and Ibn Qayyin Al-Jawziyyah, made judicial rulings against going to war in order to bring about the conversion of non-Muslims (Kalin 2005: 345).

Ibn Khaldun's point is that external wars are legitimate only when they are *Jihad*. According to classical Islam, a war is *Jihad* only when people refuse to allow Muslims to call freely for their faith in the territory of a respective non-Muslim political entity, or refuse to submit to the legal rules of the Islamic community domestically by resorting to armed dissent. Among Shi'ites, and the majority of Sunni Muslim schools of jurisprudence, an external war was legitimate only in self-defence, to defend rather than to extend the Muslim community. Peace, that is, the repelling of aggression rather than conversion to Islam, was the ultimate aim of fighting. This is clearly indicated by several verses throughout the *Qur'an* that clearly envisage a terminus *ad quem* other than conversion or annihilation. Whether Muslim rulers abided by these rules was, of course, largely a matter of political calculation rather than religious doctrine. Indeed, in the period of classical Islam societies were much more tolerant than the Christian West. Throughout the Middle Ages, one could live as a Jew in Morocco, a Christian in Cairo, or even a Zoroastrian in Shiraz, but one could not live as a Muslim in Paris or London (Jackson 2002).

In classical Islamic thought, for war to be classified as *Jihad* it must have a legitimate cause, namely, the extension or defence of the Islamic community, and be authorised by a legitimate authority, either the Caliph, who was both a religious and a political

°Mark Henley/Panos Pictures

authority in the early years of Islam, or a political authority, such as the Sultan. Most importantly, it has to be fought justly. Indeed, Islamic jurists were much more preoccupied with what in the West is known as *jus in bello*, the means to be employed, than with the issue of legitimate cause. These rules were more strict in wars against dissenting Muslim groups than non-believers; nevertheless, there developed strong codes about the treatment of prisoners and non-combatants in all wars. In particular, 'torture, mutilation and treachery were strictly forbidden'. As was cutting down trees – hence the title of this chapter (Al-Fadl 1999: 156).

In the Western tradition, 'just war' is sharply distinguished from 'holy war'. And yet a closer inspection of the meaning of the terms suggest that just war, in the Western tradition, is closer to what classical Islamic thinkers meant by *Jihad* than the term 'holy war'. St Augustine, the father of just war theory, was primarily concerned about restoration of the moral order. In Christian teachings on just war, the notion of neighbourly love and the protection of others was an important element. War was necessary, according to St Augustine, in order to 'curb licentious passions by destroying those vices which should have been rooted

out and suppressed by the rightful government' (quoted in Langan 1994: 12). According to John Langan, this 'punitive' concept of war overrides self-defence. For St Augustine, war can be authorised only by a public authority for public purposes – it is about the protection of others. Thus obedience to a rightful authority is central to his thinking, and individuals, even if they reject temporal rulings, have no right to resist. A just war also excludes passion and revenge. Following St Augustine, medieval scholars, particularly Aquinas, viewed just cause as righting an injury or a fault caused by others. In the twentieth century, just cause has come to be associated only with defensive wars – wars against aggression (Walzer 1992).

Just war was distinguished from holy war in that it was authorised by secular authorities and recognised certain *in bello* restraints. These restraints, later to be incorporated into international humanitarian law, included notions of proportionality (the means used had to be proportional to the ends – what would be gained by victory), discrimination, especially the combatant/non-combatant distinctions, rules about the treatment of prisoners and rules outlawing certain types of weapons. Holy war, by contrast, could be authorised by religious authorities and was waged

DELEGITIMISING VIOLENCE

29

In the 1980s Muslim intellectuals had not been paying attention to the international context and therefore, in the aftermath of the assassination in 1981 of Egyptian President Anwar Sadat, they were astonished to read the letter about 'neglected duty' by Abdul Salam Faraj, founder of *Jama'at al-Jihad*, the radical group responsible for the assassination. What I mean by the international context is the emergence, during the Vietnam War, of a 'just war' literature, whether for or against the concept, by authors such as Michael Walzer (1992). At the same time, ideas of 'revolutionary violence' (armed struggle) and the 'people's continuous war' were also being invoked and debated between the traditional left and the new left. The parallels between these seemingly separate debates were not fully grasped by Muslim scholars at the time.

This glorification of violence was striking, for three reasons. First is the association of violence with morality rather than necessity. This was evident in the late US President Ronald Reagan's 'evil empire' slogan with reference to the Soviet Union. It is also apparent in President Bush's presentation of the 'war on terror' as a war between right and wrong, good and evil. Second, violence is associated with religion. Just war is an old Christian concept, invoked in the late 1970s and revisited in the aftermath of September 11. Of course, its Islamic counterpart is the concept of *Jihad*, which was reintroduced about the same time and given military connotations, as distinct from its earlier spiritual, ethical and religious associations. Third, the three main proponents of violence – Islamic fundamentalists, neo-leftists and evangelicals – were not satisfied with the way international law and international organisations treated the issue. They criticised the international community's reluctance to intervene militarily in conflicts for the benefit of the oppressed, and its submission to great powers that might or might not intervene on the basis of their own interests and concerns. For evangelicals and neo-conservatives, this perceived incapacity of the United Nations justified US unilateral military intervention; for Islamic and leftist revolutionaries it was reason enough to engage in violence without waiting for the state or the international community.

Faraj's letter about 'neglected duty' raised several new issues pertinent to the evolution of the concept of *Jihad* during the 1970s. According to the traditional Sunni perspective, *Jihad* is a mandatory, but not an individual, duty. Therefore, to neglect *Jihad* is to neglect one of the pillars of Islam, which at the same time holds that *Jihad* becomes an individual duty in the case of self-defence against aggression.

Faraj had not added a new dimension to the interpretation of the concept. He argued for an extension of Jihad from defence against external aggression to internal struggle. In other words, he legitimised the resort to violence against a ruler and his associates. In so doing, he went all the way back to the interpretation of Ibn Taymiya, Ibn Al Kayyim and Ibn Kathir, medieval scholars who doubted some rulers' adherence to Islam due to their submission to and/or cooperation with invaders during the crusades and the invasions of the Moguls. Thereafter, the tendency to judge rulers to be infidels spread beyond some extremist groups to reach wide social classes, as a consequence of the growing influence of Wahhabi Salafism on Islamists in general during the 1970s and the 1980s. Salafis pay close attention to the precision of jurisprudent rulings, and they maintain a much closer association between faith and action than do traditional groups and certainly the 'Muslim Brotherhood' between the 1930s and the 1950s.

Since it is legitimate now to engage in *Jihad* against a state considered to be infidel, the third traditional Islamic condition legitimising *Jihad* no longer holds for Faraj. This condition pertains to *Jihad* always being waged by the state and always against external aggressors. And if the purpose is to resist an invader, it is legitimate for any individual to defend his land or country without permission from the state. Now *Jihad* could be pursued against the state in a modern context, according to Faraj's interpretation. Instead of delegating to political authorities, individual initiative triggered many responses against the state and also had international implications as, for example, when Muslim individuals and groups joined the *Jihad* in Afghanistan against the Russian occupation without seeking permission from their respective nation states.

The war in Afghanistan against the 'infidel' Soviet invaders bolstered the classical Islamic interpretation of *Jihad* in which everyone was devoted to fighting these occupiers of Islamic land. It is also known that Egyptian members of the Organization of *Jihad (Tandhim Al Jihad)* and the Islamic group *(Jama'a Islamiya)* that fought in Afghanistan continued in parallel to engage in operations against the state inside Egypt during the 1980s and the 1990s. It may be noted that they used the term *Jihad* in their press releases and on the Internet more in connection with the Egyptian state than with the Russians and the Americans. Yet a religious and political debate about *Jihad* took place in the rank and file of these organisations which continued to legitimise it only against rulers and their associates.

If the war in Afghanistan moved Islamic extremists away from the phase of internal *Jihad* towards that of external *Jihad*, it was the emergence of Jihadi Salafism *(salafia jihadiya)* that brought about another development around the mid-1990s. The term 'Jihadi Salafism' was first introduced by Sheikh Abdullah Azzam, a prominent Jordanian militant leader who joined the war in Afghanistan around 1987. It seems that it was intended to unify Arab and non-Arab Salafis in Afghanistan on the eve of the Russian withdrawal. Yet the term quickly proliferated, appearing in Bin Laden's press releases and then in the public statements of Algerian fighters between 1994 and 1997. However, Bin Laden and Algerian Salafis were later to disagree on priorities. Whereas Bin Laden gave priority to fighting external enemies, Algerian Salafis believed that they must first struggle against the infidel Algerian government and its associates and against those Algerians who did not rise up against the state. Consequently, Algeria experienced a long and fierce civil war after the Islamists' victory in the democratic elections was annulled by the state.

An event that occurred during the autumn of 2002, when I was teaching at Harvard, is relevant to this discussion. The Director of the Institute for American Values, together with 60 other American intellectuals, issued a statement addressed to Islamic intellectuals in which they asserted that the 'war on terror' was a just war (Institute for American Values 2002). After about a year of dialogue and debate, Arab and American scholars met in Malta to discuss various issues, among them that of just war (see Blankenhorn et al. 2005). While we moved towards agreement on several issues, including that of Palestine, we could only disagree on the issue of just war. I recall one debate between Abdullah Wald Abah from Mauritania and Jamal Baroutt from Syria on one side, and Johnson and Novak on the other. Johnson argued that a defensive war was a just war, and Wald Abah and Baroutt agreed. But there was disagreement about the definition of a defensive war. The two Arabs – one a religious scholar, the other a writer – held that a defensive war was one considered as such by international law, and would include national liberation struggles and wars waged against external aggressors. The Americans argued that a just war was defined by moral values. They went on to say that some international laws were just plain wrong while others were ineffective. Of course, that was not going to pass without a reply from the Arabs present in the meeting, who cited the Charter of the United Nations in 1945. To ignore it, and to argue ineffectiveness, was simply unacceptable. Five days after September 11, the UN Security Council unanimously adopted a resolution to attack Al-Qaeda in Afghanistan. Several nations agreed with that, and they have maintained their support, despite the fact the US went beyond the resolution by overthrowing the Afghan government and replacing it with armed gangs which it had itself contributed to ejecting from power earlier on. Justifications for the war on Iraq framed in terms of morality and self-defence were even more biased. In reality Americans equate morals with what they understand to be their national interest.

In the past two years the rhetoric of *Jihad* and just war has faded. The *Jihad* of Bin Laden and the late Al-Zarqawi is no longer accepted by scholars or by the majority of Islamic movements. Moreover, proponents of just war on the Western side have stopped calling for it, having learned hard lessons from what is happening in Iraq. It remains to be seen what alternative concepts emerge on both sides to further legitimise violence, and how global civil society can respond by reclaiming the morality of peace from those who proclaim the morality of their wars.

Ridwan Al-Sayyed, Professor of Islamic Studies, Lebanese University, Beirut

Mural of St George in an Ethiopian church
© *Pietro Cenini/Panos Pictures*

'No matter how just their complaints, a peasants' victory would mean lawlessness, disorder, bloodshed and suffering.' Thus, the rebels should be treated not as soldiers but as criminals, and Luther urged the nobility to employ their armies to 'stab, kill and strangle' the peasants as though they were rabid beasts (Kelsay 1993: 79). It was only during the American civil war that rebels began to be treated according to the rules of war.

In the Islamic tradition, by contrast, binding regulations applied to wars between Muslims.

If Muslims fight one another, the fugitive and the wounded may not be dispatched. Muslim prisoners may not be executed and women may not be intentionally killed or imprisoned. Imprisoned male Muslims must be released once the fighting, or the danger of continued fighting, ends. Furthermore, the property of Muslims may not be taken as spoils, and any property taken must be returned after the cessation of fighting. Even more, means of mass destruction such as mangonels, flame throwers or flooding may not be used unless absolutely necessary. (Al-Fadl 1999: 144–5)

These rules applied only if the rebels were considered to have a plausible reason for fighting based on a valid interpretation of the Islamic sources (*Ta'wil*). Thus, tribal reasons or greed were not plausible. The rebels also had to be sufficiently powerful (*Shawka*).

As the jurists put it, without the requirement of Shawka, anarchy and lawlessness will spread...They contend that without the requirement of Shawka, every corrupt person will invent or fabricate a Ta'wil and claim to be a Baghii (a legitimate rebel). (Al-Fadl 1999: 148)

Hence, these established rules determined under what conditions the rebels could be considered as a party with whom one could negotiate and reach settlement.

Both the Bush administration and the global jihadists have distorted the injunctions contained in these traditions and indeed reduced them to cosmetic justifications. The 'war on terror' is supposed to be a just war. It is justified as a defensive war and, according to Rumsfeld, 'we are doing everything

against non-Christians. This is why the Crusades were so bloody. It was not because they were fought against non-Europeans; rather, the Crusaders believed themselves to be fighting a holy cause, which could not be restrained by *in bello* rules. When the Crusaders sacked Jerusalem, some 65,000 'heathens' were killed. The same thing happened during the Spanish Inquisition, when Muslims and Jews were expelled or exterminated during the wars that terminated Muslim rule in Andalusia, which also marked the end of the coexistence of the three faiths (*convivencia*). In the transition to modernity, scholars like Victoria and Grotius were, according to Turner Johnson (1981), responsible for the 'dethroning of religion'. Victoria, in particular, made the point that natural law, the law imprinted by God on our consciousness, applies to non-Christians such as American Indians. Grotius identified just cause with charity, by which he meant something akin to what nowadays we would call humanitarianism.

In both traditions, internal rebellions against a rightful authority are condemned. But whereas in the Islamic tradition restraints on war applied even more stringently, because internal rebellions involved conflicts among Muslims, in the Western tradition the opposite was the case. Luther's views on the German peasants' revolt (1524–5) have been widely quoted:

32

The treatment of prisoners at Guantanamo Bay belies the idea that the 'war on terror' is a just war °Joe Coulson/Panos Pictures

humanly possible to try to avoid collateral damage' (Crawford 2003: 13). If we take the just war tradition as the starting point, the 'war on terror' fails, on the criteria both of the treatment of prisoners and of proportionality. On the one hand, the administration implies that the word 'war' is justified because Al-Qaeda can be treated as an enemy akin to a state. On the other hand, any suspected terrorist is treated like Luther's peasants with neither the protection of the laws of war nor that of criminal justice. Civilian casualties caused by the wars in Iraq and Afghanistan, even if the United States has acted discriminately according to the standards of war, now far exceed the numbers killed in terrorist attacks, with little prospect of victory in sight. But one of the problems of the just war tradition is that it is always possible to argue that military necessity overrides *in bello* constraints.

Contemporary jihadists also have a very reductionist view of what Jihad means. For them, *Jihad* is a war for the extension of Muslim identity, with no restrictions or red lines like those observed by early Muslims (cutting people's throats in front of cameras is clearly un-Islamic for any lay Muslim), whereas for classical thinkers it had much more to do with the values and political system associated with the acceptance of Islam, the ideas rather than the identity of Muslims. Indeed, there is no such thing as a holy war in Islam, because no war is holy, and nothing is more sacred than human life. Likewise, the concept and function of the realm of Islam–realm of war dichotomy, which is

mentioned frequently as established doctrine upon which the legacy of war against the opposite abode was legitimate, has been grossly exaggerated and often misrepresented. The notion of *Jahilyya*, which characterises the pre-Islamic society (realm of war), refers in classical Islam to the ignorant and uncivilised conduct of those who do not know or understand the values of Islam, and who are prone to fighting among themselves and violating the rules of war set later by Muslims. One can even say that it refers to a non-civilised society, on the assumption that Islam laid the basis of a new civility. Just like everyone else, they are born with knowledge of God's will but have not yet learned how to recognise and use that knowledge. As pointed out above, *Jahilyya* strongly resembled the Enlightenment notion of the state of nature.

Fundamentalists use the term *Jalilyya* to describe modern Muslim societies, accusing them of not abiding by Islam; they call for a 'return to Islam', but what they mean is an Islam that they have reconstructed to a great extent against many of the civilised notions of early Islamic thought and practice. Moreover, the jihadists argue that each individual has the right to judge what is legitimate and that methods are also justified by necessity.

Such stretching of terms to the extent that they lose their meaning is unacceptable in Islamic jurisprudence, which has developed a very complex and sophisticated glossary, which is subject to strict regulation and management in actual political life (Kazemi 2004: 121–39). Even the word *Shahid*, used to describe a martyr, originally meant in the Koranic language 'upholding testimony' in the religious spiritual sense, and this is synonymous with the original meaning of *Jihad*.

The question that arises is how these concepts came to be distorted by militant Islamic groups in total contradiction to the long-established and authentic traditions of Islamic jurisprudence (Lumbard 2004). This is not just a matter of theology. The Islamic heritage includes not only the religious sciences, as some scholars have rightly observed, but a wealth of rational sciences that are not considered as opposites or mutually exclusive (Nasr 1999: 217–41; 2002: 235–84). Likewise, we also need to ask how the language of the 'war on terror' has instrumentalised both Christian and secular traditions of ethical thought about war and peace.

To what extent then can we recover notions of peace and civility that were developed within those traditions? Can we learn from these traditions and use their arguments to criticise the 'war on terror' and terror? Or does the distortion of these traditions reflect a new reality – the difficulty of applying these traditions in a global era? And if terrorism in Islamic jurisprudence is defined as 'publicly directed violence against which the reasonable citizen, Muslim or non-Muslim, is unable to take safe-keeping measures' (Jackson 2001: 227–51), how is it possible in the case of the modern use of weapons in a nuclear age to differentiate between war and terrorism? And if it is impossible to make the distinction, how can a jurisprudence of disarmament and non-proliferation be developed to save high Islamic virtues and humanity?

Recovering the concepts of peace and civility

The term 'civil society' seems to have lost the civilising connotations of ancient and Enlightenment meanings. It tends to be defined as a 'third sector', between the market and the state, and is often subsumed into emerging globalising concepts like 'governance'. Increasingly, it is being judged by criteria of efficiency and competitiveness that match the measures of success in business. And it is often considered desirable to bring civil society into partnership with the state, although it is not clear whether this will help to 'civilise' the state, or whether civil society will be co-opted by governmental policies and decisions that are far from being 'civilised'.

An exploration of the classical Islamic logic of civility might contribute to developing a more critical assessment of globalisation, help to foster civility in its original meaning and to curb violence. In Islam, violence and civility, or war and peace, are human social phenomena that are bound by time and context, and are both envisioned as part of the development of human history, though peace is seen as a virtue and a goal. War and the resort to violence are seen as an evil but, because they are expected to occur, pre-emptive measures should be taken to manage and minimise them, with the aim of reaching a peaceful settlement. This is a major logic running through many aspects of the *Shari'a*, whether ruling over personal disagreements within the family or violence erupting within the community and even in times of military conflict.

This thinking has many parallels with the ideas of civil society developed by Enlightenment thinkers such as John Locke and Adam Ferguson, as well as later thinkers such as Hegel. They understood civil society as a realm of conflict characterised, according to Hegel (1820/1942: 182A), by 'waves of every passion ...regulated only by reason glinting through'. They stressed the importance of a constitutional framework for managing conflicts, of the free use of public reason by autonomous groups and individuals, and of intermediate organisations that could channel grievances and voice criticism.

Yet Western notions of civil society applied only within the framework of the Western nation state. External policies ruthlessly turned away from notions of civility and indeed, as both Rousseau and Kant pointed out, constrained the development of civility at home. Moreover, the spread of colonialism and the rise of nation states according to the Western model subjected many of the structures of classical Islam to the straitjacket of colonial, or newly created, national authorities. Later, during the second half of the twentieth century, under the slogans of secularism adopted by despotic regimes, especially in the Middle East, the structures of classical Islam were further deconstructed or put directly under the control of the state.

While in some religious traditions the notion of peace seems to imply passivity, patience and the bearing of suffering, Islam introduces a notion of peace that advocates a moral responsibility to act dynamically against the menace of evil and destruction. Here, spiritual *Jihad* comes to the forefront as an individual and collective endeavour to protect and safeguard justice ('*Adl*), which is the ultimate goal of *Shari'a* and its core values (Hanafi 2002: 56–71; Kalin 2005: 327–33). Again, there is a close parallel with Enlightenment thinkers such as Adam Ferguson, who stressed the importance of active citizenship. Muslim scholars and philosophers, such as Al-Farabi, who can be compared to Kant in his search for a notion of universal peace, imagined a global notion of humanity and civility. Today, contemporary Muslim thinkers are trying to develop ideas on civility – how to transform the concept of *Umma* in a global age, and to determine whether it can become a progressive inclusive concept with a wide and pluralistic semantic field and democratic context. These ongoing intellectual struggles could be important contributions to the attempt to build – from below – a sociology of globalisation (Mandaville 2001: 30–8). This might be the only way to avoid a clash of ignorance as described by Edward Said's response to Huntington, the former being a text that is far less famous than the latter (Said 2001).

These efforts are linked to the sociological critique of modernity. The writings of Bauman (1991) and Taylor (1991) actually resonate with the ideas of Muslim scholars and intellectuals who criticise the social malaise of modernity and the atomistic nature of modern 'togetherness'. The 'urbanized lonely crowd' is characterised by apathy, and an unwillingness or inability to bear the moral responsibility of political decisions; it is easier to go along with authority, even if it leads to violent conflict, than to express dissent or act as a moral agent in challenging the nation state. If the outcome is the 'end of public man', then civility itself is at risk (Sennett 1976/1996). Globalisation can be regarded as an extension of modernity, ever increasing the scale and anonymity of global cities, speeding up the loss of identity, allowing people's lives to be shaped by market forces, and stretching the distance between the citizen and political authority. But at the same time, by challenging the autonomy of the nation state, generating new overlapping forms of authority (global, national, local) and shifting the balance between the market and the state, globalisation offers new spaces for recovering civility. If global civil society is to play a role in combating violence and fostering civility, it has to be through revitalising public man and woman, through restoring social networks and implementing survival strategies that would allow people to claim moral responsibility and challenge the uncontested monopoly of the nation state over the relations of power, the definition of order and the use of 'legitimate' violence.

Any effort to restore the notion of civility necessitates also an understanding of death in its relation to the obligation of citizens, and modernist thinking in a time of terror (Castells 1999). Using the body as a bomb and aspiring to a better life in the hereafter is not only a simple violent act, or a notorious attitude, but the wrong answer to very real questions of alienation, disempowerment and state terrorism. Apart from condemning the killing of civilians, the phenomenon of suicide bombings needs to be understood in its modernist political context rather than a religious context. There is something akin to panic when Muslim religious scholars try to

rule on an issue like suicide bombings. They can easily end up legitimising a violent concept of *Jihad* if they condone such acts of desperate civilian disempowerment against the brutal military arsenal of occupying forces, as in the Palestine case. But, even more importantly, they are caught up in an imagined concept of war that dates back to a society where it was possible to preserve civility while justifying war. In a modern war situation, weapons of mass destruction leave no room to abide by the moral rules that applied during the period of classical Islam, as Arendt pointed out in the quotation at the beginning of this chapter. Abu Bakr, the first Caliph, talked about preserving and protecting the seeds of civility even in time of military confrontation; the idea that these seeds can be replanted in times of peace so that human societies, as well as their natural environment, can prosper again is no longer realistic. Consider, for example, the consequences of the physical destruction of Lebanon for Lebanese society.

Perhaps we should then reflect not only on terror and the 'state of war' but also on the 'war of the state' – namely, the nation state as a source of terror. With its scientific achievements applied to military industries, modernity led to total wars in which the distinction between violence and civility, soldiers and civilians, was increasingly obliterated. The 'new wars', including terror and the 'war on terror', are conducted by networks of state and non-state actors, and the main victims are civilians (Kaldor 1999). These new forms of violence developed as a way round massive concentrations of conventional military force. Because battles, that is, direct confrontations (even those between 'asymmetric' forces like the Israeli state and Hizbollah, or the US armed forces and Iraqi insurgent groups) have become so destructive, and the value placed on individual soldiers' lives so high that they are rarely risked, warring parties fight either by directly attacking unarmed civilians or by attacking at long distance through terroristic air strikes, which inevitably cause civilian casualties.

It is surely useful to draw on religious classical jurisprudence to understand how it was used or abused by terrorist groups and by the 'war of the state', and ask both religious and secular scholars to introduce progressive and civic visions of their respective traditions. In the Islamic context, it is important to grasp the conflict between the authority of the state and the authority of religious scholars, who have no independence in the secular modern state to condemn its terror policies and criticise its wars. Because they no longer enjoy autonomy from the state, they have lost the credibility that could have allowed them to challenge the claim of religious authority by the terrorists, who developed a discourse drawing on religious texts and distorting their meaning to legitimise their political ends (Lumbard 2004: xi–xv).

The late orientalist Joseph Schacht referred to Islamic law as an extreme case of 'jurists' law'. Islamic law was neither the creation nor the preserve of the early Muslim state. Rather, it developed to a large extent in conscious opposition to the latter. The introduction of Western political, legal and educational structures would bring about important and far-reaching changes, including granting the state a monopoly over the enactment and interpretation of law, a development that marginalised the traditional role of the religious jurists, and profoundly influenced the content of law in all areas except family law. Not only has modern history displaced the sources and substance of Islamic law, but the religious clerics, heirs of the classical tradition, have also forfeited their monopoly over the interpretation of Islamic law. This is partly a result of the attempt by modern Muslim states to marginalise the traditional *Ulama* (Jackson 2001).

Thus the dilemma that Muslim scholars face in an era of globalisation is the task of 'de-terrorisation' (facing militant groups) and 'de-totalitarianisation' (facing authoritarian regimes), while struggling with the consequences of 'de-territorialisation' of their faith communities, which are no longer confined in political boundaries. Moreover, in an age of rising unilateralism and global hegemony, the propaganda of fear and nightmares under the banner of war against terrorism or war against the 'war on terror' overwhelms their tasks.

And the dilemma for Western scholars lies in the fact that concepts of a territorially bounded civil society are no longer relevant. On the one hand, globalisation has brought about what Ulrich Beck calls the debounding of risk (Beck 1992). On the other hand, it has brought about a greater consciousness of genocide and human rights violations in distant places. And this greater consciousness is expressed in the growing importance of human rights and humanitarian law. Thus Western thinkers share with

their Muslim colleagues the task of de-territorisation and de-totalitarianisation, including the need to address the security measures that curb civil liberties in democratic Western countries, while at the same time they also have to foster a global concept of civility that can help to underpin new non-state layers of authority and international legal frameworks.

On pre-emptive civility: the might of the word

Islamic and Western traditions both celebrate the might of the word. In Islam the locus of the belief system is the revealed word of Allah (the *Qur'an*), in a faith that believes in the transcendental nature of the divine. In Christianity, too, the word is central and, even if the 'the word became flesh' because the divine is embodied in the human body of Jesus, the word remains the origin and the beginning[1]. The Western tradition of the Enlightenment further fostered the epistemological centrality of reason, and language was the expression of wisdom, hence philosophy as manifestation of human reason vis-à-vis the dominance of divine reason based on faith was the promised alternative to theology.

It is interesting to see how the word started losing its significance and importance with unfolding modernity (to late capitalism) due to the ascendance of both the body and the authority of science (Segel 1998). One reason, it can be argued, is the emergence of the visual, and the rising culture of television and computers, which give different forms of power precedence over the might of the word. War is a manifestation of silencing dialogue, and the sword is usually used when words lose significance in times of conflict. There is a pressing need to take the 's' away from the sword and hail the power of the word in shaping the wor(l)d.

If global civil society is to have a mission at this historical moment of humanity it would be to recapture the power of language and to regain its 'civilising' role, providing a forum for deliberative democracy, re-rooting legitimacy in civil society and highlighting the importance of the politics of presence, not merely representation. The fact that after 9/11, and in the midst of the launch of the war on terrorism, dialogues took place across boundaries, and scholars from the American and the Muslim sides

---

1 'In the beginning was the Word and the Word was with God and the Word was God' (John 1:1).

©Mark Henley/Panos Pictures

(neo-conservatives and Saudi intellectuals) exchanged statements, even if they were confrontational rather than conciliatory, contributes to the expression of conflicts through words rather than bombs. Intellectuals in Germany and France issued statements against the war in Iraq in which they defended and clarified the concept of Jihad and just war in Islam, and detached it from terrorist acts. There were also many micro-and-macro-inter-cultural and inter-faith debates that emerged and developed rapidly (Blankenhorn et al. 2005; Boase 2005). This circle of global civil society activities was often overlooked because anti-war demonstrations and other marches and campaigns attracted more attention, again due to their visual or even screen-cyber 'spectacular' nature.

The fact that individuals in their small circles and in web-chat rooms, and on the screens of local televisions, expressed messages of peace and asserted their values of civility against war and terror (or 'the war on terror') counts a great deal and should be celebrated, cherished and documented. This is the civil alternative to fear that can provide 'preventive democracy' with the needed energy to survive (Barber 2003: 218–32).

One can also find evidence that in many religious traditions, scholars and ordinary citizens are struggling with their understanding of their faith and their world. Muslim scholars have emphasised clearly that any use of weapons of mass destruction would annul the moral commandments of war and the restrictions on killing civilians (Islam On Line URL). They have been more confused about ownership of weapons of mass destruction, arguing that such weapons can be owned for deterrence purposes, although not for use. In the Jewish community, debates on the nature of the Jewish state and the democratic limitations of such an idea are conducted on the theoretical level (Walzer et al. 2000: 463–23). At the political level many Jews have started to question the logic of the use of military power by the Israeli army in the Palestinian Occupied Territory: 'Jews for Justice for Palestine' in Britain was among the first group to issue a statement against the massive Israeli military operations against Lebanon taking place in July and August 2006 (Jews for Justice for Palestinians URL). Israeli peace activists and revisionist Israeli voices condemned the deliberate Israeli attacks on civilians (Ynetnews URL) Indeed, many critical voices could be heard throughout the world especially in the West; a ceasefire petition addressed to the United Nations Security Council collected some 200,000 signatures, while many peace organisations and prominent individuals organised demonstrations and other activities. Can these campaigns provide the basis for a global peace movement that encompasses both those who aim to civilise religion and secular ideologies?

One reason for such serious efforts to piece together the puzzle to form a new image is that the old picture seems to have little relevance to the reality of war in our age. In a global world, with the increasing mobility of individuals and groups across the globe, the notion of a territory where an *Umma* is based and confined to political boundaries, is inconceivable. Whether we talk about the Christian, Muslim or Jewish *Umma*, or a secular civil society, the imaginary of a community of believers (or fellow citizens according to modern nationalism) is dramatically changing. Whether a nation or a community of believers can still claim monopoly over space (and time), and disregard all forms of diversity within its realm (including for example, a Jewish state in a form of 'ethnocracy', or an Islamic state uniting Muslims within a frame of *dar al-Islam*) is very doubtful.

This has profound implications for the legitimacy of violence. The outside has become the inside. *Dar al-Harb* no longer exists. There is no external realm of war. Hence the rules of war no longer apply, only the much more stringent rules that traditionally applied to domestic violence. Here, classical Islam has more to teach us than the just war tradition. Since the whole world is a community, everyone is, in effect, a Muslim. Thus the way force is used against dissenters is subject to severe limitations – the limitations that apply to policing in the Western tradition. In a single community, there is no such thing as foreign aggression – violent attacks are crimes or human rights violations. Force is legitimate, under domestic law, in self-defence or to save a third party. But this refers to direct defence, not the kind of 'pre-emptive' or long-distance defence claimed both for air strikes and suicide bombers. Killing of both combatants and non-combatants is wrong. Those who commit violent acts should be arrested and judged in a legal framework. Killing of non-combatants is wrong whether deliberate, as in the case of suicide bombing, or accidental, as the Americans, Israelis and Russians claim.

In general, it is the job of domestic law enforcement to uphold these rules. But even if we live in a global community, there remain separate legal jurisdictions. So what does this argument imply for territories that are occupied or where the state is repressive and acts unlawfully? One answer is that international institutions have a role to play and that, in cases of genocide or other crimes against humanity, there could be a case for an international use of force, if authorised by the United Nations or justifiable in an international court

of law, within very strict limitations about how that use of force is exercised – that is, that it must be defensive and minimise all loss of life; long-distance bombing to stop genocide, for example, is unacceptable. The adoption of the 'responsibility to protect' doctrine by the United Nations is a step in this direction but the implementation of this responsibility has not yet been specified.

The other answer has to do with domestic resistance. In principle, the argument we have put forward suggests that there may be cases where force can be used in purely defensive ways to save lives – this could count as an acceptable *Ta'wil*. In practice, however, the use of force is almost always counter-productive. Even the most extreme occupiers or repressors need legitimacy, as Arendt pointed out. Hence the most effective way to oppose occupation and repression is to withdraw legitimacy and construct a parallel legitimacy within the framework of global civil society. Creating civil spaces and safe havens even in the midst of war and occupation is a much more powerful form of resistance than violence. Indeed, the resort to violence and terrorist acts can be in part explained by the failure of networks of scholars and activists to foster a culture of peace and justice, which has allowed nation states to get away with murder and even genocide, by obscuring these crimes within the discourse of war.

One of the most recent attempts to form a global network of citizens against terror aims to encourage the silent majority of people around the world to speak up, overcome their fear and organise their efforts (Citizens Against Terror URL). More networks on many levels, in different regions, and by as many different people as possible are the only guarantee of universal peace, a goal to which both religious traditions and the Enlightenment's great philosophers aspired.

If the postmodern age is described as the age of the end of tradition, where the tradition of endings has become the fashion in intellectual discourses, global civil society can only strive to prevent one of those endings being...the end of civility.

Albrow, Martin (1996) *The Global Age: State and Society Beyond Modernity*. London: Polity Press.

Al-Fadl, Khaled Abou (1999) 'The Rules of Killing at War: An Enquiry into Classical Sources', *The Muslim World*, 89(2), 144–57.

Al-Sayyad, Nezar (2001) 'Hybrid Culture/Hybrid Urbanism: Pandora's Box of the Third Place' in N Al-Sayyad (ed), *Hybrid Urbanism: On the Identity Discourse and the Built Environment*. Westport, CT: Praeger.

– (2004) 'Urban Informality as a New Way of Life', in N Al-Sayyad, *Urban Informality: Transnational Perspectives from the Middle East, Latin America and South Asia*. Oxford: Lexington.

An-Na'im, Abdullahi (2002) 'Religion and Global Civil Society: Inherent Incompatibility or Synergy and Interdependence?' in M Glasius, M Kaldor and H Anheier (eds), *Global Civil Society 2002*. Oxford: Oxford University Press.

Arendt, Hannah (1969) 'Reflections on Violence', New York Review of Books, 12(4), 27 February. www.nybooks.com/articles/11395 (consulted 11 August 2006).

Barber, Benjamin (2003) *Fear's Empire: War, Terrorism and Democracy*. New York: W W Norton and Company.

Bauman, Zygmunt (1991) *Modernity and the Holocaust*. Cambridge: Polity Press.

Beck, Ulrich (1992) *Risk Society: Towards a New Modernity*. London: Sage.

Blankenhorn, David et al. (2005) *The Islam/West Debate: Documents from a Global Debate on Terrorism, U.S. Policy and the Middle East*. New York: Rowman and Littlefield Publishers.

Boase, Roger (ed) (2005) *Islam and Global Dialogue: Religious Pluralism and the Pursuit of Peace*. Burlington: Ashgate.

Bulliet, Richard W (2004) *The Case for Islamo-Christian Civilization*. New York: Columbia University Press.

Castells, Manuell (1999) *The Rise of the Network Society*. Massachusetts: Blackwell Publishers.

Chandhoke, N (2002) 'The Limits of Global Civil Society', in M Glasius, M Kaldor and H Anheier (eds), *Global Civil Society 2002*. Oxford: Oxford University Press.

Crawford, Neta C (2003) 'Just War Theory and the US Counter Terror War', *Perspectives on Politics*, 1: 5–25.

Eck, Diana (2005) 'Is our God listening? Exclusivism, Inclusivism and Pluralism', in R Boase (ed), *Islam and Global Dialogue: Religious Pluralism and the Pursuit of Peace*. Burlington: Ashgate.

Elias, N (2000) *The Civilizing Process*, rev. ed. Oxford: Blackwell.

Ezzat, Heba Raouf (2005) 'Beyond Methodological Modernism: Towards a Multicultural Paradigm Shift in the Social Sciences', in H Anheier, M Glasius and M Kaldor (eds), *Global Civil Society 2004/5*. London: Sage.

Falk, Richard and Strauss, Andrew (2003) 'The Deeper Challenges of Global Terrorism: A Democratizing Response', in Daniele Archibugi (ed), *Debating Cosmopolitics*. London: Verso.

Freud, Sigmund (1961) *Civilization and its Discontents*. New York: W W Norton.

Glasius, M (2005) *The International Criminal Court: A Global Civil Society Achievement*. London: Routledge.

Habermas, Jurgen (2003) 'Reconstructing Terrorism', in G Barradori, *Philosophy in a Time of Terror: Dialogues with Jurgen Habermas and Jacques Derrida*. Chicago: University of Chicago Press.

Hanafi, Hassan (2002) 'Alternative Conceptions of Civil Society: A Reflective Islamic Approach', in S Hashemi (ed), Islamic *Political Ethics: Civil Society, Pluralism, and Conflict*. New Jersey: Princeton University Press.

Hegel, F (1820/1942) *Philosophy of Right*, trans. T Knox. Oxford: Clarendon Press.

Human Rights Watch (2006a) 'Fatal Strikes: Israel's Indiscriminate Attacks against Civilians in Lebanon', *Human Rights Watch*, 18(3(E)). www.hrw.org/reports/2006/lebanon0806/ (consulted 16 August 2006).

– (2006b) 'The terrible toll of the Israeli–Lebanon conflict on civilians: ongoing human rights abuse and violations of international humanitarian law', Human Rights News, 10 August. www.hrw.org/english/docs/2006/08/10/lebano13955.htm (consulted 16 August 2006).

Huntington, Samuel (1993) 'The Clash of Civilizations?', *Foreign Affairs*, 72(3): 22–49.

Institute for American Values (2002) 'What We're Fighting For: A Letter from America'. www.americanvalues.org/html/wwff.html (consulted 15 August 2006).

Jackson, Sherman (2001) 'Domestic Terrorism in the Islamic Legal Tradition', *The Muslim World*, 91: 293–310. http://users.tpg.com.au/dezhen/jackson_terrorism.html (consulted 11 August 2006).

– (2002) 'Jihad and the Modern World', *Journal of Islamic Law and Culture*, Spring/Summer. http://users.tpg.com.au/dezhen/jihad_and_the_modern_world.html (consulted 11 August 2006).

Juergensmeyer, Mark (2000) *Terror in the Mind of God: The Global Rise of Religious Violence*. Berkeley: University of California Press.

Kaldor, Mary (1999) *New and Old Wars: Organized Violence in a Global Era*. Cambridge: Polity Press

Kalin, Ibrahim (2005) 'Islam and Peace: A Survey of the Sources of Peace in the Islamic Tradition', *Islamic Studies*, 44: 327–62.

Kazemi, Reda Shah (2004) 'Recollecting the Spirit of Jihad', in J Lumbard (ed), Islam, *Fundamentalism and the Betrayal of Tradition*. Indiana: World Wisdom.

Keane, John (1996) *Reflections on Violence*. London: Verso

– (1998) *Civil Society: Old Images, New Visions*. Cambridge: Polity Press.

Kelsay, John (1993) *Islam and War: A Study in Comparative Ethics*. Louisville, KY: John Knox Press.

Kervégan, Jean-François (2002) 'Ami ou ennemi?', *La guerre des dieux*, special issue of Le Nouvel Observateur, January.

Kramer, Martin S (2001) *Ivory Towers on Sand: The Failure of Middle East Studies in America*. Washington, DC: Washington Institute.

Langan, John (1994) 'The Elements of St Augustine's Just War Theory', *Journal of Religious Ethics*, 12: 19–38.

Lecercle, Jean-Jacques (1990) *The Violence of Language*. London: Routledge.

Lewis, Bernard (1990) 'The Roots of Muslim Rage', *Atlantic Monthly*, 266(3): 47–60.

– (1993) 'Islam and Liberal Democracy', *Atlantic Monthly*, 27(2): 89–98.

Lumbard, J. (ed) (2004) *Islam, Fundamentalism, and the Betrayal of Tradition*. Bloomington, IN: World Wisdom Inc.

Mandaville, Peter (2001) *Transnational Muslim Politics: Re-imagining the Umma*. London: Routledge.

Mouffe, C (1993) *The Return of the Political*. London: Verso.

– (2000) *The Democratic Paradox*. London: Verso.

Nasr, Seyyed Hossein (1999) 'The Western World and its Challenges to Islam', in K Ahmad (ed), *Islam: Its Meaning and Message*. Leicester: Islamic Foundation.

– (2002) *Islam and the Plight of Modern Man*. London: Islamic Texts Society.

Piscatori, J et al (2004) *Accounting for Fundamentalisms: The Dynamic Character of Movements*. Chicago: University of Chicago Press.

Said, Edward W (2001) 'The Clash of Ignorance', *The Nation*, 22 October. www.thenation.com/doc/20011022/said (consulted 11 August 2006).

Schmitt, Carl (1932/1990) *The Concept of the Political*. Chicago, London: University of Chicago Press.

– (1952) 'Die Einhiet der Welt', *Merkur*, 6(1): 1–11

– (1974) *Der Nomos der Erde*, 2nd ed. Berlin: Duncker & Humblot.

– (1976) *The Concept of the Political*. Piscataway, NJ: Rutgers University Press.

Segel, Harold B (1998) *Body Ascendant: Modernism and the Physical Imperative*. Baltimore. MD: Johns Hopkins University Press.

Sen, A (2006) *Identity and Violence*. London: Allen Lane.

Sennett, Richard (1976/1996) *The Fall of Public Man*. London: Faber and Faber.

Shaw, Martin (2004) 'New Wars of the City: Relationships of "Urbicide" and "Genocide"', in S Graham (ed), *Cities, War and Terrorism*. Oxford: Blackwell.

Taylor, C (1990) 'Modes of Civil Society', Public Culture, 3: 59–118.

– (1991) *The Malaise of Modernity*. Concord, Ontario: Anansi Press.

Tuman, Joseph S (2003) Communicating Terror. London: Sage.

Turner Johnson, James (1981) *Just War Tradition and the Restraint of War: A Moral and Historical Enquiry*. Princeton: Princeton University Press.

Walzer, Michael (1992). *Just and Unjust Wars: A Moral Argument with Historical Illustrations*. 2nd ed. New York: Basic Books

– *et al*. (eds) (2000) The Jewish Political Tradition: Authority, vol. 1. New Haven: Yale University Press.

Waltz, Susan (2002) 'Reclaiming and Rebuilding the History of the Universal Declaration of Human Rights', T*hird World Quarterly*, 23: 437–48.

Zerzan, John (2005) *Against Civilization: Readings and Reflections*. Los Angeles: Feral House.

Websites (consulted 11 August 2006)

Campus Watch, www.campus-watch.org/
Citizens against Terror, www.citizensagainstterror.org
IslamOnline.net, www.Islamonline.net
Jews for Justice for Palestinians, www.jfjfp.org/
Ynetnews, www.ynet.co.il/home/0,7340,L-8,00.html

BRINGING VIOLENCE 'BACK HOME': GENDER SOCIALISATION AND THE TRANSMISSION OF VIOLENCE THROUGH TIME AND SPACE

Jenny Pearce

Introduction

It has always surprised me how contemporary studies of violence recognise 'private (or domestic) violence' as a serious phenomenon[1] but rarely address the possibility of connections between violence in private and public spaces, or the specific contribution gender socialisation processes make to the reproduction of violences in and between those spaces and over time. Most violent acts are carried out by young men between the age of 15 and 44 on young men between the age of 15 and 44, including self-directed violence; men commit much more violence than women do - homicides, suicides and even 'accidental' violence, such as road crashes (WHO 2002). But also:

> historically and cross culturally, they make war. Men are soldiers and, as politicians and generals, those who instigate and lead the fighting. Men also engage in extreme violence: they are (mainly) the concentration camp guards, the SS, those who perpetrate genocide, mass ethnic rape, pogroms, torture, and the murder of children and old people. (Chodorow 2002: 252)

Women are implicated in violence also in numerous ways, as perpetrators as well as victims, and this certainly merits explanation; but the scale of their participation is much less than that of men (see Box 2.1). At the very least this suggests that there are valid reasons for differentiating by gender not only in explaining violence but also in addressing it. And gender is a relational variable which exists cross-culturally in all socialisation spaces where the different forms of violence are exercised.

Given the persistent blight of violence in human society, it is remarkable how relatively little attention is given to its gendered components. There are many studies pioneered by Freud on the human instinct for aggression, which often indirectly refer to gender through parental and paternal relationships. But as one exploration of the psychodynamics of extreme violence with particular attention to men and masculinity expressed it:

> I have found it impossible to rethink Civilization and its Discontents directly in relation to gender...We find an asymmetry in which psychoanalytic writing notices dynamics found predominantly in women (for Freud, narcissism and masochism), whereas dynamics that predominantly characterize men (aggression) are discussed in generic human terms...psychoanalytic books about masculinity barely mention aggression except to suggest that it can be positive and normal, and they never discuss masculine violence. (Chodorow 2002: 251)

Feminists have deconstructed patriarchy, women's oppression and exclusion, and made visible male violence against women; more recently an emerging field of masculinity studies has begun to unpack and analyse the varied patterns of male identity formation. However, the argument that violence has a gender dimension rooted in gender socialisation that might transmit and reproduce violence through time and space is surprisingly rare in mainstream discussion of violence.

There are many good reasons for this. In the first place, the sight of men committing acts of violence, either sanctioned violence as members of state institutions of coercion, or illegal social, criminal and political violences, has been conventionalised (Wagner 1993) and thereby rendered un-noteworthy. It is such a normal component of the representation of violence in literature, film, television, as well as in real life, that the gender of those who commit violent acts rarely elicits comment. Shock is produced only when we see women committing the violence, as we did in the torture images

---

1 John Keane (1996), for instance, makes no specific reference to gender, although he does make some references to violence against women. An important collection of anthropological texts on violence (Scheper-Hughes and Bourgois 2004) is powerful on violence on women, and the idea of a 'violence continuum' from the everyday to the political is a key theme, but there is relatively little analysis of acts of violence from a gender perspective which differentiates between men and women as perpetrators of those acts.

Box 2.1: **Violence and the gender divide**

According to the World Health Organization's 2002 *World Report on Violence and Health*, in the year 2000 an estimated 815,000 people died by suicide, 520,000 by homicide and 310,000 as a direct result of war-related injuries (2002: 10). 'Males accounted for 77% of all homicides and had rates that were more than three times those of females (13.6 and 4.0 respectively, per 100,000)' (2002:10). Sixty per cent of suicides occurred among males, over half among those aged 15-44. The highest rates of homicide in the world are found among males aged 15-29 years (19.4 per 100,000), followed closely by males aged 30-44 years (18.7 per 100,000). Suicide rates are also higher among males than females: 18.9 per 100,000 as against 10.6 per 100,000. 'Every year, violence leads to approximately 1.6 million deaths. Violence is among the leading causes of death for people aged 15-44 years, accounting for 14% of male deaths and 7% of female deaths' (WHO 2004: Foreword). 'Forty-70% of female murder victims are killed by their husband or boyfriend' (WHO 2002: 93), unlike in the case of male murders. A study in the United States, for example, found that only four per cent of men murdered between 1976 and 1996 were killed by their wives, ex-wives or girlfriends; in Australia, the figure was 8.6 per cent between 1989 and 1996. While there is evidence from industrialised countries that women engage in 'common couple violence', a relatively moderate form of relationship violence, 'there are few indications that women subject men to the same type of severe and escalating violence frequently seen in clinical samples of battered women' (WHO 2002: 94).

Findings from international studies conducted since 1980 show a mean lifetime prevalence of childhood sexual victimisation of 20 per cent among women and of between five and ten per cent among men (WHO 2002: 64). 'Sexual abusers of children, in the cases of both female and male victims, are predominantly men in many countries. Studies have consistently shown that in the case of female victims of sexual abuse, over 90% of the perpetrators are men, and in the case of male victims, between 63% and 86% of the perpetrators are men (2002:67). In 2004 the WHO/World Bank *World Report on Road Traffic Injury Prevention* also pointed out that young men are more likely to have a road accident than women of the same age.

Colombian boys playing © Paul Smith/Panos Pictures

of Abu Graib prison in Iraq in 2004; and the attention to the role of Lynddie England, a US army reservist, and her subsequent punishment, exemplifies this shock factor.

The kind of violence we recognise is another obfuscating dimension of the character of violence and in particular its gendered character. Pierre Bourdieu sought to explain what he termed 'misrecognition' through the way 'the dominated apply categories constructed from the point of view of the dominant to the relations of domination, thus making them appear as natural' (Bourdieu 2001: 34). Through the durable effects that the resulting social order creates, society does not recognise certain forms of violence and its effects. Emotional trauma from systematic humiliation can leave an imprint on the body as much as physical violence and be expressed through, for example, trembling, blushing, clumsiness. This is what he calls 'gentle and often invisible' violence or 'symbolic violence', of which male domination is the primary example.

Society has tended to develop categories of violence and even hierarchies of violence that legitimise and delegitimise different forms of violence. Some would privilege the condemnation of state torture of political activists over child abuse in the home; some would deny that atrocities committed by state armies could be compared to the violence of street gangs. 'Depending on one's political-economic position in the world (dis)order, particular acts of violence may be perceived as "depraved" or "glorious"' (Scheper-Hughes and Bourgois 2004: 2). These hierarchies of violence play out in different ways in distinct social, cultural and historical contexts, and the struggle to secure the universal condemnation of violence against women is emblematic of how most societies have put that particular form of violence very low on the hierarchy of recognised violences. A study of violence in two neighbourhoods of post-war El Salvador expresses this well:

It would be erroneous to suggest that there is little public awareness of the problems of 'private' violence. Individuals in the communities all agreed that domestic violence was widespread… Nevertheless, its effects appear to be minimized in comparison to the effects of other expressions of violence of a more 'public' nature, by a tacit acceptance of its perceived normality. Margarita

(32 years old, La Vía) reasoned that it was wrong for a man to hit a woman, 'except in cases of infidelity', binding notions of appropriate behaviour for women with acceptable violence. Alfonso (18 years old, La Vía) concluded that his experiences of violence as a child (including repeated physical and psychological abuse) were 'neither good nor bad, just normal'...He spoke openly about beating his partner yet, at the same time, he was critical of a local gang that had broken into his house and beaten her because '...women can't handle [violence]'. This differentiation between his use of violence against his partner and the gang's is important, and goes to the core of gendered power relations. The glaring discrepancy in his interpretation of the two acts raises huge questions about the accepted use of force, by whom and toward whom. (Hume 2004: 66)

However, there are other reasons why social constructions of masculinity remain a relatively underplayed variable in our understandings of violence. These are to do with analytical problems that arise from trying to focus differentially on the role of men and women with respect to violence. One is the sheer complexity of making correlations and weighting variables in explaining particular violences. For example, why should gender matter more than any other variable? If an injustice has been done and there is a violent response, what does it matter whether it is a man or woman who carries out the violence or is a victim of it? Another problem is that some see the *act* of violence as the main issue, while others will include *passive support for* the act of violence. The latter might include women much more than the former. There is also the danger of generalising across so many different forms of violence and appearing to reduce explanations to one factor, namely, gender, when violence is multi-causal. There is a risk of scaling up from particular kinds of explanations, for example, those at the psycho-social level, to all aspects of society and culture. Many fear accusations of gender essentialism (women are peaceful, men are warlike) when evidence clearly shows that not all men are violent and some women are. As a result of these serious difficulties, the analysis of violence often treats it as something external to us (that is, the *explaining human subject*) and gender is mostly discussed in relationship to violence against women (the *violence-receiving object*) rather than in terms of who is carrying out the violence (the *violent-acting*

subject). Violence is seen as a tragedy of the human condition or a result of our structural inequalities, for example, rather than as behaviour and attitudes which are constructed, internalised and reproduced at the same time as we all learn what it is to be a 'woman' or a 'man' within our different societies.

This chapter is not about violence against women, serious though this is. Nor is it about the role of women as perpetrators of violence. I am certainly not arguing that women cannot be violent or do not perform violent acts; there is ample evidence of this, but so far it is much less than for men[2]. Nor am I offering an explanation for all violences. I am arguing, however, that the fact that men commit more acts of violence than women is a question we should explore. My aim in this chapter is to bring violence 'back home' and to discuss the *relationship and mutually interacting character* between gendered socialisation in private and public spaces and all violence. I want to argue that gendered forms of socialisation and gendered constructions of space continue to produce and reproduce the relational dynamics which embed and perpetuate violence in our human societies. These socialisation processes increase the risks that violence will be used as an instrument to pursue a range of goals, from the worthy to the unworthy. An underlying question is how 'worthy goals' might be pursued more effectively without violence as a step towards the creation of the conditions for a society to live without violence. Gender re-socialisation, I would argue, is a necessary, if not sufficient, step in that direction.

If we do not begin to imagine and implement gender re-socialisation we will be unable to interrupt the inter-generational cycles of violence even if we do address some of the 'causes' of contemporary public and violent conflicts. The endings of war, it should be noted, have

---

2 I write 'so far', because there is anecdotal, journalistic and some scientific evidence that female participation in violent gangs, insurgencies, suicide missions and other forms of violence is increasing. This does not contradict the argument of this chapter, as it would suggest that there are contexts today in which the socialisation of girls diminishes the qualities of submission and passivity which has traditionally been one of the most cross-culturally universal models of the 'feminine'. This clearly needs further research, and we may find distinct cultural and socialisation forms in the past as well as the present which 'free' women to act violently, or where traditional gender roles are overridden by collective identities such as ethnicity and the systematic discrimination against such collective identities. The participation of women in the Rwandan genocide would be one example.

not brought an end to violence, either in the theatres in which they have been waged or in the post-war situations (Nordstrom 1997; Meintjes, Pillay and Turshen 2002; Jacobs, Jacobsen and Marchbank 2000; Pankhurst 2003). Despite our great advances in understanding nature and the transformations in public manners and behaviour, our advances in reducing violence in human interactions remain pitiful. The twentieth century is considered by many historians to have been the bloodiest in human history (Hobsbawm 1994[3]). If our goal is what Freud in an essay titled *Why War?* called 'the cultural development of mankind' (a phrase he preferred to 'civilisation', Einstein and Freud 1933:20) and involves a 'progressive rejection of instinctive ends and a scaling down of instinctive reactions', I would argue that this could be measured by our abandonment under any circumstances of the instinct to cause pain and suffering to another human being. I am assuming in this chapter, therefore (something that I acknowledge is not necessarily shared by all) that we not only want to end the many wars of our times but that we also want to end violence.

The first part of this chapter explores how our construction of space as fixed and separating, rather than about the relational interactions of which it is made up, has impeded us from making the critical connections between the private and the public in analysing violence. The second part discusses the relationship between gender identity construction and violence, drawing on my own and others' fieldwork in Latin America and elsewhere and using the psycho-social framework of James Gilligan (1997; 2001) on the relationship between gender social construction and the greater propensity of men to use violence. In the third section I return to the question of linkages between violences in different spheres of human socialisation and to the idea of a 'continuum of violence' (Scheper-Hughes and Bourgois 2004: 1). Finally, I use a gender lens to explore Hannah Arendt's (1969) proposition that power and violence are distinct. Could a new normative theory and practice of power that might emerge

from women's actions in the public arena and feminist theory help transform our analysis of violence and reduce its use?

Gendered and bounded space as obstacles to understanding violence

In an influential book, *The Sexual Contract*, political philosopher Carole Pateman (1988) discussed the gendered character of the construction of our understanding of 'private' and 'public' spheres in the course of the European project of 'modernity'. The emergence of the idea of 'civil society' bifurcated the 'public sphere' into two, that of the 'state' and that of a 'privatised' sphere of 'public' associational life, or civil society. The private domestic sphere of the 'home' was then another spatial construction that, like civil society, was to be autonomous from the state, but not subject to critical public scrutiny either by civil society or by the state. 'Civility' was a discourse for the bourgeois public sphere and the new social bonds of public associationalism that emerged in the late eighteenth century (Howell and Pearce 2001). The freedom of the individual, and of that individual in 'his' home, was established in the course of these bounded imaginings of space: 'a man's home is his castle' became a popular dictum. Another was 'a woman's place is in the home'. These sayings reflected the effort to fix the relationships within, as well as the boundaries of, the gendered space of castle/home.

As time progressed the boundaries did blur. In the course of the twentieth century, the state began to intervene in some aspects of the private, domestic world, and by the late twentieth century domestic violence and child abuse were at least recognised as a concern of the state in many parts of the world even if efforts to eliminate them have been slow and ineffective. Debates and social struggles about female participation outside the home also led to a re-gendering of spatial boundaries, and labour markets were eventually opened up of necessity to female participation. But still, in many parts of the world, spatial boundaries to the participation of women remain firmly demarcated through informal and formal mechanisms. Female participation in the public sphere of state and civil society has increased significantly in the West, at least, but that sphere is still dominated, perhaps with the exception of Scandinavia, by men. In many Muslim societies, women are separated physically from men in the public sphere either spatially and/or through dress codes.

---

3 *'Why, then, did the century end, not with a celebration of this unparalleled and marvellous progress, but in a mood of uneasiness?....Not only because it was without doubt the most murderous century of which we have record, both by the scale, frequency and length of the warfare which filled it, barely ceasing for a moment in the 1920s, but also by the unparalleled scale of the human catastrophes it produced, from the greatest famines in history to systematic genocide'. (1994:13)*

A couple at home in Morocco © Alfredo Caliz/Panos Pictures

These gendered spatial constructions have become so normal that the question is rarely posed: how does violence (and power) get transmitted from private to public and back to private, and what role does gender play in that transmission? Could the differentiated socialisation process between men and women be a transmitting mechanism? As Doreen Massey (1994; 1999) and others have reminded us, space is a 'product of interrelations. It is constituted through interactions, from the immensity of the global to the intimately tiny' (Massey 1999: 28). Gender hierarchies are just one of the interrelationships within social spaces, but there is a remarkable consistency across culture, time and space in the power men have been able to exercise over women within a range of spaces. Women almost universally enjoy less participation and power in the public sphere, and the constructions of masculinity in the intimate or domestic private space condition the character and use of power and violence outside of it, and then 'double back' to reinforce the gendered relationship in the home. There is no longer a 'starting point' for explaining this as such, although the 'home' and the intimate is arguably the formative space for gender socialisation, and the most dynamic force for replenishing the circulation and flow of power and violence over time and space.

Violence in the private sphere of the home has become an issue for the public sphere in some countries, showing that this flow can be subjected to intervention and interruption, although it remains a very difficult problem to address. Not only is the participation of women in the public sphere still limited, but the ability of women to influence public decisions around the use of violence also remains very limited. Nor does the participation of women, per se, guarantee that decisions will be different. The inclusion of women is not in itself the route to transform our understandings of violence; it is whether the women who gain power and office are able to bring new assumptions, conceptualisations, theories and behaviour that can transform the way men and women construct their relationships. Such a possibility is always there given that space is a product of 'relation-between' which 'is always in the process of becoming, it is always being made' (Massey 1999: 28). Despite spatial relationships having the appearance of structure, given that they are often very persistent over time, there is always the possibility that they can be reconstructed and relationships re-socialised.

If we go 'back home', therefore, and try to unpack the construction of gendered social differences, might we find at least some keys not only as to why the public sphere remains dominated by men, but why violence in the private and the public spheres is also perpetrated mostly by men?

Rebel fighters in El Salvador © *Fernando Moreles/Panos Pictures*

What difference might it make to our understanding of violence to do this and then to explore the connections between gendered spaces? A disadvantage might be to dilute our understanding, produce one monolithic problem of 'violence' whose multiple manifestations are ignored and therefore cannot be properly addressed. An advantage might be to recognise the magnitude of the problem of violence in human relationships in all the spaces it occurs, whether or not it is constructed as legitimate or illegitimate, and our shared responsibility in reproducing it. We might then begin to address the socialisation processes that appear to enhance the risks that men are more likely to use violence than women, though the triggers for whether they do so depend on a multiplicity of other variables. This will not stop violence in itself, given its multi-causality, but it might reduce the risk inherent in maintaining these forms of socialisation. But what is it about this socialisation that contributes to violence?

Shame, honour and pride: socialisation, men and violence

...male sociodicy owes its specific efficacy to the fact that it legitimates a relation of domination by inscribing it in a biological which is itself a biologized social construction. The double work of inculcation, at once sexually differentiated and sexually differentiating, imposes upon men and women

different sets of dispositions with regard to the social games that are held to be crucial to society, such as the games of honor and war (fit for the display of masculinity, virility) or , in advanced societies, all the most valued games such as politics, business, science, etc. The masculinization of male bodies and feminization of female bodies effects a somatization of the cultural arbitrary which is the durable construction of the unconscious. Having shown this, I shift from one extreme of cultural space to the other to explore this originary relation of exclusion from the standpoint of the dominated as expressed in Virginia Woolf's 1927 novel To the Lighthouse. *We find in this novel an extraordinarily perceptive analysis of a paradoxical dimension of symbolic domination, and one almost always overlooked by feminist critique, namely the domination of the dominant by his domination: a feminine gaze upon the desperate and somewhat pathetic effort that any man must make, in his triumphant unconsciousness, to try to live up to the dominant idea of man. Furthermore, Virginia Woolf allows us to understand how, by ignoring the illusion that leads one to engage in the central games of society, women escape the* libido dominandi *that comes with this involvement, and are therefore socially inclined to gain a relatively lucid view of the male games in which they ordinarily partake only by proxy.* (Bourdieu and Wacquant 2004: 273)

Differential power between men and women makes it more likely that male socialisation processes have a wider impact on societal development than female ones. It is not, however, the gender inequality issue per se that I am concerned with here, but the character of the socialisation that underpins it and the differential effects it produces on what individuals come to internalise in their particular societies as the 'normal' qualities of maleness and femaleness. It is the *character* of that socialisation that makes inequality between men, as much as inequality between men and women, such an important question with respect to willingness to use violence, as men strive to 'live up to the dominant idea of man'.

The need to explore the relationship between masculinity, femininity and violence has arisen from my field research in the violent contexts of Latin America and more recently in Bradford, UK, where I was part of a research team[4] looking at the riots that took place in that city in 2001, in which the overwhelming number of participants were young males of Pakistani origin. In Latin America, my experiences have taken me from the state terror and dictatorships of the Southern Cone in the 1970s to the civil wars of cold war Central America and Colombia in the 1980s, the multiple complex violences of post-Cold War Colombia, to the persistent and complex violences in indigenous communities of southern Mexico, and to the post-war contexts of Peru, Guatemala, El Salvador and Nicaragua. It is worth noting that this personal research trajectory through three decades of violence in Latin America mirrors a great deal the pathway of others who have tried to argue for linkages between everyday violences and other kinds of violence, for example, Koonings and Kruijt (1999), Moser and Clark (2001), Moser and Winton (2002), Moser and McIlwaine (2003), and Scheper-Hughes and Bourgois (2004). This is partly because Latin Americanists with this trajectory are acutely aware that the way we looked at violence in the 1970s and 1980s, a period characterised by state terror and state-promoted private violence, did not prepare us for the explosion of social violences in the course of the 1990s, both in countries which had suffered civil war and in those which had not. In El Salvador, an example of the former, an average of 6,250 people per year died from direct political violence during the 1980s, compared with 8,700 to 11,000 killed every year by criminal violence in the 1990s (Bourgois 2004: 432; PNUD 2002). But in

Brazil, which did not go through civil war, violent deaths of young men were among the highest in the world in the 1990s, with a homicide rate of 18,400 for males aged 15-29 and 10,352 for males aged 30-44 in 1995 (WHO 2002: 308).

Philippe Bourgois' anthropological reflections on this are particularly poignant as he also turned from field research in war-time El Salvador in the 1980s to the United States, his own country, to deepen his understanding of the nature of violence (Bourgois 1995). He has subsequently reflected on the forms violence takes in war time and what we call 'peace time' (2004: 425-34) by reinterpreting his ethnographic data from fieldwork in El Salvador in the 1980s. He came to recognise the violences he had ignored during a traumatic moment of army repression that he had shared with the Salvadorean peasants during fieldwork in 1981. On a return visit to post-war El Salvador in1994, the reality of life in the war, which is not easy for foreign researchers to penetrate, was finally revealed to him. He heard tales about 'misdeeds, deception and disloyalty' (2004: 430), and about the internecine violence among guerrilla fighters and executions of pro-guerrilla civilians erroneously accused of being government spies. He concluded that:

> The urgency of documenting and denouncing state violence and military repression blinded me to the internecine everyday violence embroiling the guerrillas and undermining their internal solidarity. As a result I could not understand the depth of the trauma that political violence imposes on its targets, even those mobilized to resist it ...I was unable to recognize the distinctiveness of everyday violence in revolutionary El Salvador and therefore failed to discern it to be a product of political and structural violence, despite that fact that I had effectively understood everyday violence to be at the interface of structural and symbolic violence in the US inner city. (2004: 432, 426)

I shared similar experiences to those of Bourgois, and lived for several months in 1984 in a guerrilla-controlled zone of Chalatenango, El Salvador, while undertaking an oral history of the peasant movement, and like him I have returned to El Salvador in 'peace time' and been astounded at the rise in social violence. My response to this has been different from that of Bourgois, however, in one key respect. While the other kinds of violence between and within guerrilla groups that evolved in the course of the war were certainly, as Bourgois argues, an

---

4   *The field research team included Dr Janet Bujra and Dr Marie Macey.*

Radio operator in the FMLN, El Salvador © *Mike Goldwater*

illustration of 'how the revolutionary movement in El Salvador was traumatized and distorted by the very violence it was organizing against' (2004: 431), it is the gender dimensions of the violence and abuse during the war carried out by male combatants on female combatants that led me to ask the question: what happened to men and women in this civil war? Who carried out the violence? Is there a relationship between the masculine identity of the majority of guerrilla leaders and combatants, the intra-combatant violence of the war and the role of ex-combatants in the violence of the peace? A moving set of interviews of 70 former female combatants in El Salvador illustrates the anguish of their personal and sexual lives during their time in the mountains, where 'sexuality was very present in our relationships' but 'In the personal life there was a law of silence' (Las Dignas 1996: 49)[5].

It is important to stress that by asking these gender questions I am not diminishing the categories of structural, political, symbolic and everyday violence in the Salvadorean context raised by Bourgois, and which I too would want to employ. The overwhelming amount of

5 'There was no time for affection, they came in the night and wanted sex and not to talk' (Las Dignas 1996: 51).

violence in the Salvadorean civil war was perpetrated by the state army on civilians. However, I am asking how gender interacts with each of them. I want to ask: what did women do and what did men do? It is necessary but not sufficient to explain what happened in El Salvador in terms of structural and political violence. We need to know the differential way that constructions of masculinity and femininity interacted with these forms of violence. As Bourgois and I both verified in field interviews, alcoholism and abuse of women were widespread in rural communities *before* liberation theology, revolutionary ideology, and the momentum and discipline of the armed struggle brought it under control. 'We used to put away a lotta drink and cut each other up. But then the Organization showed us the way, and we've channelled that violence for the benefit of the people', a peasant man told Bourgois (Bourgois 2004; cf. Pearce 1985: 154). It did not however, eliminate the sexual abuse of women during the war, suggesting that masculine social roles had shifted only to the requirements of armed struggle, not to any transformation in the socialisation processes. And in peacetime many young male ex-combatants, socialised in war and with few opportunities of dignified work in the countryside or cities, fell into the gang cultures that began to proliferate in San Salvador in the 1990s, mostly generated by Salvadorean migrants and sons of war refugees returning from gang experiences in Los Angeles.

Even when women are combatants in armed movements, there is some evidence that their attitude towards the violence they are engaged in differs from that of men, and this difference makes it easier for them to recuperate after the war. In Colombia, for instance, a study of ex-combatants revealed how much harder it is for male than for female ex-combatants to lay down the gun. The gun had become so much part of male identity that it was almost a part of their body, and its loss was felt almost as intensely as a loss of a body part (Castro and Diaz 1997). In Colombia, the gendered character of that country's violence has only recently begun to be recognised and visibilised, and studies are beginning to appear that explore how men and women experience violence differently, although the focus is still on women as victims rather than the men as perpetrators (see, for example, Meertens 2001). What is the origin, for instance, of the vendetta cultures that in Colombia reproduce violence throughout the generations? Revenge, or 'account settling', is a conventionalised norm among male combatants in Colombia, which leads to sons settling scores for the death of fathers, for instance, many years after the immediate act of violence[6].

If we turn to the rise of social violence throughout Latin America in the 1990s and into this millennium, we also find that young men are the overwhelming perpetrators and victims of violence. If we analyse this from the perspective of 'structural violence'[7], we can indeed relate it to economic inequality, urban unemployment and the neo-liberal restructuring that took place in the region during those years. We can also relate it to the way drugs trafficking has provided an alternative livelihood and lifestyle for marginal youth as well as organised criminal mafias. However, if we did not to ask how young men and young women differentially interact with this structural violence, we would miss some key points. What is it that young men can achieve in such conditions of inequality and impoverishment through violence and gang culture that women cannot? A thread seems to run through many studies of violent neighbourhoods and communities which suggest that the differential socialisations of men and women must offer a good source of the explanation. Mo Hume's research in El Boulevar, a marginal community in Greater El Salvador, found that:

> data from interviews and focus groups highlight the fact that exaggerated sexual prowess and violence against women were central to men's identity. Above all, for most of the male interviewees, this identity required the domination of women, children and other men. Respondents testified to feeling more manly as a result of threatening and beating women, never giving in (no se deja), being brave, having sexual relations with many women, leaving women pregnant, having lots of children, feeling more important than other men, being proud. Some men said that carrying weapons made them feel more like a man. (Hume 2004: 67)

Changing social and economic dynamics interact with gender socialisation norms and sometimes inhibit the ability of men to live up to expectations of 'manliness'. In contexts where traditional male roles have become much more difficult to live up to, such as among diaspora and migrant communities where disadvantaged ethnic positioning limits engagement with the formal labour market, violence may become a means for some males of compensating for diminishing honour and respect. Such a theme emerges in Bourgois' rich discussion of masculinities among drug dealers of Puerto Rican origin in a violent ghetto neighbourhood of East Harlem in the United States:

> A man in El Barrio can no longer 'speak' to his children, 'with his eyes' and expect to have his commands immediately obeyed. The former modalities of male respect are no longer achievable within the conjugal household or the extended kin-based community. Several generations of men caught in different phases of this fundamental cultural transformation in family forms and gender hierarchies have been crushed. Primo brought this issue to my attention. In his concern over the fate of the men in his kin network, one can discern the gender-specific form of the experience of social marginalisation in the Puerto Rican diaspora. (Bourgois 1995: 297)

Like Bourgois, work in my own country played a strong role in opening up new questions about violence. The riots that took place over 12 hours in Bradford on 7 July 2001 involved hundreds of young Pakistani males. These males come out of rural Asian and mostly Muslim socialisation cultures (although the vast majority were second-generation immigrants), in which male honour is one of the most dominant socialisation norms. These traditional cultural norms have been fertilised with Western cultural portrayals of masculinity so that the rioters described their violence in language from film and television; it was, they said:

> like a mission...James Bond...a fight to the finish...a battle...A game...I'm in the middle of a war zone...my head went...I don't take shit off nobody...I am angry...I'll take him out before he takes me out...It does mek yer feel strong, cos yer done it with a load guys and lads. (Bujra and Pearce 2005: 11)

The defence of the honour of women was a frequent justification for riot, fuelled by rumours such as 'an Asian woman had been knocked over by one of the Maria vans, the police vans' (Bujra and Pearce 2005: 11). Other comments from the young men, drew attention to the changing nature of their family socialisation and their expected roles; if his father was still alive, one

---

6 My field diary for a visit to a paramilitary-controlled commune of Medellin in 2004 records the chuckle of the paramilitary commander when I asked about revenge and vendetta among combatants: 'You mean settling accounts - of course!'

7 This concept comes originally from Johan Galtung (1996).

Box 2.2: Sincelejo, Colombia: where violence rules

1 April 2005

'What is the name of this affluent neighbourhood?', I ask the taxi driver as we reach Sincelejo, the departmental capital of Sucre on the Atlantic coast of Colombia. 'Venezia', he replies. 'Who lives here?' 'The son of the Mayor.' 'Who is the Mayor? Which party is he from? 'The Corrupts, like of all of them', he says. 'Are there paramilitary?' 'Yes. But they don't control anything. They eliminate thieves every so often. The people like it.' At the hotel I close my bedroom door and switch on the television. The press has recently revealed that at least 3,000 people of the 50,000 inhabitants from the nearby town of San Onofre are believed to have 'disappeared' since the late 1990s. But the television news was not about that San Onofre, it was San Onofre the beach resort on Colombia's beautiful Atlantic coast, San Onofre the tourist paradise! I glance up and freeze as I digest a notice pinned on the back of the door. Just above the warning that the hotel is not responsible for valuables that have not been deposited in its safe box, there is another notice: *Warning. In accordance with Article 17 of Law 679 of 2001, the HOTEL warns the GUEST that the sexual abuse and exploitation of minors in the country are punished in penal and civil law according to the prevailing legal dispositions.* What has gone on in this hotel room, I ask myself, and hardly sleep that night.

2 April 2005

The taxi driver was not exactly accurate when he claimed the paras do not control Sincelejo. I talk to the very few NGO and church workers brave enough to monitor human rights in this town. They tell me that a henchman of the town's most feared paramilitary commander, known as Cadena, or Chain, has just been captured in Venezuela and spilled the beans about the landowning, drug trafficking and political links with the paramilitary in Sincelejo. A mass grave has just been dug up in the finca (farm) El Palmar in San Onofre. They think it contains the remains of some 500 of Cadena's victims. It was from this finca that a paramilitary group set off on 17 January

moto-taxis in Sincelejo ©Jenny Pearce

2001 to massacre 27 people in El Chengue in 2001. However, only recently has Cadena become associated with the paramilitary; he has never fought the guerrillas. He murdered peasants and trafficked cocaine, I am told. Yet he is now in Santa Fe de Ralita, where President Uribe has allowed the paramilitary who wish to demobilise to gather. Most people believe that the President must be aware of Cadena's antecedents; he has many links to this region and there are rumours that he has bought land in Sucre. The paramilitary expanded into Sucre in the mid-1990s, and I visited Sincelejo at that time. The guerrillas had a strong base in the town in the 1990s. Sucre was a centre for peasant activism and also had a strong civic movement, but leaders were being killed and I sensed back then that a strategic offensive was under way, uniting landowners, political leaders, army commanders and drug traffickers against not only guerrillas but social activists generally.

Now I am told, by the head of an NGO who must remain anonymous for his own safety, that 'there is no civil society' in Sincelejo. The paramilitary have political and economic power. They own many of the shops and sell cheap; in December 2005 the queues were so huge that they had to close them. There are ten gas stations, of which the paras control five. There is real fear here; people speak in hushed voices when they mention the paras. People say they are mostly young men, aged 22-30, and Cadena is a key commander. I ask about the moto-taxis that are everywhere in the city centre - young men earning a living by giving rides on their motorbikes. I have never seen anything like it before. There are reported to be a staggering 22,000 of these in the town. They appeared suddenly in 2002 and have proliferated since then. The police let them circulate and then every three months stop and fine them. Many spy for the paras. Many have been killed. Thousands of people have come to Sincelejo, displaced by the violence in the rural areas; the moto-taxis are a way of surviving. Some students pay for their studies this way. The paras exercise social control in Sincelejo; in the neighbourhoods they kill thieves and drug addicts. They also ensure that only their friends hold political office. In Sincelejo I learn of a new form of government: *narcoparamilipolísmo*, government by drug traffickers, paramilitary and politicians. In Sincelejo, violence rules.

Source: *Extract from Jenny Pearce's field diary*

young man explained, 'I'd a been locked at home, married and with children by now' (2005:11). A complementary piece of research on a white working-class estate, in the district where a smaller disturbance had followed in the wake of the main riot, revealed a similar theme among a community deeply affected by loss of male employment and traditional male roles in the household:

> Asians...wouldn't leave [my girlfriend] alone...they touch and stuff...they haven't got any respect...the amounts of fights I've had with them when I've been out (Bujra and Pearce 2005: 12).

Where can we turn for more guidance and direction on how socialisation processes impact on masculinity, the *libido dominandi*, and its links to violent behaviour? The work of the American psychiatrist James Gilligan, whose two books, *Violence: Reflections on A National Epidemic* (1997) and *Preventing Violence* (2001), are based on his long-term studies of violent criminals, offer rich insights. I am not arguing that one can scale up from his psycho-social analysis to explanations for all violence. However, Gilligan's work led him straight to gender construction and socialisation processes:

> Understanding why men are more violent than women requires an understanding of the highly asymmetrical gender roles to which the members of each sex are assigned at birth in our patriarchal cultures, and to which they are powerfully conditioned to conform throughout the rest of the lives by virtually all institutions of our society. The relevant point here is that the differences in those gender roles makes it possible for men to ward off or undo feelings of shame, disgrace and dishonour by means of violence, whereas that is significantly less true for women. Masculinity, in the traditional , conventional sex-role of patriarchy, is literally defined as involving the expectation, even the requirement, of violence, under many well specified conditions: in times of war; in response to personal insult; in response to extramarital sex on the part of a female in the family; while engaging in all-male combat sports etc. (Gilligan 2001: 56)

Shame, honour, pride are vital components in masculine identity formation cross-culturally, as many would instinctively recognise (see Box 2.3). The next step is to see why violence might be justified for men as a response to being shamed. Shame can be induced by many factors, from a personal insult to relative poverty,

unemployment, lower caste status, ethnic discrimination (Gilligan 2001: 67), and so on. Men and women can suffer all of these and more. But the reflexes which kick in for men and for women are different when they experience inequalities and indignities and emotions of shame and dishonour. It is in these differences that men find their identity reinforced by the use of violence and women find it undermined. For a woman to be more of a woman, she is encouraged to be submissive and accepting. The opposite is true of men.

Gender and the transmission and reproduction of violence in time and space

The literature on violence tends to divide violence into various 'forms'. People differ as to the exact categories, but Philippe Bourgois' categories outlined above are sound examples of the broad consensus: Political, Structural, Symbolic and Everyday. Scheper-Hughes and Bourgois also argue for a 'continuum' between these violences (2004: 1), and the WHO study on violence as a public health issue also points to evidence of:

> links between different types of violence. Research has shown that exposure to violence in the home is associated with being a victim or perpetrator of violence in adolescence and adulthood. The experience of being rejected, neglected or suffering indifference at the hands of parents leaves children at greater risk for aggressive and antisocial behaviour, including abusive behaviour as adults. Associations have been found between suicidal behaviour and several types of violence, including child maltreatment, intimate partner violence, sexual assault and abuse of the elderly. In Sri Lanka, suicide rates were shown to decrease during wartime, only to increase again after the violent conflict ended. In many countries that have suffered violent conflict, the rates of interpersonal violence remain high even after the cessation of hostilities - among other reasons because of the way violence has become more socially acceptable and the availability of weapons. (WHO 2002: 15)

My caveat about the use of these generally useful categories of violence is that they invisibilise the gendered character of the violence. They do not necessarily conceal the victimisation of women, but they do diminish the attention drawn to the perpetration of violence by men.

I would argue, therefore, that the categorisation of forms of violence must be complemented by a spatial

Box 2.3: 'Coming of age': masculinities and male youth in Bradford, UK

A study of eight Pakistani-British and eight white English youth, carried out in Bradford between 2003 and 2006, explored their emerging ideas of masculinity and perceptions of social and anti-social behaviour.* During the ten-month fieldwork, I 'hung out' with young men, aged 10-17, facilitated a photographic 'Ladz Project', and worked as a youth worker and as a bouncer in a nightclub.

Central to the young men's emerging masculinities were their interactions and experiences with young women. While male peers were a constant influence on the development of their identity, perceptions of their power and worth evolved in relation to the opposite sex. In the nightclub, the space encircling the dance floor was appropriated by young Asian men who stood watching the young, predominantly white, women dancing in front of them. They would shout comments to attract the attention of particular girls - either to initiate a flirtatious interaction or to denigrate them sexually. Occasionally they would make forays on to the floor to chat up girls.

In the lads chillin' area (anonymous)

Poster on my bedroom door (Greg, 12)

While the space in the nightclub was very much dominated by the more confident Asian male youth (the white youth taking a backseat for fear of antagonising their Asian peers), in their geographical environment the ethnic group of the locality dominated: Asian male youth in Broadbeck, and white male, and some female, youth in Highmoor**. Both groups of young men would interact with the opposite sex in their own environs. Although the white female youth from Highmoor would enjoy public banter with local youth, and less public flirtations with the Asian lads at the nightclub, they were very hesitant about going to Broadbeck and the park where previously they had experienced being told to 'suck my dick', or had been chased by teenagers. It should be emphasised that those who expected such comments to be taken seriously, and acted upon, were in a minority. As one lad explained: 'People use that for getting to know someone...it's like a chat up....it's either to take piss out of ya or to get to know ya' (Amir, 15).

The Highmoor lads explored masculinity and sexuality through other means: several had posters or photographs of topless and scantily clad women in their bedrooms, and others had pornographic magazines. One younger lad talked me through his pile of about 30 magazines, passed on by a friend, which depicted mainly Sapphic imagery. He explained how he would hold up a particular edition to tease a girl or would sit with his mates looking at the magazines, talking about women and what they did with their girlfriends.

Strong codes were adopted by almost all the youth about what they were 'allowed' to do as young men: what was fair play or 'out of order'. It was expected that sons, brothers and friends would look out for one another, and defend the honour of family and friends.

I'll go straight in for me family....I'm there for me family always, no matter what...I'm sorry but, if they're gonna touch my family in a hurtful way, I'm gonna hurt them...in my eyes...every time if summat's ever happened...it's fully grown men that have started on [my mum] because of me real dad. Now, when these fully grown men have come to my house an' started wiv me mum, me mum's obviously retaliated because she's tryin' to look out for me. Now, I'm not sayin' I'm big an' hard. I'm not sayin' I'm leader of crew or whatever. All I'm sayin' is when that stuff kicked off I made one phone call an' I had 20 lads outside my house because there were three fully grown men outside my house kickin' off at me mum. Now I knew I couldn't take all three fully grown men on. (Tommy, 16)

*It was like the Asian folks there [at the last gang fight']. They, it's one a, one of my mates, you know...and his dad's passed away 'nt it, 'n they swore at his dad. 'N **everyone**,'n I mean everyone come, yeah. Went in, cleared it up.* (Nav, 14)

We don't like anybody messing about with us and I mean, there is a lot of racial conflict in Bradford between white and black an' we just think that [sigh] every time there's a fight we got to call our cousins, we got to call our boys, you know. (Umar, 15)

Regardless of ethnicity, a majority of young men had used violence against others within the boundaries of their clearly defined moral codes. Some had reflected on particular incidents: although they felt the use of violence had been warranted in response to racial abuse, the attacks sat heavily on their conscience. One way of disassociating their present selves from past actions was by dismissing what they did then, when they were 'boys' and 'young and stupid', thus allowing them space to be 'men' and more mature now:

We had a lot of things against him. I mean, you know...I think he was probably, he was like a racist lad. His parents are right racist as well. And every time we used to see him he used to give, you know. Like eyes and everything. So we didn't like that at all...It was just in the heat of the moment that all the boys were like yeah, let's just go, let's go whack him an' that...there was about eight or ten to ten of us...we were, we, we were only 14 so we were pretty young at that time....We were all young, an' we were just stupid. (Umar, 15)

Another young man explained his response to a racist taunt and reflected on how he feels after physical confrontation:

So I started walkin' away, 'n then he called me a white bastard again. So I turned round 'n went 'o, you called me that, didn't you, yesterday? 'N I punched him. He fell straight to floor. Now, coz he fell straight to floor I jumped on top of him, started punchin' him in the face....He tried getting' me done for assault because I punched him that many times in the eyes, 'n that hard I nearly blinded him. I wah, I wah 14 goin' on 15. I weren't that old. Now, it does scare me, coz if I carried on I could've ...made him blind for life. Or, I coulda, could, if I'd had carried on I, I'd either blinded him, broke his nose, 'owt like that. Or, I could've, worst comes to the worst, killed him....if any of those things would have happened I would've felt guilty. I don't know why, after I've had a fight I always feel guilty anyway. (Tommy, 16)

Codes also applied to neighbourhoods, for example, not 'grassing up' or carrying out crime where you lived. These were passed down through generations and 'enforced' in the white community by those living there. The philosophy on the Highmoor estate was you 'don't shit on your own doorstep' and those who transgressed this principle received retribution. In my observation only male youth or adults carried out physical retribution, the target of which was male perpetrators. However, one form of collective non-violent punishment recounted to me was the organisation of a petition and the literal driving out of a family whose son had arsoned a community facility. The Asian youth in Broadbeck recounted different reasons for not carrying out crime on their doorstep: in their experience it was simply foolhardy because they would be recognised:

Girls walking down street (Nav, 14)

Now I have my own area yeah.... It's too hot for me. Like our area's a bit hot. If I get caught or someone tells my description or somethin' they can come straight to my house 'coz they know me now. (Sajid, 15)

The research found that all those who took part in the research were either 'experiencing', 'witnessing' or 'perpetrating' violence in one form or another.*** Almost all were 'experiencing' violence either directly, as victims of street assaults, racial or 'gang' attacks, and punishment by family members for their behaviour; or indirectly, through structural violence (see Galtung 1996) wrought by poverty, poor housing, exclusion from education and harassment from the police. Two young men experienced violence through self-harm.

Paul *(Sajid, 15)*

The second most common form of violence was 'witnessing' it. The vast majority of young men had witnessed incidents in public spaces such as bullying, intimidation and attacks on youth, or had been present when 'gang' fights broke out. Fewer had witnessed violence in private spaces, such as seeing a brother punished by family members for past actions outside the home, or witnessing a parent, brother or girlfriend being assaulted in a domestic violence incident.

With regard to 'perpetrating' violence, a distinction can be made between the public and private spheres. Ten of the young men participating in this study (six Asians and four white English) told me that they had perpetrated violence in a public space through participation in, for example, street robbery, assault, intra-ethnic 'gang' attacks, vigilante-styled justice, or to defend the family or group honour (when 'dissed' or given 'dirties'). A minority in this study (two young men), acted violently in private spaces, for example, hitting their girlfriend or friend's girlfriend.

* The research presented in this box is the result of an ESRC-funded studentship on 'Discourses of the Social: A Study of Emerging Masculinities and "Anti-social" Behaviour Amongst Male Youth in Inner City Bradford', 2003-2006, supervised by Professor Jenny Pearce and Dr Janet Bujra in the Department of Peace Studies, University of Bradford.

**Highmoor and Broadbeck are pseudonyms for the two neighbouring locations in Bradford where the research was carried out. Like the aliases chosen by the youths, they are used in order to preserve the anonymity of the participants. The photographs included here were taken by the youths who wrote the captions.

*** While all the youth communicated to me that they were 'victims' of violence, they did not label their experiences in terms of the discourses used in academic literature. Terms such as 'structural violence' used to describe their experiences have been applied by me in analysis.

E J Milne, PhD researcher, Department of Peace Studies, University of Bradford

analysis if we are to refine our understanding of how in practice these kinds of violences interact with gendered socialisation processes within each space[8]. I would therefore start with the socialisation space of the home, move to the socialisation space of community, neighbourhood, school, to the socialisation space of associational life or civil society and finally to the socialisation space of nation state construction, whether as a finished or (as in many parts of the global South) incomplete and arguably unfinishable process, given the logic of globalisation. Gender socialisation is a variable in all these spaces, a likely transmitter mechanism for the reproduction and reinforcement of violence through all the spaces. This kind of analysis is open to empirical research also and thus can help us refine our tools for addressing the problems as they emerge contextually as well as cross-contextually.

This analysis looks at the character of gender domination in each of the spaces, and whether male socialisation processes in each contributes to the greater propensity of men to use violence when they feel a loss of honour, an assault on their pride and a sense of shame or inability to measure up to other social norms of manhood in the given context. For example, political violence would need to be explored through a gender lens (as well as other lenses), and the question posed: who is controlling and shaping the rules of the political game in, for instance, the space of the nation state? Why is the decision to wage war so frequently the decision of a mostly male corpus of decision makers? Is there a connection between hegemonic struggles between and within nations, the power of men in national public spheres, and the readiness to use violence to defend or promote hegemony? Gender would not explain everything (I have earlier emphasised that I am not trying to explain all violences, nor diminish the weight of other variables such as class, but to explore the implications of the evidence of the greater willingness of men to use violence). But posing the question would make us aware of potential connections between the embedding of violence in the nation state construction process, alongside the domination of men in the public political realm in the course of that construction process[9], and the persistent use of violence for certain aims. How

in turn does the publicly sanctioned use of violence relate to readiness to use violence in other socialisation spaces where male domination prevails and where masculinity is constructed in such a way as to make someone 'more of a man' for using violence? How does the flow of gendered relations between and within these spaces reinforce the normalisation, transmission and reproduction of violence across them all and through time?

Given the conventional nature of socialisation, its acceptance and internalisation in our behaviour, violence has become part of a seemingly natural human interaction. Until we question the convention and in particular its gendered components we cannot, I would argue, rid ourselves of this great source of pain and suffering. But nor would this be sufficient. We also need to think through how the acceptance of violence as a normal component of human interaction is to be challenged. And here the differences between men and women may not be so sharp. Women also often accept the normality of violence in their lives, either at home or in other spaces, as much as do men[10], and often reap the benefits of male willingness to use violence or themselves reinforce the ideal of manhood that also fosters violent responses to perceived humiliation. We need, therefore, to build a much more robust mechanism for dealing with the shame, honour, pride issues that enhance the predisposition of men to use violence in given contexts, and offer alternative constructions of masculinity. While part of the agenda would be re-socialisation, the other part is to rethink the character of power and its relationship to human interactions and violence. Feminists who have consciously re-theorised gender relationships (albeit with little

8 I would also seek a sharper refinement of the differential character and impact of physical, symbolic and structural violence. I think it is worth distinguishing between violence that can threaten your very physical existence and violence that undermines and erodes your physical existence but does not eliminate you.

9 A process which has been historically very violent throughout the world.

10 Field experience in Medellin, Colombia, reveals that girls often urge their partners to compete for power in male gangs because they reap material benefits from their partners' willingness to rob and kill.

consensus!) could potentially offer new insights and, through rethinking the exercise of power, offer women who gain the opportunity to exercise it the intellectual tools to challenge violence and the socialisation processes that foster it.

Diminishing violence through a new theory and practice of power

> ...Politically speaking, it is insufficient to say that power and violence are not the same. Power and violence are opposites; where the one rules absolutely, the other is absent. Violence appears where power is in jeopardy, but left to its own course it ends in power's disappearance. This implies that it is not correct to think of the opposite of violence as non-violence; to speak of non-violent power is actually redundant. Violence can destroy power; it is utterly incapable of creating it. (Arendt 1969: 56)

Arendt's distinction between power and violence is dependent on a particular understanding of power, one that appears counter-intuitive. Power for Arendt emerges when people decide to act together. Arendt is attempting to distinguish between human interactions that originate from a prior acceptance of the right of the Other to exist. This is a reciprocal recognition that nevertheless can lead to action to restrict the freedom of existence of the Other (ie power over, a form of power that Lukes rightly points out is not developed by Arendt), but does not deny recognition of the Other through pain on the Other's body and/or mind (the exercise of violence). Arendt's sense of power is actually profoundly different from conventional understandings of power, which I would argue derive mostly from masculine experiences and conceptualisations. For Arendt:

> Power corresponds to the human ability not just to act but to act in concert. Power is never the property of an individual; it belongs to a group and remains in existence only so long as the group keeps together. When we say of somebody that he is in power' we actually refer to him as being empowered by a certain number of people to act in their name. (1969: 44)

---

11 Lukes (2005) argues that Arendt ignores 'power over' and discusses Arendt alongside Talcott Parsons' consensual view of power. There are nevertheless vast differences between the social integrationist and functionalist propositions of Parsons on the one hand and Arendt's intellectual concern with public space and reasoned argument on the other. But Lukes is right to say that, like all conceptualisations of power, their propositions are normative (Lukes 2005:31).

I would argue that, seen through a gender lens, Arendt is trying to put forward a view of power that is much more in tune with more contemporary feminist deconstructions of power and empowerment, and the substitution of 'power over' with' power to'.

The distinction or opposition between power and violence is not as apparent to the reader of Arendt's book if both are seen through the male lens that has become conventional to us. However, the evidence that women tend to participate in public life in supportive roles, and in community-based roles, suggests that many see power very much as Arendt outlines, as about collaboration and cooperation, and are uncomfortable with exercising 'power over'. In a recent field trip to explore civil society participation in the midst of Colombia's protracted violence and war, I asked the Casa de la Mujer, a feminist group based in Bogotá, whether they had generated their own vision of power. I am struck by how their analysis echoes that of Arendt:

> Women must ask themselves, do they want to replicate exclusionary practices or encourage other types of political practices? Participation is about developing the commonality in our needs and how to negotiate individual and collective needs. Do we come together to put forward our needs or do we want to be exclusionary? Our proposals are not just for women, but for our families, for everyone. What type of political practices do we want to build? How do we not repeat other practices, including those among women? Power is denied us, how do we recognise the power of others? I don't know whether we have an alternative idea of power. We work on subjectivities. I cannot be democratic if I don't construct myself as a democratic subject. How as women do we build more democratic subjects? How do I find a balance between my personal interests and my collective interests? We need to reflect on new practices. This is a slow process. Families and schools are very authoritarian. We come from anti-democratic communities and the Church too. There is little acceptance of differences. We are very fundamentalist, left and right. The new subjectivities can materialise in new political practices. This question is in dispute in feminism. Power for what? Do we want power for human beings? Yes, but not that of men, based on

exclusion. We want a power that permits men and women to reach agreements. That doesn't mean that women are only victims. It means a construction. What is in us, which also reproduces exclusionary practices? Being victims takes away our own responsibility. In our work with women and violence, we think women are victims of violence. But we also analyse our responsibility, not for being beaten, but for not leaving the situation. We don't say women have to deal with their situation alone, we are not talking about guilt, but that something in our subjectivity makes us accept these situations. How can you transform the situation? At least you can take action and go to a doctor or a lawyer. Power is passed on through valuing the autonomy and self-esteem of women. We don't just suffer power. (Personal interview, Casa de la Mujer, Bogotá, 1 April 2005)

For these women power also has something to do with self-esteem. But it is gained through construction with others and consensus building. These reflections from differential gendered practices around power and violence could, I believe, shine a path to overcoming the destructive interaction between them that originates in gendered socialisations processes.

Conclusion

In order to end violence as well as wars, we need new ideas urgently. We need, for instance, an approach to justice claims that may recognise the justification for violent resistance or retribution in some cases, but nevertheless chooses not to use violence to pursue claims. We need to accept that non-violence is not passivity in the face of injustice. 'Civility' is an unfulfilled project in human cultural development partly because it is so unconvincing to those who experience oppression, exclusion and marginality. Such experiences generate shame and an assault on honour and pride, which in the form in which male socialisation exists, can trigger violent acts justified in terms of 'being a real man'. But to experience oppression does not mean unwillingness to oppress Others. The project of human cultural development must include an element that offers a more sustainable and universal challenge to that 'Othering', which is so often sustained or resisted by violence. It must contribute to the conditions that enable humans to live without violence.

I would argue that one of the obstacles in our pathway to reaching such a goal is gender socialisation. We need to unpack the way male and female identities have tended to foster violence and aggression in the one, and passivity and submission in the other. Through our constructions of bounded, gendered spaces, the circulation of these gendered constructions through time and space has been obfuscated. Changing our socialisation practices will not address the deep-seated inequalities which tap into the sense of shame that, it has been argued, make it more likely that men will act violently. A gendered approach to violence must, therefore, include a gendered approach to power that enables men and women to participate as equals in the public sphere where they can legitimately address the problems that have created the conditions for violence in human relationships. Unpacking the gendered components for violence is not to blame men for all violence, but to seek to understand one of the most vital components in its reproduction in order to liberate both men and women from its effects.

Arendt, H (1969) *On Violence.* San Diego and New York: Harvest Books.

Bourdieu, P (2001) *Masculine Domination.* Cambridge: Polity Press.

 – and Wacquant, L (2004) 'Symbolic Violence', in N Scheper-Hughes and P Bourgois (eds), *Violence in War and Peace: An Anthology.* Oxford: Blackwell

Bourgois, P (1995) *In Search of Respect: Selling Crack in El Barrio.* Cambridge: Cambridge University Press.
 (2004) 'The Continuum of Violence in War and Peace: Post-Cold War Lessons from El Salvador ', in N Scheper-Hughes and P Bourgois (eds), *Violence in War and Peace: An Anthology.* Oxford: Blackwell.

Bujra, J and Pearce, J (2005) 'Youth Violence: What Made them Riot?' Programme for a Peaceful City Research Hub Symposium on Young Men in the District. Unpublished.

Castro, M C and Diaz, L (1997) *Guerilla, Reinsercion y Lazo Social.* Bogota: Almudena Editores.

Chodorow, N (2002) 'The Enemy Outside: Thoughts on the Pschodynamics of Extreme Violence with Special Attention to Men and Masculinity', in Judith Gardiner (ed), *Masculinity Studies and Feminist Theory.* New York: Columbia University Press.

Einstein, A and Freud, S (1933) *Why War?* International Institution of Intellectual Coooperation, League of Nations. Reprinted, Redding, CA: CAT Publishing, 1991.

Galtung, J (1996) *Peace by Peaceful Means: Peace, Conflict in Development and Civilisation.* London: Sage.

Gilligan, J (1997) *Violence: Reflections on a National Epidemic.* New York: Ist Vintage Book Editions.

 – (2001) *Preventing Violence.* London: Thames and Hudson.

Hobsbawm, E (1994) *Age of Extremes: The Short Twentieth Century.* London: Michael Joseph.

Howell, J and Pearce, J (2001) *Civil Society and Development: A Critical Exploration.* Boulder, CO: Lynne Rienner.

Hume, M (2004) '"It's as if you don't know because you don't do anything about it": Gender and Violence in El Salvador', *Environment & Urbanization,* 16(2): 63–72.

IRIN (2004) *Our Bodies – Their Battle Ground: Gender-based Violence in Conflict Zones.* IRIN Web Special on violence against women and girls during and after conflict. September. www.irinnews.org/webspecials/gbv/gbv-webspecial.PDF (consulted 24 May 2006).

Jacobs, S, Jacobsen, R and Marchbank J (eds) (2000) *States of Conflict: Gender, Violence and Resistance.* London: Zed Press

Keane, J (1996) *Reflections on Violence.* London: Verso.

Koonings, K and Kruijt, D (1999) *Societies of Fear: The Legacy of Civil War, Violence and Terror in Latin America.* London: Zed Press.

Las Dignas (1996) *Mujeres Montana.* El Salvador: Las Dignas.

Lukes S (2005) *Power: A Radical View.* Basingstoke: Palgrave Macmillan

Massey, D (1994) *Space, Place and Gender.* Cambridge: Polity Press.
 (1999) *Power-geometries and the Politics of Space-Time.* Heidelberg: University of Heidelberg.

Meertens (2001) 'Victims and Survivors of War in Colombia: Three Views of Gender Relations', in C Berquist et al., *Violence in Colombia 1990–2000.* Wilmington, DE: Scholarly Resources.

Meintjes, S, Pillay, A and Turshen, M (eds) (2002) *The Aftermath.* London: Zed Books.

Moser, C and Clark, F (eds) (2001) *Victims, Perpetrators or Actors? Gender, Armed Conflict and Political Violence.* London: Zed Books.

 – and McIlwaine, C (2003) *Encounters with Violence in Latin America: Urban Poor Perceptions of Violence in Colombia and Guatemala.* London: Routledge.

 – and Winton, A (2002) 'Violence in the Central American Region: Towards an Integrated Framework for Violence Reduction', ODI Working Paper 171. London: ODI.

Nordstrom, C (1997) *Girls and Warzones: Troubling Questions.* Uppsala: Life and Peace Institute.

Pankhurst, D (2003) 'The "Sex War" and Other Wars: Towards a Feminist Approach to Peace-Building', *Development in Practice,* 13: 154–77.

Pateman, C (1988) *The Sexual Contract.* Cambridge: Polity Press.

Pearce, J (1985) *Promised Land: Peasant Rebellion in Chalatenango, El Salvador.* London: Latin America Bureau.

PNUD (Programa de las Naciones Unidas para el Desarrollo) (2002) Indicadores sobre violencia en El Salvador. Seminario Permanente sobre Violencia, El Salvador, PNUD. El Salvador.

Scheper-Hughes, N and Bourgois, P (2004) 'Introduction: Making Sense of Violence', in N Scheper-Hughes and P Bourgois (eds), *Violence in War and Peace: An Anthology.* Oxford: Blackwell.

Wagner, P (1993) *A Sociology of Modernity, Liberty and Discipline.* London: Routledge.

WHO (World Health Organization) (2002) *World Report on Violence and Health.* Geneva: WHO.

 – (2004) *Milestones of a Global Campaign for Violence Prevention.* Geneva: WHO.

WHO/World Bank (2004) *World Report on Road Traffic Injury Prevention.* Geneva: WHO.

CHAPTER 3

PIPE DREAM OR PANACEA? GLOBAL CIVIL SOCIETY AND ECONOMIC AND SOCIAL RIGHTS

Marlies Glasius

Introduction

The existence of hunger, homelessness, preventable disease, and illiteracy in the world can be considered variously as fate, a tragedy, a predicament, or an injustice. Each of these terms implies different value judgements about whether there is any (human or divine) culpability attached to these ills, whether there is a duty to correct them, and whether they can in fact be resolved.

This chapter considers the successes and limitations of global civil society attempts to frame access to food, housing, health and education as individual human rights; and hunger and malnutrition, homelessness and inadequate housing, and lack of access to health and education as violations of human rights. Such a framing tends to answer the questions of blame, obligation, and solubility in the affirmative. Unlike many other diagnoses, it seeks the solution at the level of the individual. But the answers to questions about where the blame lies and, more importantly, about where the obligation to guarantee the right might lie, are often confused and uncertain. This confusion and uncertainty arise from three tensions inherent in the economic and social rights frame, each of which could be considered either as a handicap or as a creative tension.

The first tension is that between the two systems of norms on which the invocation of human rights, including economic and social rights, rests. Human rights are instinctive but also contested moral norms. People are shocked by malnutrition or homelessness just as they are by torture or unfair detention. They feel it as an injustice and an infringement on human dignity, particularly when it is found alongside conspicuous wealth. Hence, statements such as 'everyone has the right to an education' or 'absolute poverty is a violation of human rights' have a resonance with poor and not-so-poor people from different parts of the world. At the same time, human rights are also legal norms, laid down, in many variations, in instruments of international and national law, with or without implementation systems.

The two normative systems have developed in tandem and are partly dependent on each other, but they are also in tension with each other (see for instance Hart 1961: 205–6; Sen 1984: 73–5). These frictions are exposed particularly forcefully when it comes to the obligations attached to economic and social rights. Morally, the concept that 'everyone has the right ...' could point towards a wide range of social actors having far-reaching responsibilities. Legally, even the precise obligations of states are far from determined, and any obligations beyond states are even more uncertain and controversial.

This brings us to the second tension and source of confusion. There is a paradox at the heart of human rights law, which again is revealed most forcefully in relation to economic and social rights. On the one hand, the very manner in which human rights are expressed signifies a breach with the tradition of absolute sovereignty, according to which each state could treat its own citizens as it pleased, and no other state had a right or responsibility to interfere. On the other hand, human rights law is also the product of an era that still thought largely in terms of stable populations sitting tight behind their borders and subject only to national political and economic forces. On the obligations side of human rights law there is a heavy assumption that every state has specific obligations to its own citizens, or at least the individuals under its jurisdiction, which go very much beyond obligations to the citizens of the rest of the world. It is when it comes to obligations to the citizens of the rest of the world ('extra-territorial obligations' in legal jargon) that international law becomes most nebulous and controversial. This finds expression in the debates surrounding humanitarian intervention, for instance, but it is also a contentious issue when it comes to the obligations of rich states in relation to the economic and social rights of the citizens of poor states. The notion that non-state actors, including inter-governmental organisations, transnational corporations or non-governmental organisations (NGOs), might have legal human rights obligations is

Figure 3.1: **The place of economic and social rights in political thought**

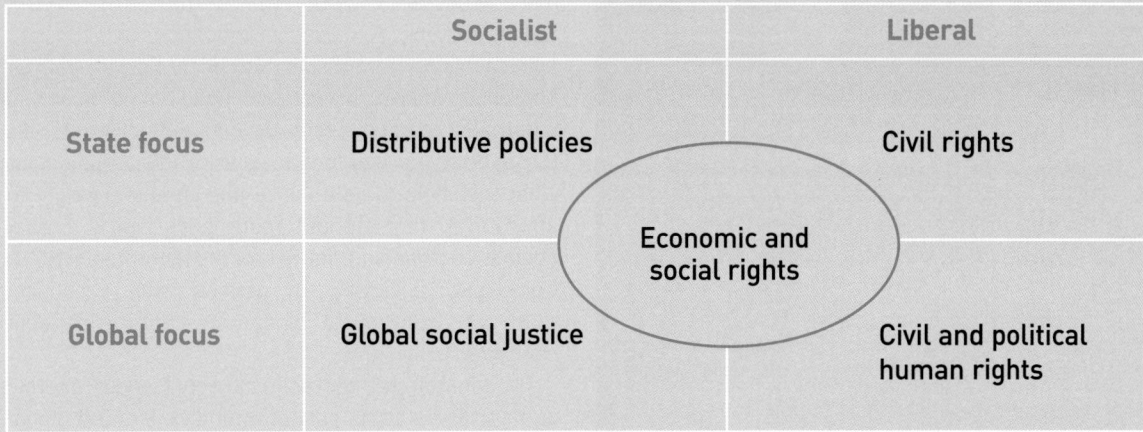

	Socialist	Liberal
State focus	**Distributive policies**	**Civil rights**
Global focus	**Global social justice**	**Civil and political human rights**

(center: **Economic and social rights**)

even more underdeveloped. The state-oriented way of thinking about obligations has the advantage of legal certainty, and it is in this area that many recent victories, described in this chapter, have been achieved. However, the exclusive reliance on obligations of the state towards its own nationals is also increasingly felt to be inadequate for addressing social justice issues in a globalised and privatised world.

The third tension exclusively concerns economic and social rights, and relates to their position in political theory. They find themselves at the crossroads, or in the crossfire, of a historic confrontation between two political ideologies, liberalism and socialism. Liberals believe that individual rights are the key to a decent political system that transcends despotism, and as such they 'trump' matters of normal political debate and policy choice. However, the classical canon of civil rights as it emerged at the heart of liberal thinking during the Enlightenment did not include rights to health, housing, or education, and many self-defined liberals would place all welfare issues in the 'policy choice' rather than in the 'inalienable rights' category. Socialism, while it comes in even more strands and variations, basically diagnoses inequality between the classes, not despotism, as the main problem to be addressed by a decent political system. Therefore, it does consider redistribution as a political imperative in order to achieve socio-economic equality. But

typically, it conceives of such schemes at the collective level, and is suspicious of the notion of individual rights, which it associates with bourgeois liberalism. Hence, the pairing of 'economic and social' with 'rights', while it need not be inherently incompatible with either system, has enemies on both sides, and few champions who root their argument in political theory. The second and third of the tensions described here are graphically represented in Figure 3.1, which suggests that economic and social rights could be seen as transcending all positions, or appealing to none.

At worst, economic and social rights can be seen as an obscure sub-discipline of international human rights law, simultaneously disconnected from realpolitik and from grassroots movements through a rarefied utopian legalism with little connection to the real world. At best, they can be seen as a value system that bridges and transcends liberalism and socialism, has a direct appeal to deprived people, and can, if it is further developed at the implementation level, deliver social justice on a global scale. This chapter explores which of these two descriptions best fits the current status and near future of economic and social rights. It sets out to do two things.

First, it describes the history of the 'economic and social rights' frame. These rights, of much more mixed ideological origin than civil and political rights, almost accidentally made their way into international

President Roosevelt was the first to set out a holistic notion of human rights © F D Roosevelt Presidential Library and Museum

human rights law and subsequently became instrumentalised, one might even say perverted, in East–West and North–South confrontations. But they were rediscovered by a small group of activists and academics in the 1980s, who clarified and strengthened their legal significance, and introduced them to new audiences in the human rights and development fields. From there, economic and social rights found increasing acceptance in a number of bilateral and multilateral fora, but also became subject to renewed co-option and bureaucratisation. They also hit a brick wall when it came to the international financial and trade institutions, and initially made little imprint on the discourse of the new global social justice movement.

Second, the chapter revisits the tensions described above, between individualist and collectivist solutions to social justice problems, between economic and social rights as legal and moral norms, and between state-focused and globally oriented ways of thinking about obligations. It does so not at a theoretical level but through the lens of actual present-day activities of global civil society actors, describing new synergies and new methodologies in their work as well as remaining controversies, blind spots and limitations.

Recent history

The first elevation into international politics
Economic and social rights are commonly believed to derive primarily from socialist ideologies that came to the fore in the late nineteenth and early twentieth century, in contrast to civil and political rights, which are associated with the eighteenth-century Enlightenment. A closer examination of European political history contradicts this notion. Edward Palmer Thompson shows, for instance, how 'rioting' poor and paternalist pamphleteers in England joined forces throughout the eighteenth century to campaign for what they held to be a moral and customary right to affordable, high-quality food, particularly bread, against encroaching market forces (Thompson 1971). Conversely, achieving the general vote, a political right, was central to nineteenth-century socialist concerns (Ishay 2004: 135).

The idea of civil and political rights and economic and social rights as part of an indivisible and global value system was first set out in Franklin Delano Roosevelt's famous 1941 Four Freedoms speech, which looked forward to 'a world founded upon four essential human freedoms: freedom of expression; freedom of worship; freedom from fear; and freedom from want'. His freedom from want was also intended to confer international obligations: 'translated into world terms, [it] means economic understandings which will secure to every nation a healthy peacetime life for its inhabitants' (Roosevelt 1941). What these 'understandings' should amount to was not elaborated. The holistic notion of human rights was subsequently expressed in the Universal Declaration of Human Rights of 1948, which included the right to social security, to work, to rest and leisure, to an adequate standard of living, including food, clothing, housing and medical care, and to education.

Labour rights have had rather a different political trajectory from other economic and social rights through their close relation with the history of trade unionism, and do not form the focus of the rest of this chapter. Neither will 'cultural rights', such as the right to speak one's own language or to take part in communal cultural life. While economic and social rights often have cultural aspects, cultural rights do raise specific issues, to do with minority groups and identity, which are separable from the main concerns of economic and social rights.

Soon after the adoption of the Universal Declaration, the Cold War divide made itself felt in human rights, as everywhere else in international politics. Each bloc appropriated its own version of human rights. According to Western states, led by the

United States, only civil and political rights were legally enforceable, whereas economic and social rights were of a programmatic nature, requiring state intervention and therefore to be realised progressively rather than immediately enforceable. The Soviet bloc countered that civil and political rights were a reflection of the interests of the ruling class in capitalist societies. They were meaningless to citizens without the realisation of economic and social rights. But while Western states emerged as opponents, in reality the Soviet bloc was not a wholehearted supporter of economic and social rights qua rights; it merely used them rhetorically in its opposition to civil and political rights (Arambulo 1999: 15–18). The concept of rights, which places entitlement and empowerment at the individual level, went against the Marxist–Leninist model. After more than 20 years of wrangling, two separate human rights treaties were adopted by the United Nations: the International Covenant on Civil and Political Rights (ICCPR) and the International Covenant on Economic, Social and Cultural Rights (ICESCR; see Box 3.1). They finally came into force in 1976. ICESCR was the Cinderella of the UN human rights system: it had no monitoring committee of experts, the politicised but influential Commission on Human Rights was kept away from it, and few, if any, civil society organisations paid any attention to it.

Meanwhile, developing countries sought to add another right to the international catalogue: a United Nations resolution adopted in 1979 said that 'the right to development is a human right *and that equality of opportunity for development is as much a prerogative of nations as of individuals of nations*' (quoted in Sengupta 2002: 863, emphasis added). Given the confusion between 'states' and 'nations' that is inherent in the very name of the United Nations, this statement transformed development from a human into a state right, more specifically a right of poor states. Thus, it was closely related to the idea of the New International Economic Order. The 1986 Declaration on the Right to Development, adopted by the UN General Assembly, puts more emphasis on the individual level, while also spelling out that there are multiple duty-bearers in relation to human rights. But the Declaration has little legal status and little implementable detail. To this day, independent experts, open-ended working groups and UN task forces are making little-noticed attempts to clarify (or obfuscate) the right to development (Salomon 2005).

Thus, for more than 40 years after the announcement of a world 'free from want' by the president of the United States, economic and social rights remained a dead letter. With the exception of labour rights, they failed to inspire global civil society activity. Steering a course that transcended the bitter Cold War dispute on human rights was, as an organisation like Amnesty International found, difficult enough. The language of economic and social human rights fitted so badly with any of the major ideologies of the day that it appears to have been beyond the political imagination of the actors and thinkers in civil society. Nor did the 'right to development' capture the imagination. Such rights were therefore easily hijacked by a variety of state agendas, which were in reality directed against civil and political rights, or against economic inequality between states.

Eventually, a number of 'like-minded' Western states such as Australia, Canada, Denmark, Germany and the Netherlands, which somewhat dissented from 'Western thought' as formulated by the United States, became interested in improving the shamefully inadequate procedures to monitor the Covenant. Also, in this new stage of the Cold War, the Soviet Union and its satellites warmed to the idea of an enhanced status for economic and social rights, just as Reaganite America became increasingly ideologically opposed to them (Alston 1987: 345–9). So, in 1986, 18 'independent' experts (some more independent than others) were installed on a new UN Committee on Economic, Social and Cultural Rights. Still, in 1987, Philip Alston, the most dedicated member of the new committee, wrote that 'for a variety of historical, ideological, pragmatic, and other reasons, there remains considerable reluctance on the part of many, if not most, human rights NGOs to become involved' in economic and social rights (Alston 1987: 371–2). This was to change dramatically in the next 15 years.

Discovery by global civil society

In the early 1980s, small groups of activists, philosophers and lawyers were simultaneously but separately beginning to rediscover the most vital and compelling of all economic and social rights: the right to food.

Two very different but novel arguments were advanced in short books by two leading academics,

Box 3.1: The rights to food, health, housing and education in the International Covenant on Economic, Social and Cultural Rights

Article 11
1. The States Parties to the present Covenant recognize the right of everyone to an adequate standard of living for himself and his family, including adequate food, clothing and housing, and to the continuous improvement of living conditions. The States Parties will take appropriate steps to ensure the realization of this right, recognizing to this effect the essential importance of international co-operation based on free consent.

2. The States Parties to the present Covenant, recognizing the fundamental right of everyone to be free from hunger, shall take, individually and through international co-operation, the measures, including specific programmes, which are needed:

(a) To improve methods of production, conservation and distribution of food by making full use of technical and scientific knowledge, by disseminating knowledge of the principles of nutrition and by developing or reforming agrarian systems in such a way as to achieve the most efficient development and utilization of natural resources;

(b) Taking into account the problems of both food-importing and food-exporting countries, to ensure an equitable distribution of world food supplies in relation to need.

Article 12
1. The States Parties to the present Covenant recognize the right of everyone to the enjoyment of the highest attainable standard of physical and mental health.

2. The steps to be taken by the States Parties to the present Covenant to achieve the full realization of this right shall include those necessary for:

(a) The provision for the reduction of the stillbirth-rate and of infant mortality and for the healthy development of the child;

(b) The improvement of all aspects of environmental and industrial hygiene;

(c) The prevention, treatment and control of epidemic, endemic, occupational and other diseases;

(d) The creation of conditions which would assure to all medical service and medical attention in the event of sickness.

Article 13
1. The States Parties to the present Covenant recognize the right of everyone to education. They agree that education shall be directed to the full development of the human personality and the sense of its dignity, and shall strengthen the respect for human rights and fundamental freedoms. They further agree that education shall enable all persons to participate effectively in a free society, promote understanding, tolerance and friendship among all nations and all racial, ethnic or religious groups, and further the activities of the United Nations for the maintenance of peace.
2. The States Parties to the present Covenant recognize that, with a view to achieving the full realization of this right:

(a) Primary education shall be compulsory and available free to all;

(b) Secondary education in its different forms, including technical and vocational secondary education, shall be made generally available and accessible to all by every appropriate means, and in particular by the progressive introduction of free education;

(c) Higher education shall be made equally accessible to all, on the basis of capacity, by every appropriate means, and in particular by the progressive introduction of free education;

(d) Fundamental education shall be encouraged or intensified as far as possible for those persons who have not received or completed the whole period of their primary education;

(e) The development of a system of schools at all levels shall be actively pursued, an adequate fellowship system shall be established, and the material conditions of teaching staff shall be continuously improved.

3. The States Parties to the present Covenant undertake to have respect for the liberty of parents and, when applicable, legal guardians to choose for their children schools, other than those established by the public authorities, which conform to such minimum educational standards as may be laid down or approved by the State and to ensure the religious and moral education of their children in conformity with their own convictions.

4. No part of this article shall be construed so as to interfere with the liberty of individuals and bodies to establish and direct educational institutions, subject always to the observance of the principles set forth in paragraph I of this article and to the requirement that the education given in such institutions shall conform to such minimum standards as may be laid down by the State.

Article 14
Each State Party to the present Covenant which, at the time of becoming a Party, has not been able to secure in its metropolitan territory or other territories under its jurisdiction compulsory primary education, free of charge, undertakes, within two years, to work out and adopt a detailed plan of action for the progressive implementation, within a reasonable number of years, to be fixed in the plan, of the principle of compulsory education free of charge for all.

Source: *ICESCR (1966)*

which had a seminal impact on the economic and social rights frame. In *Poverty and Famines,* published in 1981, economist Amartya Sen analyses a number of famines with a view to demolishing the then-existing paradigm among developmental economists, which held that famines were caused by a general decline in the availability of food. Instead, he argues, 'A person's ability to command food – indeed, to command any commodity he wishes to acquire or retain depends on the entitlement relations that govern possession and use in that society. It depends on what he owns, what exchange possibilities are offered to him, what is given to him free, and what is taken away from him' (Sen 1981: 154–5). Hence, the global focus on increasing agricultural productivity, which had reigned hitherto, was inadequate for solving problems of starvation and famine. Nor could market mechanisms be relied upon to relieve famines because markets respond to 'entitlements': individuals' property and possibilities of exchange, not their physical needs as such. Therefore, policies designed to prevent or relieve famines should tackle the socio-political and legal conditions that govern entitlements in a particular society, not just provide more food. 'The focus on entitlements', Sen concludes in his essay, 'has the effect of emphasizing legal rights...The law stands between food availability and food entitlement' (Sen 1981: 165–6). At this point Sen does not make a case for a 'right to food'. 'Entitlements', his key concept, are not moral rights but a label for a person's actual ownership and exchange capabilities. But his argument – that hunger needs to be tackled at the level of entitlements, and that market mechanisms alone will not do this – does point in the direction of policies that alter legal and socio-political structures. The invocation of a right to food can be such an instrument. In a later article, Sen defends the idea of a moral 'metaright' to policies that would help make the right to food realisable (Sen 1984). Sen's argument – that famine (and by extension, as he elaborates in later work, other forms of deprivation) is not caused by absolute scarcity but by legal and political circumstances – was not wholly original even at the time. But it was groundbreaking for a mathematically trained economist armed with data and equations to present such an analysis, and it profoundly affected the hitherto rather technical thinking about development in international institutions. It laid the foundations for the later adoption of 'rights-based approaches' to development.

Political philosopher Henry Shue's *Basic Rights: Subsistence, Affluence, and U.S. Foreign Policy* (1980) is more directly concerned with policy, but has in fact had a more indirect effect on policy makers. It attacks the distinctions made between civil and political rights, constructed as requiring a duty only of non-interference, and economic and social ones, constructed as requiring positive intervention. Instead, Shue argues that the three most basic rights, which underlie all others, are those to physical security, to subsistence (fear and want again), and to liberty. The first two of these he subjects to the exact same analysis of correlative (negative and positive) duties. He distinguishes three types of duties: to avoid depriving people of their rights, to protect them against such deprivation by others, and to aid those whose rights have already been deprived (Shue 1980: 35–64). This tripartite categorisation of obligations, later adapted to 'respect/protect/fulfil', has been a tremendous inspiration to subsequent generations of legal scholars trying to establish exactly what obligations economic and social rights entail. The trinity of obligations has been widely cited by judges (see Box 3.2) and has made its way into the wording of the South African Constitution.

At the same time, some grassroots membership groups of Amnesty International were beginning to feel frustrated with the organisation's limited mandate. In 1982 the Heidelberg group in Germany sent a letter to other Amnesty groups suggesting a new orientation on economic and social rights, and got positive responses from groups in Austria, Switzerland and Italy. The right to food – most concrete, most directly connected to life and death, but also most defensible from a resource perspective – soon became the focus. The national and international leadership made it clear that it was not prepared to move in this direction, so individual members took their actions outside Amnesty and started networking with development and solidarity groups. Sometimes these organisations were reluctant to adopt a human rights approach to food, but there were always some individuals who were enthusiastic. After three years, the network was transformed into a formal human rights organisation, the Foodfirst Information and Action Network (FIAN). Inspired by the Amnesty approach, it focused on blatant violations such as famines related to forced relocation, and undertook Urgent Actions, writing letters to governments, 'even though we did not quite know what was a violation of the right to food, we were finding that out as we were doing it' (Interview Künnemann). Today, FIAN has around 3,300 members in 60 countries, only 12 paid staff, and continues to rely largely on voluntary work by its 40 or so active groups. It continues to write protest letters and send fact-finding missions, and also campaigns for agrarian reform, lobbies the UN, and undertakes human rights education (FIAN URL).

Finally, international lawyers began to take notice of economic and social rights, organising conferences on the right to food in Norway in 1981 and the Netherlands in 1984, and generating associated publications (Eide et al. 1984; Alston and Tomasevski 1984). A third meeting, in 1986, went beyond the right to food. In this four-day conference in Maastricht, a group of 29 experts, including four members of the brand-new UN Committee on Economic, Social and Cultural Rights, succeeded in drafting and unanimously agreeing the Limburg Principles on the Implementation of the International Covenant on Economic, Social and Cultural Rights (Limburg Principles 1987). These 103 principles provided the new committee with a point of reference for interpreting the sometimes obscure and contradictory legal text of the Covenant.

Deepening and widening the focus on economic and social rights

In academia, the Limburg Principles sparked innumerable articles and a spate of doctoral dissertations, constituting a new field of expertise within human rights scholarship. This began to address objections against economic and social rights as 'too vague', 'too costly', or 'not amenable to judicial review'. The objection often raised against the justiciability of economic and social rights – namely, that the Covenant allows the rights to be 'progressively realised' rather than immediately guaranteed – was met with the notion that each right has a 'minimum core content' (and a related, operationalised and context-dependent 'minimum threshold') that does require immediate implementation. Shue's tripartite division of obligations was elaborated for different rights, and supplemented with another categorisation into

'four As': food, health or housing must be available, accessible, acceptable and adaptable. Again, there are variations on this theme. More recently, scholars have taken their cue from activists' work by transferring their focus from the nature of the obligations to a 'violations approach', working outwards from the most egregious violations.

Increasingly, academic and practising lawyers have also begun to test the justiciability of economic and social rights by bringing lawsuits before domestic courts, with some remarkable results (discussed in the next section). Many legal scholars are now also lobbying for an individual complaints procedure at the international level (also discussed below).

In the NGO field, the foundation of FIAN was followed in 1987 by Habitat International Coalition, which transformed itself in that year from a rather lifeless federation of housing corporations and local authorities into an organisation committed to the right to adequate housing, based in the South and focused on lobbying at the UN (Habitat International Coalition URL). It was followed in 1992 by the establishment of the Centre on Housing Rights and Evictions (COHRE URL) and in 1993 by the establishment of the Center for Economic and Social Rights (CESR URL), founded by recent Harvard graduates in New York. All have grown from kitchen-table initiatives into medium-sized international NGOs. In their wake have come hundreds of other, mainly domestic, organisations working specifically in the area of economic and social rights.

The second elevation into international politics

The human rights community

At the 1993 World Conference on Human Rights in Vienna – the first big human rights conference after the Cold War – the formula first adopted in 1968, that human rights and fundamental freedoms are indivisible, was expanded to 'all human rights are universal, indivisible and interdependent and interrelated'. This mantra has been much repeated and celebrated by economic and social rights advocates, but it was a victory only at the rhetorical level, and against relatively little opposition. At the time the human rights debate had moved on to a challenge to the universality of human rights by so-called Asian values propagated by Indonesia, Malaysia and Singapore. Economic and social rights were not a major bone of contention.

Another innovation agreed at the Vienna conference may have been of more practical relevance to the status of economic and social rights. It was decided that the UN should have a global 'face' of human rights in the form of a high commissioner. The second incumbent of this post, the vocal Mary Robinson, committed herself to redressing the imbalance of attention between civil and political versus economic and social rights. She emphasised time and again that extreme poverty was the worst kind of human rights abuse. This constituted a paradigm shift. Most human rights experts at that time, and perhaps still, would have identified situations of genocide or ethnic cleansing as the worst form of human rights abuse. Most development experts would have been inclined to think of extreme poverty as an intractable problem, not a human rights violation.

From the mid-1990s, global mainstream human rights organisations slowly and gingerly began to take up the economic and social rights agenda. Some, such as the International Commission of Jurists, have always supported them at an abstract level, but devote relatively little attention to them. Others, such as Human Rights Watch, gradually incorporated more work on economic and social rights into their daily practices, but maintain a very narrow view on what is appropriate economic and social rights advocacy for an organisation such as theirs (see Box 3.4). Amnesty International finally and famously incorporated economic, social and cultural rights into its mandate in 2001. The organisation still considers itself to be in a learning phase in relation to economic and social rights, and is only gradually expanding its focus from 'respect' violations directly connected to earlier campaigns on civil and political rights, such as for instance the denial of access to work, health and education that has resulted from the building of the wall in the Palestinian Occupied Territories (Amnesty International 2005).

At the global level, campaigning for a UN complaints procedure for individuals, to be established via an 'optional protocol' to the Covenant, has since 1993 become one of the main focuses of the human rights community. Numerous unofficial drafts exist. Nonetheless, it was not until 2003 that the UN Human Rights Commission established an 'Open Ended Working Group', that is, a talking shop, to consider such a protocol. The year 2006 will be crucial for the individual complaints procedure. After three years of deliberation, the working group will hold its last session, and the first session of the new Human Rights Council, convening in June 2006, is expected to decide whether or not to go ahead with drafting a protocol. If there is not enough support, there will be no individual complaints procedure in the foreseeable future (ESCR Protocol Now URL).

The development community

Human rights and development were separated at birth, given over to different organisations and mechanisms within the United Nations system. At the non-governmental level, too, separate organisations developed in these fields, which, particularly at the global policy-making level, had little contact. Human rights entered the radar screen of development organisations only with the Vienna conference of 1993. For instance, this spurred Novib, now the Dutch member of Oxfam International, to support the foundation of the Platform for Human Rights, Democracy and Development (PIDHDD URL) in Latin America, now one of the strongest actors on economic and social rights.

In preparation for the 1995 World Summit for Social Development in Copenhagen, a coalition of disparate, especially Southern, groups, again funded by Novib, collaborated in a bid to get states to make concrete commitments on economic and social issues. After much discussion, especially virtual discussion via the nascent Alliance for Progressive Communications (APC) network, the coalition came to employ a 'merger between a "rights-based" approach and a macro-economic approach', out of which the Social Watch network was born (Van Reisen 2000). This network, as the name suggests, takes the human rights tradition of monitoring state performance according to specific benchmarks into the social development realm (Social Watch URL).

Another impetus came from UNDP, which, with the publication of the annual Human Development Report in 1990, had relaunched itself as a laboratory of new ideas in development thinking. In 2000, having explored participation, human security and gender in previous editions, it gave a new push to the incorporation of human rights into development theory and practice with its report *Human Rights and Human Development* (UNDP 2000).

Seeing extreme poverty as a human rights violation, rather than an intractable problem, represented a paradigm shift ©*Mark Henley/Panos Pictures*

However, human rights are not the only new concept to have seeped into development thinking in recent years; they compete with many others. The development field has a remarkable capacity for absorbing paradigms that challenge it. In the 1990s development variously became sustainable development, gender-sensitive development, and more recently conflict-sensitive development, as well as rights-based development. But to what extent is development practice affected by these changes in terminology? Peter Uvin (2002) distinguishes three levels of adoption of the rights-based paradigm: a purely rhetorical–formulaic incorporation, an add-on leading to the incorporation of some human rights programmes and projects in the overall operations of an organisation, and, most rarely, 'a fundamental rethinking of the development paradigm itself', ideally leading to transformation at the operational level.

At the level of rhetoric, Uvin identifies two devices. The first is to claim that development organisations have always been in the business of fulfilling human rights, and more specifically economic and social rights. Thus he quotes the World Bank, which claims that 'its lending over the past 50 years for education, health care, nutrition, sanitation, housing, environmental protection and agriculture have helped turn rights into reality for millions' (World Bank 1999: 3-4). Even such rhetorical adoption of human rights may not be entirely without consequences. Katarina

Tomasevski, the UN Special Rapporteur on the Right to Education, has described how the Bank has been persuaded to shift from a position of charging fees for primary education to championing free education (Tomasevski 2005: 719–20).

The second and opposite rhetorical trick is found much more often in the publications and websites of development NGOs.

It consists of suggesting that major, epochal changes are now underway in the development enterprise, and they follow directly from the blinding realization of the crucial importance of human rights in development practice. The key human rights contribution to development practice, as repeated in countless documents, is the need for the engagement and participation of the poor in the processes that affect their lives. This argument is breathlessly presented as a major breakthrough that we all ought to feel truly pleased about, as if development practitioners had not been proposing exactly the same thing for decades now, with very little to show for it. (Uvin 2002: 4)

However, most organisations have not confined their commitment to human rights purely to rhetoric. The majority have reached Uvin's second level of adoption, having begun to institute some human rights programmes. International organisations such as UNDP, the bilateral development agencies of

In the 1990s UN summits helped catalyse the development of economic and social rights © Anders Gunnartz/Panos Pictures

Canada, Denmark, Norway and Sweden, and NGOs including Save the Children Fund and Care all fall into this category (Darrow and Tomas 2005: 480; Piron 2005). Typically, this adoption translates simply into financial support for projects of local and international human rights organisations, which sometimes include new specialised economic and social rights organisations or hybrids between traditional fields.

Has any organisation reached the third level of engagement, namely, rethinking the development paradigm and transforming development practice at the operational level? Only a few organisations might claim genuinely to have achieved this. ActionAid, Oxfam and UNICEF have most explicitly revamped their entire mandate, basing it on human rights. UNICEF explicitly bases its work first and foremost on the widely ratified Convention on the Rights of the Child (UNICEF URL). ActionAid and Oxfam do not specifically refer to human rights treaties (a point of criticism by traditional human rights advocates), but instead base themselves on a self-defined set of rights. In the case of ActionAid these are 'women's

rights, the right to education, the right to food, the right to human security during conflicts and emergencies, the right to a life of dignity in the face of HIV and AIDS and the right to just and democratic governance' (ActionAid International 2005). Oxfam bases all its programmes on five more holistically expressed 'rights': the right to a sustainable livelihood, the right to basic social services, the right to life and security, the right to be heard, and the right to an identity (Oxfam International 2001).

It is rather early to tell to what extent these commitments are transforming the practices of the organisations. Various pitfalls can be identified. The first is that, having incorporated human rights, development organisations, ever in pursuit of the moral high ground, move on to the next fashionable concept (as Uvin, 2002: 4, points out). Certainly in the latest Oxfam publications, there seems to be a shift towards 'economic and social justice'. The second danger is a facile relabelling of existing projects to fit with the new objectives. In ActionAid's right to education, or in Oxfam's right to basic social services, old service-delivery mandates are easily recognised, while the right 'to be heard' reflects more recent preoccupations with participation and accountability. The third and most pervasive problem is a very limited understanding of the obligations that flow from human rights. Time and again, documents on rights-based development assert either that rights-based projects can help developing country governments meet basic human rights or, more confrontationally, that they help the citizens of developing countries hold their governments accountable. Some have viewed this cynically, as reintroducing conditionality through the back door, via the beneficiaries (Cornwall and Nyamu-Musembi 2005: 14). Others look upon it more benignly as a tool to empower the poor and marginalised. Even so, the state, and in particular the developmental state, cannot be the be-all and end-all for the fulfilment of economic and social rights. Other states, international financial institutions and transnational corporations may have to assume obligations in order to guarantee effective fulfilment. But the buck does not stop there. Development organisations, whether non-governmental, bilateral or inter-governmental, often have a bigger presence in the health or education sector of developing countries than the state itself. The rhetoric of rights-based development has gone hand in hand with the rhetoric of accountability, but no donor agency has yet spelled out that, in the name of rights-based development, it can henceforth be held accountable by beneficiaries or non-beneficiaries on a specific, self-defined or - better still - legally documented set of human rights obligations. In rights-based development, the rights are for the poor, but the obligations are born by the poor state alone. Development agencies do not recognise themselves as power-holders with possible obligations, and let themselves off the hook.

National and regional successes

Perhaps the greatest advances in economic and social rights, or at least the ones most visible to actual victims of economic and social rights violations, have been made at the national level. Parliaments have adopted laws and constitutional changes that directly recognise economic and social rights, and attendant state obligations; and courts have been increasingly active in interpreting national and international law in such a way that they can judge whether a violation of a right has taken place, and recommend state action to redress the situation. Mostly, both the new laws and the legal judgements have come about after sustained civil society campaigns. There are too many examples of such national victories to describe them all here. Box 3.2 gives a brief overview of the most significant developments.

Three cases are described in greater detail: the Grootboom case on the right to housing in South Africa, the Right to Food Campaign in India, and the intervention on the right to health in free trade negotiations in Ecuador. The first was a landmark advance in justiciability, the second showed a Supreme Court becoming proactively engaged in implementation, and the third is an initiative with both legal and political, and both national and international aspects.

South Africa's new post-Apartheid constitution, inaugurated in 1996, contains a comprehensive bill of rights that includes explicit recognition and concrete descriptions of a number of economic and social rights. In 1998, Mrs Irene Grootboom lived with her family and her sister's family in a shack about 20 metres square in Wallacedene, an informal settlement without water, electricity, sewage or rubbish collection services. Most of the residents had been on the waiting list for subsidised housing for

years. Mrs Grootboom and a few hundred others decided to take matters into their own hands and occupied a vacant farm that was privately owned and had been earmarked for low-cost housing. They were evicted through a court order, their new-built homes were bulldozed and their possessions burned. When a High Court judgment initially granted them government shelter, the government appealed to the Constitutional Court. The court had to interpret article 26 of the new South African Constitution (Republic of South Africa 1996), which provides that (a) 'everyone has the right to have access to adequate housing'; (b) 'the state must take reasonable legislative and other measures (such as policy and programmes) to achieve the progressive realisation of this right'; and (c) 'within its available resources'. The court decided to test whether the Cape Metropolitan Council's housing programme was 'reasonable'. It found that, while the long-term policies were laudable, because there was 'no express provision to facilitate access to temporary relief for people with no access to land, no roof over their heads, for people living in intolerable conditions and crisis situations', the programme was not reasonable and therefore unconstitutional (Thipanyane n.d).

The Grootboom case was hailed by human rights lawyers all over the world. It gave life to the far-reaching provisions in the South African Constitution and demonstrated that a judicial court could review and enforce even the 'obligation to fulfil' economic and social rights, by using a standard of 'reasonableness' that is familiar to many legal systems (Pieterse 2004). Yet it also raises questions about how much lawsuits can actually achieve. After the case the state purchased the squatted farm and some surrounding land to develop low-cost housing for the Grootboom group and others. But the only amenity on the site now named 'Grootboom', where several thousand people live, is a foul-smelling sanitary block with about 12 toilets and some showers and washbasins, most of which are blocked (Schoonakker 2004; Whittal et al. 2004). Box 3.3, which describes the story of the Pom Mahakan community in Bangkok, demonstrates a very different form of community activism and negotiation to prevent eviction.

In India, the Supreme Court has long since established that the right to life protected by the Constitution incorporates aspects of the rights to food and health. There is also a long-established system of public distribution of food to the needy in India. But a 2001 petition to the Supreme Court revealed just how badly this system was functioning. The petition revealed that, 20 years after Sen's *Poverty and Famines*, there was still widespread hunger in the country, especially in the drought-affected areas of Rajasthan and Orissa, while more than 50 million tonnes of food grain were lying idle on the premises of the Food Corporation of India. Both the identification of families living below the poverty line and the actual distribution at village level were so erratic and unreliable that less than five rupees worth of food per person per month was being distributed.

The court confirmed that the coexistence of surplus stocks with deaths from starvation constituted a violation of the right to food, and issued an interim order directing the states included in the petition to implement eight different schemes for food security. Since then, the case has been extended to both the central government and all the states of India, and the court has issued a number of other interim orders to improve both the identification of the beneficiaries and the implementation of food schemes and employment programmes. Village councils have been authorised to conduct social audits of all food and employment schemes implemented in their area. The court has given binding force to existing famine codes, and directed state governments to cancel the licences of retail ration shop dealers that did not open on time, overcharged, made false entries or engaged in black marketing. Uniquely, the court also appointed its own commissioners to monitor progress in executing its rulings.

State implementation of the right to food remains lacklustre and even the court's commissioners are still routinely denied access to relevant documents. However, while the initial petition was brought only by a small group of lawyers from the People's Union for Civil Liberties (PUCL), the Supreme Court's proactive stance has galvanised a much wider campaign. Besides public interest litigation, the Right to Food Campaign organises marches, rallies and fasts, initiates public hearings, conducts research, and engages in media advocacy and lobbying. Provision of midday meals to schoolchildren has been a particularly effective campaign target. On 9 April 2002, the campaign coordinated a national day of action for midday meals. Across some 100 districts in nine states, activists organised a host of activities – schoolchildren lined roads with empty plates in hand,

copies of the Supreme Court's order were distributed, and local communities, NGOs and people's organisations fed children in public places in order to embarrass the government for not doing so. Some members of the campaign have since expanded their work to include the right to employment, in particular in relation to cash-for-work or food-for-work schemes. The campaign remains largely a volunteer effort, which accepts only individual donations in rupees with no strings attached (Right to Food Campaign URL; Interview Patnaik).

Ecuador, with Colombia and Peru, has been negotiating a bilateral free trade agreement for the Andes countries with the United States since 2004. While draft texts are secret, Ecuadorian civil society groups have been particularly concerned about a clause on intellectual property rights, which could block access to cheap generic drugs. In July 2004, the president tried to smooth the negotiations with a decree on intellectual property that would have the same effect. The Centro de Derechos Económicos y Sociales (CDES), an offshoot of CESR in New York, wrote to the government, citing pronouncements by the UN Committee on the Rights of the Child and the Committee on Economic, Social and Cultural Rights to demonstrate that the decree was contrary to the right to health. Within two weeks, Ecuador's head negotiator wrote back, agreeing that the draft decree was unconstitutional and in violation of the right to health, endangering access to affordable medicine. The decree was not passed, and Ecuador's trade team has begun using human rights language in the negotiations, which at the time of writing are ongoing ('Ecuador' 2004; CDES URL).

Brick walls: the unconverted
The United States, historically one of the staunchest opponents of economic and social rights, remains one of a handful of states that has not ratified the International Covenant on Economic, Social and Cultural Rights, on the basis that 'these are not rights but aspirations'. Under the Bush Administration, any specific objections to economic and social rights have become rather obscured by its record on civil and political rights, particularly in relation to 'the war on terror'. But domestically in the United States, economic and social rights are gaining friends and prominence, against relatively little resistance, as they have elsewhere. A new human rights coalition

founded in 2003, whose members range from International groups like Amnesty, Human Rights Watch and CESR to major domestic groups like the American Civil Liberties Union, the National Association for the Advancement of Colored People and the American Friends Service Committee, has the advancement of economic and social rights as one of its core principles (Lobe 2003). Grassroots groups such as the Kensington Welfare Rights Union (URL), an organisation of the homeless, and the affiliated University of the Poor (URL), are also using economic and social rights language and making transnational connections.

But the main adversaries of economic and social rights are no longer to be found in state governments. They are the international financial and trade organisations. As seen above, the World Bank is a partial exception, seeking to co-opt rather than oppose rights language along the lines of 'we've always done it'. The International Monetary Fund (IMF) has been more explicit in its hostility. It has stated that 'IMF was not a signatory to the Covenant … IMF did not specifically take States' obligations under the Covenant into consideration when negotiating or consulting with them…' (UN CESCR 1999). Thus, the IMF refuses to take a position on how states are supposed to mediate between their human rights obligations and the obligations imposed on them in respect of loans. Various governments, including those of Argentina and Egypt, have made it clear to the UN Committee on Economic, Social and Cultural Rights that, when negotiating with the IMF, they do not have the power or leeway to resist particular measures in the name of human rights (Dowell-Jones 2004: 80). So far, despite all the protests against the financial institutions in recent years, civil society pressure specifically in relation to its (legal, political or moral) human rights obligations has been fairly minimal. The first legal study of possible human rights obligations of the Bank and Fund was published only in 2001 (Skogly). What little pressure there has been has had no noticeable effect at all.

The record of the World Trade Organiization (WTO) is in many ways similar. The organisation's powerful Dispute Settlement Mechanism is obliged to take any treaty obligations between disputing states into account, but has not so far applied this provision in relation to human rights treaties. Nor has it allowed non-state actors to submit materials. Economic and social rights activists do not have a common position on how trade should relate to these rights. While some would like to see the WTO take human rights obligations on board (Howse and Mutua 2000), others treat the idea of a 'merger and acquisition' (Alston 2002) of human rights by trade lawyers with suspicion, for the same reasons that Uvin treats the co-option of rights by the World Bank with scepticism. For the time being, they need not worry. The official stance of WTO has not shifted. Nonetheless, an important concession to what can only be described as a regard for the right to health has been made, as the result of massive civil society pressure, at the WTO negotiations in Doha: developing countries are allowed 'flexibility' in importing and exporting generic drugs when they can demonstrate that a national health crisis requires it (WTO 2003).

The private sector cannot actually be described as 'hostile' to economic and social rights: by and large, it has simply not been asked to take a position yet. Mainstream human rights organisations have begun work on the human rights obligations of corporate entities only recently, and have generally done so cautiously, striking a more cooperative note than in their relations with governments because of the much weaker legal basis for these obligations. Of course, for decades there have been civil society initiatives characterised by their aggressive attitude towards corporations, but, as will be discussed below, they have generally not used human rights language, let alone economic and social rights language. Yet the private sector can become implicated in economic and social rights issues in many ways: through use of child labour in factories or, conversely, through sponsoring community education or health centres not directly related to its for-profit activities, but most importantly, through its growing role in service-provision (Malby 2002). For most of the twentieth century, states were the primary providers of services such as health and education. This meant that they had a double accountability in relation to these services: a legal accountability to respect, protect and fulfil economic and social rights under international and occasionally also national law, and a rather stronger political accountability to the citizens benefiting (or not) from these services. When health, education, electricity, water or sanitation services are contracted out to the private sector, the state

Box 3.2: Recent developments in national and regional law and jurisprudence on economic and social rights

2004

Constitutional Court of Colombia: the state must draw up a time-bound plan to allocate resources to meet economic and social rights of internally displaced people (Tomasevski 2005).

2002

Indian Parliament: the constitution is amended explicitly to oblige the state to provide free and compulsory education to all children aged 6–14 years (Tomasevski 2005).

Supreme Court of South Africa: Treatment Action Campaign case. The Court assesses that there is sufficient medical evidence that Nevirapine is safe and effective in preventing mother-to-child transmission of HIV/AIDS, that the pilot schemes are unreasonably rigid, and that there are sufficient resources to provide the drug to all who need it. The state must therefore provide the drug (Pieterse 2004).

Supreme Court of Venezuela: retrenchment of an anti-retroviral (ARV) treatment programme violates the right to health (Yamin 2005).

2001

African Commission: Ogoni case. The Nigerian government has violated rights to life, property, health, family protection, and a healthy environment. The Commission also recognises a right to food and a right to housing, which are not in the African Charter, as following from the rights above. The right to dispose freely of one's natural resources has been violated by the government because it did not exercise due diligence in monitoring oil companies. However, no direct complaint can be brought against them (Chirwa forthcoming 2006).

Inter-American Court: in response to the death of five street children in Guatemala, the Court declares that the right to life does not only comprise the right not to be deprived of life arbitrarily, but also the right to access to the conditions needed to lead a dignified life (Case Law Database, ESCR-Net URL).

African Commission: Zaire case. The government of Zaire violates the right to health by not providing drinking water, electricity or sufficient medicine. But the exact nature of the government's obligations is not spelled out (Chirwa forthcoming 2006).

Supreme Court of India: right to food case. On confirming that the co-existence of surplus food stocks with deaths from starvation constituted a violation of the right to food, the court ordered the states of Orissa and Rajasthan to implement various schemes to ensure food security. Later, the directive was extended to all states of India, and the court issued a number of interim orders designed to improved the implementation of food schemes, including appointing its own commissioners to monitor progress.

2000

Supreme Court of South Africa: Grootboom case. Government measures to meet its positive obligations to fulfil the constitutional right to housing must be 'reasonable' in the Court's judgment. The failure to provide any relief to those in most urgent need is held to be not reasonable and thus unconstitutional

(Pieterse 2004).

Revised Swiss Constitution: provides that 'Whoever is in distress without the ability to take care of him- or herself has the right to help and assistance and to the means indispensable for a life led in human dignity' (Case Law Database, ESCR-Net URL) .

House of Lords, United Kingdom: holds that cases concerning asbestos exposure of South Africans implicating a UK-registered company can be heard in the UK (Case Law Database, ESCR-Net URL).

1998
Supreme Court of Argentina: having announced a policy to provide a child vaccine, the government is obliged to manufacture and distribute the vaccine (Yamin 2005).

Europe: The Additional Protocol to the European Social Charter Providing for a System of Collective Complaints enters into force, allowing trade unions, employers' organisations and accredited international NGOs to make complaints to a committee of independent experts about violation of the rights in the charter.

1997
Supreme Court of Costa Rica: the right to life in the constitution implies the right to health. The state's social security institute is therefore obliged to provide ARV treatment (Yamin 2005).

1996
South Africa: adopts a new constitution that includes a range of directly enforceable economic and social rights, which the state must 'respect, protect, promote and fulfill' (Pieterse 2004).

1993
Supreme Court of the Philippines: the issuance of timber licences violates the constitutional right, specifically of children and future generations, to 'a balanced and healthy ecology' (Case Law Database, ESCR-Net URL).

1992
Supreme Court of India: having already recognised in earlier judgments the right to housing, the right to a livelihood and the right to health as integral to the 'right to life' enshrined in the constitution, the court now holds that the right to education flows directly from the right to life as recognised by the constitution, and hence the charging of a 'capitation fee' by private medical schools is unconstitutional. A later judgment restricts the right to free education to those under 14 (Case Law Database, ESCR-Net URL).

1990
Supreme Court of Canada: the right to have one's children educated in the minority language (English or French) in the Canadian Charter of Rights and Freedoms creates a 'sliding scale' of obligations, where the state's duties will vary depending on the number of students involved (Case Law Database, ESCR-Net URL).

Box 3.3: Averting the threat of eviction: the Pom Mahakan community in Bangkok

Pom Mahakan is a community of around 300 residents located next to Mahakan Fort, between the old city wall and the canal in central Bangkok. In January 2003, the Bangkok Metropolitan Administration (BMA) served the residents with a notice to vacate their homes. Residents were offered relocation to a place called Minhburi, on the outskirts of Bangkok, 45 kilometres away. The proposed relocation was part of the government-sponsored 'Rattanakosin Island Plan'. The community would make way for a manicured urban park. The announcement of the planned eviction heightened the fears of many similar communities in Rattanakosin that they might also be in line for removal.

A home in Pom Mahakan © *Jean du Plessis, Centre on Housing Rights and Evictions (COHRE)*

Pom Mahakan has been occupied by the residents and their forebears for up to six generations. Michael Herzfeld, professor of anthropology at Harvard University, who has done intensive work in Pom Mahakan, described it as a 'vibrant, cohesive community with a remarkable sense of collective responsibility and mutual support', housed in 'a rare complex of vernacular architecture' (Herzfeld 2003), well worth preserving in rapidly modernising Bangkok.

Residents began holding protests, building barricades and organising a night-watch system. They also acted pre-emptively: assisted by a coalition of academics, NGOs and human rights activists, including the Centre on Housing Rights and Evictions (COHRE), they put forward a highly innovative land-sharing plan as an alternative to eviction and relocation. The plan included the renovation of the older buildings and the integration of the residences into an historical park. The residents even started implementing part of this plan, and many outsiders rallied to the call to support them in this process.

Despite these efforts, in August 2003 an administrative court ruled that the eviction was legal and could go ahead. In January 2004, the authorities started work on the unoccupied areas of Pom Mahakan, including moving the canal pier and excavating certain areas. While the authorities confirmed that the community would be evicted, it was not clear when this would happen. In April 2004, the authorities again announced that they would implement the eviction. That month, the owner of the oldest wooden house in the community, an ancient double-storey teak structure that had become a symbol of the anti-eviction struggle, lost hope and sold it to an outside buyer. Within a few days, this 100-year-old house had been dismantled and taken away. The community had been using the house as a museum and as an exhibition area for their development plans. They had hoped to buy it to establish a permanent community museum.

Global context

Every year, millions of people are forcibly evicted and plunged into homelessness. This practice entrenches patterns of poverty, discrimination and social exclusion. International law explicitly recognises the right to adequate housing. It also clearly prohibits forced eviction, and has repeatedly condemned this practice as a gross and systematic violation of human rights.

Nevertheless, forced evictions are truly a global phenomenon, occurring in both developing and developed countries, and in democracies and dictatorships alike. They are generally caused by one, or any combination, of the following:

- development and infrastructure projects, often funded by major international financial institutions;
- large international events, including global conferences and international sporting events such as the Olympic Games

- urban redevelopment and 'beautification' initiatives, aimed at drawing investment into previously neglected areas and creating 'world-class' cities

- property market forces, often supported by government intervention, resulting in systematic 'gentrification' of areas, usually at the direct expense of the poorer residents

- the absence of state support to the poor under deteriorating economic conditions

- political conflict resulting in 'ethnic cleansing' of entire communities and groups.

In the overwhelming majority of these cases, the evicted people receive no relocation assistance or compensation, and end up poorer than before. The numbers are extraordinary: many evictions are counted not in thousands but in hundreds of thousands of people. The total number of forced evictions in any given year is impossible to determine but here are some recent examples of mass evictions:

- In July 2000, nearly 1 million people were evicted in Rainbow Town, Port Harcourt, Nigeria.

- In India's Narmada River Valley, the ongoing Narmada Sagar and Sardar Sarovar dam projects, when finally completed, will have displaced over 250,000 people.

- In 2003-4 in Jakarta, as part of an effort to clear various areas of informal occupation, over 100,000 people were either evicted or threatened with eviction.

- In early 2004, some 150,000 people were evicted in New Delhi and 77,000 in Kolkata (Calcutta), India.

- In Beijing, China, over 300,000 people have reportedly lost their homes as a result of preparations for the 2008 Olympic Games.

- In various locations in Zimbabwe an estimated 300,000 residents of informal settlements were forcibly evicted in June and July 2005, as part of the government's 'Operation Restore Order'. In addition, up to 30,000 informal traders were arrested.

Pom Mahakan preserved

Under the threat of the bulldozer, the Pom Mahakan community continued to attempt to negotiate with the authorities in a bid to prevent eviction. After a further scare that the eviction would finally be implemented during December 2005, followed by community resistance and pressure from many quarters, the Governor of Bangkok finally agreed to resolve the issue through negotiations. On 19 December 2005, he wrote to COHRE to confirm that negotiations between the community, the Bangkok Metropolitan Administration and Silapakorn University had resulted in an agreement to preserve and develop the area as an 'antique wooden house community'.

Jean du Plessis, Centre on Housing Rights and Evictions (COHRE)

remains legally responsible for the rights of the citizens, but the company is most directly involved, and may be more powerful. Its first accountability is to its shareholders. Both its legal and its political accountability to service-users (or non-users, those excluded by price, for instance) are much weaker, more controversial and harder to enforce than those of the state. Focusing on the obligations of corporations will be one of the greatest challenges for the economic and social rights movements in the near future.

The early social justice movement

The anti-globalisation or anti-capitalist movement, now definitively rebranded as the global social justice movement, famously burst on the scene at the World Trade Organisation meeting in Seattle in 1999. As discussed in many places, it had roots in anti-imperialist thinking and specific struggles in the South, such as the Zapatista uprising and the Ogoni movement, as well as in environmental and labour rights movements in the North. While the mix of groups and intellectual traditions was rich, human rights activism was remarkably absent from it. For instance, neither the anti-World Bank coalition 50 Years is Enough nor the loose anti-corporate and anti-WTO network Peoples' Global Action had any participation from human rights groups, or, for that matter, from specialised economic and social rights groups (50 Years is Enough URL; Peoples' Global Action URL).

The absence may be explained by a combination of suspicion and moving in parallel circuits, simply not knowing each other. Although the human rights community and the social justice community do not neatly correspond to the older political labels 'liberal' and 'socialist' respectively, each had a tendency, informed by the Cold War and the period immediately afterwards, to understand each other according to these labels.

The suspicion towards human rights, and human rights advocates in particular, can be understood in the light of the appropriation of human rights rhetoric by the 'victors' of the Cold War. The fall of the Berlin Wall was widely presented as a triumph for market capitalism and 'liberal values', that is, civil and political rights, simultaneously. The Clinton Administration was the most human-rights-friendly US government in two decades, and the World Bank

too embraced its own version of human rights in the post-Washington consensus, conflating neo-liberal orthodoxy with respect for human rights in statements like: 'by helping to fight corruption, improve transparency, and accountability in governance, strengthen judicial systems, and modernize financial sectors, the Bank contributes to building environments in which people are better able to pursue a broader range of human rights' (World Bank 1999: 3). The human rights movement did little to dispel the notion that human rights and free market reforms were two sides of the same coin. This was not because it necessarily endorsed this notion, although some individuals and groups probably did and still do, but rather because it was in some ideological disarray. It would condemn state violence used against Ogoni or Zapatista leaders, for instance, but it would not comment in any way on their political struggle.

Its traditional insistence that human rights were above politics, so useful during the Cold War, was getting in the way of gaining a political voice. Enemies in the form of traditional dictatorships, left and right, were fast disappearing from the scene, whilst human rights values were being embraced by controversial new friends. New demands were being made on the human rights mandate: to take up abuses by armed groups, by corporate actors, by men upon women in the private sphere, as well as to embrace economic and social rights. The human rights movement is still sorting its way through this expanded agenda. Moreover, human rights organisations had become very professionalised and legally oriented. The activists forming a human chain around the centre of Birmingham to protest against Third World debt in May 1998 and the lobbyists pushing to establish an international criminal court at a UN conference in Rome a month later, for instance, had little or nothing in common in terms of tactics or networks.

Arguably, the specialised economic and social rights groups such as FIAN, COHRE or CESR would have made much more natural allies for the anti-capitalist movement. Their world view was much closer to that of the protestors, they had grassroots links as well as experience of international fora such as the UN, and they had a language at their disposal that might have appealed to the anti-capitalist movement, which was at the time justly accused of knowing much better what it was against than what it was for. But the fact is these groups were not there at the beginning. Only in the early twenty-first century did social justice groups begin to forge links with economic and social rights groups as well as mainstream human rights organisations.

New departures

New forums

The World Social Forum (WSF) has in recent years become a place of convergence and crossover between different types of global civil society activists (Glasius and Timms 2006). As described above, the early social justice movement may have distrusted the human rights paradigm, and made no use of the economic and social rights frame. This has definitely begun to change with the spread of the social forums. The 2005 WSF made human rights one of its 11 themes, and about one third of the events held in the human rights space had economic and social rights-related themes (Forum Social Mundial 2005). Still, the evidence of a convergence between human rights activists and the social justice movement around economic and social rights remains somewhat mixed. Many social justice activists continue to make no reference to economic and social rights, speaking more broadly of justice and equality versus the criminality, greed and destructiveness of the neo-liberal paradigm instead. Even when they do, their concerns and approaches and those of the human rights community sometimes remain completely separate.

Three different workshops at the 2005 WSF in Porto Alegre, all attended by the author, illustrate this mixed record of convergence. Just prior to the forum, a thematic World Social Forum on Health took place, attended by 800 people, which adopted the 'right to health' as its lead theme (World Social Forum on Health URL). A follow-up session to this during the WSF, entitled 'Right to Health: Neoliberalism or Social Movements', saw participants from Argentina, India, Colombia and Burundi describing the consequences of privatisation, austerity measures and military conflict for the right to health in their respective countries, and describing the social movement action being undertaken against this. Other participants from Argentina and Mexico stressed the need to give medical students a more 'people-oriented education' and to protect the use of alternative medicine by indigenous groups from state

repression and corporate interests. The principal terms in the discourse of this workshop were 'neoliberalism' and 'struggle'. Participants used their own, self-defined concept of the right to health, and no reference was made to the Covenant or to any national lawsuits or legal provisions concerning the right to health.

The next day, another workshop on economic and social rights took place in the human rights space, entitled 'Economic, social and cultural rights in the international system: shadow reports to the ESC Rights Committee and the challenges of the Working Group on the Optional Protocol'. Apart from the author of this chapter and one Belgian development worker, there was no overlap between participants in this workshop (which included the French member of the UN Committee on Economic, Social and Cultural Rights, as well as other primarily Latin American and European lawyers) and the previous workshop. As the title would suggest, the discussion focused on sharing experiences regarding the practice of submitting civil society reports, parallel to the state reports, to the UN Committee, and on the negotiations on the Optional Protocol. Key terms in the discourse of this workshop were 'justiciability', 'strategising', and 'lobbying'. The phrases 'neoliberalism' and 'struggle' were not used.

At a workshop on the right to housing, however, the dynamics were rather different. Here, participants ranged from a Geneva-based international lawyer who described the existing international provisions and legal avenues regarding the right to housing, national-level activists from Egypt and Brazil who described a variety of tactics (from legal appeals or political negotiations to direct action and use of the media) to a Brazilian from São Paolo who had recently become the victim of slum clearance, and had come to the forum looking for help. An instant petition was drafted, and further discussions held about how to address the situation of his community.

While social forum sessions have all the advantages and drawbacks of embedding economic and social rights activism in a much wider movement, a specific network on economic and social rights has also recently been founded. The International Network for Economic, Social and Cultural Rights (ESCR-Net) was officially inaugurated in June 2003, after years of deliberation, with a founding conference attended by 250 activists from over 50 countries. ESCR-Net is primarily a facilitating platform rather than a campaigning coalition (ESCR-Net URL).

During the long gestation period of the network, members were already going ahead with joint activities, setting up a case law database and various listservs, lobbying jointly for the Optional Protocol, and drafting principles on women's economic and social rights. Since then, working groups on corporate accountability and on how to involve and connect grassroots groups and movements have been added, as well as smaller initiatives on budget analysis and export credit agencies (see below), and various discussion groups. These activities are essentially self-managed by different groupings of members, backed by a tiny secretariat in New York.

Both individuals and NGOs can join ESCR-Net. Members include a wide variety of organisations including usual suspects such as FIAN and COHRE, traditional human rights organisations, a social justice think tank like Focus on the Global South, sections of Amnesty International and ActionAid, and much more radical grassroots groups like the Movimento Sem Terra from Brazil or the Kensington Welfare Rights Union from the United States. Minutes of the inaugural meeting show the latter type of groups to be particularly interested in learning how to use international law to their advantage, while human rights lawyers emphasised that a human rights culture with popular support needed to be built.

New synergies

At the new forums where previously unconnected actors meet over economic and social rights, new synergies are being discovered. One of the biggest growth areas of the economic and social rights movement has been the right to health. Its cause célèbre has been the success of the South African Treatment Action Campaign, first in persuading the South African Supreme Court that the right to health required national roll-out of a particular anti-retroviral (ARV) drug, and then, in coalition with international NGOs, in persuading the WTO that there needed to be an exemption to the TRIPS agreement that would allow the manufacture and distribution of cheap versions of ARV drugs to combat HIV/AIDS in developing countries. But health rights activists have also achieved many other successes, primarily but not exclusively related to HIV/AIDS treatment, in Thailand, Brazil and other countries (Seckinelgin 2002: 123-5).

Patients (especially people living with HIV/AIDS), health professionals, human rights lawyers, development organisations and anti-privatisation activists are all part of this growing movement. Where only ten years ago the right to health was generally met with the sceptical comment that one cannot claim a right to be healthy, now a right to 'the highest attainable standard of health' is widely accepted in both medical and development circles.

Another momentous area of synergy is over the right to water. This right was initially formulated largely outside the human rights movement. It has caught the attention of development organisations, particularly of Care International. But it also has connections with anti-dam campaigns, with political conflicts such as that between Palestine and Israel, and with anti-privatisation campaigns, the most famous case being that of Bechtel in Bolivia (see Chapter 5 in this Yearbook). Like food, water is so vital to human life that to claim it as a right has intuitive appeal. But until recently it had no explicit basis in international law. Gradually, it has been embraced by the human rights community as being constituted by particular aspects of the existing rights to food and health, culminating in the adoption of a 'General Comment' on the right to water by the UN Committee on Economic, Social and Cultural Rights in November 2002 (UN CESCR 2002; Filmer-Wilson 2005; Nelson and Dorsey 2003).

New methodologies

A recent trend in global civil society has been the growth of budget analysis, which aims generally to make government conduct more transparent and accountable. It is particularly relevant to economic and social rights because the Covenant and other legal texts oblige states to take steps to fulfil these rights 'to the maximum of their available resources'. Where that maximum lies in a particular context is of course contested, but budget analysis can be a powerful political tool, demonstrating a government's commitment to a particular right, or lack thereof. An analysis of the Mexican budget over four years from the point of view of the right to health found that resource allocation for the control and prevention of disease was declining; a disproportionate share of the health budget went to those employed in the formal sector, and more 'pro-poor' spending of the federal budget went to the better-off rather than the poorest states. This pioneering project was published in book form in 2004 (Centro de Analisis e Investigacion et al. 2004). A handful of other such projects are under way, and in March 2005 Dignity International organised a first 'linking and learning' programme for human rights activists and budget analysis groups (ESCR-Net URL). Rights-based budget analysis is bound to be further refined and become a more widely used tool in coming years.

Less developed than budget analysis is the use of economic and social rights indicators. Traditionally, human rights activists have often been wary of quantifying human rights abuses, voicing doubts over both the availability of accurate data and their validity. But in the area of economic and social rights developing 'indicators' has its attractions. First, as many aspects of economic and social rights are to be 'progressively realised', indicators are needed to establish whether there is progress. Moreover, development indicators that at least have a bearing on economic and social rights already exist, for instance on nutrition, literacy, enrolment in schools, and many aspects of health. But these existing indicators have several drawbacks from a rights-based perspective. They may measure the enjoyment of rights; but, if they indicate lack of enjoyment, they do not pinpoint blame. Statistical indicators do not discriminate well between political will and the capacity to fulfil rights. Hence, human rights activists argue that, next to enjoyment indicators, compliance indicators would have to be developed for states and other actors. They might have to be supplemented with more qualitative indicators on legislation and policy. Second, statistical indicators give averages: they cannot tell us whether the rights of each individual are respected (Green 2001).

Despite these unresolved questions, some organisations are beginning to do work on indicators of economic and social rights, figuring out along the way which existing indicators they can borrow from related fields, and which they will need to develop themselves. The Philippine Human Rights Information Center, for instance, has been testing the usability of grassroots-based indicators on economic and social rights at the national level, while Physicians for Human Rights is globally pioneering the use of health-related indicators for the right to health (Yamin 2005; Philrights URL).

Finally, economic and social rights actors are only just beginning to look at extra-territorial and non-state obligations. This is a vast area, and largely unexplored terrain from both an academic and an activist perspective. One of the most interesting recent initiatives in this respect, at the borderline between inter-state and private accountability, is that on export credit agencies. Export credit agencies (ECAs) are a particularly untransparent instrument of rich countries to stimulate private sector exports or make overseas investments through the use of loans, guarantees, and insurance. Some progress has already been made pushing ECAs to institute minimum environmental standards. A workshop in September 2005, coordinated by ESCR-Net, aimed to explore the possibilities for economic and social rights activists to begin applying the same sort of pressure, bringing together human rights experts, ECA-watchers and local activists affected by controversial ECA-funded projects (ESCR-Net URL).

Unresolved issues

Through the categorisation of obligations, the identification of a minimum core content, and the violations approach, the nature of the obligations exacted by economic and social rights had become much more clear by the end of the 1990s than they had been even ten years earlier. Since then, new networks, synergies and methodologies have emerged that begin to enable global civil society to push for implementation. Nonetheless, some complex questions remain that cannot be resolved simply by calling either for more legal–academic clarification or for more political activism. They require urgent answers from global civil society actors if they are to make any progress in exacting universal enjoyment of economic and social rights.

Rights as instruments of struggle or instruments of law

As argued in the introduction, rights can be interpreted as legal guarantees or as moral claims. Their power lies precisely in the fact that, much of the time, they are both simultaneously. But, as more actors enter the economic and social rights arena, there is a divergence of views on what exactly a rights frame entails. Human rights lawyers typically base their rights claims on international law, while

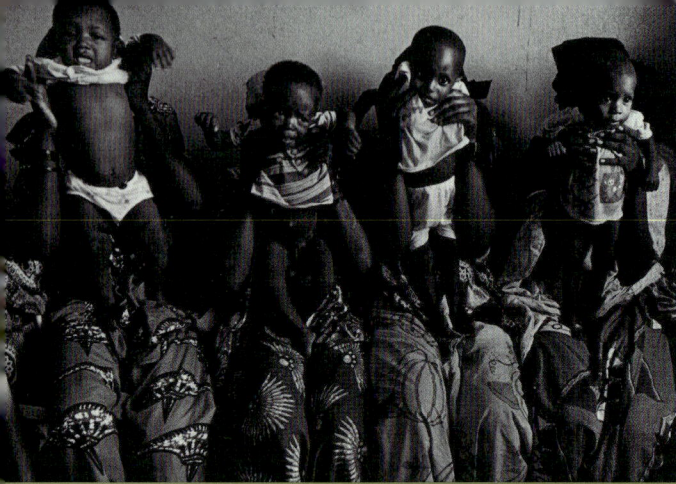

Campaigns on the right to health have been among the most successful in the economic and social rights movement
© Alvaro Leiva/Panos Pictures

social justice activists typically take a self-defined right, based on collectively identified primary needs, as their point of departure. So far, this distinction has often remained unspoken. Human rights lawyers have been keen to bring grassroots groups the message that they have legally defined rights, but usually prefer not to emphasise that these rights may be rather more limited than the affected communities envisage.

It is questionable whether the dominant civil society practice to date, of fudging the distinction between legal rights and moral–political claims, is sustainable. Some bottom-up rights coincide with those in international law and some, such as the 'right to water', are relatively easy to reconcile with it. But others, such as the 'right to the city', the latest claim to emerge from social forums, will stretch the tolerance and imaginativeness of lawyers.

In the area of the right to food, FIAN has made the distinction explicit, clarifying why it insists on using the 'right to food' as its framing, rather than the broader concept of 'right to food sovereignty' championed by Via Campesina, the worldwide coalition of small peasants' organisations. 'The political expansion of the rights-based language contains the risks for those rights, which are already legally binding, of being seen more as political demands' (Windfuhr and Jonsen 2005). This difference of opinion has not prevented FIAN and Via Campesina from being joint leading partners in a global campaign for agrarian reform.

If such distinctions are not more openly discussed and negotiated, cracks are bound to appear in the brand-new coalitions now sprouting up, and some

of the old suspicions, particularly between human rights lawyers and social justice activists, that the other party are capitalist lap-dogs or socialist revolutionaries respectively, may re-emerge.

Hierarchy of rights and political choices

Economic and social rights are being embraced not only by grassroots activists and lawyers but increasingly by judges. Local, national and international courts have become much more inclined to find a legal basis not only for upholding economic and social rights but also for upholding their own competence to judge whether there has been a violation. Protection of citizens' rights through law courts is a mechanism deeply rooted in different legal systems, going back to Enlightenment thinking and even earlier practice. But the doctrine of 'checks and balances', which accounts for the competence of courts to judge state laws and policies against a set of rights, and if necessary overturn them, was premised on the notion of an over-zealous state interfering in the lives of its citizens. It did not have an underperforming or neglectful state in mind.

Starting with Henry Shue's seminal work, political theory has moved on from the notion that civil and political rights confer only negative obligations, to leave citizens alone, while economic and social rights confer only positive obligations to provide. Even in the most classic libertarian tradition, the state would have obligations to protect property from threats by third parties, and to put systems in place to enable some political participation. Hence, courts are also universally considered competent to adjudicate on such issues – for instance on the recounts in the 2000 US presidential election.

Nonetheless, economic and social rights raise much more trenchantly the issue of how far judges can go in not just proscribing but prescribing specific policies. The right to food case in India, described above, is a case in point. The Supreme Court has become very hands-on in telling the provincial states how to manage food distribution. In 1998, the Argentinian Supreme Court handed down a similarly prescriptive decision, ruling that the government was under an obligation to roll out a vaccine programme. This particular decision was based on earlier stated policy, but, in general, should a court be able to decide that a vaccine programme is a necessary component of the right to health? In the case of the right to education, one could go even further. Many economic and social rights lawyers would argue on the basis of the principle of 'non-retrogression' that, if secondary or tertiary education has once been free, introduction of fees becomes a human rights violation. A judiciary panel could go along with such a decision and forbid reintroduction or raising of fees. If so, what space does that leave for democratic debate and political choice on educational policy? A government endeavouring to honour all human rights obligations would have very little democratic manoeuvring space left. Should the electorate not have any say in how to implement the right?

In order to answer these questions, it may be necessary to re-examine the idea of a hierarchy of human rights, or, more accurately, a hierarchy of aspects of rights. Human rights lawyers, traumatised by the competing rights ideologies put forward in the Cold War, have generally shied away from the idea that some rights might be more imperative than others. They have hidden behind the formula that all human rights are universal, indivisible, interdependent and interrelated, and posited that each of them overrides the normal cut and thrust of political decision-making.

Yet it is intuitive, on the basis of needs, that not all rights, or more accurately not all aspects of rights, are equally vital. Paid holidays are not as essential as food. The reluctance to barter with human rights, and particularly with economic and social rights, has laid human rights activists open to the charge of being maximalist and unrealistic, writing 'letters to Santa Claus' (Orwin and Pangle 1984: 15). Yet in practice, choices are made. It is not accidental that most global civil society activity in the area of economic and social rights began with the right to food. The 'minimum core content' idea is another concession to the idea of hierarchy, but there has been little discussion of what might be legitimate forms of hierarchy or prioritisation for more developed states, and whether their margin of political choice widens accordingly.

This might be a task not just for lawyers, but also for moral and political philosophers. One of the most controversial questions to answer in this respect would be whether hierarchy must be established solely on the basis of need, or whether questions of cost can also play a role. It is no longer disputed that the world does, in principle, have not only sufficient food stocks but also sufficient resources to deal with allocation and distribution, so that no-one should go hungry. Where people go hungry nonetheless, there is no need for philosophical speculation or economic calculation, only for political activism. But it becomes more difficult when it comes to housing, health and education. The right to health may be a particularly good test case, as aspects of it do deal in life and death, but fulfilment can be much more costly than fulfilment of the right to food.

Resource implications

According to the Covenant, states are obliged to 'progressively realise' economic and social rights, 'individually and through international assistance', 'to the maximum of their available resources' (ICESCR, 1966). This is at the heart of the Roth–Rubenstein controversy, described in Box 3.4. Roth argues from the assumption that, at least at state and possibly at inter-state level, there are not enough resources. Therefore, human rights advocates should stay away from resource issues, because their recommendations would interfere with other legitimate forms of spending (Roth 2004a: 65). Rubenstein, on the other hand, claims that 'the amounts needed are high but within reach' (Rubenstein 2004a: 856). Neither really has a sufficient empirical basis for his claim. It certainly seems clear that, in the realm of international assistance, states are not spending to the maximum of their available resources, but to what extent are they doing so at the national level? The Supreme Court of South Africa, one of the richer states on the continent, has rejected the doctrine of minimum core content on the - again arbitrary - judgment that South Africa is not at this point financially able to fulfil even these minimum demands. The doctrine of 'progressive realisation' is equally problematic. The 'non-retrogression principle', described above, is based on a developmentalist assumption that all states are gradually becoming better off. How is this to apply to a country like Argentina after the financial crisis, or to the Democratic Republic of Congo after a decade of war?

At the same time, the questions that are being asked about the cost of economic and social rights were never asked about civil and political rights. In fact, we have no idea how to cost human rights in general, as may be illustrated through the example of the right to form trade unions and engage in collective bargaining, a hybrid between a civil and an economic

While the vast majority of human rights organisations have now recognised work on economic and social rights as a legitimate part of their mandate, there continues to be lack of clarity, and indeed controversy, on what that means in practice. Such differences of opinion were highlighted by a series of exchanges between Ken Roth, executive director of Human Rights Watch, and Leonard Rubenstein of Physicians for Human Rights, in a series of exchanges in *Human Rights Quarterly* in 2004.

Roth (2004a) contends that international human rights organisations are best at 'naming and shaming', and that they can effectively do so only when there is relative clarity about violation, violator, and remedy. Therefore, they should restrict their work on economic and social rights to cases where governments are guilty of arbitrary or discriminatory conduct: for instance the US policy of evicting convicts from public housing, or South Africa's ideologically based denial of the morning-after pill to rape victims. International human rights organisations should stay away from economic and social rights issues that primarily concern the allocation of resources. Residents of the country in question have the clearest understanding of how to allocate resources, and international human rights organisations are poorly placed to comment on government action plans. Rubenstein (2004a) argues that human rights organisations must not rely on naming and shaming alone, but with local partners they should also engage in affirmative strategies that influence the design of systems and services so that they fulfil economic and social rights. They have long done so in the area of civil and political rights by, for instance, building up detailed knowledge of weapons capabilities or designing an effective court system. If human rights organisations are not yet very good at identifying rights aspects of health or education policies, they will need to get better at it. 'By the time bad social programs are designed and in place and the naming and shaming occurs, resources will have been misspent and human rights violated in a way that is not easily undone' (2004a: 856). Roth later concedes that this can be a legitimate task of human rights organisations, but will not be the main focus of Human Rights Watch.

Rubenstein (2004a) also argues that human rights organisations must base their monitoring, that is, their 'naming and shaming', not only on arbitrary and discriminatory conduct but on the legal obligations of different actors under the Covenant. First, the Covenant does have something to say about resource use: the state must spend on economic and social rights 'to the maximum of its available resources'; and other states have a duty of 'international assistance and cooperation'. It is therefore legitimate for human rights organisations to advocate more resources. They routinely do so in the field of civil and political rights: Human Rights Watch advocacy to defend the freedom rights of the mentally ill in the United States, for instance, implies a considerable outlay of funds. Moreover, such a frame will have more resonance with the communities affected: HIV/AIDS victims who are denied treatment want to demand anti-retrovirals on the basis of their right to survive, not on the basis of arbitrary government conduct.

Roth (2004b) disagrees on both counts. He argues that some developing countries simply lack the means to meet even the 'minimum core' standards set by the Covenant and its implementing Committee. If human rights organisations demand that such expenditures are nevertheless made, they inevitably get involved in trade-offs between legitimate investments in rights.

Rubenstein (2004b: 879) argues that advocating resources for economic and social rights is not a zero-sum game: pressure for resources typically increase the size of the pot. At the domestic level, it is legitimate for them to get involved in budget analysis, and at the international level it is imperative that they engage in advocacy to increase resources. Others have since contributed to the debate. Most recently Katarina Tomasevski (2005) has asked why, instead of arguing over what poor countries could or could not afford, Roth and Rubenstein do not concentrate more on advocating effectively for the implementation of economic and social rights in their own rich country, the United States.

right. It is generally considered as a 'negative right', without cost implications. But, as Dowell-Jones (2004: 48) argues, while this right may carry no direct cost for the state, it may drive up wages and therefore carry a cost for employers and the national economy. On the other hand, the same collective bargaining freedoms may also prevent wildcat strikes and smooth cooperation between employers and employees, improving the predictability and output of productive processes in a country. There is no definitive answer to the question whether the right to form trade unions should be considered cost neutral, costly or profitable to the state.

So, what approach should economic and social rights advocates take to the resource issue? One approach would be to emphasise the hidden benefits of policies that respect, protect and fulfil human rights, arguing that they lead to a virtuous cycle of social well-being and financial stability for all. Such reasoning would be contestable to say the least. Another approach is to take the moral high ground and argue that human rights must be fulfilled regardless of the cost, as has always been the approach to civil and political rights. A third, more pragmatic approach is taken by those who engage in budget analysis. In analogy with the violations approach, they begin by trying to establish not the maximum available resources of a state, but which budget allocations are most blatantly not using maximum available resources, that is, diverting money to less legitimate causes. From there it may be possible over time to close in on the 'difficult cases'.

Extra-territorial and non-state obligations

There is general consensus that, whatever the 'maximum available resources' of developing countries might be, they are insufficient to realise fully economic and social rights. Therefore, these rights can only ever be fulfilled if it is accepted that the obligations emanating from economic and social rights go beyond the state of citizenship or residence.

The idea that obligations – moral, political or legal – fall on more than one actor is not in itself problematic. Obligations are not a zero-sum game. The fact that a school might undertake part of a child's social and moral education, for instance, does not absolve parents from the same task. Moral philosophy is quite at ease with the idea of concurrent obligations. Domestic legal systems, too, are entirely comfortable with the idea of concurrent obligations. When a teacher sexually molests a child, besides his own criminal liability the school or its board may be liable for not having checked whether he was a known sex offender, and the authorities might be liable for not having shared appropriate information with the school. Such multiple liabilities are the bread and butter of domestic litigation.

Therefore, there are neither philosophical nor legal objections to the idea of human rights obligations, including economic and social rights obligations, falling on actors other than the state. But there are huge political and practical obstacles. As Künnemann says, 'obligations are trapped between the nation state and the international community...The result is a situation where the maximum of available resources is neither reached internationally nor nationally, with a convenient excuse the blame the other side' (quoted in Hennessey 2002: 87-8). The Covenant insists that states have an obligation to realise economic and social rights beyond their borders 'through international assistance and cooperation', but the extent and nature of such obligations remain obscure. Development assistance allocations suggest that rich states do recognise some kind of responsibility to help meet global social needs, but this may be conceived as a moral requirement or political expediency rather than a legal obligation, and the sums are paltry in comparison both with rich country GDPs and with poor country needs.

It is too easy to blame this solely on ill will on the part of rich states. The duty 'to take steps...especially economic and technical' has been enshrined in the Covenant for 30 years, but economic and social rights advocates have done little if anything to clarify what those steps might be. Economic and social rights activists have been overly focused on the state. They are only now beginning to inquire into the nature of 'extra-territorial obligations' on the part of states and of inter-governmental organisations. The obligations of transnational corporations or non-governmental organisations, whether political, moral or legal, are even less elaborated. This is an area where economic and social rights advocates need to catch up quickly if their work is to have any relevance to those deprived of health, housing or education in a globalised and privatised world.

Elena was 25 years old and it was her third pregnancy. As is common for indigenous women in the Andes of southern Peru, Elena gave birth at home, attended only by her husband. The next morning, Elena was obviously ill and her husband spoke with the village's community health worker who went to fetch the nearest doctor from a health centre over an hour away. The young doctor only arrived at Elena's house in the early afternoon, and he attempted to extract manually the remains of the placenta. He had never performed this procedure, but he said that he believed Elena was haemorrhaging internally and that he could do no more. The health worker then set out for a different health centre, which had an ambulance. However, the ambulance – a pick-up truck with a double cab – had broken down and became operational only hours later. The ambulance arrived at Elena's house when it was already evening, but without the more experienced doctor from the second health centre, who was nowhere to be found at that hour. The first doctor had hoped his more senior colleague would arrive with the ambulance to administer stabilising drugs that might enable Elena to travel the many hours to a district hospital, which was more likely to have surgical and blood bank capacities. The young doctor, Elena's husband and brother-in-law, and the health worker began debating in Spanish what to do. Throughout, neither Elena nor her sisters-in-law, who only spoke Aymara, were consulted. Her husband was told that he would at least have to pay for the pick-up truck's fuel – which could add up to more than the price of a cow – and, if Elena died at the hospital, he would have to pay to have the body brought back, too. Her husband and brother-in-law decided not to move Elena, and she died a few hours later of a post-partum haemorrhage.

Elena's story is far from an isolated case; Peru has the second-highest maternal mortality ratio in South America and it is estimated that a woman or girl dies approximately every four hours from pregnancy-related causes. There are many ways to analyse Elena's story, as well as those facts about maternal mortality in Peru. Policy making and advocacy in public health – just as in education, housing, and many other social arenas – have been going on for years without the lens or rhetoric of human rights. A human rights lens underscores that death from pregnancy-related causes is not 'natural', but rather a product of social priorities and policy decisions; it changes why Elena's death matters from a question of productivity lost or personal tragedy to one of injustice. But it raises many questions.

Who is responsible?

If Elena's death is a violation of the right to health, who is responsible for the violation? A human rights perspective would first point in the direction of state accountability, look at what Peru has done to make perinatal care more easily available to women like Elena, ask whether expert staff or appropriate medication should have been provided closer to Elena's home, and whether charging petrol for the ambulance was acceptable. But other actors may bear responsibility, too. Over half of the financing for maternal, infant, and reproductive health in Peru comes from foreign sources, primarily in the form of loans, which means assuming further debt. Projects financed by loans from the World Bank and the Inter-American Development Bank, as well as aid from the US Agency for International Development (USAID) were largely designed, funded, and managed apart from the Ministry of Health, and yet, in considerable measure, they determined the scope of Elena's right to health and, ultimately, also her right to life. Finally, there are elements of cultural and gender discrimination in Elena's case. Her relatives and the medical staff confer about her situation in Spanish, a language she does not understand, without consulting her.

What kind of responsibility?

What kind of responsibility do the different actors bear? Does the state bear a legal responsibility under national and international law? Even if that can be established, it would be much harder to argue that the actions or neglect by the international financial institutions or USAID are also subject to legal scrutiny. Perhaps political responsibility can be attributed to them, but how can they be made politically accountable? What of the relatives and medical staff – could they have legal responsibility for letting Elena die, or just moral responsibility for not consulting her?

What is to be done?

A classic human rights approach to Elena's case would be to seek redress from the state on behalf of her relatives. But, although this might set an important legal precedent, it is not the only or necessarily the most useful way to help women in her situation. Human rights advocates tend to assume either deliberate abuse or at least culpable neglect behind human rights violations. But, especially in the case of economic and social rights, the state may not always know what to do. In Peru, throughout most of the 1990s – as in much of the world – the government did not have a clear or consistent understanding of the epidemiology of maternal mortality. The human rights community often does not have a clear idea of the most appropriate form of action on economic and social rights either. It needs to foster alliances with health or education professionals as well as grassroots groups.

Priorities for the future include the human rights community becoming much more sophisticated in the use of both process and outcome indicators. It also needs to go beyond court-centric approaches to strategies that range from expert advice to the government, to consciousness-raising (concientización) of individuals and communities, and it needs to take participation much more seriously. Ultimately, human rights need to be understood as operating in the arena of political contestation, not just neutral interpretation of the law.

Abstracted from Yamin (2005)

Conclusion

Economic and social rights advocates began as a very small group. Gradually, in the 1990s they overcame the Cold War legacies of government manipulation and rhetoric. Surprisingly, convincing major players in global civil society of the economic and social rights frame was as much of a challenge as convincing global institutions. When mainstream human rights and development organisations, governmental and non-governmental, had to some extent begun to adopt the economic and social rights frame, a danger arose that the movement would become exclusively oriented towards global policy makers, either very legally oriented or co-opted into development-speak.

But in the last few years, the field appears to have been thrown wide open, and new collaborations are being forged between all sorts of global civil society actors, from different regions, levels and fields. The excitement is palpable. There will undoubtedly be friction and misunderstanding between these different actors in coming years, but this will hopefully lead to a more explicit understanding of each other's points of departure, strengths and weaknesses.

At the same time, the reality is that, in the face of a growing movement for economic and social rights, 850 million people live with chronic hunger, 27 million children are not immunised against preventable diseases, millions suffer forced evictions, and one in five adults in the world is illiterate (FAO 2005: WHO 2005: COHRE 2003: UIS 2005).

Apart from the old and still largely unfulfilled mandate of pushing economic and social rights onto government agendas through litigation and political actions, the movement now faces the much more complex and controversial challenge of engaging the agendas of global economic actors, such as the international financial institutions and corporate entities. It is in this area that global civil society has most catching up to do, from establishing legal norms to exerting political pressure on a host of different actors, and it needs to do so rapidly if it is to have an impact.

The attractions of the economic and social rights frame are firstly, the simplicity and moral appeal of the idea that 'everyone has the right to' have their most basic needs met; secondly, the flexibility that this framework, vesting rights universally in the individual, allows for the identification of a variety of obligation-holders beyond the state; and thirdly, the –

admittedly rudimentary – international legal basis for such obligations. The greatest contributions to economic and social rights have so far been made by a coalition of legal experts and grassroots activists. They will need to continue to negotiate their differences and define modes of cooperation, as well as solicit new inputs from moral philosophers, political economists and technical experts on food, education, health and housing to deepen as well as widen the meaning of economic and social rights obligations. Driven by a diverse, imaginative and determined set of global civil society actors, the economic and social rights frame could become the instrument of choice for achieving social justice in a globalised and privatised world.

The author would like to thank all participants in the Bellagio seminar on global civil society and economic and social rights for their input into this chapter, during and after the event, and would like to thank the Rockefeller Foundation for facilitating the seminar.

ActionAid International (2005) *Rights to End Poverty: ActionAid International Strategy 2005/2010.*
www.actionaid.org/wps/content/documents/INT%20STRAT(Long)%20.pdf

Alston, Philip (1987) 'Out of the Abyss: The Challenges Confronting the New U.N. Committee on Economic, Social and Cultural Rights', *Human Rights Quarterly* 9: 332-81.

– (2002) 'Resisting the Merger and Acquisition of Human Rights by Trade Law: A Reply to Petersmann', *European Journal of International Law* 13: 815-44.

– and Tomasevski, Katarina (eds) (1984) *The Right to Food.* Utrecht: Martinus Nijhoff and SIM.

Amnesty International (2005) *Human Rights for Human Dignity: A Primer on Economic, Social and Cultural Rights.*
http://web.amnesty.org/library/index/engPOL340092005

Arambulo, M K C (1999) *Strengthening the Supervision of the International Covenant on Economic, Social and Cultural Rights: Theoretical and Procedural Aspects.* Antwerp: Intersentia.

Centro de Analisis e Investigacion (FUNDAR), International Budget Project (IBP) , International Human Rights Internship Program (IHRIP) (2004) *Dignity Counts: A Guide to Using Budget Analysis to Advance Human Rights.*
www.iie.org/IHRIP/Dignity_Counts.pdf

Chirwa, Danwood Mzikenge (forthcoming 2006) 'The Protection of Socio-Economic Rights in the African Regional System', in M Langford (ed), *Socio-economic Rights Jurisprudence: Emerging Trends in Comparative and International Law.* Cambridge: Cambridge University Press.

COHRE (Centre on Housing Rights and Evictions) (2003) *Global Survey on Forced Evictions No 9.*
www.cohre.org/downloads/survey9.pdf

Cornwall, Andrea and Nyamu-Musembi, Celestine (2005) 'Why Rights, Why Now? Reflections on the Rise of Rights in International Development Discourse', *IDS Bulletin* 36(1): 9-18.

Darrow, Mac and Tomas, Amparo (2005) 'Power, Capture, and Conflict: A Call for Human Rights Accountability in Development Cooperation', *Human Rights Quarterly* 27: 471-538.

Declaration on the Right to Development (1986)
www.ohchr.org/english/law/rtd.htm

Dowell-Jones, Mary (2004) *Contextualising the International Covenant on Economic, Social and Cultural Rights: Assessing the Economic Deficit.* Leiden: Martinus Nijhoff.

'Ecuador: International Trade, Health, and Children's Rights' (2004) *3D Country Briefing.* September.
www.3dthree.org/pdf_3D/3DCRCEcuadorBrief_Sept04.pdf

Eide, A, Eide, W B, Goonatilake, S, Gussow, S and Omawale, J (eds) (1984) *Food as a Human Right.* Tokyo: United Nations University.

FAO (Food and Agricultural Organisation) (2005) *The State of Food Insecurity in the World 2005.*
ftp://ftp.fao.org/docrep/fao/008/a0200e/a0200e.pdf

Filmer-Wilson, Emily (2005) 'The Human Rights-Based Approach to Development and the Right to Water', *Netherlands Quarterly on Human Rights* 23: 213-41.

Forum Social Mundial (World Social Forum) (2005) *Programmacao.*
www.forumsocialmundial.org.br/dinamic.php?pagina=programa_fsm2005_ing

Glasius, Marlies and Timms, Jill (2006) 'Social Forums: Radical Beacon or Strategic Infrastructure?' in Marlies Glasius, Mary Kaldor and Helmut Anheier (eds), *Global Civil Society 2005/6.* London: Sage.

Green, Maria (2001) 'What We Talk About When We Talk About Indicators: Current Approaches to Human Rights Measurement', *Human Rights Quarterly* 23: 1062-97.

Hart, H L A (1961) *The Concept of Law.* Oxford: Clarendon Press.

Hennessy, Roisin (2002) 'Defining States' International Legal Obligations to Cooperate for the Achievement of Human Development: One Aspect of Operationalising a Human Rights-Based Approach to Development', in Martin Scheinin and Markku Suksi (eds), *Human Rights in Development Yearbook 2002.* Leiden: Brill.

Herzfeld, Michael (2003) 'Pom Mahakan: Humanity and Order in the Historic Center of Bangkok', *Thailand Human Rights Journal* 1: 101-19.

Howse, Robert and Mutua, Makau (2000) 'Protecting Human Rights in a Global Economy: Challenges for the World Trade Organization', *Rights & Democracy.* January.
www.ichrdd.ca/site/publications/index.php?subsection=catalogue&lang=en&id=1271

ICESCR (International Covenant on Economic, Social and Cultural Rights) (1966) www.ohchr.org/english/law/cescr.htm

Ishay, Micheline (2004) *The History of Human Rights: From Ancient Times to the Globalization Era.* Berkeley: University of California Press.

Limburg Principles on the Implementation of the International Covenant on Economic, Social and Cultural Rights (1987) UN Doc. E/CN.4/1987/17. www.unimaas.nl/bestand.asp?id=2453

Lobe, Jim (2003) 'Ending Exceptionalism: New Human Rights Network Denounces Selectivity in Bush Administration's Human Rights Agenda', *Foreign Policy In Focus.* 11 December.
www.globalpolicy.org/wtc/liberties/2003/1211exceptionalism.htm

Malby, Steven J (2002) 'Education and Health: a Role for Private Actors in Meeting Human Rights Obligations?', *International Journal for Human Rights* 6(3): 1-36.

Nelson, Paul J and Dorsey, Ellen (2003) 'At the Nexus of Human Rights and Development: New Methods and Strategies of Global NGOs', *World Development* 31: 2013-26.

Orwin, C and Pangle, T (1984) 'The Philosophical Foundation of Human Rights' in M F Plattner (ed), *Human Rights in Our Time: Essays in Memory of Victor Baras.* Boulder, CO: Westview Press.

Oxfam International (2001) *Towards Global Equity: Strategic Plan 2001-2004.* www.oxfam.org/en/files/strat_plan.pdf

Pieterse, Marius (2004) 'Possibilities and Pitfalls in the Domestic Enforcement of Social Rights: Contemplating the South African Experience', *Human Rights Quarterly* 26: 882-905.

Piron, Laure-Hélène (2005) 'Rights-Based Approach and Bilateral Aid Agencies: More than a Metaphor?', *IDS Bulletin* 36(1): 19-30.

Republic of South Africa (1996) Constitution.
www.polity.org.za/html/govdocs/constitution/saconst.html?rebookmark=1

Roosevelt, Franklin Delano (1941) 'Annual Message to Congress' (known as the Four Freedoms Speech). 6 January. *The Franklin & Eleanor Roosevelt Institute.*
www.feri.org/common/news/details.cfm?QID=2089&clientid=11005

Roth, Kenneth (2004a) 'Defending Economic, Social and Cultural Rights: Practical Issues Faced by an International Human Rights Organization', *Human Rights Quarterly* 26: 63-73.

– (2004b) 'Response to Leonard S Rubenstein', *Human Rights Quarterly* 26: 873-8.

Rubenstein, Leonard S (2004a) 'How International Human Rights Organizations Can Advance Economic, Social and Cultural Rights: A Response to Kenneth Roth', *Human Rights Quarterly* 26: 845-65.

– (2004b) 'Response by Leonard S Rubenstein', *Human Rights Quarterly* 26: 879-81.

Salomon, Margot (2005) 'Towards a Just Institutional Order: A

Commentary on the First Session of the UN Task Force on the Right to Development', *Netherlands Quarterly of Human Rights* 23: 409-38.

Schoonakker, Bonny (2004) 'Treated with Contempt'. *Sunday Times* (South Africa), 21 March.

Seckinelgin, Hakan (2002) 'Time to Stop and Think: HIV/Aids, Global Civil Society and People's Politics' in Marlies Glasius, Mary Kaldor and Helmut Anheier (eds), *Global Civil Society 2002*. Oxford: Oxford University Press.

Sen, Amartya (1981) *Poverty and Famines: An Essay on Entitlement and Deprivation*. Oxford: Clarendon.

– (1984) 'The Right Not to be Hungry', in Philip Alston and Katarina Tomasevski (eds), *The Right to Food*. Utrecht: Martinus Nijhoff and SIM.

Sengupta, Arjun (2002) 'On the Theory and Practice of the Right to Development', *Human Rights Quarterly* 24: 837-89.

Shue, Henry (1980) *Basic Rights; Subsistence, Affluence, and U.S. Foreign Policy*. Princeton: Princeton University Press.

Skogly, Sigrun (2001) *The Human Rights Obligations of the World Bank and the International Monetary Fund*. London: Cavendish.

Thipanyane, Tseliso (n d) 'Housing for the Poor: Constitutional Court Judgement on the Grootboom Complaint'. South African Human Rights Commission. www.sahrc.org.za/housing_for_the_poor.htm

Thompson, E P (1971) 'The Moral Economy of the English Crowd in the Eighteenth Century', *Past and Present* 50: 76-132.

Tomasevski, Katarina (2005) 'Unasked Questions about Economic, Social, and Cultural Rights from the Experience of the Special Rapporteur on the Right to Education (1998-2004): A Response to Kenneth Roth, Leonard S Rubenstein, and Mary Robinson', *Human Rights Quarterly* 27: 709-20.

UIS (UNESCO Institute for Statistics) (2005) 'International Literacy Day 2005: Women Still Left Behind in Efforts to Achieve Global Literacy'. Fact Sheet 06-05. September. www.uis.unesco.org/ev.php?ID=6264_201&ID2=DO_TOPIC

UN CESCR (United Nations Committee on Economic, Social and Cultural Rights) (2002) *General Comment No. 15: The Right to Water*. UN Doc. E/C.12/2002/11, 20 January 2003. www.unhchr.ch/tbs/doc.nsf/(Symbol)/a5458d1d1bbd713fc1256 cc400389e94?opendocument

– (1999) Twenty-first session, Summary Record of the First Part (Public) of the 37th Meeting. UN Doc. E/CN.12/1999/SR.37, paragraph 35.

Universal Declaration of Human Rights (1948) www.unhchr.ch/udhr/lang/eng.htm

UNDP (United Nations Development Program) (2000) *Human Development Report 2000: Human Rights and Human Development*. http://hdr.undp.org/reports/global/2000/en/

Uvin, Peter (2002) 'On High Moral Ground: The Incorporation of Human Rights by the Development Enterprise', *Praxis: The Fletcher Journal of Human Security* 17. http://fletcher.tufts.edu/praxis/archives/xvii.html

Van Reisen, Miriam (2000) 'The Prehistory of Social Watch: the Transformation of NGO Networking in Ongoing International Negotiations', *Social Watch*. March. www.socialwatch.org/en/acercaDe/dientesDelLeon.htm

Whittal, Jennifer, Muzondo, Ivan, Dewar, David, and Barry, Michael (2004) 'Informal Settlements: Breeding Grounds of Conflict', *Reconciliation Barometer* 2(2): 5-8. www.ijr.org.za/politicalanalysis/reconcbar/Aug2004.pdf

Windfuhr, Michael and Jonsen, Jennie (2005) *Food Sovereignty: Towards Democracy in Localized Food Systems*. Rugby: ITDG Publishing.

World Bank (1999) *Development and Human Rights: The Role of the World Bank*. Washington, DC: World Bank.

World Health Organization (2005) *Progress Towards Global Immunization Goals -2004. Summary Presentation of Key Indicators*. www.who.int/immunization_monitoring/data/SlidesGlobalIm munization.pdf

World Trade Organization (2003) 'Implementation of Paragraph 6 of the Doha Declaration on the TRIPS Agreement and Public Health Decision of the General Council of 30 August 2003'. www.wto.org/english/tratop_e/trips_e/implem_para6_e.htm

Yamin, Alicia (2005) 'The Future in the Mirror: Incorporating Strategies for the Defense and Promotion of Economic, Social and Cultural Rights into the Mainstream Human Rights Agenda', *Human Rights Quarterly* 27: 1200-44.

Interviews

Küennemann, Rolf, founding Director of FIAN. Telephone interview, 15 December 2005.

Patnaik, Biraj, adviser to the Commissioners of the Supreme Court of India on the Right to Food. Interview 21 November 2005.

Websites (consulted 13 March 2006)

50 Years is Enough, www.50years.org

CDES (Centro de Derechos Economicos y Sociales), www.cdes.org.ec

CESR (Center for Economic and Social Rights), www.cesr.org

COHRE (Centre on Housing Rights and Evictions), www.cohre.org

ESCR-Net (International Network of Economic, Social and Cultural Rights), www.escr-net.org/

ESCR Protocol Now, www.escrprotocolnow.org/

FIAN (FoodFirst Information and Action Network), www.fian.org

HIC (Habitat International Coalition), www.hic-net.org

KWRU (Kensington Welfare Rights Union), www.kwru.org

PGA (Peoples' Global Action), www.nadir.org/nadir/initiativ/agp/

PhilRights (Philippine Human Rights Information Center), www.hrnow.org/about/a000218_au_prights.htm

PIDHDD (Plataforma Interamericana de Derechos Humanos Democracia y Desarrollo (Inter-American Platform for Human Rights, Democracy and Development), www.pidhdd.org/

Right to Food Campaign, www.righttofoodindia.org

Social Watch, www.socialwatch.org

UNICEF, www.unicef.org

University of the Poor, www.universityofthepoor.org

World Social Forum on Health, www.fsms.org.br/ingles

CHAPTER 4

WAR AND PEACE: THE ROLE OF GLOBAL CIVIL SOCIETY

Mary Kaldor, Denisa Kostovicova and Yahia Said

Only the dead have seen the end of war.

Plato

The genocide (in Rwanda) in 1994 would not have been possible or taken such gruesome dimensions without the complicity of civil society groups. The ideology of hate was not only propagated by the state, but also actively supported by some civil society groups, including segments of the press.

Timothy Longman, 1999

Kant was right when he said that a state of peace had to be 'established'. What perhaps even he did not discern that this is a task which has to be tackled afresh every day of our lives; and that no formula, no organisation and no political or social revolution can ever free mankind from this inexorable duty.

Michael Howard, 1978

Introduction

There is a widespread view that the way to end wars is to promote global civil society. In places like Iraq, Afghanistan, the Democratic Republic of Congo, or Colombia, external donors provide money and training to help build civil society as a bulwark against violence.

Civil society is, of course, the antithesis of war. Historically, civil society referred to a secular constitutional order, where the rule of law, based on an explicit or implicit social contract, replaced force as a method of governance. Thus it referred to domestic peace. Nowadays, global civil society is often equated with international NGOs, as the space between the state, the market and the family operating at a global level. In this chapter, when we use the term global civil society we mean a space (local, national and global) where individuals, groups and organisations come together voluntarily to debate public affairs and to exert political influence. Even though this space is more or less free of violence and relatively free of fear, it includes a complex range of different positions – those who oppose all wars, those who favour some wars and oppose others, and those who try to manage or mitigate the effects of war.

In this chapter, our aim is to outline these different positions. We do not reject the notion that the promotion of global civil society can contribute to peace. But we suggest that there needs to be greater understanding of the different strands of opinion, of who should be supported and how. We also argue that global civil society cannot be artificially created. Civil society is about agency – it is about the ideas and activities of individual human beings in different circumstances who choose to link up across borders or in other ways to magnify their capacities to act. While war tends to polarise and reduce the space where people can debate freely, it can also, paradoxically, promote civil society – many significant groups and organisations were founded in reaction to war.

In developing this argument, we start with a brief historical discussion, outlining the relationship between civil society and war in the past and how this has changed as a consequence of globalisation. We then provide a framework for understanding different positions within civil society in relation to war. And in the last section, we illustrate this framework through case studies of Serbia and Iraq.

The authors would like to thank Eman Ebed, Chloe Davies and Tahirih Lyon for their assistance on this chapter.

Historical context

According to Michael Howard (2000), 'peace' is a modern invention. The idea of discrete periods of peace and the imagined possibility of universal peace came into being after the Treaty of Westphalia in 1648 when modern states began to establish a monopoly of legitimate violence. This process was associated with the process of internal pacification, which involved the construction of civil societies. Wars became definable events, disruptions to normal 'peaceful' social intercourse, in place of more or less continuous violence. They were, by and large, external events, against other states. And they had beginnings and endings. Hence the distinction between war and peace was both a geographical distinction between what was external and internal and, at the same time, a temporal distinction, that is, wars were contained in time. The definition of internal wars as 'civil wars' reflected this distinction between domestic civil society and international anarchy. Wars also became increasingly destructive as professional armies were established, and science and technology was applied to warfare. We may be in a 'civil state as regards our fellow citizens', noted Jean-Jacques Rousseau, 'but in the state of nature as regards the rest of the world'; and he asked, have we not 'taken all kinds of precautions against private wars only to kindle national wars a thousand times more terrible?' (quoted in Kaldor 1999: 17).

Thus the earliest modern peace movements are to be found in those areas characterised by modern states. Of course, a peace tradition can be traced back to much earlier periods. The early Christians were pacifists but, after Christianity was adopted by the Roman Empire and war was legitimised by the teaching of St Augustine, Christianity became one of the most belligerent religions. Nevertheless there continued to be debates within the Christian Church. Thus, for Lollards, the followers of the Oxford reformer John Wyclif, who died in 1384, war was a contradiction of true religion. In the early fifteenth century, these first British pacifists included university-trained theologians and members of the gentry, peasants and artisans, but they became a repressed sect at the time when a cult of war appeared untouchable (Brock 1970). Cooper points out that these Christian pacifists, such as Quakers or Mennonites and Brethren on the continent, never became a model for widespread opposition to war, despite their clear anti-war message that only drew vicious persecution upon them. Instead of proselytising, they made limited arrangements with the authorities, such as performing alternative services during the war (Cooper 1991: 5).

Unlike in early Christianity, in classical Islam war could be justified in certain circumstances; Muhammad himself was a warrior in the Medina period. Nevertheless, there were pacifist strands of thinking in the period of classical Islam, especially among Shi'ites who argued that war was justifiable only in self-defence. Likewise, although Buddhism is widely considered a pacifist religion, Buddha was not against all wars. The Buddha 'does not teach that those who are involved in war to maintain peace and order, after having exhausted all means, to avoid conflict, are blameworthy' (More Questions and Answers on Buddhism URL).

Peace movements first made their appearance in the English civil war but became a significant component of European and North American civil society only after the Napoleonic Wars. By then, peace was understood as peace between nations. The Society for the Promotion of Permanent and Universal Peace was established in England in 1916. The American Peace Society was founded the same year. Its aim was:

To increase and promote the practice already begun of submitting national differences to amicable discussion and arbitration and...of settling all national controversies by an appeal to reason, as becomes rational creatures....this shall be done by a Congress of Nations whose decrees shall be enforced by public opinion that rules the world...Then wars will cease... (Quoted in Howard 1978: 40–1)

The first International Peace Convention was held in London in 1843 and the second in Brussels in 1848. Thereafter there were annual peace congresses in different European cities until the enterprise collapsed under the impact of the Crimean War and the subsequent bout of warfare in Europe.

Towards the end of the nineteenth century the peace movement was revived. The liberal case for an international authority and an international civil society was supplemented by more radical arguments about social factors that lead to war. The early nineteenth-century liberals like Cobden or J S Mill had believed that free trade would increase international intercourse and eventually end wars. In the late nineteenth century, socialists argued that the expansionary nature of capitalism, especially imperialism, led to war, and in particular the armaments industry fomented war so as to increase its profits. Basil Zaharoff, the salesman of Vickers warships, became the personification of this idea (Scott 1962).

From 1892, universal peace congresses were held annually. In 1900, according to F S L Lyons, there were 425 peace organisations – 46 in Britain, 72 in Germany, 16 in France, 15 in the US, 1 in Russia and 211 in Scandinavia (Lyons 1963). At the Hague Peace Conferences of 1899 and 1907, Baroness Bertha von Suttner organised a daily newsletter and daily salons where activists could mix with diplomats, in a foretaste of today's parallel civil society summits.

Along with the peace movement came the rise of humanitarian agencies. Indeed, the first peace societies had been composed of people who had provided humanitarian assistance during the Napoleonic Wars. Later in the century, Henri Dunant was to found the Red Cross after he witnessed the horrors of the Battle of Solferino. The efforts of the Red Cross and peace groups were to lead to the codification of international humanitarian law as a result of The Hague and the Geneva Conventions.

But peace and humanitarianism was only one strand of civil society thinking. Another important strand was nationalism and, until the end of the nineteenth century, nationalism was equated with freedom. Many civil society thinkers, such as Hegel, believed that patriotism was necessary to hold civil society together. War, argued Hegel, is necessary to preserve the 'ethical health of peoples.... Just as the movement of the ocean prevents the corruption which would be the result of perpetual calm, so by war people escape the corruption which would be occasioned by a continuous or eternal peace'(Hegel 1829/1996: 331). Later in the century, Mazzini, one of the liberators of Italy, was to argue that war was necessary for liberation:

Insurrection – by means of guerrilla bands – is the true method of warfare for all nations desirous of emancipation....It forms the military education of the people and consecrates every foot of the native soil by memory of some warlike deed. (Quoted in Howard 1978: 49–50)

And the free trade argument was turned on its head by Friedrich List, who argued that protection and even war strengthened the nation state. There was huge sympathy, especially in Britain, for the plight of the smaller nationalities under the Turkish or Austrian yoke. *The Daily Mail* talked of 'gallant little Serbia' before the onset of the Balkan wars. The cause of Greek independence or of Bulgarian liberation from Turkish oppression was widely taken up.

Yet another important position in civil society was the notion that imperialism was a way to extend the benefits of civilisation. William Gladstone, the British Prime Minister, justified the occupation of Egypt in terms that anticipated Bush and Blair's defence of the Iraq War after their failure to obtain the consent of the UN Security Council:

We should not fully discharge our duty if we did not endeavour to convert the present interior state of Egypt from anarchy and conflict to peace and order. We shall look during the time that remains to us to the co-operation of the Powers of civilised Europe. But if every chance of obtaining co-operation is exhausted, the work will be undertaken by the single power of England.

And he added that he had:

laboured to the uttermost to secure that if force were employed against the violence of the Arabs it should be force armed with the highest sanction of law; that it should be force authorised and restrained by the united Powers of Europe, who in such a case represent the civilised world. (Quoted in Howard 1978: 56)

By 1914, the growth of militarism, nationalism and imperialism had overwhelmed the growth of peace opinion. The widely held view that civil society favoured peace was overturned by the nationalist enthusiasms of the mass of the European population.

The short twentieth century (as Eric Hobsbawm, 1994, calls it) from 1914 to 1989 was probably the bloodiest century in history. The 'civilised' powers of Europe were responsible for two world wars and the Cold War. The First World War claimed 15 million lives. The Second World War claimed 35 million lives (half of which were civilian). The Cold War maintained an uneasy, no war–no peace in Europe through the threat of planetary destruction; outside Europe, some

In addition to peace and human rights groups, humanitarian agencies proliferated during the Cold War © Sven Torfinn/Panos Pictures

5 million people were killed every decade of the Cold War in conflicts fought in its name. The merger of nationalism and the state, and socialism and the state, gave rise to totalitarianism in which civil society was effaced. 'Hegel was mutating into Hitler; Mazzini into Mussolini', wrote Michael Howard (2000: 55), and, he might have added, Marx into Mao (and Stalin though it lacks the alliterative ring).

But the twentieth century also spawned a peace movement, larger and more global than its nineteenth century predecessor. In the First World War, the Union of Democratic Control established by those who opposed the war, such as Bertrand Russell, Charles Trevelyan and E D Morel, generated the ideas that led to US President Wilson's Fourteen Points. The Women's International League for Peace and Freedom (WILPF) was established after two meetings in The Hague of women from different sides in the war, as well as neutrals. WILF was to play a key role in promoting the League of Nations, as was the International Chamber of Commerce, which was concerned about the disruption to trade represented by war. The League of Nations Union proliferated local groups in the aftermath of the First World War. These efforts were to be deeply disappointed both by the rise of fascism and the failure of the League to respond to Italy's invasion of Abyssinia and Germany's march into the Rhineland.

A mass transnational peace movement developed during the Cold War outside the Communist bloc. It was opposed both to nuclear weapons and particular wars such as Vietnam. It began in Japan and the Pacific as a reaction to Hiroshima and Nagasaki and in opposition to atomic testing. It reached its height in Europe in the 1980s when some 5 million people demonstrated against a new generation of nuclear weapons in 1981 and again in 1983. By the end of the 1980s, small independent peace movements had also developed in the Eastern bloc.

The Cold War period also marked the rise of human rights groups, along with the various human rights conventions and the Helsinki Agreement of 1975. Although some human rights activists were also peace activists, there was always a tension between peace and freedom that arose from the internal–external divide between civil society and war, which was similar to the tension between peace and national emancipation in the nineteenth century. Peace was about the international arena – peace between states. Freedom, or human rights, was considered a domestic responsibility – peace within states. Some human rights activists, particularly dissidents in Communist countries, believed that war or the threat of war was the only way to liberate themselves. A significant contribution to the ending of the Cold War was the dialogue between peace and human rights groups across the Cold War divide, which produced an emerging consensus that freedom is more likely to be achieved within a framework of international peace and vice versa – international peace is more likely to be achieved in democracies (see Kaldor 2003: ch. 3). In addition to peace and human rights groups, humanitarian agencies also proliferated in response to conflicts in the so-called

Third World. NGOs such as Oxfam and CARE, which had been founded during the Second World War, continued their work during the Cold War.

The Cold War and the arms race ended not with a war but with the victory of civil society. This, it can be argued, marked a profound rupture in international relations. It is no accident that the term 'globalisation' entered public discourse in the aftermath of the Cold War. Globalisation is often considered an economic phenomenon; free trade and free capital movements have greatly increased economic interconnectedness and this has eroded the autonomy of the nation state to make economic policy. Many scholars argue that globalisation also means interconnectedness in other fields – political, military, cultural or social (Held et al. 1999; Giddens 1990). But perhaps the most significant change since the end of the Cold War has been that in the character of the nation state as a result of the loss of the monopoly of legitimate violence. As a consequence, the inside–outside contrast between internal peace and external war, between a domestic rule of law and international anarchy, has become blurred so that the idea of peace as international peace or domestic peace no longer has the same significance.

This change is the consequence both of transnationalism and of fragmentation, as well as changing norms. The Kellogg–Briand Pact of 1928 and the Nuremberg trials after the Second World War made aggression an international crime. Today, the use of military force by states is illegal, unless in self-defence or authorised by the UN Security Council. This new norm is paralleled by the declining capacity of states to wage war unilaterally. Military forces are increasingly interconnected through military alliances such as NATO, various partnerships, arms control arrangements, joint peacekeeping forces and exercises, not to mention the arms trade, the provision of military training and the transnationalisation of military production. Moreover, the huge increase in the destructiveness and accuracy of conventional arms means that any use of military force even against technologically inferior enemies, as in Iraq or Afghanistan, is very risky.

But if the capacity to maintain a monopoly of legitimate violence is challenged from above by interconnectedness and new global norms, it is also challenged from below by the privatisation, fragmentation and informalisation of military forces in many parts of the world. It is often argued that, while

inter-state war has declined, there has been an increase in civil wars. This terminology reflects a continuing preoccupation with the inside–outside distinctions of the nation-state era. What has been increasing are 'new wars', in which the distinctions between public and private, and between internal and external, break down. These wars are fought by a combination of state and non-state actors. They are both global and local; often violence is highly localised and may or may not spill over borders, although the actors may include foreign mercenaries, diaspora volunteers, transnational criminal groups, and international governmental and non-governmental agencies.

The changing nature of war has been paralleled by a change in the meaning of civil society. During the Cold War, civil society activities were defined largely in relation to the nation-state; today global civil society is engaged in a dialogue with different levels of authority – local, national and global. Indeed, during the demise of the Cold War, the coming together of peace and human rights groups who addressed their concerns to governments, NATO and the Helsinki process, as well as local authorities, represented the emergence of a new type of public space.

In the next section, we discuss various interpretations of contemporary wars and how these influence civil society action for peace or for war.

Different civil society positions on war

According to the Human Security Report 2005, the number of conflicts has declined in the first few years of the twenty-first century and, moreover, conflicts have become less deadly with declining numbers of casualties (Human Security Centre URL). The main reasons given are the end of colonialism and of the Cold War, and a more active role by the international community. It can be argued that the rise of global civil society, in particular the growing importance of peace and human rights groups, has contributed to this trend. In places where global civil society has been quiescent, for example in Darfur and Rwanda, or where global civil society is deeply divided, as in the Middle East, tragedies continue to take place.

However, although the number of conflicts appears to be declining, there are disturbing counter-trends. These include the 'war on terror' and the escalating violence in the Middle East, the increase in civilian casualties directly from violent attacks and indirectly

Table 4.1: Global civil society positions on war and peace

Interpretation of war		Anti-war	For some wars
'Old wars'	Power politics	**Who:** Peace movements **How:** Opposition to militarism and aggression	**Who:** Neo-conservatives, realists, Russian conservatives, anti-imperialists **How:** War is sometimes justified in the national or ideological interest
	Ancient rivalries	**Who:** Conflict resolution groups, multiculturalists or consociationalists **How:** Negotiated final settlement	**Who:** Nationalist and religious groups, clash of civilisations **How:** Interest in war to win power on the basis of identity
'New wars'	Political economy	**Who:** Global Witness, Campaign Against the Arms Trade, Revenue Watch, Development NGOs **How:** Undermining war economy and building an alternative	**Who:** Criminals, smugglers, mercenaries, adventurers **How:** Interest in war as a source of revenue
	New nationalist, religious and other ideologies	**Who:** Human rights groups, women's groups, cosmopolitan networks **How:** Alternative identities, cosmopolitan ideologies and legitimate public authority	**Who:** Liberal internationalists, extreme secularists, those who favour 'Responsibility to protect' **How:** Just war for human rights, and/or managing conflict and protecting civilians

from hunger and disease associated with war, the rise of terrorism and organised crime, and the spread of nuclear weapons. Moreover, in many of the areas where ceasefires have been reached, for example in large parts of Africa, the Balkans, the South Caucasus and Central Asia, people continue to experience high levels of insecurity as a result of human rights violations and crime; and the risk of conflict remains high.

Whether these conditions can be addressed, and the secular decline in war-related violence continues, depends in large part on global civil society and the positions it adopts. Although a case can be made for global civil society's contribution to this decline, there are instances where global civil society has contributed to conflict. Therefore, it is important to analyse the various positions adopted by different actors and how these influence conflict trends.

Table 4.1 provides a framework for identifying different strands of opinion within global civil society.

The first column refers to different ways of interpreting contemporary conflicts, which might be shared by both pro-war and anti-war groups. The second and third columns show the kind of groups that represent each position. In addition to these groups, there are humanitarian agencies that do not take positions but try to mitigate the effects of war. Of course, the myriad civil society positions is difficult to capture in a framework of this kind; within groups, movements and organisations, a variety of different views and strategies, both overlapping and contradictory, can be found. So the framework should be treated as a heuristic device; no doubt it is possible to find many ideas that do not neatly fit the framework.

Old wars

The first two positions are described as 'old war' positions. Those who hold these views see war as something that takes place between two states, or coalitions of states or non-state actors who aspire to statehood, based on some deep-seated grievances or conflicts of interest.

Power politics

The first position is about 'power politics' – the idea that war is pursued by states for geopolitical reasons, to protect their national interest and extend their power. This interpretation is usually applied to inter-state war but there is a widespread view that other types of war are manipulated by outside powers. Thus, in Yugoslavia there were many who argued that US and NATO intervention was motivated by self-interest such as the establishment of new military bases or access to oil pipeline routes. At best, intervention in the Balkans was described as a typical imperialist undertaking of 'imposing progress upon those in the cross hairs' (Cockburn 1999). In the South Caucasus, the clash between the United States and Russia over control of the region is often cited, with some reason, as a key factor in the persistence of frozen conflicts. Russia played a role in fomenting as well as freezing all the conflicts, and Russian conservatives argue that instability in the area helps to preserve the region as a Russian zone of conflict (Karagiannis 2002). The United States has been keen to build relations with oil-rich Azerbaijan, and has insisted on the construction of the Baku–Ceyhan pipeline, at great cost, which avoids Iran and Russia. Now it is sponsoring the 'Caspian Guard' initiative, which includes the construction of radar facilities and assistance to the Azeri navy to prevent proliferation and protect the pipeline – objectives that can be perceived as targeted against Russia and Iran.

Those who see war as power politics and support some wars include neo-conservatives in the US who believe in the use of force to extend America's global hegemony, and in the mission to extend democracy worldwide, based on the American model. This approach was embodied in the Project for the New American Century, which brought together a group of policy makers and intellectuals who later became known as the neo-conservatives. They include Elliott Abrams, Dick Cheney, Francis Fukuyama, Donald Rumsfeld and Paul Wolfowitz, most of whom are or have been prominent members of the Bush administration. According to PNAC's Statement of Principles:

America has a vital role in maintaining peace and security in Europe, Asia, and the Middle East. If we shirk our responsibilities, we invite challenges to our fundamental interests. The history of the 20th century should have taught us that it is important to shape circumstances before crises emerge, and to meet threats before they become dire. The history of this century should have taught us to embrace the cause of American leadership. (PNAC 1997)

Organisations such as the Heritage Foundation and American Enterprise Institute also embody this perspective.

This position also includes realists who believe force should be used to protect national interest. Realists tend to be less belligerent than neo-conservatives, who believe in America's mission to spread democracy. Realists argue that national interests can often be protected better using peaceful rather than violent means. Thus, leading American realists opposed the war in Iraq (Scowcroft 2006). Think tanks such as the International Institute for Strategic Studies in London and the Centre for Defence Studies in Delhi play a significant political role in promoting this way of thinking about war.

Since most conceptions of war are shaped by the idea of clashes between states, groups that describe themselves as peace movements are usually those opposed to the war-like policies of states, especially the US. Peace movements have always been internationalist, and a number of important global peace coalitions campaign for peace and against armaments, especially weapons of mass destruction. These include some that were formed earlier in the twentieth century such as the International Peace Bureau or the Women's International League for Peace and Freedom. A significant recent initiative was the Hague Appeal for Peace (URL), which was established on the centenary of the 1899 Hague Peace Convention, when thousands of peace activists gathered in Brussels. The organisation brings together a network of peace groups and international organisations from around the world.

Of course, many different positions are to be found among activists. The dominant view in the global movement that opposed the war in Iraq has been based on a similar interpretation of conflict as 'power politics'. The war in Iraq is perceived as the means by which the United States seeks to control sources of oil and territory for military bases. The global anti-war demonstration of 15 February 2003, involving 8 million people around the world, was unprecedented in size and coordination. One of the most popular banner/slogans of the action was 'No Blood for Oil'. Speakers at the London rally, which brought 1.5 million people to the streets of London, rejected US and British justifications for the war on the grounds of weapons of mass destruction, deposing tyranny, or the war on terror, insisting instead that the pursuit of Iraq's vast oil wealth was the main motive. Noam Chomsky of MIT is one of the most prominent representatives of this perspective:

..they have an international program, which has been announced, dominating the world by force, permanently, preventing any challenge, and in particular, controlling the very crucial energy resources of the world. Mostly in the Middle East, secondarily in Central Asia and a few other places. (Chomsky 2003)

Similarly, Tariq Ali lists three motives for the US war in Iraq: 're-colonization'– oil, support for Israel and intimidation of strategic rivals such as China and Japan (Ali 2003a).

This view could be regarded as a reverse echo of the pro-war realist view. Both agree on a particular interpretation of conflict. The different stances towards the war in Iraq depend on whether American control over oil fields or military bases is considered good or bad. In the first Gulf War, both the US and UK governments justified the war in terms of the need for oil.

A paradox of this perspective is the tendency for anti-war activists to justify and support violent resistance against what they view as imperialist aggression, thus legitimising war of another kind. Many activists support, or refuse to condemn, Palestinian violence even when it is aimed at civilian targets. Some have described the insurgency in Iraq as an Intifada (Klein 2004). George Galloway, a British MP and leading figure in the UK Stop the War Coalition, called for an Iraqi Intifada in a speech delivered only two months after the invasion. In April 2003 Tariq Ali (2003b) referred to an Arab-wide Intifada as the only thing that could have prevented the invasion of Iraq. It is sometimes unclear whether the main goal of these activists is ending the war or the defeat of the United States and its allies.

Among peace activists and realists there are those who regard power politics as a significant source of conflicts but nevertheless believe these can be managed through diplomacy and multilateral organisations of states such as the United Nations. The International Crisis Group, which conducts research and advocacy on conflict and brings together former foreign policy officials with peace and human rights activists, often reflects this approach, although its invaluable reports on particular conflicts adopt a range of perspectives.

Ancient rivalries

The second position is ancient rivalries – the idea that there are long-standing divisions based on culture, race or religion that can, at best, be managed or suppressed. Thus Communist rule was supposed to have 'kept the lid' on ethnic and religious divisions boiling underneath in the former Soviet Union and Yugoslavia. Likewise, colonialism in Africa is said to have contained tribal rivalries in Africa or masked religious difference in South Asia. The notion of ancient rivalries is applied both to inter-state conflict and to civil wars. The most well-known example of the former is Samuel Huntington's *Clash of Civilisations* (2002); while Robert Kaplan's *Coming Anarchy* (2001) and *Balkan Ghosts* (2005) put forward an ancient rivalries thesis to explain wars in the Balkans and Africa.

In the scholarly literature, a distinction is drawn between primordial or essentialist understandings of nationalism and religious fundamentalism on the one hand, and constructed or instrumental approaches on the other. The former see nations and religions as deeply rooted in society, givens that cannot be changed. The latter argue that nationalist or religious identities are imagined, constructed or used as forms of political mobilisation through various means, especially the media. The ancient rivalries position is based on an interpretation of identity politics that is closer to the essentialist view than the constructionist or instrumental view. Nationalist and religious groups tend to present themselves as enduring phenomena, whose right to power derives from history. Therefore, those who perceive war as based on ancient rivalries and support war for that purpose are the more extreme nationalist and religious fundamentalist groups. Such groups include Seselj's Serbian Radical party, militant Zionists or Al-Qaeda (Kaldor and Muro 2003).

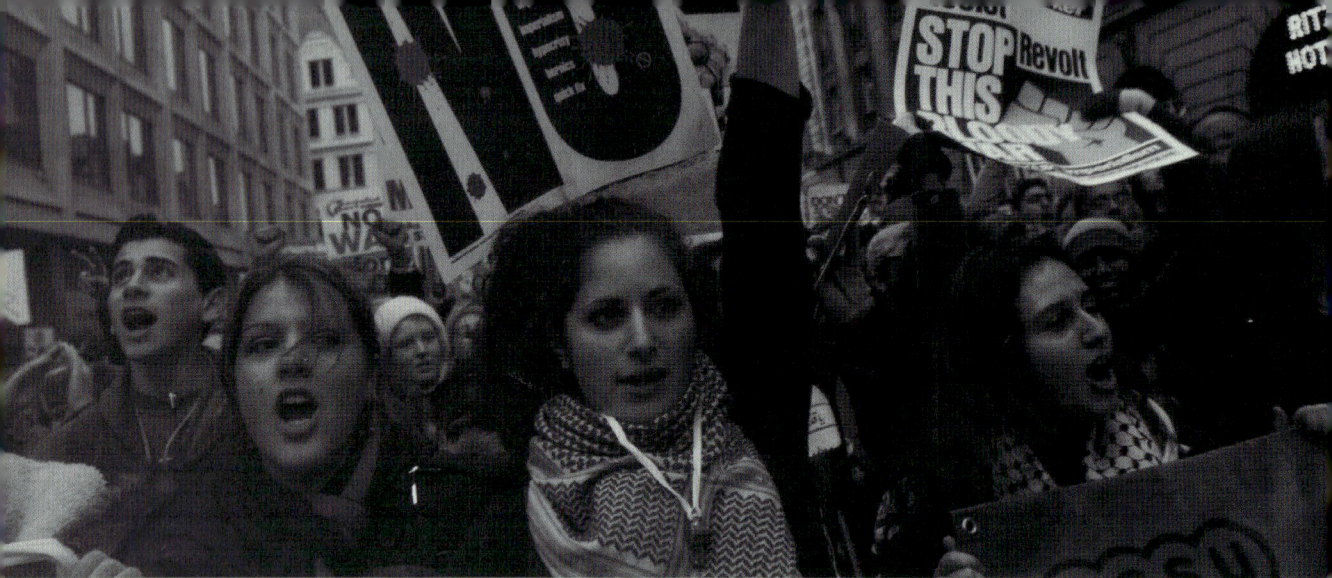

'No blood for oil': anti-war protesters express a 'power politics' interpretation of the war in Iraq © *Andrew Testa/Panos Pictures*

Contemporary secular ideological positions can also be treated as a version of the 'ancient rivalries' position. In the aftermath of the 11 September 2001 terrorist attacks, the neo-conservative rhetoric intensified to describe an existential struggle between 'us', the 'civilized nations', and 'Terrorists who hate us for what we are and who are bent on destructing our way of life' (Bush 2001); between democracy and religious fundamentalism; between good and evil. The rhetorical framework of the 'global war on terror' is not unlike other religious and ethnic ideologies that depict an eternal cosmic struggle, and it is unsurprising that the two often overlap with American Christian Right groups or Jewish extremists in the United States and Israel.

There are also, of course, moderate nationalist and religious political currents that oppose war but nevertheless favour access to power on the basis of national or religious identity. Thus, the moderate SDLP in Ireland consists of nationalists who favour a united Ireland but pursue their aims peacefully. The Bosnian Muslim Party, the SDA, favoured a multi-ethnic Bosnia, organised by ethnic parties in a peaceful way. And some nationalist groups veer from pro-war to pro-peace positions; this is probably true of both Likud in Israel and Hamas in Palestine. Moderate nationalist or religious groups often favour partition and/or consociational arrangements, whereby ethnic or religious interests are built into constitutional arrangements (Lijphart 1977). The Dayton Agreement, the Lebanese Constitution, and the Good Friday Agreement are examples of consociationalism. Partition has been widely applied in

former British colonies – India and Pakistan, Israel and Palestine, Cyprus, Northern Ireland, and most recently in the former Yugoslavia (Kumar 1997).

Among scholars, there are those who argue that a strong civil society that crosses identity divisions helps to bring about peaceful coexistence of different ethnicities or religion. Thus Varshney (2002) shows that in India pre-existing cross-sectarian links help diffuse the conflict. This line of thought underlies the approach of those peace activists who accept the framing of conflict in terms of long-standing ethnic, religious or other identity-based rivalries and who support conflict resolution approaches. Thus Conciliation Resources, International Alert and other 'second track' initiatives seek peaceful resolutions of conflict by facilitating dialogue between the warring sides through confidence-building exercises and placing protagonists in a neutral environment. The Israel–Palestine conflict, the most visible, emotive and senseless conflict for many people around the world, attracts many conflict resolution activists. One of these initiatives culminated in the 1993 Oslo Peace Accord after a process of informal meetings at the Norwegian Institute for Applied Social Science, which involved academics, intellectuals and grassroots activists from Israel and Palestine. At the heart of this model consociational arrangement is partition along ethnic lines which, by accepting that Palestinians and Israelis cannot share the same country, implicitly recognises a version of the ancient hatreds argument.

Cther examples of the conflict resolution approach are 'interfaith dialogues' or 'dialogue of civilisations'. These initiatives seek to dispel the notion of ancient hatreds, clash of faiths, civilisations and other identities by emphasising commonalities and dialogue. Unlike the conflict resolution approach, such initiatives attract anti-conflict ethnic and religious representatives, and are thus more likely to achieve agreement in the form of appeals and declarations for peace. However, the effectiveness of such outcomes is circumscribed by the fact that they emphasise the identities underpinning the conflict and tend to exclude alternative cross-cutting identities.

Since the 11 September 2001 attacks in the United States there have been many initiatives involving Muslim, Jewish and Christian clerics calling for dialogue and condemning the targeting of civilians in the name of religion. On the assumption that most terrorists are unlikely to heed appeals from 'moderate' clerics, and that the vast majority of Muslims do not need such appeals to refrain from attacking civilians of other faiths, the most significant result of such initiatives is to exonerate Islam from the violence perpetrated in its name.

The actions of civic and religious leaders during the Acholi conflict in northern Uganda, many of whom have demonstrated a remarkable commitment to reconciliation, offers an example of identity-based civil society organisations playing a decisive and valuable role in pushing for the peaceful settlement of conflict. As Carlos Rodriguez says:

> During the early years of the war in Acholiland, religious leaders in the region focused primarily on providing moral and practical support to their parishioners and Church institutions became centres of support for thousands seeking shelter from the violence. Over time a greater consensus emerged amongst church leaders in the North on the need to be proactive in 'bearing witness' about the conflict and to engage directly in peacebuilding. This transformation has resulted in a number of initiatives that have placed religious leaders at the heart of efforts to support a political resolution of the conflict and to address the consequences of the war... (Rodriguez 2002)

The Acholi Religious Leaders Peace Initiative was formally inaugurated in February 1998 with Nelson Onono-Onweng, the Anglican Bishop of northern Uganda, as its founding chair. Its first major event was the Bedo Piny pi Kuc (sitting down for peace)

conference. It drew more than 150 Acholi, who discussed the causes and effects of the insurgency, the reasons for its persistence and possible strategies to end it. They concluded that 'the insurgency cannot be won by the gun' and subsequently called for dialogue between the government and the Lord's Resistance Army, an amnesty and efforts at reconciliation through the Acholi traditional practice of mato oput.

New wars

In contrast to the first two positions, those who hold 'new war' positions see the conflicts of today as complex socio-economic phenomena that transcend traditional concepts and categories. New wars sustain and reproduce themselves primarily with the help of war economies and the manufacturing of identities (Kaldor 1999). Instead of assuming deep-seated grievances or conflicts of interests, the warring parties may have shared interests in conflict in order to strengthen political and economic positions.

Political economy

Paul Collier analyses civil wars from an economic perspective, and points to the low opportunity cost of conflict in the absence of other forms of employment. According to this line of thinking, under certain conditions fighting is the only, or best available, form of employment. This situation is self-sustaining since a lack of security decreases the likelihood of other, more gainful, forms of employment emerging. Therefore, recruitment of combatants may be relatively easy, although warlords or rebel leaders still have to provide political justification. Once the fighting starts, however, the cycle of killing and revenge reproduces grievances and, together with the cycle of economic destruction, makes such conflicts difficult to stop. Collier emphasises dependence on primary commodities as a significant contributing factor to conflict because they provide a convenient economic base and/or prize for the rebellion (Collier and Hoeffler 2004).

The availability of arms, especially small arms, linked to unemployment, is also considered one of the conditions that make violence an attractive option (see Box 4.1). In West Africa, gangs of young men armed with weapons made available as a result of the Cold War and regional conflicts provide a 'nomadic army' for conflicts in different countries (see UNOWA 2005).

Political economists such as David Keen (1998), Mark Duffield (2001), David Malone and Mats Berdal (Berdal and Malone 2002) consider that warring parties, who may comprise state and non-state actors, have a vested interest in war primarily for economic reasons, and therefore simultaneously collude and conflict with each other. Loot and pillage, control of primary commodities, smuggling and trafficking, or trade in arms may be the primary objective of predatory rulers, warlords and rebel leaders. In practise it is often difficult to distinguish between the Such activities may also be an expedient way to finance political causes, but with time the war economy takes over and it becomes less and less clear whether the political or the economic is the primary objective.

There are two main interpretations about what creates the conditions for war economies and what the remedies might be. Liberals argue that authoritarian regimes and command economies cause shortages and market distortions that foster corruption, black markets and trafficking. Thus the solution is liberalisation, including the promotion of civil society as a counterbalance to the state. This line of thinking sees civil society engaged in the provision of social and humanitarian services as an alternative to the overbearing state (see the section on promoting civil society below).

Others argue the exact opposite: liberal prescriptions restrict fiscal spending, creating unemployment that provides armies of recruits for warlords. Also, liberal economic policies undermine state legitimacy, thus contributing to war. The solution is a stronger, more accountable state and more rather than less state spending to provide essential services and create an alternative economic base to a war economy.

One area where there is agreement is that of natural resources. Economists such as Sachs (Sachs and Warner 1995) and Collier (Collier and Hoeffler 2004) have found robust evidence to support what political economists have asserted all along: a direct correlation between resource dependence and conflict in less developed countries. Although there is no consensus on how resource dependence contributes to conflict – for example, geopolitics, state weakness or the provision of an income stream – there is agreement that transparency in the resource sector is central to addressing this issue.

Several civil society activities focus on introducing greater transparency in the extractive industries. The Revenue Watch (URL) network aims to bring transparency to the payments made by corporations to governments. The idea is that a public equipped with this information is better capable of holding government to account for the misuse of natural resource wealth. Similarly, some civil society groups are dedicated to breaking the link between natural resources and conflict (see Box 4.2). These initiatives have brought together both local and global civil society activists with governments, international organisations and companies.

New nationalist and religious identities

Those who believe that political interests drive war argue that nationalist and religious groups are an important factor, but that these ethnic and religious divisions are deliberately fostered for the purpose of winning power. Political leaders in formerly authoritarian states, new aspirants to power in moments of transition, and adventurers and criminals seeking legitimacy try to mobilise on the basis of sectarian identities, promoting exclusivist ideologies through the media and indeed through violence itself. The new wave of nationalist and religious ideologies, whether nationalist parties in the former Yugoslavia, Sunni–Shi'a divisions in Iraq, communalism in India, or the Hutu–Tutsi division in Rwanda, may appeal to memories of past violence, but they need to be understood as new phenomena, new religious and nationalist ideologies that have developed in response to the complex changes associated with globalisation.

If sectarian identities are constructed rather than givens, then this position represents an implicit critique of diplomacy and conflict resolution approaches because such approaches legitimise exclusive ideologies by treating them as the key partners in peace processes.

Those who interpret these conflicts as the consequence of new, rather than ancient, rivalries argue that what needs strengthening in civil society are those actors who promote a non-sectarian identity – cosmopolitan groups, human rights groups and women's groups, for example. In situations of violence, it might be necessary to talk to those who promulgate extremist ideologies but within a framework that engages and involves those who oppose such ideologies.

Groups in this category combine work on peace and

Box 4.1: NGOs, global civil society and the UK arms trade

The international arms trade, in its legal, illegal and illicit forms, has attracted increasing attention in recent years because of issues such as the use to which recipients put weapons, the purported role of small arms in conflicts, and government subsidies for arms production and export. The UK was the world's fifth largest exporter and fourth largest importer during 2000–4 (SIPRI 2005: 418, 449). It participates in various arms control mechanisms, and is particularly active in small arms control, working to strengthen controls on their supply, to reduce their availability and to address the demand for them (FCO 2005). In this it is supported by a number of NGOs, including Amnesty International (URL), British American Security Information Council (BASIC URL), International Alert (URL), Oxfam GB (URL) and Saferworld (URL). Yet its activity in the wider international arms trade continues to attract the criticism of these same organisations, as well as Campaign Against Arms Trade (CAAT URL) which does not work on small arms issues in any depth).

These NGOs differ in their objectives and strategies, but are all active on one or more aspects of the arms trade. NGOs are not the only global civil society actors to be concerned with the arms trade; direct action groups, such as Disarm DSEi and Ploughshares, seek to disrupt it, while industry lobby groups such as the Defence Manufacturers' Association and Society of British Aerospace Companies seek to promote it. In addition, weapons manufacturers are integrated into the machinery of the UK state through their representation on military advisory bodies and a 'revolving door' that operates between the arms industry and government. For example, the head of the Defence Export Services Organisation, the branch of the Ministry of Defence that promotes arms sales, is drawn from the arms industry (see CAAT 2005). This means that arms capital is structurally privileged over NGOs and direct action groups, and is therefore much more likely to ensure that the state acts in its interests.

UK arms exports are ostensibly controlled by an eight-part set of guidelines, which amalgamates the EU Code of Conduct on Arms Exports (June 1998) with UK government criteria (July 1997). These guidelines are politically but not legally binding, and do not greatly restrict the level of exports. They set out the conditions under which the government will refuse arms export licences; for example, the UK government claims it will not issue a licence 'if there is a clear risk that the proposed export might be used for internal repression' and 'will not allow exports which would provoke or prolong armed conflicts or aggravate existing tensions or conflicts in the country of final destination' (Ministry of Defence, FCO and DTI 2000). However, the guidelines are so interpreted that high levels of exports are licensed to countries such as Indonesia despite the evidence presented by NGOs, campaign groups and activists, of the use of military equipment in human rights abuses in East Timor, Aceh, West Papua and elsewhere in Indonesia. 'Risk' is clearly a relative concept.

Although the guidelines are sometimes invoked to refuse licences and serve to legitimise claims that the UK is a responsible exporter, arms exports receive considerable support from, among others, government ministers (including the Prime Minister), defence attachés and the royal family, who promote arms sales on behalf of major arms companies, such as BAE Systems. As well, arms exports are subsidised via the Export Credit Guarantees Department (ECGD), which guarantees companies against the risk of recipients defaulting. NGOs active in the arms trade cover a variety of issues and adopt a variety of conceptual approaches and strategies. For example, CAAT is opposed to the arms trade per se, but the other organisations are not. This reflects a key difference in campaign strategy: CAAT operates with a much stronger 'outsider' approach than the other organisations. Whereas Amnesty, Oxfam and Saferworld are leading organisations in the Control Arms Campaign (URL), which is calling for an international arms trade treaty to codify states' existing responsibilities under international law, CAAT prefers to focus on its own Call the Shots campaign, which focuses on the relationship between arms companies and the UK government as the main reason for the high levels of support for arms exports.

The ultimate test of the effectiveness of NGO campaigns on arms trade issues is the pattern of UK exports, which has not changed substantially under the Blair Administration, despite the so-called and (hurriedly dropped) 'ethical dimension' to foreign policy and the proclaimed commitment to the arms export guidelines. However, NGO activity has served to publicise the operation and effects of the arms trade, signalling to industry and government that their actions are being scrutinised. In this sense, the activities of the various NGOs have a cumulative effect. CAAT's protests and demonstrations at arms company AGMs can serve to raise the political temperature and thus complement the work of the other, more insider NGOs.

However, it is also possible that mainstream NGO initiatives have a negative impact on outsider groups' effectiveness: while NGOs such as Amnesty, Oxfam and Saferworld have a reputation for being 'engaged' and 'constructive', CAAT is seen as less 'realistic' and 'reasonable'. This means the government, and on occasion industry, can engage with mainstream NGOs and claim to be taking NGO concerns into account, while sidelining the more far-reaching demands of outsider groups. Given that mainstream efforts have had little effect on the overall pattern of exports, perhaps the more extensive demands and alternative strategies of outsider groups hold greater potential for more transformational change; but they are being muffled by insider activity. For scholars and activists alike, this raises the uncomfortable possibility that much NGO activity is too close to government and industry for comfort.

Anna Stavrianakis, University of Bristol

human rights. The activities of the Helsinki Citizens Assembly (HCA) in the Balkans and the Caucasus were emblematic of this approach. It brought together activists, academics and policy makers who rejected the ethno-nationalists' narratives used to perpetuate the conflict. Unsurprisingly, many of those involved have developed an immunity to imposed identities as dissidents under communism. As an international network, the HCA linked them with peace activists in the West in a relationship based on mutual solidarity rather than support. Activists in the West were empowered by the information they obtained from their colleagues in the region, which enabled them to conduct advocacy and mobilisation in their own countries. Through this relationship, activists in Balkans and Caucasus were more aware of policy thinking in Western capitals, and were empowered and protected by their membership of an international movement. The network was thus able to devise ideas and policies, from peace corridors and prisoner exchanges in the Caucasus to protectorates in the Balkans, which played an important role in reducing conflicts and helped to create more space for non-ethnic narratives.

Women's groups, often formed in response to wars, often play a critical role in promoting non-sectarian identities. For example, in northern Uganda the Gulu District Women's Development Committee played a significant role in 1989 by mobilising other women in

a peaceful demonstration at a time when no other groups dared to speak out about the war:

Wearing rags and singing funeral songs, the women marched through Gulu town demanding an end to the violence. At the same time, many from the LRA gave up fighting and returned home. Although there are no available statistics to substantiate the outcome of the demonstration, a period of relative calm followed...(Manivannan URL)

Similar examples can be found in other conflicts, especially Sierra Leone and Liberia, where women's groups were instrumental in bringing about ceasefires, although, despite playing a key role in peace-making, women are often sidelined from the political process afterwards. Women in Black, an international network, began staging vigils in Israel in 1988 against the occupation of the West Bank and Gaza. The network has hubs in Italy, Spain, Germany, England, Azerbaijan, Colombia, and in the former Yugoslavia, where during the war women held weekly vigils against the Serbian regime's policies of nationalist aggression. Women in Black groups have formed in many cities in the United States since 11 September 2001 (Women in Black URL).

Local action is another means of stemming conflict and creating 'islands of civility'. Civil society activists working with international partners created such islands in Tuzla in Bosnia and Herzegovina, and in Kazakh-Echevan on the border between Armenia and Azerbaijan. The people of San Jose de Apartado in Colombia have been recognised worldwide for bravely banning armed actors from their village, whether they are paramilitaries, guerrillas or the Colombian army. Residents who declared their village a 'Peace Community' have pledged not to participate in conflict, directly or indirectly, nor to provide information to any parties involved in the conflict. The perceived threat of such a stance is perhaps indicated by the retaliation against the people of San Jose de Apartado: since 1997, armed groups have murdered 160 people – out of a total population of 2,000.

In September 2005 members of the Colombian Solidarity Campaign and the European Network of Fraternity and Solidarity with Colombia joined 100 people from Colombia and abroad at a gathering of the Network of Communities in Resistance (RECORRE url). The meeting was hosted by the Peace Community, a founding member of the network.

Among those who believe that constructed religious and nationalist identities are important factors in conflict, some favour the use of force on the grounds that this is the only way to avoid legitimising extremist or sectarian positions – they perceive diplomacy as a form of appeasement. Thus, liberal internationalists favour humanitarian intervention – the 'responsibility to protect' as a way of enforcing human rights. There is a civil society argument as well. In sectarian wars, the first victims are those who hold cosmopolitan positions – those who favour human rights and democracy. Such a position depends on being able to express opinion without fear; therefore, some would support the use of force to create public spaces – safe havens, protectorates or trusteeships – where alternative inclusive ideas can be strengthened. The risk of liberal internationalism is that it can be used to justify wars that have more to do with geo-politics than humanitarianism. Thus the strongest case for invading Iraq and Afghanistan was made on humanitarian grounds.

Humanitarian groups and their role in conflict

A significant global civil society actor in conflict zones is humanitarian NGOs, which do not take a political position on the conflicts in which they work. Regardless of their apolitical stance, the presence and activities of humanitarian agencies can be a

Women in Black demonstration: women's groups play a significant role in peacemaking © Penny Tweedie

factor in the duration, intensity and outcome of conflict, whether intended or not.

Groups that work with refugees and internally displaced people (IDPs), agencies that provide food, water, medicine and other services to people in war zones have first-hand knowledge about conflict and are often the first to warn of impending escalation. Therefore their presence can prevent and reduce suffering, and with it the grievances that perpetuate conflict.

Warring parties, including state and non-state actors, often use the humanitarian aid infrastructure to pursue their goals, for example by intercepting supplies, forcing NGOs and international agencies to pay for access to injured civilians or displaced persons, and even using refugee assistance as a vehicle for ethnic cleansing.

Often, UN, NATO and US forces seek to coordinate closely with humanitarian NGOs in order to provide services for civilians in their areas of operations. This reduces the burden on the military and casts it in a more favourable light. However, NGOs have been uneasy about this 'encroachment on the humanitarian space', especially in the case of Iraq, where the legitimacy of the war is in question.

Some argue that humanitarian and service-delivery NGOs absolve state actors from their obligations to protect and care for civilians, and this perpetuates state weakness and war economies. Others suggest that humanitarian agencies can make use of the legitimacy established by providing aid to influence the conflict and create situations free of fear.

Box 4.2: Campaigning against the causes of conflict, corruption and human rights abuses

Global Witness investigates the use of natural resources and their revenues to fund conflict, corruption and human rights abuses, and then works to stop it. Founded in London in 1995, it initially investigated the relationship between the genocidal Khmer Rouge in Cambodia and illegal timber exports across the Thai border. Although the border was closed in 1995, it soon became clear that the Khmer Rouge was only part of a wider problem in Cambodia and in many other resource-rich countries: the deliberate exploitation of political and economic disorder by elites to loot the state's assets.

This was proven when Global Witness received confidential letters in early 1996 from Cambodia's co-prime ministers to the Thai prime minister, which agreed to circumvent an export ban to allow some 1.1 million cubic metres of timber to be exported by 18 Thai companies that had based their logging operations in pro-Khmer Rouge areas. The bulk of the revenue (between US$35 million and $90 million) would probably have gone directly to the Khmer Rouge war effort, although lucrative kickbacks were envisaged for all the other parties. The government itself would have made money from the deal too, of course (Global Witness 1996: 14).

This looting is an extreme version of the 'resource curse' – the common failure of the political structures that accrete around 'bonanza' economies, which are based on the extraction of natural resources to convert that wealth into long-term social development. This is especially common when public institutions are relatively young. If a government has direct access to substantial rents from natural resources, typically from foreign investors, it is freed from the pressures for public accountability that emerge in a state dependent on broad-based domestic taxation. Instead of trying to appeal to a broad domestic constituency, ruling elites may focus on controlling resource rents. 'Crony capitalism' soon develops, with government officials diverting revenues away from the public purse into systems of patronage to line their own pockets, and to fund internal security control and military adventurism. Domestic politics becomes a struggle between different constituencies for access to these sources of revenue.

This 'rentier' model of state (mis)behaviour is inherently unstable and vulnerable to dissolution into armed conflict as competing groups may resort to violence (see Collier 1998; Collier and Hoeffler 1998; 2000/1; 2002). Indeed, easily exploited natural resource rents encourage 'political-military entrepreneurship': where there is little chance to prosper outside of the ruling elite, enterprising individuals may seek to gain wealth, power and status through the prosecution of armed conflict (Le Billon 2005). Tangible riches in the form of natural resources also alter the mindset of combatants, turning war and insurgency from a purely political activity into an economic one; conflicts become less about grievance and more about greed. Political alliances mutate and battlefield enemies often then collaborate to make money.

Global Witness has perhaps done more than any other organisation to highlight and investigate this problem in the field. The methodology that we developed in Cambodia was simple and tries to marry some of the elements of investigative journalism with the more typical NGO method of dogged campaigning. We aim to gather detailed, first-hand evidence of the problem, seeking to name and shame those responsible for mismanagement and misappropriation of revenues from natural resources. Often a determined investigation is necessary to establish the facts, the reliability of our sources and to interpret the documents we have obtained. In drafting our reports we have to address significant libel concerns too.

Once completed, we publicise our reports and lobby relentlessly for long-term solutions. This often means arguing for a reconfiguration of the international marketplace to reduce the opportunities to profit from illicit natural resource exploitation. Although closing a border (as in Cambodia) may be effective in the short term, eventually that border will reopen and the same problem may recur. The industry as a whole has to be sensitised to the problem and its working practices altered. In addition, local institutions need to be strengthened so as to manage ethically their side of the trade.

Not all our findings are original; many may be 'open secrets amongst the knowing, but the knowing are few' (to quote Felix Frankfurter, a legal adviser to US President Roosevelt on much of his New Deal legislation in the 1930s) (cited in Douglas 1934). The aim of our investigations is often to pressure governments, companies or institutions into tackling problems that they may be aware of but have chosen not to deal with. As Frankfurter said (Douglas 1934): 'there is a shrinking quality to such transactions; to force knowledge of them into the open is largely to restrain their happening. Many practices safely pursued in private lose their justification in public.'

This is the essence of the Global Witness approach. A classic example of this was our investigation and campaign on 'conflict diamonds', for which we were nominated for the Nobel Peace Prize in 2002. Prior to this campaign, it was seen as acceptable for major companies such as De Beers, its proxies and its competitors, in the name of sustaining the world diamond price, to buy diamonds directly or indirectly from conflict zones in countries such as Angola and Sierra Leone. Global Witness's main contribution was to expose these actions and their brutal consequences, which included bankrolling rebel groups like the Revolutionary United Front, notorious in Sierra Leone for mass rape, extrajudicial executions and other terror tactics such as amputating limbs. We and partner organisations then worked with industry and government to establish a regime to detect and remove conflict diamonds from the world trade. We lobbied through the UN for immediate sanctions on rebel groups, and pushed for a diamond trade licensing system known as the Kimberley Process.

In many ways, the Global Witness approach has travelled well. A key refinement has been to work much more closely with local civil society groups. Unsurprisingly, many African, Latin American and Asian organisations – both grassroots and national – are well aware of the problems but are unable to document and expose them because of lack of resources or the threat of retaliation. Because we are international, we tend to have more room for manoeuvre: we can help assemble a more coherent paper trail and follow the leads from local NGOs to build a bigger picture of the problem, and use our knowledge of the international policy system to achieve more effective results.

By publishing the information ourselves and publicising the wider problem, we can also act as a lightning conductor, drawing the heat of retaliation away from local groups while creating a domestic political space for them to occupy. An example of this approach is our collaboration with more than 300 NGOs in more than 50 countries (of which about three-quarters are developing countries) to launch a campaign for revenues from the oil, gas and mining industries to be disclosed and managed in a more open manner. We have extensively documented how a lack of transparency has facilitated the embezzlement of vast sums from the public purse by the ruling elites in many resource-rich countries, while the people as a whole remain in dire poverty. In Angola during the late 1990s, for example, against the background of the arms-to-Angola scandal in France, about a quarter of the oil dollars were missing from the state's accounts (mostly diverted into offshore structures linked to the president and his allies). Meanwhile a quarter of the children were dying of preventable diseases before the age of five (Global Witness 2004).

Our efforts encouraged companies and governments to cooperate with international and local NGOs to establish a process to improve disclosure and tracking of revenues into national exchequers, called the Extractive Industries Transparency Initiative (EITI). It remains a work in progress, with the support of about 20 resource revenue-dependent countries. It will allow local civil society groups to improve oversight of revenues, and facilitate debate about how those revenues are managed. Real progress has been made in this regard in countries such as Nigeria and Azerbaijan; in others, including Indonesia, Ghana and Trinidad, the commitment has been more rhetorical than real. In Congo Brazzaville and Equatorial Guinea, the government has shamelessly persecuted the very groups it is supposed to be working with. An international evaluation process within the EITI is necessary in order to reward countries that are making progress and to highlight and redress failures.

Global Witness came into being because the misuse of natural resource revenues, which was beyond the control of citizens, was deepening corruption and fomenting conflict. Ultimately, our aim is to create ways for citizens to exercise control over revenues from their countries' natural resources so that they are a benefit rather than a curse. Once we have achieved that, Global Witness will become obsolete – but we are not there yet.

Gavin Hayman, Campaign Coordinator, Global Witness

Table 4.2 provides an overview of selected civil society actors in conflicts – their different roles and positions.

Promoting democracy and 'creating' civil society

The promotion of civil society as a tool to prevent and reduce conflict is an extension of the liberal notion of civil society as counterbalance to the state. This is quite logical since the market and civil society are closely related in liberal thinking. Thus, Western donors have embraced the idea of supporting civil society both as a non-violent way of resolving conflict among competing interests and as part of a liberalising agenda that will prevent authoritarianism by restraining the state.

If a normative understanding is applied, and 'civility' is conceived as the opposite of 'violence', then it follows that promoting 'civil' society will undermine the threat of conflict. As Adekson says:

The 'civility myth' directly originates from the phrase 'civil society,' which mistakably assumes that there is a section of society that is predominantly civil and another that is not. Following from this view, the state is regarded as a monstrous, corrupt, and inept leviathan that only could be resisted by a coherent, morally superior and orderly civil society. (Adekson 2004)

In many parts of the world, there has been a backlash against donor support for civil society in conflict zones on the grounds that this has created an artificial 'fifth column', which promotes the interests of donors. Authors like Ikelegbe argue that these NGOs are dominated by Western ideology and unable to manage conflicts effectively.

If we look at what constitutes the present flowering of civil society groups, their direction and energy, it would seem that western liberal ideology and donor funding dictate them... Thus, numerous questions arise in the consideration of the constitution of civil society as an alternative platform for managing conflicts. (Ikelegbe 2003)

Others critics, such as Chabal and Daloz (1999), argue that the blossoming of NGOs is not a sign of Western-style civil society but an opportunistic adaptation by political actors to the changing complexion of the international aid agenda, leaving unequal power relations intact and, again, offering little hope for effective conflict resolution.

The policies of donor agencies, particularly the Bretton Woods institutions, often result in what Richard Joseph (1998) terms 'virtual democracy', which is arguably largely cosmetic, designed to gain respectability in the court of world opinion and thus access to resources, rather than a genuine political liberalisation. For Chabal and Daloz, 'There is as yet no evidence of functionally operating civil society in Africa'. They argue that:

The emergence of a properly institutionalised civil society, led by politically independent citizens, separate from government structures, is only possible where there is a strong and strongly differentiated state. Only then is it meaningful to speak of a counter-hegemonic civil society.

Instead, they suggest:

What we observe in Black Africa is the constant interpenetration, or straddling, of the one by the other...Understanding politics in Africa is a matter of identifying the complexities of the 'shadow boxing' that takes place between state and society. But above all, it is a matter of explaining the myriad ways in which political actors, within both 'state' and 'civil' society, link up to sustain the vertical, infra-institutional and patrimonial networks which underpin politics on the continent. (Chabal and Daloz 1999: 17)

In some cases civil society promotion is taken even further and activists are given political roles, by-passing the political process. Civilian political actors drawn from civil society formed the first interim government in Liberia after the conflict, the Interim Government of National Unity (IGNU), and have been represented to some degree in the various interim arrangements up to leadership level since then, including the recent National Transitional Government of Liberia and its National Transitional Legislative Assembly. While this role has provided an important counterbalance to the power of the military factions, it has also served to compromise the supposed neutrality of those civil society actors who become part of the state, resulting in a local loss of legitimacy of even highly internationally respected individuals, as they have become identified more with their own political ambitions, interests, prejudices and beliefs than with the more broadly representative role that they claimed initially (pers .comm, Philippa Atkinson). Thus, the key reasons against 'importing' civil society to resolve conflict can be summarised as follows:

- civil society is not an object but a complex set of relations that emerged historically in compromises made between Western publics and emerging state powers
- in itself, civil society is not capable of catalysing a functioning and legitimate statehood necessary to ease violence
- when civil society is imported, in the form of NGOs, it is tied to and serves particular interests that may themselves exacerbate conflict (for example, the dictates of international donors)
- imported civil societies are often viewed as illegitimate 'peace profiteers'
- imported civil society can crowd out indigenous and rooted activists who may contribute to reducing conflict.

On the other hand, where there are groups and organisations seeking to influence their own societies, as described above, then transnational links that allow these groups to strengthen their position through greater visibility, access to power holders or even funding outside assistance can be critical.

Civil societies and conflict: a comparison of former Yugoslavia and Iraq

Despite the obvious differences between the wars in the former Yugoslavia and Iraq, it is possible to identify some commonalities that help to illustrate the relationship between global civil society and war. Both countries were totalitarian states, which did not allow a free articulation of a political alternative and its organisation. In both countries, the creation of civil society paralleled a process of bloody disintegration, although the roots of civil society were in autonomous, often secret, spaces that, in Yugoslavia, became sites for a critical and free discussion carved out by liberal intellectuals, and, in Iraq, involved the opposition in exile, in Kurdistan, as well as underground. These nascent civil societies failed to defuse sectarian tensions. On the contrary, civil society actors influenced the framing of conflict in each country, which in turn shaped their profile and activities in relation to violence. In fact, it is more accurate to talk about civil societies rather than 'a civil society' in former Yugoslavia and Iraq. Different civil society actors and groups served either to promote or to counteract the conflicts in Yugoslavia and Iraq.

In Yugoslavia, the 'authentic' indigenous groups were instrumental in creating the notion that the Yugoslav conflict was caused by centuries-old ethnic hatreds, and was the outcome of competing and conspiratorial interests by great powers. By contrast, the emerging human rights, anti-war and women's groups challenged this deterministic interpretation of the conflict. They exposed the 'production of hatred' and supported multi-ethnic tolerance on the ground and as a political vision. The outbreak of war in Iraq began as a result of foreign invasion; but Islamist and tribal leaders, together with the former exiled opposition, played a critical role in fomenting 'resistance', which metamorphosed into sectarian conflict. As in Yugoslavia, human rights and humanitarian groups, women's organisations, progressive clergy, intellectuals, and artists held a different perspective, which promoted the Iraqi public interest and a non-sectarian Iraqi identity. Both conflicts are new wars, which cannot be separated from the plethora of global forces that moulded them; the nascent civil societies of Yugoslavia and Iraq, whether their actors promoted or opposed conflict, were part of a global network or were influenced by the global context.

Former Yugoslavia

With the waning of Communism in former Yugoslavia, the divergent ideological paths taken by the dissident intellectuals gathered around the journal Praxis illustrate the contradictory roles that segments of Yugoslav civil society played in relation to the conflict. Established in 1964, Praxis was the initiative of a group of Marxist scholars, who emerged as critics of the implementation of Marxist doctrine in Yugoslavia, specifically of the authoritarian and bureaucratic aspects as well as some elements of the market-oriented economic reforms. They advocated 'socialist humanism', a more humane version of Communism, and hence did not question the system as such by calling for democracy. Nonetheless, they represented the centre of autonomous thought, which would spread with the decreasing legitimacy of the Communist Party during the 1970s and 1980s. However, this initial core of opposition would divide along two lines: nationalist and liberal (Dragovic-Soso 2002: 22–63; Magas 1993: 49–73).

Table 4.2: Selected global civil society actors

● Predominant
◐ Significant
○ To some extent

	Organisation					Activity					Position				
	Organisation	NGO/group	Movement/network	Think tank/academia	Media/website	Inform/educate	Lobby	Mobilise	Serve	Riot/celebrate	Power politics	Ancient rivalries	Political economy	Ideologies	
Acholi Religious Leaders Peace Initiative			●			◐	●				●	●			www.interfaithpeace.net/showorg.php?orgid=15
American Enterprise Institute				●		◐	●				●	◐			www.aei.org
Amnesty International	●	◐									○		◐	●	www.amnesty.org
Carnegie Endowment for International Peace				●		●	◐				●		○		www.carnegieendowment.org
Centre for Defence Studies, Delhi				●		●	◐				●		◐	○	www.cdiss.org
Christian Aid	●					○	◐		●						www.christian-aid.org.uk
Communidad de Paz de San Jose de Apartado			●					●						●	www.cdpsanjose.org
Communita Di San Egidio	●							●				●			www.sanegidio.org
Conciliation Resources	●						◐	●			◐	●			www.c-r.org
Gaza Community Mental Health Project	●					○	◐				○		◐	●	www.gcmhp.net
Global Witness	●		◐										●		www.globalwitness.org
Gulu District Women's Development Committee			●				◐	●						●	
Gush Shalom (Israel)			●					●			●				gush-shalom.org
Helsinki Citizens' Assembly			●	◐		○	◐	●			○		◐	●	www.hyd.org.tr/en/hca.asp
Hague Appeal for Peace			●				◐	●			●			◐	www.haguepeace.org
Institute for Security Studies (Africa)	◐			●		●	◐						◐	●	www.iss.co.za
Inter-Church Peace Council (Netherlands)	●	◐				●	●	○			◐			●	www.ikv.nl
International Alert	●						◐		●		●	●	●		www.international-alert.org
International Crisis Group			●	◐	●	●	◐				●		○	◐	www.crisisgroup.org
International Institute for Strategic Studies				●		●	◐				●		◐	○	www.iiss.org
International Peace Bureau			●				◐	●			●			◐	www.ipb.org
Iraqi Women's Network			●								◐			●	www.whrnet.org
*Italian Consortium of Solidarity		◐	●				◐		◐						www.icsitalia.org
*Médecins Sans Frontières (MSF)		●				○	◐		●						www.msf.org
Nairobi Peace Initiatives		●										●			www.npi-africa.org
Noam Chomsky	●					◐	◐				●	◐			www.chomsky.info
Network of Communities in Resistance (RECORRE)			●				◐	●						●	http://www.prensarural.org/recorre/index.html
Norwegian Institute for Applied Social Science (FAFO)				●		●	◐				◐	●			www.fafo.no
*Oxfam		●				○	◐		●						www.oxfam.org
Pax Christi (international)			●				◐	●				●			www.paxchristi.net
Paz Colombia		●	●					●					●		www.galeon.com/pazcolombia
Peace Brigades International		●	●						●				●		www.peacebrigades.org
Peace Now (Israel)			●					●			◐	●			www.peacenow.org.il
Project for the New American Century				●			●				●	◐			www.newamericancentury.org

	Organisation					Activity					Position				
	Organisation	NGO/group	Movement/network	Think tank/academia	Media/website	Inform/educate	Lobby	Mobilise	Serve	Riot/celebrate	Power politics	Ancient rivalries	Political economy	Ideologies	
Publish What You Pay		●		●		●	●				●		●		www.publishwhatyoupay.org
Pugwash Conferences on Science and World Affairs			●			●	●				●				www.pugwash.org
Revenue Watch Institute		●		●		●	●				●		●		www.revenuewatch.org
Stockholm International Peace Research Institute				●		●					●			●	www.sipri.org
Stop the War Coalition			●				●	●		●	●				www.stopwar.org.uk
Women in Black			●				●	●						●	www.womeninblack.net
Womens International League for Peace and Freedom	●					●	●							●	www.wilpf.org/
West Africa Network for Peace-Building (WANEP)	●	●				●	●		●		●	●			www.wanep.org

* humanitarian agencies are concerned with mitigating the effects of conflict rather than taking a position

The use of civil society as a platform for fanning exclusive Serbian nationalism is best illustrated by the Belgrade-based Serbian Association of Writers and the debates about Kosovo it hosted in the late 1980s. Kosovo's autonomous status was disputed in heated emotional language that vilified the Albanian majority population, portrayed the Serb emigration from Kosovo as an 'exodus', and lamented their fate as 'genocide' and 'ethnic cleansing'. While these protest evenings focused on Kosovo established Serbs as victims at the hands of the Albanians, the Serbian sense of martyrdom in the federal Yugoslav context was articulated in the draft Memorandum of the Serbian Academy of Sciences and Arts, which was leaked to the public in 1986. Signatories described the Serbs as Yugoslavia's perennial losers – in economic, political and cultural terms – summed up in the phrase 'weak Serbia, strong Yugoslavia'. The impact of the Memorandum was far-reaching, as it legitimised Serbian grievances, from Kosovo, through Bosnia and Herzegovina to Croatia (Thomas 1999: 32–51).

This increasingly strident sector of civil society articulated Serbian grievances as an historical injustice. Portraying Serbs as martyrs at the hands of other national groups in Yugoslavia in exclusive nationalist terms foreclosed the possibility of a democratic and peaceful resolution of outstanding political and economic issues plaguing the federation, at a time when the Communist Party was losing the mantle of undisputed arbiter. According to the Serbian Association of Writers and the Serbian Academy of Sciences and Arts – two 'authentic' Serbian voices that were perceived as independent and reputable – the Serb battles of the late 1980s and early 1990s echoed those they had fought with their Balkan foes from time immemorial. Civil society had created a powerful vision of Serbian 'plight'; all that the rising Serbian leader, Slobodan Milosevic, had to do was turn it into a political platform, summed up in the slogan 'all Serbs in one state' (Gow 2003). Crucially, the implementation of this political programme entailed the use of force.

As the clouds of war gathered over the former Yugoslavia, the 'other' civil society was galvanised in a direct rejection of exclusive nationalism emanating from the non-state sector. Belgrade, Zagreb, Sarajevo and Prishtina became hubs of a new kind of activism focused on opposing the looming conflict. A number of human rights, anti-war and women's groups were founded and challenged the vision of closed societies propagated by nationalist civil society actors. Three interconnected features characterised their activism:

• they supported an open, individual and human rights oriented vision of a multiethnic society
• they harboured transnational linkages in former Yugoslavia

• they connected and collaborated with global civil society in its opposition to the war in Yugoslavia.

Liberal civil society's support for multi-ethnicity was informed by its interpretation of the looming ethnic conflict and bloodshed that followed: violence was a result of the instrumentalisation of ethnicity, rather than an inevitable and predetermined outcome of ancient hatreds. After the forced abolition of Kosovo's autonomy, civil society in Prishtina mounted a non-violent response. In 1990, 400,000 Albanians signed a declaration. 'For Democracy, Against Violence'; thousands of candles were lit in protest; pots and pans were banged at the beginning of the curfew; factory whistles and car horns were hooted at a specific hour to commemorate the dead (Kostovicova 1997: 24–5; Clark 2000: 57–8). In April 1992, thousands of citizens of Sarajevo thronged to the city to protest against ethnic divisions and affirm the city as a model of inter-ethnic coexistence and tolerance (Silber and Little 1995: 250–2). These mass grassroots anti-war manifestations were not enough to stop state repression nor, eventually, war in Kosovo and Bosnia and Herzegovina. However, they did provide a foundation for a variety of autonomous civil society activities during the war, from documenting war crimes to supporting the idea of multi-ethnicity.

Alongside their liberal vision, transnational connections maintained among civil society groups in former Yugoslavia during the war also sent a strong message. They kept alive the meaning of multiculturalism while nationalists were trying to erase it – ideologically, through the political platform of a homogenous nation state and practically, through an ethnic cleansing campaign on the ground. During the war in Bosnia and Herzegovina, a number of anti-war activists from Serbia gathered around the project 'Living in Sarajevo'. This initiative attracted more than a dozen NGOs and civic groups which pleaded with international agencies to facilitate a trip to Sarajevo. The Serbian activists considered their dispatches of food, clothes parcels and letters to their Sarajevo counterparts insufficient. Serbian activists wanted to meet Sarajevans to demonstrate that there was another Belgrade and another Serbia that did not accept national divisions. Eventually, in April 1994 a group of 38 anti-war activists from Serbia travelled for 48 hours from Belgrade to Sarajevo. Following the trails over Mount Igman, they entered the city through its infamous tunnel, under heavy artillery and sniper fire from the Bosnian Serb Army. Such transnational horizontal links dating from the war provided a foundation for the future post-conflict reconciliation in the region.

Connections with global civil society were equally significant. They provided an external legitimisation of multiculturalism when such ideas were under attack in former Yugoslavia. Also, they were a valuable gesture of solidarity when local peace activists, labelled national traitors, found themselves under tremendous pressure. The Peace Caravan organised by the Helsinki Citizens' Assembly in 1991 was one such initiative. The high point of the Caravan's voyage, which took it from Trieste through Slovenia, Croatia, Serbia, Bosnia and Herzegovina, and Macedonia, was a human chain formed around four places of worship in Sarajevo – Orthodox, Catholic, Muslim and Jewish. It did not stop the conflict, but was a powerful boost for peace activists. It also helped forge links between NGOs, peace groups and movements in Europe, and their counterparts emerging in former Yugoslavia, as well as among groups in Yugoslavia. These links would be a symbolic lifeline for local anti-war groups and activists who were increasingly marginalised, ostracised and threatened by their nationalist establishments, as the human and material cost of war grew. Such, for example, was the impact of Susan Sontag's stay in Sarajevo during the siege in 1993, where, under flashlights and candles due to a lack of electricity, she staged the Bosnian version of Samuel Beckett's *Waiting for Godot*, with a multi-ethnic cast – a symbol of the city's resistance to exclusive nationalism.

However, transnational interaction with global civil society also provided external legitimisation to nationalist civil society in former Yugoslavia. The parade of 'foreign friends' who visited and supported Serbian nationalists in Serbia and in Bosnia and Herzegovina during the war and its aftermath affirmed the portrayal of the conflict as one caused by 'ancient hatreds' and great power rivalry. The frequent contacts of Russian émigré writer Eduard Limonov with a variety of civil society groups in the early 1990s, such as the Belgrade media and the Serbian Literary Society, are illustrative. His support for the Serbs was inspired by the pan-Slavic Orthodox solidarity in the battle against 'the fascism of the new world order'. His support for the 'Serb cause' was caught on camera on a visit to Bosnian Serbs, when he fired a round at besieged Sarajevo from an anti-aircraft machine gun from one of the hills surrounding the city (Reljic et al. 1992).

At the same time, as war continued the civil society landscape in former Yugoslavia became increasingly crowded by local and global NGOs whose activity focused on the delivery of humanitarian aid. Their engagement was based on the premise that the conflict could be mitigated through service provision, reconstruction, and stimulation of alternative livelihoods, in line with the political economy approach to conflict. Despite their narrow focus on humanitarian aid, these groups were often closely aligned to business or political interests; for example, 'The Third Child' charity headed by Svetlana Raznatovic, aka Ceca, a folk singer and widow of the assassinated war criminal Zeljko Raznatovic, aka Arkan. Since 1994, the charity, which is closely linked with Arkan's extreme nationalist Party of Serbian Unity, has supported needy families with three or more children, many of them refugees and war veterans, in an effort to rehabilitate a traditional notion of Serbian family, and wrest Serbia from the perceived dangers of a low birth rate. Like many other local charities, it built its credibility on the fact that it had nothing to do with the West or Western NGOs.

It was only after the war that the international community launched an 'offensive' to create a civil society in the Balkans. During the war, outside support had been given to established grassroots initiatives. But this funding was an insufficient incentive for new groups to become involved in risky anti-war advocacy and activism. The outcome of post-war funding was the artificial creation of a multitude of NGOs, whose contribution to democratisation and good governance has been ambiguous. In the first five months of 2001, after Milosevic's fall the previous year, about 800 new NGOs were registered in Serbia owing to the surge in donations (NGO Policy Group 2001: 22–3). As elsewhere in former Yugoslavia, their key weakness has been instability of their mission, intermittently working on human rights, ethnic reconciliation, and environmental issues, and so on. Their activism was influenced by conditions attached to foreign donations, rather than by persuasion. The fate of Otpor, a group of fearless youths driven by a human rights agenda, who opposed Milosevic's regime, is telling. With a clenched fist spray-painted on the walls and streets of Serbia, it became a symbol of resistance

and alternative to xenophobic nationalism. However, Western support did not sustain its vigour beyond Milosevic's fall, when the group transformed into a political party that has failed to attract general support.

In sum, the emergence of the civil society(ies) in former Yugoslavia contests the notion of civil society as a barrier to conflict. In fact, it shows that the interrelationship between local civil society, its global counterparts and conflict is much more complex. Different segments of civil society promoted and mitigated the conflict in Yugoslavia. At the same time, interaction with global civil society encouraged both integration and disintegration of the multi-ethnic societies in the Balkans, as civil society liberals and nationalists drew strength from contacts abroad. Lastly, in so far as the end of Communism overlapped with the beginning of the Yugoslav conflict, it is precisely the foreboding of a bloody war and its outbreak that prompted the emergence and growth of liberal, human rights and anti-war groups. Although they were marginalised by the pact between nationalist elites and nationalist civil society, liberal civil society established during the war has provided the foundation for building democracy and advancing reconciliation in the region after its end.

Iraq

In Iraq the interaction between civil society and conflict takes place within a context of pervasive fear and increasing sectarian polarisation. Some civil society actors helped shape the narratives that sustain the conflict while others struggle to dispel them. International efforts at promoting civil society have had limited success in creating sustainable, locally rooted groups, let alone reducing conflict. Segments of civil society contributed to the conflict in different ways: some actors promoted sectarian narratives that inflamed tensions; others, those in exile who were non-sectarian, identified the regime with the state, thus helping to precipitate state collapse after the US–UK-led invasion. In the aftermath, rule by the Coalition Authority served to entrench extremist narratives.

After the regime-state collapse and pervasive fear

The invasion did not only remove the regime, it also precipitated the collapse of the remnants of the Iraqi state. The army, security services and media were dissolved. De-Ba'athification crippled the rest of the bureaucracy by forcing many civil servants out of the public sector. And an unwillingness and inability to prevent rioting allowed the destruction of most state assets. Most damaging, however, were the images of rioting broadcast for weeks after the invasion. Coalition forces may have stood by in order to allow long-oppressed Iraqis to 'let off some steam', and to emphasize news of the regime's demise. The quip by US Defence Secretary Donald Rumsfeld, 'stuff happens', supports this view. The effect of the televised images of rioting was to engender a new fear among ordinary Iraqis about the rise of lawlessness. Indeed, criminal and terrorist networks took advantage of the security vacuum rapidly.

Thus after the invasion, Iraqis were exposed to a new order of fear. The threat of repression by the regime was replaced by a myriad of other dangers: Coalition violence, suicide bombs, abduction gangs, religious zealots and sectarian vigilantes. If one could escape the regime's reach in the past by eschewing politics, today there is no guarantee of safety. Since 2003, ordinary Iraqis have become targets in a state of pervasive Hobbesian violence: Shi'a and Sunni, secular and religious, academics and labourers, collaborators and nationalists, women and children; even the dead are targeted by religious and sectarian fanatics who desecrate holy shrines. In such an atmosphere it is difficult to speak of civil society. Yet it is possible to argue that some civil society actors create and maintain the narratives that underpin some of the violence, while others struggle to contain it.

Justifying violence

The violence in Iraq is sustained by several overlapping narratives, most of which are generated by civil society. Indeed, these narratives were shaped by the experience of opposition groups both underground and in exile during the years of Saddam Hussein. The exiled opposition was largely divided between those who pursued a nationalist agenda and those who pursued Kurdish and Shi'ite agendas, and it is these groups that formed the main political parties. After the invasion of Kuwait the regime's Ba'athist ideology was largely discredited and Saddam Hussein turned to both Sunni Islam and tribalism to mobilise political support. At the same time, the regime was too weak to rule by repression alone and thus it combined co-optation with toleration for milder forms of opposition. This strategy

left enough space for the Hawza – the Shi'a religious hierarchy – to expand its role as the main moral authority, especially among the poor.

Today the insurgency is largely Islamic, Sunni, yet nationalist in discourse, and targeted mostly at Coalition forces with the aim of driving them out of the country. Another discourse concerns the need to protect traditional Islamic, Arab and tribal values, and communities, from corruption by Westerners and their Iraqi allies. As the violence acquires a sectarian character, insurgents are being depicted increasingly as protectors of the Sunni community.

Nationalist political and religious activists not only recognise resistance as a legitimate right, they advocate it as a religious and civic duty. While some caution that in the current circumstances it may be more appropriate to pursue resistance by peaceful means, most advocate or justify the use of force. Sunni clerics play a key role in providing the narrative for the insurgency, although they do not lead it. They are also involved in mobilising support for insurgents and civilian victims of counter-insurgency efforts and sectarian reprisals. Activists promoting the right to resist foreign occupation, including through violent means, are engaged in transnational networks through which they receive support from anti-imperialist and anti-capitalist campaigners, both in the region and in the West.

Related to but distinct from the nationalist insurgents are the 'holy warriors' associated with Al-Qaeda. They view Iraq as a battleground in a cosmic struggle against 'Crusaders and Zionists'. In addition to attacking Coalition forces they target the Iraqi military and civilians, whom they deem legitimate targets due to their association with the foreign 'infidels'. Al-Qaeda has set out to provoke civil war by targeting Iraq's Shi'a community; it also targets Sunnis who engage in the political process and anyone who does not subscribe to its extremist Wahhabi version of Islam. Al-Qaeda employs spectacular violence to provoke an over-reaction that helps mobilise support in Iraq and across the Islamic world. Al-Qaeda benefits from transnational networks that facilitate funding, recruit fighters and conduct advocacy for the cause. Some of these networks include legitimate actors such as Islamist and Arab nationalist activists, who celebrate Al-Qaeda suicide bombers as martyrs.

The official argument advanced by the Coalition and expatriate political leaders has evolved from liberation and regime change to the need to combat terrorism and protect the democratic project in Iraq. As violence has intensified, the rhetoric focuses on the need to protect Shi'a and Kurdish communities from Sunnis who have, according to this narrative, associated themselves with Saddam's remnants and Arab Al-Qaeda fighters. This is exactly the intended consequence of Al-Qaeda's violence against the Shi'a community. It is also a logical evolution of the policies of returning exiles. Lacking a popular base, expatriate politicians saw sectarianism and ethno-nationalism as a means to attract popular support. They argued that the Shi'a and Kurdish communities were the victims of the regime, and the Sunnis were the regime's main constituency. This absolved their respective communities from culpability for the crimes of the regime and entitled them to power and resources in compensation for past suffering. Transitional justice is being used to redistribute power and resources on the basis of identity.

Coalition forces have helped entrench the sectarianism of their expatriate allies. They introduced ethnic and sectarian quotas in the division of power and relied on sectarian and ethnic militias in counter-insurgency operations. Even in its attempts to redress sectarian tensions, the Coalition Authority is deepening them by reaching out to sectarian Sunni leaders as a counterbalance to perceived bias in favour of the Kurds and the *Shi'a*, thus encouraging politicians on all sides to identify themselves in sectarian terms.

The economic agenda

An important catalyst for the violence in Iraq is money. Criminal networks and traffickers of oil, weapons, drugs, people and money thrived before the war. In the aftermath of the invasion, the volume of criminal activity increased significantly, as a result of the collapse of state institutions on one hand and the massive influx of dollars, which have not been accounted for properly, on the other. Crime is intertwined with the violence on all sides. Sometimes it is difficult to know whether the political is a facade for economic enterprise, or crime is a tool to finance the political project.

Civil society

Whether any of the groups described above – former opposition parties, Islamists, tribal and criminal networks – can be construed as civil society is of course contested. Normative or value-based approaches to civil society may not accept them. Postmodern or multicultural approaches may consider all but the criminal networks as local manifestations of civil society (see Kaldor 2003). Some may even consider smuggling and corruption as forms of social capital. However, there is no doubt that these groups have grassroots presence, represent the interest of cross-sections of society and compete to impose their vision of how Iraqis should live their lives.

The combination of pervasive violence and extreme exclusivist narratives leaves little space for non-sectarian, non-violent and democratic activism. Some of the groups and initiatives operating in this space were active before the invasion; they included artists, political debating societies, and groups of professionals, academics and civil servants acting within the folds of the state bureaucracy to promote a civil democratic alternative to the regime (Said 2005). Even within state-controlled NGOs, such as the Woman's Union and Dar Al-Hikma think tank, spaces were emerging for independent, if not dissident, thought, although these were more limited in size and influence than identity-based groups. The invasion and its aftermath weakened them further.

There were also NGOs operating in exile and in Kurdistan, associated to varying degrees with the exile opposition, and providing humanitarian assistance, campaigning against the regime and/or sanctions. Conflict, including the invasion, has created both cleavages and transformations among these activists. Not all exiled campaigners against the regime were prepared to provide moral justification for the war. After the invasion, activists who sought redress for the regime's crimes were divided between those who argued for the redistribution of access to power and resources and those who adopted a transitional justice and human rights perspective.

After the invasion Coalition forces and other international actors expended enormous resources on the development of civil society. US funds for the promotion of civil society amounted to US$3 billion (US Department of State 2006)[1], in addition to the millions of dollars contributed by other Coalition governments, the UN and the European Union.

The area of civil society investment was liberalisation.

---

1 *Three categories in the Iraq Relief and Reconstruction Fund (IRRF) could be used for the promotion of civil society: Justice, Public Safety and Civil Society; Democracy; and Education, Refugees, Human Rights and Governance. These categories amount to US$2.75 billion.*

Box 4.3: **Iraq's Mahdi army**

The oscillation of Muqtada al-Sadr's Mahdi army between a social movement and an armed militia, and between Islamic nationalism and Shi'a sectarianism, is emblematic of the processes taking place in Iraq today. Shortly after the invasion and the fall of the Ba'athist regime in 2003, the Sadrists emerged as a movement of young, poor Shi'a in the slums of Baghdad and the southern countryside, who were led by a populist cleric and engaged in a variety of contradictory activities.

Some of al-Sadr's followers were involved in the looting that followed the regime's fall; and they were the first to organise neighbourhood watch committees and help restore some of the stolen property. They attracted many Shi'a ex-Ba'athists and yet engaged in vigilante violence against former Ba'athist officials. They established vigilante Sharia courts and prosecuted gypsies and Christians for selling alcohol. They were the first Shi'a group to clash with the Americans, losing thousands of fighters in Najaf and Sadr city in 2004. They declared solidarity with the Sunni insurgents in Falluja when the city was attacked in April 2004, but not when it was attacked again in November that year. The Sadrists continue to demand US withdrawal and deride the exiles for their association with the occupation, while participating actively in a government in which they have several ministers. They oppose the mainstream Shi'a parties, in part for their closeness to Iran, yet are suspected of receiving Iranian assistance, including weapons and training. Today, Mahdi army activists are accused of being at the forefront of Shi'a sectarian violence, while their leaders continue to engage with Sunni clerics with whom they maintain a better relationship than any of the other *Shi'a* groups.

With their extensive grassroots network, the Sadrists are a microcosm of Iraqi society. Their convulsions reflect the fears and pains endured by a people racked by unimaginable violence. They lurch from one extreme to the other in search of answers, and in the process become part of the problem.

Yahia Said, Centre for the Study of Global Governance, LSE

The Coalition Provisional Authority saw liberalisation as a conflict prevention tool. It sponsored civil society initiatives aimed at promoting small and medium enterprises, micro-lending, entrepreneurship and the delivery of social services. Beyond creating hundreds of donor-dependent civil society groups and entrepreneurs, it is difficult to test the sustainability and impact of these efforts.

A handful of Iraqi and international groups focusing on humanitarian assistance, culture, development and human rights continue to resist sectarianism by promoting cross-cutting identities and interests, and engaging with global civil society networks to influence policy makers. They face enormous challenges and threats: their members are subjected to sectarian violence, and they may face political oppression for breaking the mould.

These increasingly beleaguered actors include spiritual leaders, activists and professionals who refuse to be swept up by the sectarian fever. Among them are powerful figures such as Ayatollah Sistani –

a leading force of moderation in Iraqi society whose standing is being weakened by parasitic politicians using his name for their divisive politics. There are clerics who take a stand against terrorist actions in the name of resistance or Islam. There are women activists who refuse to accept a constitution that puts them at the mercy of clerics. There are civil servants and professionals who are trying to save whatever is left of the state from destruction by short-sighted politicians. These are individuals who refuse to be reduced to their ethnic identity but rather identify themselves through their values and convictions. Although they may be politically isolated in an atmosphere of growing fear and hatred, they enjoy the trust of Iraqis with whom they stay connected, in contrast to politicians and holy warriors. These people are best equipped to negotiate and design Iraq's future and the political programme that will end conflict. To stand a chance of achieving this they will need the protection and empowerment by the international community.

Conclusion

A Yearbook chapter cannot possibly do justice to the complex myriad of groups, movements and individuals engaged in debates about war. In a sense, the emergence of global civil society parallels the decline in violence between states as more and more decision-making taken at global, national and local levels reflects the outcomes of new forms of global politics involving states, international organisations and non-state actors. What we have argued, however, is that the capacity of civil society to address new forms of local and transnational violence in different parts of the world depends on the composition of civil society – the mix of different positions and different interpretations of contemporary warfare. While the emergence of actually existing global civil society is a necessary condition for a decline in war, an alternative method of managing conflict at global, national and local levels, it is by no means a sufficient condition. The very meaning of global civil society is the antithesis of war and violence, but actually existing global civil society is complex and contradictory, containing elements that can both contribute to peace and play a pivotal role in fomenting the conflict.

The cases in Iraq and Yugoslavia show that any support for civil society has to be based on an understanding of the conflicts as 'new wars', and has to be directed at transforming the war economies and constructing non-sectarian identities. In both these cases, conflict emerged in situations where there was little space for civil society. Fear caused by authoritarianism and totalitarianism, or by the insecurity that collapsing authoritarian and totalitarian states leave behind, is anathema to civil society or at least to those manifestations of civil society which can counteract conflict. Often these regimes leave behind perverse forms of civil society like religious and nationalist groups, which survive and thrive in the atmosphere of fear; but these can and often do engage in creating narratives for conflict.

Once conflicts are under way there is even less space for activism of any kind. In such conditions investment in the promotion of civil society can at best be a futile exercise, especially when the models promoted are alien to the local environments. At worse they can further exacerbate conflict through feeding into war economies or further eroding state legitimacy.

The vulnerable remnants of non-sectarian, public interest-based activism in conflict zones, as well as those new groups, like women activists, that emerge in response to conflict, are critical to ending war, since they carry the seeds of rebuilding of legitimate public authority. Supporting them is therefore critical. So are proposals for addressing the underlying political economy of war, through, for example, revenue transparency or alternative legitimate livelihoods.

In a global era the creation and development of civil society is no longer confined to local circumstances, if it ever was. With democracy promotion programmes focused on civil society building, with ties to diasporas and other connections, the outside world is deeply implicated in shaping non-state capacities and voices. In many cases external support has been critical in offering a lifeline to non-sectarian groups when their states clamped down on them. However, it is also true that outside assistance carries its own risks – the risks of co-optation and even delegitimisation. The most important form of support is engagement, which helps to create spaces free of fear and want where such groups can thrive, and which facilitates access to the key centres of power.

The argument of this chapter has implications for the broader confrontation between terror and the war on terror, and the different positions to be found in global civil society. There are the neo-conservatives and liberal internationalists who support the war on terror as a way of confronting terror. There are the peace movements that give priority to opposing the war on terror. And there are those who understand the confrontation as an expression of ancient rivalries, both the global Islamists and those Western secularists who promote the idea of a 'clash of civilisations'. A 'new war' approach to the confrontation would promote a non-sectarian cosmopolitan identity that opposes both terror and the war on terror, and that creates new public spaces at local, national and global levels.

REFERENCES

Adekson, Adedayo Oluwakayode (2004) *The Civil Society Problematique: Deconstructing Civility and Southern Nigeria's Ethnic Radicalisation*. London: Routledge.

Ali, Tariq (2003a) 'Re-colonizing Iraq', *New Left Review*, 21(May–June).

– (2003b) 'World Politics After Iraq.' Webcast. http://www.workingtv.com/tariqali.html (consulted 27 June 2006).

Amnesty International UK (URL) http://www.amnesty.org.uk (consulted 17 July 2006).

BASIC (URL) http://www.basicint.org (consulted 17 July 2006).

Berdal, M and Malone, D (eds) (2002) *Greed and Grievance: Economic Agendas in Civil Wars.* Boulder, CO: Lynne Rienner Publishers.

Brock, Peter (1970) *Twentieth Century Pacifism*. London and New York: Van Nostrand-Reinhold.

Bush, G (2001) 'Address to the Joint Session of Congress, 20 September.' http://www.whitehouse.gov/news/releases/2001/09/20010920-8.html (consulted 7 July 2006).

CAAT (Campaign Against Arms Trade) (2005) *Who Calls the Shots? How government-corporate collusion drives arms exports* (London: CAAT).

– (URL) http://www.caat.org.uk (consulted 17 July 2006).

Chabal, Patrick and Daloz, Jean-Pascal (1999) Africa Works: Disorder as Political Instrument. Oxford: James Currey.

Chomsky, N (2003) 'An Hour with Noam Chomsky on Iraq, War, Profiteers and the Media.' 26 December. http://www.democracynow.org/article.pl?sid=03/12/26/1451251 (consulted 29 June 2006).

Clark, Howard (2000) *Civil Resistance in Kosovo*. London and Sterling, VA: Pluto Press.

Cockburn, Alexander (1999) 'Beat the Davel', *The Nation*, 10 May.

Collier, Paul (2000) 'Doing Well out of War: An Economic Perspective', in Mats Berdal and David M. Malone (eds), *Greed and Grievance: Economic Agendas in Civil Wars.* Boulder, CO: Lynne Rienner

– and Hoeffler, Anke (1998) 'On Economic Causes of Civil War', *Oxford Economic Papers*, 50: 563–73:

Collier, Paul and Hoeffler, Anke (2000/1) *Greed and Grievance in Civil War*. Washington, DC: World Bank Development Research Group.

– (2004) 'Greed and Grievance in Civil Wars', *Oxford Economic Papers*, 56: 563–95.

Control Arms Campaign (URL) http://www.controlarms.org (consulted 17 July 2006).

Cooper, Sandi E (1991) *Patriotic Pacifism: Waging War on War in Europe, 1815–1914*. New York: Oxford University Press.

Criteria ('Consolidated Criteria') (26 October 2000), HC 199-203W, reprinted in Douglas, W (1934) 'Directors Who Do Not Direct', *Harvard Law Review*, 47: 1305–34.

Dragovic-Soso, Jasna (2002) *'Saviours of the Nation': Serbia's Intellectual Opposition and the Revival of Nationalism*. London: Hurst & Company.

Duffield, Mark (2001) *Global Governance and the New Wars*. London: Zed Books.

FCO (Foreign and Commonwealth Office) (2005) *Conflict Prevention – Small Arms and Light Weapons*. http://www.fco.gov.uk (consulted 17 July 2006).

Giddens, A (1990) *The Consequences of Modernity*. Cambridge: Polity Press in association with Blackwell.

Global Witness (1996) *Corruption, War & Forest Policy - The Unsustainable Exploitation Of Cambodia's Forests*. February. http://www.globalwitness.org/reports/index.php?section=cambodia (consulted 9 February 2006).

– (2004) *Time for Transparency. Coming Clean on Oil, Mining And Gas Revenues*. March. http://www.globalwitness.org/reports/show.php/en.00049.html (consulted 9 August 2006).

Gow, James (2003) *The Serbian Project and its Adversaries: A Strategy of War Crimes*. London: Hurst & Company.

Hague Appeal for Peace (URL) http://www.haguepeace.org (consulted 1 August 2006).

Hegel, G. W. F. (1820/1996) *The Philosophy of Right*, trans. S. W. Dyde. London: Prometheus Books.

Held, D, McGrew, A, Goldblatt, D and Perraton, J (1999) *Global Transformations: Politics, Economics and Culture*. Cambridge: Polity Press.

Hobsbawm, Eric (1994) *The Age of Extremes: The Short Twentieth Century, 1914–1991*. London: Michael Joseph.

Howard, Michael (1978) *War and the Liberal Conscience*. London: Temple Smith.

– (2000) *The Invention of Peace*. Oxford: Blackwell.

Human Security Centre (URL) http://www.humansecurityreport.info/index.php?option=content&task=view&id=28&Itemid=63 (consulted 1 August 2006).

Huntington, Samuel (2002) *Clash of Civilizations and the Remaking of World Order.* New York: Free Press.

Ikelegbe, O A (2003) 'Civil Society and Alternative Approaches to Conflict Management in Nigeria', in A Imobighe (ed), *Civil Society and Ethnic Conflict Management in Nigeria*. Lagos: Spectrum Books.

International Alert (URL) http://www. http://www.international-alert.org (consulted 17 July 2006).

Joseph, Richard (1998) 'Africa, 1990–1997: From Abertura to Closure', *Journal of Democracy*, -9(2): 3–17.

Kaldor, Mary (1999) *New and Old Wars: Organised Violence in a Global Era*. Cambridge: Polity Press.

– (2003) *Global Civil Society: An Answer to War*. Cambridge: Polity Press.

Kaplan, R D (2001) *The Coming Anarchy: Shattering the Dreams of the Post Cold War*. US: Vintage Books

– (2005) Balkan Ghosts: *A Journey Through History*. US: Picador.

Karagiannis, Emmanuel (2002) *Energy and Security in the Caucasus*. London: Routledge.

Keen, David (1998) *The Economic Functions of Violence in Civil Wars*. Adelphi Paper 320. London: International Institute of Strategic Studies.

Klein, Naomi (2004) 'An Iraqi Intifada', *Guardian*, 12 April. http://www.guardian.co.uk/Iraq/Story/0,2763,1190300,00.html (accessed 1 August 2006).

Kostovicova, Denisa (1997) *Parallel Worlds: Response of Kosovo Albanians to Loss of Autonomy in Serbia*, 1989–1996.

Research Paper 2. Southeast Europe Series, Keele European Research Centre, Keele University.

Kumar, Radha (1997) *Bosnia in the Annals of Partition*. London and New York: Verso.

Le Billion (2005) *Fuelling War: Natural Resources and Armed Conflict*. Adelphi Paper 357. London: International Institute for Strategic Studies.

Lijphart, Arend (1977) *Democracy in Plural Societies: A Comparative Exploration*. New Haven and London: Yale University Press.

Longman, T (1999) 'State, Civil Society and Genocide in Rwanda', in Richard Joseph (ed), *State, Conflict and Democracy in Africa*. Boulder, CO: Lynne Rienner Publishers.

Lyons, F S L (1963) *Internationalism in Europe 1815–1914*. Leidens: Sythoff.

Magas, Branka (1993) *The Destruction of Yugoslavia: Tracking the Break-up 1980–92*. London and New York: Verso.

Manivannan, R. (URL) 'Traditions of Nonviolence.' http://www.npeurope.org/documents/PDFTraditionsofNonviolencecombined.pdf (consulted 4 August 2006).

Ministry of Defence, FTO (Foreign and Commonwealth Office) and DTI (Department of Trade and Industry) (2000) *The Consolidated EU and National Arms Export Licensing Criteria* ('Consolidated Criteria'), HC 199–203W, reprinted in FCO (2002), *Strategic Export Controls, Annual Report 2001*. London, FCO, Appendix F.

More Questions and Answers on Buddhism (url) http://web.singnet.com.sg/~alankhoo/MoreQA.htm#War (consulted 9 August 2006).

NGO Policy Group (2001) *Third Sector in Serbia: Status and Prospects*. Belgrade: NGO Policy Group. http://www.un.org.yu/download/60/460-ngo_survey.pdf (consulted 4 August 2006).

Oxfam GB (URL) http://www.oxfam.org.uk (consulted 17 July 2006).

PNAC (Project for the New American Century) (1997) *Statement of Principles*, June 3, 1997. http://www.newamericancentury.org/statementofprinciples.htm (consulted 2 July 2006).

RECORRE (Network of Communities in Resistance) (URL) http://www.prensarural.org/recorre (consulted 3 February 2006).

Reljic, Dusan, Markovic, Predrag, Sebor, Janko and Mijovic, Vlastimir (1992) 'False Witnesses: Limonov & Co.', Vreme News Digest Agency, 16 November. http://www.scc.rutgers.edu/serbian_digest/60/t60-3.htm (consulted 10 April 2006).

Revenue Watch (URL) http://www.revenuewatch.org/ (consulted 1 August 2006).

Rodriguez, Carlos (2002) 'The Role of the Religious Leaders.' Conciliation Resources. http://www.c-r.org/our-work/accord/northern-uganda/religious-leaders.php (consulted 4 August 2006).

Sachs, Jeffrey D and Warner, Andrew M (1995) *Natural Resource Abundance and Economic Growth*. Working Paper No. 5398. Cambridge, MA: National Bureau of Economic Research.

Saferworld (URL) http://www.saferworld.org.uk (consulted 17 July 2006).

Said, Y (2005) 'Civil Society in Iraq', in H Anheier, M Glasius and M. Kaldor (eds), *Global Civil Society 2004/5*. London: Sage

Scott, J D (1962) *Vickers: A History*. London: Weidenfeld and Nicholson.

Scowcroft, Brent (2006) 'Don't Attack Saddam', *Wall Street Journal*, 15 August http://ffip.com/opeds081502.htm (consulted 30 June 2006).

Silber, Laura and Little, Allan (1995) *The Death of Yugoslavia*. London: Penguin Books.

SIPRI (2005) *SIPRI Yearbook 2005*. Oxford OUP.

Thomas, Robert (1999) *Serbia under Milosevic: Politics in the 1990s*. London: Hurst & Company.

UNOWA (United Nations Office for West Africa) (2005) *Youth Unemployment and Regional Insecurity in West Africa*. http://www.iydd.org/documents/iydd_docs/unemployment-insecurity%5B1%5D.pdf (consulted 9 August 2006).

US Department of State (2006) 'Iraq Weekly Status Report, July 5, 2006.' http://www.state.gov/documents/organization/68747.pdf (consulted 4 August 2006).

Varshney, A (2002) *Ethnic Conflict and Civic Life: Hindus and Muslims in India*. New Haven and London: Yale University Press.

Women in Black (URL) http://www.womeninblack.net (consulted 1 August 2006).

CHAPTER 5

WATER: A GLOBAL CONTESTATION

Edited by Willemijn Dicke and Fiona Holland with contributions from Patrick Bond, Fadia Daibes-Murad, Sanjeev Khagram, Alessandro Palmieri, Carlos B Vainer, Zoë Wilson and Patricia Wouters

Introduction

Willemijn Dicke

Everyone needs water, for drinking and for growing food, and in many cases we need protection from it, primarily against flooding. Each of these human needs requires the active management of water resources that, as this chapter illustrates, is a site of increasing contestation between politicians, scientists, corporations, civil society activists and water managers.

The worldwide community of water professionals has spoken of a water crisis at least since the 1990s (Gleick 1993). Water resources have become more scarce, and the risks of flooding have increased. Political conflict over water has grown steadily. As a result, water issues have moved into the domain of 'high' politics (Bernauer 1997: 192), ambassadors have been recalled in protest and heads of government have become embroiled in water crises.

Water professionals say that these crises will multiply and intensify in coming decades as a consequence of both environmental factors and political developments. First, the effects of climate change, a burgeoning world population, and expanding industrialisation and urbanisation will make clean water increasingly scarce. As Gleick (1993: 10) points out, a key issue in the twenty-first century will be 'how to satisfy the food, drinking water, sanitation and heath needs of ten or twelve of fifteen billion people, when we have failed to do so in a world of five billion'. Second, climate change and rising sea levels will demand new measures for protection against flooding. The idea has taken root that higher dikes and firmer dams are insufficient to guarantee long-term safety under these changing conditions. A new and more sustainable approach is needed.

With greater awareness of the seriousness of the crisis has come an increased demand for more effective governance. Professionals and scientists agree that water should be managed in a more comprehensive manner. Underpinning this approach is the belief that every major intervention in the water system will have effects elsewhere (Kooiman and Warner 2000): pollution, floods, dams, drinking water, bathing water and irrigation are interrelated. 'Comprehensive water management' requires that the entire water system is taken into account (see Figure 5.1). According to this perspective, water is a global resource (Abu-Zeid 2000), a global public good (Kaul, Grunberg and Stern 1999), a global common (Buck 1998), or even a common heritage of humankind (Abu-Zeid 2000; Petrella 1999).

This global perspective on water resources has important consequences for their governance. In the past, nation states claimed sovereignty over the water resources within their territory, and management was organised within territorial boundaries. The notion of 'comprehensive water management', requiring a holistic approach, has challenged the pivotal position of the nation state. If the nation state is rejected as the natural unit of governance of water, how then should it be managed? Whose water is it anyway, if national boundaries no longer define 'ours' against 'theirs'? What is the appropriate unit of governance? What values should water management espouse? Often, if not always, values such as public health, safety, and sustainability conflict with the various uses of water, for example, irrigation, drinking water supplies and shipping. How, if at all, can these uses be prioritised?

In the search for answers to these questions, scientists, water managers and politicians have something in common: increasingly they are turning to global civil society. The underlying reason is recognition of the global dimension of water resources (Dicke 2001). When water resources were considered a national public good, the nation state was thought to be the appropriate agent for their provision to the citizenry. But in the case of global public goods, collectivity cannot be equated with the citizens of a country. The benefits of global public

Figure 5.1: The natural water cycle

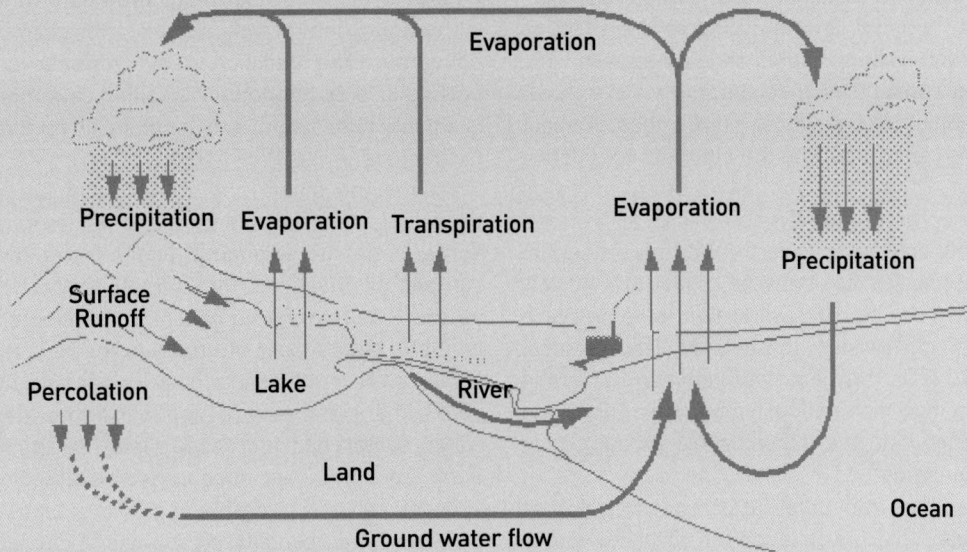

Source: Erich Roeckner, Max Planck Institute for Meteorology

This diagram depicts the water cycle in which rain and snow is transported through lakes, rivers and ground water to the ocean, where evaporation leads to precipitation again. Linked to this natural system is the chain of uses and users of water. The first step of the water chain is composed of securing, treating and distributing water. The second step is consumption of water - for drinking, irrigation or cooling industrial machinery. In the third step, water is collected, again for treatment, and also for draining off. Eventually, the water is led back to the environment, where step one starts again. Besides water for drinking and industrial purposes, other uses of water, such as for fishing, recreation and navigation, influence the natural system.

Water management comprises supervision of both the natural cycle and the chain of use(r)s, a task complicated by many, often conflicting interests, involved, from agriculture, conservation and fisheries to drinking water supply, security from flooding, and navigation. They are intimately linked through the natural water cycle and therefore safeguarding one interest will affect another. For example, drainage should be balanced in order to avoid depletion of the soil, yet at the same time drinking water delivery needs to be guaranteed; farmers prefer a ground water level that is not optimal for the adjacent nature reserve.

goods are quasi-universal in terms of countries, people and generations (Kaul, Grunberg and Stern 1999:3), and this necessitates a redefinition of collectivity: no longer the inhabitants of a country, but humankind as a whole.

Perhaps the most visible evidence of these attempts to redefine collectivity in water management is the growing importance of NGOs (see Record 16) and the existence of cross-border water regimes governing many rivers and coastal zones. Yet another instance of global civil society consists of transnational corporations (TNCs) that are responsible for drinking water supply and sewage services. For many, TNCs are not part of global civil society. For this author, however, global civil society consists of the interplay between various forces and institutions including nation states, private agents, transnational corporations, transboundary organisations, financial institutions and international organisations.

The global contestation over water includes many issues. Global and local movements collide with nations and intergovernmental bodies over ocean-related issues (for example, protection of the environment, fishery, shipping, prevention of floods); TNCs compete for contracts to provide drinking water and sewage services to local markets; local and global movements conflict over large infrastructure projects, most notably dams; and the worldwide community of water professionals disagree about climate change - is it happening and if so what would be the effect on flood risks and what measures should be taken? The list of issues could be much longer.

In this chapter we have chosen three debates about water resources to illustrate the attempts to redefine collectivity. These themes have been selected because they are relatively accessible to a broad audience, not only water experts, and they reflect the variety of issues at play between global civil society and the global contestation over water. To name a few: the North-South division, the tension between local and global NGOs, the interplay between state and non-state actors, the relationship between public and private parties, and the difficulties of accountability and representation.

Several authors with different perspectives debate three issues: the privatisation of drinking water supplies, water resources as a source of international conflict, and the construction of dams. In each instance, the importance of the nation state is shown to have declined, while that of global civil society has increased, with varying degrees of involvement and influence in water management.

I provide a short introduction to each topic, and in the conclusion to the chapter lessons are drawn from the three debates about how, to what extent and under what conditions, global civil society can contribute to solving the water crises.

Privatisation and transnational corporations

The first debate, privatisation, is about drinking water: can its provision be commodified? Some groups argue that water is a public good while others argue that public funds often do not suffice to provide this public service, and that both developed and developing countries would be better off privatising drinking water services.

Theoretically speaking, there are no reasons why water should or should not be privatised. Only collective goods cannot be privatised. Collective goods are defined partly by their non-excludability: no one can be excluded from receiving them. The provision of drinking water is not a pure collective good: customers can literally be disconnected from drinking water. But theory cannot solve the issue of privatisation. In practice, so-called private goods can be provided by the state. These are often called

merit goods. They are socially so desirable that public laws authorise their provision to citizens without payment or with subsidy - for example, free education. The decision about whether or not a particular private good is classified as a merit good is a political decision, and is not based on the nature of the good (Rose 1987: 219).

Around the globe, and in historical perspective, the provision of drinking water varies widely. In some countries drinking water companies are completely privatised, for example in the UK, while others require drinking water companies to remain in public hands, as is statutory in the Netherlands.

Due to several factors (see Finger and Allouche 2002), financial pressure on public authorities in the water sector has increased since the mid-1990s. Such pressures have encouraged privatisation, both in developed and in developing countries, as private firms are often considered sources of capital.

The debate about the privatisation of drinking water illustrates how global civil society has put the role of the national state in perspective. Increasingly, drinking water and sewage services are provided by privatised companies. Often, these companies are part of a transnational corporation, such as Veolia and Suez. In reaction, local and global NGOs and especially social movements have entered the scene, and their activities and influence are discussed by Patrick Bond and Zoë Wilson.

Water conflicts

Although the intensity and length of water conflicts around the world vary, transboundary water disputes are a serious problem, and, due to the increasing scarcity of fresh water in combination with the growth in world population, will remain so in the next decades. The question is, as water conflicts move into the realm of 'high politics', will there be less space for civil society politics? The debate over water as a source of conflict reveals two important aspects of global civil society in relation to water. First, global civil society has manifested itself through international law. NGOs have played a major role in developing and implementing international law. Second, there are important cross-border water regimes. These are non-nation state agencies, such as river authorities, in which collectivity is no longer equated with the nation state. Instead of territorial boundaries, water itself has become the ordering principle in the formation of the collectivity. Alongside ministries and provinces, NGOs contribute to the governance of the river. Cross-border water regimes are shaped by the interplay between state actors and NGOs. One example is La Plata River Basin, one of the most important river basins of the world, draining approximately one-fifth of the South American continent, extending over some 3.1 million km², and conveying waters from central portions of the continent to the south-western Atlantic Ocean (OAS 2005:1). Another example of cross-border river regimes is the International Commission for the Protection of the Rhine (ICPR URL), which cooperates with states, other intergovernmental organisations and NGOs. Through the ICPR, the Rhine-bordering countries of Germany, France, Luxemburg, the Netherlands, and Switzerland, and the European Community are united in order to discuss problems of water protection and to seek common solutions.

Dams

NGOs play a role not only in cross-border water regimes. They are very influential in other debates over water, for example, the construction of dams. Here, grassroots organisations, regional movements and international NGOs (see Record 16) have become increasingly important players in recent years.

'Narmada' has become almost iconic as an example of civil society influence. The Save the Narmada Movement opposed the construction of large dams on the River Narmada in central India because it would have affected the millions of people living in the valley.

For some, civil society has contributed positively to the debate; for others it has 'fuelled' it through vehement protests against the construction of the dams. Whether for or against the movement, both sides share the view that NGOs have reshaped the way in which decision making over such large and radical measures should take place. Both advocates and opponents of the anti-dam movements claim that the campaigns of these organisations have opened up spaces and processes for the involvement of stakeholders, and for a broader and integrated decision-making process on dams. Some criticise the influence of Northern issues and Northern NGOs on local, Southern anti-dam movements. The authors in this

debate discuss whether the influence of NGOs is, on the whole, a good or a bad thing.

Debate1

Overall, ordinary people and civil society benefit from the privatisation of drinking water supplies and sewage systems

Patrick Bond

No one can deny that drinking water in the Third World, as well as many Northern cities, requires vast new investments and better management. An estimated 2.6 billion people lack adequate sanitation, and 1.1 billion lack access to 'improved' water sources. There is an urgent need for dramatic improvements in water investment, management and affordability. Third World states have shrunk during the past quarter-century of sustained structural adjustment, addled by debt payment outflows, capital flight and foreign aid cutbacks, as well as neo-liberal ideology.

Given that the resources required for water and sanitation cannot often be found, due to prevailing power relations in the budgetary process, arguments for privatisation usually start with the capital infusions that large transnational firms (such as Veolia, Suez, Biwater and Bechtel) can supply. In addition, these firms bring technological capacities and have an incentive to reduce system leaks and inefficiencies.

In contrast, the strategy adopted by the more radical civil society groups - especially 'water warriors' in major anti-privatisation campaigns - has been to defend the state as the key institution for delivering water. To be sure, there are vast problems with relying on the state (whether national or municipal), given Third World governments' propensity to ignore the needs of poor citizens. Yet in most societies it remains the main institution with the capacity to organise purified, high-pressure water in sufficient quantities to serve gender equity, public health and other broader eco-social goals. Privatised water suppliers have no interest in such public goods, and the cost of the imported capital includes heavy profit outflows in often very scarce foreign currency. Critics also argue that the trend towards private outsourcing - including some examples of NGO delivery - has been destructive because standards are lower, prices are higher, disconnections are more common, maintenance is worse and accountability is harder to establish.

The water privatisation trend became dominant around 1992, when both the Rio Earth Summit and Dublin World Water Forum espoused the principle that water is 'an economic good'. However, by the time of the Hague World Water Forum in 2000, enough adverse experiences had accumulated in commercialised water systems that a broad-based set of water movements emerged to fight back (Box 5.1). By 2003 in Osaka and 2006 in Mexico City, the Forums witnessed large-scale demonstrations by civil society activists.

Often the water battles boil down to the controversial role of specific corporations, such as Bechtel in Cochabamba or Suez in Buenos Aires and Johannesburg. In early 2006 Bechtel finally dropped its World Bank compensation lawsuit against the Bolivian people following its expulsion six years earlier, but the intervening period demonstrated how hard it was for a Third World municipal supplier without sufficient resources to extend the grid, no matter how progressive the management of the water agency. The 2005 election of an anti-neo-liberal, indigenous-led Bolivian government is likely to improve Cochabamba's water system.

Likewise, Suez was kicked out of Buenos Aires in 2005 because it insisted on increasing water tariffs beyond consumers' ability to pay. In 2006 the firm's Johannesburg affiliate was sued by South Africa's Campaign Against Water Privatisation for violating constitutional water rights, on the grounds that prepaid water meters installed in Soweto are 'self-disconnection' devices.

In early 2006, the European Union's attempt to have water included within the World Trade Organisation's General Agreement on Trade in Services appeared to falter, based largely on strong alliances between Third World movements and Scandinavian activists. Water activists are also fighting against commodification more generally, even when a foreign business or the World Bank are not the main enemies.

These are the kinds of campaign that will resonate for years and in the process generate a formidable transnational network of water warriors who share information and campaigns, given that in so many cases they find themselves up against the same global financial institutions, aid agencies and corporations. But it is also likely that, notwithstanding some occasional defensive victories, the movements' more durable successes will only follow shifts in national power and the redirection of increased state resources into water and sanitation, among other needed social goods and services. International solidarity by global civil society is a crucial ingredient along the way, as Bolivia shows.

Because these movements have, since the late 1990s, often generated superb examples of sectoral cooperation across borders, in the process addressing gendered, racialised, class and ecological inequalities in overlapping and interlocking ways, their campaigning against commodified water will continue to serve as a model for global civil society. In sum, I disagree with the proposition and anticipate that by combining defensive reactions against privatisation with growing state influence over governments (such as in Bolivia and Venezuela), civil society will enhance the ability of states to supply water and sanitation properly, and with increasing elements of community and worker control.

Zoë Wilson

In face of the looming global water scarcity and contamination crisis and related development targets, such as the Millennium Development Goals, it is important to complicate our understanding of public and the private sectors and steer clear of over-stylised 'privatisation' debates. Helpful also is a pragmatic focus on delivery and treatment systems, and the potential for private sector and civil society actors to contribute to solutions at multiple points in the water access and sewage treatment cycles - at various scales and under various conditions of potable water scarcity. There are three main reasons. First, water and sanitation solutions require technologies and infrastructures. This is, in fact, the key challenge. Second, conventional water systems were developed 'when little was known about the fundamental physics and chemistry of the subject and when practically no applicable microbiology had been discovered' (Feachem et al. 1983: 63-4), and have since revealed their deep ecosystem impacts. Thus, systems are also in need of innovation. Third, in the developing world, it is hard to escape the fact that relying on government alone to solve urgent water and sanitation problems has not been successful. In this light, there are at least five key limitations to the anti-privatisation position.

First, the movements that Bond refers to tend to draw distinctions between 'public' and 'private' in ideal

Box 5.1: Contestants in the water privatisation debate

For

The pro-privatisation lobby often assembles at the triennial World Water Forum - at The Hague in 2000, Kyoto in 2003 and Mexico City in 2006 - and related meetings of the water establishment such as the World Trade Organization. The major lobbies include the Global Water Partnership, created by the World Bank, UNDP and Swedish aid; the World Water Council, founded by Suez, Canadian aid and the Egyptian government, and joined by 300 private companies, government ministries and international organisations; the International Private Water Association, formed of companies, the World Bank, US Credit Export Agency and Overseas Private Investment Corporation, and the European Bank for Reconstruction and Development. Other key pro-privatisation lobbies include the World Bank, which imposed privatisation as a loan condition in a third of water projects worth $20billion during the 1990s; Britain's Department for International Development, repeatedly accused of using the Adam Smith Institute to privatise Third World water; Mikhail Gorbachev's Green Cross, in ongoing dispute with the Council of Canadians over global-scale water rights and property rights in the UN; Aquafed, a federation set up by a former Suez managing director; and the World Panel on Financing Infrastructure. The latter was chaired by former IMF managing director Michel Camdessus in 2002-3, with major multilateral development banks, Citibank, Lazard Freres, the US Ex-Im Bank, private water companies, state elites from Egypt, France, Ivory Coast, Mexico, and Pakistan, and two NGOs, Transparency International and WaterAid. Its main advice was to make much greater amounts of public money available to privatisers, including via a risk-insurance mechanism to safeguard companies like Suez against currency crises that devastated the firm's Argentina operations after 2001. Finally, some NGOs, such as WaterAid, members of Freshwater Action Network, the Pacific Institute or South Africa's Mvula Trust, find themselves uncomfortably straddling the divide between the establishment and mass popular movements, given that they have been accused occasionally by activists of betraying the struggle to reduce water prices and raise standards and institutional delivery systems.

Against

Civil society forces opposed to the privatisation of water supplies include the Council of Canadians in Ottawa (Barlow and Clarke 2002), Public Citizen (2003a; 2003b) in Washington, and the World Development Movement and War on Want in Britain. Trade unions, indigenous people's movements and environmental groups, particularly the International Rivers Network and Friends of the Earth (2003), are also active on the issue. A host of think tanks are involved, including the PSI Research Unit at Greenwich University, Polaris Institute (2003) in Ottawa, the Transnational Institute's (2005) Corporate Europe Observatory in Amsterdam, the Municipal Services Project in South African and Canadian universities (McDonald and Ruiters 2005), Parivartan, and the Centre for Science and the Environment in New Delhi, Food and Water Watch in Washington (Grusky and Fiil-Flynn 2004), and the International Forum on Globalization in San Francisco. In addition, high-profile community leaders, politicians and intellectuals have become involved, many from urban community revolts against privatisation, from Detroit, Atlanta and several French cities, to Accra, Dar es Salaam and Soweto in Africa, Cochabamba and El Alto in Bolivia, and the cities of Buenos Aires, Manila, Jakarta and Auckland (Petrella 2001; Shiva 2002). In Vancouver, a 2001 'Blue Planet' conference gathered activists. In Delhi the 2004 People's World Water Forum (2004) aligned the various movements on analysis and common targets. The Red Vide network of anti-privatisation activists links Latin America, as demonstrated convincingly at the 4th World Water Forum in Mexico City where the Reclaiming Public Water global network was born. The World Social Forum (in Porto Alegre, Mumbai and Nairobi), as well as regional social forums, provide spaces for water activist assemblies. Email listserves such as 'water warriors', 'reclaiming public water' and 'right to water' permit information exchange and coordination.

terms, and in the process exaggerate similarities between Northern and Southern states while failing to fully engage with developing country states on their own terms. It is true, as Bond notes, that both Cold War geo-politics and the debt crisis of the 1980s and 1990s constrained developing country resources and priorities, and in the process intensified the split between 'the public' and those 'who in fact rule'. Yet developing countries also have endogenous social, political and economic configurations and processes to bear in mind. Landscapes of power and influence differ significantly from those of the water-rich industrialised world in ways that are not well captured in the analyses of 'water-warrior' movements that assume that, under popular mobilisation pressures, developing country governments will simply realise their obligation to roll out sustainable, piped pressurised water and sanitation services to all.

This lesson has been hard learned, as Berkeley environmental physicist Ashok Gadgil (2004: 214) has noted. The paradox of water sector development assistance is that, while since the mid-1980s key multilateral forums and national strategy documents have recognised water as a human right, investment and aid are still being 'funneled into supplying water to those who had political access or political voice in the developing world'. Free-flowing budget support rarely translates into a lived experience of water rights, and at this stage the case for strengthening the role of already failing bureaucracies, which Bond advocates, is uneven at best. Rather, as Gadgil notes, such strategies have 'led to huge incompetence and inefficiency in the supply management of water systems in the developing countries' (2004: 214).

Attesting to the complicated relationship between idealism and realism is the sad postscript to perhaps the most celebrated anti-privatisation action, which in 2001 saw the Bolivian government cancel its contract with water giant Bechtel.

> Today, water is again as cheap as ever, and a group of community leaders runs the water utility, Semapa. But half of Cochabamba's 600,000 people remain without water, and those who do have the service enjoy it only intermittently - some as little as two hours a day, the fortunate no more than 14. 'I would have to say we were not ready to build new alternatives', said Oscar Olivera, who led the movement that forced Bechtel out. (Forero 2005)

The second limitation is that the anti-privatisation critique rests mainly on contentious evaluations of 'first tier' companies, such as Suez, Vivendi and Bechtel, and their high-profile, high-risk interventions into domestic water service provision (notwithstanding, for example, Vivendi's successful water recycling partnerships). In the process, the lobby tends to misrepresent the landscape and overlook other forms and scales of private sector involvement - as well as the intricate interplay between various types of actors.

In the Northern fringes, these include a wide variety of small- to medium-sized enterprises that inject dynamism and innovation into the sector, fill supply-chain gaps and serve as a reservoir of competitive expertise on everything from rainwater harvesting to water-free sanitation options. Private sector actors lead the way in waterless and composting toilets while challenging deeply entrenched social norms - at both individual and institutional levels - around waterborne sanitation, while boasting lower installation, water and sewer, and maintenance costs than conventional waterborne technologies. Similarly, alternative technology industry-trade associations such as World Toilet Organisation and Dry Toilet clubs are at the forefront of lobbying for more latitude for ecologically friendly and water-free technologies in Scandinavian and European Union regulatory frameworks.

In the South, alternative technologies are often closer to the core of people's experience. Commercial technologies such as the Treedle pump, simple water filtration units and rainwater harvesting and storage units are important everyday technologies finding wide support among international civil society and media, including *National Geographic*, the *International Herald Tribune* and *Scientific American;* philanthropic organisations such as the Ford Foundation; international NGOs such as International Development Enterprises and WaterAid; and multilaterals such as the International Water Centre. Inventors and entrepreneurs also have a role. For example, in India, following the Grameen phone model, Emergence Energy is exploring the viability of fostering networks of entrepreneurs to make affordable and widely available the Slingshot - a water purification device that separates clean water, even from black water, by vaporising it. The informal sector also has innovations not to be dismissed lightly. In Mozambique, for example, entrepreneurial informal-sector operators now serve close to 50 per cent of households with piped water in and around the capital of Maputo. Thus, privatisation cannot be equated with 'Suez' or 'Vivendi'.

Third, as Box 5.1 illustrates, anti-privatisation debates tend to overlook actors that threaten to blur distinctions between private sector and civil society found in a range of innovative partnerships and networks. These include relatively new forms, such as social entrepreneurship and other unorthodox cross-sectoral partnerships and multidisciplinary global knowledge networks. These work to develop important 'off the grid' options against the grain of sometimes misguided state interventions, as well as innovative solutions useful at multiple levels, including the small community and individual levels. Here, engineering and architectural firms form part of an important technical and innovation system. While frontier technologies are open to the accusation of being second-class technologies, importantly they also work to provide solutions where no other actors, including the state, operate, and where existing mainstream technologies are inappropriate. They also, increasingly, produce ambitious results at scale, in both developing and developed worlds, attested to by the development of eco-villages such as China's Tangye New Town, which is being designed to house 180,000 people and provide services to one million more. Global supply chains for alternative technologies also help make possible North America's estimated thousand 'intentional communities' and hundred or so 'eco-villages', as well as the roll-out of urgent alternative and appropriate water and sanitation options in municipalities in the South, as in South Africa's eThekwini Muncipality.

Fourth, the anti-privatisation debates underestimate the urgent need for innovation and dynamism - a key strength of the private sector - in a field where the energy to problem-solve the world's most immediate health question has been slow to develop. Here, emergent movements beyond the public-private divide are evident in the immense popularity of, for example, the annual Global Social Entrepreneurship Forum run by Oxford University's Skoll Business School, MIT's Emerging Technologies Conference, the multidisciplinary and sectoral university-based networks related to water and sanitation, such as Loughborough University's Water Engineering Development Centre, and other quasi-academic networks such as Ecosanres and Sanitation Connection. Other sources of innovation that transcend the public-private divide include new university courses such as Stanford University's Entrepreneurial Design for Extreme Affordability, and the work of foundations such as the Lemelson Foundation, which supports pro-poor invention and entrepreneurship in, among other areas, the water sector.

Finally, anti-privatisation debates tend to assume that developing countries will follow the industrialised country model. Yet there are serious environmental and health problems associated with the spread of water-guzzling and ecosystem-polluting water and sanitation technologies evolved in industrialising Europe. Conventional waste-water systems are increasingly seen as systems where drinking water is misused to transport waste into the water cycle. Conventional water systems also consume large amounts of energy in delivery and treatment processes, and in many ways are over-engineered, not reflecting innovations that make smaller cheaper pipes efficient, and still designed to firefighting, rather than drinking water delivery, specifications.

The world's poor require simple time- and cost-saving solutions they can implement today. In the medium term, human and environmental health will benefit from more innovation. At the very least, the practice of flushing massive quantities of black water into the global water system has to change. In the longer term, while the world is growing more homogenised, globalisation is also giving rise to new social and political forms that increasingly look to ways to link to 'the grid' on their own terms. These challenges suggest that an organic synthesis of technological innovations springing from the work of a host of individuals, organisations and institutions, which span the public-private sector divide in new ways, offers the best route forward.

Debate 2

Global civil society has contributed positively to the debate on dams and has improved decisions about them and the construction of them

Sanjeev Khagram

Global Village Cameroon (GVC), a local NGO, and International Rivers Network (IRN) condemned the proposed Lom-Pangar dam in Cameroon in a joint report released in January 2006 (Kinsai 2006). The paucity of public information on the decision-making process, resource mechanisms and proper grievance procedures for affected people, as well as the absence of social and environmental plans for the project, was considered unacceptable by GVC and IRN, given the World Commission on Dams' findings of 2000.

The Lom-Pangar dam project featured prominently in President Paul Biya's address to the nation on 31 December 2005 (Kinsai 2006), as one of the major long-term development initiatives envisaged by government. In a vigorous defence of the project, the Ministry of Energy and Water Resources dismissed claims by GVC and IRN of gross lack of transparency, noting that all documents pertaining to the project were still in preparation. The GVC-IRN report claims that alternatives to the Lom-Pangar dam have not been examined, though it does not provide any systematic investigation of what these options for sustainable development might be. The report does cite further risks from flooding of protected forests, farmlands and pastoral zones; anticipated strains on resources, health and livelihoods; unclear benefits to affected communities; and widespread suspicion that multinational companies will get the lion's share of the electricity generated by the project.

The conflict over the Lom-Pangar dam is hardly unique. Rather, it is part of a historical trend of mounting contestation over big dam building that has spread throughout the world. Since the 1950s, and especially the 1970s, critics of big dams led by civil society organisations and networks have forced the reform, postponement and cancellation of these projects in countries such as the United States, Sweden and France; in the former Communist bloc, Soviet successor states and eastern Europe; and from Chile to Uganda and Nepal.

During the 1980s and 1990s, government agencies, international organisations and companies slowly began to reform their policies and practices on the construction of major dams around the world. Partly these reforms were motivated by the scientific and practical knowledge base that had accumulated from the tremendous amount of research into and experience of dam building since the 1950s. But these actors were also pushed persistently and progressively to initiate, expedite, modify, and broaden reform efforts, or even halt the building of dams by growing numbers of transnationally allied critics, who coalesced from a multitude of struggles and campaigns waged at the local, national and international levels.

Domestic civil society groups such as the Movement of Dam Affected Peoples in Brazil and the Save the Narmada Movement in India empowered themselves to block or substantially reform unequal and unsustainable big dam projects. They often did so by forming partnerships with like-minded foreign supporters such as Survival International or Environmental Defense. At the same time, civil society groups from the developed world such as European Rivers Network or the Sierra Club not only focused their energies on halting the global growth in the building of big dams abroad but also lobbied for their decommissioning and for river restoration domestically.

Transnational civil society critics of big dam projects have both promoted and been strengthened by the worldwide and multi-level spread of norms regarding human rights, environmental protection, anti-corruption, and others. The institutionalisation of these principles by states, international organisations and multinational corporations has been the result, in part, of civil society lobbying and monitoring activities, and substantially contributed to the effectiveness of these allied groups. The unprecedented changes in World Bank policies on resettlement, indigenous peoples and so on since the 1980s, while hardly perfect, are highly visible examples of these trends.

But transnational civil society critics of big dams do not have the same impact everywhere. First, these actors and the range of tactics they employ are likely to be most effective in democratic institutional contexts that offer opportunities to organise and gain access to decision-making processes, and that significantly reduce the ability of big dam proponents to violently repress resistance. Second, and perhaps most important, the ability of the opponents of big dams to shape outcomes is greatly enhanced when composed of, and especially if led by, domestic peoples' groups and social movements that are capable of generating sustained grassroots mobilisation and advocacy from the local to global levels.

Most countries had similar, relatively successful records of big dam building between the 1950s and the 1970s. However, the more recent case of Lesotho and South Africa's effort to build the largest dam scheme in Africa, the Lesotho Highlands Project, demonstrates that the impact of transnational organising, the existence of supportive norms, and even domestic democratisation will be lessened without the presence of strong, grassroots mobilisation. The project has gone forward despite the potential of less costly development alternatives and negative social and environmental effects. On the other hand, the ability of the Lesotho High Court to find major multinational corporations guilty of corruption, and to trigger (with civil society support) World Bank anti-bribery sanctions on those firms, provides powerful evidence of the altered dynamics of big dam building.

In Indonesia during the 1980s and 1990s, big dam projects continued to be promoted but under different circumstances from those in southern Africa. Although strong lobbying by domestically federated non-governmental organisations and grassroots anti-dam mobilisation resulted in some minor reforms, Indonesia's authoritarian regime gave big dam proponents a relatively unchecked licence to repress opponents. Even with the adoption of environmental norms and principles, the subversion of human rights and judicial and other democratic procedures limited effective transnational linkages and therefore successful anti-dam struggles. As a result, as in the case of Brazil, many transnational civil society groups promoted democratisation in Indonesia as a strategy for more sustainable development.

In China, the absence of both grassroots mobilisation and the existence of an authoritarian regime resulted in even less change in the dynamics of dam construction than in Indonesia or southern Africa. Although transnational activism has prevented foreign donors and international development agencies from supporting China's mammoth Three Gorges Project, construction has not been halted. However, the case of the Three Gorges shows that even when this increasingly global movement encountered a hostile domestic regime it has had an impact - in China today domestic critics of large dams are among the most effective advocates for democratisation.

The stance of the Chinese government in the World Commission on Dams (WCD) from 1998 to 2000 was largely sceptical in part because domestic critics were not as organised as they are now becoming. But transnational activists were crucial to the creation of this path-breaking multi-stakeholder innovation in (more) transparent and participatory global governance. The WCD conducted the first independent global review of major dams, yet its report (WCD 2000) did not decry all big dam building. For example, it found that most big dams did not displace indigenous peoples (though the projects that did had devastating effects on these communities) and a significant minority did not substantially damage the environment (some projects were socially and environmentally beneficial). However, it found that between 40 and 60 per cent of big dams had failed to generate the financial and economic benefits expected by advocates and thus should not have been built solely on those grounds.

Correspondingly the WCD did propose a profoundly different approach, linking big dam projects to sustainable water resource development and management. This called for a greater focus on adaptive management and better utilisation of the often untapped potential of the 45,000 big dams already constructed around the world. It also recommended transparent, participatory and accountable decision-making, multi-criteria options assessment, equitable distribution of benefits and costs, and greater compliance with already accepted social and environmental safeguards whenever big dams were involved (the latter being one of the continuing failures of partially reformed government agencies, international organisations, and corporations). These constructive recommendations would never have been possible without the active and concerted involvement of transnationally allied civil society in the WCD process.

In the future, transnational civil society organisations and alliances can improve their capacities and strengthen their activities in a number of areas. First, the larger, often international or Northern-based groups must continue to improve their accountability mechanisms, particularly to local communities even if the latter are not effectively organised. Second, the most ardent opponents must recognise that big dams are not inherently unacceptable, even though a large portion of those proposed should not be built (often solely on economic grounds independent of their social and environmental effects). Finally, and most important, transnational civil society networks must focus more on promoting equitable and sustainable alternatives to big dams, including improving the functioning of those projects that have already been completed.

Carlos B Vainer

Sixty per cent of the world's rivers are affected by dams or by some kind of diversion, leading to between 40 million and 80 million forced evictions (WCD 2000). More than 4 million people were displaced by the 300 large dams that, on average, entered into construction each year during the 1990s (World Bank 1996). National governments, dam builders and financial agencies usually emphasize the contribution of dams to development: energy, irrigation, drinkable water, flood control. Environmentalists, human rights advocacy organisations and, last but not least, the grassroots movements in the valleys, point out the social and environmentally destructive impacts of dams, and their contribution to increasing social or ethnic inequalities.

After a comprehensive independent review of dams, which included a multi-stakeholder participatory process, the WCD (2000) concluded:

- Decisions-making processes on building dams have not consulted affected people; cost-benefit analysis have very often overestimated benefits and underestimated costs.

- Dams have contributed to increased inequalities, since the benefits have largely gone to the richest social groups.

- Displaced persons - families, communities - have faced extreme economic hardship and community disintegration. Indigenous, tribal, and peasant and fisher communities have been particularly hard hit by forced eviction and the loss of natural resources upon which their livelihoods depend.

Criticism of and resistance to large dams spread during the 1980s. In the fancy palaces of global forums, conferences and meetings, human rights advocacy organisations and environmentalists, mostly Northern-based, campaigned, lobbied and pressured governments and international financial institutions to consider more seriously the social and environmental impacts of dams. In the poor hamlets, villages and towns of the valleys, and on the banks of the rivers, affected communities struggled as much as they could to avoid these mega-projects, for recognition of their individual and collective rights, and to obtain fair reparation for material and immaterial losses.

Responding to this growing pressure, many national governments, and the majority of international financial institutions, have hired experts and created new departments. Innovative legal tools, criteria and guidelines have been devised to deal with social impacts. Have they been enforced? Have governments and financial institutions complied with their own policies? Has the international pressure of so-called global civil society achieved its goals?

In this contribution we suggest that campaigns and lobbying led by Northern-based international non-governmental organisations and networks have proved mostly ineffective. International activism has given material, political, and moral support to local and national resistance, but it could not and cannot ensure new practices and compliance with the new social and environmental policies. So far, grassroots and community-based movements have been, and probably will remain, the main way to stop dams and ensure that the economic, cultural, social and environmental rights of people affected by dams are recognised. Why is that?

Scene 1: 14 January 2006

About 400 people attend a meeting at St Xavier College, an austere and traditional Jesuit institution in Mumbai. They are celebrating 20 years of the Narmada Bachao Andolan (NBA, Save the Narmada Movement). After some militant songs, Medha Patkar speaks. She is the incarnation, personalisation and symbol of this movement. She talks about the suffering of the villagers, of the farmers, of the tribals displaced, or about to be displaced, by the Sardar Sarovar Project.

The international campaign to stop the dams in the Narmada Valley, and in defence of the human rights of farmers and tribals to fair compensation and adequate rehabilitation, is the most quoted example of transborder activism (Keck and Sikking 1998; Khagram 2004). In 1993, after an independent report revealed its failure to address social issues, the World Bank withdrew from the Sardar Sarovar Dam project. Nevertheless, in the valley things have not changed as we might have imagined. And the World Bank will probably fund new dam projects in India in coming years.

I asked Medha Patkar, leading NBA activist and a member of the World Commission on Dams, about the relevance of global forums and international cooperation between anti-dam movements.

In India we still have the same problems and there are no relevant concrete changes in the projects. But the WCD process has been important to raise awareness about the poor performance of dams, both economically and technically, and its tragic environmental and social performance. The Indian government rejected the WCD report and its recommendations, but in fact this report became a reference. Also very important have been the international meetings of anti-dams movements in Curitiba (Brazil, 1997) and Rasi Salai (Thailand, 2003). (Interview with the author, Mumbai, January 2006. Emphasis added)

Scene 2: 23 January 2006

A meeting is held on the main square of a village settled to receive about 140 families displaced by the Sardar Sarovar Project in the Narmada Valley. Fifty men tell NBA activists based in Baroda, the nearest city, that they don't have enough water, the land isn't good and there isn't enough grazing land for their cattle. Many of these men hold documents that they cannot read. These are letters from the authorities explaining that the oldest sons of the displaced families have the right to become 'beneficiaries' of the resettlement, that is, they have right to receive two acres of land...once they can prove that in 1987 they were 18 years old. The problem: once, in their villages, there were no schools, no official agencies nor civil registers; and so the only way to prove their age is by the witness of relatives and neighbours. But the authorities do not accept this and demand formal, written proof.

This is happening now, when governments are supposedly constrained by rules and laws, and national and multilateral financial institutions have established criteria that require resettlement and rehabilitation as a condition of their support for any large dam project. It evokes the 1960s and 1970s, when social impacts were not an issue. It evokes the sad story of the Sobradinho Dam, which forcibly displaced 70,000 people in north-east Brazil, the poorest region of the country. Many people were still in their houses when the water arrived. It evokes the ongoing legal process against the government of Guatemala in the InterAmerican Court of Justice over the Chixoy Dam, where in 1982 444 peasants and indigenous people were killed for protesting against its construction on their ancestral territory.

There are so many examples that show the ineffectiveness of words and documents, agreements, protocols and memorandums! So many examples

show that the main resource of poor communities affected or threatened is their ability to organise themselves and fight, that is, their capability to become collective political actors.

Dipti, born in India, went to the United States with her family and studied social sciences at Berkeley. She came to the Narmada Valley and decided to become a full time activist of the Narmada Bachao Andolan.

You want to know whether 'global civil society' has been important to improve the conditions of the people affected by dams? I will tell you. **If villagers, farmers, adivasi [tribals] are 'global civil society', I can say that yes:** *'global civil society' made a big difference. If we have now some resettlements - even with their problems - it is because this 'global civil society' organised itself and challenged state governments, the government of India, the World Bank, the dam builders. If today we have some rights recognised, this is because of our struggle.* (Interview with the author, Baroda, January 2006. Emphasis added)

Global, local. Some villagers told me that before the dams they had never heard about the other side of the mountains, let alone about the rest of India. The dam and the struggle gave them another perspective on their lives - in other words, another scale of understanding. Now, many of them know that dam builders are not only local or national actors. Many left their village or region for the first time when they joined an NBA march or rally. The dam and the resistance are making them more national and global than strictly local, and they are keen to strengthen their connections with other grassroots anti-dam movements. But they still believe that the decisive front is in the local and national sphere. Of course, they think of NGOs and international networks as allies - but they believe that the decisive battles will be won or lost on the banks of the rivers, challenging leading political groups in each country.

Some questions

So far, non-governmental representations in the global conferences, meetings, and seminars have been dominated by Northern NGOs. The same can be said about international coalitions and networks, whose constituency is the urban middle classes, both in the North and in the South. Recent experience shows that their campaigns and support are helpful to local and national movements.

These NGOs and transnational networks have the material and other resources (language, symbolic tools and cultural references) to be partners in the international forums dominated by developed countries. But they do not have the legitimacy to represent indigenous people, farmers and fishermen and women, affected by dams in the South. Will popular movements fighting locally and nationally for the rights of the affected people - the NBA in India, Movement of People Affected by Dams in Brazil, the Assembly of the Poor in Thailand - become relevant to global actors? Will they be able to overcome the challenge of languages, resources and mobility to build their own coalitions and networks? Will this perspective make 'global civil society' more inclusive and more effective in changing the logic and procedures of decision-making processes surrounding the construction of dams? We do not have a definitive answer but the World Social Forum and the experience of Via Campesina, the international peasants movement, show that it is not utopian to wonder about international coalitions of community and locally based movements.

Alessandro Palmieri [1]
The role of storage in adapting to climate variability

The true source of water is meteoric precipitation, be it in the form of rain or snow. There is agreement, at scientific level, that global warming is taking place. At the same time there is no consensus on the effect of global warming on climate change. The only agreement is that there will be more precipitation variability and even more extreme variations in surface run-off. Sporadic, spatial and temporal distribution of precipitation rarely coincides with demand. Whether the demand is for natural processes or human needs, the only way water supply can match demand is through storage. Storage capacity in natural systems (lakes, wetlands, groundwater, snow pack, and so on) and in man-made reservoirs mitigates extremes in hydrological variability. The gloomy subject of climate variability and the huge energy needs of the planet, especially in fast-developing countries, demand serious responses, based on science, not on ideology or advocacy. The medium-term future of renewables lies in a synergy between hydropower and other forms of renewable energy sources, especially the intermittent ones (wind and solar).

People need a range of tools for their water and energy security

To achieve water and energy security, humanity needs efficient services for irrigation, domestic and industrial water supplies, security against droughts, protection from floods, and power generation. Infrastructures aimed at providing those services must not only be developed, they also need to be efficiently managed; hence the concomitant need for capable water institutions. Water infrastructure is just a tool, and its benefits should be aligned with the needs of the people.

Investments in institutions and infrastructures require significant financial resources. At the same time, community-level activities require a widespread presence on the territory. The two dimensions – large investments and community-level activities – are equally important in meeting people needs, but they are often presented in an 'either-or' context. Very often we hear arguments such as 'small is beautiful' and 'large is bad'; other stakeholders come up with opposite arguments. Sometimes such statements refer to dams.

In reality, large investments in institutions and infrastructure, and community-level activities represent a continuum of complementary tools whereby one tool builds on the results of the others.

There is no such thing as a bad small dam or a good big dam or vice versa. The response to poor countries' water demands should be based on a customised approach, because a one-size-fits-all solution does not exist. It is sad to observe that international NGOs almost never, at least in the writer's experience, bring this honest and constructive message to communities in developing countries in dire need of water and energy. To a large extent, this observation is also true for some government organisations that still think they can act in the 'decide-hide-defend' mode. What people really need are transparent decision-making processes in which they can participate effectively. The ultimate question is: who is going to represent my needs?

---

[1]
The findings, interpretations, and conclusions expressed herein are those of the author and do not necessarily reflect the views of the IBRD/ World Bank and its affiliated organisations, or those of the executive directors of The World Bank or the governments they represent.

Box 5.2: The hidden benefits of dams

Villagers in Huangshui and Hehu in China's Zhejiang province have taken shares in the Huangshui hydroelectric power plant instead of one-off cash compensation payments. The building of the Huangshui plant will submerge some 40 hectares of farmland. According to Interfax (2004), a local government official said that such an arrangement between the developers of the plant and villagers was very rare in China. It is estimated that the villagers could receive dividends worth US$24,163 every year.

Meanwhile, the Yellow River has begun to flow to the North China Sea again after construction of the Xialongdi multipurpose dam. The water body had been virtually consumed by extractions. Now, the water downstream of the dam is silt-free, as are the irrigation canals. The hydropower component replaces the burning of 1.9 million tons of coal per year, saving emissions of 4.6 million tons of carbon dioxide, 33,000 tons of sulphur dioxide and 18,700 tons of nitrogen oxide. Yet these very real benefits do not appear on the balance sheet of the project, whose income is derived entirely from hydropower production.

The El-Cajon Dam in Honduras is the only reservoir in that country to play any significant role in flood control. It is designed with capacity to route floods, so raising its height and enabling it to flood more land. When Hurricane Mitch hit Honduras in October 1998, the peak discharge of the flood at the entrance to the El-Cajon Reservoir was estimated to be about 10,000 m3/s, which the reservoir reduced to about 1,000 m3/s. Two highly populated alluvial plains lie at the end of a 10 km-long, narrow gorge downstream of the dam. The flood had a serious economic effect but caused no casualities. The effect of an uncontrolled flood ten times higher scarcely bears thinking about. But the value of the dam's disaster prevention function could not have been envisaged at the planning stage (UNEP-DDP 2004: 60).

Decision making on dams and their alternatives

Stakeholder participation is a key instrument for identifying and managing risks and uncertainty. Indeed, this is one area where social, economic and commercial considerations converge. It is in the interest of all concerned parties (governments, developers, lenders, project-affected communities, and intended beneficiaries) that issues be resolved early in the project development process.

Water infrastructure programmes can be designed to enhance their impact on poverty alleviation. Local populations, and first among them project-affected communities, should share the benefits of water infrastructure programmes. One way is through revenue sharing. Under this mechanism, some of the revenues are redistributed to local or regional authorities in the form of royalties tied to power generation or to water charges. Development funds financed from power sales, water charges, or government grants may be established to provide seed money for fostering economic development in the project-affected area. A variety of mechanisms may allow local or regional authorities to partly or fully own an infrastructure project. Local or regional authorities may negotiate free energy or preferential electricity rates with the hydropower producer, which benefit all electricity consumers in their constituency and contributes to local and regional economic development. Taxes to be paid to regional and local authorities can also be defined in state legislation, sometimes as a percentage of project sales or net income. Several countries, such as China, Colombia, Brazil, Korea, and Japan, among others, have incorporated revenue sharing into legislation.

Rights, risks and responsibilities

The difficulties that countries face in developing water infrastructure are not only financial but relates also to public acceptance of such large and often controversial investments. A large part of the controversy concerns how the costs and benefits of infrastructure projects are evaluated. Box 5.2 contains several examples that demonstrate how difficult it is to quantify, in monetary terms, the environmental and social costs associated with large dams.

Stakeholder involvement processes are viewed by many as the way to achieve consensus on the implementation of much needed projects. At the same time stakeholder involvement processes are not free from disadvantages. Much needs to be done to improve commitment and responsiveness, mainly in terms of timely outcomes, if the approach is to find more widespread application.

The World Commission on Dams report (WCD 2000) advocates a 'Right at Risk' approach for stakeholder identification. The concept of 'responsibility' should be added, giving the 3Rs approach, for at least two reasons: (a) it identifies additional stakeholders that have a stake in good public decision making, and (b) it helps select from the wider group of stakeholders those willing to assume responsibility for informing public decision making. A multi-stakeholder approach cannot succeed without an underlying programme of activities that is time bound, cost effective and supported by committed governments. Aiming at negotiated agreements rather than consensus is probably a more realistic way to achieve such results.

Moving ahead

Increasing involvement of civil society groups in decision-making processes on important infrastructure projects, including dams, can be regarded as a sign of discomfort with the way in which civil society's needs have traditionally been represented. This discomfort has brought international NGOs to play a representation role together with, but most often in opposition to, government institutions. At the same time, it is not always the most vocal of those international NGOs that have shown themselves to be 'close enough' to the real needs of people. In too many cases the priorities of some international NGOs, especially single-issue ones, do not necessarily coincide with those needs. Increasing evidence indicates that what is usually presented as 'the civil society voice' is in reality only a segment of that voice, a segment that legitimately delivers a message about negative impacts of water infrastructures but remains silent about positive impacts. It is becoming increasingly clear that a better job needs to be done to include and engage 'civil society' in options assessment. That job is a hard one: it requires reaching out to stakeholders who are not vocal but have a lot to contribute to the quality of projects. In most cases, those stakeholders are not organised to speak with a common voice. On this issue, I share the view of Carlos Vainer regarding the value of community-based organisations (CBOs). For example, consumer associations are promising civil society initiatives for getting the dialogue focused on real needs and for achieving effective self-representation. Ultimately, good

decision making is a political issue that, by definition, is rooted in good representation. Increased national and international support for CBOs would allow the latter to play a more effective role, including free and informed selection of development-oriented NGOs with which CBOs can confidently share common interests.

Debate 3

Global civil society and international law have contributed positively to the debate on and solutions to conflicts and tensions over shared water resources

Fadia Daibes-Murad

On earth there are an estimated 200 international river basins where approximately 40 per cent of the world's population lives. Of those basins, more than 50 straddle three or more countries. Cross-border groundwater is used virtually in every continent of the world and is subject to high competition for its use as a main source of supply. There is an impressive record, both historical and contemporary, of treaties and agreements between and among sovereign states over the development, management and protection of the water resources of rivers and lakes that cross international borders. These treaties cover many of the major rivers of the world, including the Niger, Nile, Danube and Mekong, and, as of late, some aquifers such as the Geneva aquifer, which is shared between Switzerland and France.

This contribution attempts to identify the role of global civil society organisations (GCSOs) and international law in the sphere of international watercourses, and their contribution to the debate on finding solutions to conflicts. As a point of departure, and despite the ambiguous or contested relationship of law to civil society, the author strongly believes that such organisations have been a very important source of international water law. Despite their informal nature, GCSOs around the world have developed creative solutions to water shortages and resource sharing, exercising their skill in, for example, developing applicable codes and principles, as drafters of treaties or codes, and as judges or advocates at international tribunals. Their contribution to cooperation in the field of international watercourse management is reflected in certain agreements such as the India-Nepal Mahakali River Treaty, which refers to the 'determination to cooperate in development of water resources and by agreement'; and in the Indus Water Treaty, which divides, rather than shares, the waters between India and Pakistan. The reiteration of very similar expressions of the same principles, such as the principle of equitable and reasonable utilisation and the duty of pollution prevention, coupled with increasing acceptance by the international community of agreements such as the 1966 Helsinki Rules on the Utilization of International Rivers, demonstrates an increased awareness of the current and emerging water crises, the risks of uncontrolled use of waters that cross borders between two or more states, and the importance of international cooperation in resolving conflicts over international waters.

Despite the prodigious efforts by GCSOs such as the International Law Association and the International Law Institute, it is must be acknowledged that the problems associated with the equitable and reasonable utilisation, development and protection of international watercourses remain unresolved. The alarming rate of population growth, coupled with the effects of climate change, is expected to result in severe water scarcities. Moreover, the limited access to shared water of the weaker party to the conflict is expected to intensify. The latter could be referred to as 'political scarcity'. These two conditions will undoubtedly contribute to global political instability and conflict. This is true of the Middle East, where political and natural scarcities may create new water conflicts and escalate existing ones. The conflict over water between Israel and the Occupied Palestinian Territory is one of the most contentious in the region. The essence of the conflict lies in the serious disparity between the Palestinians' access to international water resources and that of the Israelis because, as the occupying power, Israel has absolute control over all the water in the Occupied Palestinian Territory. Although the links between tension over water and the ongoing political violence in the Occupied Territory are unclear, it seems reasonable to conclude that water scarcity and its consequent economic effects contribute to the unrest in the Occupied Palestinian Territory. Many specialists (Shuval, Daibes-Murad, Wouters) believe that water in the Middle East could be a catalyst for conflict or a vehicle for cooperation. However, equitable agreements to share water remain hard to achieve because the magnitude of political conflicts and problems outpaces current efforts at cooperation.

Evidence of the role of global civil society in the evolution of international water law is manifold. The work of organisations such as the International Law Association is a good example of how global civil society has influenced the development of international law and used United Nations mechanisms for achieving distributive justice in the utilisation of these resources. Until 1997, the Helsinki Rules on the 'Uses of the Waters of International Rivers', which were adopted in 1966 by the International Law Association, were the only set of written rules to be referred to by experts, officials and state representatives. These rules provide that a basin state is entitled to an equitable and reasonable share of the beneficial uses of the international waters. The extensive interaction and debate between this organisation and the UN system culminated in the codification, in 1997, of the rulings that represent customary international practice in the field of international watercourses, which are binding to all.

The 1997 United Nations Convention on Non-Navigational Uses of International Watercourses (UNGA 1997) represents not only the outcome of the UN International Law Commission but the culmination of most of the attempts by various countries' representatives, scientists and lawyers to find the best means of sharing international watercourses. Consequently, the UN convention has attempted to incorporate, in an improved manner, most of the principles derived from the work of some organisations, such as the Helsinki rules, and even the essence of some theories of allocation, to benefit not only one state in particular but the interests of all states. The objective of the convention is to refrain from the unilateralism of some upstream states and to provide preventive mechanisms for the resolution of disputes that result from the inequitable utilisation of international watercourses.

The impact of the 1997 UN Convention and the 1966 Helsinki Rules is being felt around the world. For example, the 14-member Southern African Development Community (SADC) developed its revised protocol on shared watercourses in 2000 based on the principles and rules embraced within the UN Convention. The Palestinian Authority formally adopted the UN Convention and the 1966 Helsinki Rules in its framework position on negotiations on water with Israel in 2000. In the case of Israel, international law has had a limited role in resolving the water conflict between Israel and Palestine. Israel appears not to have intended to employ these rules and principles to resolve the existing water conflict. From the author's perspective there is enough ground to confirm that Israel is unlikely to be ready for a binding agreement relating to international water on the basis of international law.

This brief analysis demonstrates that in the past three decades global civil society has contributed significantly to creating peaceful solutions to potential and existing tensions over sharing water resources through the codification and progressive development of international water law. However, the analysis demonstrates equally the need to do much more. There remains a gap between the efforts and achievements of global civil society organisations and realities on the ground. Their efforts need to be complemented by cooperation, mutual trust, political will and commitment. States have a moral and ethical responsibility and a legal obligation to support the efforts of global civil society as part of their duty to maintain global peace and prosperity. Countries must be encouraged to adopt a cooperative approach rather than using violence in an attempt to solve problems over the shared waters. Global civil society organisations must continue their scholarly efforts to evaluate the important possibility that water cooperation may bring peace. Governments must give scholars enough recognition and sustained support. This is the only means to ensure that such efforts are comprehensive and conducive to transforming or resolving conflicts, and that countries' fears of future water wars will disappear.

Patricia Wouters

Access to safe water is a fundamental human need and, therefore, a basic human right. Contaminated water jeopardises both the physical and social health of all people. It is an affront to human dignity.
Kofi Annan, World Water Day, 22 March 2001

Serious drought threatens drinking water for 14 million people in northern China, and the annual mid-year flooding has engulfed a large swathe of central and eastern China, with storms claiming the lives of 22 people in Guizhou province in early May 2006. Numerous countries in Africa, from Ethiopia to Sudan, Kenya, Niger and Malawi, suffer from severe water scarcity, with the attendant adverse impacts for millions of people. These examples, a handful among many, demonstrate the growing potential of water to cause tension. A billion people lack access to safe drinking water, and approximately one-third of the world of the world's population face severe water shortages in the next two decades. At the local level, governments around the world struggle to reform water policies and laws, seeking new ways to address increasingly complex issues related to the management of water resources - both within and beyond national borders. The issue is complex and raises issues beyond water per se - including matters concerning human dignity, economic prosperity and regional security.

Recently, water has returned to the international agenda: more than 20,000 people attended the 4th World Water Forum in Mexico, in March 2006, and the UN General Assembly declared 2005-2015 to be the 'International Decade for Action - Water for Life' (UNGA 2003). Among the Millennium Development Goals is a global commitment to reduce by half the number of people without access to safe drinking water and adequate sanitation by 2015 - a target that the international community now recognises will be missed.

With an estimated 4 billion people relying upon water that originates outside national borders, and more than 3,500 treaties governing the world's shared watercourses around the world, I would argue that the aim of international water law is clear - the peaceful management of shared transboundary freshwaters within responsive, transparent and enforceable frameworks. But the efficacy and operational potential of international law to reduce tension and prevent conflict is not always understood and consequently not applied to its best advantage - a reflection of shortcomings in the current water resource management paradigm.

Water knows no boundaries. Thus the Blue Nile, originating in the Ethiopian highlands, flows downstream across Sudan and enters the Mediterranean Sea via Egypt. However, Ethiopia's plans to use more of the Nile's upstream waters led to angry responses from Egypt, including exchanges of diplomatic notes. Who will benefit from the use of such waters? More important, will this be fair and equitable to all - especially to the poorest, the voiceless and the weakest?

Recall the severe consequences of upstream management of the Zambezi, the fourth largest river in Africa, which some considered responsible for the

Box 5.3: A framework for international law on water

International water law can be best understood through the following five-point analytical framework, which identifies the key legal issues that need to be addressed (with interdisciplinary inputs) in each transboundary watercourse regime:

• Scope - what waters are covered? What uses are covered? What states are covered?
• Substantive rules - what are the rules that determine 'who gets what', ie those laws that determine the legality of existing or proposed new uses.
• Procedural rules - what are watercourse states required to do when they undertake new or increased uses?
• Institutional mechanisms - what is mandate of the joint bodies or river basin organisations established to manage the transboundary watercourse?
• Dispute avoidance/settlement and compliance - what rules facilitate compliance with the agreement (or regime) and promote dispute avoidance? Where disputes arise, how are these resolved?

We now develop indicators to assess the relative impact of succeeding in, or, failing to, effectively address these five core areas in the development of an agreed regime to manage transboundary waters.

Source: Vinogradov, Wouters and Jones (2003: 15-21)

devastating floods in Mozambique in 2003. Was Zambia responsible for the consequent loss of life in Mozambique? In November 2005 a blast ripped through a PetroChina benzene factory in China's north-eastern Jilin province, resulting in an 80-kilometre slick escaping into the Songhua River, which left 4 million people without water services in Harbin, and polluted the main source of drinking water for the 600,000 residents of the Russian city of Khabarovsk, as well as devastating a fishery downstream. These are just two of many international incidents caused by activities in one country that affect another, the conduit for which is transboundary watercourses. How are such conflicts to be prevented or resolved? It is within this context that we must examine the relevance and role of international water law, and in 'new' ways; not, as some wrongly consider it, a notion of law that conjures up entrenched adversaries who fight over 'rights', but of law as an enabling mechanism that promotes the peaceful management of transboundary waters and provides a framework within which needs can be identified, protected and reviewed. I would argue that law is a vehicle for managing change, offering, in fact, a 'meta-framework' for examining all the relevant factors and circumstances, and providing a transparent, responsive and legitimate means to ensure that there is 'water for

all', especially the weakest.

How does international water law work in practice? In line with the Statute of the International Court of Justice, when we seek the 'sources' of the rules of international law we have four areas to consider: treaty law, customary law, general principles and, as a secondary source, academic research and writing in this area. Regardless of the existence of a treaty governing a particular transboundary watercourse, all states are governed by the overarching rule of customary international law - that each state is entitled (and obliged) to an equitable and reasonable 'use' of its shared waters. The only global treaty that captures this rule - the 1997 United Nations Convention on the Non-Navigational Uses of International Watercourses (UNWC; UNGA 1997) - is not yet in force, but there is a renewed UN campaign to encourage ratification worldwide, a move that is to be commended.

However, despite scholarly research, including rigorous comparative work on state practice (including treaty practice), there remains serious shortcomings in appreciating the many strengths of the UNWC. For example, a recent UNEP report (2006) claims that the UNWC and the 1992 United Nations Economic Commission for Europe (UNECE) Helsinki

Box 5.4: Bridging the chasm

Working across disciplines is very challenging but some progress has been made. The UNESCO Hydrology for the Environment Life and Policy (HELP) programme offers a stakeholder-driven multidisciplinary approach to managing the world's water resources, with some 67 HELP basins around the world. One example is the Murrumbidgee basin in Australia, a 'demonstration basin' that exemplifies the HELP approach. This new integrated approach to management brings together water law and policy experts, water resource managers and water scientists. Their combined expertise makes it possible to monitor hydrological, climatological and ecological factors as well as sociological, economic, administrative and legal issues in a HELP catchment area. These findings will help address the policy and management issues identified by users. The programme requires the active involvement of both policy and facilitating groups to set the policy agenda and to ensure that the scientific results address community needs.

This work inspired one of the books seeking to analyse the interface between water law and science, an exercise that identifies some of the successes and problems involved in attempting to work across disciplines (Wallace and Wouters 2006). Such an approach requires a courageous leap of faith, and is built upon the assumption that each side is willing to bring its expertise to the table and to engage with others from different disciplines. This may necessitate the creation of a new common language, as we discovered when trying to develop the Legal Assessment Model as a tool to help transboundary watercourse states to develop national water policies in line with their entitlements and obligations in international law (Wouters et al. 2005). A good example is the South Africa Water Act, which outlines an equitable and reasonable allocation plan for water, with vital human and environmental needs protected under the 'reserve' (Wouters 2005).

Source: UNESCO Hydrology for the Environment Life and Policy (URL)

Convention on Transboundary Rivers and Lakes, lack 'practical application' due to 'their vague and sometimes contradictory language and the lack of proper enforcement mechanisms', and that '...the impact they have made on international water management has not met expectations' (UNEP 2006: 35). Yet, contradicting this statement, the report suggests that treaties and institutions have played the most important roles in influencing watercourse state relations! I would argue that treaties and river basin organisations derive their origins and legitimacy from international law - it is the platform that enables, facilitates and develops these instruments and joint bodies. The misunderstanding about the relevance and role of international law illustrated in the UNEP report is, unfortunately, pervasive.

What is the more enlightened approach? First, the UNWC and the UNECE Helsinki Convention are not 'vague'; they each represent multilateral international agreements that provide identifiable and transparent substantive and procedural rules, including the creation of joint institutions as core components of a regime designed to facilitate the peaceful management of shared water resources.

Second, as framework instruments these treaties provide basic guidelines that serve as a baseline for (perhaps) more detailed basin-specific agreements, to be negotiated and agreed by watercourse states on a case-by-case basis. Third, the suggestion that these agreements suffer from 'failed implementation' is simply wrong - serious obstacles have been overcome allowing for effective management of the Indus, the Mekong, the Colorado, the Danube (to name just a few), and hundreds of watercourses shared by two or more countries around the world.

Global warming, climate change, and devastating natural occurrences have conspired to exacerbate tension over water resources, which affect all corners of the globe and threaten to worsen. What can international law, international lawyers and policy makers do now to prevent 'water wars'? It is essential that water lawyers are part of both rapid and long-term response teams, collaborating with politicians, scientists and stakeholders to devise a framework for anticipating and dealing with these issues. The body of rules that have evolved under international water law, outlined in Box 5.3, provides the foundation for the peaceful management of the world's shared resources, establishing a level playing field and a forum for all parties.

The problems with operationalising this framework arise from a lack of human and financial resources at the local level. We need a new generation of local water leaders with appropriate education, mentoring and networks, enabling them to identify, articulate and act upon local issues in a way consistent with regional and international interdependencies.

A new conceptual approach to international water law must be developed and disseminated beyond the legal community. To some extent, this enlightened paradigm is already emerging - Box 5.4 outlines the UNESCO Hydrology for the Environment, Life and Policy (HELP) programme, a pioneering interdisciplinary approach that is stakeholder driven.

In conclusion, the global water challenge presents new opportunities for interdisciplinary research, including water law as an integral component. Together we must find innovative ways to educate our next generation of 'water champions', as an enlightened new community, supported at the local level. This is not unrealistic: it can be realised through the creation and long-term support of 'water knowledge hubs' around the world, targeted at engaging existing stakeholders and regional institutions, especially universities. How the international community manages transboundary waters will be pivotal in avoiding and resolving conflicts over water. International water law provides a transparent and dynamic legal framework to tackle these issues and should be considered an integral part of the solution.

Conclusion

Willemijn Dicke

Global civil society is often equated with NGOs, but the case of water reveals all its various agents. The debate about privatisation involved transnational corporations alongside local and global NGOs. In the debate over international water conflicts, we have seen local and global NGOs, international law, nation states and (non-state) cross-border water authorities. The debate over dams was led initially by Northern NGOs and later joined by local groups and networks. In the latter case, the World Bank and other global institutions played a role of major importance.

In scrutinising the three debates, can we assess the role of global civil society in helping to solve the water crisis? With such a diversity of actors involved, the answer is bound to be ambiguous. The debate over dams illustrates this point well. Initially, the most vociferous and visible anti-dam proponents were Northern NGOs. But local dwellers felt their views were inadequately represented by these organisations, and took matters into their own hands. In the debate about conflicts over water resources, the manifold shape of global civil society is even more apparent, with local and global NGOs, international law and cross-border water management schemes playing a part.

The three debates illustrate that the extent of global civil society's influence is dependent on the interplay between various forces and institutions, including nation states, private agents, transnational corporations, transboundary organisations, financial institutions and international organisations. While a definitive assessment of the role of global civil society in water management is impossible, this chapter suggests that the interplay serves to stimulate solutions to problems, and articulates values and issues that would otherwise remain hidden.

However, we have also seen that new problems are identified as a result of the involvement of global civil society, such as legitimacy - who is representing whom and on what grounds? Another issue is competition and conflict among various global civil society actors, which points to the challenges of organising civil society.

Despite these issues, this chapter illustrates the increasingly vital role global civil society plays in the management of water - and how this potential could be strengthened, not only because of its merits, as shown in the debates, but also because there is no alternative, whether we like it or not. In order to achieve sustainable and resilient water governance, collectivity has to be redefined in ways which restore the relation between water and society. Global civil society is pivotal in this redefinition of collectivity because its involvement in the governance of water is not supranational, but based on subsidiarity and decentralised action, all prerequisites of effective and sustainable management (Bernauer 1997; van Ast 2000).

REFERENCES

Abu-Zeid, M A (2000) 'Word from the President of the World Water Council', in W J Cosgrove and F R Rijsberman (eds), *World Water Vision. Making Water Everybody's Business*. London: Earthscan Publications.

Ast, J van (2000). *Interactief Watermanagement in Grensoverschrijdende Riversystemen* [Interactive Water Management in Transboundary River Systems]. Delft: Eburon.

Barlow, M and Clarke, T (2002) *Blue Gold: The Fight to Stop the Corporate Theft of the World's Water.* New York: New Press.

Bernauer, T (1997) 'Managing International Rivers', in O R Young (ed), *Global Governance: Drawing Insights from the Environmental Experience*. Cambridge, MA: MIT Press.

Buck, S (1998) *The Global Commons: An Introduction*. Washington DC: Island Press

Dicke, Willemijn (2001) *Bridges and Watersheds. A Narrative Analysis of Water Management in England, Wales and the Netherlands*. Amsterdam: Aksant.

Feachem, R, Bardley, D, Garelick, H and Mara, D (1983) *Sanitation and Disease: Health Aspects of Excreta and Wastewater Management*. World Bank Studies in Water Supply and Sanitation No. 3. New York: John Wiley & Sons.

Finger, Matthias and Allouche, Jeremy (2002) *Water Privatisation: Trans-National Corporations and the Re-Regulation of the Water Industry*. Cambridge: Cambridge University Press.

Forero, Juan (2005) 'Who Will Bring Water to the Bolivian Poor? Multinational Is Ousted, but Local Ills Persist', *New York Times*, 15 December.

Friends of the Earth International (2003) *Water Justice for All: Global and Local Resistance to the Control and Commodification of Water*. Amsterdam: Friends of the Earth International.

Gadgil, Ashok (2004) 'Ashok Gadgil on Safe Drinking Water', in Bruce Mau and the Institute Without Boundaries (ed), *Massive Change*. London: Phaidon Press Limited.

Gleick, P H (1993) *Water in Crisis. A Guide to the World's Freshwater Resources*. Oxford: Oxford University Press.

Grusky, S and Fiil-Flynn, M (2004) *Will the World Bank Back Down?* Water Privatization in a Climate of Global Protest. Washington, DC: Public Citizen.

ICPR (International Commission for the Protection of the Rhine) (URL) www.iksr.org/index.php?id=328 (consulted April 2006).

Interfax (2004) 'Stakes in Hydropower Projects Offered to Villagers as Compensation.' 9 January. http://my.reset.jp/~adachihayao/040110J.htm (consulted 18 May 2006).

Kaul, Inge, Grunberg, Isabelle, and Stern, Mark (1999) 'Defining Global Public Goods', in I Kaul, I Grunberg and M Stern (eds), *Global Public Goods: International Cooperation in the 21st Century*. Oxford: Oxford University Press.

Keck, Margaret E and Sikking, Kathryn (1998) *Activist Beyond Borders: Advocacy Networks in International Politics*. Ithaca, NY: Cornell University Press.

Khagram, Sanjeev (2004) *Dams and Development: Transnational Struggles for Water and Power*. Ithaca and London: Cornell University Press.

Kinsai, Nformi Sonde (2006) 'Lom-Pangar Dam Project: NGOs Decry Lack of Transparency.' The PostNewsLine.com. 13 January.

www.postnewsline.com/2006/01/lompangar_dam_p.html (consulted 31 May 2006).

Kooiman, J and Warner, J (2000) 'Three is a Crowd? Reintroducing Civil Society in Water Governance.' Paper presented at the fourth international research symposium on public management, Erasmus University, Rotterdam.

McDonald, D and Ruiters, G (2005) *The Age of Commodity: Water Privatization in Southern Africa*. London: Earthscan.

OAS (Organization of American States) (2005) *La Plata River Basin*. Water Project Series, Number 6. Washington, DC: Office for Sustainable Development, OAS. www.oas.org/dsd/News/english/Documents/OSDE_6LaPlata .pdf (consulted 31 May 2006).

People's World Water Forum (2004) *Declaration of the People's World Water Movement*. 14 January, New Delhi. www.citizen.org/cmep/Water/conferences/articles.cfm?ID=1 1053 (consulted 15 June 2006).

Petrella, R (1999) *Le Manifeste de L'Eau. Pour un contrat mondial*. Lissabon: Club of Lisbon.

–(2001) *The Water Manifesto: Arguments for a World Water Contract*. London: Zed Books

Polaris Institute (2003) *Global Water Grab: How Corporations are Planning to Take Control of Local Water Services*. Ottawa: Polaris Institute.

Public Citizen (2003a) *The Evian Challenge: A Civil Society Call for the EU to Withdraw its GATS Water Requests*. Washington, DC: Public Citizen.

–(2003b) *Water Privatization Fiascos: Broken Promises and Social Turmoil*. Washington, DC: Public Citizen.

Rose, R (1987) 'Giving Direction to Permanent Officials: Signals from the Electorates, the Market and Expertise', in J-E Lane (ed), *Bureaucracy and Public Choice*. London: Sage.

Shiva, V (2002) *Water Wars: Privatization, Pollution and Profit*. Boston: South End Press.

Transnational Institute (2005) *Reclaiming Public Water*. Amsterdam: Transnational Institute.

UNEP (United Nations Environment Programme) (2006) *Challenges to International Waters; Regional Assessments in a Global Perspective*. UNEP.

UNEP-DDP (Dams and Development Project) (2004) *Financing Dams and Sustainable Development*. Issue-based Workshop No. 3: Proceedings and Submissions. Nairobi: DDP. www.unep.org/dams/files/Issue-basedWorkshops/ Financing_procgs.pdf (consulted18 May 2006).

UNESCO (URL) Hydrology for the Environment Life and Policy. http://portal.unesco.org/sc_nat/ev.php?URL_ID=1205&URL_ DO=DO_TOPIC&URLSECTION=201 (consulted 5 June 2006).

UNGA (United Nations General Assembly) (1997) *Convention on the Law of the Non-Navigational Uses of International Watercourses*. Resolution 51/229 of 21 May. Reproduced in UN document A/RES/51/229 of 8 July 1997.

–(2003) *International Decade for Action, 'Water for Life', 2005-2015*. Resolution 58/217 of 23 December. Reproduced in UN document A/RES/58/217 of 9 February 2004. www.unesco.org/water/water_celebrations/decades/water_f or_life.pdf (consulted 16 May 2006).

Vinogradov, Sergei, Wouters, Patricia and Jones, Patricia (2003) *Transforming Potential Conflict into Cooperation Potential: The Role of International Water Law*. Paris: UNESCO.

http://unesdoc.unesco.org/images/0013/001332/133258e.pdf (consulted 21 May 2006).

Wallace, Jim and Wouters, Patricia (eds) (2006) *Hydrology and Water Law: Bridging the Gap*. London: IWA Publishers.

WCD (World Commission on Dams) (2000) *Dams and Development: A New Framework for Decision-Making*. London and Sterling, VA: Earthscan Publications. www.dams.org/report (consulted 31 May 2006).

World Bank (1996) *Resettlement and Development: The Bankwide Review of Projects Involving Involuntary Resettlement 1986-1993*. Working Paper No. 32. Washington, DC: Environment Department, World Bank.

Wouters, Patricia (2005) '*Water Security: What Role for International Water Law?*', in Felix Dodds and Tim Pippard (eds), *Human and Environmental Security: An Agenda for Change*. London: Earthscan.

Wouters, Patricia, Vinogradov, Sergei, Allan, Andrew, Jones, Patricia and Rieu-Clarke, Alistair (2005) *Sharing Transboundary Waters. An Integrated Assessment of Equitable Entitlement: The Legal Assessment Model*. Paris: International Hydrological Programme, UNESCO.

CHAPTER 6

THE CHURCH, THE MOSQUE, AND GLOBAL CIVIL SOCIETY
Mark Juergensmeyer

Introduction

Religion has always been global. Its ideas and adherents have never been easily contained within the boundaries of polities, whether they were kingdoms, empires, or nation-states. The old cartographic ploy of colouring a map with blue for this religion and green for that one has never really worked. There have always been dense centres of religious communities in a few particular places, and a wondrous mixing of hues almost everywhere else. Yet, as Map 6.1 indicates, many of the sacred centres of the world's religious traditions have been significant global markers for members of their faiths and have served as transnational loci, places of interactive encounter on both social and symbolic levels.

One should not presume, however, that these global centres are the 'headquarters' of the religious traditions with which they are associated. Only the Vatican really performs that function, and even in the case of the papacy its administrative control is more symbolic than real. Within a mile of the Vatican quarters in modern Rome many members of the Roman Catholic faith cheerfully ignore the church's edicts regarding birth control, abortion, homosexuality and the like. Yet most would affirm the significance of the papal see as their religious community's transnational home.

In other cases it is not so much the comfort of home that attracts as the awesome force of spiritual power. Shrines like those at Lourdes or Najaf may become places of pilgrimage because of their mystical or historical significance. In other cases, such as the mega-churches of modern evangelical Protestantism, it is the excitement of the crowds and the charisma of the preachers that attract. The largest religious gathering on the planet is the Kumbh Mela at the confluence of the Ganga and Yamuna rivers in India, where every 12 years tens of millions of devotees converge. At the most recent event in 2003 it is said that numbers approached 70 million. Annually over 2 million come to Mecca on the Haj, the pilgrimage required of all faithful Muslims. Like other transnational sacred centres it attracts devotees not only because of the historical significance of the site but also because of its mystery and the sheer force of the multitudes.

It would be easy to dismiss the political and social implications of these transnational religious centres and assert that, like rock concerts, they give the illusion of transnational community without the substance of it. To some extent this is true, in that worshippers come and go with the reward of personal spiritual transformation, but without necessarily undergoing any changes that would affect the socio-political sphere. Moreover, the appeal of some of the most potent new religious movements is precisely because they do not have traditional religious centres. As Box 6.1 indicates, many new religious movements are seen almost like rogue states, potentially dangerous in part because they are so hard to pin down geographically.

Even those religious traditions that have a global centre are not necessarily agents of the status quo. Many rebel against the forces of modernity and secular globalisation, and have more of a transforming social effect than might initially meet the eye (see Berger and Huntington 2003; Beyer 1994; 2006; Hopkins 2001; Juergensmeyer 2004; 2005; 2006). For one thing, the appearance of a global community can lead to a sense of transnational identity. When Malcolm X, the American political activist, came to Mecca on pilgrimage in 1964 he was deeply affected by the fact that his fellow Muslims came in every shade of skin colour, from the whitest white to the deepest black. He abandoned some of the more racist teachings of his Black Muslim faith soon after.

Moreover, these transnational centres of religion can become bases of social and political power that can enhance the importance of the clergy and leaders associated with them. In the current political climate, where cultural affiliations can purchase political influence, religious leaders with significant followings can make striking claims on public life. When their following has a transnational character, the leaders can have a broad and potentially global impact (see Berger 1999; Beyer 1994; 2006; Rudolph and Piscatori 1997; Thomas 2005).

In this chapter I want to examine this multi-levelled significance of places of worship in global civil society by focusing on two very specific sites in two quite different parts of the world. I might have chosen Mecca and the Vatican, but it seemed to me that it would be more useful to focus on two somewhat less famous sites, and to find sacred locations that carry political and social significance both locally and in their transnational connections.

One of the two examples that I have chosen is the Imam Ali Mosque associated with Grand Ayatollah Sayyid Ali Husaini Sistani in Najaf, Iraq. The other is the Windsor Village United Methodist Church, a mega-church led by the Reverend Kirbyjon Caldwell in Houston, Texas, in the United States. Despite the many differences between the two religious centres and their leadership, both are influenced by the winds of global cultural change, and both contribute to the growing transnational character of their respective religious traditions.

One can find parallels to the Imam Ali Mosque in Najaf and the Houston mega-church in virtually every society – including leading Hindu temples of Banares and Vrindavan and their attendant Brahmin leaders; the Dalada Maligawa Temple in Kandy, Sri Lanka, with its adjacent coterie of influential Theravada Buddhist monks; and the Golden Temple of Sikhism at Amritsar, Punjab, with its powerful panchayat of religious leadership installed in the Akal Takht located in the temple's precincts. As Map 6.1 shows, every religious tradition has significant religious sites with attendant communities and leadership roles, though the way that religious organisations function within their traditions can be quite different.

The roles of mosque and church, for example, are not equivalent. There are no priests or pastors in the Islamic tradition. Rituals do not mediate in one's salvation in the Islamic tradition in the way they do in Roman Catholic Christianity, nor does the mosque constitute local communities of faith in the same way that churches function in Protestant Christianity. Muslim clergy lead worship, and they adjudicate the laws and norms of the tradition, but they do not play the same role in a follower's path to salvation that a Christian priest or pastor does. Yet, as we shall see,

Iman Ali Mosque © *Caroline Penn*

the reputation of local religious centres and the charisma of some Muslim leaders put them in positions of influence and authority not unlike those of their powerful Christian counterparts. And like them, they play an expanding role in the public life of the societies of which they are a part, and in the globalisation of the religious culture of their traditions.

The mosque

The Imam Ali Mosque in Najaf is one of the most remarkable sites in Shi'a Islam. Though only a small percentage of the world's Muslims are Shi'a – the rest are almost all associated with the dominant Sunni version of Islam – they constitute the majority in southern Iraq. Shi'ites are also found in southern Lebanon, Pakistan, and especially in Iran, where 90 per cent of the population is Shi'a of a particular form. Like the Shi'a in Iraq they are followers of the Ithna Ashari (Twelver) brand of Shi'ism, which is based on the belief that there will be 12 great leaders, or imams, in world history.

What makes the Najaf mosque significant is that it is not only a place of worship but also a location for pilgrimage, since it serves as the tomb of the founder of the Shi'a line of leadership. It holds the mortal remains of Ali Ibn Abi Talib, son-in-law of the prophet Mohammed, who is regarded by Shi'ites as the first imam and the first caliph in Islamic history. For this reason it is one of the most important sites in the Shi'a tradition.

Shi'a clerics that are associated with the Imam Ali Mosque understandably are accorded a great deal of reverence in Shi'a society. At present the Mosque's most visible clerical celebrity is the Grand Ayatollah

Map 6.1: World religions, religious centres and religious freedom, 2005

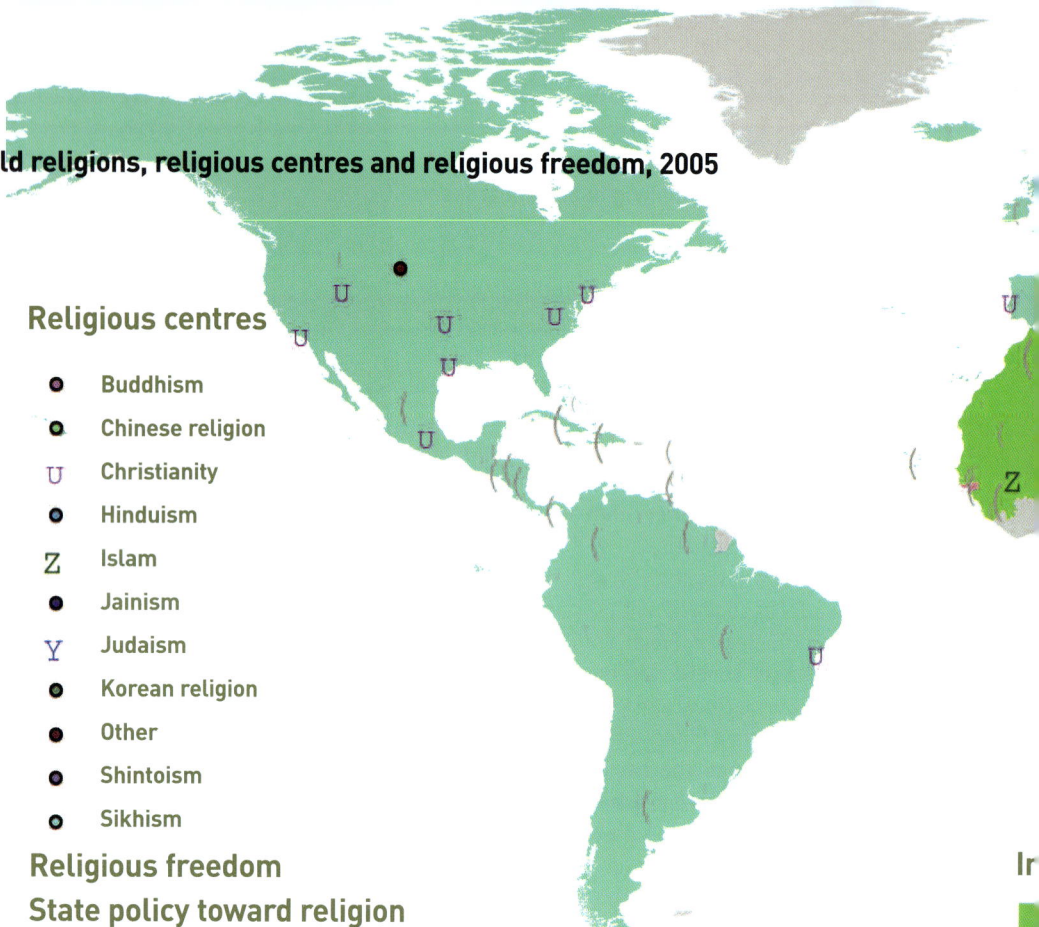

Religious centres

- **Buddhism**
- **Chinese religion**
- U **Christianity**
- **Hinduism**
- Z **Islam**
- **Jainism**
- Y **Judaism**
- **Korean religion**
- **Other**
- **Shintoism**
- **Sikhism**

Religious freedom
State policy toward religion

(**Major interference**

(**Minor interference**

(**Neutral**

(**Minor support**

(**Major suport**

Predominant religion

- (no data)
- **Buddhist**
- **Chinese universist**
- **Christian**
- **Enthno-religionist**
- **Hindu**
- **Jew**
- **Muslim**
- **Non-religious**

Top 10 Religious Groups

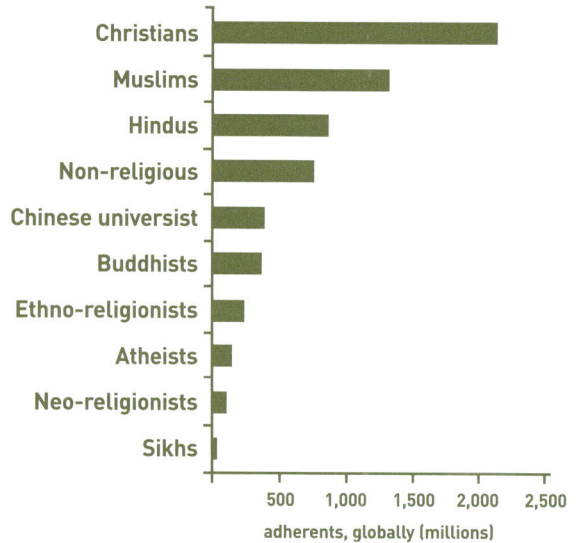

adherents, globally (millions)

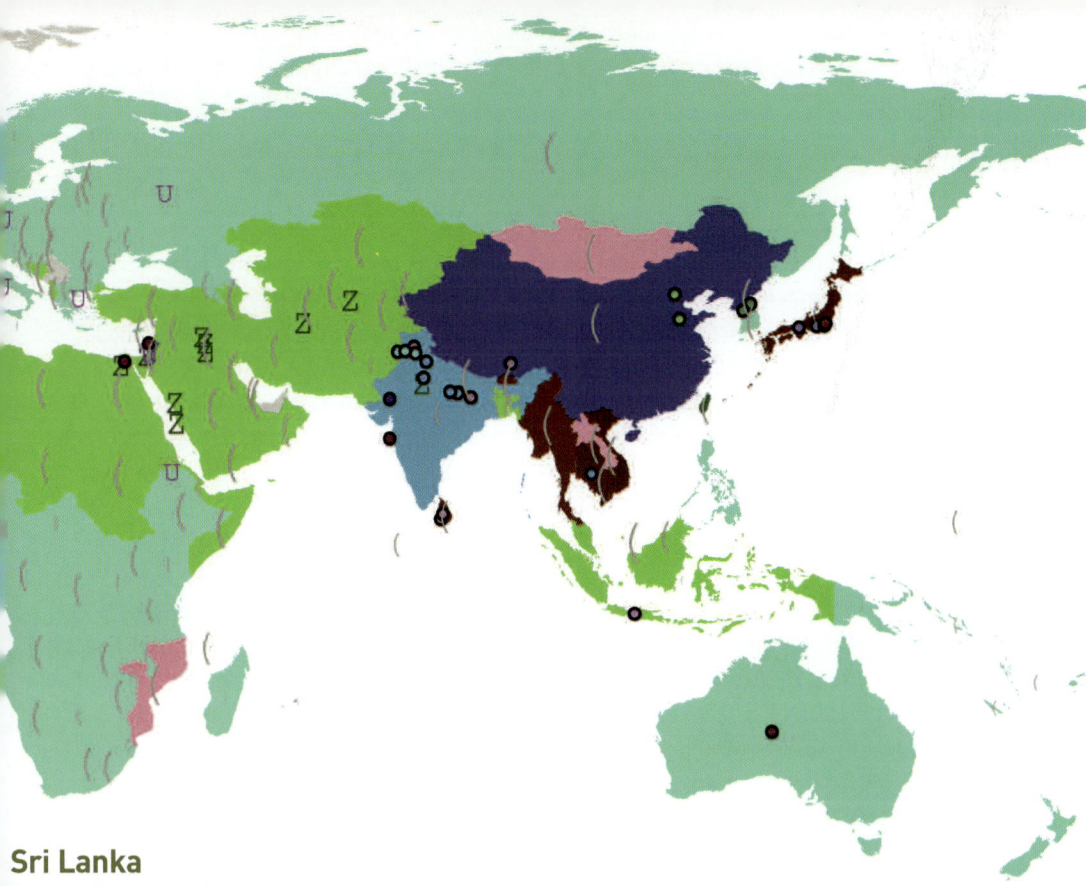

Sri Lanka

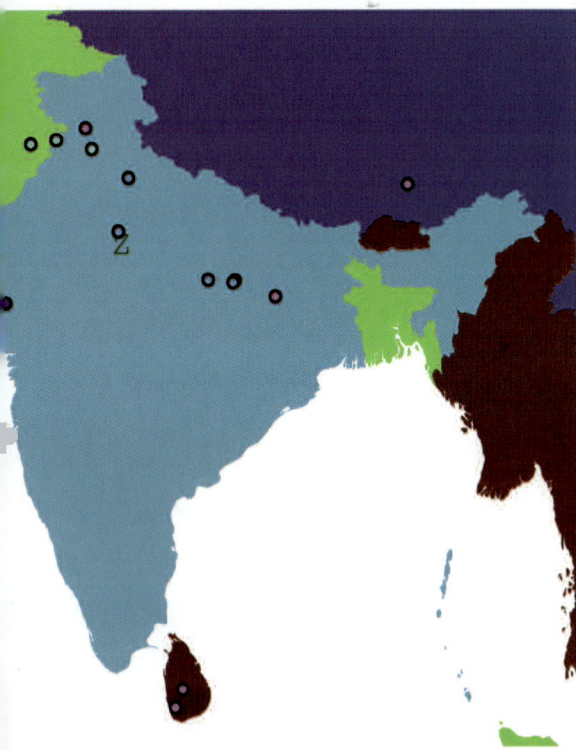

Israel and Palestinian Authority

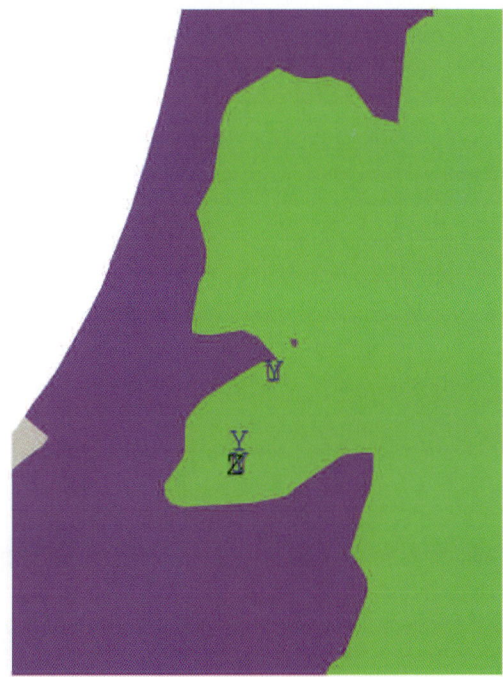

Box 6.1 Transnational religious movements

Outside the mainstream organisations of the world's religious traditions are a plethora of religious movements that are not governed by traditional authorities, nor do they subscribe to the orthodox versions of religious beliefs. Many of these are transnational in character, and gain their legitimacy through their worldwide following. For this reason they are often regarded with suspicion by traditional religious authorities. Political authorities sometimes regard them as rogue movements that are difficult to control.

Within Sunni Islam, for example, the Ahmaddiyya movement has spread from its origins in India to Pakistan and elsewhere in the Muslim world, especially Africa. Though outlawed in Pakistan and persecuted in other Muslim countries it still claims tens of millions of adherents worldwide. The Bahai faith that emerged from Shi'ite Islam is also reviled, especially in Iran, where members of Bahai have been jailed and tortured. The largest percentage of its 7 million members worldwide is in India and the United States, and it has an international centre in Haifa, Israel.

Within Christianity, the Mormons endured decades of persecution in the United States before stabilising as a socially conservative community in the state of Utah. Increasingly, however, the Church of Jesus Christ of Latter Day Saints – as the movement is officially called – is becoming one of the largest religious movements worldwide, where it is sometimes treated with suspicion. Though it is based in Salt Lake City, since 1996 over half of its members live outside the United States. Some 65 per cent of its 12 million members live in South and Central America. Other Christian movements that have developed a transnational network include the Jehovah's Witnesses, Seventh Day Adventists, and Pentacostal movements. In some cases their aggressive missionary attempts at conversion have put them at odds with local authorities.

The Chinese government has banned Falun Gong, a transnational religious movement also known as Falun Dafa. Founded in the 1990s by Li Hongzhi, who now lives in New York, the teachings of the movement are based on traditional Chinese Buddhist concepts and practices. The worldwide membership is probably around several million (though the movement claims 200 million followers). It includes many non-Chinese living in Europe and America, though most followers are in China. In 1999 the movement was able to use its Internet connections to quickly organise a rally of some 10,000 members who protested at the buildings housing the offices of several Chinese leaders. The Chinese government, impressed by the organisational power of the movement, permanently banned it from the country and attempted to block access to its websites.

The Japanese government also considered proscribing the Aum Shinrikyo, a new religious movement with transnational connections, after the 1995 sarin nerve gas attack in the Tokyo subway. Shoko Asahara, the leader of the movement, was implicated in the terrorist act and sentenced to death by the Japanese courts. At its height many of its members were located outside Japan, including Russia, where the movement's apocalyptic prophesies were taken seriously. Since 2000 the movement has renamed itself Aleph.

Hindu religious movements gained worldwide prominence in the 1970s. George Harrison, a member of the Beatles, helped to publicise the movement led by Maharishi Mahesh Yogi and ensure it a worldwide following. The movement led by Rajneesh, another guru, gained notoriety by establishing communes in the United States and Europe that were secretive and said to flout conventional social and moral standards. The Hare Krishna Movement (the International Society of Krishna Consciousness) has consisted largely of non-Indian devotees outside India. In the twenty-first century, the largest growing Hindu movement worldwide has been the Swaminarayan Movement, which appeals largely to expatriate Indians living around the world. It has some 9,000 centres in 45 countries.

Other transnational religious movements have no ties with traditional religion. Some of these movements are controversial. The Church of Scientology was founded in 1952 by L Ron Hubbard, an American science fiction writer, based on his practice of dianetics, which is a kind of alternative self-help therapy. By the dawn of the twenty-first century the movement had acquired a global following of several hundred thousand, according to non-church estimates (within the movement the estimate is 10 million). The movement has been banned in Germany, where it is considered an unscrupulous commercial organisation.

Although the Al-Qaeda network associated with Osama bin Laden and similar radical jihadi movements are obviously revolutionary political movements, they might also be considered which transnational religious movements, are perceived as rogue bands by governmental authorities. Though these movements are clearly political in that they critique the secular nation-state system and Western political and economic intrusion into the Middle East, they are also religious in their ideology and have gained influence through mosques and religious-based websites. Through their transnational network of affiliations they offer a prototype of an alternative religious-based view of globalisation that is a challenge to the Western-dominated paradigm of global world order in the post-cold war era.

Sayyid Ali Husaini Sistani. Another leading cleric, Sayed Mohammed Baqir al-Hakim, might have been significant competition for Sistani's clerical authority, but he was killed in a bomb blast at the Najaf mosque on 29 August 2003, soon after the US-led military coalition's invasion that toppled Saddam Hussein's regime. Al-Hakim had been living in Iran to escape Saddam's persecution of Shi'ite Islamic leaders, and returned to what was assumed would be a mantle of political and religious leadership before the blast terminated his life. It was widely assumed that Abu Mus'ab al-Zarqawi, or some other jihadi Sunni extremist, was behind the terrorist attack, which took approximately 100 other lives as well.

A year later, in August 2004, the Najaf mosque was occupied by members of the Badr Brigade, a military cadre associated with the young Muqtada al Sadr, another clerical competitor. The members of the brigade sought safe haven in the mosque from troops dispatched by the US occupation forces and the interim Iraq government to bring al Sadr to justice for a series of crimes with which he had been charged. Sistani was out of the country at the time, seeking treatment for a heart condition in London. When he returned, a ceasefire was arranged, and the keys of the mosque were turned over to him.

The Grand Ayatollah Sistani was born in 1930 in Mashhad, Iran. Early in his life he went to Najaf to study, and stayed there indefinitely. His mentor in Najaf was the Grand Ayatollah Abdul-Qassim Khoei, who managed to steer clear of the vicissitudes of Iraqi politics by declaring a separation between religion and state. Before his death, Khoei had designated Sistani as his successor. Sistani has largely adopted the position of his mentor in steering clear of direct involvement in politics, a position that likely provided a certain amount of personal security under the Saddam regime.

Since the fall of Saddam, however, Sistani has been involved in politics in several ways – directly through issuing fatwas with political overtones, though never publicly supporting particular candidates, and indirectly through behind-the-scenes political discussions. He is especially close to members of the Supreme Council for the Islamic Revolution in Iraq (SCIRI), the dominant Shi'a political organisation.

Even before the fall of Saddam, Sistani had issued a fatwa calling on the Shi'a community to avoid resisting the US military invasion. In the new Iraq, Sistani

pressured the US occupation authorities by calling for early democratic elections that would ensure Shi'a political control in the country. He has also issued fatwas urging Shi'ites to vote, and to avoid responding in kind to the attacks by radical Sunni activists.

The church

In searching for a Christian analogy to the Najaf mosque, one might immediately think of St Peter's Cathedral at the Vatican and the role of the Pope, or an important Catholic constituency in a Latin American country where the Church hierarchy and political leadership are closely intertwined. Or one might think of a comparable pilgrimage centre, such as Lourdes or Jerusalem. For the purpose of this chapter and our attempt to understand the role of religion in contemporary public life, however, I have settled on a distinctly US example – the Windsor Village United Methodist Church of Houston, Texas, and its pastor, the Reverend Kirbyjon Caldwell.

The first thing to be said about the Windsor Village United Methodist Church in Houston is that it is a long way from the Imam Ali Mosque in Najaf – and that the Reverend Caldwell is no Grand Ayatollah Sistani. This distance is more than geographic. As I have mentioned, the congregational role that the Church plays in Protestant Christianity is quite different from the more public role of the mosque in Shi'a Islam, and the role of the clergy is also quite different in the two traditions. A Shi'ite Muslim ayatollah is a leader and scholar but his role is not quite that of a Protestant Christian pastor, and even less that of a Roman Catholic priest. One could also cite other dissimilarities in the organisation of religious life, the significance of sacred sites, and the social significance of religious affiliation.

Yet there are also some interesting similarities. Both religious centres are at the heart of the societies in which they are set. Protestant Christianity is, like Shi'a Islam, the minority branch of its tradition but Houston is firmly in Protestant country, just as Najaf is in Shi'a territory. The Reverend Caldwell, the reigning cleric of the Houston Church, is, like Sistani, enormously popular in his region. Both religious centres have impressive numbers of followers. Caldwell has built his community church into mega-church status with some 14,000 listed members and thousands more as part of a public ministry nurtured through publications and radio and television programmes. When he accepted the call to the pastorate at the Windsor Village church, its membership numbered only 25 souls. It is now the largest Methodist church in the United States.

Though it began as a small African-American community church without any particular significance – certainly nothing with the historical weight of the Imam Ali Mosque – it has become something of a place of pilgrimage in contemporary Protestant life. In addition to Sunday services that attract an enormous multicultural and international following, the church has its own radio and television programmes. The elaborate website of the church lists an array of affiliated organisations, including nine separately charted non-profit organisations that are administered under the rubric of the Power Connection.

Like Sistani, Caldwell is politically influential in an indirect way. Tom DeLay, the once-powerful member of the US House of Representatives, has participated in executive meetings of the church's Power Connection organisation, as have many other local political leaders. Much of Caldwell's political clout is due to his relationship with another Texas politician, George W Bush, the current President of the United States, who frequently attends the church in Houston and who has called on Caldwell to be an adviser on faith-based initiatives organised by the federal government. Caldwell, who calls Bush 'Brother President', has explained his friendship by reference to their common interest in business entrepreneurship. Caldwell, who has an MBA from the Wharton School of Business, in addition to a theological degree, has published a book titled *Entrepreneurial Faith*, which is a sequel to his first popular book, *The Gospel of Good Success* (Caldwell 2000; Caldwell and Kallestad 2004). Since the African-American community in the United States tends to favour the Democratic Party, Caldwell was roundly criticised by other African-American clergy for preferring Bush to Al Gore, Bush's rival in his first-term election. Caldwell, who claims to be an independent, defended his support for Bush by citing the president's positive record on involving African-American aides in his campaign and for promising blacks a role in capitalism's success. Caldwell was invited to introduce Bush to the Republican Convention that nominated Bush as its presidential candidate; and at Bush's first inaugural ceremony

Caldwell was asked to give the benediction. Since then he has been a frequent visitor to the White House.

Mosque and church in the public sphere

This brief look at two influential centres of religious life in Iraq and the United States, provides an opportunity to make several observations about the role of religion in society at this moment of late modernity and the dawn of the era of globalisation. The first is that religious institutions are increasingly aware of the role that they play in the public sphere (see Appadurai 1996; Robertson 1992).

One could say that religion has always played a significant role in public life and that there is nothing new about the politicisation of religion or the religionisation of politics. While this is no doubt true, it is also the case that religion has taken a back seat politically ever since the secular values of the European Enlightenment were imposed on Western societies in the eighteenth century and thrust upon the rest of he world as part of the inheritance of colonial influence in the nineteenth and twentieth centuries (Masuzawa 2005). During this period the doctrine of the separation of church and state was often interpreted as meaning that religious influence had no role in the shaping of public policy or the choice of political leadership. In the last decades of the twentieth century and the beginning of the twenty-first, however, religion has roared back into public life with a vengeance. Sometimes it has laid claim to public attention through acts of violence; at other times its assertions are made more quietly through the ultimately more far-reaching impact of political influence. What this means for religion is the awareness that it has the potential to make an impact on public life (see Cowan 2002).

The political success of Caldwell and Sistani indicates that this impact can be considerable indeed. It can also be beneficial to the careers of religious leaders. One could observe that Sistani and Caldwell have used the platforms of mosque and church to shrewd political advantage. Indeed, they are prime examples of the powerful role that religious leaders can play in an indirect way in democratic societies.

Sistani's power in the post-Saddam era has grown considerably. This has meant that he has extraordinary influence in the making and breaking of candidates for political leadership, and that his concerns about the role of religion in Iraqi society can be expressed in statements of public policy. It also means that his authority has been entrenched within his own leadership circles. Religious-based charities directly under his control have expanded considerably with government support. He has used the positive public response to his religious-based social service institutions to remind the Iraqi community that religion is often able to provide services and support when the government will not or cannot do so.

In the nearby setting of Palestine, the Hamas movement used the goodwill that it generated within the Palestinian community through a network of health clinics and other social service agencies to create political power. This electoral power enabled the party to triumph over Fateh, its secular rival, at the January 2006 elections, to become the majority party in the Palestinian National Assembly.

In the United States it cannot be said that the Reverend Caldwell has anything like the political influence of Hamas or Grand Ayatollah Sistani. Some political observers have commented that no evangelical leader can have much political power under the Bush administration since President George W Bush is himself a sort of religious leader. In this sense he has replaced such religious politicians as the Reverend Jerry Falwell and Pat Robertson, who have sometimes resorted to making extreme political statements as a way of retaining public attention. If President Bush is the leader of the religious right, Caldwell is his faithful lieutenant. Nothing in Caldwell's statements indicates anything other than a kind of blind loyalty to Bush's leadership. When Bush was criticised for claiming that God had instructed him to wage war in Iraq and try to bring peace to Palestine and Israel, it was Caldwell, along with the head of Bush's office to promote federal support for faith-based initiatives, who was brought to a press conference to assure the public that Bush was not claiming to be hearing voices from God and that he was indeed quite normal.

Though Caldwell's influence on most aspects of public policy in the White House may be limited to that of a cheerleader, he has made a contribution to one of President Bush's pet projects, the federal funding of faith-based community programmes. In fact, Caldwell's own organisation and his stable of nine community-based non-profit organisations would have much to benefit from such federal support. His

non-profits deal with a variety of community services including low-cost housing, business loans, health care and educational support.

Most Methodist pastors do not have the popularity or influence of the Reverend Kirbyjon Caldwell; and most local Shi'ite clerics do not have the political muscle of the Grand Ayatollah Sistani. Yet the recognition of Sistani's and Caldwell's roles does raise awareness about the potential of the influence of religion in public life. Though one might conclude that Sistani and Caldwell largely function in a self-serving way, they demonstrate that religion can make a difference in public life. In many cases this public role of religion can be quite positive.

By enhancing the image of religion's potential for leadership in areas of political and social service in society, these visible leaders may be making a significant contribution. By their examples they might indirectly be encouraging other religious activists to be involved in the public sphere in similar ways, or in ways that are less narrow and self-serving. There have indeed been instances in the past in which the influence of religion on the state has helped governments to become more humane. During the civil rights struggle in the United States, for example, the moral authority of the Church was a significant factor in pressing for the expansion of rights for members of minority racial and ethnic groups. At the same time there are instances where being touched by political power has been a good thing for religious institutions. In some cases it has made them more concerned about issues of social equality and justice. Because the Roman Catholic Church is aware of its potential for political influence it is more attentive than otherwise to public issues and more prone to comment about ethical issues in society, including censuring warfare and condemning the death penalty. Thus, though the newly discovered public role of religion can be narrow and self-serving, it can also expand religion's social awareness and help society to address moral issues.

The multicultural and transnational dimensions of local institutions

The second observation to be made about religion's renewed public role is its international and transnational perspective. It might be suggested that in choosing to focus on the Imam Ali Mosque and the Windsor Village United Methodist Church I have not provided very good examples of global thinking, and that may be true. But what is impressive about these examples is that even such locally powerful institutions as these, to a certain degree, have an ethnically and internationally inclusive world view. Despite the fact that al Sistani's mosque and Caldwell's church are potent local forces, they both have transnational ties.

The Imam Ali Mosque is almost by definition transnational. Because of its prime historical importance it is a place of pilgrimage and worship for pious Shi'ite Muslims from around the world. As a result the site is something of an international community. Sistani himself comes from Iran, where Farsi was his native tongue, and he still able to speak Farsi as well as Arabic. The very fact that Islam has a liturgical language that is common to Muslims of all nationalities is something of a transnational cultural tie. At Najaf, Sistani is able to communicate and serve as a spiritual leader to all Shi'ite Muslims, not only Arabic-speaking Iraqis but also Farsi-speaking Iranians, Urdu-speaking Pakistanis, and the occasional English-speaking Shi'ite from somewhere else in the world. The interfaith and multicultural constituency of Najaf's pilgrimage community has helped to provide something of a diverse and even international flavour to the neighbourhood of the Imam Ali Mosque. It is in microcosm an example of the globalisation of Islam (see Bayes and Tohedi 2001; Doumato and Posusney 2001; Mottahedeh, Schaebler and Stenberg 2004).

The Imam Ali shrine is also respected by many Sunni Muslims both inside and outside Iraq, a fact that has not gone unnoticed by leaders such as Sistani, who have made efforts to meet with Sunni as well as Shi'ite leaders. Sistani and SCIRI, the party with which he is largely associated, have gone out of their way to make the point that they welcome support from Sunni as well as Shi'a Muslims, and from members of other religious communities as well. They claim that SCIRI does not have a pro-Shi'a political agenda.

This point was made even more emphatically by Abu Israa al-Malika, a member of the politburo of the Shi'ite-based Islamic Da'awa Party in Iraq, which met with an international delegation of scholars, including Mary Kaldor and Yahia Said of the London School of Economics, and myself, in May 2004. Al-Malika pointed out that the alleged Sunni–Shi'a divide in Iraq was greatly exaggerated. He said that many families

Poster of Grand Ayatollah Ali Husaini Sistani
© Farah Nosh/Panos Pictures

inter-married, that many tribes, including the tribe of interim Iraq President al-Yawar, had both Sunni and Shi'a elements within it, and that Sunni Arabs comprised 15 per cent of the support of his own Islamic Da'awa Party, which is regarded as Shi'ite. In the 2005 elections, both the Islamic Da'awa Party and SCIRI made an effort to reach out to Sunni and other communities and include non-Shi'ites in their organisations.

Thus, political power – or perhaps more correctly the quest for greater political power – has caused local religious institutions and groups to reach out beyond their own constituencies. Perhaps without quite his realising how it happened, the Grand Ayatollah Sistani has become not just a Shi'a leader but an Iraqi one, and a spokesperson not just for Iraq but for moral values that relate to persons from a variety of ethnic and national backgrounds.

Something of the same could be said of the Reverend Kirbyjon Caldwell. Though his Windsor Village United Methodist Church is almost entirely American, it is largely African American, and the ethnicity of most of its members is a strong reminder that US society is not totally European in ethnic composition. Caldwell is attentive to the needs of his African-American constituency and quite conscious of his connections to it, especially in addresses and messages aimed primarily at members of the church and the local community. He is fond of quoting from the sermons of the Reverend Martin Luther King Jr.

and associating himself by implication with America's civil rights movement, which that brought more rights to African Americans. But outside this circle Caldwell speaks as a public servant and a representative of the moral dimension of society in general, with no specific ethnic reference. He seems to make a special effort to reach out to the majority community in society in recruiting new members to his church and in gaining public support for his Power Connection and its non-profit ventures.

The ambivalent relationship to global civil society

The fact that religious leaders such as Caldwell and Sistani reach out to a constituency beyond their own small ethnic and national circles does not mean that they have become more broad-minded or global in their thinking. In fact, one could argue that in their attempts to harness their multicultural and international constituencies they are exploiting global civil society rather than nurturing it. But it does indicate that, for good or for ill, socially and politically active religious groups in the contemporary milieu must take into account the increasing multicultural and international character of the societies of which they are a part. It also means that to some extent, perhaps despite themselves, they become more transnational in their thinking than they themselves realise.

In accessing Sistani's website, www.sistani.org, one is presented with an elaborately designed Internet location available to the reader in a variety of languages, including English. Since the site is filled with complicated graphics it takes a while for it to fully load up on one's computer screen. The first image to appear is a shaded outline map of the continents of the world with no national boundaries. The fact that Najaf appears to be located at the centre of this map would seem to signify that this is a rather imperialistic view of the world, with Sistani's Shi'a community at the epicentre of worldwide cultural meaning and social significance. But it is indeed a global vision.

The very fact that Sistani has a website – and a quite sophisticated one at that – indicates that he or members of his inner circle recognise the importance of this transnational means of communication. Indeed, as Box 6.2 indicates, religious organisations are increasingly reaching out to new followers through electronic means. In some cases the religious constituency consists entirely of those who have logged on to a site or who engage in conversation in a web-based chat room. Such associations can sometimes take on a kind of intense intimacy especially in the busy sites of jihadi Muslim ideologies or millenarian Christian visionaries. These are cases where cyber-communication has led to cyber-community.

The Reverent Kirbyjon Caldwell also has a website, which is located at www.kingdombuilders.com. Interestingly, unlike the sites of most non-profit institutions, the entrepreneurially minded Caldwell has designated it as a dot.com rather than a dot.org site. It is the Internet location not only for the Windsor Village Methodist Church but also for the nine non-profit organisations associated with the Power Connection NGO administrative umbrella. It is also the site for several other affiliated organisations, including the Christian Entrepreneurial Organization (CEO) and an organisation called Caring for the Nations.

Caring for the Nations is Caldwell's way of updating the old missionary enterprise that for over two centuries has characterised the Protestant approach to the world. One might say that the Roman Catholic branch of Christianity is by its nature transnational, since it has a central administrative allegiance to the Pope and a hierarchical organisational structure that unites all parishes and church agencies, wherever they are in the world, to the transnational network of the Roman Church. This is not the case with the Protestant branch of Christianity, in which organisational control is vested into local hands and the cultural context of the church communities tends to be national, sometimes stridently so, and

Box 6.2: Global religious websites

Increasingly the Internet provides a transnational locale for religious communication and interaction. Religious websites enable traditional organisations to reach out to their membership, publicise their activities, and attract new followers. At the same time many of the new websites have been launched by non-traditional groups. In these cases the respondents and followers who access the sites, enter web-chat rooms, and post messages on web-bulletin boards constitute new forms of transnational religious communities. At the extreme end of this development are the militant Christian and jihadi Muslim sites, many of them with active chat rooms and bulletin board listings, which recruit new followers and propagate their activist ideologies. The most secretive sites are password-protected and shift locations frequently to avoid government monitoring.

In part to counteract the jihadi sites, a moderate south-east Asian Muslim group supported by the Malaysian government has set up its own cyber mosque. It reaches out to the culturally and politically curious through several languages, and advocates an essentially non-political version of Islam (http://cybermosque.mpsj.gov.my). Perhaps the most informative of the Muslim websites is Islam on Line, which offers news of developments in the Islamic world in addition to theological and devotional resources (www.islamonline.net).

Several non-denominational sites provide chat rooms for Christians interested in engaging in discussion of theological and moral issues. Usually, no attempt is made to limit the discussion, though the tenor of the sites is often evangelical without being overtly political or millenarian. One such site is located at www.christianforums.com. Another Christian site is somewhat more theologically liberal and reaches out to agnostics and Christians who are unaffiliated with any church. It calls itself the First Church of Cyberspace, (www.godweb.org). A Jewish site similar to the First Church of Cyberspace aims at a non-committed Jewish audience and calls itself a CyberSynagogue. (www.synagogue3000.org).

Among the many informative religious websites is a useful Buddhist cyber centre, Tricycle (www.tricycle.com). A site that provides news and general information on all religious communities and their organisations worldwide is www.beliefnet.com, which claims to be the Internet's 'largest spiritual website' and which supports itself largely through advertising. A site that provides a reasonably objective attempt to determine the actual numbers of adherents of religious communities worldwide is located at www.adherents.com.

occasionally with a xenophobic vengeance. The great missionary movement of the Protestant Churches in the nineteenth and twentieth centuries that brought thousands of eager American and European missionaries to Africa, India, China, and south-east Asia, were therefore on a double mission. On the one hand they were extensions of national influence, a sort of cultural parallel to economic and political colonialism. But at the same time they established networks of transnational affiliation, thereby anticipating the era of globalisation and competing with the global influence of the Catholic Church.

Caring for the Nations supported by the Windsor Village United Methodist Church of Houston, Texas, reflects both of these dimensions of missionary internationalism. It replicates the missionaries' patronising approach to other parts of the world in presuming that people in other nations need and would welcome the 'caring' that the Houston Church's Caring for the Nations programme provides. Evangelism is one of the activities promoted by Caring for the Nations, and one can only assume that the form of Christianity that it encourages people from other nations to adopt is strikingly similar to the cultural values and religious beliefs of the members of the Windsor Village United Methodist Church. Yet at the same time the organisation is pledged to provide social benefits, including disaster relief, health services and education. Many of the social services promoted by Caldwell's non-profit agencies associated with the Power Connection provide social welfare support for the needy in Houston. Thus in some ways the Caring for the Nations movement is a way of thinking of the Church's relation to society in transnational terms.

In this respect the Caring for the Nations programme of the Houston church has much in common with other transnational efforts of Christian organisations that have a positive impact on global civil society. As Box 6.3 indicates, international non-profit non-governmental organisations are associated with every religious tradition (see Smock 2001; Simkhada and Warner 2005). The Protestant global agency for social service and emergency relief, for example, is Church World Service, an agency supported by the United Methodist Church and other Protestant denominations through the World Council of Churches, the international Protestant coordinating body. Particular church groups, such as the American Friends Service Committee, which is sponsored by the Quakers, have also provided an important supportive role for global civil society, especially in the area of international conflict-resolution negotiation. One might suggest that the Windsor Village United Methodist Church's international agencies are simply carrying on a tradition of social service that is a part of every religious organisation's image of itself as an agency of humane benefit to the world.

Thus even the most parochial and nationalistic of religious organisations have the potential to reach out and think in terms of transnational service and influence. There is, of course, a great diversity of opinions within the communities associated with the Windsor Village United Methodist Church and the Imam Ali Mosque. Leaders such as the Reverend Kirbyjon Caldwell and the Grand Ayatollah Sistani represent a significant element of the community, but not all of it. Yet their broader aspirations for political influence and social impact help to shape the role of religious institutions in the contemporary world. This role increasingly is one that interacts – in both exploitive and supportive ways – with transnational networks and an emerging global civil society.

Box 6.3: Transnational religious NGOs

Almost every religious tradition has organisations that provide emergency relief and social services. Some of these are local, in that they are directly connected to churches, mosques, temples and synagogues in a particular locale. But many of these organisations are transnational, providing social services around the world to anyone in need regardless of faith.

Some of the Christian relief organisations have been accused of using their social services as a means of securing conversions or selectively serving only members of their own religious community. Some evangelical Protestant Christian groups have been banned in India and elsewhere for this reason. The Salvation Army provides social services to all who need it, but also conducts adjacent religious activities. World Vision International, an independent charity with a Christian orientation provides services in 96 countries; it reserves 5 per cent of its funds for religious activities in countries where religious proselytising is allowed. Catholic organisations, including Catholic Relief Service and Catholic Agency for Overseas Development serve all in need, but often utilise existing church organisational networks to facilitate the distribution of relief supplies. Church World Service, the Protestant international relief service associated with the World Council of Churches, also uses existing church networks as well as providing relief directly in emergency situations. Other groups, such as the Quakers' American Friends Service Committee, are committed to international relief and conflict mediation regardless of religious affiliation, and do not utilise local Christian organisations to provide their services.

A similar tension (between social services that are linked to local religious networks and those that are offered directly to all in need) exists within the charitable organisations associated with other religious traditions. In Islam, one of the five pillars of the faith is Zakat (charitable offerings). These are sometimes imposed as a kind of tax and distributed by governments in Islamic countries, administered sometimes through local mosque-related organisations and sometimes through charitable organisations specifically created for humanitarian relief. Islamic Relief is an international organisation operating in 25 countries; it was established by a Muslim doctor living in the UK to provide services similar to those delivered by Christian charitable organisations. Muslim Aid also offers non-denominational relief and social services, as does Merhamet, which is active in Bosnia and Turkey.

One of the largest Muslim charities, the Holy Land Foundation, was outlawed in the United States in December 2001. The charity claimed to be established solely to provide relief for refugees, particularly displaced Palestinians. It also provided funds to assist refugees in Bosnia and elsewhere, including aid for homeless people in the United States after tornadoes in Texas and floods in Iowa. But the US government noted that its founders included leaders of Hamas, and the charity was alleged to have been a conduit for funds to the militant Palestinian movement, which has been involved in suicide attacks in Israel.

World Jewish Aid was established by the UK Jewish community to provide emergency relief and development aid to those who need it throughout the world. A similar mission is stated by Shanti Volunteer Association, an international Buddhist NGO based in Japan. In India, the Sarvodaya Movement was established as an NGO providing village-level development and relief following the tradition of Mohandas Gandhi. In Sri Lanka, a Buddhist version of the movement called Sarvodaya Shramadana has been established by A T Ariyaratne, a Sinhalese Buddhist. BAPS Care International, an international relief organisation, has been established in association with the worldwide Hindu Swaminaryanan movement.

Some organisations that bear a religious name are not directly related to any religious organisation or community. The Christian Children's Fund, though founded by a Presbyterian minister, has no connection with any religious organisation. The International Red Cross and the Red Crescent, its associated organisation in the Middle East, are not affiliated with any religion, despite the cross and crescent symbolism in their names.

REFERENCES

Appadurai, Arjun (1996) *Modernity at Large: Cultural Dimensions of Globalization*. Minneapolis: University of Minnesota Press.

Bayes, Jane and Tohedi, Nayereh (eds) (2001) *Globalization, Religion and Gender: The Politics of Implementing Women's Rights in Catholic and Muslim Countries*. New York: Palgrave Macmillan.

Berger, Peter (ed) (1999) *The Desecularisation of the World: Resurgent Religion and World Politics*. Minneapolis: Eerdmans.

– and Huntington, Samuel (eds) (2003) *Many Globalizations: Cultural Diversity in the Contemporary World*. New York: Oxford University Press.

Beyer, Peter (1994) *Religion and Globalization*. Thousand Oaks: Sage Publications.

– (2006) *Religion in a Global Society*. London: Routledge.

Caldwell, Kirbyjon (with Seal, Mark) (2000) *The Gospel of Good Success: A Road Map to Spiritual, Emotional, and Financial Wholeness*. New York: Fireside Press.

Caldwell, Kirbyjon and Kallestad, Walt (with Sorensen, Paul) (2006) *Entrepreneurial Faith: Launching Bold Initiatives to Expand God's Kingdom*. Colorado Springs, CO: WaterBrook Press.

Cowan, Tyler (2002) *Creative Destruction: How Globalisation is Changing the World's Cultures*. Princeton: Princeton University Press.

Doumato, Eleanor and Posusney, Marsha (eds) (2001) *Women and Globalisation in the Arab Middle East*. Boulder, CO: Lynne Reiner Publishers.

Hopkins, Dwight N (2001) *Religions/Globalizations: Theories and Cases*. Durham: Duke University Press.

Juergensmeyer, Mark (ed) (2004) *Global Religions: An Introduction*. New York: Oxford University Press.

– (ed) (2005) *Religion in Global Civil Society*. New York: Oxford University Press.

– (ed) (2006) *The Oxford Handbook of Global Religions*. New York: Oxford University Press.

Masuzawa, Tomoko (2005) *The Invention of World Religions Or, How European Universalism Was Preserved in the Language of Pluralism*. Chicago: University of Chicago Press.

Mottahedeh, Roy, Schaebler, Birgit and Stenberg, Leif (eds) (2004) *Globalisation and the Muslim World: Culture, Religion, and Modernity*. Syracuse: Syracuse University Press.

Robertson, Roland (1992) *Globalization: Social Theory and Global Culture*. Thousand Oaks, CA: Sage Publications.

Rudolph, Susanne H and Piscatori, James (eds) (1997) *Transnational Religion and Fading States*. Boulder, CO: Westview Press.

Simkhada, Shambhu Ram and Warner, Daniel (eds) (2005) *Religion, Politics, Conflict and Humanitarian Action: Faith-Based Organisations as Political, Humanitarian or Religious Actors*. Program for the Study of International Organizations Occasional Paper. Geneva: Graduate Institute of International Studies.

Smock, David (2001) *Faith-Based NGOs and International Peacebuilding*. Washington, DC: US Institute of Peace.

Thomas, Scott (2005) *The Global Resurgence of Religion and the Transformation of International Relations: The Struggle for the Soul of the 21st Century*. London: Palgrave Macmillan.

CHAPTER 7

THE ODD COUPLE: FOOTBALL AND GLOBAL CIVIL SOCIETY
David Goldblatt

America TV...made a giant flag approximately 150 metres wide and costing $40,000 which was 'donated' to an 'Argentine supporter' to be used at the home match against Ecuador. The flag was in Argentine colours, with the logo of the channel printed in its lower half; along with a legend saying 'Argentina is passion' the motto of the television channel is 'America is passion'. It was shown at the beginning of the game and during the intermezzo, filling a whole terrace of the stadium...Meanwhile sheltered from view beneath the flag, spectators were threatened by dozens of pickpockets who demanded that they hand over their belongings. Thus, between the sponsorship of patriotism and delinquency, our national story continues.

Pablo Alabarces and Maria Rodriguez (2000)

Introduction

Football and global civil society may seem odd bedfellows. After all, world football is primarily organised around competitions between representative national teams that mimic, if they do not always mirror, the order of power and modes of interaction common in the inter-state system. When football is not enmeshed in the competitiveness, rivalries and occasional acts of violence that pass for polite conduct between states, it appears similarly deformed by the global economic system, in which the poor are subject to the rule of the rich. The fabric of the game appears deeply penetrated by the logos and interests of multinational corporations, intent on reducing the spectacle to another variant of sanitised universal consumerism. The culture of global football, though changing, remains overwhelmingly masculine; its dressing rooms and stadiums are not only demographically defined by men but often actively exclude women, and remain in most societies a repository of racism and homophobia. Football consorts with the enemies of global civil society rather than being its ally. In the face of these empirical realities I propose an alternative and utopian line of argument.

- First, football, as a diverse and complex cultural practice, is actually constitutive of global civil society. Its institutional networks and regularised competitions provide an infrastructure of interaction. Its values, narratives, aesthetics and pleasures provide a real and universal shared global cultural heritage.
- Second, football serves as both a practical problem and a lucid metaphor for the wider relationship between civil society and economic and political power, nationally and globally.
- Third, the pathologies of football are primarily the result of the unchecked power of authoritarian and corrupt political institutions, and gormless corporations that have supported and managed its commercialisation and global spread.
- Fourth, football can fulfil its potential as a central element of a universal, equitable and progressive global culture only if the forces within global civil society are mobilised to challenge the current system of football governance and economics.

Football as global culture and world heritage

When Brazil beat Germany 2-0 in Japan to win the 2002 World Cup, more than half the planet was watching. Has humanity ever gathered in such a way, in such numbers before? As a way of gauging the global cultural significance of the occasion, it is worth pausing for a moment to consider the historical setting and origins of the World Cup final, a task that the global cultural and heritage agencies such as UNESCO have failed to do. They are not alone: the key writings on cultural globalisation barely mention football (Held et al. 1999, for example), and the few monographs on the matter focus on sport in general (Miller et al. 2001; Bairner 2001).

At the 1928 Amsterdam Olympics, football proved by far and away the most popular event. The tournament was won by Uruguay, in front of a crowd which would have been ten times the size had everyone obtained the tickets they asked for. FIFA, the global organising body for football founded in 1904, was finally propelled into action, forming its first World Cup organising committee. Until then there had been some interest in hosting the event from a number of European countries, but the practicalities, the risks and the costs dissuaded them all. The field was left open for

A five-a-side women's football team in Iran ° Caroline Penn/Panos Pictures

the only country prepared to put its money on the table: Uruguay. And Uruguay had money. Its wool, hide and beef industries had boomed throughout the 1920s. Eager to entrench and advertise the country's status as football world champion, Uruguay's government offered to pay visiting teams' expenses, proposed that the tournament begin in July 1930 - 100 years on from the inauguration of Uruguay's first independent constitution - and promised to build a new and fitting stadium for the occasion.

It was without doubt the finest football stadium yet built. In some ways it still is. The Centenario's capacity was less than that of Hampden Park or Wembley, but at 90,000 it was the largest outside the British Isles. Architecturally it was in a different league. Flush with overseas investment, government spending and rich, architecturally cultured patrons, the late 1920s had seen a building boom in Montevideo. Uruguay's architectural elite had been among the first and most enthusiastic students of the emergent minimalism and modernism of inter-war Europe.

It was in this context that Juan Scasso drew up his plans for the Centenario. It was to be Latin America's first reinforced concrete stadium, built as a double-tiered ellipse broken into four stands that fanned out like the multilayered petals of an art-deco

flower. The detailing of walkways, walls and seats stayed faithful to a core aesthetic of flush surfaces and simple patterns. For these structures alone, the Centenario was an exceptional stadium, but on the north side of the ground Scasso added his tour d'hommage, a nine-story tower rising 100 metres above the sunken pitch. It was and remains an extraordinary statement of modernist optimism.

At its base, the square walls of the tower sprouted the elegant aerodynamic wings of an aeroplane. At the front, the prow of a sleek, steel-hulled ship pitched upwards. The eye, following the prow of the ship, turned immediately up along the rectangular concrete fluting that ran all the way to the high flagpole at the very top of the tower. In the shadow of the tower, before a crowd that numbered more than 100,000 (20 per cent of the adult male population of the country), Uruguay and Argentina played the first World Cup final.

In spring 2004 I was lucky enough to be standing at the top of the tour d'hommage with Juan Capalan, the Director of the Museo de Futbol, and in a state of some excitement. 'This is where it all began. This is the spot. The single greatest collective human experience is watching the World Cup final. Global eclipses must slowly cross the earth's surface, but satellite television transmission is instantaneous.'

FOOTBALL

Girls playing football in the playground of the Islamic Alnahda Elementary School ° Stefan Boness/Panos Pictures

Box 7.1: Women and football

Though the evidence is on occasion rather thin, it seems clear that women played some of the many variants of global folk football. Accounts from native North America, the Japanese medieval court and English Shrove Tuesday games all suggest women playing either in mixed games or among themselves. The same cannot be said of the early development of association football. Women had no immediate access to the sport, which was nurtured in the exclusively male institutions of public school, university, old boys' clubs and the armed forces. Just as impartially, modern football was from its very inception tied to a vast ideological raft of Victorian masculinities that all presumed that sport, like the rest of the public realm, was a matter for men alone (on the history of women's football, see Williams 2003; Hong 2004).

In the face of structural and ideological constraints, upper-class women in Britain took to the field anyway. The first women's football match in England was played in 1895 when the South of England beat North London 7-1 in Crouch End. The Football Association and its European counterparts were quick to ban women from using their facilities or those of any clubs affiliated to them. The same strategy of exclusion was used in the 1920s to marginalise the women's football scene that had emerged from the munitions factories of the First World War. Football crowds, though never exclusively so, were overwhelmingly male.

Independent attempts to organise women's football began with the creation of the International Ladies Football Association in 1957 and the holding of a women's European Championship won by Manchester Corinthians. The Italian-based CIEFF was formed in 1969 and held informal women's world cups in Italy in 1970 and in Mexico in 1971. Driven by fear of losing control and by some dim recognition that women's football was a significant sporting force, FIFA and UEFA acted. UEFA called on all member nations' football associations to incorporate women's football into the mainstream.

In terms of participation and sporting success, women's football has three strongholds - North America, China and northern Europe, and it is gaining ground in sub-Saharan Africa. In America and China the relative weakness of men's football has created the space in which the game can grow. The United States boasts the only fully professional women's football league, though a year after its launch in 2003, the Women's United Soccer Association (WUSA) was in deep and irrevocable financial trouble. In northern Europe the egalitarianism and social engineering of social democratic governments has helped promote women's football. FIFA organised the first women's World Cup in 1991, and it has been played every four years since.

Table 7.1: Who plays where: registered football players by football confederation and gender, 2000

	FIFA	AFC	CAF	CONCAFAF	CONMEBOL	OFC	UEFA
PLAYERS/JUGADORES JOUERS/SPIELER	242,378	105,290	22,585	38,560	22,056	1,276	52,611
% OF POPULATION	4.1	3.0	2.9	8,4	6.5	4.4	6.7
MALE/MASCULINA/ HOMMES/MANNER	220,494	99,192	21,140	28,047	21,357	1,182	49,567
FEMALE/FEMENINA/ FEMMES/FRAUEN	21,884	6,098	1,445	10,513	690	94	3,044

Source: *FIFA (2000)*

Capalan nodded. 'In a thousand years, if we make it, people are going to make the same journey that I made to see the place where the most global phenomenon of the modern era of globalisation began,' I said. 'A shame,' Capalan replied, 'because the stadium will not be here. Its experimental concrete was not designed to resist the salty air of a coastal city'. 'Then it must be preserved. Shouldn't it be a UNESCO World Heritage site?'

Well, shouldn't it? Is there any cultural practice more global than football? Rites of birth, death and marriage are universal, but infinite in their diversity. Football is played by the same rules everywhere. No single world religion can match its geographical scope. The use of English and the vocabularies of science and mathematics must run football close for universality, but they remain the lingua francas of the world's elites, not of its masses. Only the most anodyne products of America's cultural industries can begin to claim a reach as wide as football, and then only for a fleeting and vacuous moment in those parts of the world that can afford

them. Football has not merely been consumed by the world's societies, it has been embraced, embedded and then transformed by them.

The World Cup, therefore, is the greatest regular opportunity for the peoples of the world to look at each other, however bizarre the lens of football makes us appear. Whether you are in the audience or not, football is a precious global cultural resource held in common, however much FIFA and the rest of the global football bureaucracy, the global media industries and multinational sponsors try to run it, own it or buy it. Football, in all its many guises, is one of the many webs of institutions and practices that create the fragile networks of global civil society. It is the pre-eminent mass global cultural phenomenon of the early twenty-first century and, for all its manifold faults and pathologies, is an enduring source of autonomous and universal ethics, aesthetics and moral values. At the very least, we should preserve the scintillating architecture of the stadium where its globalisation as a shared experience began.

The FIFA Football World Cup™, to give it its full title, is held every four years. Only the hosts now qualify automatically; everybody else must compete for the other 31 places in a two-year series of qualifying rounds; 15 places are allocated to UEFA, five to Africa, four to South America and three to Asia and CONCACAF*, the final place decided in play-off between a Latin American country and Oceania. It was first held in 1930 in Uruguay and, after missing 1942 and 1946 due to the Second World War, has been played ever since (on the history of the World Cup see Freddi 2006; Glanville 2006).

Uruguay 1930: Uruguay 4 Argentina 2. A national celebration and global publicity for Uruguay's' golden era in the magical Estadio Centenario.

Italy 1934: Italy 2 Czechoslovakia 1. Mussolini's Italy plays host, and ahead of the Berlin Olympics is the innovator in turning global sporting competition into a highly politicised spectacular.

France 1938: Italy 4 Hungary 2. France, after the fall of the Popular Front, is the host. The darkening shadows of the Second World War arrive as the Italian team is jeered by anti-fascists and exiles as they get off the train at Marseilles and again at all of their matches.

Brazil 1950: Uruguay 2 Brazil 1. The Brazilians use the World Cup to convince the world and themselves that post-Vargas Brazil has modernised and industrialised, and is ready to take its place in the world. In the greatest act of sporting hubris ever, Brazil effectively announces its victory before the final, only to lose to Uruguay.

Switzerland 1954: West Germany 3 Hungary 2. The first World Cup to be televised sees the West German team triumph in Switzerland, serving as a founding cultural moment of the Federal Republic and a relieved return to international normality for the pariah nation.

Sweden 1958: Brazil 5 Sweden 2. The whole world takes notice, Brazil wins the World Cup in Sweden and sets a benchmark for attractive football.

Chile 1962: Brazil 3 Czechoslovakia 1. World Cup hosting rights are becoming an increasingly political matter - the Chileans beg FIFA 'give us the World Cup for we have nothing else'. The last World Cup without global live television coverage.

England 1966: England 4 West Germany 2. Football comes home. England, after refusing to participate and then participating poorly, wins the World Cup at home. The arrival of slow-motion replays helps fuel controversy over England's winning goal.

Mexico 1970: Brazil 4 Italy 1. The first World Cup final to be televised live and in colour sees Brazil beat Italy in a defining moment for world football. Brazil plays the game that everyone wants to watch and play.

West Germany 1974: West Germany 2 Holland 1. The skies darken. Chilean dissidents protest over the Pinochet regime all through the first round, the tournament lives in fear of a repeat of the kidnappings at the 1972 Munich Olympics.

Argentina 1978: Argentina 3 Holland 1. Argentina's junta empties the country's coffers, and fills the nation's jails to put on the World Cup and pull out all the stops to win it. Its miraculous 6-0 victory over Peru remains heavily tainted.

Spain 1982: Italy 3 West Germany 1. Spain gets its turn in the sun at the first expanded World Cup: 24 teams in a Byzantine playing system that sees the first burst of rampant commercialism inside and outside the stadiums, and FIFA's own expenses exceed those of all the 24 squads put together.

Mexico 1986: Argentina 3 West Germany 2. Columbia holds the hosting rights but the endless civil war makes affording and staging the World Cup impossible. In the biggest stitch-up of the century, Mexico gets a second crack at the tournament, whisking the rights away from the super-organised but hopelessly naive Americans.

Italy 1990: West Germany 1 Argentina 0. Beyond the glitz, the essential dynamic of Italia 90's management is a shameless commercialism whose neo-liberal business school argot did not prevent the uptake of vast quantities of public subsidy. The Italian state spends billions of lire on the World Cup, the local organising committee raise another 60 billion lire in sponsorship and services from Italian companies, and they still lose money.

USA 1994: Brazil 0 Italy 0 (Brazil win on penalties 3-2). Football conquers America, or not. Despite vast crowds, global coverage and a reasonable national team performance, most of America manages to completely ignore the World Cup in its midst.

France 1998: France 3 Brazil 0. France's multi-ethnic national team wins at home, prompting an outpouring of French self-congratulation over their rainbow team and rainbow nation - an aura short-circuited by the riots and disorder in the *banlieue* in 2005.

South Korea-Japan 2002: Brazil 2 Germany 0. Asia's first World Cup. Japan and South Korea chosen as co-hosts after two years of intensely bitter and politicised lobbying. FIFA takes the soft option by asking them to split the tournament. Like an estranged couple they manage to operate in the same space without even looking at each other.

---

* Confederation of North, Central American and Caribbean Association Football. See Box 7.3 for explanations of abbreviations used in this chapter

AFC (Asian Football Confederation): the Asian football confederation spent its first 30 years trying to grapple with the impossible size and diversity of the continent that made regular international football difficult. Only since the mid-1990s has it been able to attract sponsorship that made international tournaments feasible. Now experiencing massive economic growth in the Far East.

CAF (Confédération Africaine de Football): formed in 1957 with just the four independent African nations of the era - Ethiopia, Egypt, South Africa and Sudan. South Africa's refusal to field multi-ethnic teams saw them banned. From its inception CAF had been infused with a sense of pan-African identity and pride. Currently dominated by francophone West Africans.

CONCACAF (Confederation of North, Central American and Caribbean Association Football): The Americas minus CONMEBOL puts North America, Mexico, the Caribbean and Central America together.

CONMEBOL (CONfederación sudaMEricana de FútBOL): the oldest football confederation, it consists of all of South America apart from Guyana, French Guiana and Surinam, whose size and footballing backwardness properly places them in the Caribbean. The pioneers of bloc voting and organisation within FIFA.

FIFA (Fédération Internationale de Football Association): founded in 1904, the unelected global INGO that runs football from its Swiss fortress.

IAFB (International Association Football Board): originally established by the four British 'home nations' in 1886, it now shares membership of the ultimate rule-making body for football with four FIFA members.

OFC (Oceania Football Confederation): the slightly ludicrous geography of global football created OFC in 1966, putting Australasia together with the tiny island archipelagos of the Pacific. Australia in particular has found membership to be highly restrictive and even damaging to its teams' chances, and, in parallel with the country's Asia-orientated diplomacy and trade, has recently joined AFC for World Cup qualifying purposes.

UEFA (Union of European Football Associations): europe's governing body, though this includes states as far east as Kazakhstan and ,since 1992, Israel (diplomatically removed from the Asian Zone). As the organiser of the European Champions League, it is easily the most wealthy and powerful of the confederations, and is run more transparently than any other too. Its recent record on anti-racism is also very strong.

David Beckham in China © Qilai Shen/Panos Pictures

Football and civil society

What we are witnessing may be quite simply the death of the cherished, though rather flimsily based assumption that sport can remain permanently superior to the society it serves. If that belief is indeed shown to be a delusion, we are all in trouble...Without idealism, sport does not exist. Romance and honesty and fair play are not outmoded concepts but the basic apparatus of its survival. If sport ceases to be a slightly fantastic metaphor for life...and becomes just another sleazy part of it, sport is a waste of time. (McIlvanney 1999)

The assumption that sport might permanently remain superior to the societies that play it was never tenable. In this, McIlvanney is a sociological rather than a sporting romantic. Spectaculars require backers. The circus must be organised and paid for, and no more so than in football. Football attracts and must therefore deal with power and money, which will always be looking to buy or take their share of glory. But glory bought or stolen turns to dust. The drama and its outcome cannot be decided by the forces of money and power. Victory should not be bought. Allegiances should not be imposed. Love is not

tradeable, nor can it be ruled. Yet so often in its transition from a chaotic folk ritual to a sector of the global entertainment industry, football has sunk to the level of venality and instrumentalism prevalent in wider society. Referees have been bought, linesmen have been corralled and games have been thrown. Players, clubs and fans have been exploited, liquidated, mistreated and thrown on the scrap heap. Across the world, football's bureaucracies have been run as personal fiefdoms and political campaign machines. Violence, racism and bigotry have constantly staked their place on and off the pitch.

Yet, for all the historical evidence, the potency of McIlvanney's claim is undeniable. Football offers something else. Intrinsically it resists these deformations because in the end football is just a game. Indeed, that is its essential virtue. It is bound by rules and structured by values that are its own autonomous creation. As a game it insists on a universalism of access and the rule of law. The multiple bottom lines for those who play and follow football are not calculated in money or power but in victories and pleasures. But the meaning of victory in

Box 7.4: Football - game rules of a conflict

One event many analysts identify as the first act of ethnically motivated violence in wars in former Yugoslavia took place not on a battlefield but on a football field. On 13 May 1990, more than one year before the 'real war' began, supporters of Serbia's Red Star Belgrade and Croatia's Dynamo Zagreb clashed in a stadium in Zagreb, Croatia, prior to the Yugoslavian league game (which never took place), with dozens of injuries on both sides. The initial causes of the incident remain murky as all sides blame one another, but how the violence began is not really important. What is important is that all sides in the then still united Yugoslavia became aware of the extent of the tragedy soon to follow. Rivalry that started as classical football hooliganism and 'machismo' soon acquired an ethnic and nationalist identity. Coupled with the growing anti-Communist hysteria of the late 1980s, organised football supporters claimed the unofficial title 'the voice of people', the people who were not afraid to speak out against the regime.

With weakening Communist rule and growing calls for democratisation, newly formed political parties with nationalist platforms, populist leadership, and opportunist individuals in all former Yugoslavian republics provided funds and logistics to the organised football supporters. The potential to attract sympathisers of political interests gained momentum in the context of a deteriorating economic situation and rising ethnic tensions in the country in the late 1980s and early 1990s. Since the media were still under the government's control and public gatherings either forbidden or strictly monitored, football games with thousands of spectators and nationwide live television and radio coverage seemed the most promising recruitment grounds and propaganda venues. Banners and flags with nationalist symbols banned under Communist rule began appearing at football stadiums in the late 1980s. Despite the risk of persecution and severe punishment, local authorities first ignored and later even encouraged such symbols during games. Slogans and songs praising one ethnic group's historical figures and expressing nationalist insults became part of the now mandatory football choreography, especially if clubs played on 'foreign' territory. Eventually, the nationalists successfully awakened extreme ethnic consciousness in thousands of young men, and used images from stadiums throughout Yugoslavia to show others the strength of their support or the threats other groups posed. Thousands of chanting supporters, songs, banners, flags, fireworks, all constituted an important part of nationalist political propaganda in the guise of football fans' routines.

In spring 1991, during the Yugoslavian football cup game in the city of Split, Croatia, supporters of another Croatian club, Hajduk, snatched the Yugoslavian national flag from the mast and burned it in front of television cameras. Millions of people from all ethnic groups finally realised that the Yugoslavia they used to know was no more. Opportunists seized the moment and used it for their own purposes, and instead of downplaying the incident they chose to magnify it to an extent that would suit all sides' different interests. Croats used the burning of the flag to mark the beginning of their struggle for an independent Croatia, while Franjo Tudjman, the late Croatian President, publicly endorsed it and used the wave of public support for the incident to boost his political party's popularity. Serbs, in turn, blamed the Croats for deliberately trying to destroy the Yugoslavian unity.

The deteriorating economic and security situation in former Yugoslavia in 1990-1 failed to keep people from football stadiums. Violence followed almost every major game played during that period, and some analysts go as far as to suggest that football hooliganism was probably the spark that started the war.

Already, with the first gunshots in the early summer of 1991, football fans eager to show off their 'courage' voluntarily joined the ranks of the regular military, the police, or notorious paramilitary groups such as 'Arkan's Tigers'. Zeljko Raznatovic, widely known as 'Arkan', the most feared and notorious paramilitary commander in the Balkans, who was later indicted for war crimes at the International Criminal Tribunal for the former Yugoslavia (ICTY) in the Hague, was also the leader of Red Star Belgrade Fan Club 'Delije', or 'the tough guys'. Prior to his assassination in January 2000, attributed to Serbia's organised crime gangs, Arkan used his influence and 'fame' as a tough guy to recruit young, impulsive, and passionate individuals into the ranks of his paramilitary group. None of that would have been possible without the knowledge and the approval of Serbia's political leadership. Furthermore, Croatia's Dynamo fans, better known as 'Bad Blue Boys' (BBBs), also joined the military and paramilitary forces. Outside Dynamo's stadium in Zagreb, one can spot a monument for the BBBs who died during the war and who are honoured not on Croatia's independence day but on 13 May. Delije and BBBs made the 'honourable' decision that, instead of continuing the fight using fists, rocks and baseball bats on streets and parks around Yugoslavian stadiums, they should put on uniforms and take up weapons.

Within a few months after the outbreak of war, the UN Security Council imposed sports sanctions, among others, upon Serbia and Montenegro, which included a prohibition on playing international football. However, the reality is that most of those who used football for selfish political ends never experienced the violence themselves. Some of these leaders are now dead, while some of those who survived are sitting in ICTY's detention centre in The Hague, facing war crimes charges for their role in the bloodshed. Inmates reside on the same floor regardless of their ethnic origin, watch television together, cook and spend time in a fitness centre. Ironically, their favourite pastime is football, and so far no incidents have been reported from the detention centre. If only there had been a way to put them all together in one place where they could play football with each other before the war started. Maybe then football would have gained a value beyond its instrumentalisation for political violence. It might seem an odd coincidence, but only a few months before the war in Yugoslavia reached the point of no return, Red Star Belgrade won the national title as well as UEFA's Champions League title in May 1991. Red Star was and still is from Belgrade, but its star players came from all ethnic backgrounds, and the star player was Robert Prosinecki, a Croat. Prosinecki played a crucial role in the final of UEFA Champions League on 29 May 1991 and was given a hero's welcome in Belgrade.

Haled Al-Hashimi, Technical University of Berlin, and Carolin Goerzig, Ludwig Maximilians University, Munich

this realm cannot be compared with that on the real battlefields of the world. Football matches do not change social structures; no victory, however comprehensive, can shift the real balance of power or change the actual distribution of wealth and status. But they offer glory. For winning, and winning in style. For winning because you were the best, the quickest, the cleverest. Because, when it came to it on the pitch, when the whistle blew and money, power, status, reputation and history were all sent to the dugout, you wanted it more. You rode your luck and you took your chances when they came.

And its pleasures? There is the love of playing the game. Because, before the great club colours were chosen and the monumental stadiums were raised and filled, people just played anywhere. There is the love of watching the game. Because, before the pitch was circled with fences and turnstiles, before the earth was circled with television satellites, before there were giant screens and action replays, people just came to watch. There is the love of following the game. Because the game is not just an art, it's drama, too. It has great metropolitan and minor provincial theatres, with free-spending and penny-pinching impresarios and their megalomaniac, obsessive directors. It has legions of critics and a fantastical rotating cast of angels and devils, geniuses and journeymen, fallen giants and rising stars. It offers the spotlight for individual brilliance while relishing the

defiance and heart of collective endeavour. It has staged tragedy and comedy, epic and pantomime, unsophisticated music hall and inaccessible experimental performances. It does imperious triumph, lucky escapes, impossible comebacks and stubborn stalemates. It captures the brilliance of unpredictability, the uncertainties of the human heart and human skill, of improvisation and chance. And those that follow it are not merely the crowd, they are the chorus. Consumers and commentators, spectators and participants, without whom every goal is just a ball in the back of the net, every victory just three points in the bag.

But if football does reflect the most genial and appealing dimension of civil societies it also displays and nurtures its darker side, and no more so than in its capacity to generate human solidarity - surely the sine qua non of any civil society. Football offers love of us and hatred of them. Because, before clubs became global brands, before club crests competed with corporate logos, football had become entwined with every conceivable social identity and the social divisions that surely follow them: Derby Day in Glasgow; Belfast and Dundee pitches Catholic against Protestant; in Calcutta it aligns Hindu Mohan Bagun against Muslim Mohammedan Sporting. In Athens, AEK are the migrant refugees from the Greco-Turkish war contesting the turf, 80 years later, with the locals of Olympiakos. Through the multiple acts of playing, organising,

Figure 7.1: FIFA membership, 1910-2000

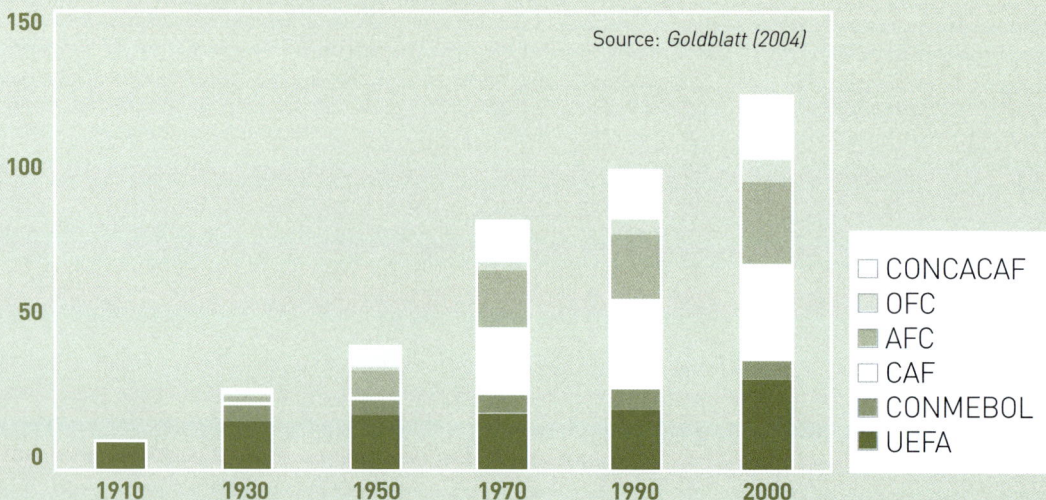

Source: Goldblatt (2004)

Originally built for the Olympic Games of 1936, the Berlin stadium has been renovated for the 2006 football World Cup
© *Stefan Boness/Panos Pictures*

watching and following, people have defined and expressed who they think they and their neighbours are.

Football possesses its own autonomous networks and organisation. It is oriented towards values and pleasures, aesthetic and dramatic standards that can be judged only on their own terms, and whose authenticity and integrity are undermined by their excessive alignment with money and power. Like every civil society, football is a source of the most profound forms of solidarity and imagined communities - though it offers no guarantees of harmony and peace. Football thus serves as both practical problem and lucid metaphor for the complex relationship between civil societies and the formal spheres of economic and political power. In the following section I want to focus on how this interrelationship has been organised at a global level and with what consequences.

The globalisation of football: a very brief history

Under the auspices of Britain's public schools and elite universities, and their strange alliance of muscular Christians, imperial ideologues and old-boy gentleman players, the rules, techniques and culture of many modern sports were first determined:

football, cricket, rugby, tennis, not to mention hockey, polo, rounders, table tennis and croquet. The transformation of football into a regularised, rule-bound, national amateur passion must therefore be seen in the wider context of Britain's unique place in the invention and codification of modern sport (Murray 1994; Goldblatt 2006).

In the two decades that followed the creation of the resolutely aristocratic and amateur Football Association (FA) and its rules in 1863, football spread like wildfire, carried by evangelical emissaries in Sunday schools, teachers' colleges and boys' clubs. The game travelled from England to the Celtic nations, from London and the south to the Midlands and the north, from the elite to the Victorian middle and working classes, from just playing the game to watching and following it. By the mid-1880s games were attracting five-figure crowds; fierce local loyalties and enmities were being established.

British football parallels the course of Britain's Industrial Revolution. Blessed and cursed by being first, its Industrial Revolution overwhelmed the world's economies. In the 1880s its football, based on the massive, extraordinary weight of working-class

Figure 7.2: World Cup television audience (millions), 1986-2006

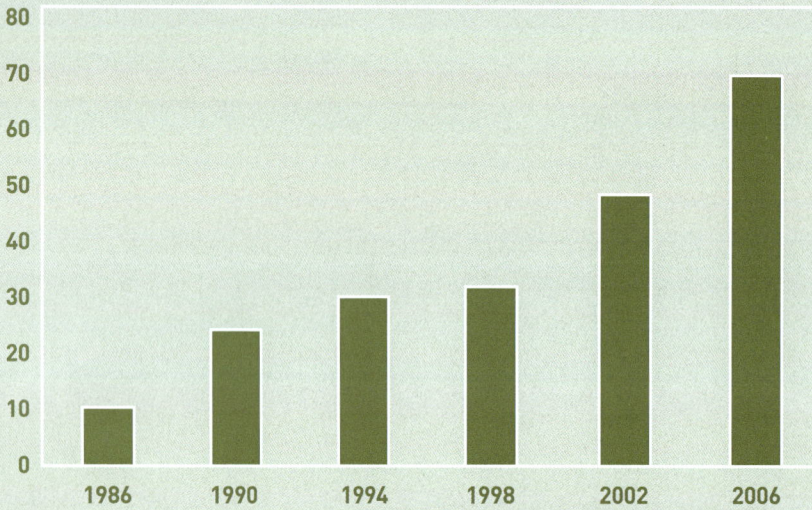

Source: *FIFA (2002)*

Figure 7.3: Value of World Cup television rights (in millions of Swiss francs), 1986-2006

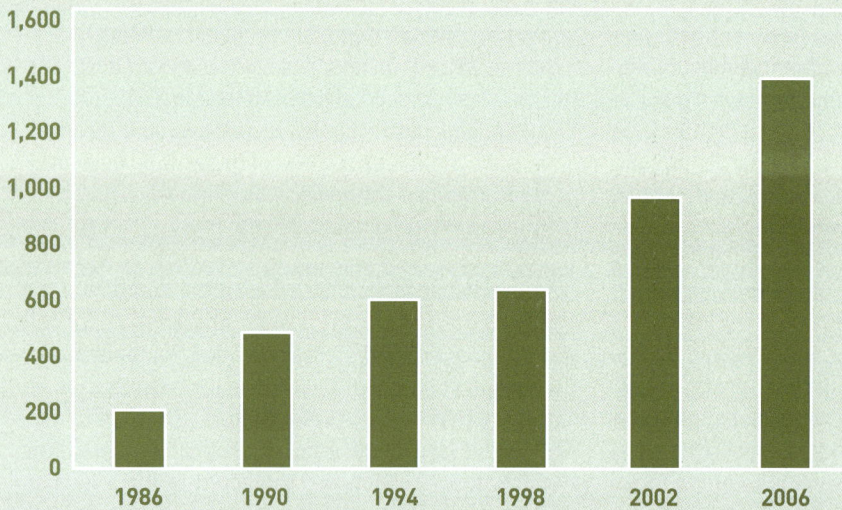

Source: *FIFA (2002)*

The national stadium, Freetown, Sierra Leone ©*Pep Bonet/Panos Pictures*

participation and support, hurtled inevitably towards professionalisation. Increasing free time, income and confidence among the organised working classes, allied to the ambitious new money of northern traders and entrepreneurs, saw competitive football attract fans, money and investment.

From the late 1860s Britons were everywhere: migrant textile workers in the Netherlands, embassy staff in Stockholm, Scottish gardeners in Vienna, English teachers in Bruges, colonial officials and cartographers in Rangoon, factory managers in Moscow, expatriate coffee merchants in Sao Paulo. All took football with them, and everywhere, with a passion and fascination unimaginable now in a world suffused with football, people started playing. First among the significant expatriate communities in Buenos Aires, Vienna, Montevideo and Mexico City; then among the local urban elites and professionals, who in a matter of years had taken the game over; and finally among the urban masses, who not only played the game but followed it too. By the eve of the First World War football associations were established in every region of the earth. The majority of the world's leading clubs had been founded by this date.

The origins of international football are remarkably parochial. It is only in the geography of football (and rugby) that England versus Scotland constituted an international encounter. During the four years after 1863 the only such games were between England and Scotland, then in 1876 the Welsh took on the Scots for the first time and an Irish team first played in 1882. International football, it appeared, was to be conducted between stateless nations rather than nation-states or empires. But then there was no one else to debate the technicalities of the matter. At the end of the nineteenth century Britain alone made the rules on and off the pitch. In 1882 representatives of the four home nations' (as they were collectively referred to) football associations met and created the International Association Football Board (IAFB), which was to serve as the ultimate football law-making body. As early as 1896 Canada and the USA had set up a number of thinly attended international fixtures. In Latin America, Argentina and Uruguay began to play each other - officially - in 1901. Austria and Hungary followed suit in 1902. Both pairings created a public spectacle and rivalry that was of at least equal social intensity to the England-Scotland clash.

Alongside this emergent network of international

Box 7.5: **Football against racism**

Football has a long and dishonourable relationship with racism. In Brazil in the early twentieth century, black players were barred from the leading clubs, and the president actually insisted that no black players represent the nation at the Copa America. When black players forced their way into the game in the 1920s, they still had to endure 'Jim Crow'-style regulation to keep them out. White Europeans, for the most part, adopted a form of sporting apartheid in their African and Asian colonies (on racism in football, see Back, Crabbe and Solomos 2001; Merkel and Tokarski 1996; Vasili 2000).

Black players were rare in, though not wholly absent from, European football before the 1970s. Pioneers in England include West African Arthur Wharton, who played in goal for Preston North End in 1887 and later for Rotherham, Walter Tull at Tottenham in the 1920s, and Jack Leslie at Plymouth in the 1930s. The leading black players of the 1960s, South African Albert Johansson at Leeds and Barbadian Clive Best at West Ham, had to endure from both the press and the crowd an assumption of inconsistency and lack of fibre and fighting spirit. In the early 1970s, the first generation of British-born black players, drawn almost entirely from Afro-Caribbean communities, broke into professional football. Their ascent is all the more remarkable when one considers the degree of open and institutionalised racism that they encountered. Many crowds, and not just those segments where the skinheads and National Front organisers were present, demonstrated the depth of racist attitudes in England. The wave of abuse that could be heard in the nation's stadiums sprang effortlessly from a ready-made vocabulary of invective and a deep historical reservoir of ignorance and prejudice. Most crude and gruesome of all was the booing and monkey chanting of players on the ball and the playground spite of 'get back on your jam jar'. And showering the pitch with bananas; one of the more cowardly weapons in the armoury of racist abuse. Meantime, the FA saw nothing, and the television coverage and commentary teams miraculously rendered it all invisible.

It was against this background that the first anti-racist campaigns in world football were launched. The Let's Kick Racism Out of Football campaign was started by the Commission for Racial Equality and the Professional Footballers' Association in 1993 (www.kickitout.org). In the UK, it is supported by all the game's governing bodies, supporters' organisations and local authorities. It has been joined by the more grass roots-oriented Football Unites, Racism Divides (www.furd.org), which was started in 1995 by a group of Sheffield United fans. They have been pioneers in educating, campaigning and acting on the issue of racism in football. In the late 1990s, as the numbers of black players and black migrants to European countries increased, revealing a deep and unreflective strain of Continental racism, similar campaigns were established, and they are now grouped as Football Against Racism in Europe (FARE), a network of organisations from 13 European countries set up in February 1999 (www.farenet.org). FARE's members, who all conduct their own domestic anti-racism campaigns, include, in Austria, Fair Play (www.fairplay.or.at); in Germany, Flutlicht - Verein für antirassistische Fussballkultur (www.flutlicht.org); in France, Ligue Internationale Contre le Racisme et l'Antisémitisme (LICRA) (www.licra.org/licrasport); in Poland, Never Again Association - Stowarzyszenie Nigdy Wiecej (http://free.ngo.pl/nw/); in Italy, Progetto Ultrà - UISP Emilia Romagna (www.progettoultra.it) and Unione Italiana Sport Per Tutti (UISP) (www.uisp.it); and the leading campaign group against homophobia in sport, European Gay & Lesbian Sport Federation (EGLSF) (www.gaysport.info).

Since the turn of the Millennium, UEFA has become much more actively involved in challenging racism in European football, and its ten-point plan developed with FARE for tackling racism (UEFA 2002) gives a good indication of all of their work:

1. Issue a statement saying the club will not tolerate racism, spelling out the action it will take against those engaged in racist chanting. The statement should be printed in all match programmes and displayed permanently and prominently around the ground.
2. Make public address announcements condemning racist chanting at matches.
3. Make it a condition for season-ticket holders that they do not take part in racist abuse.
4. Take action to prevent the sale of racist literature inside and around the ground.
5. Take disciplinary action against players who engage in racial abuse.
6. Contact other clubs to make sure they understand the club's policy on racism.
7. Encourage a common strategy between stewards and police for dealing with racist abuse.
8. Remove all racist graffiti from the ground as a matter of urgency.
9. Adopt an equal opportunities policy in relation to employment and service provision.
10. Work with all other groups and agencies, such as the players' union, supporters, schools, voluntary organisations, youth clubs, sponsors, local authorities, local businesses and police, to develop pro active programmes and make progress to raise awareness of campaigning to eliminate racial abuse and discrimination.

Colombians watching Colombia versus Argentina on television °Jeremy Horner/Panos Pictures

football, the early twentieth century also saw the development of transnational football. In the cultural and political spaces not yet overrun by homogenous centralising, border-closing nation states, the international football scene was full of pleasing anomalies. In Britain, Scottish, Welsh and Irish teams were often participants in the notionally English FA Cup. The best teams from Hungary and Bohemia were invited to Vienna to play in Der Challenge Cup. Stade Helvetica, the team of Swiss expatriates in Marseilles, won the French championship, while teams from south-western France and northern Spain played in the cross-border Pyrenean Cup before a national tournament existed in either country. Milan and other leading northern Italian clubs crossed the Alps to play the Chiasso Cup in Switzerland from 1901. Yet Milan would not meet a team from Rome till 1911.

The development of cross-border postal networks, telegraph lines and railways, all in the later half of the nineteenth century, were the infrastructural preconditions of regularised international sport of any kind. These new networks of communication necessitated the creation of international institutions of regulation and technical standardisation, such as the International Telegraph Union, created in 1865,

and the Universal Postal Union, established in 1874. Against that background it was obvious to a small group of Western European football administrators that some kind of international regulation and systematisation of football was required. On 21 May in Rue St Honaire in Paris, FIFA, or, in its full Gallic glory, Fédération Internationale de Football Association, was formed by delegates from seven countries: Belgium, Denmark, France, the Netherlands, Spain, Switzerland, and Sweden. Initially, the British stayed aloof but joined later (only to leave twice in the 1920s). Germany, Austria, Italy and Hungary signed up immediately.

European and American elites thought attitudes to international sport and international politics in the first half of the twentieth century split three ways: that they were best kept well apart; that sport was war or at least politics by other means; or that sport could underpin a utopian politics of peace. In the great arc of world history between the foundation of FIFA in 1904 and the 1934 World Cup, the Olympian vision of football, indeed of any sport, as a universalist peacemaker was reduced to tatters. Nationalist politics crushed these hopes, hijacking both the staging of sporting contests and the meaning that they were invested with among domestic publics and

Box 7.6: Independent football supporters and fan projects

Football Supporters International is a web portal and a network of unofficial and grass-roots supporters clubs and fan projects that are collaborating to provide fan embassies at major tournaments, and facilitate carnivalesque celebrations (www.footballsupportersinternational.com). Members of the network include: in England, the Football Supporters' Federation (www.fsf.org.uk); in Germany, Koordinationsstelle Fan-Projekte (www.kos-fanprojekte.de); in the Netherlands, Landelijk Informatiepunt Supportersprojecten (LIS) (www.lisnet.nl) and Eurosupport (www.footballsupporters.info); in Switzerland, Fanprojekt Basel (www.fanprojekt-basel.ch). All of these groups have become involved with campaigning nationally and at a European level on issues around ticket prices, racism, policing and safety.

in the international political arena. By the time of the grotesque propaganda exercise that was the 1936 Berlin Olympics, any residual hope that the Olympian spirit was sufficiently powerful to neutralise the pathological passions of nationalism was looking threadbare. The British position - that politics was simply not appropriate or relevant to the conduct of the game whatever its actual worth - became impossible to sustain in the face of opponents who increasingly invested football matches and football prowess with cultural and political weight.

Despite the best intentions of FIFA and its heartfelt gentlemanly, progressive liberalism, international football became deeply politicised, a process that reached its pre-war apogee in Mussolini's Italy at the 1934 World Cup. In retrospect perhaps this was inevitable, for international football came of age at precisely the moment that mass ultra-nationalist politics was at its height in Europe and Latin America. More finally attuned to the manipulation of popular taste, more ready and able to intervene in mass culture than the bubbling empires of fin-de-siècle Europe, the new dictators and populists of the 1920s and 1930s took a close and active interest in the game.

When FIFA reconstituted itself at the end of the Second World War, it had just 54 members – over half of them European and around another fifth from Latin America. By 1974 membership had grown to 140, with Europeans and Latin Americans making up less than a third of the total. Europe, whose borders seemed permanently frozen by the Cold War, had added an extra Germany and the ex-British micro-colonies of Cyprus and Malta. In Latin America, Colombia was expelled and then let back in, and Venezuela, always the continent's most backward football nation, finally

joined. The other 90 or so new members came from three regions: Africa, Asia and the Caribbean. This in turn was the result of a deluge of state formation that followed the almost total dismantling of every remaining European empire but the Portuguese, whose final ignominious collapse came in 1975. Yet despite this remarkable global expansion, FIFA remained what it had always been: a minuscule, cash-strapped, understaffed, micro-bureaucracy, institutionally dominated by Europeans, challenged by Latin Americans and dismissive of everyone else. All of this was transformed in 1974 when the incumbent President Sir Stanley Rous lost his office to Joao Havelange, President of the Brazilian Football Federation.

The Brazilian had run a lengthy and expensive campaign against Rous in the early 1970s, mobilising developing-world dissent and offering a programme of expansion and aid. Havelange's accession to the throne ushered in an era in which football would be globalised and commercialised. The decisive moment in Havelange's reign came over dinner with Horst Dassler, the son of Adi Dassler, the founder of the sports goods conglomerate Adidas, and then chief executive of Adidas France. The question was: how could they catalyse the intersection of the World Cup, the growing global television market, and corporate sponsorship to generate a vast revenue stream for all of them? The answer they came up with, and the model of global sporting commercialisation that evolved over the next decade, has provided the template for every major exercise in global sports sponsorship. When this model was combined with the global transformations of live television broadcast, as well as the diffusion of television sets to every last corner of the planet, the scale and profile of the World

Children with a home-made football, Mashimoni Squatters' Primary School, Nairobi. *°Crispin Hughes/Panos Pictures*

Box 7.7: The football and social development network

Over the last 20 years, aid agencies and development ministries have become increasingly aware of the potential of football as an instrument of social development and community building in the developing world. The Nordic governments have been at the forefront of this. Streetfootballworld is a UN-supported web portal and organisation linking and supporting a network of development and football projects across the world (www.streetfootballworld.org). The World Cup in Germany has, for the first time, hosted street footballers from across the world in a tournament running parallel to the 2006 FIFA World Cup.

One of the best examples of this kind project is the Mathare Youth Sports Association (MYSA) from Nairobi, Kenya. The MYSA project started in 1987 as the first street football project in Africa. Boys and girls from more than 60 slum areas now take part in the programmes, where they combine environmental work, cleaning up Mathare, with education and organised football (see the excellent field work on the project in Hognestad and Tollinson 2004).

Cup and regional football tournaments between national teams like the European Championships, the Asian Cup and the African Cup of Nations grew stupendously.

Under Havelange, FIFA's membership continued to rise as the organisation mopped up the new states emerging from the now defunct Portuguese empire. In keeping with the president's political fondness for small associations (whose votes were equal in power to that of the largest nations, but whose poverty made them much more coaxable), FIFA added the micro-states and Lilliputian islands of the world. Between 1976 and 1990 FIFA accepted the membership of Grenada, Belize, St Lucia and St Vincent from the Caribbean; San Marino and the Faroe Islands in Europe; the Solomon Islands, Vanuatu, Samoa and Tahiti in the Pacific; and, just for good measure, Macao, Rwanda, Oman, the Seychelles and the Maldives. The disintegration of the Soviet empire and Yugoslavia would add another set of new states in the 1990s. FIFA's membership now easily exceeds that of the UN.

An empire of such global proportions required a new capital, and Havelange supplied it when he replaced the sleepy Swiss villa-office of the Rous era with the gleaming but angular white concrete and glass of the new FIFA house, which held over 100 full-time staff. The emperor himself was acquiring a new level of significance and power, too. In the fearsome battle between the Swiss and the French for the rights to host the 1998 World Cup, the Swiss Football Federation nominated Havelange for the Nobel Peace Prize. The standing ovation that followed the announcement would have shamed Kim Il Jung II. Not that the French were above such sycophancy; Mitterrand awarded Havelange the Légion d'honneur. Havelange did not receive, and has not received, the Nobel Peace Prize, but that can hardly have bothered the dark lord who articulated the transformation of his, and FIFA's, global status with remarkable candour:

> I've been to Russia twice, invited by President Yeltsin. I've been to Poland with their President. In the 1990 World Cup in Italy I saw Pope John Paul II three times. When I go to Saudi Arabia, King Fahd welcomes me in a splendid fashion. In Belgium, I had a one-and-a-half hour meeting with King Albert. Do you think a head of state will spare that much time for just anyone? That's respect. That's

the strength of FIFA. I can talk to any President, but they'll be talking to a President too on an equal basis. They've got their power and I've got mine; the power of football, which is the greatest power there is. (Quoted in Yallop 1999)

The balance sheet

Havelange was not kidding. He is not a man to kid around. He can rightly argue that under his presidency, FIFA was transformed from a sleepy sporting association into one of the most important cultural INGOs in the world. FIFA has pioneered and refined the core model of sports sponsorship and global television coverage that has transformed the economics and presentation of the world's sporting spectaculars. FIFA can also claim that it has opened those spectaculars to the developing world and the previously excluded by organising and promoting the Women's World Cup, creating a World Youth Cup, expanding the World Cup itself, and, finally, awarding hosting rights to Africa. It has paid out significant development monies to peripheral football associations and aligned itself with the UN and its core agencies in areas as diverse as childcare, conflict resolution and health promotion campaigns. None of which means that the power of football is Joao Havelange's, FIFA's or anyone else's alone. Such unrepentant and patrician self-importance is the first of many structurally ingrained problems with the global governance of football.

It is not merely a question of pomp and pomposity but an institutionally ingrained style of governance that is authoritarian and secretive. In the twenty-first century, the custodians of one the world's most significant shared cultural properties simply cannot be allowed to operate in this way. The legitimacy of FIFA and indeed all international sporting organisations rests on nothing more than having got there first and having the support of national football associations whose own legitimacy and authority are similarly threadbare. This structural inadequacy had been made worse by the autocratic and duplicitous behaviour of the organisation. FIFA's level of transparency and accountability make the World Bank look good. Its internal political machinations, if not quite the Kremlin under Communism, would not pass muster of the kinds of international group that observe national elections. Beholden only to itself and hidden behind Swiss criminal and banking law, FIFA's democratic credentials are zero (for a blow-by-blow account of

Austria celebrate their victory in the 2003 Homeless World Cup Championship ©*The Homeless World Cup*

Box 7.8: **Alternative world cups**

The Homeless World Cup (www.streetsoccer.org) has been running since 2003. It brings together street football teams from around the world, especially those linked to the global network of street papers like *The Big Issue* in the UK. It has created an opportunity to globalise and publicise the issue of homelessness, and offers homeless people a unique opportunity for travel and personal development.

The Mondiali Antirazzisti (Anti-racist World Cup, www.mondialiantirazzisti.org) was started in 1996 in Italy and has been held annually ever since. In 2006 it hosted more than 200 teams from all over the world. It combines football with festivals, conferences and music, publicising the anti-racist issue in football and creating new links and networks among progressive forces in the football world.

The Unrepresented Nations and Peoples Organization (UNPO, www.unpo.org) is an international organisation made up of indigenous peoples, occupied nations, minorities and independent states or territories that have joined together to protect their human and cultural rights, preserve their environments, and find non-violent solutions to conflicts that affect them. The UNPO Football Cup is a tournament for teams formed from nations, minorities and indigenous peoples that are prevented from participating in the official world of sports. The first tournament took place in 2005 prior to a meeting of the General Assembly of UNPO.

FIFA's mode of operations, see Yallop 1999; Sugden and Tomlinson 1998; 2003).

That said, even were FIFA to be profoundly reformed there remains at the core of global football's dilemmas the conflict between cosmopolitanism and internationalism. On the one hand, football clearly functions as a kind of universal language. Like other visual arts it does not suffer from problems of translatability. Perhaps most importantly, despite its English origins, it is not perceived to be the game or the property of any particular nation or region. On the other hand, this kind of cosmopolitan framework is counterpoised against the national organisation of football associations and football teams, whose interaction is closer to a sporting Hobbesian war of all against all than a global cooperative network or community. The irredeemably national and competitive qualities of international football has, despite its promise of mutual understanding and shared cultural horizons, made it a limited instrument of détente, diplomacy and conflict resolution, most famously recounted by Ryzard Kapuscinski in *The Soccer War* (1990), in which a World Cup qualifying game between Honduras and El Salvador provides the spark for the already dry tinder of hostilities and conflict over illegal migration and land squatting on the border.

The various international encounters between the two Germanies at the 1974 World Cup and between Iran and the USA in the 1998 World Cup, friendlies between the two Koreas, and the co-hosting of the 2002 World Cup by the still embittered neighbours South Korea and Japan have, for all the hype made little or no contribution to improving international relationships. Indeed, in the case of East Germany's victory over West Germany in 1974, it mainly served to reinforce the separation of the states. In Korea-Japan 2002, the atmosphere of mutual collaboration was so strong that the gigantic opening ceremony in Seoul managed a two-hour spectacular visual display without a single reference to the Japanese co-hosts.

Experiments with international football as an instrument of conflict resolution have also proved mixed. In 2003 the Brazilian UN peacekeeping force in Haiti brought the national team to Port-au-Prince to play a game against its hosts. The column of white armoured cars and Brazil's leading players won a great deal of goodwill and attracted a peaceful multitude onto the streets, but its contribution to halting the miserable disintegration of Haitian politics was nugatory. In Liberia, specially arranged football games, including those of the national team, have provided the opportunity for well-observed truces among combatants, but fighting has resumed afterwards with monotonous regularity.

In the end, competitive football does not and cannot stop wars, nor will it make the peace, and we should not expect it to. Rather, what could give real content and life to the cosmopolitan solidarities that football promises is its potential as an instrument of global youth work, social work and community capacity building. For example there is a growing band of alternative and parallel World Cups that bring together global causes including the homeless, anti-racism and migrant groups, and unrepresented peoples and nations (Box 7.5). Across the developing world there are thousands of projects and local NGOs engaged in this kind of work, some supported by international development agencies. Street football is providing a network and umbrella to bring them together (Box 7.7). FIFA's record in this area is rather mixed. Clearly significant sums, most recently through the Goal Programme, have passed from the centre to the peripheries. However, those funds have been almost exclusively channelled through national football associations and orientated towards elite football. As a consequence, hardly any monies have trickled down into the area of greatest sporting need in the developing world. More alarmingly, there is a rising tide of evidence to suggest that national football associations and their officers are corrupt (Jennings 2002; 2003).

Democratising the global game

Football offers a glimpse of democracy. Its simplicity and flexibility make it open to all. Its unpredictability and variability suggest the possibility that the force of better play might prevail over any extraneous considerations. But in reality the social organisation and culture of football have always been marked by inequalities of power. In authoritarian societies national football associations have been invariably controlled from above. In more democratic societies they have acquired more autonomy from the state, but are monopolised by closed, conservative and self-replicating elites whose relationship to transparency and accountability is passing at best. For most of the twentieth century clubs and directors held a fearsome whip hand over professional players with a combination of restrictive contracts and maximum wages. Players' unions have used strike action to break some of these restrictions and create a free labour market in which the highly skilled now hold all the cards.

The most excluded group from football's decision-making processes has been the supporters. Fans' loyalty to their clubs and the intensity of their pleasures have made mobilising their main instrument of power - staying away and not paying up - peculiarly hard to organise. Fans strikes and stay-aways, although occasionally organised successfully, have been few and far between. The socio model of club organisation in Iberia and Latin America, in which paid-up club members vote for the president and the board, offers the illusion of democracy. However, like the politics of those states for much of the century, elections have been managed and fixed; clientelism and patronage networks have always eluded the formal structures of representative democracy. The public floatation of football clubs on stock markets and the promise of shareholder democracy have proved equally illusory.

In response to this systematic pattern of exclusion, since the mid-1970s there has been in Western Europe a discernable movement towards self-organisation among fans. This has taken innumerable forms, not all of them particularly savoury. English and Scottish hooligan firms organised around ritualised displays of force and fashion and semi-structured street-fighting. The Italian ultra movement of the 1970s reinvented European football carnival while consorting with violence and intimidation. The travelling support of the Scottish, Dutch and Danish national teams combined post-industrial sports tourism with an informal ambassadorial role as purveyors of alcohol-drenched bonhomie.

In the 1990s, among small and initially disconnected groups, a whole wave of more politicised self-organisation began to emerge. First, a Europe-wide movement against racism in football has developed in response to the shocking levels of racial abuse in football stadiums, which made them recruiting grounds for the European far right in the 1980s. Other previously excluded or hidden football groups have also begun to emerge - for example, the European gay and lesbian network, which is taking on one of the major public repositories of open homophobia.

Most football supporters, in then end, want to support their club, and it is at the local and club level that alternative forms of supporter organisation have been busiest. In Germany, starting in the late 1980s, these organisations were catalysed by German local government through fan projects - a complex mixture of low-key youth work, preventive social work and community capacity building. This experiment has been repeated with some success in the Netherlands, Austria and Switzerland. In Britain, these kinds of energies have been mobilised in a number of directions. They have spawned an independent fanzine and website culture of rare, if uneven, wit and insight. Following the recent rash of failing and bankrupt clubs in the lower leagues, the same energies have been directed into development of supporters trusts, a form of cooperative or social ownership in which fans take a part or whole stake in their club. At an international level some of these organisations have come together to provide fan embassies and cultural events at major tournaments.

These kinds of organisation, network and action are the kernel of football's global civil society. Whether a movement can be created that can counter the global football authorities with even a modicum of the force mobilised by, for example, the World Social Forum against global capital is another matter. One way of creating unity is to negotiate a shared agenda for change (see Katwala 2000 for an excellent attempt to do so across all sports). Let's start with these five things:

1. Mobilising from below

First and foremost, the European vanguard of self-organisation of football needs to support, nurture and connect with similar organisations in the rest of the world. While European fans have much to complain about, it is as nothing compared with the inequalities and indignities foisted upon the football players and supporters of the developing world.

2. Changes at the top

The leadership of global football - centred on FIFA and its regional confederations - must be reformed. The abdication of Sepp Blatter, President of FIFA, from his throne would be a welcome and innovative way of initiating the process. It would help mark the passing of the Havelange-Samaranch era of global sports governance in which the interests of global bureaucrats and multinational corporations prevailed over all, and in which modes of governance forged in the autocratic polities of Franco's Spain and Brazil under the generals cease to be the norm. Blatter's resignation could perhaps be accompanied by an agreed amnesty for all FIFA and senior football officials who spill the beans on global football's own truth and returning payments commission.

Whether Mr Blatter goes now or later, all such posts should have fixed terms. There should be no repeat of the Havelange-Samaranch era when entrenched administrators maintained their rule for more than two decades. There are few enough checks and balances in international sporting governance as it is, without supporting the creation of dynasties. When elections for these posts happen they should be subject to external monitoring. Candidates should be encouraged to do more than meet other football administrators in expensive hotels, but go public with their manifestos and intentions, engage in debate on the global media and perhaps argue it out on television publicly.

3. Transparency

Next is the simple matter of financial transparency. All of the global football institutions must publish extensive, detailed and open accounts. Although matters of commercial secrecy must be acknowledged, there should be as much detail as possible about the nature of commercial contracts and sponsorship deals, and a careful inventory of personal expenses and gifts.

4. Accountability

If FIFA and its friends are, as they claim, among the leading INGOs in the new world order, then they should be subject to a much greater degree of scrutiny and accountability. The most immediate and important reform in this area must be bringing to an end the self-investigation and self-regulation that passes for probity in world football. It simply cannot be right that successive scandals and incidents of major financial mismanagement are investigated formally only by FIFA itself. The already frayed trustworthiness and legitimacy of the organisations will not sustain this as a plausible mode of operation. Alongside this the organisation should consider the various ways in which the players' and fans' voices can actually be

heard in the debate. This cannot be remedied by promises, rhetoric or charters. Possibilities include:

- pubic consultation exercises on major rule changes and other initiatives
- deliberative polling of fans and players
- public meetings at major tournaments in which officials can be subject to public scrutiny.

5. Anti-corruption measures

The issue of corruption in global football is multifaceted. The Danish organisation Play the Game, which researches and campaigns on these issues and gathers the world sports' media together to discuss them, has published its own anti-corruption charter, which is a pretty good starting point for tackling this immensely difficult question (Play the Game 2005).

Finally, FIFA should just loosen up. Its insufferable self-importance and pomposity may be all very well for most of the international governance circuit, but it will not do for football. If we wanted stuffed shirts, the worlds of formal economics and politics have them in their legions. But this is football. This is a game. This is the world's game and the world's carnival. FIFA may hold it in trust for the rest of us, but it cannot be allowed to continue to do so without openness, without dialogue and without some fun.

Alabarces, P and Rodriguez, M (2000) 'Football and Fatherland: The Crisis of National Representation in Argentinian Soccer', in G Finn and R. Giulianotti (eds), *Football Culture: Local Conflicts, Global Visions*. London: Frank Cass.

Back, L, Crabbe, T and Solomos, J (2001) *The Changing Face of Football: Racism, Identity and Multiculture in the English Game*. Oxford: Berg.

Bairner, A (2001) *Sport, Nationalism and Globalization: European and North American Perspectives*. 2001. New York: SUNY.

FIFA (2000) *The Big Count*. Nyon: FIFA.

– (2002) *FIFA Fact Sheet: The World Cup and Television*. Nyon: FIFA.

Freddi, C (2006) *Complete Book of the World Cup 2006*. London: Collins Willow.

Glanville, B (2006) *The Story of the World Cup*. London: Faber.

Goldblatt, D (2004) *Football Yearbook 2004-05*. London: Dorling Kindersly.

– (2006) *The Ball is Round: A Global History of Football*. London: Penguin.

Held, D, McGrew, A, Goldblatt, D and Perraton, J (1999) *Global Transformations: Politics, Economics and Culture*. Cambridge: Polity Press.

Hognestad, H and Tollinson, A (2004) 'Playing against Deprivation: Football and Development in Nairobi, Kenya', in G Armstrong and R Giulianotti (eds), *Football in Africa: Conflict, Conciliation and Community*. London: Palgrave Macmillan.

Hong, F (ed) (2004) Soccer, Women, Sexual Liberation: Kicking off a New Era. Special issue of *Soccer and Society* 2(2/3).

Kapuscinski, R (1990) *The Soccer War*. London: Granta. Katwala, S (2000) Democratising Global Sport. London: Central Books.

Jennings, A (2002) 'Ripping up Soccer: The Story Behind the FIFA Scandals'. 12 November. www.playthegame.org/Home/Knowledge%20bank/ Articles/Ripping%20up%20Soccer,-c,%20The%20 Story %20Behind%20the%20FIFA%20Scandals .aspx (consulted 7 May 2006).

– (2003) 'Blatter's Secret Bonus that FIFA tried to Cover Up', *Daily Mail*, 3 March.

McIlvanney, H (1999) *McIlvanney on Football*. Edinburgh: Mainstream.

Merkel, U and Tokarski, W (eds) (1996) *Racism and Xenophobia in European Football*. Aachen: Meyer and Meyer.

Miller, Toby, Lawrence, Geoffrey, McKay, Jim and Rowe, David (2001) *Globalization and Sport: Playing the World*. London: Sage.

Murray, B (1994) *The World's Game: A History of Soccer*. Urbana: University of Illinois Press.

Play the Game (2005) 'Statement For Integrity and Anti-Corruption in Sport', www.playthegame.org/Home/News/Up%20To %20Date/Statement.aspx (consulted 7 May 2006).

Sugden J and Tomlinson, A (1998) *FIFA and the Contest for World Football: Who Rules the People's Game?*

Cambridge: Polity.

– (2003) *Badfellas: FIFA Family at War*. Edinburgh: Mainstream.

UEFA (Union of European Football Associations) (2002) 'UEFA Backs Anti-racism Plan'. 10 October. www.uefa.com/uefa/news/kind%3D128/new sid%3D37750.html (consulted 15 May 2006).

Vasili, P (2000) *Colouring Over the White Line: The History of Black Footballers in Britain*. Edinburgh: Mainstream.

Williams, J (2003) *A Game for Rough Girls: A History of Women's Football in England*. London: Routledge.

Yallop, D (1999) *How They Stole the Game*. London: Poetic Publishing.

FUZZY SET APPROACHES TO THE STUDY OF GLOBAL CIVIL SOCIETY
Hagai Katz, Helmut Anheier and Marcus Lam

Introduction

This chapter builds on the comparative-historical approach to studying global civil society presented in *Global Civil Society 2005/6* (Anheier and Katz 2005). There, we suggested this approach in order to remedy some of the methodological problems that plague the study of transnational aspects and processes: the complexity of the phenomena involved, the limited number of cases available for analysis, the paucity of data in terms of coverage and quality, and the tendency of conventional statistical methods to emphasise the outcome rather than the process of causality.

Drawing on the work of Ragin (1987) and others, we suggested that the qualitative comparative method (QCA) and the basic set theory it builds on could be a useful tool for the analysis of global civil society. Yet QCA has its limitations in the sense that it treats social phenomena as dichotomous, meaning that in QCA a case either demonstrates or doesn't demonstrate a certain trait, and the methodology is not sensitive to subtle differences in the strength of the trait between cases. This could be seen as reductionism: classifying manifestations of global civil society as dichotomous rather than gradual or continuous phenomena can result in loss of information and hence in measurement errors, which, ultimately, can limit theory testing and conceptual development. In response, fuzzy set approaches seek to overcome these limitations by applying set theory to non-dichotomous data. This chapter outlines the logic and procedures of fuzzy set QCA (fs/QCA), and illustrates its utility by analysing the necessary conditions for the globalisation of civil society.

Crisp and fuzzy sets[1]

As we outlined in *Global Civil Society 2005/6*, QCA uses Boolean algebra, which allows us to assess 'combinatorial complexity when comparing relatively small numbers of cases that involve multiple causal factors' (Anheier and Katz 2005: 290). It evaluates different combinations of causal factors leading to the presence or absence of a particular outcome. To recall the social forum example in Anheier and Katz (2005): The outcome 'social forum success' (with 1 = successful, and 0 = unsuccessful) could be caused by factors such as the presence of local leadership (1 = presence, 0 = absence); the degree of coordination with related causes (1 = presence, 0 = absence); and the availability of financial and human resources for organising and holding the forum (1 = presence, 0 = absence).

This approach assumes dichotomous outcome and causal factors, or 'crisp' sets, in the sense that membership in each is unequivocal and non-ambiguous: a particular case either shows the characteristics of set membership (and hence is given a score of 1) or it does not (and hence is given a score of 0). While crisp sets can uncover complex causal relationship among multiple causes and a specified outcome (see also Ragin 2004), the 'crisp' membership assumption can nonetheless be homogenising, even overly simplifying, and ultimately misses much of the diversity and causal complexity involved. Indeed, many phenomena and relations in global civil society are a matter of degree and cannot be forced into simple dichotomies (Anheier and Katz 2005: 293; generally see Ragin 1987; 2000).

By contrast, a fuzzy set approach allows for both different degrees of membership as well as dichotomous distinctions, thus capturing the inherent 'dual nature of diversity'[2]. In the social forum example above, presented more fully in Anheier and Katz (2005),

1 *This chapter draws strongly on the work of Charles Ragin, and particularly on Fuzzy Set Social Science (Ragin, 2000), which is the definitive text for the methodology.*

2 *Ragin argues that there are two aspects to diversity exhibited by social phenomenon: (a) differences in kind, that is, the difference between two extremes, whether a social phenomenon does or does not exhibit the characteristic of interest. This is similar to crisp membership described above; and b) differences in degree, that is, differences between the categories that fall in the interval between the two extreme states. For a fuller discussion of diversity as it relates to fuzzy set methodology, see Ragin (2000).*

cases (here: social forum locations) can vary: some may have stronger leadership or more resources than others. Fuzzy set approaches can take account of such variations in causal factors and outcomes.

Basic fuzzy set analysis

Clearly, a critical issue for fuzzy set approaches is defining scales or criteria that set the number of categories or degrees and their boundaries between 'a lot' of local leadership and 'no' local leadership, or between 'plenty' and 'no' resources, and so on. A first step in approaching the scaling issue is to look at the dual meaning of membership in fuzzy sets. Such sets exhibit both qualitative (that is, a case either is or is not a member in the set) and quantitative aspects (that is, the various degrees of membership ranging between 0 and 1). A simple fuzzy set can have a membership scale with only three values: 0, 1/2 and 1; it can also have more values, as would be the case for a stepwise scale of 0, 0.2, 0.4, 0.6, 0.8 and 1; and it can even approach a continuous scale with values ranging from 0.00, 0.01, ..., 0.99 to 1.00.

In practice, determining fuzzy set membership is based on a correspondence between theoretical concepts and data. For example, if a theory suggests intermediate positions between the two extreme qualitative states of full member and full non-member, we may proceed as follows, taking into account available empirical information: full set membership has a score of 1; strong, partial membership has a score close to 1 (for example, 0.75); membership scores of 0.5 indicate maximum ambiguity with cases 'neither in nor out' of the set; scores close to zero (such as 0.25) indicate weak membership in the set; and a score of 0 indicates full non-membership.

Setting and calibrating membership scores is a creative challenge for users of fuzzy set approaches. To appreciate this challenge, consider the meaning of a 'heap of sand' (Verkuilen 2005). How much sand constitutes a heap? Few people would say that a few grains of sand on a carpet constitute a heap, yet most would agree that a bucket of sand dumped in their living room is a heap. The problem is that locating the cut-off point between heap and not-heap is to some extent arbitrary, and involves interpretation. The translation of numerical variables into fuzzy set membership scores, therefore, requires theoretically informed decisions.

Next is the selection of cases for analysis. While case selection may be limited by data availability, theoretical rather than statistical considerations of representativeness are important. Specifically, cases should be selected with non-zero scores in the outcome set. For example, analysing the causes of generous welfare regimes, Ragin (2000: 290–5) selects developed nations that have at least some degree of 'welfare generosity'. Given the relatively small number of cases involved, all empirical observations rather than some probability sample would enter the actual analysis. More generally, given that selected cases are non-probability samples, Katz, Vom Hau and Mahoney (2005) suggest identifying cases from homogenous populations to help control for unknown contextual variations that may affect the relationship between causes and outcome.

With scales established and membership scores calculated for cases selected, the analysis proceeds by looking at the causal relationship between the outcome set and the sets of conditions, including combinations among the latter. This analysis begins with tests of necessity to determine which factors have to be present for the outcome to occur. Conditions found to be necessary are then compared with other causal conditions to evaluate different combinations that are sufficient for producing the outcome. As a result, the analysis reveals the various combinations of necessary and sufficient causes that form different paths leading to the outcome. In a similar fashion to QCA, sufficient combinations are then reduced using Boolean mathematics to create a parsimonious statement of the cause and effect relations involved. Let us look at some of these steps more closely.

Operations on fuzzy sets

Because fuzzy sets are represented by numerical values, they can be analysed using algebraic operations, the most common of which are negation, logical *AND*, logical *OR*, concentration, and dilation[3]. For negation, we subtract the case's fuzzy set score from 1: $\sim A = 1 - A$ (Ragin 2000: 172), where $\sim$ indicates 'not' and A refers to a membership score in the fuzzy

---

3 *In this brief overview, we are unable to deal with the last two operations that involve additions of quantitative modifiers to verbal constructs of fuzzy sets. For a full discussion, see Ragin (2000).*

set. It is important to keep in mind, however, that the negation of a fuzzy set means only the degree to which the case is not in a specific set A, and it does not indicate any membership degree in any opposing sets. For example, if the fuzzy set is 'rich' and the cases are individuals, then the negation of the membership scores in the set of 'rich' individuals does not indicate their score in the set of 'poor' individuals. To determine the membership scores in the set of 'poor' individuals requires a separate fuzzy set with its own scores.

Logical *AND* operations refer to joining two or more fuzzy sets, also known as compound sets or the intersection[4]. *AND* operations are ruled by the minimum of the two fuzzy set scores. For example, suppose a case has the following membership scores in two fuzzy sets: 'local leadership' with 0.65 and 'financial resources' with 0.35. The minimum rule states that the membership score in the combined set of 'local leadership *AND* financial resources' is the minimum of the two scores, that is, 0.35, because the higher value in one fuzzy set cannot compensate for lower values in another.

Logical *OR* operations also refer to joining two fuzzy sets, but indicate union rather than their intersection[5]. In this operation we take the maximum of the two scores. For example, for the two hypothetical fuzzy sets mentioned above, the membership score in 'local leadership *OR* financial resources' would be 0.65 because the score of the combined set would be at least as high as score in the set where membership is highest. The logical *AND* and *OR* operations also hold for any number of component fuzzy sets (that is, three, four or five components).

Necessary and sufficient causes

The difference between necessary and sufficient conditions is best introduced by the following hypothetical examples:

1. S = AC + BC means that condition C is necessary for S to occur but not sufficient in the sense that C needs the presence of either A or B in producing S.

2. S = AC shows that both A and C are necessary but not sufficient as they have to be co-present for the outcome S to occur.

3. S = A + BC indicates that A is sufficient but not

necessary as the absence of A and the presence of BC can bring about the outcome S.

4. S = A states that A is both necessary and sufficient cause of S.

A first step in identifying necessary and sufficient conditions is to select cases that exhibit the outcome of interest and assess the presence of common conditions. Necessary causes are identified with the help of the subset principle. It states that when membership in the outcome is less than or equal to membership in the cause, then the cause can be considered a necessary condition for the outcome. The scores for necessary conditions set a ceiling on the degree of membership in the outcome (Ragin 2000: 218). For multiple causal conditions, the subset principle would apply to the intersection (minimum score) of the factor sets, which would then be compared with the membership scores in the outcome set.

Like necessary conditions, sufficient conditions can also be expressed in the form of an arithmetic relationship: membership scores in causal condition should be less than or equal to membership scores in the outcome. That is, according to the subset principle, sufficient causal conditions are a subset of the outcome. Notice that this is the inverse to the rule for necessary conditions. In terms of research design, the study of sufficient conditions is also the inverse of the study of necessary conditions; instead of selecting cases based on the outcome, researchers select cases based on causal conditions, which are determined a priori.

Finally, if there are more than one causal combination with scores less than or equal to the outcome scores, the next step is to simplify the list and see whether any causal combinations are redundant according to the containment rule. This rule, based on Boolean minimisation, states that more complex casual expressions can be absorbed by less complex ones as along as all the elements that appear in the latter also appear in the former. In other

---

4 Logical 'and' operations are annotated as a multiplication and written as 'AB' or 'A*B' which is interpreted as A AND B or the intersection of A and B.
5 Logical 'or' operations are annotated as an addition and written as 'A + B' which is interpreted as A OR B or the union of A and B.

Figure M1: Global civil society and globalisation

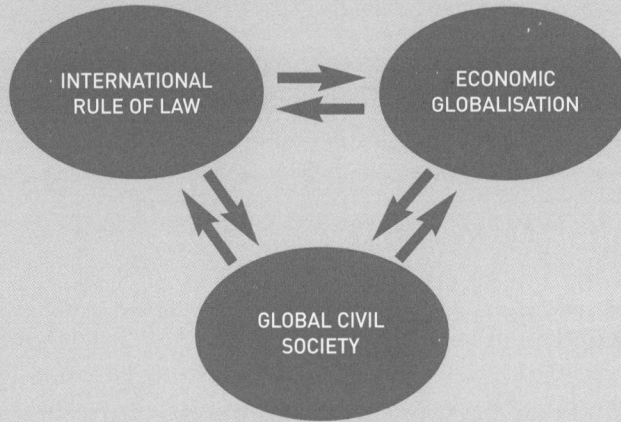

words, the containment rule weeds out redundancies among conditions. The final step in fuzzy set analysis is to form a summary statement describing the causal combination (see Ragin 2000: 245).

Applying the method: the necessary conditions of global civil society

To demonstrate the utility of fuzzy set approaches for the study of global civil society, we offer a brief analysis of the 'causal chemistry' of phenomena linked to the development of global civil society. Since space does not permit a full illustration of a fuzzy set application, we concentrate on an admittedly rather simplistic analysis of the necessary conditions of global civil society development.

Fuzzy set analysis is strongly guided by theory, and requires clear and well-formulated theoretical argument for testing causal statements. For the following illustration, we return to the model presented in *Global Civil Society 2002* (Anheier and Stares 2002). This model situates global civil society in the context of two other complexes: economic globalisation (finance, production, trade) and international law (treaty ratification, human rights, and so on). Hence, there is a threefold connection between global civil society, economic globalisation and the international rule of law, as shown in Figure M1.

Considering this theoretical model further, we hypothesise specific causal relationships among these three elements. One such hypothesis sees economic globalisation and the international rule of law as causal preconditions for the emergence of a globalised civil society at the country level. The integration of national civil society in a global civil society, as expressed in national involvement in international NGOs and the adoption of cosmopolitan values, would depend on open access to financial markets and trade, and on the acceptance of international laws, conventions and norms such as human rights. Together, these factors would provide a shared causal platform from which global civil society could emerge.

But are economic globalisation and the acceptance of the international rule of law indeed causal conditions for the development of global civil society? This question can be answered using a fuzzy set methodology. First, we assess whether economic globalisation and the acceptance of the international rule of law (the two conditions) are necessary for the emergence of global civil society (the outcome). We can then determine whether in all the cases where a globalised civil society has emerged we also find both a globalised economy and an acceptance of international law. Next, we would inquire whether the conditions are sufficient for the emergence of the outcome, that is, whether in all cases where these conditions are met global civil society has emerged.

Determining fuzzy set membership

Fuzzy set analysis begins with the selection of indicators. For the global civil society set, we use the Global Civil Society Index (GCSI) developed by Anheier

Table M1: Defining membership for fuzzy set 'countries accepting international rule of law'

Raw scores of international rule of law source data	Verbal fuzzy membership score label	Fuzzy membership score
Low on all 4 indices	Fully out	0
Low on 3 indices and medium on 1 index	Almost fully out	0.125
Low or medium on all 4 indices	Mostly out	0.25
Low or medium on 3 indices and high or very high on 1 index	More or less out	0.375
Low or medium on 2 indices and high or very high on 2 indices	Neither in nor out	0.5
High or very high on 3 indices and low or medium on 1 index	More or less in	0.625
High or very high on all 4 indices	Mostly in	0.75
Very high on 3 indices and high on 1 index	Almost fully in	0.875
Very high on all 4 indices	Fully in	1

and Stares (2002). This index comprises variables measuring organisational and individual aspects of civil society, such as participation, cosmopolitan values and membership in international organisations. For the set 'economic globalisation' we use the index developed by the Swiss Institute for Business Cycle Research (URL), which incorporates on the one hand data on actual flows, including trade, foreign direct and portfolio investment, and income payments to foreign nationals, and on the other financial and trade restrictions such as import barriers, tariffs, taxes on international trade and capital account restrictions (Dreher 2006). For the set 'acceptance of an international rule of law' we took into account both intent and action by using (a) data on the number of human rights, humanitarian and environmental international treaties ratified, and (b) data on actual human rights practices.

Empirically, these indicators determine the membership scores of countries in each of the three sets in the model – the set of economically globalised nations, the set of countries accepting the international rule of law, and the set of countries with a globalised civil society. Determining fuzzy set membership scores is a crucial step. In this case, we had to determine three critical scores:

- full membership, represented by the score 1.0, to be assigned to cases that are undoubtedly and fully members in the set

- full non-membership, represented by the score of 0, for cases that are clearly not members in the set

- maximum ambiguity, where cases are neither clearly in nor out of the set.

For space reasons, we illustrate the assignment of membership scores only for the condition 'acceptance of the international rule of law'. Four variables from two sources were used to compile fuzzy membership scores for this set. The first two were the number of humanitarian and human rights treaties and the number of environmental treaties ratified by each country. The second source used was the CIRI Human Rights Data Project (CIRI URLa), which produces indices of human rights violations from the human rights reports of the US Department of State and Amnesty International. The two indices used here are CIRI's Physical Integrity Rights Index (Cingranelli and Richards 1999), which measures actual human rights violations, and Empowerment Rights Index (Richards, Gelleny and Sacko 2001), which measures governments' respect for various political, economic and social rights (short descriptions of these two indices are available on CIRI's website, CIRI URLb).

The raw scores for each of these indicators were grouped into four levels: low, medium, high and very high, and the combination of scores used to determine fuzzy set membership. As shown in Table M1, a country that scored low on all four indices is

Table M2: **Fuzzy set membership scores**

Country	Global Civil Society Index	Economic globalisation	International rule of law
Argentina	0.125	0.625	0.75
Austria	0.625	0.875	0.75
Belgium	0.75	0.875	1
Bulgaria	0.125	0.625	0.625
Chile	0.125	0.625	0.75
Croatia	0.25	0.25	0.625
Czech Republic	0.5	0.875	0.75
Denmark	0.875	0.875	1
Estonia	0.25	0.875	0.75
Finland	0.75	0.875	1
France	0.625	0.875	0.875
Germany	0.375	0.875	1
Greece	0.375	0.75	1
Hungary	0.125	0.625	0.875
Iceland	0.875	0.875	0.875
Ireland	0.625	0.875	0.875
Italy	0.5	0.875	1
Latvia	0.25	0.875	0.75
Lithuania	0.125	0.75	0.75
Netherlands	0.875	0.875	1
Poland	0.125	0.375	0.75
Russian Federation	0.125	0.375	0.625
Slovakia	0.375	0.625	0.625
Slovenia	0.375	0.625	0.75
Spain	0.375	0.875	0.875
Sweden	1	0.875	1
Switzerland	0.625	0.875	1
Ukraine	0.125	0.375	0.5
United Kingdom	0.625	0.875	0.875
United States	0.375	0.875	0.375

fully out of the set of countries accepting the international rule of law (no country in our data received this score), while a country that scored very high on all four indices is fully in the set of countries accepting the international rule of law. Countries that scored low or medium on two indices and high or very high on the other two were located at the point of complete ambiguity – neither in nor out of the set. The level of detail of the index scores yielded a 9-point scale, as Table M1 shows.

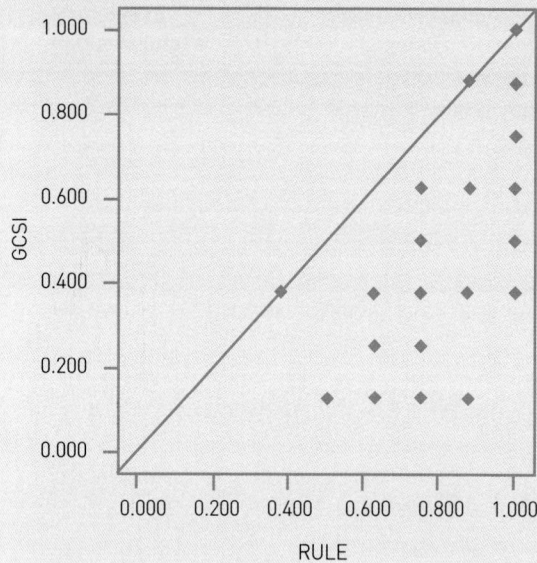

Figure M2: Plot of GCSI against RULE

We applied the same approach to constructing fuzzy sets for 'economic globalisation' and 'global civil society'. Table M2 shows the resulting scores for each country. These scores provide the input for the actual fuzzy set analysis, that is, for establishing whether economic globalisation and the international rule of law are necessary and/or sufficient conditions for global civil society. Note that one country, Mexico, scored 0 on the outcome, and was therefore excluded from further analysis.

Analysing necessary conditions

As mentioned above, determining necessary conditions is based on the subset principle. If set A is fully contained in set B, A is a subset of B, and membership in set B is a condition for membership in set A. In other words, all cases of set A must also be cases of set B, and membership of set B is necessary for membership of subset A.

Are economic globalisation and the international rule of law necessary conditions for global civil society? Following the principles described above, we need to compare the membership scores of the cases in the outcome set (GCSI) with those in the condition sets (ECON and RULE). If membership scores in the outcome set are consistently lower than membership scores in each of the conditional sets, we can conclude that the answer to this question is 'yes'.

It is useful to present this as a bi-plot, in which cases are plotted as a function of their membership scores in the outcome set (Y axis) and condition sets (X axis). If indeed the outcome is a subset of the conditions, all the cases will be on or below the diagonal of the plot. As is shown in Figure M2, GCSI is indeed a subset of RULE. This can be interpreted as a confirmation of the hypothesis that an acceptance of the international rule of law is required for the emergence of a globalised civil society.

By contrast, the relationship between economic globalisation and global civil society seems more complex. As is shown in Figure M3a, in one case (Sweden) membership score in the fuzzy set GCSI is higher than in the fuzzy set ECON. In light of this one aberrant case, are we to conclude that economic globalisation is not a necessary condition for global civil society? From a strict set-theoretical viewpoint, we should. However, Ragin (2000: 223–6) suggests two possible ways to resolve this problem. The first addresses measurement and translation imprecision. Aberrant cases may be caused by measurement errors or by imperfect translation of data into fuzzy set membership. If the accuracy of data is an issue, adjustment factors can be introduced to correct for measurement biases.

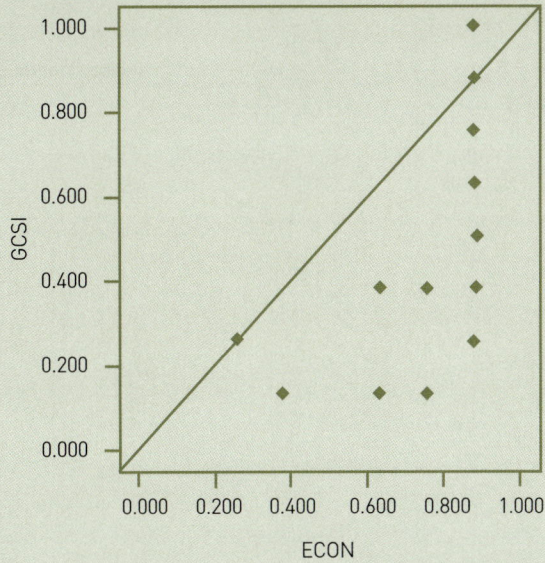

Figure M3a: **Plot of GCSI against ECON**

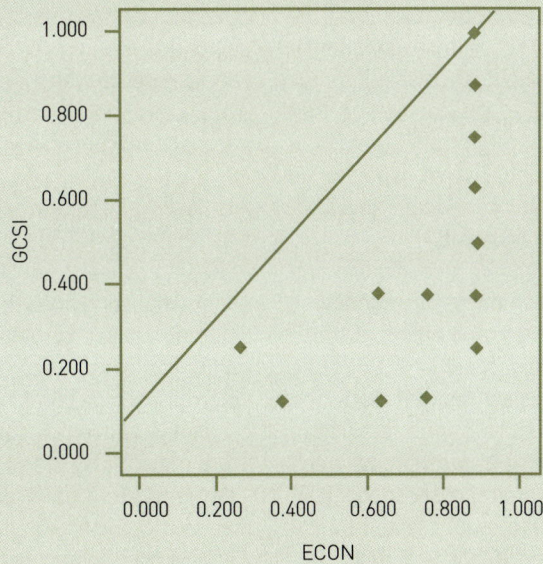

Figure M3b: **Plot of GCSI against ECON with adjustment factor**

Hence, to substitute for better measures, one makes the criteria for evaluating the subset relationship more lenient. By moving the diagonal upwards, as shown in Figure M3b, 'near misses' are no longer a violation of necessity.

The second cause of aberrant cases or near misses may be the randomness inherent in social science data. Even with near perfect measures, many effects are outside specified models and difficult to control and account for. One way to address this problem is to set probabilistic rather than absolute criteria for necessity. For example, a benchmark criterion of 80

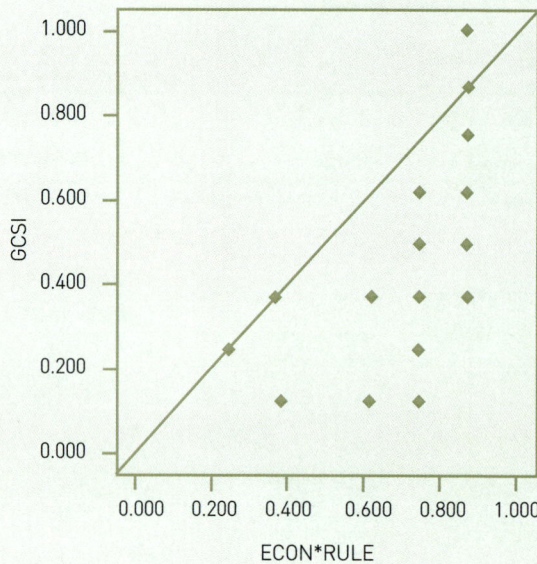

Figure M4: **Plot of GCSI against intersection of ECON and RULE**

per cent means that necessity will be accepted if 80 per cent of the cases support it, with a confidence level of 95 per cent (or a .05 significance level). In our case such a benchmark leads to the conclusion that the hypothesis that economic globalisation is a necessary condition for global civil society is supported: within a 95 per cent confidence level, 29 out of 30 of the cases indicate necessity.

So far we have seen that economic globalisation and international rule of law are each necessary conditions for global civil society. But is the combination of these two conditions also a necessary condition? Does the emergence of global civil society require both the acceptance of international norms and economic interconnectedness? To answer this question, we need to compare the membership scores of cases in the GCSI set with membership scores in the set created by the intersection of these two sets: ECON and RULE. As mentioned above, the set intersection is applied by taking the minimum membership score of the case in the original sets. The result is shown in Figure M4.

Again, the 'near miss' case of Sweden doesn't prevent us from concluding that necessity is supported with an 80 per cent benchmark and 95 per cent confidence level. It would seem, therefore, that it takes a combination of economic globalisation and the international rule of law for global civil society to

emerge, and we can alter our theoretical model to depict this relationship (Figure M5): global civil society cannot emerge without at least some level of economic globalisation and some level of adherence to the international rule of law.

Analysing causal complexity - testing sufficient conditions

Analysing causal complexity requires knowing not only under what conditions the outcome occurs but also the different causal combinations involved. With this in mind, the next steps in fuzzy set analysis are to determine which combinations of factors are sufficient conditions and which combinations explain cases that score more highly than others in the outcome set.

An important difference between sufficient and necessary causes is that the former must logically involve a combination of causal conditions, not just one. The number of causal combinations is guided by the formula $3^k - 1$, where k is the number of dichotomies in the property space. In our example, there are eight possible causal combinations to test:

1. ECON
2. RULE
3. ~ECON
4. ~RULE
5. ECON*RULE
6. ECON*~RULE
7. ~ECON*RULE
8. ~ECON*~RULE

Figure M5: Necessary conditions for global civil society

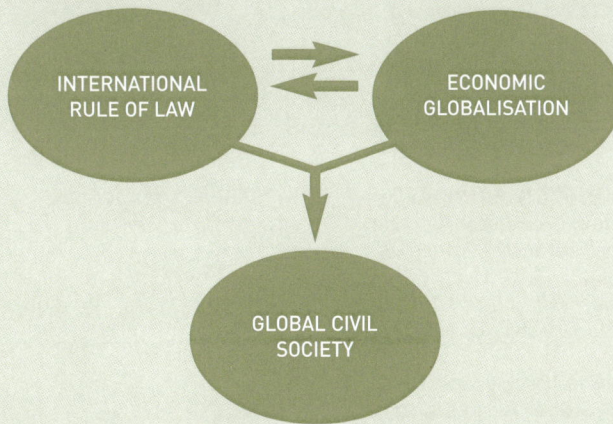

The case scores for each combination are determined using the operations on fuzzy sets outlined above, that is, subtracting from 1 for negation, and finding the minimum for intersection. Once this is done, we compare the scores for each causal condition with the scores for the outcome, and choose the combinations that are subsets of the outcome set by finding combinations with scores less than or equal to the outcome scores. Note that in the analysis of sufficiency, the logic of the subset principle is the reverse of that in the necessity test.

If there are two or more sufficient causal combinations, the next step is to simplify the list and establish whether any causal combinations are redundant according to the containment rule, in a similar fashion to what we demonstrated in *Global Civil Society 2005/6* (Anheier and Katz 2005). The end result is a succinct statement of the combinatorial relationship between causes and outcome. Space limitations, however, prevent us from presenting this part of the analysis, but the general thrust of the fuzzy set approach should have become clear.

Conclusion

The purpose of this chapter is to explore further the applicability of comparative historical research methods, and particularly fuzzy set approaches, for examining aspects of global civil society. In this chapter we have only scratched the surface of what is a complex yet very promising analytical approach in social research. Further work could incorporate other factors that presumably affect the emergence of global civil society, such as regime type, economic development and availability of resources. It would be beneficial to complete the analysis, in particular pinpointing both 'necessity' and 'sufficiency' factors in an effort to unveil the full 'causal chemistry' of global civil society.

However, fuzzy set approaches are not suitable for all research questions. For some topics, other techniques are more appropriate; for example, large-N studies concerned with the 'effects of a cause' rather than the 'causes of an effect', would benefit from the application of regression models (Katz, Vom Hau and Mahoney 2005: 569). Moreover, using a fuzzy set analysis requires a well-grounded theoretical basis to inform the relevant variables (or sets) included in the analysis, and the expected causal relationships in terms of conditions and outcomes. Thus, the 'property space' and the variables included in the analysis are theoretically derived. Unfortunately, many areas of global civil society research lack the theoretical basis for establishing the property space for the kind of analysis proposed here.

Nonetheless, we hope that this brief illustration has highlighted the benefits of applying fuzzy set qualitative comparative methods to the study of global civil society. We hope that scholars of global civil society will consider adding this method to their repertoire, taking advantage of its unique approach to conceptualising, measuring and analysing social phenomena. As a result, we should see an improved understanding of the causal connections of global civil society and its many manifestations.

Anheier, Helmut and Katz, Hagai (2006) 'Learning from History? Comparative Historical Methods and Researching Global Civil Society', in Marlies Glasius, Mary Kaldor and Helmut Anheier (eds), *Global Civil Society 2005/6*. London: Sage.

Anheier, Helmut and Stares, Sally (2002) 'Introducing the Global Civil Society Index', in Marlies Glasius, Mary Kaldor and Helmut Anheier (eds), *Global Civil Society 2002*. Oxford: Oxford University Press.

Cingranelli, David L and Richards, David L (1999) 'Measuring the Level, Pattern, and Sequence of Government Respect for Physical Integrity Rights', *International Studies Quarterly*, 43: 407–18.

Dreher, Axel (2006) 'Does Globalisation Affect Growth? Evidence from a New Index of Globalization', *Applied Economics*, 38: 1091–110.

Katz, Aaron, Vom Hau, Matthias and Mahoney, James (2005) 'Explaining the Great Reversal in Spanish America: Fuzzy-Set Analysis versus Regression Analysis', *Sociological Methods & Research*, 33: 539–73.

Ragin, Charles (1987) *The Comparative Method: Moving Beyond Qualitative and Quantitative Strategies*. Berkeley: University of California Press.

– (2000) *Fuzzy Sets Social Science*. Chicago: Chicago University Press.

– (2004) *From Fuzzy Sets to Crisp Truth Tables*. COMPASSS Research Group. www.compasss.org/RaginFSForthcoming.PDF (consulted 25 July 2006).

Richards, David L, Gelleny, Ronald and Sacko, David (2001) 'Money with a Mean Streak? Foreign Economic Penetration and Government Respect for Human Rights in Developing Countries', *International Studies Quarterly*, 45: 219–39.

Verkuilen, Jay (2005) 'Assigning Membership in a Fuzzy Set Analysis', *Sociological Methods & Research*, 33: 462–96.

Websites (consulted 6 July 2006)
Swiss Institute for Business Cycle Research. www.kof.ch/globilization
CIRI (URLa). http://ciri.binghamton.edu/index.asp
– (URLb). http://ciri.binghamton.edu/documentation/ciri_variables_short_descriptions.pdf

Note on Data

Relation to the Data Programme in previous editions of the Global Civil Society Yearbook

We have updated the information presented in previous editions of the Yearbook wherever possible. Those indicators repeated from previous editions represent more recent or updated figures. In order to facilitate comparisons, country data are grouped by income and region where possible, using World Bank classifications.

We have added new indicators where we judge them to be valuable, sometimes representing a departure from those presented last year. Such indicators are found in our records on social justice; political rights and civil liberties; air travel; governance and accountability; NGOs and global governance; political rights, civil liberties, press freedom and economic freedom; attitudes towards the US; and attitudes towards globalisation. This year we include two new records: economic and social rights, and religion. Thus we introduce the following data sources to the Yearbook: Bread for the World, *Hunger Report*; ESCR-net: International; Gallup International Millennium Survey; International Air Transport Association (IATA), *World Air Transport Statistics*; International Labour Organization, LABORSTA database; SustainAbility Ltd and WWF UK; The Heritage Foundation; UN Millennium Development Goal Indicators Database; UNAIDS; UNESCO; EFA Global Monitoring Report; UNFPA State of World Population Report; Union of International Associations (UIA), *Yearbook of International Organizations*; United Nations Housing Rights Programme; United Nations Human Settlements Programme (UN-HABITAT); United Nations, Office on Drugs and Crime (UNODC); *Trafficking in Persons - Global Patterns Report*; World Bank, Social Development Papers; and World Christian Database.

We continue using graphical formats for presentation of some data, for example the records on world trade, and economic and social rights. For some elements of last year's data programme we have been unable to obtain updated or equivalent data. Thus, we have decided not to reproduce the data on students abroad and attitudes to NGOs. Reproducing data on tsunami relief was irrelevant, so more general information of international disaster relief was included in the international philanthropy record instead. All data from previous Yearbooks remain available on our website at
www.lse.ac.uk/Depts/global/researchgcspub.htm

Sources and explanatory notes

Brief references to sources are found at the end of each record. All major terms used in the records are briefly defined in the Glossary. As will become clear, comparative information is not available for some countries and variables. Data reported is the most up to date available. A blank entry indicates that the data are not available, not comparable, or otherwise of insufficient quality to warrant reporting. To improve readability of the data and to facilitate interpretation, each record is preceded by a brief description of the information presented and points to some of the key findings.

Countries

Countries in these tables are generally independent states with more than 100,000 inhabitants according to the most recent population estimates. Short or conventional country names are used. It is not the intention of the editors to take a position with regard to the political or diplomatic implications of geographical names or continental groupings used.

China, Hong Kong, Macao, Taiwan, and Tibet

Hong Kong became a Special Administrative Region (SAR) of China in 1997 after formal transfer from the UK. Macao became a SAR of China in 1999 after formal transfer from Portugal. Data for China before these dates do not include Hong Kong and Macao; thereafter they do unless otherwise stated. Tibet was annexed by the People's Republic of China in 1949. Data for Tibet are included in those for China and Tibet. Taiwan became the home of Chinese nationalists fleeing Communist rule on the mainland and claims separate status from the People's Republic of China. An attempt is made to include data for Taiwan, which is not recognised by the United Nations as an independent country, where this is possible.

Czechoslovakia

Czechoslovakia ceased to exist (in UN terms) on 31 December 1992. Its successor states, the Czech Republic and the Slovak Republic, became UN members in 1993. Figures predating 1993 are given for the Czech Republic and Slovakia separately where possible, or otherwise not at all.

Ethiopia and Eritrea

Eritrea became independent from Ethiopia in 1993. Data for Ethiopia until 1993 include Eritrea, later data do not.

Indonesia and East Timor

The Indonesian occupation of East Timor ended in late 1999. After a transitional period under the authority of the United Nations, East Timor became independent on 20 May 2002. Data for 1999 and after are presented separately for Indonesia and East Timor wherever possible. All data for Indonesia also include Irian Jaya (West Papua), the status of which has been in dispute since the 1960s.

Israel and the Palestinian Authority

An attempt was made to present separate data entries for Israel and the Palestinian Authority where such data is available. Where not possible this is made evident in the table footnotes.

Morocco and the Western Sahara

The Western Sahara (formerly Spanish Sahara) was annexed by Morocco in the 1970s. Unless otherwise stated, data are amalgamated for 'Morocco and the Western Sahara'.

Yugoslavia and Serbia & Montenegro

The Socialist Federal Republic of Yugoslavia dissolved in 1991 into Bosnia and Herzegovina, the Republic of Croatia, the Republic of Slovenia, the former Yugoslav Republic of Macedonia, and the Federal Republic of Yugoslavia. In February 2003 the Federal Republic of Yugoslavia was renamed Serbia and Montenegro, reflecting the implementation of constitutional change to a looser federation of its two republics. For ease of presentation, the name 'Serbia and Montenegro' is used throughout these records, where the 'Federal Republic of Yugoslavia' would have applied pre-2003. Wherever possible, data are given separately for Serbia & Montenegro and the other constituent states of the former Yugoslavia.

Aggregations

Where possible we present data for groups of countries (by region and economy) as well as for individual countries. These groups are generally classified according to World Bank definitions. Preference is given to aggregations calculated in the source where such aggregations are available. The aggregations are weighted differently depending on the data presented, usually using population or GDP. To give an example, in Record 1 we present figures for trade as a percentage of GDP. The aggregate figure for South Asia is calculated as the sum of trade for Afghanistan, Bangladesh, Bhutan, India, Maldives, Nepal, Pakistan and Sri Lanka, divided by the sum of GDP for those countries, and multiplied by 100 to generate a percentage, ie

Trade as % GDP for South Asia =

$$\frac{(\text{Afghan trade} + \text{Bangladeshi trade} +)}{\text{Afghan GDP} + \text{Bangladeshi GDP} + ...} \times 100$$

Some aggregations are simple sums, as in the data on air travel, international food donations, ISO 1400 accredited companies, natural disaster relief, remittances, refugee population totals, total military personnel and peacekeeping forces, numbers of international organisations and membership thereof, NGOs participating in WTO ministerial conferences and INGOs holding participatory status with the Council of Europe. In such cases each country's contribution to the regional or world figure is given equal weight under this method of aggregation.

Record 1: Global economy

The first table contains data on the globalisation of domestic economies. It shows total trade, foreign direct investment (FDI), receipts of official development aid, and the dollar value of remittances. It also includes information on changes over time between 1994 and 2004, with the latest figures available. We try to show the extent to which national economies are part of an emerging global economy, and where growth or contraction has been most pronounced in this respect since the mid-1990s. The table shows significant increases in trade and direct investments between 1994 and 2004 for most countries, and substantial increase in the international flows of remittances. In contrast, official development aid has decreased in most countries, with the exception of some middle- and low-income economies in Europe and Central Asia where aid has increased - though in only a few of those countries does it exceed 5% of gross national income.

Country	Trade — Total trade in % GDP			Official development aid* — Aid (% GNI)			Foreign direct investment — Inward FDI stock (% GDP)			Outward FDI stock (% GDP)			Remittances — Outgoing total (US$ millions, current)			Incoming total (US$ millions, current)		
	1994	2004	1994-2004 % change	1994	2004	1994-2004 % change	1994	2004	1994-2004 % change	1994	2004	1994-2004 % change	1994	2004	1994-2004 % change	1994	2004	1994-2004 % change
East Asia & Pacific																		
Low income economies																		
Cambodia	65	141	118	12	10	-14	7	47	552	5	6	11	38	139	267	11	177	1,513
Indonesia	52	58	11	1	0	-96	9	4	-52	3				913		449	1,866	316
Korea, Dem. Rep.							8	11	40									
Laos	65	71	9	14	11	-18	8	27	236	0	1	558	1	1	-50	10	1	-90
Mongolia	143	162	13	30	16	-45	3	45	1,335					49			203	
Myanmar	3						4	8	89					25		42	118	180
Papua New Guinea	94	*131*	*39*	6	8	19	29	56	91	4	8	85	20	17	-15	20	6	-70
Solomon Islands	148	*86*	*-42*	17	48	189	39	50	30				6	6	0		2	
Vietnam	77	140	81	6	4	-28	33	66	101								3,200	
Middle income economies																		
China**	47	65	38	1	0	-85	14	15	9	3	2	-17	19	2,067	10,781	986	21,283	2,060
Fiji	116			2	3	9	31	10	-68	13	2	-84	28	40	43	30	24	-20
Malaysia	180	221	23	0	0	177	31	39	28	11	12	10	187	3,464	1,752	455	987	117
Micronesia				47	36	-23												
Philippines	74	102	38	2	1	-68	8	15	81	1	2	48	89	16	-82	3,452	11,634	237
Samoa	73	74	2	26	8	-68	13	18	37					4		37	45	22
Thailand	83	136	65	0	0	-100	11	30	173	1	2	108				1,281	1,622	27
Tonga	73			21	9	-57	4	19	400				2	16	700	21	66	214
Vanuatu	102			22	12	-43	101	136	34		4		15	17	13	18	9	-50

Country	Total trade in % GDP 1994	Total trade in % GDP 2004	Total trade in % GDP 1994-2004 % change	Aid (% GNI) 1994	Aid (% GNI) 2004	Aid (% GNI) 1994-2004 % change	Inward FDI stock (% GDP) 1994	Inward FDI stock (% GDP) 2004	Inward FDI stock (% GDP) 1994-2004 % change	Outward FDI stock (% GDP) 1994	Outward FDI stock (% GDP) 2004	Outward FDI stock (% GDP) 1994-2004 % change	Outgoing total (US$ millions, current) 1994	Outgoing total (US$ millions, current) 2004	Outgoing total 1994-2004 % change	Incoming total (US$ millions, current) 1994	Incoming total (US$ millions, current) 2004	Incoming total 1994-2004 % change
High income economies																		
Australia	39	*38*	-3				28	41	48	14	27	95	586	1,955	234	1,277	2,744	115
Brunei							2	136	8,881	6	9	34						
Japan	16	*22*	37				0	2	426	6	8	38	1,583	1,411	-11	874	931	7
Korea, Rep.	54	84	55	0	0	-63	2	8	297	2	6	213	541	2,545	370	1,038	832	-20
New Caledonia	42			13			4	4	6									
New Zealand	60	58	-3				43	52	21	11	10	-17	379	911	140	995	1,132	14
Europe & Central Asia																		
Low income economies																		
Armenia	112	92	-18	15	8	-44	6	28	351		1			127		65	336	417
Azerbaijan	154	124	-20	4	2	-50			157			31	9	200	2,122	3	228	7,500
Georgia	167	79	-53	7	6	-17		35	2,070					26			303	
Kyrgyzstan	74	95	29	10	12	16	4	26	503				66	73	11	1	189	18,800
Moldova	82	133	61	3	4	25	3	36	1,292	2	1	-38	10	52	420	1	703	70,200
Tajikistan	95	111	17	5	12	140	4	24	481					119			252	
Ukraine	74	115	56	1	1	1	2	14	711	0	0	27		20			411	
Uzbekistan	37	73	97	0	2	839	2	11	446									
Middle income economies																		
Albania	50	64	28	8	5	-43	7	20	200	2	1	-40		4		307	889	190
Belarus	155	143	-8	1	0	-75	1	9	1,417	3	*0*	-99	17	80	371	29	244	741
Bosnia & Herzegovina	102	81	-20	36	8	-79		20		0	1	10		26			1,824	
Bulgaria	91	127	40	2	3	58	4	32	767	1	*1*	-37		11			103	
Croatia	92	103	12	1	0	-53	2	39	1,469	5	7	53	69		376	1,222	225	
Czech Republic	104	144	39	0	0	-24	10	53	415	1	3	329	55	1,337	2,331	164	454	177
Estonia	154	165	7	1	1	16	21	85	314	3	13	340	1	27	2,550	3	164	5,367
Hungary	64	132	106	1	0	-36	17	61	259	1	5	548	146	128	-12	152	307	102
Kazakhstan	84	101	20	0	1	176	16	55	239		1		503	1,353	169	116	167	44
Latvia	91	104	14	1	1	15	12	33	175	8	2	-79	2	13	550		230	
Lithuania	117	116	-1	1	1	14	8	29	281	0	2	46,039	1	28	2,700	1	325	32,350
Macedonia	87	101	16	3	5	49	1	25	3,397		0			16			213	
Poland	45	80	76	2	1	-66	4	25	592	0	1	146	155	460	197	581	2,710	366

Country	Trade — Total trade in % GDP			Official development aid* — Aid (% GNI)			Foreign direct investment — Inward FDI stock (% GDP)			Outward FDI stock (% GDP)			Remittances — Outgoing total (US$ millions, current)			Incoming total (US$ millions, current)		
	1994	2004	1994-2004 % change	1994	2004	1994-2004 % change	1994	2004	1994-2004 % change	1994	2004	1994-2004 % change	1994	2004	1994-2004 % change	1994	2004	1994-2004 % change
Romania	52	84	61	1	1	146	1	25	1,785	0	0	13	5	8	60	11	132	1,100
Russian Federation	51	57	12	0	0	-51	1	17	1,974	0	14	11,656	3,695	5,534	50	4,563	2,668	-42
Serbia & Montenegro		76			5		2	16	661								4,129	
Slovakia	114	156	37	1	1	13	4	35	822	1	2	111	6	15	150	48	425	785
Slovenia	115	120	5	0	0	-12	9	15	59	3	8	196	20	60	200	273	290	6
Turkey	42	64	52	0	0	-25	11	12	8	1	2	129				2,627	804	-69
Turkmenistan	175	124	-29	1	1	-38	4	12	199									
High income economies																		
Austria	68	97	43				7	22	191	5	23	382	292	2,013	589	845	2,475	193
Belgium***	130	165	26				42	74		28	71		3,660	2,623	-28	4,613	6,840	48
Cyprus	96			1	0	-32		53		1	17	2,197	34	263	674	81	243	199
Denmark	66	82	25				12	41	240	13	41	218	200	1,226	513	439	1,075	145
Finland	64	69	7				7	30	349	13	44	247	42	164	290	67	577	761
France	43	52	21				12	27	119	13	38	182	4,280	4,882	14	3,954	12,663	220
Germany	46	71	54				7	13	94	11	31	185	9,241	10,442	13	4,409	6,497	47
Greece	42	50	21				10	13	33	3	6	121	222	497	124	2,886	1,242	-57
Iceland	68	80	17				2	14	580	2	31	1,171	18	47	161	48	112	133
Ireland	132	145	10				85	126	48	25	53	109	162	856	428	324	358	10
Italy	44	52	19				6	13	122	9	17	91	2,229	4,745	113	2,419	2,172	-10
Luxembourg***	202	271	34					575			555			6,009			1,170	
Netherlands	104	125	21				27	74	177	41	94	130	2,512	5,153	105	984	2,164	120
Norway	70	73	4				13	20	55	14	29	101	475	916	93	170	392	13
Portugal	64	69	9				20	39	99	3	27	891	386	1,024	165	3,806	3,212	-16
Spain	41	55	33				19	35	86	6	34	472	716	5,411	656	2,631	6,900	162
Sweden	66	85	27				11	47	343	28	59	108	231	672	191	249	643	158
Switzerland	66	81	23				19	51	172	43	110	155	8,723	12,796	47	1,212	1,760	45
United Kingdom	54	53	-2				18	36	100	27	65	144	2,072	2,957	43	1,969	6,350	222

Country	Trade: Total trade in % GDP			Official development aid*: Aid (% GNI)			Foreign direct investment: Inward FDI stock (% GDP)			Outward FDI stock (% GDP)			Remittances: Outgoing total (US$ millions, current)			Incoming total (US$ millions, current)		
	1994	2004	1994-2004 % change	1994	2004	1994-2004 % change	1994	2004	1994-2004 % change	1994	2004	1994-2004 % change	1994	2004	1994-2004 % change	1994	2004	1994-2004 % change
Latin America & Caribbean																		
Low income economies																		
Haiti	17	63	268	24	7	-72	8	7	-11	0						43	876	1,937"
Nicaragua	48	80	68	24	28	18	10	50	411	0	1	62,556				50	519	938
Middle income economies																		
Argentina	18	43	140	0	0	9	9	35	306	4	14	306	177	151	-15	62	288	365
Barbados	108	103	-4	0	1	-2,300	12	16	29	2	2	-11	9	18	103	46	109	138
Belize	102	117	15	5	1	-87	28	66	137	5	4	-10	7	9	21	13	25	95
Bolivia	49	57	17	10	9	-7	24	0	-100	0	0	56	10	43	330	5	158	3,060
Brazil	19	31	68	0	0	4	10	25	143	8	11	35	252	401	59	2,068	3,575	73
Chile	57	66	15	0	0	-83	25	58	136	4	15	329	7	3	-57	13		
Colombia	36	43	20	0	1	462	6	23	268	1	5	384	146	50	-66	968	3,190	230
Costa Rica	77	96	25	1	0	-90	21	26	22	1	1	108	7	192	2,643	17	320	1,782"
Cuba	28						0	0	11									
Dominican Republic	68	98	43	1	1	-16	9	44	358	0	0	78	7	24	243	798	2,471	210
Ecuador	51	55	8	1	1	-54	17	42	145	0	1	43	5	7	30	276	1,610	483
El Salvador	55	71	29	4	1	-64	3	23	579	1	1	46		33		972	2,564	164
Grenada	110	114	3	7	4	-44	69	141	106	0			1	2	100	13	23	77
Guatemala	42	49	17	2	1	-53	16	17	4	0			11	36	227	285	2,591	809
Guyana	223	201	-10	16	19	17	69	121	75	0	0	-46	11	57	416	1	100	9,920"
Honduras	82	91	11	9	9	0	17	32	92					1		89	1,142	1,183"
Jamaica	109	98	-10	2	1	-61	30	66	124	5	12	145	55	425	672	522	1,623	211
Mexico	38	62	62	0	0	-83	8	27	242	1	2	241				4,122	18,143	340
Panama	195	128	-35	0	0	-30	39	67	71	55	83	50	25	87	248	112	127	13
Paraguay	87	73	-16	1	0	-100	10	15	45	2	2	-5				148	260	76
Peru	29	39	35	1	1	-4	10	20	98	0	1	436	89	123	38	473	1,123	137
St. Lucia	137	125	-9	6	-3	-156	94	163	74	0			1	1	0	2	4	100
St. Vincent & the Grenadines	117	110	-6	4	3	-32	62	170	175	0			1	1		2	4	75
Suriname	49	91	85	10	2	-76							3	14	367	4	9	125

Country	Trade — Total trade in % GDP			Official development aid* — Aid (% GNI)			Foreign direct investment — Inward FDI stock (% GDP)			Outward FDI stock (% GDP)			Remittances — Outgoing total (US$ millions, current)			Incoming total (US$ millions, current)		
	1994	2004	1994-2004 % change	1994	2004	1994-2004 % change	1994	2004	1994-2004 % change	1994	2004	1994-2004 % change	1994	2004	1994-2004 % change	1994	2004	1994-2004 % change
Trinidad & Tobago	79	108	37	0	0	-101	67	83	25	0	6	1,262	9			27	87	221
Uruguay	40	58	43	0	0	-62	6	18	215	1	1	-6		1			57	
Venezuela	53	56	6	0	0	-7	12	41	226	5	9	61	609	214	-65	2	20	900
High income economies																		
Bahamas				0			21	40	92	34	26	-24	40	119	198			
Netherlands Antilles											1		18	52	189	9	5	-44
Middle East & North Africa																		
Low income economies																		
Palestinian Authority	91	59	-35	13	25	101	27									486	692	42
Yemen	110	59	-46	5	2	-59	8	8	-6	0	0	291	68	108	59	1,059	1,283	21
Middle income economies																		
Algeria	49	66	36	1	0	-46	4	9	131	1	1	44				1,395	2,460	76
Djibouti				9			3	13	381				17			14		
Egypt	51	58	13	5	2	-64	23	27	16	1	1	110	255	13	-95	3,672	3,341	-9
Iran	53	62	18	0	0	-40	2	2	14	0						1,200	1,032	-14
Jordan	118	127	8	6	5	-21	10	32	227				93	272	192	1,094	2,287	109
Lebanon	74	63	-15	2	1	-48	1	12	903	3	3	2				2,165	2,700	25
Libya	53				0		3	3	-5	3	7	154	283	790	179		10	
Malta	204	159	-22	2	0	-92	15	66	332	1	7	545	3	18	493	24	16	-33
Morocco	56	72	30	2	1	-34	18	36	104	1	1	42	17	42	147	1,827	4,221	131
Oman	78	100	28	1	0	-69	16	14	-15	0	0	-13	1,365	1,826	34	39	40	3
Saudi Arabia	60	78	28	0	0	4	13	8	-37	1	1	-37	18,078	13,555	-25			
Syria	78	69	-13	7	0	-93	13	53	298				11	42	282	535	855	60
Tunisia	93	93	0	1	1	71	63	62	-3	0	0	2	19	19	-3	629	1,432	128
High income economies																		
Bahrain	155	147	-6	1	1	19	35	71	99	19	37	92	431	1,120	160			
Israel	81	93	16	2	0	-75	5	28	453	4	14	229	919	2,116	130	1,602	398	-75
Kuwait	93	93	0	0	0	-65	0	1	100	15	5	-70	1,331	2,402	80			
Qatar	79				0		5	15	201	0								

Country	Trade — Total trade in % GDP			Official development aid* — Aid (% GNI)			Foreign direct investment — Inward FDI stock (% GDP)			Foreign direct investment — Outward FDI stock (% GDP)			Remittances — Outgoing total (US$ millions, current)			Remittances — Incoming total (US$ millions, current)		
	1994	2004	1994-2004 % change	1994	2004	1994-2004 % change	1994	2004	1994-2004 % change	1994	2004	1994-2004 % change	1994	2004	1994-2004 % change	1994	2004	1994-2004 % change
United Arab Emirates	139	148	6	0	0	-128	4	5	27	0	2	484						
North America																		
High income economies																		
Canada	68	73	8				20	31	54	19	37	98						
United States	22	24	8				7	13	83	9	17	96	20,366	38,751	90	1,943	3,038	56
South Asia																		
Low income economies																		
Afghanistan					38		0	1	53									
Bangladesh	23	36	59	5	2	-53	1	6	553	0	0	65		8		1,151	3,584	211
Bhutan	68			29	12	-59	1	2	119									
India	20	42	104	1	0	-86	1	6	446	0	1	758	351	1,008	187	5,857	21,727	271
Nepal	50	49	-3	11	6	-42	1	2	175				9	64	607	50	823	1,545
Pakistan	35	31	-13	3	2	-51	6	9	46	0	1	107	2	11	450	1,749	3,945	126
Middle income economies																		
Maldives		178		10	4	-59	15	23	49				22	62	180	2	3	45
Sri Lanka	79	82	3	5	3	-48	10	11	4	0	1	140	16	236	1,376	715	1,590	122
Sub-Saharan Africa																		
Low income economies																		
Angola	161	126	-22	23	7	-71	60	89	47	0	1	1,688	149	296	99			
Benin	50	42	-17	18	9	-47	25	7	-71	0	1	230	23	6	-75	89	55	-38
Burkina Faso	37	32	-15	22	13	-43	4	2	-53	1	1	-29	51	44	-14	80	50	-38
Burundi	39	33	-14	34	55	60	3	8	152	0	0	685	4	4	0			
Cameroon	42	51	23	10	5	-46	16	7	-53	3	2	-40	62			11	11	0
Central African Republic	54	27	-49	20	8	-61	9	8	-14	5	3	-34	27			0		
Chad	50	88	74	19	12	-36	25	73	188	6	2	-74	15			1		
Comoros	67	47	-30	21	7	-68	10	7	-31	1	0	-52	6			15	12	-20
Congo, Dem. Rep.	43			5	29	497	10	29	196									
Congo, Rep.	133	142	7	24	4	-85	51	67	31				23	24	4	4	1	-75
Côte d'Ivoire	70	87	24	21	1	-95	16	25	51	6	4	-27	355	635	79	110	148	35

Country	Trade — Total trade in % GDP			Official development aid* — Aid (% GNI)			Foreign direct investment — Inward FDI stock (% GDP)			Foreign direct investment — Outward FDI stock (% GDP)			Remittances — Outgoing total (US$ millions, current)			Remittances — Incoming total (US$ millions, current)		
	1994	2004	1994-2004 % change	1994	2004	1994-2004 % change	1994	2004	1994-2004 % change	1994	2004	1994-2004 % change	1994	2004	1994-2004 % change	1994	2004	1994-2004 % change
Equatorial Guinea	161			26			95	124	30	0	0	-69						
Eritrea	111	98	-11	30	29	-4		68										
Ethiopia	30	58	96	20	23	17	3	31	962		5		1	9	840	25	133	434
Gambia	103	94	-8	19	16	-18	49	86	75	9	13	56				17	8	-53
Ghana	62	89	43	10	15	50	13	22	64		4		5	6	20	16	82	413
Guinea	48	44	-10	11	7	-33	4	13	232		1		22	48	118	1	42	4,100**
Guinea-Bissau	51	84	66	79	28	-64	9	18	108		0		13	7	-50	0	23	
Kenya	71	58	-19	10	4	-60	10	8	-22	1	2	64	4	34	750	137	494	260
Lesotho	135	152	13	10	6	-35	19	32	69	0	0	1,290	75	29	-61	320	355	11
Madagascar	52	80	54	10	29	182	5	12	116	0	0	-44	8	7	-13	13	16	23
Malawi	91	76	-17	41	26	-37	17	20	23		1		1	1	0	1	1	0
Mali	66	64	-2	25	12	-52	13	18	38	1	2	35	37	58	57	103	154	49
Mauritania	88	99	13	27	11	-60	9	64	640	0	0	-19	25			5	2	-60
Mozambique	62	68	10	61	21	-65	7	39	439	0			19	20	5	55	58	5
Niger	43	42	-4	25	17	-29	24	12	-52	8	4	-42	47	9	-81	7	26	264
Nigeria	83	92	11	1	1	7	36	44	22	7	7	3	4	21	423	550	2,273	313
Rwanda	71	37	-48	96	26	-73	30	15	-50	0	0	30	1	31	2,960	4	10	145
São Tomé & Príncipe	106	133	25	114	56	-50	25	123	384					1			1	
Senegal	77	68	-11	18	14	-24	9	14	51	3	2	-27	60	57	-5	114	511	348
Sierra Leone	55	62	12	35	34	-1		6						3		24	25	3
Somalia							0	1	1,101									
Sudan		39		6	4	-21	1	26	2,069				1	2	100	107	1,403	1,211
Tanzania	64	47	-26	22	16	-27	13	48	265				1	33	3,150	1	11	990
Togo	65	81	24	13	3	-77	27	31	15	3	3	4	4	28	600	15	149	893
Uganda	28	41	48	19	17	-9	3	24	699	3	2	-27	231				306	
Zambia	73	47	-36	23	21	-8	43	56	28					24				
Zimbabwe	71	80	13	8	4	-53	3	21	535	2	4	140	7				44	
Middle income economies																		
Botswana	88	72	-18	2	0	-78	24	15	-38	12	20	69	146	206	41	70	39	-44
Cape Verde	70	95	35	30	15	-50	3	23	703	1	1	-30	3	1	-67	85	92	8

Country	Trade — Total trade in % GDP			Official development aid* — Aid (% GNI)			Foreign direct investment — Inward FDI stock (% GDP)			Outward FDI stock (% GDP)			Remittances — Outgoing total (US$ millions, current)			Incoming total (US$ millions, current)		
	1994	2004	1994-2004 % change	1994	2004	1994-2004 % change	1994	2004	1994-2004 % change	1994	2004	1994-2004 % change	1994	2004	1994-2004 % change	1994	2004	1994-2004 % change
Gabon	100	101	1	5	1	-88		3		5	3	-48	156	115	-26	4	6	50
Mauritius	121	112	-7	0	1	48	7	15	125	3	4	47	1	11	1,000	118	215	82
Namibia	100	91	-8	4	3	-26	49	33	-34	0	0	-59	11	18	60	15	15	1
South Africa	42	54	28	0	0	34	9	22	134	14	14	-4	658	935	42	99	521	426
Swaziland	170	176	4	5	5	-5	44	39	-11	9	5	-48	6	131	2,083	77	89	15

Region	Trade — Total trade in % GDP			Official development aid* — Aid (% GNI)			Foreign direct investment — Inward FDI stock (% GDP)			Outward FDI stock (% GDP)			Remittances — Outgoing total (US$ millions, current)			Incoming total (US$ millions, current)		
	1994	2004	1994-2004 % change	1994	2004	1994-2004 % change	1994	2004	1994-2004 % change	1994	2004	1994-2004 % change	1994	2004	1994-2004 % change	1994	2004	1994-2004 % change
Low income	34	51	51	5	3	-38	10			2			1,395	3,049	119	11,882	43,967	270
Middle income	49	67	37	1	0	-35	12			5			8,937	22,929	157	40,665	117,127	188
Low & middle income	47	65	38	1	1	-28	12	26	114	6	13	118	10,332	25,978	151	52,547	161,094	207
East Asia & Pacific	59	82	39	1	0	-71							408	6,770	1,559	6,798	41,250	507
Europe & Central Asia	61	84	37	1	1	-35							4,013	9,725	142	8,682	19,431	124
Latin America & Caribbean	33	49	48	0	0	-4							1,445	1,895	31	11,124	41,051	269
Middle East & North Africa	60	67	12	2	2	-24							2,128	3,112	46	14,115	20,353	44
South Asia	24	41	71	2	1	-54		6			1		384	1,388	261	9,524	31,671	233
Sub-Saharan Africa	60	66	10	7	5	-27	16			10			1,954	3,089	58	2,304	7,339	218
High income	39	45	*18*				14	21	43	9	27	207	79,798	128,092	61	39,145	66,485	70
World	40	*48*	*19*	0	0	-17	9	22	137	10	24	141	90,130	154,070	71	91,692	227,579	148

Where data for a particular year are not available, figures are taken from the year before or after as an estimate. These figures, and estimates based on them, are presented in italics.
* Official development aid includes both official development assistance and official aid.
** Data for Hong Kong, Macao and Taiwan are not included in this table.
*** FDI data for Belgium and Luxembourg are available as a combined figure in 1994 and separate in 2004. Hence a 1994-2004 comparison has not been calculated. The 1994 joint FDI figure is listed under Belgium.

Sources: World Development Indicators 2005, WDI Online, World Bank, http://devdata.worldbank.org/dataonline; UNCTAD Foreign Direct Investment database, http://stats.unctad.org/FDI/TableViewer/tableView.aspx, UNCTAD World Investment Report 2005 http://www.unctad.org/en/docs/wir2005annexes_en.pdf

Record 2: **Global trade**

This record shows the unevenness of economic globalisation as measured by trade flows. The network graph offers a simplified and consolidated view of trade flows among major world regions for 2004. The diagram should be interpreted by reference to the thickness of the lines between regions (indicating volumes of trade), the position of the regions (spatial centrality reflecting a central position in the trading system), and the size of the regions' nodes (reflecting total trade flows into and out of each region). There is a clear distinction between core, semi-periphery and periphery in the world trade system. Thus, the US, European Union (EU) and East Asia and the Pacific occupy the most central positions within this network, with the greatest amounts of trade flowing between the EU and the US. Japan, Europe and Central Asia, the Middle East and North Africa, and South Asia are at the semi-periphery, and Sub-Saharan Africa and Latin America are at the outer periphery.

The accompanying table illustrates a general trend of increased overall centralisation in the network of world trade between 2000 and 2004 (calculated on the basis of the gap between the most centralised and least centralised nodes in the network). This means that trade is becoming more concentrated in the rich regions. A growing share of world trade is channelled between the US, the EU, and East Asia and the Pacific. South Asian countries are becoming more central while Japan's centrality has declined due to its continuing economic crisis (centrality in the global trade network is determined not only by a particular region's share of total world trade but also the 'strength' of the regions it trades with).

Direction of flow (export region → import region)*	Amount of trade in % world trade** 2004
East Asia & Pacific → Europe & Central Asia	0.4
East Asia & Pacific → European Union	1.8
East Asia & Pacific → Japan	1.5
East Asia & Pacific → Latin America & Caribbean	0.2
East Asia & Pacific → Middle East & North Africa	0.2
East Asia & Pacific → South Asia	0.3
East Asia & Pacific → Sub-Saharan Africa	0.2
East Asia & Pacific → United States	2.2
Within East Asia & Pacific	1.3
Europe & Central Asia → East Asia & Pacific	0.2
Europe & Central Asia → European Union	3.6
Europe & Central Asia → Japan	0.1
Europe & Central Asia → Middle East & North Africa	0.2
Europe & Central Asia → South Asia	0.1
Europe & Central Asia → United States	0.3
Within Europe & Central Asia	1.8
European Union → East Asia & Pacific	1.1
European Union → Europe & Central Asia	3.6
European Union → Japan	0.6
European Union → Latin America & Caribbean	0.5
European Union → Middle East & North Africa	0.8
European Union → South Asia	0.3

Direction of flow (export region → import region)*	Amount of trade in % world trade** 2004
European Union → Sub-Saharan Africa	0.5
European Union → United States	3.3
Within European Union	24.3
Japan → East Asia & Pacific	1.5
Japan → Europe & Central Asia	0.1
Japan → European Union	1.0
Japan → Latin America & Caribbean	0.2
Japan → Middle East & North Africa	0.1
Japan → South Asia	0.1
Japan → Sub-Saharan Africa	0.1
Japan → United States	1.5
Latin America & Caribbean → East Asia & Pacific	0.2
Latin America & Caribbean → Europe & Central Asia	0.1
Latin America & Caribbean → European Union	0.7
Latin America & Caribbean → Japan	0.1
Latin America & Caribbean → Middle East & North Africa	0.1
Latin America & Caribbean → United States	2.9
Within Latin America & Caribbean	0.8
Middle East & North Africa → East Asia & Pacific	0.2
Middle East & North Africa → Europe & Central Asia	0.1
Middle East & North Africa → European Union	0.9
Middle East & North Africa → Japan	0.1
Middle East & North Africa → United States	0.1
Within Middle East & North Africa	0.1
South Asia → East Asia & Pacific	0.1
South Asia → European Union	0.3
South Asia → Middle East & North Africa	0.1
South Asia → United States	0.2
Within South Asia	0.1
Sub-Saharan Africa → East Asia & Pacific	0.2
Sub-Saharan Africa → European Union	0.4
Sub-Saharan Africa → Japan	0.1
Sub-Saharan Africa → South Asia	0.1
Sub-Saharan Africa → United States	0.4
Within Sub-Saharan Africa	0.2

Direction of flow (export region → import region)*	Amount of trade in % world trade** 2004
United States → East Asia & Pacific	0.7
United States → Europe & Central Asia	0.1
United States → European Union	1.9
United States → Japan	0.6
United States → Latin America & Caribbean	0.7
United States → Middle East & North Africa	0.1
United States → South Asia	0.1
United States → Sub-Saharan Africa	0.1

* European Union countries: Austria, Belgium, Denmark, Finland, France, Germany, Greece, Ireland, Italy, Luxembourg, Netherlands, Portugal, Spain, Sweden, United Kingdom. All other regions represented in the diagram comprise the countries listed in World Bank classifications of these regions.

** Only flows amounting to at least 0.1% of total world trade are included in this table. Flows not associated with a region are also excluded from the table. Figures do not therefore sum to 100%.

Source: World Bank, World Development Indicators 2006: Table 6.3. Direction and growth of merchandise trade; Direction of trade 2004; http://www.worldbank.org/wdi2006/contents/index2.htm.

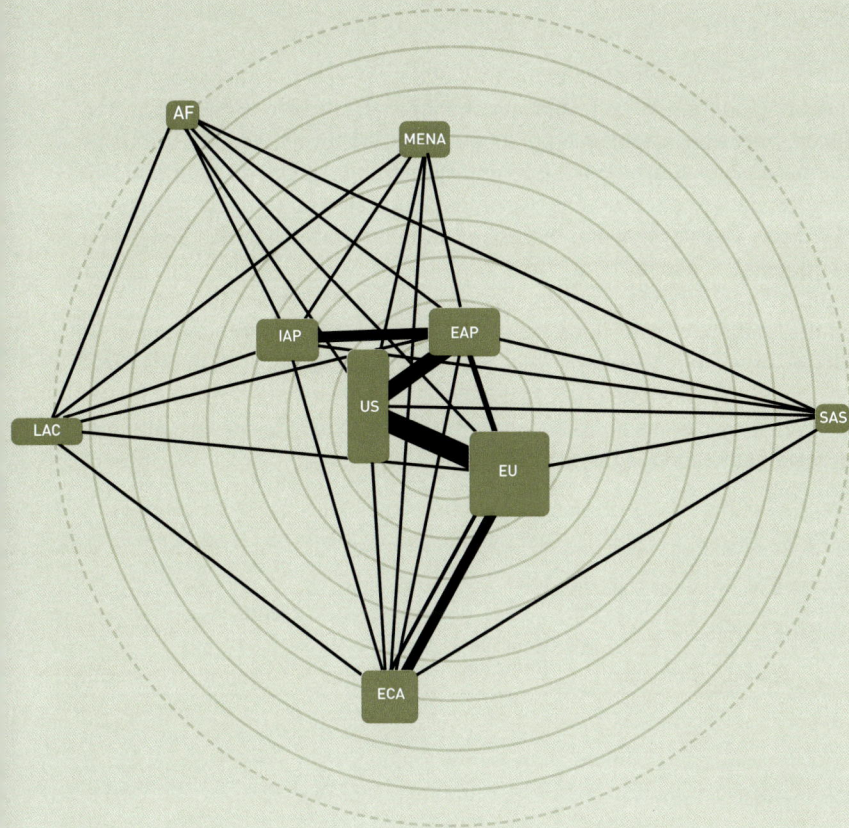

EAP — East Asia & Pacific

ECA — Europe & Central Asia

EU — European Union

JAP — Japan

LAC — Latin America & Caribbean

MENA — Middle East & North Africa

SAS — South Asia

USA — United States

Changes in trade network centrality, 2000-2004

Node	Region	Network centrality		Change in centrality (% change) 2000-2004
		2000	2004	
LAC	Latin America & Caribbean	9.5	9.1	-4
AF	Sub-Saharan Africa	7.7	9.1	18
SAS	South Asia	9.5	9.3	-2
MENA	Middle East & North Africa	12.0	10.7	-11
ECA	Europe & Central Asia	9.5	10.7	12
JAP	Japan	13.0	11.9	-8
EAP	East Asia & Pacific	13.0	13.1	1
US	United States	13.0	13.1	1
EU	European Union	13.0	13.1	1
Network centralisation		2.1	2.2	7

Record 3: Trafficking in persons

One of the major vehicles and consequences of globalisation is the flow of people across national boundaries. One such flow, albeit a negative aspect of globalisation, is trafficking of people. Trafficking is defined as 'the recruitment, harbouring, transportation, provision, or obtaining of a person for labour or services, through the use of force, fraud or coercion for the purpose of subjection to involuntary servitude, peonage, debt bondage, or slavery'. While no accurate quantitative data exists (the US government estimates up to 900,000 people are trafficked annually worldwide), the US State Department and the United Nations Office on Drugs and Crime (UNODC) issue reports that provide a qualitative assessment of the forms and scope of trafficking by country. In the table below, a country is designated 'yes' if the report lists it as an origin of trafficking, as a transit country for trafficked people, or as a destination for trafficking. The US report also identifies countries where internal trafficking exists, and the UN's *Trafficking in Persons – Global Patterns 2006* report, also rates the level of each from 'very low' (1) to 'very high' (5). The data show that human trafficking is pervasive globally. Differences between developed and developing nations in the nature of trafficking are also shown, with the former acting mostly as transit and destination, and the latter as the source.

Country	US Department of State Report				UNODC Report		
	International trafficking			Internal trafficking	Source	Transit	Destination
	Source	Transit	Destination				
East Asia & Pacific							
Low income economies							
Cambodia	yes	yes	yes		4	1	4
Indonesia	yes	yes	yes	yes	3	2	2
Korea, Dem. Rep.	yes				3		
Laos	yes	yes	yes		4	2	2
Mongolia	yes	yes		yes			
Myanmar	yes		yes	yes	4	4	3
Vietnam	yes		yes	yes	4	1	3
Middle income economies							
China	yes	yes	yes	yes	5	1	4
Fiji					1		1
Malaysia	yes	yes	yes		3	3	3
Philippines	yes	yes	yes	yes	4	1	3
Thailand	yes	yes	yes	yes	5	5	5
High income economies							
Australia			yes				4
Brunei					1	2	2
Hong Kong					3	3	4
Korea, Rep.	yes	yes	yes		2	1	3
Japan			yes			1	5
Macao					1		3

Country	US Department of State Report				UNODC Report		
	International trafficking			Internal trafficking	Source	Transit	Destination
	Source	Transit	Destination				
New Zealand			yes			2	3
Singapore			yes		3	3	3
Taiwan					3		4
Europe & Central Asia							
Low income economies							
Armenia	yes	yes	yes		4		
Azerbaijan	yes	yes		yes	3	2	
Georgia	yes	yes	yes		4	3	1
Kyrgyzstan	yes	yes	yes	yes	3	1	2
Moldova	yes	yes			5	2	1
Tajikistan	yes				3		1
Ukraine	yes	yes		yes	5	4	3
Uzbekistan	yes	yes		yes	4		2
Middle income economies							
Albania	yes	yes			5	5	3
Belarus	yes				5	3	
Bosnia & Herzegovina	yes	yes	yes		3	4	4
Bulgaria	yes	yes	yes	yes	5	5	3
Croatia	yes	yes	yes		3	3	3
Czech Republic	yes	yes	yes	yes	4	4	4
Estonia	yes	yes		yes	4	1	3
Hungary	yes	yes	yes	yes	4	5	3
Kazakhstan	yes	yes	yes	yes	4	3	3
Latvia	yes	yes		yes	4	2	3
Lithuania	yes	yes	yes		5	2	3
Macedonia		yes	yes	yes	3	4	3
Poland	yes	yes	yes	yes	4	5	4
Romania	yes	yes			5	4	2
Russian Federation	yes	yes	yes	yes	5	3	3
Serbia & Montenegro	yes	yes	yes	yes	3	4	3
Slovakia	yes	yes			4	4	1
Slovenia	yes	yes	yes		3	2	2
Turkey		yes	yes	yes	3	4	5
Turkmenistan					3		

	US Department of State Report				UNODC Report		
	International trafficking			Internal trafficking			
Country	Source	Transit	Destination		Source	Transit	Destination
High income economies							
Austria		yes	yes			2	4
Belgium		yes	yes			4	5
Cyprus				yes		3	4
Denmark		yes	yes				4
Finland		yes	yes			1	3
France			yes			4	4
Germany		yes	yes			4	5
Greece		yes	yes			4	5
Iceland							3
Ireland						1	2
Italy		yes	yes			5	5
Luxembourg			yes				2
Netherlands		yes	yes	yes	1	3	5
Norway			yes			1	3
Portugal		yes	yes				3
Spain		yes	yes			2	4
Sweden		yes	yes			1	3
Switzerland		yes	yes			2	4
United Kingdom		yes	yes			3	4
Latin America & Caribbean							
Low income economies							
Haiti	yes	yes	yes	yes	3		2
Nicaragua	yes	yes			2		
Middle income economies							
Argentina	yes		yes	yes	2		3
Belize		yes	yes	yes		1	2
Bolivia	yes	yes		yes			
Brazil	yes		yes	yes	4		1
Chile	yes	yes	yes	yes	1		1
Colombia	yes	yes		yes	4	1	
Costa Rica	yes	yes	yes	yes	1	2	2
Cuba	yes			yes	3		
Dominican Republic	yes	yes	yes		4		3
Ecuador	yes	yes	yes		3		2
El Salvador	yes	yes	yes	yes	3	1	3

Country	US Department of State Report				UNODC Report		
	International trafficking			Internal trafficking	Source	Transit	Destination
	Source	Transit	Destination				
Guatemala	yes	yes	yes	yes	4	1	3
Guyana	yes	yes	yes				
Honduras	yes	yes		yes	3		1
Jamaica	yes	yes		yes	1	1	1
Mexico	yes	yes	yes	yes	4	3	3
Panama	yes	yes	yes	yes	2	1	3
Paraguay	yes			yes	1		2
Peru	yes	yes		yes	3		
Suriname		yes	yes	yes			
Trinidad & Tobago							1
Uruguay	yes	yes	yes		1	1	
Venezuela	yes	yes	yes	yes	3		3
High income economies							
Netherlands Antilles							3
Middle East & North Africa							
Low income economies							
Yemen	yes		yes	yes	1		2
Middle income economies							
Algeria		yes		yes	3	2	1
Djibouti					2		1
Egypt		yes			1	3	2
Iran	yes	yes	yes	yes	2		3
Iraq					2		2
Jordan					2	1	
Lebanon			yes		2	1	3
Libya							2
Morocco	yes	yes	yes	yes	4	2	1
Oman			yes				2
Saudi Arabia			yes			1	4
Syria			yes		1		3
Tunisia					2		
High income economies							
Bahrain			yes			1	3
Israel			yes				5
Kuwait			yes	yes			3
Qatar			yes				3

Country	US Department of State Report				UNODC Report		
	International trafficking			Internal trafficking	Source	Transit	Destination
	Source	Transit	Destination				
United Arab Emirates			yes				4
North America							
High income economies							
Canada		yes	yes	yes	2	3	4
United States					2		5
South Asia							
Low income economies							
Afghanistan	yes	yes		yes	3		
Bangladesh	yes	yes			4	1	2
Bhutan					2		1
India	yes	yes	yes	yes	4	3	4
Nepal	yes			yes	4	1	
Pakistan	yes	yes	yes	yes	4	1	4
Middle income economies							
Maldives					2		1
Sri Lanka	yes			yes	3		2
Sub-Saharan Africa							
Low income economies							
Angola	yes			yes	3		
Benin	yes	yes	yes	yes	4	3	3
Burkina Faso	yes	yes	yes	yes	3	3	3
Burundi	yes				2		1
Cameroon	yes	yes	yes	yes	3	2	3
Chad	yes			yes	1	1	1
Congo, Dem. Rep.					2		1
Congo, Rep.	yes			yes	3		2
Côte d'Ivoire	yes	yes	yes		3	3	3
Equatorial Guinea					2	1	3
Eritrea					2		
Ethiopia	yes			yes	3		1
Gambia	yes	yes	yes	yes	2		1
Ghana	yes	yes	yes	yes	4	2	3
Guinea	yes	yes	yes	yes	2		
Kenya	yes	yes	yes	yes	3		3
Lesotho					2	1	
Liberia		yes	yes		3		1

| Country | US Department of State Report | | | | UNODC Report | | |
| | International trafficking | | | Internal trafficking | Source | Transit | Destination |
	Source	Transit	Destination				
Madagascar	yes			yes	2		
Malawi	yes	yes		yes	3	1	1
Mali	yes	yes	yes	yes	3	1	2
Mauritania	yes		yes				
Mozambique	yes				3	1	1
Niger	yes	yes	yes	yes	3	1	2
Nigeria	yes	yes	yes		5	2	3
Rwanda	yes			yes	2		
Senegal	yes	yes	yes	yes	3	1	1
Sierra Leone	yes	yes	yes	yes	3		1
Somalia					2		
Sudan	yes				2		1
Tanzania	yes	yes	yes	yes	3	1	2
Togo	yes	yes	yes		3	3	3
Uganda	yes		yes		3		2
Zambia	yes	yes			3	1	1
Zimbabwe	yes	yes			2	1	1
Middle income economies							
Botswana					2	2	
Cape Verde					2		
Gabon			yes		2	3	3
Mauritius	yes		yes				
South Africa	yes	yes	yes	yes	3	3	3

Lack of data for a country does not necessarily mean that it does not have a trafficking problem: rather it may be that credible information regarding trafficking is not available. Hence, missing data should be treated with caution. Countries excluded from this list or for which blank cells are presented may or may not have a trafficking problem, but credible information regarding trafficking is not provided by the sources in this record.

Source: US Department of State, (June 2005). Victims of Trafficking and Violence Protection Act of 2001: Trafficking in Persons Report, 2005. Office of the Under Secretary for Global Affairs, Office to Monitor and Combat Trafficking in Persons, Publication 11252, www.state.gov/g/tip/rls/tiprpt/2004; United Nations Office on Drugs and Crime (UNODC), Trafficking in Persons - Global Patterns, April 2006, http://www.unodc.org/unodc/en/trafficking_persons_report_2006-04.html

Record 4: Air travel

Air travel facilitates global activism and creates economic as well as social ties. The table data from the International Air Transport Association (IATA) comprises 2004 statistics from airlines about the number of passengers carried and the number of kilometres they fly. It includes the ratio of international to domestic travel (numbers exceeding 1 indicate that international travel surpasses domestic travel), and allows us to move away from the nation state as the only unit of analysis. The table shows that the gap in air travel between high income and low-to-middle income economies remains substantial.

Country	Air Transport				
	International		Domestic		
	Passengers carried (number)	Passenger-kilometres flown (1000s)	Passengers carried (number)	Passenger-kilometres flown (1000s)	Ratio of Passengers carried: int'l to domestic
			2004		
East Asia & Pacific					
Low income economies					
Indonesia					
Garuda	2,368,657	8,165,767	7,288,167	5,972,019	0.3
Mongolia					
MIAT	162,266	616,304	91,933	76,298	1.8
Papua New Guinea					
Air Niugini	146,023	388,447	612,947	276,784	0.2
Solomon Islands					
Solomon Airlines	30,293	62,388	52,543	14,345	0.6
Middle income economies					
China					
China Yunnan Airlines	159,975	318,992	4,475,960	4,903,220	0.0
Air China Limited	4,907,994	20,900,463	19,226,856	25,151,797	0.3
China Airlines	8,716,789	29,081,176			
China Cargo Airlines					
China Southern Airlines	2,663,894	8,006,570	36,373,692	46,083,180	0.1
China Eastern Airlines	2,768,164	9,918,460	16,741,288	19,212,167	0.2
China Northwest Airlines	598,535	987,005	3,494,900	4,243,324	0.2
Shanghai Airlines	113,728	240,399	5,607,763	7,232,371	0.0
Hainan Airlines	52,987	215,157	10,508,025	14,077,384	0.0
Xiamen Airlines	159,721	460,360	6,058,786	6,345,499	0.0
Shandong Airlines	21,038	57,100	2,987,144	3,293,192	0.0
Shenzhen Airlines			4,836,932	6,400,692	

	Air Transport				
	International		Domestic		
Country	Passengers carried (number)	Passenger-kilometres flown (1000s)	Passengers carried (number)	Passenger-kilometres flown (1000s)	Ratio of Passengers carried: Int'l to domestic
			2004		
Fiji					
Air Pacific	586,719	2,388,962			
Malaysia					
Malaysia Airlines	8,370,229	37,871,685	8,936,578	4,789,275	0.9
Micronesia					
Continental Micronesia	1,283,857	3,095,533	168,479	1,037,206	7.6
Philippines					
Philippine Airlines	2,372,591	11,265,319	3,153,537	2,061,325	0.8
Samoa					
Polynesian Airlines	92,438	314,082	90,970	12,008	1.0
Thailand					
Bangkok Airways	465,641	321,936	1,394,773	739,453	0.3
Thai Airways	13,277,358	47,480,333	5,487,966	3,238,200	2.4
High income economies					
Australia					
Austral	13,683	3,198	1,532,940	1,761,267	0.0
Air Austral	491,210	2,064,398	140,331	170,574	3.5
Qantas	7,789,056	50,825,075	16,475,762	22,760,519	0.5
Regional Express			972,032	375,954	
Brunei					
Royal Brunei	1,079,837	3,853,827			
Korea, Rep.					
Korean Air Lines Co. Ltd.	10,203,937	41,490,557	11,050,629	3,863,704	0.9
Asiana Airlines	5,955,187	16,862,173	5,913,414	2,055,387	1.0
Japan					
Japan Airlines International	12,732,038	64,625,875	39,004,253	30,180,548	0.3
Nippon Cargo Airlines	0	0	0	0	
All Nippon Airways	3,605,577	17,687,428	42,844,548	37,303,404	0.1
New Zealand					
Air New Zealand	4,337,944	21,536,109	6,967,457	3,173,396	0.6
Singapore					
Silkair	1,036,811	1,853,661			
Singapore Airlines	15,877,066	77,082,200			

	Air Transport				
	International		Domestic		
Country	Passengers carried (number)	Passenger-kilometres flown (1000s)	Passengers carried (number)	Passenger-kilometres flown (1000s)	Ratio of Passengers carried: int'l to domestic
			2004		
Taiwan					
EVA Air	5,228,183	21,367,402			
TransAsia	584,911	559,253	2,577,335	802,847	0.2
Europe & Central Asia					
Low income economies					
Armenia					
Armenian Int'l Airways	71,332	190,890			
Armavia	424,749	756,329			
Ukraine					
Air Ukraine	21,460	54,716			
Ukraine Int'l Airlines	472,180	896,781	66,374	36,434	7.1
Aerosvit Airlines	684,759	2,004,610	136,780	65,624	5.0
Middle income economies					
Albania					
Albanian Airlines	188,890	144,659	0	0	
Belarus					
Belavia	274,046	398,753	139	31	1,971.6
Bulgaria					
Hemus Air	65,070	73,070	45,732	16,482	1.4
Croatia					
Croatia Airlines	866,215	796,334	470,196	144,256	1.8
Czech Republic					
Czech Airlines	3,931,988	5,685,889	62,805	17,585	62.6
Estonia					
Estonian Air	509,560	547,321			
Hungary					
MALEV	2,546,234	3,509,695			
Kazakhstan					
Air Astana	316,059	1,233,127	526,778	700,393	0.6
Latvia					
Air Baltic	585,297	556,043			
Lithuania					
Lithuanian Airlines	381,894	507,095	736	225	518.9

Country	Air Transport				
	International		Domestic		
	Passengers carried (number)	Passenger-kilometres flown (1000s)	Passengers carried (number)	Passenger-kilometres flown (1000s)	Ratio of Passengers carried: int'l to domestic
	2004				
Macedonia					
Macedonian Airlines	210,875	275,612			
Poland					
LOT	2,677,507	5,622,039	815,587	238,640	3.3
Romania					
Tarom S.A.	875,385	1,260,135	186,338	68,738	4.7
Russian Federation					
Aeroflot Russian Airlines	4,561,322	15,872,756	1,939,915	4,471,724	2.4
Samara Airlines	90,992	187,026	301,129	354,629	0.3
Pulkovo Aviation Enterprise	891,623	1,963,746	1,337,552	2,003,639	0.7
Siberia Airlines	677,668	1,804,011	2,427,603	6,207,076	0.3
Transaero	549,229	1,522,473	301,052	1,222,066	1.8
Volga-Dnepr Airlines	0	0	40,497	29,920	
Vladivostok Air JSC	152,848	187,649	414,758	1,493,115	0.4
Serbia & Montenegro					
Montenegro Airlines	115,332	114,661	221,714	76,089	0.5
Jat Airways	827,984	1,022,421	248,489	72,546	3.3
Slovenia					
Adria Airways	764,991	710,973	0	0	
Turkey					
Turkish Airlines	5,585,540	14,178,227	5,791,099	3,204,179	1.0
High income economies					
Austria					
Austrian	7,173,832	17,399,319	445,287	120,426	16.1
Lauda Air S.p.A.	336,928	2,928,680			
Belgium					
TNT Airways S.A.	71,903	181,831			
EAT					
SN Brussels Airlines	3,192,679	4,556,025			
Cyprus					
Cyprus Airways	1,702,258	3,421,285			
Helios Air	310,996	812,225	0	0	
Denmark					

Country	Air Transport				
	International		Domestic		
	Passengers carried (number)	Passenger-kilometres flown (1000s)	Passengers carried (number)	Passenger-kilometres flown (1000s)	Ratio of Passengers carried: int'l to domestic
	2004				
Maersk Air A/S	1,425,491	1,714,066	0	0	
Finland					
Finnair	3,738,947	9,343,236	2,289,174	1,132,864	1.6
Blue1 (Blue1 Ltd.)	987,802	659,320	151,833	71,751	6.5
France					
Air France	26,904,455	96,958,488	18,488,184	10,405,374	1.5
Corse Air International	334,765	1,094,396	985,683	7,459,408	0.3
Compagnie Aérienne Corse	604,129		1,194,968		
Germany					
Air Berlin	9,754,424	14,203,547			
Dba Luftfahrtgesellschaft mbH	148,016	111,665	2,530,929	1,256,152	0.1
European Air Express	29,536	20,012	49,674	23,372	0.6
Eurowings	2,691,200	2,555,265	777,703	367,656	3.5
Hapag Lloyd	6,546,714	15,325,732	202,476	473,992	32.3
Hahn Air Lines GmbH	10,008	2,884	0	0	
Lufthansa	34,407,167	103,866,418	13,860,520	5,604,524	2.5
LTU					
Greece					
Aegean Airlines S.A.	711,370	953,247	2,492,787	805,997	0.3
Olympic Airlines	2,596,902	5,849,487	3,197,486	938,868	0.8
Hellas Jet	278,409	618,600			
Iceland					
Icelandair	1,381,626	3,702,424			
Ireland					
Aer Lingus	6,959,356	11,136,104	0	0	
CityJet	1,206,215	910,707			
Italy					
Air One S.p.A.	10,205	4,684			
Alitalia	11,486,222	26,162,725	10,502,219	4,084,535	1.1
Blue Panorama S.p.A.	30,493	39,483			
Meridiana	446,451	535,863	3,150,619	1,900,383	0.1

	Air Transport				
	International		Domestic		
Country	Passengers carried (number)	Passenger-kilometres flown (1000s)	Passengers carried (number)	Passenger-kilometres flown (1000s)	Ratio of Passengers carried: int'l to domestic
			2004		
Luxembourg					
Cargolux					
Luxair	855,840	572,582			
Netherlands					
KLM	20,285,860	63,012,988	100,327	14,332	202.2
Norway					
Braathens	593,614	1,231,535	4,158,692	2,404,950	0.1
Widerøe	376,744	207,019	1,440,805	347,708	0.3
Portugal					
PGA - Portugália Airlines	714,043	828,312	271,496	75,204	2.6
TAP - Air Portugal	4,670,347	12,240,823	1,949,086	1,465,381	2.4
Air Luxor	352,648	517,549	158,648	157,525	2.2
SATA Air Açores			391,581	69,005	
Spain*					
Iberia	11,428,499	35,935,013	14,822,560	9,830,634	0.8
Spanair	673,027	1,214,922	5,601,176	4,562,158	0.1
Binter Canarias	1,269	659	2,420,296	426,968	0.0
Air Europa	1,525,971	4,990,041	5,282,565	4,770,511	0.3
Air Nostrum	1,019,238	929,446	2,808,264	1,066,438	0.4
Sweden					
Falcon Air					
Skyways	299,211	145,134	888,207	362,559	0.3
SAS Scandinavian Airlines	12,822,970	20,925,308	7,555,598	3,124,872	1.7
Malmö Aviation	185,066	205,574	842,083	388,292	0.2
Switzerland					
SWISS	8,619,199	20,454,187	659,866	144,643	13.1
United Kingdom					
British Airways	28,567,380	102,857,803	6,895,156	3,642,909	4.1
Bmi	5,358,442	4,537,490	4,528,178	2,006,768	1.2
Flybe	1,071,567	936,531	2,890,251	986,438	0.4
GB Airways	2,120,574	3,672,011			
Virgin Atlantic	4,328,628	30,222,744			

	Air Transport				
	International		Domestic		
Country	Passengers carried (number)	Passenger-kilometres flown (1000s)	Passengers carried (number)	Passenger-kilometres flown (1000s)	Ratio of Passengers carried: int'l to domestic
	2004				
Latin America & Caribbean					
Middle income economies					
Argentina					
Southern Winds S.A.	70,361	702,209	667,488	711,418	0.1
Aerolíneas Argentinas	1,738,099	8,318,987	2,574,697	2,912,364	0.7
Bolivia					
LAB	538,305	1,244,384	671,936	226,730	0.8
Brazil					
TAM Linhas Aéreas	727,433	3,244,548	11,236,582	8,575,629	0.1
Varig	2,999,311	18,041,247	10,180,239	9,813,720	0.3
Chile					
Lan Airlines	4,100,278	12,975,330	2,452,760	2,694,800	1.7
Lan Chile Cargo S.A.	0	0			
Colombia					
Avianca	1,827,226	4,180,546	3,569,724	1,484,151	0.5
El Salvador					
TACA	4,231,572	7,861,443	122,228	39,830	34.6
Jamaica					
Air Jamaica	2,007,765	5,060,257			
Mexico					
AEROMEXICO	2,115,893	6,572,005	7,075,597	7,180,827	0.3
Mexicana	3,379,291	8,324,430	4,815,962	4,463,831	0.7
Lineas Aereas Azteca S.A.de C.V.	48,780	100,154	691,210	1,092,170	0.1
Panama					
Copa	1,500,673	4,100,452			
Paraguay					
Transportes Aéreos Del Mercosur	366,021	431,475	7,435	1,893	49.2
Uruguay					
PLUNA	564,149	1,075,934			
Venezuela					
Aeropostal Alas De Venezuela C.A.	589,807	803,170	2,025,170	828,751	0.3

	Air Transport				
	International		Domestic		
Country	Passengers carried (number)	Passenger-kilometres flown (1000s)	Passengers carried (number)	Passenger-kilometres flown (1000s)	Ratio of Passengers carried: int'l to domestic
	2004				
Middle East & North Africa					
Low income economies					
Palestinian Authority					
Palestinian Airlines	5,284	909			
Middle income economies					
Algeria					
Air Algérie	1,913,438	2,651,545	1,322,926	701,421	1.4
Egypt					
Egyptair	3,188,744	8,145,869	1,349,887	614,877	2.4
Iran					
Iran Air	1,214,212	3,238,783	5,751,377	3,895,849	0.2
Mahan Airlines	189,455	646,465	574,750	515,829	0.3
Jordan					
Royal Jordanian	1,660,235	5,327,059			
Lebanon					
T.M.A.	0	0			
Libya					
MEA-AirLliban	1,086,730	2,197,171			
Afriqiyah Airways	161,000	453,722	0	0	
Malta					
Air Malta	1,365,223	2,281,788			
Morocco					
Royal Air Maroc	2,363,007	5,341,002	641,345	209,968	3.7
Oman					
Oman Air	809,756	1,358,609	172,785	142,260	4.7
Saudi Arabia					
Saudi Arabian Airlines	5,250,533	14,896,606	9,692,100	7,660,463	0.5
Tunisia					
Tunis Air	1,961,541	2,918,592			
High income economies					
Bahrain					
DHL International E.C.					
Gulf Air	5,265,577	16,963,912	1,588,063	899,342	3.3

Country	Air Transport				
	International		Domestic		
	Passengers carried (number)	Passenger-kilometres flown (1000s)	Passengers carried (number)	Passenger-kilometres flown (1000s)	Ratio of Passengers carried: int'l to domestic
	2004				
Israel					
C.A.L. Cargo Airlines Ltd.	0	0			
Arkia Israeli Airlines	22,719	55,734	594,446	181,156	0.0
El Al	2,947,061	14,325,661			
Kuwait					
Kuwait Airways	2,316,668	6,680,916			
Qatar					
Qatar Airways	4,453,071	12,171,615	0	0	
United Arab Emirates					
Emirates	12,029,779	48,748,922			
North America					
High income economies					
Canada					
Air Canada	11,024,137	45,796,170	10,330,801	20,183,534	1.1
Cargojet Airways	3,703	123	3,348	64	1.1
United States					
United Parcel Service	0	0	0	0	
Atlas Air					
American Airlines	18,841,318	70,036,066	72,728,685	139,219,507	0.3
Aloha Airlines	26,883	102,036	4,154,890	3,646,244	0.0
Alaska Airlines	1,988,401	3,734,629	15,087,061	23,205,320	0.1
Continental Airlines	9,664,238	41,061,875	30,883,386	60,031,922	0.3
America West Airlines	967,109	2,059,993	20,152,047	35,463,956	0.0
US Airways	4,451,106	16,978,982	37,948,915	48,216,607	0.1
Delta Air Lines	7,493,418	40,265,350	79,289,197	117,516,072	0.1
Federal Express	0	0	0	0	
Northwest Airlines	9,903,614	51,703,803	46,525,037	66,276,564	0.2
United Airlines	9,367,800	67,484,064	61,868,417	116,835,792	0.2
South Asia					
Low income economies					
Bangladesh					
Biman Bangladesh	1,285,452	4,825,587	361,214	76,467	3.6
India					

Country	Air Transport				
	International		Domestic		
	Passengers carried (number)	Passenger-kilometres flown (1000s)	Passengers carried (number)	Passenger-kilometres flown (1000s)	Ratio of Passengers carried: int'l to domestic
	2004				
Jet Airways	95,363	69,052	7,754,160	6,676,991	0.0
Air India	3,362,217	17,420,855	942,160	892,520	3.6
BWIA West Indies Airways	1,088,242	3,009,440	44,150	3,787	24.6
Indian Airlines	1,731,999	4,047,967	6,716,339	6,359,426	0.3
Sahara Airlines	85,390	60,724	2,490,459	2,863,160	0.0
Pakistan					
Pakistan International	2,984,678	11,837,430	2,112,749	1,742,501	1.4
Middle income economies					
Sri Lanka					
Srilankan Airlines	2,412,889	8,310,070			
Sub-Saharan Africa					
Low income economies					
Ethiopia					
Ethiopian Airlines	1,109,776	4,269,555	293,517	124,123	3.8
Kenya					
Kenya Airways	1,512,843	5,104,968	424,662	177,959	3.6
Madagascar					
Air Madagascar	166,612	735,666	346,896	175,429	0.5
Malawi					
Air Malawi	81,087	83,912	33,241	61,937	2.4
Mozambique					
LAM	105,652	148,781	193,381	239,631	0.5
Nigeria					
Albarka Air			140,783	64,760	
Senegal					
Air Senegal International	378,559	756,187	42,049	11,894	9.0
Zambia					
Zambian Airways Limited	28,894	9,636	20,474	9,730	1.4
Zimbabwe					
Air Zimbabwe	140,334	528,494	97,508	47,450	1.4
Middle income economies					
Mauritius					
Air Mauritius	1,009,324	5,694,723	80,132	48,168	12.6

	Air Transport				
	International		Domestic		
Country	Passengers carried (number)	Passenger-kilometres flown (1000s)	Passengers carried (number)	Passenger-kilometres flown (1000s)	Ratio of Passengers carried: int'l to domestic
			2004		
Namibia					
Air Namibia	234,965	884,542	45,581	26,505	5.2
South Africa					
SA Airlink	35,169	13,493	555,610	333,803	0.1
Inter Air	44,161	98,523			
Safair			0	0	
Comair	115,884	117,282	2,316,630	2,350,370	0.1
SAA-South African Airways	2,882,883	19,390,108	3,857,146	3,690,102	0.7

* Spain Air transport data includes the Canary Islands.

	Air Transport				
	International		Domestic		
Region	Passengers carried (number)	Passenger-kilometres flown (1000s)	Passengers carried (number)	Passenger-kilometres flown (1000s)	Ratio of Passengers carried: int'l to domestic
			2004		
Low income	18,544,101	66,045,394	30,262,486	25,969,269	0.61
Middle income	128,962,320	398,099,768	217,127,065	229,357,356	0.59
Low & middle income:					
East Asia & Pacific	49,318,897	182,156,438	137,589,239	155,159,739	0.36
Europe & Central Asia	29,321,029	62,077,041	15,335,273	20,423,392	1.91
Latin America & Caribbean	26,804,964	83,036,570	46,091,028	40,026,115	0.58
Middle East & North Africa	21,169,158	49,458,120	19,505,170	13,740,667	1.09
South Asia	13,046,230	49,581,125	20,421,231	18,614,852	0.64
Sub-Saharan Africa	7,846,143	37,835,869	8,447,610	7,361,861	0.93
High income	400,446,549	1,388,686,396	632,617,371	805,220,404	0.63
World	547,952,970	1,852,831,558	880,006,922	1,060,547,030	0.62

Source: IATA International Air Transport Association, World Air Transport Statistics (WATS), 49th Edition.

Record 5: Media and communication

Communications and news are major facilitators of globalisation, as well as of dissent from it. This record offers an indication of people's exposure to media as well as their local and transnational communication with each other, all for the latest available year and with a time comparison where feasible. The table shows that exposure to media and communications in the developed world is reaching a point of saturation and beginning to wane, while in the developing world it continues to grow. People in developing countries are increasingly better connected, thanks partly to the rapid expansion of cellular communications. Data on computer and internet use reveal growing global connectedness, but they also indicate the 'digital divide' between developed nations and the rest of the world, alongside vast variations in internet access among developing countries in different regions.

Country	Television sets per 1,000 people		Cable television subscribers per 1,000 people		Daily newspaper circulation per 1,000 people		Main telephone lines per 1,000 people		Cellular telephone subscribers per 1,000 people		As % of telephone subscribers 2004	Personal computers per 1,000 people		Internet users per 1,000 people	
	1993	2003	1993	2003	1997	2000	1994	2004	1994	2004		1994	2004	1994	2004
East Asia & Pacific															
Low income economies															
Cambodia	8.0						0.6	2.7	0.9	36.8	93.2		2.8		3.0
Indonesia	88.2			24.5			13.0	45.9	0.4	137.9	75.0	3.7	13.9	0.0	66.7
Korea, Dem. Rep.	23.1	160.4					24.2	44.0	0.0						
Laos	6.7						4.0	12.9	0.1	35.3	73.1		3.8		3.6
Mongolia	32.0	80.7		20.5	24.2	17.6	30.8	55.7	0.0	128.7	69.8		124.		79.5
Myanmar	5.0	7.0			9.2		3.1	8.5	0.0	1.8	17.9		6.5		1.3
Papua New Guinea	2.7	23.1					8.8	12.1	0.0	6.9	19.5		63.6		29.5
Solomon Islands	5.8	10.5					17.0	13.7	0.4	3.3	19.3		42.9		6.4
Vietnam	45.1						6.2	70.3	0.2	60.4	32.9	0.7	12.7		71.4
Middle income economies															
China	209.0		25.1		35.4	59.3	22.9	241.1	1.3	258.3	51.8	1.7	40.9	0.0	72.5
Fiji	53.2	117.5					78.4	122.4	1.5	131.8	51.9		52.3	0.1	72.5
Malaysia	156.2				105.3	95.3	144.3	178.6	28.8	587.0	76.7	32.3	196.8	1.0	396.8
Philippines	101.0				66.1		16.6	42.1	2.6	403.5	90.5	7.9	45.1	0.1	53.9
Samoa	109.3	148.2					44.4	72.9	0.0	57.6	44.1				32.7
Thailand	170.0				74.3		47.7	106.7	12.8	429.9	80.1	11.8	58.3	0.5	109.5
Tonga	20.7	70.4					67.1		0.0		23.0		49.0		29.4
Vanuatu	10.1	13.0					26.3	32.6	0.4	50.7	60.8		14.5		36.2
High income economies															
Australia	594.7	722.1			174.5	161.0	492.9	540.6	67.9	817.9	58.6	238.8	682.2	22.3	646.4
Brunei	256.0						214.5	251.7	54.4			27.8	84.8	153.1	

Country	Television sets per 1,000 people		Cable television subscribers per 1,000 people		Daily newspaper circulation per 1,000 people		Main telephone lines per 1,000 people		Cellular telephone subscribers per 1,000 people		As % of telephone subscribers 2004	Personal computers per 1,000 people		Internet users per 1,000 people	
	1993	2003	1993	2003	1997	2000	1994	2004	1994	2004		1994	2004	1994	2004
Korea, Rep.	242.6	458.2	102.3	282.2			397.0	541.9	21.6	760.9	57.9	87.2	544.9	3.1	656.8
Japan	649.1		74.0	193.4	576.3	566.0	485.7	460.1	34.7	716.0	60.9	92.0	541.6	8.0	587.0
New Zealand	495.5	573.7			223.6	202.2	458.0	443.4	66.1	745.4	62.7	179.6	473.8	31.8	788.0
Singapore	319.7				277.7	272.9	389.3	439.6	68.9	910.5	67.4	146.2	763.2	11.7	571.1
Taiwan											62.7				
Europe & Central Asia															
Low income economies															
Armenia	214.4						178.3	192.5	0.0	67.2	25.9		66.1	0.1	49.6
Azerbaijan	217.1	334.0					83.6	118.4	0.1	214.6	58.7		17.9	0.0	49.1
Georgia	220.6					4.9	102.5	151.2	0.0	186.1	55.2		42.5		38.9
Kyrgyzstan	24.6			3.6			74.6	78.6	0.0	58.9	38.7		17.1		51.6
Moldova	294.1			24.6			125.4	204.7	0.0	186.6	47.7		26.6	0.0	96.3
Tajikistan	195.0						47.1	38.6	0.0	7.5	16.3			0.8	
Ukraine	335.4				68.7	174.8	155.4	255.9	0.1	289.5	53.1	6.9	28.0	0.1	79.0
Uzbekistan	183.0						69.3	66.5	0.0	20.8	24.1			33.6	
Middle income economies															
Albania	95.2						13.1	90.0	0.0	64.3	81.2				24.1
Belarus	273.3				141.2		184.8	328.8	0.2	249.4	41.4			0.0	162.9
Bosnia & Herzegovina	92.3						70.8	239.4	0.0	268.0	52.8				57.6
Bulgaria	272.7			133.5	153.0	172.9	295.0	356.9	0.8	609.4	63.4	14.2	59.4	0.2	283.5
Croatia	235.7		11.8		114.1	133.8	259.2	424.9	4.7	639.8	57.7	18.3	189.5	2.7	293.3
Czech Republic	377.5		40.4				210.7	337.7	2.9	1,054.3	75.9	43.5	239.8	12.6	469.8
Estonia	389.0	507.0	9.8	117.0	184.9	191.6	258.3	329.2	9.4	930.9	73.9		920.7	11.6	496.7
Hungary	424.3		72.6	190.7	171.8	162.3	171.5	353.9	13.8	863.5	70.9	34.1	146.0	4.9	267.1
Kazakhstan	226.8						123.5	166.7	0.0	184.0	52.5			0.0	26.7
Latvia	430.9	858.9		176.8	116.7	137.8	261.8	272.8	3.3	664.4	70.3	3.1	216.6		350.2
Lithuania	342.1			76.9	32.1	30.9	245.4	238.7	1.2	995.9	80.7	5.5	155.1		281.8
Macedonia	179.5				44.2	53.5	172.6	308.2	0.0	382.9	59.6		68.9		78.3
Poland	274.8	228.8	15.6	94.0	503	101.6	129.9	321.8	1.0	604.9	65.3	22.1	192.8	3.9	235.7
Romania	200.3			172.5			123.4	202.4	0.1	471.1	69.9	11.0	113.0	0.3	207.5
Russian Federation	377.6						162.5	255.8	0.2	517.3	65.3	11.5	132.2	0.5	111.2
Serbia & Montenegro	170.4						187.3	329.6	0.0	580.6	63.8	13.3	47.7		147.3

Country	Television sets per 1,000 people		Cable television subscribers per 1,000 people		Daily newspaper circulation per 1,000 people		Main telephone lines per 1,000 people		Cellular telephone subscribers per 1,000 people		As % of telephone subscribers 2004	Personal computers per 1,000 people		Internet users per 1,000 people	
	1993	2003	1993	2003	1997	2000	1994	2004	1994	2004		1994	2004	1994	2004
Slovakia	359.3		28.9		188.1	130.8	187.7	232.3	1.1	794.3	77.4	28.1	296.0	3.2	422.9
Slovenia	296.4	365.5	100.5		171.8	168.4	290.2	407.0	8.2	951.4	68.2	75.4	352.5	10.6	475.7
Turkey	268.9		2.2	14.8			201.2	266.6	2.9	483.9	64.5	13.0	51.6	0.5	142.5
Turkmenistan	187.9					6.8	74.3	80.1	0.0	2.0	2.4				7.6
High income economies															
Austria	471.8		77.4	156.9	308.9	309.0	465.6	460.4	35.1	977.6	67.8	113.5	418.4	13.9	477.2
Belgium	453.8		353.2	377.7	157.5	153.0	449.2	456.4	12.7	876.3	65.5	158.2	348.0	6.9	403.0
Cyprus	345.7				69.5		458.8	506.5	31.9	775.5	60.5	34.7	301.5	1.1	360.8
Denmark	549.2		119.3	236.7	307.0	283.2	600.0	643.0	96.7	955.8	59.7	192.1	655.6	13.4	696.2
Finland	502.2	679.1	153.6	210.6	451.8	445.0	550.4	452.9	132.8	954.1	67.8	159.2	481.1	49.1	628.5
France	580.7		22.4		145.1	142.1	549.8	560.9	15.3	737.9	56.8	135.3	487.1	9.0	414.0
Germany	479.5	674.9	166.0	250.8	305.1	291.0	476.0	661.1	30.6	864.3	56.6	150.9	561.1	272	9.2
Greece	211.9						471.5	466.5	14.5	998.9	59.4	28.4	89.2	3.8	176.8
Iceland	434.1		4.2		365.9	322.3	557.6	652.1	82.1	997.5	60.4	169.2	472.4	67.7	772.4
Ireland	322.5		120.6	134.0	149.8	147.7	347.3	496.3	24.6	929.1	65.2	156.8	494.3	5.6	265.4
Italy	427.7				103.0	109.0	429.7	450.9	39.2	1,089.9	70.7	71.8	315.3	1.9	501.4
Luxembourg	565.3	598.0	100.5	334.4	290.1	275.7	551.9	800.2	31.9	1,197.9	60.0		653.0	5.0	597.4
Netherlands	490.9		346.1		303.9	279.5	511.0	482.8	20.9	910.3	65.3	169.0	682.4	32.5	614.2
Norway	423.1		144.8		590.8	569.0	553.8	668.7	135.7	861.0	65.1	229.7	572.8	41.5	390.3
Portugal	370.0		0.9	128.2	31.7	102.4	347.5	403.5	17.4	980.8	71.0	43.0	133.5	7.2	281.0
Spain	417.0		3.3	24.3		98.2	375.2	415.8	10.5	904.7	68.3	48.5	256.7	2.8	335.7
Sweden	467.7		208.7		438.1	409.5	679.6	708.1	157.3	1,034.5	60.3	182.2	763.0	34.2	756.2
Switzerland	407.3		320.8		374.1	371.7	608.7	710.5	47.5	849.2	54.4	228.8	826.2	27.2	473.6
United Kingdom	446.8		10.5		317.5	326.4	487.6	562.9	67.7	1,020.6	64.4	170.2	599.5	10.3	628.1
Latin America & Caribbean															
Low income economies															
Haiti		60.1		7.2			6.9	16.7	0.0	47.6	74.1				59.5
Nicaragua	104.5		6.1				19.5	39.9	0.5	137.4	77.5	8.0	37.2	0.1	23.3
Middle income economies															
Argentina	270.2		108.1		65.4	40.5	142.1	226.7	7.0	352.1	60.8	34.4	96.4	0.4	133.4
Barbados	280.8						327.0	504.8	11.4	744.3	59.6		126.5		557.9
Belize	155.8						133.6	119.5	3.9	345.9	73.1				123.9

Country	Television sets per 1,000 people		Cable television subscribers per 1,000 people		Daily newspaper circulation per 1,000 people		Main telephone lines per 1,000 people		Cellular telephone subscribers per 1,000 people		As % of telephone subscribers 2004	Personal computers per 1,000 people		Internet users per 1,000 people	
	1993	2003	1993	2003	1997	2000	1994	2004	1994	2004		1994	2004	1994	2004
Bolivia	113.2			7.4	110.4		33.2	69.4	0.6	199.9	74.2	3.0	35.5		38.8
Brazil	219.7	369.4		13.4	41.8	45.9	77.2	230.4	3.6	356.7	60.8	11.3	105.2	0.4	119.6
Chile	232.4						112.1	205.8	8.2	593.3	74.2	26.1	132.6	1.4	266.7
Colombia	187.7	319.0			28.8		92.9	195.2	2.3	231.6	57.2	13.2	66.7	1.0	79.8
Costa Rica	224.9					70.0	126.8	315.8	2.1	217.0	40.7		238.4	2.8	235.1
Cuba	188.4					53.6	32.3	68.3	0.1	6.7	9.0		26.7		13.3
Dominican Republic	86.6				15.9	27.5	73.5	106.8	2.8	289.0	73.0				91.2
Ecuador	113.8	252.1		13.9	48.1	98.2	58.8	123.6	1.7	348.5	68.7	9.8	55.5	0.3	47.9
El Salvador	148.4				37.2		42.5	131.3	0.9	271.0	67.4		43.9		86.9
Guatemala	55.5						25.1	92.1	1.1	257.7	73.7	2.1	18.8		61.5
Guyana	40.3					74.8	60.3	136.9	1.7	191.9	50.5		36.0		193.3
Honduras	75.1						24.0	52.7	0.0	100.3	64.4		15.6		31.5
Jamaica	288.4						101.8	189.1	10.6	831.9	84.9	3.5	62.8	0.4	403.5
Mexico	184.2		11.6			93.5	94.8	174.1	6.4	370.5	68.0	23.5	108.0	0.4	135.2
Panama	169.4						109.8	118.4	0.0	269.5	69.5		40.9	0.1	94.5
Paraguay	64.5						32.1	50.4	1.6	293.8	86.3		59.2		24.9
Peru	132.5		0.1				33.0	74.4	2.2	148.5	66.6		97.6	0.1	116.8
St. Lucia	211.7						175.3		3.7	568.3	64.5	0.6	158.9		336.1
Suriname	144.9			4.2	68.7		123.0	182.1	3.4	476.7	72.4				67.2
Trinidad & Tobago	333.1						162.9	246.9	2.1	497.9	67.0	16.0	105.3		123.0
Uruguay	514.4						182.2	290.7	2.1	174.4	37.5		125.0	0.6	197.7
Venezuela	162.6			32.4			108.2	128.1	14.8	322.3	71.6	23.2	82.1	0.6	88.5
High income economies															
Bahamas	237.5						287.5	439.0	8.9	583.5	57.1				291.8
Middle East & North Africa															
Low income economies															
Yemen	266.2						11.8	39.3	0.6	52.7	57.3		14.8		8.9
Middle income economies															
Algeria	101.1				26.4		40.5	70.7	0.0	144.7	67.2	2.6	9.0	0.0	26.1
Djibouti	53.9						12.6	14.3	0.0	*30.1*	75.6		27.0		11.6
Egypt	140.0	247.6					40.9	130.3	0.1	105.2	44.7	3.2	31.7	0.1	53.7
Iran	87.0						74.5	*219.5*	0.2	64.2	22.8	13.8	109.6	0.0	82.1

Country	Television sets per 1,000 people		Cable television subscribers per 1,000 people		Daily newspaper circulation per 1,000 people		Main telephone lines per 1,000 people		Cellular telephone subscribers per 1,000 people		As % of telephone subscribers 2004	Personal computers per 1,000 people		Internet users per 1,000 people	
	1993	2003	1993	2003	1997	2000	1994	2004	1994	2004		1994	2004	1994	2004
Iraq	75.3						31.0	36.9	0.0	20.5	35.7				1.3
Jordan	142.6				76.2		78.0	113.5	0.4	293.1	72.1	7.4	55.1		110.3
Lebanon	354.1					63.3	141.5	178.0	0.0	250.8	58.5	12.9	113.0		169.5
Libya	99.9						56.0	133.2	0.0	22.6		14.5			35.7
Malta	374.6	556.2	54.6				435.6	522.0	20.1	726.8	59.7	66.8	314.0		750.1
Morocco	149.3				23.7	29.1	38.8	43.9	0.5	313.1	87.7	2.7	20.8		117.4
Oman	644.2						74.7	94.9	3.2	317.7	76.8	8.0	46.6		96.7
Saudi Arabia	251.9						92.0	154.3	0.9	383.1	71.3	29.6	353.9		66.2
Syria	68.3						47.8	143.1	0.0	126.2	46.9	5.6	32.3	0.0	43.1
Tunisia	161.7					18.9	53.8	121.2	125	0.3	358.7	74.8	47.5	0.1	84.1
High income economies															
Bahrain	427.1						240.2	267.6	31.2	907.7	77.2		169.0		213.4
Israel	278.1		131.6	1,467.7			396.0	441.3	24.7	1,057.3	70.7	101.9	741.0	5.6	470.7
Kuwait	344.7							202.1		813.2	80.1		183.0		243.9
Qatar	401.1	426.2	7.7	115.5			224.7	245.7	22.4	631.1	72.0	48.5	171.2		212.4
United Arab Emirates	238.1						277.5	274.9	41.3	852.6	75.6	43.3	115.7		320.6
North America															
High income economies															
Canada	659.8	706.8	274.4		166.3	167.9	592.6	634.5	64.1	468.6	42.1	195.8	700.2	23.7	625.5
United States	778.8		228.0		205.6	196.3	583.2	606.0	91.7	616.7	50.6	294.5	749.2	49.4	630.0
South Asia															
Low income economies															
Afghanistan	9.8						1.5	1.7	0.0	21.0	92.3				0.9
Bangladesh	14.2						2.3	5.9	0.0	31.1	77.0		11.9		2.2
Bhutan				15.4			6.8	33.0	0.0	19.9	38.7		12.3		22.3
India	50.1		8.1		48.1		10.7	40.7	0.0	43.8	51.8	0.9	12.1	0.0	32.4
Nepal	2.6						3.6	15.1	0.0	6.7	21.8	0.7	4.4	0.0	6.6
Pakistan	38.3			26.7	29.7	39.3	15.3	29.6	0.2	33.0	52.7	2.9			13.2
Middle income economies															
Maldives	50.1						48.5	98.1	0.0	352.6	78.2		112.1	0.0	59.2
Sri Lanka	58.5	125.2	114		29.1	28.8	10.2	51.0	1.6	113.9	69.0	1.0	27.3	0.0	14.4

Country	Television sets per 1,000 people 1993	Television sets per 1,000 people 2003	Cable television subscribers per 1,000 people 1993	Cable television subscribers per 1,000 people 2003	Daily newspaper circulation per 1,000 people 1997	Daily newspaper circulation per 1,000 people 2000	Main telephone lines per 1,000 people 1994	Main telephone lines per 1,000 people 2004	Cellular telephone subscribers per 1,000 people 1994	Cellular telephone subscribers per 1,000 people 2004	As % of telephone subscribers 2004	Personal computers per 1,000 people 1994	Personal computers per 1,000 people 2004	Internet users per 1,000 people 1994	Internet users per 1,000 people 2004
Sub-Saharan Africa															
Low income economies															
Angola	6.6				11.3		4.4	6.2	0.2	47.8	90.7		3.2		11.1
Benin	15.8						4.0	8.9	0.0	*29.8*	84.2		3.7		12.2
Burkina Faso	8.8	12.2			1.3		2.8	6.3	0.0	31.0	83.0	0.2	2.2		4.1
Burundi	1.5	35.1			2.5		2.6	*3.4*	0.1	9.1	72.8		4.7	0.0	3.4
Cameroon	31.1				6.5		4.5	6.9	0.1	95.8	94.2		10.0		10.4
Central African Rep.	4.8				1.7		2.2	2.5	0.0	15.1	85.7		2.8		2.3
Chad	3.1				0.2		0.7	1.4	0.0	13.0	90.4		1.6		6.4
Comoros	13.2						9.0	*23.0*	0.0	3.5	13.1		8.5		13.6
Congo, Dem. Rep.	1.4				2.8		0.8	0.2		36.8	99.0				
Congo, Republic	6.8				6.5		7.3	3.6	0.0	98.8	96.5		4.4		9.3
Côte d'Ivoire	23.5				15.7		7.2	12.6	0.0	85.7	86.6		14.7		16.8
Equatorial Guinea	66.0				4.7		6.5	*20.0*	0.0	112.8	85.3		14.2		10.2
Eritrea	5.7	53.0					4.9	9.3	0.0	4.7	33.7		3.5	0.0	11.8
Ethiopia	3.4				0.4		2.5	*6.3*	0.0	2.5	29.0		3.2		1.6
Gambia	1.0				1.7		17.0		0.8	118.4	82.0	0.3	15.6		33.2
Ghana	40.4				13.9		2.9	14.5	0.2	78.2	84.4	0.9	5.2		17.0
Guinea	14.0						1.3	*2.9*	*127*	0.1	12.4	81.0	4.8	0.0	5.0
Guinea-Bissau					4.8		6.0	7.1	0.0	0.9	10.8	16.9			
Kenya	18.1				9.2		8.6	8.9	0.1	76.1	89.5	0.6	13.2		44.8
Lesotho	6.7	36.8	446		9.0		9.4	20.7	120	0.0	88.4	81.0			23.9
Liberia	20.1				15.0		2.2			0.0	14.7		.		
Madagascar	9.8				4.6		2.5	3.4	36	0.0	18.4	85.0	5.0		5.0
Malawi					2.4		3.3	7.4	0.0	17.6	70.5	1.6			3.7
Mali	11.4				1.1		1.5	5.7	0.0	30.5	84.2	3.2			3.8
Mauritania		43.6					3.8	*13.2*	0.0	175.3	93.1	14.1			4.7
Mozambique	3.1				2.6		3.7	*4.1*	0.0	36.4	90.1		5.8		7.1
Niger	7.7				0.2		1.3	1.8	0.0	11.0	86.0		0.7		1.8
Nigeria	39.6				26.0		3.6	8.0	0.1	71.1	89.9	4.3	6.7		13.7
Rwanda					0.1		1.8	2.6	0.0	15.6		85.8			4.3
São Tomé & Príncipe							19.6	*46.6*	0.0	*32.2*					130.7

Country	Television sets per 1,000 people		Cable television subscribers per 1,000 people		Daily newspaper circulation per 1,000 people		Main telephone lines per 1,000 people		Cellular telephone subscribers per 1,000 people		As % of telephone subscribers 2004	Personal computers per 1,000 people		Internet users per 1,000 people	
	1993	2003	1993	2003	1997	2000	1994	2004	1994	2004		1994	2004	1994	2004
Senegal	22.8						8.1	20.6	0.0	90.3	82.1	5.1	21.3		42.3
Sierra Leone	10.9						3.8	4.9	0.0	22.3	82.5			0.0	1.9
Somalia	13.2	20.2					2.4	25.1	0.0	62.8	71.4		6.3		25.1
Sudan	85.0						2.2	29.0	0.0	29.5	50.5	0.2	17.1	0.0	32.1
Tanzania	10.2						2.9	4.0	0.0	43.6	91.7		7.4		8.9
Togo	6.7					2.2	4.9	10.4	0.0	37.7	78.4		28.6	0.0	36.9
Uganda	6.1					2.7	1.5	2.6	0.0	41.9	94.2		4.3		7.2
Zambia	36.1					21.9	8.6	7.6	0.0	26.1	77.2		9.8	0.1	20.1
Zimbabwe	27.5						11.6	24.5	0.0	30.7	57.2	1.9	77.3	0.0	63.4
Middle income economies															
Botswana	20.8				24.9		31.9	77.1	0.0	318.7	80.7	6.3	45.2		33.9
Cape Verde	2.7						47.1	148.3	0.0	132.8	47.3		96.9		50.5
Gabon	78.8				28.9		28.9	28.4	2.4	359.2	92.7	2.8	29.4		29.4
Mauritius	192.5				76.5	116.4	116.3	286.7	5.1	413.2	59.0	18.0	278.7		145.8
Namibia	33.0				7.2		43.6	63.7	0.0	142.4	69.1		109.5		37.3
South Africa	105.8				28.4	25.4	98.6	105.2	8.9	428.5	80.2	22.9	82.2	2.6	78.4
Swaziland	27.1						20.8	41.8	0.0	100.9	71.0		32.1		32.1

Region	Main telephone lines per 1,000 people			Cellular mobile telephone subscribers per 1,000 people			Personal computers per 1,000 people			Internet users per 1,000 people		
	1994	2004	% change 1994–2004	1994	2004	% change 1994–2004	1994	2004	% change 1994–2004	1994	2004	% change 1994–2004
Low income	9.4	30.0	220	0.0	42.1	93,209	1.3	11.3	741		24.3	
Middle income	59.6	191.5	221	2.2	293.6	13,003	7.3	60.9	730	0.3	90.2	26,084
Low & middle income	38.9	121.4	212	1.3	185.5	13,698	5.3	40.7	671	0.2	62.0	24,757
East Asia & Pacific	22.4	187.9	739	1.9	243.5	12,921	2.9	38.2	1,224	0.0	73.8	160,738
Europe & Central Asia	156.9	*241.7*	*54*	1.0	457.5	44,209	14.0	109.7	686	1.2	138.0	11,013
Latin America & Caribbean	82.4	178.9	117	4.4	318.4	7,082	17.0	92.4	445	0.5	114.5	22,821
Middle East & North Africa	49.1	90.6	85	0.2	128.6	62,536	6.7	48.5	628	0.0	41.5	140,240
South Asia	10.1	35.1	248	0.0	41.3	90,767	1.1	12.1	1,003	0.0	26.1	237,642
Sub-Saharan Africa	10.6	10.3	-2	0.7	74.1	10,353		15.1			19.4	
High income	496.9	537.0	8	52.9	771.7	1,360	169.0	574.1	240	21.7	544.9	2,413
World	115.3	191.4	66	10.0	279.3	2,692	36.8	129.8	253	4.6	139.1	2,930

Empty cells indicate that data were unavailable. In such instances, where possible, figures are taken from the year before or after as an estimate. These figures, and estimates based on them, are presented in italics.

Sources: World Bank, World Development Indicators 2005 (WDI-Online); International Telecommunications Union (ITU),
ICT – Free statistics homepage, www.itu.int/ITU-D/ict/statistics

The first section of this record presents people's evaluations of the UN's performance and their rating of its future priorities from the Gallup International Millennium Survey 2000. No limits were put on the number of priorities respondents could choose. The second section presents three indices – Corporate Ethics, Public Sector Ethics and Corporate Governance – that show people's perceptions of ethics, averaged for each country, based on the World Bank's *Global Competitiveness Report 2004/5*. A low score indicates negative evaluations of ethics in government and the corporate world, a high score indicates positive evaluations. The third section of this record examines the disclosure of companies about their lobbying practices, based on the findings of SustainAbility and WWF UK in *Influencing Power: Reviewing the conduct and content of corporate lobbying*. Based on the quality of information and approach adopted by each company it was given one of the following ratings:

None: no information provided on lobbying, or the company makes general references, such as a simple statement of compliance with the law on political contributions, but provides no insight into activities or impacts.

Basic: recognises the relevance of lobbying to corporate responsibility issues.

Developing: as above, but with evidence that systems and processes are being developed to actively manage and disclose lobbying and public policy activities. The company is likely to discuss at least one 'material' issue in some depth.

Systematic: systems exist to actively manage and disclose lobbying and public policy activities. The company is likely to discuss policy positions on several material issues in some depth. However, the approach to lobbying is still not fully integrated with company values and business decision- making.

Integrated: as above and in addition an explicit link is made between corporate values and principled, core business decision-making (including corporate governance) processes, and the company's approach to public policy. This rating was not given to any of the companies analysed.

This record shows that the achievements of the UN do not rank very highly for people in many countries in the Gallup survey, which may explain why support for the UN becoming a global government in the future is relatively low. Corporate ethics in the private and the public sector are consistently ranked higher in high income economies, and European and US corporations are more transparent concerning their lobbying practices than companies in other parts of the world.

Global governance: evaluation and the roles of the UN

| Country | How satisfactory do you find results achieved by the UN up until now? % responding... | | What would you say should be the most important aims for the UN in the future? % respondents selecting... | | | | | | |
	Satisfactory	Unsatisfactory	To improve the health of human beings	To give humanitarian aid in times of natural disasters	To give humanitarian aid in times of war/conflict	To prevent war by intervention	To maintain peace by armed forces	To develop into a world government	To protect human rights
Austria	40	37	14	26	32	46	20	9	44
Bolivia	57	28	25	15	12	11	4	3	26
Bosnia	55	38	35	18	17	44	18	9	50
Chile	46	35	39	50	40	47	17	13	67
Dominican Republic	42	38	25	21	5	7	7	3	28
Ecuador	67	28	31	32	23	21	16	9	43
Iceland	68	19	93	96	96	79	52	31	98
Paraguay	62	21	14	9	6	15	3	7	41
South Africa	42	10	28	25	23	26	17	9	33
Taiwan	40	52	19	42	34	43	21	21	43
Thailand	83	15	17	42	62	25	9	7	44
Turkey	33	43	17	21	21	34	16	9	34
Ukraine	36	24	20	25	14	23	8	4	37
United Kingdom	60	36	19	31	21	41	18	6	42
United States	64	31	22	35	24	31	17	6	42
Uruguay	30	36	28	29	16	42	5	4	44

Source: Gallup International Millennium Survey2000, http://www.gallup–international.com/contentfiles/survey.asp?id=6

Accountability

Country	Corporate Ethics Index	Public Sector Ethics Index	Corporate Governance Index
East Asia & Pacific			
Low income economies			
Indonesia	40.3	47.3	44.7
Vietnam	34.1	29.7	38.1
Middle income economies			
China*	46.5	42.1	35.3
Malaysia	56.9	58.6	66.7
Philippines	14.1	7.6	48.9
Thailand	28.7	36.3	49.7
High income economies			
Australia	71.1	78.6	88.4
Japan	62.4	62.0	79.2
Korea, Rep.	36.4	40.9	55.4
New Zealand	82.5	89.7	90.2
Singapore	83.0	92.7	80.9
Taiwan	57.0	65.9	72.1
Europe & Central Asia			
Low income economies			
Georgia	16.5	10.9	27.0
Ukraine	20.3	18.8	22.4
Middle income economies			
Bosnia & Herzegovina	19.6	21.5	20.1
Bulgaria	28.5	25.2	20.5
Croatia	24.2	27.7	25.4
Czech Republic	31.5	35.4	42.8
Estonia	56.8	57.9	61.2
Hungary	32.6	40.7	46.7
Latvia	28.8	32.3	43.1
Lithuania	31.2	35.1	45.0
Macedonia	22.8	26.0	28.8
Poland	19.8	19.1	26.4
Romania	20.2	28.4	39.5
Russian Federation	20.5	20.4	29.9
Serbia & Montenegro	24.2	21.3	18.7

Country	Corporate Ethics Index	Public Sector Ethics Index	Corporate Governance Index
Slovakia	28.0	38.0	56.4
Turkey	25.5	27.5	36.4
High income economies			
Austria	69.7	67.8	78.4
Belgium	65.0	64.1	85.9
Cyprus	45.9	54.8	31.5
Denmark	85.9	93.6	94.8
Finland	84.8	93.8	95.4
France	59.7	61.4	73.7
Germany	73.7	74.3	90.8
Greece	36.5	39.8	44.6
Iceland	82.4	92.6	78.6
Ireland	60.3	64.1	80.4
Italy	40.9	33.9	32.6
Luxembourg	69.2	83.6	68.4
Malta	50.9	46.3	39.7
Netherlands	85.2	84.3	88.5
Norway	84.9	90.1	83.8
Portugal	55.1	60.4	49.5
Slovenia	41.2	49.3	46.2
Spain	51.0	59.4	52.4
Sweden	77.0	84.0	92.6
Switzerland	74.2	81.7	82.8
United Kingdom	80.3	79.7	87.9
Latin America & Caribbean			
Low income economies			
Nicaragua	27.7	18.6	17.1
Middle income economies			
Argentina	23.1	21.8	36.2
Bolivia	19.1	14.5	14.6
Brazil	35.4	35.2	56.3
Chile	66.0	62.9	62.2
Colombia	36.7	22.6	42.0
Costa Rica	40.1	34.2	47.8
Dominican Republic	24.6	15.8	24.9
Ecuador	20.4	12.1	19.9

Country	Corporate Ethics Index	Public Sector Ethics Index	Corporate Governance Index
El Salvador	46.7	38.2	36.3
Guatemala	19.2	16.7	24.3
Honduras	17.7	11.3	16.7
Jamaica	29.8	21.1	47.8
Mexico	31.1	23.3	38.4
Panama	25.0	20.3	30.6
Paraguay	21.2	10.2	11.2
Peru	29.6	23.5	32.8
Trinidad & Tobago	27.9	26.7	44.1
Uruguay	51.3	40.9	24.3
Venezuela	24.6	12.9	26.0
Middle East & North Africa			
Middle income economies			
Algeria	39.4	27.0	34.4
Egypt	44.8	35.0	49.3
Jordan	63.2	58.8	38.1
Morocco	37.5	46.1	43.5
Tunisia	57.2	62.0	46.0
High income economies			
Bahrain	59.6	57.3	52.4
Israel**	58.4	64.3	73.2
United Arab Emirates	73.0	76.2	48.7
North America			
High income economies			
Canada	63.1	59.7	84.4
United States	57.4	70.1	89.8
South Asia			
Low income economies			
Bangladesh	15.6	9.0	24.3
India	34.6	31.7	55.4
Pakistan	22.8	10.3	31.3
Middle income economies			
Sri Lanka	29.8	20.2	43.8
Sub-Saharan Africa			
Low income economies			
Angola	24.5	13.7	15.4

Country	Corporate Ethics Index	Public Sector Ethics Index	Corporate Governance Index
Chad	16.6	11.6	17.3
Ethiopia	28.9	24.6	31.4
Gambia	40.4	33.1	47.7
Ghana	46.5	36.9	52.9
Kenya	34.8	22.3	47.4
Madagascar	17.9	16.0	32.2
Malawi	36.9	22.6	42.3
Mali	28.0	18.1	31.5
Mozambique	17.7	12.7	26.4
Nigeria	26.1	15.1	45.7
Tanzania	23.4	18.4	35.5
Uganda	28.9	17.7	36.4
Zambia	34.1	29.1	50.9
Zimbabwe	41.2	20.3	56.9
Middle income economies			
Botswana	50.8	55.9	45.2
Mauritius	26.8	27.1	39.7
Namibia	48.8	37.8	50.2
South Africa	59.0	42.2	80.9

* China excludes Hong Kong and Macao.
** Israel excludes the Palestinian Authority.

Source: Corruption, Governance and Security: Challenges for the Rich Countries and the World, by Daniel Kaufmann (September 2004), in the Global Competitiveness Report 2004/2005, www.worldbank.org/wbi/governance/pubs/gcr2004.html: the data are available at http://www.worldbank.org/wbi/governance/pdf/ETHICS.xls

Lobbying disclosure practices among 100 of the world's largest companies, by country

Country	Systematic	Developing	Basic	None
East Asia & Pacific				
Australia			BHP Billiton	
Japan			Toyota	Bridgestone
				Canon
				Fujifilm
				Hitachi
				Honda
				Ito-Yokado
				Matsushita Electric
				Mitsubishi Tokyo FG
				Nissan
				Sony
				Toshiba
Korea, Rep.				Samsung
Europe				
Belgium			Fortis	
Finland			Nokia	
France		Total	France Telecom	Alcatel
			Suez	AXA
				BNP Paribas
				Carrefour
				L'Oreal
				Sanofi-Aventis
				Vivendi Universal
Germany	BASF		DaimlerChrysler	Allianz
			Deutsche Telekom	Deutsche Bank
			Volkswagen	E.On
			Bayer	Siemens
Italy				Assicurazioni Generali
Netherlands		Philips	ING	ABN Amro
		Royal Dutch / Shell	Unilever	Aegon
Spain			BBVA	Banco Santander
			Repsol	Telefonica
Sweden				Ericsson
Switzerland		Swiss Re	Credit Suisse	Novartis
			Nestle	UBS
United Kingdom	BP	AstraZeneca	Barclays	HSBC
	GlaxoSmithKline	Diageo		Reuters
				Vodaphone

Country	Systematic	Developing	Basic	None
North America				
Canada			Alcan	
United States	Chevron	Altria	Birstol-Myers Squbb	Nortel Networks
	Dow	Microsoft	Citigroup	3M
	Ford	Pfizer	Coca Cola	American Int'l. Group
	General Motors	Time Warner	Colgate-Palmolive	AT&T
	HP		Dell	EMC
			DuPont	General Electric
			ExxonMobil	Gillette
			IBM	Intel
			Johnson & Johnson	JPMorgan Chase
			McDonald's	Kimberly-Clark
			Merck	Luccent Technologies
			Morgan Stanley	News Corporation
			Procter & Gamble	PepsiCo
			Texas Instruments	Tyco
			United Technologies	Wal-Mart

Lobbying disclosure practices among 100 of the world's largest companies, by sector

Sector	Systematic	Developing	Basic	None
Materials	BASF Dow		BHP Billiton Bayer Alcan DuPont	
Energy	BP Chevron	Total Royal Dutch / Shell	Repsol ExxonMobil	
Health Care	GlaxoSmithKline	AstraZeneca Pfizer	Birstol-Myers Squbb Johnson & Johnson Merck	Sanofi-Aventis Novartis
Consumer Discretionary	Ford General Motors	Philips Time Warner	Toyota DaimlerChrysler Volkswagen McDonald's	Bridgestone Fujifilm Honda Matsushita Electric Nissan Sony Vivendi Universal Reuters News Corporation
Information Technology	HP	Microsoft	Nokia Dell IBM Texas Instruments	Canon Hitachi Toshiba Samsung Alcatel Ericsson Nortel Networks EMC Intel Luccent Technologies
Financials		Swiss Re	Fortis ING BBVA Credit Suisse Barclays Citigroup Morgan Stanley	Mitsubishi Tokyo FG AXA BNP Paribas Allianz Deutsche Bank Assicurazioni Generali ABN Amro Aegon Banco Santander UBS HSBC American Int'l. Group JPMorgan Chase

Sector	Systematic	Developing	Basic	None
Consumer Staples		Diageo Altria	Unilever Nestle Coca Cola Colgate-Palmolive Procter & Gamble	Ito-Yokado Carrefour L'Oreal Gillette Kimberly-Clark PepsiCo Wal-Mart
Telecommunications			France Telecom Deutsche Telekom	Telefonica Vodafone AT&T
Industrials			United Technologies	Siemens 3M General Electric Tyco
Utilities			Suez	E.On

Source: Beloe, Seb, Jules Peck and Jodie Thorpe, 2005. Influencing Power: Reviewing the conduct and content of corporate lobbying. London: © 2005 SustainAbility Ltd and WWF UK

Global civil society is both dependent on the international rule of law and one of the main actors pushing for the adoption and enforcement of it. The table indicates which countries have ratified the major human rights, humanitarian, disarmament, and environmental treaties, and in which years, according to the most recent data available. It shows how many countries have ratified each treaty, and how many of the listed treaties each country has ratified. The number of listed treaties ratified by each country since 2000 is also shown. In terms of the number of treaties ratified, it seems that low- and middle-income countries in Europe and Central Asia, Latin America and Africa are catching up with high-income economies. The highest numbers of recent ratifications are of humanitarian and environmental law treaties.

Key

ICESCR	International Covenant on Economic, Social and Cultural Rights (As of 26 January 2006)
ICCPR	International Convenant on Civil and Political Rights (As of 26 January 2006)
ICCPR-OP1	Optional Protocol to the International Convenant on Civil and Political Rights (As of 26 January 2006)
ICCPR-OP2	Second Optional Protocol to the International Convenant on Civil and Political Rights (As of 26 January 2006)
CERD	International Convention on the Elimination of all forms of Racial Discrimination (As of 26 January 2006)
CEDAW	Convention on the Elimination of All Forms of Discrimination Against Women (As of 2 March 2006)
CAT	Convention against Torture and Other Cruel, Inhuman or Degrading Treatment or Punishment (As of 26 January 2006)
Gen	Convention on the Prevention and Punishment of the Crime of the Genocide (As of 26 January 2006)
ILO 87	Freedom of Association and Protection of the Right to Organise Convention (Accessed 22 March 2006)
CSR	Convention relating to the Status of Refugees (Accessed 22 March 2006)
ICC	Rome Statute on the International Criminal Court (Accessed 22 March 2006)
CWC	Chemical Weapons Convention (As of 26 March 2006)
BWC	Biological Weapons Convention (Accessed 22 March 2006)
LMC	Convention on the Prohibition of the Use, Stockpiling, Production and Transfer of Anti-Personnel Mines and on their Destruction (Accessed 22 March 2006)
Geneva	Geneva Conventions (Accessed 30 March 2006)
Prot 1	First Additional Protocol to the Geneva Conventions (Accessed 30 March 2006)
Prot 2	Second Additional Protocol to the Geneva Conventions (Accessed 30 March 2006)
BC	Basel Convention on the Control of Transboundary Movements of Hazardous Wastes and Their Disposal (Accessed 22 March 2006)
CBD	Convention on Biological Diversity (Accessed 22 March 2006)
UNFCCC	United Nations Framework Convention on Climate Change (Accessed 22 March 2006)
KP	Kyoto Protocol to United Nations Framework Convention on Climate Change (Accessed 22 March 2006)
VCPOL	Vienna Convention for the Protection of Ozone Layer (Accessed 22 March 2006)

Country	Human Rights											Humanitarian Law						Environmental Law					Total	Ratified since 2000
	ICESCR	ICCPR	ICCPR-OP1	ICCPR-OP2	CERD	CEDAW	CAT	Gen	ILO 87	CSR	ICC	CWC	BWC	LMC	Geneva	Prot 1	Prot 2	BC	CBD	UNFCCC	KP	VCPOL		
East Asia & Pacific																								
Low income economies																								
Cambodia	92	92			83	92	92	50	99	92	02	05	83	99	58	98	98	01	95	95	02	01	20	5
East Timor	03	03		03						03	02			03		05	05				04		9	9
Indonesia					99	84	98		98			98	92		58			93	94	94		92	11	0
Korea, Dem. Rep.	81	81			01			89					87		57	88			94	94	05	95	11	2
Laos					74	81		50				97	73		56	80	80		96	95	03	98	12	1
Mongolia	74	74	91		69	81	02	67	69		02	95	72		58	95	95	97	93	93	99	96	19	
Myanmar						97		56	55						92				94	94	03	93	8	1
Papua New Guinea					82	95		82		00	86	94	80	04	76			95	93	93	02	92	14	3
Solomon Islands	82					82	02			95		04	81	99	81	88	88		95	94	03	93	14	3
Vietnam	82	82			82	82		81				98	80		57	81		95	94	94	02	94	14	1
Middle income economies																								
China & Tibet	01				81	80	88	83		82		97	84	56	83	83		91	93	93		89	15	1
Fiji					73	95		73	02	72	99	93	73	98	71				93	93	98	89	14	1
Malaysia						95		94				00	91	99	62			93	94	94	02	89	11	2
Philippines	74	86	89		67	81	86	50	53	81		96	73	00	52		86	93	93	94	03	91	19	2
Samoa						92				88	02	02		98	84	84	84	02	94	94	00	92	13	4
Thailand	99	96			03	85					02		75	98	54			97	03	94	02	89	13	4
Tonga					72			72				03	76		78	03	03		98	98		98	10	3
Vanuatu						95						03	90	05	82	85	85		93	93	01	94	11	3
High income economies																								
Australia	75	80	91	90	75	83	89	49	73	54	02	94	77	99	58	91	91	92	93	92		87	21	1
Brunei												97	91		91	91		91	02			90	7	1
Korea, Rep.	90	90	90		78	84	95	50		92	02	97	87		66	82	82	94	94	93	02	92	19	2
Japan	79	79			95	85	99		65	81		95	82	98	53	04	04	93	93	93		88	17	2
New Zealand	78	78	89	90	72	85	89	78		60	00	96	72	99	59	88	88	94	93	93	02	87	21	2
Singapore						95		95				97	75		73			96	95	97		89	9	0
Europe & Central Asia																								
Low income economies																								
Armenia	93	93	93		93	93	93	93	06	93		94	94		93	93	93	99	93	94	03	99	19	2
Azerbaijan	92	92	01	99	96	95	96	96	92	93		00	04		93			01	00	95	00	96	18	6
Georgia	94	94	94	99	99	94	94	93	99	99	03	95	96		93	93	93	99	94	94	99	96	21	1

Country	Human Rights											Humanitarian Law						Environmental Law					Total	Ratified since 2000
	ICESCR	ICCPR	ICCPR-OP1	ICCPR-OP2	CERD	CEDAW	CAT	Gen	ILO 87	CSR	ICC	CWC	BWC	LMC	Geneva	Prot 1	Prot 2	BC	CBD	UNFCCC	KP	VCPOL		
Kyrgyzstan	94	94	95		97	97	97	97	92	96		03			92	92	92	96	96	00	03	00	18	4
Moldova	93	93			93	94	95	93	96	02		96		00	93	93	93	98	95	95	03	96	18	3
Tajikistan	99	99	99		95	93	95		93	93	00	95		99	93	93	93		97	98		96	17	1
Ukraine	73	73	91		69	81	87	54	56	02		98	75	05	54	90	90	99	95	97	04	86	20	3
Uzbekistan	95	95	95		95	95	95	99				96	96		93	93	93	96	95	93	99	93	17	0
Middle income economies																								
Albania	91	91			94	94	94	55	57	92	03	94	92	00	57	93	93	99	94	94	05	99	20	3
Belarus	73	73	92		69	81	87	54	56	01		96	75	03	54	89	89	99	93	00	05	86	20	4
Bosnia & Herzegovina	92	93	95	01	93	93	93	92	93	93	02	97	94	98	92	92	92	01	02	00		93	21	5
Bulgaria	70	70	92	99	66	82	86	50	59	93	02	94	72	98	54	89	89	96	96	95	02	90	22	2
Croatia	91	92	95	95	92	92	92	92	91	92	01	95	93	98	92	92	92	94	96	96		91	21	1
Czech Republic	93	93	93	04	93	93	93	93	93	93		96	93	99	93	93	93	93	93	93	01	93	21	2
Estonia	91	91	91	04	91	91	91	91	94	97	02	99	93	04	93	93	93	92	94	94	02	96	22	4
Hungary	74	74	88	94	67	80	87	52	57	89	01	96	72	98	54	89	89	90	94	94	02	88	22	2
Kazakhstan	06	06			98	98	98	98	00	99		00			92	92	92	03	94	95		98	16	5
Latvia	92	92	94		92	92	92	92	92	97	02	96	97	05	91	91	91	92	95	95	02	95	21	3
Lithuania	91	91	91	02	98	94	96	96	94	97	03	98	98	03	96	00	00	99	96	95	03	95	22	6
Macedonia	94	94	94	95	94	94	94	94	91	94	02	97	96	98	93	93	93	97	97	98	04	94	22	2
Poland	77	77	91		68	80	89	50	57	91	01	95	73		54	91	91	92	96	99	02	90	20	2
Romania	74	74	93	91	70	82	90	50	57	91	02	95	79	00	54	90	90	91	94	94	01	93	22	3
Russian Federation	73	73	91		69	81	87	54	56	93		97	75		54	89	89	95	95	94	04	86	19	1
Serbia & Montenegro	01	01	01	01	01	01	01	01	00	01	01	01		03	01	01	01		02	01		01	20	20
Slovakia	93	93	93	99	93	93	93	93	93	93	02	95	93	99	93	93	93	93	94	94	02	93	22	2
Slovenia	92	92	93	94	92	92	93	92	92	92	01	97	92	98	92	92	92	93	96	95	02	92	22	2
Turkey	03	03			02	85	88	50	93	62		97	74	03	54			94	97	04		91	16	5
Turkmenistan	97	97	97	00	94	97	99		97	98		94	96	98	92	92	92	96	96	95	00	93	20	2
High income economies																								
Austria	78	78	87	93	72	82	87	58	50	54	00	95	73	98	53	82	82	93	94	94	02	87	22	2
Belgium	83	83	94	98	75	85	99	51	51	53	00	97	79	98	52	86	86	93	96	96	02	88	22	2
Cyprus	69	69	92	99	67	85	91	82	66	63	02	98	73	03	62	79	96	92	96	97	99	92	22	2
Denmark	72	72	72	94	71	83	87	51	51	52	01	95	73	98	51	82	82	94	93	93	02	88	22	2
Finland	75	75	75	91	70	86	89	59	50	68	00	95	74		55	80	80	91	94	94	02	86	21	2
France	80	80	84		71	83	86	50	51	54	00	95	84	98	51	01	84	91	94	94		87	20	2

Country	Human Rights											Humanitarian Law						Environmental Law					Total	Ratified since 2000
	ICESCR	ICCPR	ICCPR-OP1	ICCPR-OP2	CERD	CEDAW	CAT	Gen	ILO 87	CSR	ICC	CWC	BWC	LMC	Geneva	Prot 1	Prot 2	BC	CBD	UNFCCC	KP	VCPOL		
Germany	73	73	93	92	69	85	90	54	57	53	00	94	72	98	54	91	91	95	93	93	02	88	22	2
Greece	85	97	97	97	70	83	88	54	62	60	02	94	75	03	56	89	93	94	94	94	02	88	22	3
Iceland	79	79	79	91	67	85	96	49	50	55	00	97	73	99	65	87	87	95	94	93	02	89	22	2
Ireland	89	89	89	93	00	85	02	76	55	56	02	96	72	97	62	99	99	94	96	94	02	88	22	4
Italy	78	78	78	95	76	85	89	52	58	54	99	95	75	99	51	86	86	94	94	94	02	88	22	1
Luxembourg	83	83	83	92	78	89	87	81	58	53	00	97	76	99	53	89	89	94	94	94	02	88	22	2
Netherlands	78	78	78	91	71	91	88	66	50	56	01	95	81	99	54	87	87	93	94	93	02	88	22	2
Norway	72	72	72	91	70	81	86	49	49	53	00	94	73	98	51	81	81	90	93	93	02	86	22	2
Portugal	78	78	83	90	82	80	89	99	77	60	02	96	75	99	61	92	92	94	93	93		88	21	1
Spain	77	77	85	91	68	84	87	68	77	78	00	94	79	99	52	89	89	94	93	93	02	88	22	2
Sweden	71	71	71	90	71	80	86	52	49	54	01	93	76	98	53	79	79	91	93	93	02	86	22	2
Switzerland	92	92		94	94	97	86	00	75	55	01	95	76	98	50	82	82	90	94	93	03	87	21	3
United Kingdom	76	76		99	69	86	88	70	49	54	01	96	75	98	57	98	98	94	94	93	02	87	21	2
Latin America & Caribbean																								
Low income economies																								
Haiti		91			72	81		50	79	84		06		06	57			96	96	05	00		13	4
Nicaragua	80	80	80		78	81	05	52	67	80		99	75	98	53	99	99	97	95	95	99	93	20	1
Middle income economies																								
Argentina	86	86	86		68	85	86	56	60	61	01	95	79	99	56	86	86	91	94	93	01	90	21	2
Barbados	73	73	73		72	80		80	67		02		73	99	68	90	90	95	93	94	00	92	18	2
Belize		96			01	90	86	98	83	90	00	03	86	98	84	84	84	97	93	94	03	97	19	4
Bolivia	82	82	82		70	90	99	05	65	82	02	98	75	98	76	83	83	96	94	94	99	94	21	2
Brazil	92	92			68	84	89	52		60	02	96	73	99	57	92	92	92	94	94	02	90	19	2
Chile	72	72	92		71	89	88	53	99	72		96	80	01	50	91	91	92	94	94	02	90	20	2
Colombia	69	69	69	97	81	82	87	59	76	61	02	00	83	00	61	93	95	96	94	95	01	90	22	4
Costa Rica	68	68	68	98	67	86	93	50	60	78	01	96	93	99	69	83	83	95	94	94	02	91	22	2
Cuba					72	80	95	53	52			97	76		54	82	99	94	94	94		92	15	1
Dominican Republic	78	78	78		83	82			56	78	05		73	00	58	94	94	00	96	98	02	93	18	4
Ecuador	69	69	69	93	66	81	88	49	67	55	02	95	75	99	54	79	79	93	93	93	00	90	22	2
El Salvador	79	79	95		79	81	96	50		83		95	91	99	53	78	78	91	94	95	98	92	19	0
Guatemala	88	92	00		83	82	90	50	52	83		03	73	99	52	87	87	95	95	95	99	87	20	2
Guyana	77	77	93		77	80	88		67		04	97		03	68	88	88	01	94	94	03	93	18	4
Honduras	81	97	05		02	83	96	52	56	92	02	05	79	98	65	95	95	95	95	95	00	93	21	5

Country	Human Rights											Humanitarian Law						Environmental Law					Total	Ratified since 2000
	ICESCR	ICCPR	ICCPR-OP1	ICCPR-OP2	CERD	CEDAW	CAT	Gen	ILO 87	CSR	ICC	CWC	BWC	LMC	Geneva	Prot 1	Prot 2	BC	CBD	UNFCCC	KP	VCPOL		
Jamaica	75	75			71	84		68	62	64		00	75	98	64	86	86	03	95	94	99	93	18	2
Mexico	81	81	02		75	81	86	52	61	00	05	94	74	98	52	83		91	93	93	00	87	20	4
Panama	77	77	77	93	67	81	87	50	58	78	02	98	74	98	56	95	95	91	95	95	99	89	22	1
Paraguay	92	92	95	03	03	87	90	01	62	70	01	96	76	98	61	90	90	95	94	94	99	92	22	4
Peru	78	78	80		71	82	88	60	60	64	01	95	85	98	56	89	89	93	93	93	02	89	21	2
St. Lucia					90	82			80			97	86	99	81	82	82	93	93	93	03	93	14	1
St. Vincent & the Grenadines	81	81	81		81	81	01	81	01	93	02	02	99	01	81	83	83	96	96	96	04	96	21	6
Suriname	76	76	76		84	93			76	78		97	93	02	76	85	85		96	97		97	16	1
Trinidad & Tobago	78	78			73	90		02	63	00	99	97		98	63	01	01	94	96	94	99	89	18	4
Uruguay	70	70	70	93	68	81	86	67	54	70	02	94	81	01	69	85	85	91	93	94	01	89	22	3
Venezuela	78	78	78	93	67	83	91	60	82		00	97	78	99	56	98	98	98	94	94	05	88	21	2
High income economies																								
Bahamas					75	93		75	01	93			86	98	75	80	80	92	93	94	99	93	15	1
Middle East & North Africa																								
Low income economies																								
Yemen	87	87			72	84	91	87	76	80		00	79	98	70	90	90	96	96	96	04	96	19	2
Middle income economies																								
Algeria	89	89	89		72	96	89	63	62	63		95	01	01	62	89	89	98	95	93	05	92	20	3
Djibouti	02	02	02	02		98	02		78	77	02	06		98	78	91	91	02	94	95	02	99	19	9
Egypt	82	82			67	81	86	52	57	81					52	92	92	93	94	94	05	88	16	1
Iran	75	75			68			56		76		97	73		57			93	96	96	05	90	13	1
Iraq	71	71			70	86		59					91		56								7	0
Jordan	75	75			74	92	91	50			02	97	75	98	51	79	79	89	93	93	03	89	18	2
Lebanon	72	72			71	97	00	53					75		51	97	97	94	94	94		93	14	1
Libya	70	70	89		68	89	89	89	00			04	82		56	78	78	01	01	99		90	17	4
Malta	90	90	90	94	71	91	90		65	71	02	97	75	01	68	89	89	00	00	94	01	88	21	5
Morocco & Western Sahara	79	79			70	93	93	58		56		95	02		56			95	95	95	02	95	15	2
Oman					03	06						95	92		74	84	84	95	95	95	05	99	12	3
Saudi Arabia					97	00	97	50				96	72		63	87	01	90	01	94	05	93	14	4
Syria	69	69			69	03	04	55	60						53	83		92	96	96	06	89	14	3
Tunisia	69	69			67	85	88	56	57	57		97	73	99	57	79	79	95	93	93	03	89	19	1
High income economies																								
Bahrain					90	02	98	90				97	88		71	86	86	92	96	94	06	90	14	2

Country	Human Rights											Humanitarian Law						Environmental Law					Total	Ratified since 2000
	ICESCR	ICCPR	ICCPR-OP1	ICCPR-OP2	CERD	CEDAW	CAT	Gen	ILO 87	CSR	ICC	CWC	BWC	LMC	Geneva	Prot 1	Prot 2	BC	CBD	UNFCCC	KP	VCPOL		
Israel & Occupied Territiories	91	91			79	91	91	50	57	54					51			94	95	96	04	92	14	1
Kuwait	96	96			68	94	96	95	61			97	72		67	85	85	93	02	94	05	92	17	2
Qatar					76		00					97	75	98	75	88	05	95	96	96	05	96	13	3
United Arab Emirates					74	04		05				00			72	83	83	92	00	95	05	89	12	5
North America																								
High income economies																								
Canada	76	76	76	05	70	81	87	52	72	69	00	95	72	97	65	90	90	92	92	92	02	86	22	3
United States		92			94		94	88				97	75		55					92		86	9	0
South Asia																								
Low income economies																								
Afghanistan	83	83			83	03	87	56	57	05	03	03	75	02	56			02	02			04	16	8
Bangladesh	98	00			79	84	98	98	72			97	85	00	72	80	80	93	94	94	01	90	18	3
Bhutan					81							05	78	05	91			02	95	95	02	04	10	5
India	79	79			68	93		59				96	74		50			92	94	93	02	91	13	1
Nepal	91	91	91	98	71	91	91	69				97			64			96	93	94	05	94	15	1
Pakistan					66	96			57	51		97	74		51			94	94	94	05	92	12	1
Middle income economies																								
Maldives					84	93	04	84				94	93	00	91	91	91	92	92	92	98	88	15	2
Sri Lanka	80	80	97		82	81	94	50	95			94	86		59			92	94	93	02	89	16	1
Sub-Saharan Africa																								
Low income economies																								
Angola	92	92	92			86			01	81				02	84	84			98	00		00	12	4
Benin	92	92	92		01	92	92		60	62	02	98	75	98	61	86	86	97	94	94		93	19	2
Burkina Faso	99	99	99		74	87	99	65	60	80	04	97	91	98	61	87	87	99	93	93	05	89	21	2
Burundi	90	90			77	92	93	97	93	63	04	98		03	71	93	93	97	97	97	01	97	19	3
Cameroon	84	84	84		71	94	86		60	61		96		02	63	84	84	01	94	94	02	89	18	3
Central African Republic	81	81	81		71	91			60	62	01			02	66	84	84	06	95	95		93	16	3
Chad	95	95	95		77	95	95		60	81		04		99	70	97	97	04	94	94		89	17	2
Comoros					04	94			04	78				02	85	85	85	94	94	94		94	12	3
Congo, Rep.	83	83	83		88	82	03		60	62	04		78	01	67	83	83		96			94	16	3
Congo, Dem. Rep.	76	76	76		76	86	96	62	01	65	02	05	75	02	61	82	02	94	94	95	05	94	21	6
Côte d'Ivoire	92	92	97		73	95	95	95	60	61		95		00	61	89	89	94	94	94		93	18	1
Equatorial Guinea	87	87	87		02	84	02		01	86		97	89	98	86	86	86	03	94	00	00	88	19	6

Country	Human Rights											Humanitarian Law						Environmental Law					Total	Ratified since 2000
	ICESCR	ICCPR	ICCPR-OP1	ICCPR-OP2	CERD	CEDAW	CAT	Gen	ILO 87	CSR	ICC	CWC	BWC	LMC	Geneva	Prot 1	Prot 2	BC	CBD	UNFCCC	KP	VCPOL		
Eritrea	01	02			01	95			00			00		01	00			05	96	95	05	05	13	10
Ethiopia	93	93			76	81	94	49	63	69		96	75	04	69	94	94	00	94	94	05	94	19	3
Gambia	78	79	88		78	93		78	00	66	02	98	91	02	66	89	89	97	94	94	01	90	20	4
Ghana	00	00	00		66	86	00	58	65	63	99	97	75	00	58	78	78	03	94	95	03	89	21	7
Guinea	78	78	93		77	82	89	00	59	65	03	97		98	84	84	84	95	93	93	00	92	20	3
Guinea-Bissau	92					85				76			76	01	74	86	86	05	95	95	05	02	13	4
Kenya	72	72			01	84	97			66	05	97	76	01	66	99	99	00	94	94	00	88	18	5
Lesotho	92	92	00		71	95	01	74	66	81	00	94	77	98	68	94	94	00	95	95	00	94	21	5
Liberia	04	04		05	76	84	04	50	62	64	04	06		99	54	88	88	04	00	02	02	96	20	10
Madagascar	71	71	71		69	89	05		60	67		04		04	63	92	92	99	96	99	03	96	18	4
Malawi	93	93	96		96	87	96		99	87	02	98		98	68	91	91	94	94	94	01	91	19	2
Mali	74	74	01		74	85	99	74	60	73	00	97	02	98	65	89	89	00	95	94	02	94	21	5
Mauritania	04	04			88		04		61					00	62	80	80	96	96	94	05		13	5
Mozambique		93		93	83	97	99	83	96	83		00		98	83	83	02	97	95	95	05	94	18	3
Niger	86	86	86		67	99	98		61	61	02	97	72	99	64	79	79	98	95	95	04	92	20	2
Nigeria	93	93			67	85	01		60	67	01	99	73	01	61	88	88	91	94	94	04	88	19	4
Rwanda	75	75			75	81		75	88		75	04	75	00	64	84	84	04	96	94	04	01	18	5
Sao Tome & Principe						03			92	78		03	79	03	76	96	96		99	99		01	12	4
Senegal	78	78	78		72	85	86	83	60	63	99	98	75	98	63	85	85	92	94	94	01	93	21	1
Sierra Leone	96	96	96		67	88	01		61	81	00	04	76	04	65	86	86		94	95		01	18	5
Somalia	90	90	90		75		90			78					62							01	8	1
Sudan	86	76			77			03	74	74		99	04	03	57	06		06	95	93	04	93	15	6
Tanzania	76	76			72	85		84	00	64	02	98		00	62	83	83	93	96	96	02	93	18	4
Togo	84	84	88		72	83	87	84	60	62		97	76	00	62	84	84	04	95	95	04	91	20	3
Uganda	87	95	95		80	85	86	95	05	76	02	01	92	99	64	91	91	99	93	93	02	88	21	4
Zambia	84	84	84		72	85	98		96	69	02	01		01	66	95	95	94	93	93		90	18	3
Zimbabwe	91	91			91	91		91	03	81		97	90	98	83	92	92		94	92		92	16	1
Middle income economies																								
Botswana		00			74	96	00		97	69	00	98	92	00	68	79	79	98	95	94	03	91	18	5
Cape Verde	93	93	00	00	79	80	92		99			03	77	01	84	95	95	99	95	95	06	01	19	6
Gabon	83	83			80	83	00	83	60	64	00	00		00	65	80	80		97	98		94	17	4
Mauritius	73	73	73		72	84	92		05		02	93	72	97	70	82	82	92	92	92	01	92	19	3
Namibia	94	94	94	94	82	92	94	94	95	95	02	95		98	91	94	94	95	97	95	03	93	21	2

Country	Human Rights											Humanitarian Law						Environmental Law					Total	Ratified since 2000
	ICESCR	ICCPR	ICCPR-OP1	ICCPR-OP2	CERD	CEDAW	CAT	Gen	ILO 87	CSR	ICC	CWC	BWC	LMC	Geneva	Prot 1	Prot 2	BC	CBD	UNFCCC	KP	VCPOL		
South Africa		99	02	02	98	95	98	98	96	96	00	95	75	98	52	95	95	94	95	97	02	90	21	4
Swaziland	04	04			69	04	04		78	00		96	91	98	73	95	95	05	94	96	06	92	18	7
Total States in table	147	149	102	52	163	167	135	134	139	134	93	158	140	136	175	152	147	155	171	171	142	173	3,134	
Total States Parties*	152	155	105	56	170	182	141	138	145	143	100	178	155	150	192	164	159	168	188	189	162	190	3,382	
Ratified since 2000 (States in table)	11	12	11	13	13	11	22	9	17	9	88	37	5	57	2	8	10	30	11	9	127	14		526

* Total States Parties refers to the total number of ratifications for each treaty, including from those countries with populations of less than 100,000 that are not included in this table.

Sources:
Office of the United Nations High Commissioner for Human Rights:
http://www.ohchr.org/english/law/index.htm
http://www.ohchr.org/english/countries/ratification/4.htm
http://www.ohchr.org/english/countries/ratification/5.htm
http://www.ohchr.org/english/countries/ratification/12.htm
http://www.ohchr.org/english/countries/ratification/2.htm
http://www.un.org/womenwatch/daw/cedaw/states.htm
http://www.ohchr.org/english/countries/ratification/9.htm
http://www.ohchr.org/english/countries/ratification/1.htm

International Labor Organization:
http://www.ilo.org/ilolex/cgi-lex/ratifce.pl?C087

United Nations Treaties:
http://untreaty.un.org/ENGLISH/bible/englishinternetbible/Bible.asp#partI
http://untreaty.un.org/ENGLISH/bible/englishinternetbible/partI/chapterV/treaty5.asp
http://untreaty.un.org/ENGLISH/bible/englishinternetbible/partI/chapterXVIII/treaty11.asp
http://untreaty.un.org/ENGLISH/bible/englishinternetbible/partI/chapterXXVI/treaty8.asp
http://untreaty.un.org/ENGLISH/bible/englishinternetbible/partI/chapterXXVII/treaty18.asp
http://untreaty.un.org/ENGLISH/bible/englishinternetbible/partI/chapterXXVII/treaty35.asp
http://untreaty.un.org/ENGLISH/bible/englishinternetbible/partI/chapterXXVII/treaty32.asp
http://untreaty.un.org/ENGLISH/bible/englishinternetbible/partI/chapterXXVI/treaty10.asp
http://untreaty.un.org/ENGLISH/bible/englishinternetbible/partI/chapterXXVII/treaty11.asp
http://untreaty.un.org/ENGLISH/bible/englishinternetbible/partI/chapterXXVII/treaty18.asp

The Biological and Toxin Weapons Convention Website:
http://www.opbw.org/

International Committee of the Red Cross:
http://www.icrc.org/IHL.nsf/TOPICS?OpenView#Victims%20of%20Armed%20Conflicts
http://www.icrc.org/IHL.nsf/WebSign?ReadForm&id=470&ps=P
http://www.icrc.org/IHL.nsf/WebSign?ReadForm&id=470&ps=P

Record 8: Human rights violations

Global civil society is instrumental in exposing human rights violations. At the same time, human rights violations form one of the main threats to the survival of local civil societies. While Record 7 shows the extent to which states have committed to abide by international law, this table shows the extent to which they actually respect international human rights law. The table displays information on human rights abuses by country, covering extrajudicial executions and disappearances, arbitrary detentions, torture, freedom of expression, and the situation of minorities, using the latest information available from three sources: Amnesty International (report of 2006), the US State Department (reports of 2005) and Human Rights Watch (report of 2006). The table shows that human rights are violated globally, especially in low- and middle-income economies, the most common violation being torture. In developed nations, torture and discrimination against minorities is not uncommon.

Country	Disappearances & extrajudicial executions			Arbitrary detentions			Torture			Discrimination against minorities			Restricted freedom of expression & association		
	AI	SD	HRW	AI	SD	HRW	AI	SD	HRW	AI	SD	HRW	AI	SD	HRW
East Asia & Pacific															
Low income economies															
Cambodia		yes	*yes*		yes	*yes*		yes	yes		yes	yes	yes	yes	yes
East Timor					yes		yes	yes	yes		yes				
Indonesia	yes	yes	yes	yes	yes	yes	yes	yes	yes	yes	yes	yes	yes	yes	yes
Korea, Dem. Rep.	yes	yes			yes	yes	yes	yes	yes		yes	yes	yes	yes	yes
Laos	yes	yes			yes		yes			yes	yes		yes	yes	
Mongolia		*yes*			yes		yes	*yes*					yes	yes	
Myanmar		yes	yes	yes	yes		yes	yes	yes	yes	yes	yes	yes	yes	yes
Papua New Guinea	*yes*	yes	yes			yes*	*yes*	yes	yes		yes	yes*			yes*
Solomon Islands										yes	yes				
Vietnam					yes	yes	*yes*	yes		yes	yes	yes	yes	yes	
Middle income economies															
China & Tibet	*yes*	yes			yes		yes	yes		yes	yes	yes	yes	yes	yes
Fiji											yes			yes	
Malaysia		*yes*		yes		yes	*yes*		yes	yes	yes	yes	yes		
Philippines	*yes*	yes		yes	yes		yes	yes			yes		yes	yes	
Samoa															
Thailand		yes	yes	yes	yes		yes	yes	yes	yes	yes	yes			yes
Tonga														yes	
Vanuatu															
High income economies															
Australia										yes	yes				
Brunei					yes						yes			yes	
Korea, Rep.										yes	yes				
Japan											yes		yes		

Country	Disappearances & extrajudicial executions			Arbitrary detentions			Torture			Discrimination against minorities			Restricted freedom of expression & association		
	AI	SD	HRW	AI	SD	HRW	AI	SD	HRW	AI	SD	HRW	AI	SD	HRW
New Zealand															
Singapore				yes						yes	yes		yes	yes	
Europe & Central Asia															
Low income economies															
Armenia					yes		*yes*	yes	yes	yes	yes	yes	yes	yes	yes
Azerbaijan		*yes*			yes		yes	yes	yes		yes		yes	yes	yes
Georgia					yes		yes	yes	yes	yes	yes	yes	yes	yes	yes
Kyrgyzstan					yes			yes	yes		yes		yes	yes	
Moldova			yes		yes		yes	*Yes*			yes		yes		
Tajikistan							yes	yes			yes		yes	yes	yes
Ukraine		*yes*			yes		yes	yes	yes	yes	yes	yes			
Uzbekistan	yes	yes	yes	yes	yes		yes	yes	yes	yes	yes	yes	yes	yes	yes
Middle income economies															
Albania					yes		yes	*yes*			yes				
Belarus		*yes*		yes	yes		yes	*yes*			yes		yes	yes	yes
Bosnia & Herzegovina								*yes*			yes				
Bulgaria	*yes*	yes		yes			yes	yes		yes	yes				
Croatia								*yes*			yes	yes			
Czech Republic							*yes*	yes		yes	yes				
Estonia							*yes*	yes		yes					
Hungary								yes		yes	yes				
Kazakhstan					yes			yes			yes		yes	yes	yes
Latvia							yes	*yes*		yes	yes				
Lithuania											yes				
Macedonia								yes			yes			yes	
Malta							yes								
Poland							*YES*			yes	yes			yes	
Romania		yes						yes		yes	yes				
Russian Federation	yes	yes	yes	yes	yes	yes	yes	yes	yes	yes	yes	yes		yes	
Serbia & Montenegro		*yes*			yes		yes	yes		yes	yes	yes		yes	
Slovakia										yes	yes				
Slovenia								*yes*		yes	yes				
Turkey	yes	yes	yes		yes		yes	yes	yes	yes	yes	yes	yes	yes	yes
Turkmenistan		*yes*			yes		*yes*	yes		yes	yes	yes		yes	yes
High income economies															
Austria				yes				*yes*			yes				

Country	Disappearances & extrajudicial executions			Arbitrary detentions			Torture			Discrimination against minorities			Restricted freedom of expression & association		
	AI	SD	HRW	AI	SD	HRW	AI	SD	HRW	AI	SD	HRW	AI	SD	HRW
Belgium										yes	yes				
Cyprus							yes	yes			yes				
Denmark															
Finland											yes				
France								yes		yes	yes				
Germany							yes				yes			yes	
Greece							yes			yes	yes			yes	
Iceland											yes				
Ireland										yes	yes				
Italy		yes					yes				yes			yes	
Luxembourg															
Netherlands											yes				
Norway															
Portugal	yes						yes	yes							
Spain	yes	yes			yes		yes	yes			yes				
Sweden											yes				
Switzerland							yes	yes			yes				
United Kingdom	yes		yes				yes	yes	yes		yes				
Latin America & Caribbean															
Low income economies															
Haiti	yes	yes	yes		yes	yes	yes	yes	yes				yes	yes	yes
Nicaragua	yes	yes			yes		yes	yes			yes		yes	yes	
Middle income economies															
Argentina		yes			yes		yes	yes	yes	yes	yes				
Barbados								yes							
Belize		yes		yes	yes		yes	yes							
Bolivia		yes			yes			yes		yes	yes				
Brazil	yes	yes	yes	yes	yes	yes	yes	yes	yes	yes	yes	yes		yes	
Chile								yes			yes	yes			yes
Colombia	yes	yes	yes	yes	yes		yes	yes	yes		yes		yes	yes	yes
Costa Rica															
Cuba				yes	yes		yes				yes		yes	yes	yes
Dominican Republic	yes	yes			yes		yes	yes		yes	yes			yes	
Ecuador		yes			yes		yes	yes		yes	yes				
El Salvador		yes			yes			yes			yes				
Guatemala		yes	yes		yes			yes	yes		yes			yes	yes

Country	Disappearances & extrajudicial executions			Arbitrary detentions			Torture			Discrimination against minorities			Restricted freedom of expression & association		
	AI	SD	HRW	AI	SD	HRW	AI	SD	HRW	AI	SD	HRW	AI	SD	HRW
Guyana	yes	yes						*yes*						yes	
Honduras	yes	yes			yes		yes	yes			yes				
Jamaica	yes	yes			yes		yes	*yes*		yes	yes				
Mexico		yes		yes	yes	yes	yes	yes	yes	yes	yes		yes	yes	yes
Panama											yes			yes	
Paraguay		yes	yes		yes		yes	yes			yes				
Peru							yes	yes	yes		yes	yes		yes	yes
St. Lucia								yes							
Suriname								yes			yes			yes	
Trinidad & Tobago	yes	*yes*					yes	*yes*			yes				
Uruguay							*yes*				yes				
Venezuela	yes	yes	yes		yes		*yes*	yes		yes	yes		yes	yes	yes
High income economies															
Bahamas					yes		*yes*	yes		yes	yes				
Middle East & North Africa															
Low income economies															
Yemen	yes	yes		yes	yes		*yes*	yes		yes	yes		yes	yes	
Middle income economies															
Algeria	yes	*yes*			yes		yes	yes					yes	yes	
Djibouti		*yes*			yes			*yes*			yes			yes	
Egypt	*yes*	*yes*		yes	yes	yes	yes	yes	yes			yes	yes	yes	yes
Iran	yes	yes		yes	yes		yes	yes	yes	yes	yes	yes	yes	yes	yes
Iraq	*yes*	yes	yes	yes	yes	yes	yes	yes	yes		yes		yes	yes	
Jordan				yes	yes	yes	yes	yes	yes		yes		yes	yes	yes
Lebanon	yes	yes		yes	yes		yes	yes			yes		yes	yes	
Libya							yes	yes		yes	yes	yes	yes	yes	
Morocco & Western Sahara	*yes*	yes			yes		*yes*	yes	yes		yes		yes	yes	yes
Oman					yes					yes				yes	
Saudi Arabia	*yes*		yes	yes	yes	yes	yes	yes		yes	yes		yes	yes	
Syria		yes	yes		yes	yes	yes	yes	yes	yes	yes	yes	yes	yes	yes
Tunisia	*yes*	yes			yes		yes	yes	yes				yes	yes	
High income economies															
Bahrain					yes		yes	*yes*			yes		yes	yes	
Israel & Occupied Territories	yes		yes	yes		yes	*yes*	yes	yes	yes		yes			
Kuwait	*yes*	yes					yes	yes		yes	yes			yes	
Qatar				yes						yes	yes			yes	

Country	Disappearances & extrajudicial executions			Arbitrary detentions			Torture			Discrimination against minorities			Restricted freedom of expression & association		
	AI	SD	HRW	AI	SD	HRW	AI	SD	HRW	AI	SD	HRW	AI	SD	HRW
United Arab Emirates					yes		yes	yes			yes	yes	yes	yes	yes
North America															
High income economies															
Canada															
United States	yes			yes		yes	yes		yes	yes		yes	yes		
South Asia															
Low income economies															
Afghanistan	*yes*	yes	yes	yes	yes		yes	yes			yes		yes	yes	
Bangladesh		yes	yes		yes	yes	yes	yes	yes	yes	yes	yes	yes	yes	yes
Bhutan											yes			yes	
India	yes	yes	yes	yes	yes	yes	yes	yes	yes	yes	yes	yes	yes	yes	yes
Nepal	yes	yes	yes	yes	yes	yes	yes	yes	yes	yes	yes	yes	yes	yes	yes
Pakistan	yes	yes	yes	yes	yes	yes	yes	yes	yes		yes	yes	yes	yes	yes
Middle income economies															
Maldives				yes	yes		yes	*yes*						yes	
Sri Lanka	yes	yes			yes		yes	yes			yes			yes	
Sub-Saharan Africa															
Low income economies															
Angola	yes	yes		yes	yes		*yes*	yes	yes		yes			yes	yes
Benin					yes			*yes*						yes	
Burkina Faso		yes			yes			yes						yes	
Burundi	yes	yes	yes	yes	yes	yes	yes	yes	yes		yes			yes	yes
Cameroon	*yes*	yes		yes	yes		yes	yes		yes	yes		yes	yes	
Central African Republic	yes	yes			yes			yes			yes		yes	yes	
Chad		yes			yes			yes			yes		yes	yes	
Comoros											yes				
Congo, Dem Rep.	yes	yes		yes	yes		yes	yes		yes	yes		yes	yes	
Congo, Rep.	*yes*	yes		yes	yes			yes			yes			yes	
Côte d'Ivoire	yes	yes	yes	yes	yes	yes	yes	yes	yes	yes	yes	yes	yes	yes	yes
Equatorial Guinea	yes	*yes*		yes	yes		yes	yes			yes		yes	yes	
Eritrea		yes	yes	yes	yes	yes	yes	yes	yes	yes	yes	yes	yes	yes	yes
Ethiopia	yes	yes	yes	yes	yes	yes	yes	yes	yes	yes	yes		yes	yes	yes
Gambia					yes			yes			yes			yes	
Ghana		yes			yes			yes			yes			yes	
Guinea		*yes*			yes		yes	yes			yes		yes	yes	
Guinea-Bissau	*yes*	*yes*		yes	yes		*yes*	yes					yes	yes	

Country	Disappearances & extrajudicial executions			Arbitrary detentions			Torture			Discrimination against minorities			Restricted freedom of expression & association		
	AI	SD	HRW	AI	SD	HRW	AI	SD	HRW	AI	SD	HRW	AI	SD	HRW
Kenya	yes	yes			yes		yes	yes			yes		yes	yes	
Lesotho		*yes*						yes			yes				
Liberia					yes			*yes*		yes	yes				
Madagascar		yes			yes			yes			yes			yes	
Malawi	yes	*yes*		yes	yes		yes	yes			yes		yes	yes	
Mali															
Mauritania		yes			yes		yes	yes			yes			yes	
Mozambique	yes	yes			yes		yes	yes			yes		yes	yes	
Niger								*yes*			yes			yes	
Nigeria	*yes*	yes	yes		yes	yes		yes	yes	yes	yes	yes	yes	yes	yes
Rwanda		yes		yes	yes	yes		yes			yes		yes	yes	
Sao Tome & Principe															
Senegal		yes			yes			yes			yes		yes	yes	
Sierra Leone	*yes*	*yes*	yes		yes	yes	*yes*	*yes*	yes	yes	yes		yes	yes	yes
Somalia		yes		yes	yes			yes		yes	yes		yes	yes	
Sudan	*yes*	yes		yes	yes			yes		yes	yes		yes	yes	
Tanzania	*yes*	yes		yes	yes		*yes*	yes			yes		yes	yes	
Togo	yes	yes		yes	yes		yes	yes			yes		yes	yes	
Uganda		yes	yes		yes		yes	yes	yes		yes	yes	yes	yes	yes
Zambia	*yes*	yes			yes		*yes*	yes			yes		yes	yes	
Zimbabwe	*yes*	yes			yes		*yes*	yes	yes		yes		yes	yes	yes
Middle income economies															
Botswana								yes			yes			yes	
Cape Verde								*yes*						yes	
Gabon		yes			yes			yes			yes			yes	
Mauritius								*yes*							
Namibia		*yes*			yes			yes			yes			yes	
South Africa		*yes*	yes		yes		yes	yes	yes	yes	yes				
Swaziland	*yes*	yes			yes		yes	yes			yes		yes	yes	

'yes' denotes a violation. Absence of data indicates either that no violations have been recorded or that no data are available.
'*yes*' denotes a violation using Global Civil Society Yearbook definitions (see glossary) but the report itself does not mention or denies it.
* HRW report on Papua New Guinea focuses on human rights violations due to police violence.

Sources: Amnesty International Report 2006, http://web.amnesty.org/report2006/index-eng; U.S. State Department 2005 Country Reports on Human Rights Practices http://www.state.gov/g/drl/rls/hrrpt/2005/index.htm; Human Rights Watch World Report 2006, http://hrw.org.wr2k6

Record 9: Social justice

This record illustrates another element of the spread of the international rule of law, namely, social justice. Growing inequality appears to be one of the characteristics of globalisation. It can be seen as inhibiting the emergence of global civil society, but it is also one of global civil society's major causes. This record contains indicators of poverty, inequality, and social exclusion. In addition to the Human Development Index, which combines GDP per capita, educational attainment, and life expectancy at birth, this record includes the percentage of people living with HIV, rates of unemployment, the ratio of girls to boys in education, and the burden of debt servicing on national economies. While the first five indicators are common assessments of quality of life, the last two focus on equality, gender equality and inequality between nations respectively.

The data show that health, education and equality outcomes in Sub-Saharan Africa are extremely low, affected to a great extent by the HIV and AIDS pandemic, though the HDI in two of every three Sub-Saharan countries in the table improved slightly compared to the figures we reported last year. People's financial security declined as unemployment increased in many countries. Unemployment decreased mostly in developed nations. The burden of debt on national economies increased in many countries, but particularly in the transition economies of East and Central Europe and Central Asia.

Country	Human Development Index (HDI)			GDP per capita, PPP in current international $			Net primary school enrolment ratio (%)			Total unemployment			People living with HIV*	Ratio of girls to boys in primary education (%)			Debt service as % flows from abroad		
	value 1995	value 2003	% change 1995-2003	1994	2004	% change 1994-2004	2000	2004	% change 2000-2004	Total rates 1993	Total rates 2003	% change 1993-2003	Per 1,000 residents end 2003	2000	2004	% change 2000-2004	1993	2003	% change 1993-2003
East Asia & Pacific																			
Low income economies																			
Cambodia	0.533	0.571	7	1,252	2,423	94	91	98	8				12.6	87	92	5	9.6	0.9	-91
East Timor		0.513																	
Indonesia	0.663	0.697	5	2,536	3,609	42	94	96	2		*9.1*		0.5	97	*98*	2	21.4	12.8	-40
Laos	0.487	0.545	12	1,082	1,954	81	82	84	3				0.3	85	88	3	8.3	10.3	24
Mongolia	0.633	0.679	7	1,077	2,056	91	91	84	-7				0.2	104	102	-2	6	4.4	-27
Myanmar		0.578					82	*85*	4				6.7	99	*101*	2	12.4	3.8	-69
Papua New Guinea	0.515	0.523	2	2,398	2,543	6							2.8	90	88	*-3*	9.3	7.3	-22
Solomon Islands		0.594		2,133	1,814	-15		80						92	97	5	5.7		
Vietnam	0.66	0.704	7	1,311	2,745	109	95				2.25		2.7	94	93	-1		3.3	
Middle income economies																			
China**	0.683	0.755	11	2,217	5,896	166				2.6	4.3	65	0.7	*101*	100	*-1*	10.2	2.8	-73
Fiji	0.741	0.752	1	4,386	6,066	38	100	96	-3	5.9			0.7	98	98	-1	5.7		
Malaysia	0.76	0.796	5	6,474	10,276	59	97			*3*	3.6	20	2.1	*100*			6.2	4.7	-24
Philippines	0.736	0.758	3	3,294	4,614	40	*93*	94	*1*	8.9	10.2	15	0.1	*100*	99	*-1*	23.3	13.8	-41
Samoa	0.742	0.776	5	3,780	5,613	48	93							100	100	0	8.7		
Thailand	0.749	0.778	4	5,406	8,090	50	84	87	3	1.5	1.54	3	9.0	95	96	1	4.3	8	86
Tonga		0.81		5,230	7,870	50	*100*	98	*-2*					97	95	-2	4.5	*5.8*	29
Vanuatu		0.659		3,211	3,051	-5	93	94	1					98	97	-1	1.4	1.2	-14

Country	Human Development Index (HDI)			GDP per capita, PPP in current international $			Net primary school enrolment ratio (%)			Total unemployment			People living with HIV*	Ratio of girls to boys in primary education (%)			Debt service as % flows from abroad		
	value 1995	value 2003	% change 1995-2003	1994	2004	% change 1994-2004	2000	2004	% change 2000-2004	Total rates 1993	Total rates 2003	% change 1993-2003	Per 1,000 residents end 2003	2000	2004	% change 2000-2004	1993	2003	% change 1993-2003
High income economies																			
Australia	0.933	0.955	2	19,624	30,331	55	93	95	3	10.7	6	-44	0.7	100	100	0			
Brunei													0.6	99	100	1			
Korea, Rep.	0.855	0.901	5	11,392	20,499	80	97	100	3	2.8	3.6	29	0.2	101	99	-1			
Japan	0.925	0.943	2	22,218	29,251	32	100	100	0	2.5	5.3	112	0.1	100	100	0			
New Zealand	0.905	0.933	3	16,049	23,413	46	100	100	0	9.5	4.7	-51	0.3	101	100	-1			
Singapore	0.861	0.907	5	16,797	28,077	67				2.7	5.4	100	1.0						
Taiwan										1.45	4.99	244							
Europe & Central Asia																			
Low income economies																			
Armenia	0.698	0.759	9	1,530	4,101	168	81	97	19				0.9	100	103	4	1.1	8.7	691
Azerbaijan		0.729		1,872	4,153	122	86	84	-2				0.2	101	98	-2		6	
Georgia		0.732		1,213	2,844	134	100	93	-7		11.5		0.7	100	100	0		9.9	
Kyrgyzstan		0.702		1,167	1,935	66					12.5		0.8	99	100	1	0.4	7.7	1,825
Moldova	0.682	0.671	-2	1,384	1,729	25	79	78	-2		7.9		1.3	99	99	0	2	6.6	230
Tajikistan	0.629	0.652	4	854	1,202	41		98					0.0	93	95	3	0.2	7.7	3,750
Ukraine	0.747	0.766	3	4,314	6,394	48	81	86	7		9.1		7.5	99	100	1	1.5	5.5	267
Uzbekistan	0.679	0.694	2	1,241	1,869	51							0.4		99			19.6	
Middle income economies																			
Albania	0.702	0.78	11	2,328	4,978	114	100	96	-4		15.175			99	99	-1	3.2	3.6	13
Belarus	0.751	0.786	5	3,494	6,970	100	94	95	1					99	97	-2	0.6	1.7	183
Bosnia & Herzegovina		0.786		1,535	7,032	358							0.2					6.4	0
Bulgaria	0.784	0.808	3	5,202	8,078	55	97	94	-3	21.4	17.6	-18	0.1	97	98	1	6.2	7.5	21
Croatia	0.799	0.841	5	6,357	12,191	92	86	87	2		14.3		0.0	99	99	1	2.4	7.9	229
Czech Republic	0.843	0.874	4	11,820	19,408	64	90	87	-4	4.3	7.8	81	0.2	99	98	-1	6.5	3	-54
Estonia	0.795	0.853	7	5,866	14,555	148	98	95	-4	6.6	10	52	5.8	97	96	0	1.3	0.8	-38
Hungary	0.812	0.862	6	9,159	16,814	84	88	89	1	11.9	5.7	-52	0.3	98	99	0	34.7	6.8	-80
Kazakhstan***	0.721	0.761	6	3,481	7,440	114	89	98	11	7.5	8.8		1.1	100	99	-2		3	
Latvia	0.765	0.836	9	5,164	11,653	126	92	87	-6		10.6		3.3	98	97	-1	0.7	4	471
Lithuania	0.787	0.852	8	5,857	13,107	124	98	92	-6	17.4	12.4	-29	0.4	99	99	0	0.3	11.3	3,667
Macedonia		0.797		4,922	6,610	34	93	92	-1		36.7		0.1	99	100	1		8.7	
Poland	0.816	0.858	5	6,973	12,974	86	97	98	1	14	19.6	40	0.4	99	99	1	8.2	6.5	-21

Country	Human Development Index (HDI)			GDP per capita, PPP in current international $			Net primary school enrolment ratio (%)			Total unemployment			People living with HIV*	Ratio of girls to boys in primary education (%)			Debt service as % flows from abroad		
	value 1995	value 2003	% change 1995–2003	1994	2004	% change 1994–2004	2000	2004	% change 2000–2004	Total rates 1993	Total rates 2003	% change 1993–2003	Per 1,000 residents end 2003	2000	2004	% change 2000–2004	1993	2003	% change 1993–2003
Romania	0.768	0.792	3	5,204	8,480	63	94	90	-4	8.2	7	-15	0.3	98	98	0	4.4	10.4	136
Russian Federation	0.77	0.795	3	5,952	9,902	66				5.9	8	36	5.9	99	99	1	4.4	8.3	89
Slovakia		0.849		8,028	14,623	82	89	85	-5	13.7	17.4	27	0.0	99	99	0	8.2	6.9	-16
Slovenia	0.853	0.904	6	11,792	20,939	78	96	96	0	9.1	6.6	-27	0.3	102	99	-2			
Turkey	0.709	0.75	6	5,040	7,753	54		89		8.8	10.5	19		91	94	3	25.4	20.3	-20
Turkmenistan		0.738			2,896								0.0				0.4	5.7	1,325
High income economies																			
Austria	0.914	0.936	2	22,179	32,276	46				4.3	4.3	0	1.2	99	99	0			
Belgium	0.929	0.945	2	21,215	31,096	47	100	100	0	8.2	8.2	0	1.0	99	99	0			
Cyprus	0.858	0.891	4	14,587	22,805	56	95	96	1		4.1			100	100	0			
Denmark	0.913	0.941	3	22,593	31,914	41	99	100	1	8	5.5	-31	0.9	100	100	0			
Finland	0.914	0.941	3	18,588	29,951	61	100	100	0	16.2	9	-44	0.3	99	99	0			
France	0.921	0.938	2	20,264	29,300	45	100	100	0	11.5	9.7	-16	2.0	99	99	0			
Germany	0.913	0.93	2	20,526	28,303	38				9.5	10	5	0.5	99	100	0			
Greece	0.876	0.912	4	13,129	22,205	69	94	98	4	9.67	8.9	-8	0.8	100	100	-1			
Iceland	0.919	0.956	4	21,514	33,051	54	99	99	0	5.3	3.3	-38	1.7	98	98	0			
Ireland	0.894	0.946	6	15,796	38,827	146	93	96	3	15.7	4.4	-72	0.7	99	99	0			
Italy	0.907	0.934	3	20,358	28,180	38	100	99	0	9.8	8.7	-11	2.4	100	99	0			
Luxembourg	0.911	0.949	4	34,854	69,961	101	96	90	-6				1.1	101	99	-2			
Netherlands	0.928	0.943	2	21,564	31,789	47	100	99	0	6.2	4.3	-31	1.2	98	98	0			
Norway	0.936	0.963	3	25,877	38,454	49	100	99	0	6	4.5	-25	0.5	100	100	0			
Portugal	0.878	0.904	3	13,175	19,629	49				5.4	6.3	17	2.1	96	95	-1			
Spain	0.904	0.928	3	16,532	25,047	52	100	100	0	22.64	11.5	-49	3.3	98	98	0			
Sweden	0.929	0.949	2	19,744	29,541	50	100	100	0	8.2	4.9	-40	0.4	102	103	0			
Switzerland	0.921	0.947	3	26,661	33,040	24	96	94	-2	3.7	4.1	11	1.8	99	99	0			
United Kingdom	0.921	0.939	2	20,325	30,821	52	100	100	0	10.3	4.8	-53	0.9	100	100	0			
Latin America & Caribbean																			
Low income economies																			
Haiti	0.45	0.475	6	1,630	1,844	13							33.8				2.7	10.8	300
Nicaragua	0.641	0.69	8	2,796	3,634	30	80	88	9		12.2		1.2	101	98	-3	32.7	11.7	-64

Country	Human Development Index (HDI)			GDP per capita, PPP in current international $			Net primary school enrolment ratio (%)			Total unemployment			People living with HIV*	Ratio of girls to boys in primary education (%)			Debt service as % flows from abroad		
	value 1995	value 2003	% change 1995-2003	1994	2004	% change 1994-2004	2000	2004	% change 2000-2004	Total rates 1993	Total rates 2003	% change 1993-2003	Per 1,000 residents end 2003	2000	2004	% change 2000-2004	1993	2003	% change 1993-2003
Middle income economies																			
Argentina	0.833	0.863	4	10,544	13,298	26				10.1	15.6	54	3.4	100			26.5	34.7	31
Barbados	0.852	0.878	3				100	100	0	24.5	11	-55	9.3	98	99	0	11.2	5.6	-50
Belize	0.768	0.753	-2	4,547	6,747	48	96	99	3	9.8	10	2	13.2	96	98	2	6	24.9	315
Bolivia	0.636	0.687	8	1,995	2,720	36	95	95	0	6	8.69	45	0.6	99	99	1	33.4	20.1	-40
Brazil	0.747	0.792	6	6,108	8,195	34	95			6.2	9.7	56	3.6	94			12.2	38.6	216
Chile	0.816	0.854	5	6,693	10,874	62	87	86	-1	4.5	7.4	64	1.6	98			14.9	5.5	-63
Colombia	0.752	0.785	4	5,642	7,256	29	89	83	-6	7.8	14.2	82	4.3	100	99	-1	26.6	34.6	30
Costa Rica	0.811	0.838	3	6,372	9,481	49	92	92	0	4.1	6.7	63	2.9	98	99	1	14.9	8.9	-40
Cuba		0.817					99	96	-3				0.3	95	95	0			
Dominican Republic***	0.7	0.749	7	4,209	7,449	77	86	86	0	19.9	16.7		10.2	97	95	-2	5.8	7.4	28
Ecuador	0.73	0.759	4	3,015	3,963	31	99	99	1	8.3	11.5	39	1.6	99	100	0	21	19.7	-6
El Salvador	0.689	0.722	5	3,771	5,041	34	88	91	3	9.94	6.9	-31	4.4	95	96	1	20.4	11.7	-43
Guatemala	0.617	0.663	7	3,226	4,313	34	86	93	8		3.4		6.5	89	92	3	12.5	9.8	-22
Guyana	0.685	0.72	5	3,245	4,439	37	99	99	1				14.7	97	99	2	17.2	9.5	-45
Honduras	0.64	0.667	4	2,269	2,876	27	88	91	4	3.1	5.1	65	9.1	102	100	-2	28.4	9.4	-67
Jamaica	0.723	0.738	2	3,420	4,163	22	90	88	-2	16.3	10.9	-33	8.4	100	100	0	20.8	21.4	3
Mexico	0.782	0.814	4	7,343	9,803	33	99	100	1	2.4	2.1	-13	1.6	98	98	0	18.9	11.3	-40
Panama	0.772	0.804	4	4,798	7,278	52	98	100	2	13.3	13.6	2	5.1	97	97	0	3	9.2	207
Paraguay	0.739	0.755	2	4,339	4,813	11	92			5.1	11.2	120	2.6	96			7.7	6.6	-14
Peru	0.734	0.762	4	3,890	5,678	46	100			9.9	10.3	4	3.0	99			58.8	20.8	-65
St. Lucia		0.772		4,893	6,324	29	94	98	3	17.1				99	96	-4	3.3	7.4	124
Suriname		0.755					93	92	0	14.7			11.7	104	102	-1			
Trinidad & Tobago	0.789	0.801	2	6,316	12,182	93	93	92	-1	19.8	10.4	-47	22.4	99	97	-2	30.6	3.6	-88
Uruguay	0.817	0.84	3	7,611	9,421	24	90			8.3	16.9	104	1.8	98			17.6	23.1	31
Venezuela	0.767	0.772	1	5,477	6,043	10	88	92	5	6.7	15.8	136	4.3	98	98	0			
High income economies																			
Bahamas	0.81	0.832	3	13,524			87	84	-4	13.1	10.8	-18	17.8	98	100	2			
Middle East & North Africa																			
Low income economies																			
Yemen	0.436	0.489	12	647	879	36	60	75	26				0.6	63	71	12	7.2	4	-44

Country	Human Development Index (HDI)			GDP per capita, PPP in current international $			Net primary school enrolment ratio (%)			Total unemployment			People living with HIV*	Ratio of girls to boys in primary education (%)			Debt service as % flows from abroad		
	value 1995	value 2003	% change 1995–2003	1994	2004	% change 1994–2004	2000	2004	% change 2000–2004	Total rates 1993	Total rates 2003	% change 1993–2003	Per 1,000 residents end 2003	2000	2004	% change 2000–2004	1993	2003	% change 1993–2003
Middle income economies																			
Algeria	0.671	0.722	8	4,380	6,603	51	92	97	6		23.7		0.3	92	93	1			
Djibouti	0.477	0.495	4		1,993		28	33	19				11.9	73	79	8	3.3		
Egypt	0.611	0.659	8	2,670	4,211	58	93	94	2	10.9	11	1	0.2	92	*95*	*3*			
Iran	0.694	0.736	6	4,739	7,525	59	80	89	11				0.5	95	110	15	3	3.5	17
Iraq							83	88	5		28.1			82	83	1			
Jordan	0.708	0.753	6	3,596	4,688	30	93	*93*	*0*				0.1	100	*101*	*0*	19.4	22.6	16
Lebanon	0.727	0.759	4	3,689	5,837	58	95	93	-2				0.8	95	96	1	6.2	81.5	1,215
Libya		0.799											1.8	98	*100*	2			
Malta	0.852	0.867	2	12,336	18,879	53	98	94	-4		7.6		1.3	101	*99*	*-2*			
Morocco**	0.579	0.631	9	3,132	4,309	38	77	87	13	15.9	19.3	21	0.5	84	90	7	45.4	25.7	-43
Oman	0.738	0.781	6	10,651	15,259	43	81	78	-3				0.5	97	100	3	10.1	5.3	-48
Palestinian Authority		0.729					100	86	-13		25.4			101	100	0			
Saudi Arabia	0.741	0.772	4	11,480	13,825	20	59	53	-10		*5.2*			96	96	0			
Syria	0.672	0.721	7	2,770	3,610	30	93	98	5		*11.7*		0.0	92	95	3	2.6	3	15
Tunisia	0.698	0.753	8	4,594	7,768	69	94	97		15.6	14.3	-8	0.1	95	96	*1*	21.2	13.7	-35
High income economies																			
Bahrain	0.826	0.846	2	13,520	20,758	54	95	97	1				0.9	101	100	-1			
Israel	0.88	0.915	4	18,091	24,382	35	100	*99*	*-1*	10	10.7	7	0.4	99	*100*	1			
Kuwait	0.813	0.844	4		19,384		83	86	4					102	100	-2			
Qatar		0.849					95	90	-5					97	98	1			
United Arab Emirates	0.814	0.849	4	19,364	24,056	24	77	71	-8					96	97	0			
North America																			
High income economies																			
Canada	0.934	0.949	2	20,892	31,263	50	98			11.2	7.6	-32	1.8	100					
United States	0.929	0.944	2	27,079	39,676	47	95	94	*-1*	6.9	6	-13	3.3	98	*100*	2			
South Asia																			
Low income economies																			
Afghanistan														0	35				
Bangladesh	0.452	0.52	15	1,163	1,870	61					4.3			100	*102*	2	16.8	8.3	-51
Bhutan		0.536																7.7	
India	0.546	0.602	10	1,704	3,139	84	83	*87*	5	3.62			4.8	82	94	*14*	26.7	18.1	-32

Country	Human Development Index (HDI)			GDP per capita, PPP in current international $			Net primary school enrolment ratio (%)			Total unemployment			People living with HIV*	Ratio of girls to boys in primary education (%)			Debt service as % flows from abroad		
	value 1995	value 2003	% change 1995-2003	1994	2004	% change 1994-2004	2000	2004	% change 2000-2004	Total rates 1993	Total rates 2003	% change 1993-2003	Per 1,000 residents end 2003	2000	2004	% change 2000-2004	1993	2003	% change 1993-2003
Nepal	0.466	0.526	13	1,056	1,490	41	66						2.3	79	88	11	9	10	11
Pakistan	0.492	0.527	7	1,584	2,225	40		66		4.73	*8.3*	75	0.5		73		24.5	16.8	-31
Middle income economies																			
Maldives		0.745					96							100	*98*	*-3*	3.7	3.5	-5
Sri Lanka	0.727	0.751	3	2,492	4,390	76		99		14.7	9.2	-37	0.2		99		11.2	7.8	-30
Sub-Saharan Africa																			
Low income economies																			
Angola		0.445		2,128	2,180	2							16.0				2.9	14.8	410
Benin	0.395	0.431	9	780	1,091	40	52	83	59				8.6	69	77	12	5.3	6.3	19
Burkina Faso	0.311	0.317	2	829	1,169	41	36	40	13				24.2	71	78	11	11.5	12.5	9
Burundi	0.324	0.378	17	674	677	0	43	57	32				35.5	80	83	4	35.5	63.6	79
Cameroon	0.494	0.497	1	1,497	2,174	45							35.6	85	85	0	18.3	8.7	-52
Central African Rep.	0.367	0.355	-3	990	1,094	11							66.0	*68*	69	*0*	3.8		
Chad	0.344	0.341	-1	800	2,090	161	54	*57*	*6*				21.9	61	64	6	7.9	5.4	-32
Comoros	0.517	0.547	6	1,611	1,943	21	55							85	88	4	3.8		
Congo, Dem. Rep.	0.393	0.385	-2	867	705	-19							20.3				8.9		
Congo, Rep.	0.531	0.512	-4	733	978	33							23.9	92	93	2	8.3	3.8	-54
Côte d'Ivoire	0.427	0.42	-2	1,360	1,551	14	53	*56*	*6*				32.4	75	79	6			
Equatorial Guinea	0.518	0.655	26	1,301			84	59	-30					95	94	-1	1.8		
Eritrea	0.409	0.444	9	890	977	10	41	48	17				14.8	82	80	-2	13		
Ethiopia	0.323	0.367	14	501	756	51	36	46	29	22.9			21.9	67	81	21	17.9	7.3	-59
Gambia	0.424	0.47	11	1,463	1,991	36	67						4.7	85			11.1	14	26
Ghana	0.531	0.52	-2	1,513	2,240	48	61	58	-5				16.5	93	94	1	22.8	5.2	-77
Guinea		0.466		1,583	2,180	38	47	64	36				15.6	70	81	16	10.8	10.7	-1
Guinea-Bissau	0.341	0.348	2	810	722	-11	45							67			13.1	9.4	-28
Kenya	0.524	0.474	-10	956	1,140	19	67	76	14				36.7	99	94	-4	20.4	14.4	-29
Lesotho	0.573	0.497	-13	1,470	2,619	78	82	86	5				177.8	104	100	-4	5.3	8.9	68
Liberia							66						31.0	73			0.2		
Madagascar	0.458	0.499	9	750	857	14	65	89	37	4.5			7.9	96	96	0	14.4	4.7	-67
Malawi	0.412	0.404	-2	439	646	47		95					72.9	96	102	7	22.2	23.1	4
Mali	0.307	0.333	8	607	998	64		46					11.0	75	79	5	16.1	5.8	-64

Country	Human Development Index (HDI)			GDP per capita, PPP in current international $			Net primary school enrolment ratio (%)			Total unemployment			People living with HIV*	Ratio of girls to boys in primary education (%)			Debt service as % exports of flows from abroad		
	value 1995	value 2003	% change 1995-2003	1994	2004	% change 1994-2004	2000	2004	% change 2000-2004	Total rates 1993	Total rates 2003	% change 1993-2003	Per 1,000 residents end 2003	2000	2004	% change 2000-2004	1993	2003	% change 1993-2003
Mauritania	0.424	0.477	13	1,486	1,940	31	63	74	19				3.3	94	98	4	29.2	15.7	-46
Mozambique	0.328	0.379	16	622	1,237	99	56	71	28				68.2	76	83	10	31.2	3.9	-88
Niger	0.256	0.281	10	666	779	17	25	39	55				5.4	69	72	4	16	6.4	-60
Nigeria	0.418	0.453	8	782	1,154	48		88					28.6	82	85	4	12.8		
Rwanda	0.335	0.45	34	630	1,263	101	72	73	2				28.5	97	102	5	14.8	10	-32
São Tomé & Principe		0.604												95				24.6	
Senegal	0.421	0.458	9	1,177	1,713	45	54	66	22				4.0	87	95	10	8.7	23.4	169
Sierra Leone		0.298		728	561	-23		71									17.5	10.9	-38
Somalia																			
Sudan	0.465	0.512	10	1,152	1,949	69	43						11.5	85	87	2	5.4	1.3	-76
Tanzania	0.422	0.418	-1	440	674	53	51	86	67				43.3	99	96	-3	26.3	5.8	-78
Togo	0.51	0.512	0	1,230	1,536	25	77	79	3				18.8	78	84	8	6	1.9	-68
Uganda	0.412	0.508	23	876	1,478	69		98				3.2	19.7	94	99	5	50.5	7.8	-85
Zambia	0.424	0.394	-7	736	943	28	63	80	27	19.7			81.5	93	96	2	14.1		
Zimbabwe	0.589	0.505	-14	2,381	2,065	-13	82	82	0	5			139.9	97	98	1	24.3		
Middle income economies																			
Botswana	0.659	0.565	-14	5,362	9,945	85	80	82	3				197.6	100	99	-1	3.6	1.3	-64
Cape Verde	0.677	0.721	6	3,400	5,727	68	98	92	-6					97	95	-2	11.9	7.2	-39
Gabon		0.635		5,431	6,623	22	77			18			35.8	100	99	0	4.2		
Mauritius	0.747	0.791	6	6,867	12,027	75	96	95	-1	3.9	10.2	162		100	100	1	5.5	4.7	-15
Namibia	0.693	0.627	-10	5,196	7,418	43	74	74	-1				105.7	102	102	0			
South Africa	0.742	0.658	-11	7,959	11,192	41	90	89	-2		29.7		115.6	96	97	1	0	4.3	
Swaziland	0.603	0.498	-17	3,925	5,638	44	76	77	1				199.0	94	95	0	2.5		

Region	Human Development Index (HDI) value 2003	GDP per capita, PPP in current international $			Net primary school enrolment % ratio			Ratio of girls to boys in primary education (%)		
		value 1994	value 2004	% change 1994–2004	value 2000	value 2004	% change 2000-2004	2000	2004	% change 2000-2004
Low income	0.593	1,366.2	2,296.8	68	75.1	*78.9*	5	83.4	*88.6*	6
Middle income	0.774	3,780.6	6,756.8	79				*98.4*	*98.1*	0
Low & middle income:										
East Asia & the Pacific	0.768	2,352.9	5,353.6	128				*99.8*	*98.7*	-1
Europe & Central Asia		5,080.9	8,584.8	69				*97.3*	*97.9*	1
Latin America & Caribbean	0.797	5,991.1	7,957.6	33	94.0			96.9		
Middle East & North Africa		3,918.8	5,816.9	48	84.5	88.5	5	89.2	*92.9*	4
South Asia	0.628	1,626.6	2,867.0	76	82.9	*87.6*	6	82.2	*89.6*	9
Sub-Saharan Africa	0.515	1,434.2	1,938.2	35		*64.1*		84.1	87.1	4
High income	0.910	21,442.4	30,990.9	45	95.2	*94.5*	-1	99.0	*99.5*	0
World	0.741	5,878.2	8,907.6	52				89.5	*93.7*	5

Where data for a particular year are not available, figures are taken from the year befor or after as an estimate. These figures, and estimates based on them, are presented in italics.

* These estimates include all people with HIV infection, whether or not they have developed symptoms of AIDS. For some countries the AIDS cases source data only states that number of cases is smaller than 200 or 500. For such countries the per capita data in this table was calculated using 200 and 500 as an estimated maximum. Per capita figures presented here are therefore maximum figures.

** Data for China excludes Hong Kong and Macao; data for Morocco excludes Western Sahara.

*** The two unemployment data points for Dominican Republic and Kazakhstan come from different surveys and may not be comparable. Therefore we did not calculate percentage changes for these countries.

Sources: Human Development Report 2005, Cultural Liberty in Today's Diverse World, New York: Oxford University Press, http://hdr.undp.org/statistics/data/indicators.cfm;World Bank, World Development Indicators (WDI-Online) 2005, http://devdata.worldbank.org/dataonline; UN Millennium Development Goal Indicators Database http://millenniumindicators.un.org/unsd/mi/mi_indicator_xrxx.asp?ind_code=44; Internationa Labor Organization, LABORSTA database, http://laborsta.ilo.org/; UNAIDS 2004 Report on the global AIDS epidemic http://data.unaids.org/Global-Reports/Bangkok/Table_countryestimates_GlobalReport2004_en.xls.

Record 10: Economic and social rights

This new record focuses on four major categories of economic and social rights, which are discussed in Chapter 3 of this edition: the right to food, health, housing and education. Data is supplied on the status of these rights around the world, what is being done to address them and how effective such policies are. On the right to food, we contrast the level of dietary energy supply and under-nourishment with international food donations. On the right to health, the rates of tuberculosis, its detection and treatment are compared. On the right to housing, the prevalence of slum dwelling is contrasted with relevant legislation. On the right to education, we consider the quality of education (using pupil/teacher ratio) and compare it to government investment in education and enrolment in private schools.

The second part of this record analyses ESCR-net, a global network of organisations that work on economic, social and cultural rights (www.escr-net.org/EngGeneral/home.asp). The table lists the international composition of the network's members and its working groups. The third part of this record presents a diagrammatic analysis of the thematic focus of member organisations of ESCR-net, based on correspondence between organisations in different countries and the various themes addressed by member organisations. The closer two countries are, the greater the overlap in areas on which they work; the closer a country and theme are, the closer is the focus of ESCR-net members in this country on this theme. Consider, for example, the closeness between Tanzania and HIV/AIDS. Countries are identified in the diagram using the international country internet suffix (see www.computerhope.com/jargon/num/domains.htm).

The data in the first table demonstrate the deep gaps in the status of social and economic rights between the developed and developing world, with some exceptions, such as in education in formerly communist European and Asian countries.

While definitely a global network, ESCR-net membership reflects the North-South gap in participation in global civil society. The country/theme correspondence diagram indicates that ESCR-net member organisations view most themes as closely related, while other themes, for example, education, AIDS and indigenous peoples, are addressed by only a few of the network's members, which tend to have a narrow focus and specialise in those themes.

	Food					Health Tuberculosis				Housing				Education		
Country	Per capita dietary energy supply (calories/day) 2002	Proportion of the population under-nourished (%) 2000-2002	International food donations received (cereals, metric tons) 1993	International food donations received (cereals, metric tons) 2003	% change 1993-2003	Prevalence per 100,000 population 2003	Detection rate % 2003	Treatment success % 2003	Death rate per 100,000 population 2003	People lacking sufficient living area (%) 2001	People lacking durable housing (%) 2001	Urban population living in slums (%) 2001	Constitution containing reference to housing rights 2002	Private enrolment as % total enrolment in primary education 2001	Expenditures primary student (% GDP per capita) 2003**	Pupil to teacher ratio 2001
East Asia & Pacific																
Low income economies																
Cambodia	2,046	33	39,096	33,667	-14	742	60	92	81			72.2	yes	0.9	5.9	56
East Timor				6,251		753	53	81	95			12.0				51
Indonesia	2,904	6	51,774	186,875	261	674	33	86	65		12.7	23.1			16.0	3.7	21
Korea, Dem. Rep.	2,142	36				187	91	88	16			0.7	yes			
Laos	2,312	22	2,350	3,471	48	327	47	78	26			66.1			2.0	7.9	30
Mongolia	2,249	28	25,019	48,692	95	237	68	87	32			64.9			2.3	38.3	32
Myanmar	2,937	6				183	73	81	24			26.4					33
Papua New Guinea						527	15	53	47			19.0	yes	1.4	12.4	36
Solomon Islands	2,265					60	107	90	4			7.9				
Vietnam	2,566	19	76,342	24,027	-69	238	86	92	22		7.4	47.4	yes		0.3		26
Middle income economies																
China*	2,951	11	193,333	8,808	-95	245	43	93	18			37.8	yes			20
Fiji	2,894				38	63	85		4		67.8		yes		28	
Malaysia	2,881					135	69	76	16			2.0			3.8	17.0	20
Philippines	2,379	22	52,452	106,100	102	458	68	88	49	27.3	4.3	44.1	yes	7.1	11.6	35
Samoa						44	51	84	5			9.8			16.6		25
Thailand	2,467	20				203	72	74	17		7.1	2.0			13.6	16.5	19
Tonga						44	80	83	5			1.0			9.2		21
Vanuatu						71	70	79	8			37.0			3.8		29
High income economies																
Australia	3,054					6	9	78	1			1.6			27.6	16.6	
Brunei	2,855					61	138	84	5			2.0			33.8		14
Korea, Rep.	3,058					118	23	83	10			37.0	yes		1.4	16.6	32
Japan	2,761					42	40	76	4			6.4			0.9	21.5	20
New Zealand	3,219					11	57	60	1			1.0			2.0	18.9	18
Singapore						42	44	87	5								

Country

	Food					Health Tuberculosis				Housing				Education		
	Per capita dietary energy supply (calories/day) 2002	Proportion of the population under-nourished (%) 2000–2002	International food donations received (cereals, metric tons) 1993	International food donations received (cereals, metric tons) 2003	% change 1993–2003	Prevalance per 100,000 population 2003	Detection rate % 2003	Treatment success % 2003	Death rate per 100,000 population 2003	People lacking sufficient living area (%) 2001	People lacking durable housing (%) 2001	Urban population living in slums (%) 2001	Constitution containing reference to housing rights 2002	Private enrolment as % total enrolment in primary education 2001	Expenditures primary student (% GDP per capital) 2003**	Pupil to teacher ratio 2001

Europe & Central Asia

Low income economies

Country																
Armenia	2,268	34	276,140	41,676	-85	89	43	79	11			2.0	yes	0.5	9.6	19
Azerbaijan	2,575	15	58,202	11,075	-81	109	28	84	11	5.3		7.2			7.3	16
Georgia	2,354	27	655,370	117,168	-82	95	52	65	13			8.5		1.8		14
Kyrgyzstan	2,999	6	156,082	1,222	-99	140	57	82	18	4.7	0.3	51.8	yes	0.3	6.1	24
Moldova	2,806	11	110,674	34,888	-68	177	39	61	20		5.6	31.0		1.0	18.1	20
Tajikistan	1,828	61	82,576	75,685	-8	267		79	32			56.0			6.8	22
Ukraine	3,054	3	151,213	200,000	32	133			12		5.6	6.1	yes	0.4	11.9	20
Uzbekistan	2,241	26		82,100		156	20	80	16	7.8	2.1	50.7				

Middle income economies

Country																
Albania	2,848	6	225,083	26,568	-88	33	29	90	4			7.0		2.2		22
Belarus	3,000		128,208			59	44		7		5.6	5.6		0.1		17
Bosnia & Herzegovina	2,894	8	900			63	48	95	8			7.8	yes			
Bulgaria	2,848	11	155,560			47	81	86	6		5.6	5.6		0.3	16.9	17
Croatia	2,799	7	8,224			68	0		7			7.8		0.2	48.7	18
Czech Republic	3,171					12	63	73	1		5.6	5.6		1.0	11.8	17
Estonia	3,002	5				53	69	67	7		5.6	12.2	yes	1.9	20.1	14
Hungary	3,483					33	41	55	4		5.6	5.6	yes	5.2	20.3	10
Kazakhstan	2,677	13	59,981			152	86	78	19	1.8	0.3	29.7		0.6	8.1	19
Latvia	2,938	4				78	83	76	11		5.6	5.6		0.8	22.0	14
Lithuania	3,324		77,100			73	85	72	9		5.6	5.6		0.4		16
Macedonia	2,655	11				37	49	79	6			7.8				21
Poland	3,374					34	56	86	4		5.6	5.6	yes	1.2	34.4	15
Romania	3,455		75,205			194	38	76	20		5.6	18.8		0.2		17
Russian Federation	3,072	4	2,484,820	24,373	-99	157	9	67	19		5.6	5.6	yes	0.4		17
Serbia & Montenegro			431,808	1	-100	44	37	91	5			4.6			38.3	20
Slovakia	2,889	5				29	34	85	4	0.0	5.6	5.6	yes	4.0	11.4	19

Country	Food					Health Tuberculosis				Housing				Education		
	Per capita dietary energy supply (calories/day) 2002	Proportion of the population under-nourished (%) 2000–2002	International food donations received (cereals, metric tons) 1993	International food donations received (cereals, metric tons) 2003	% change 1993–2003	Prevalance per 100,000 population 2003	Detection rate % 2003	Treatment success % 2003	Death rate per 100,000 population 2003	People lacking sufficient living area (%) 2001	People lacking durable housing (%) 2001	Urban population living in slums (%) 2001	Constitution containing reference to housing rights 2002	Private enrolment as % total enrolment in primary education 2001	Expenditures primary student (% GDP per capital 2003**	Pupil to teacher ratio 2001
Turkmenistan	2,742	9	45,720			83	49	77	10		0.8	2.0				
High income economies																
Austria	3,673					12			1			5.6	yes	4.3	23.8	14
Belgium						12	57	69	1			14.9	yes	54.3	18.7	12
Cyprus	3,255					4	91	75	0			0.0		5.2		19
Denmark	3,439					6	75	77	1	5.6		5.6		11.0	24.4	10
Finland	3,100					10			1	5.6		5.6	yes	1.2	17.8	16
France	3,654					12			1			5.5		14.6	17.8	19
Germany	3,496					7	55	69	1			4.1	yes	2.6	16.9	14
Greece						22	0		2			5.6		7.1	14.5	13
Iceland						3	28	100			5.6	5.6		1.3		11
Ireland	3,656					12	0		1		0.8	0.8		1.1	12.0	20
Italy	3,671					6	79	79	1			5.6		6.7	24.7	11
Luxembourg						10	126		1			5.6		6.7		12
Netherlands	3,362					6	50	68	1			9.1	yes	68.4	16.6	10
Norway	3,484					5	46	80	1	5.6		5.6		1.7	27.1	
Portugal	3,741					37	87	82	5			14.0	yes	10.5	23.3	11
Spain	3,371					27	0		3			5.6	yes	33.6	18.9	14
Sweden	3,185					4	62	73		5.6		5.6	yes	4.6	22.5	12
Switzerland	3,526					7	0		1			5.6	yes	3.6	23.2	14
United Kingdom	3,412					12			1	5.6		5.6		4.9	15.1	17
Latin America & Caribbean																
Low income economies																
Haiti	2,086	47	115,972	59,282	-49	386	46	78	50	34.9	12.1	85.7	yes			
Nicaragua	2,298	27	54,666	34,227	-37	78	91	82	8	38.0	29.3	80.9	yes	16.0	8.9	37
Middle income economies																
Argentina	2,992					55	65	58	6			33.1	yes	20.0	12.4	20
Barbados						14	34		2			1.0		11.3		16
Belize	2,869					56	98	85	4			62.0		87.1		23

Country	Food					Health Tuberculosis				Housing				Education		
	Per capita dietary energy supply (calories/day) 2002	Proportion of the population under-nourished (%) 2000–2002	International food donations received (cereals, metric tons) 1993	International food donations received (cereals, metric tons) 2003	% change 1993–2003	Prevalence per 100,000 population 2003	Detection rate % 2003	Treatment success % 2003	Death rate per 100,000 population 2003	People lacking sufficient living area (%) 2001	People lacking durable housing (%) 2001	Urban population living in slums (%) 2001	Constitution containing reference to housing rights 2002	Private enrolment as % total enrolment in primary education 2001	Expenditures primary student (% GDP per capita) 2003**	Pupil to teacher ratio 2001
Bolivia	2,235	21	205,729	116,915	-43	301	71	84	33	32.7	10.1	61.3	yes	20.7	15.5	25
Brazil	3,049	9	25,227			91	18	75	8	9.9	2.6	36.6	yes	8.1	11.3	23
Chile	2,863	4	1,178			17	115	86	1			8.6		45.5	15.8	32
Colombia	2,585	13	30,799			80	7	84	8	13.8	2.5	21.8	yes	18.8	15.9	26
Costa Rica	2,876	4	5,731			18	117	85	1			12.8	yes	6.8	16.2	24
Cuba	3,152	3	10,748			13	93	92	1			2.0	yes		32.3	14
Dominican Republic	2,347	25	6,788	800	-88	123	65	78	15	17.0	2.5	37.6	yes	14.4	8.9	39
Ecuador	2,754	4	12,329	5,350	-57	209	37	84	27			25.6	yes	27.4	3.0	25
El Salvador	2,584	11	80,413	11,968	-85	78	53	88	9			35.2	yes	10.8	10.0	26
Guatemala	2,219	24	150,239	40,656	-73	104	44	84	12	30.0	20.6	61.8	yes	12.8	6.7	30
Guyana	2,692	9	36,992			178	31	85	21			4.9	yes	0.9		26
Honduras	2,356	22	149,397	63,840	-57	102	78	87	12	4.0		18.1	yes			34
Jamaica	2,685	10	157,086			9	90	49	1			35.7		4.8	15.1	34
Mexico	3,145	5	97,292			45	81	84	5			19.6	yes	7.9	13.8	27
Panama	2,272	26	2,005			52	92	73	4			30.8	yes	10.0	10.4	24
Paraguay	2,565	14	726			105	18	92	12			25.0	yes	14.9	13.0	
Peru	2,571	13	406,660	25,591	-94	231	81	92	22	28.0	22.8	68.1	yes	13.5	7.0	29
St. Lucia						22	71	25	2			11.9	yes	2.8		24
Suriname	2,652	11	26,400			102			12			6.9	yes	47.8		20
Trinidad & Tobago	2,732	12				13			1			32.0		5.7	16.1	19
Uruguay	2,828	4				33	80	82	3			6.9	yes	12.7	11.0	21
Venezuela	2,336	17				52	80	82	5			40.7	yes	14.4		
High income economies																
Bahamas						52	52	59	6			2.0		24.6		17
Middle East & North Africa																
Low income economies																
Yemen	2,038	36	88,441	118,726	34	151	43	82	12	13.8	15.5	65.1		1.3		
Middle income economies																
Algeria	3,022	5	18,354	18,982	3	53	113	89	2			11.8			11.1	28

Country	Food Per capita dietary energy supply (calories/day) 2002	Proportion of the population under-nourished (%) 2000–2002	International food donations received (cereals, metric tons) 1993	International food donations received (cereals, metric tons) 2003	% change 1993–2003	Health Tuberculosis Prevalence per 100,000 population 2003	Detection rate % 2003	Treatment success % 2003	Death rate per 100,000 population 2003	Housing People lacking sufficient living area (%) 2001	People lacking durable housing (%) 2001	Urban population living in slums (%) 2001	Constitution containing reference to housing rights 2002	Education Private enrolment as % total enrolment in primary education 2001	Expenditures primary student (% GDP per capita) 2003**	Pupil to teacher ratio 2001
Djibouti	2,220		8,054	5,334	-34	988	53	82	98					11.0		34
Egypt	3,338	3	230,222	22,016	-90	36	56	88	3		4.2	39.9		8.1		23
Iran	3,085	4	54,115	23,797	-56	36	59	85	3			44.2	yes	3.8	11.3	24
Iraq			86,616	1,203,020	1,289	236	20	91	33	3.1		56.7				21
Jordan	2,673	7	223,201	139,714	-37	5	89	89	1	11.7	0.1	15.7	yes	29.4	15.0	20
Lebanon	3,196	3	9,975	10,000	0	13	67	91	1			50.0	.	63.5	5.4	17
Libya	3,320					21	147	61	1			35.2		2.5	3.0	8
Malta						6	19	60	1			5.6		37.1		19
Morocco**	3,052	7	124,060			105	83	89	10	27.8	1.2	32.7		4.9	18.9	28
Oman						12	81	92	1			60.5		4.1	17.7	23
Palestinian Authority			52,590			37	4	100	4			60.0		8.3		31
Saudi Arabia	2,844	3				57	38	76	5			19.8		6.7	32.6	12
Syria	3,038	4	36,152	7,235	-80	52	45	87	5	3.1		1.4		4.4	13.8	24
Tunisia	3,238		46,358			24	91	92	2			3.7		0.8	15.8	22
High income economies																
Bahrain						52	49	88	5			2.0	yes	21.1		16
Israel	3,666		3,000			8	55	81	1			2.0			21.7	12
Kuwait	3,010	5				31	67	55	3	1.0		3.0		30.4	16.1	14
Qatar						72	57	75	7			2.0		41.2		12
United Arab Emirates	3,225					26	32	79	2			2.0		50.7	6.9	15
North America																
High income economies																
Canada	3,589					4	76	81	1		5.8	5.8		6.5		17
United States	3,774					3	89	70			5.8	5.8		10.3	21.2	15
South Asia																
Low income economies																
Afghanistan			69,676	116,375	67	671	18	87	93			98.5	yes			43
Bangladesh	2,205	30	626,032	238,908	-62	490	33	84	57	42.2	39.9	84.7	yes	38.7	8.9	55
Bhutan			362	3,638	905	194	32	86	21			44.1		1.4		40

Country	Food					Health Tuberculosis				Housing				Education		
	Per capita dietary energy supply (calories/day) 2002	Proportion of the population under-nourished (%) 2000–2002	International food donations received (cereals, metric tons) 1993	International food donations received (cereals, metric tons) 2003	% change 1993–2003	Prevalence per 100,000 population 2003	Detection rate % 2003	Treatment success % 2003	Death rate per 100,000 population 2003	People lacking sufficient living area (%) 2001	People lacking durable housing (%) 2001	Urban population living in slums (%) 2001	Constitution containing reference to housing rights 2002	Private enrolment as % total enrolment in primary education 2001	Expenditures primary student (% GDP per capita) 2003**	Pupil to teacher ratio 2001
India	2,459	21	288,426	36,406	-87	287	47	87	31	20.2	9.6	55.5		15.5	12.4	40
Nepal	2,453	17	13,250	9,545	-28	316	60	86	28	33.1	34.4	92.4	yes	7.0	12.0	40
Pakistan	2,419	20	67,187	14,000	-79	358	17	77	43	59.0	23.7	73.6	yes			44
Middle income economies																
Maldives	2,548		1,370	22,004	1,506	39	106	95	2					2.0		23
Sri Lanka	2,385	22	338,885	42,844	-87	89	70	81	9	13.8		13.6	yes	1.9		
Sub-Saharan Africa																
Low income economies																
Angola	2,083	40	222,189	172,624	-22	256	118	74	20			83.1		5.2		35
Benin	2,548	15	23,648	18,239	-23	141	94	80	12	17.8	20.3	83.6		7.3	9.7	53
Burkina Faso	2,462	19	28,682	21,878	-24	303	18	64	33	15.5	7.6	76.5	yes	12.0		47
Burundi	1,649	68	55,817	45,360	-19	519	30	79	59			65.3		1.3	12.5	49
Cameroon	2,273	25	2,220	23,931	978	221	86	70	21	10.1	18.9	67.0		24.9	8.5	61
Central African Republic	1,980	43	1,809	3,410	89	493	6		54	13.0	72.9	92.4				74
Chad	2,114	34	13,009	20,454	57	439	11	72	48	31.1	85.4	99.1		27.8	9.7	71
Comoros	1,754		5,871			103	37	96	8			61.2		10.1		39
Congo, Dem. Rep.	1,599	71	17,505	72,803	316	537	63	78	59			49.5	yes			
Congo, Rep.	2,162	37	1,050	5,088	385	489	57	71	57			90.1		19.0	8.1	56
Côte d'Ivoire	2,631	14	45,480	24,226	-47	618	39	67	68	22.6	0.8	67.9		10.9	14.6	44
Equatorial Guinea			5,011			351			39			86.5	yes	32.8		43
Eritrea	1,513	73	247,215	175,825	-29	431	18	82	52		34.9	69.9		8.3	11.8	44
Ethiopia	1,857	46	590,299	941,976	60	507	36	76	60	38.1	65.9	99.4	yes	6.0		57
Gambia	2,273	27	7,335	9,491	29	337	70	74	39			67.0		2.0	11.9	38
Ghana	2,667	13	113,353	51,431	-55	369	40	60	41	21.2	0.9	69.6		18.3		32
Guinea	2,409	26	46,187	30,094	-35	394	51	72	43	24.0	8.5	72.3		20.6	9.2	47
Guinea-Bissau	2,024		8,885	8,602	-3	300	55	48	34			93.4		19.4		44
Kenya	2,090	33	262,113	56,572	-78	821	46	79	89	21.7	20.0	70.7		5.6		32
Lesotho	2,638	12	25,242	20,932	-17	390	70	52	46	10.6		57.0			23.8	47
Liberia	1,900	46	151,873	70,388	-54	484			53			55.7				38

Country	Food					Health Tuberculosis				Housing				Education		
	Per capita dietary energy supply (calories/day) 2002	Proportion of the population under-nourished (%) 2000–2002	International food donations received (cereals, metric tons) 1993	International food donations received (cereals, metric tons) 2003	% change 1993–2003	Prevalance per 100,000 population 2003	Detection rate % 2003	Treatment success % 2003	Death rate per 100,000 population 2003	People lacking sufficient living area (%) 2001	People lacking durable housing (%) 2001	Urban population living in slums (%) 2001	Constitution containing reference to housing rights 2002	Private enrolment as % total enrolment in primary education 2001	Expenditures primary student (% GDP per capita) 2003**	Pupil to teacher ratio 2001
Madagascar	2,005	37	34,242	40,680	19	325	77	74	36	43.9	9.2	92.9		21.7	8.2	48
Malawi	2,155	33	28,260	22,736	-20	469	35	72	52	23.7	31.5	91.1				63
Mali	2,174	29	23,631	746	-97	582	18	50	64	21.7	37.6	93.2	yes		15.2	56
Mauritania	2,772	10	58,205	58,587	1	664			73	33.8	42.3	94.3		3.3	14.0	39
Mozambique	2,079	47	264,609	175,490	-34	557	45	78	62	24.9	38.1	94.1		1.8		66
Niger	2,130	34	24,655	18,254	-26	272	54		30	30.2	35.4	96.2		3.8	15.5	41
Nigeria	2,726	9				518	18	79	57	26.5	11.2	79.2	yes			40
Rwanda	2,084	37	86,146	24,115	-72	628	27	58	69	13.8	38.2	87.9			6.9	59
São Tomé & Principe			7,215	3,509	-51	256			28			2.0	yes			33
Senegal	2,279	24	35,853	16,218	-55	429	59	66	47	27.3	6.4	76.4		11.0	13.6	49
Sierra Leone	1,936	50	29,202	43,683	50	794	33	81	88			95.8			16.8	37
Somalia			79,443	21,512	-73	748	29	89	118			97.1				
Sudan	2,228	27	255,263	158,592	-38	355	34	78	54			85.7		4.7		
Tanzania	1,975	44	27,034	112,324	315	476	43	80	52	16.5	35.4	92.1		0.2		46
Togo	2,345	26	10,706	8,000	-25	673	17	68	74	19.7	4.8	80.6		40.9	5.7	35
Uganda	2,410	19	18,932	90,030	376	621	44	60	71	19.2	26.4	93.0		4.9		54
Zambia	1,927	49	3,360	44,999	1,239	508	65	83	61	24.4	14.9	74.0			7.1	45
Zimbabwe	1,943	44	9,037	343,019	3,696	500	42	67	61	15.9	2.8	3.4		87.3	16.2	38
Middle income economies																
Botswana	2,151	32	8,211			342	68	71	34			60.7		4.7	6.1	27
Cape Verde	3,243		57,555	32,747	-43	328			39			69.6				29
Gabon	2,637	6				242	93	47	23	11.8	8.8	66.2		29.0	4.7	49
Mauritius	2,955	6	1,925			136	28	92	11					24.0	9.0	25
Namibia	2,278	22		2,846		477	86	62	52	20.4	9.6	37.9	yes	4.2	21.0	32
South Africa	2,956			74,600		341	118	68	28	12.1	6.5	33.2	yes	2.0	14.3	37
Swaziland	2,322	19	8,362	14,470	73	683	35	47	83				11.2	32	12	16

Region	Food					Health Tuberculosis				Housing	Education	
	Day capita dietary energy supply (calories/day) 2002	Proportion of the population undernourished (%) 2000-2002	Int'l food donations received (cereals, metric tons) 1993	Int'l food donations received (cereals, metric tons) 2003	% change 1993-2003	Prevalence per 100,000 population 2003	Detection rate % 2003	Treatment success % 2003	Death rate per 100,000 population 2003	Urban population living in slums (%) 2001	Private enrolment as % total enrolment in primary education 2001	Pupil to teacher ratio 2001
Low income	2,393	22	5,879,436	4,453,722	-24	382.0	42.6	80.4	41.7	59.7	12.1	38.1
Middle income	2,904	9	6,653,796	2,050,579	-69	180.1	47.3	83.3	15.1	31.7	3.7	20.7
Low & middle income:												
East Asia & the Pacific	2,856	12	440,366	417,891	-5	303.1	47.6	90.5	25.6	34.7	2.7	21.4
Europe & Central Asia	2,998	6	5,186,524	614,756	-88	109.8	23.3	53.3	12.4	16.2	0.8	13.6
Latin America & Caribbean	2,859	10	1,576,377	358,629	-77	90.1	50.0	79.1	9.2	33.1	12.2	23.3
Middle East & North Africa	2,747	5	978,138	1,548,824	58	70.3	62.2	86.3	6.9	35.2	5.4	21.6
South Asia	2,387	21	1,405,188	483,720	-66	318.2	42.6	85.6	35.4	60.9	15.5	41.3
Sub-Saharan Africa	2,238	30	2,946,639	3,080,481	5	483.7	46.2	71.2	54.1	76.1	8.3	43.7
High income	3,274	0	3,000	0		18.1	50.7	56.7	1.7	7.1	9.9	15.5
World	2,751	13	12,536,232	6,504,301	-48	238.8	45.9	78.0	24.1	39.4	8.1	27.0

Where data for a particular year are not available, figures are taken from the year befor or after as an estimate. These figures are presented in italics.

Blank cells do not necessarily indicate 'zero', but may indicate lack of data, so should be interpreted with caution.

Regional summaries are regional averages weighted by population, using only countries in the table. Food donations regional summaries are simple regional sums.

* Data for China excludes Hong Kong and Macao; Data for Morrocco excludes Western Sahara.

** Most recent data point in last seven years.

Sources: Bread for the World, Hunger report 2006, table 2: Global food, nutrition and education and table 3: Hunger, Malnutrition and Poverty, http://www.bread.org/learn/hunger-reports/hunger-report-2006-download.html; United Nations Statistics Division (2005), http://millenniumindicators.un.org; United Nations Housing Rights Programme, Report No.1, 2002, Nairobi; United Nations Human Settlements Programme (UN-HABITAT), 2003, Slums of the World: The face of urban poverty in the new millennium?, Nairobi: UN-HABITAT, http://www.unhabitat.org/publication/slumreport.pdf; UNFPA state of world population 2005, http://www.unfpa.org/swp/2005/images/e_indicator2.pdf; UNESCO, EFA Global monitoring report, 2005, table 14:Private enrolment and education finance and table 17: Trends in basic or proxy indicators, http://portal.unesco.org/education/en/ev.php-URL_ID=36027&URL_DO=DO_TOPIC&URL_SECTION=201.html; Food and Agriculture Organisation of the United Nations, statistical databases, http://faostat.fao.org/faostat/collections?version=ext&hasbulk=0

ESCR-net global presence

Country	Network Membership			Corporate Accountability Working Group						Budgets Analysis Discussion Group					Social Movements Working Group			
	Individual	Organisation*	All occurrences	Co-ordinator	Steering Committee**	Active member	Other member	Participants	All occurrences	Co-ordinator	Training programme organisers	Training programme participants	Participants	All occurrences	Co-ordinators	Leading group	Other involved groups	All occurrences
East Asia & Pacific																		
Low income economies																		
Cambodia	1		1					1	1									
Indonesia		1	1					1	1			1	4	5				
Mongolia													1	1				
Middle income economies																		
China***	3	1	4					4	4			1	2	3				
Malaysia		2	2					1	1									
Philippines					1	1		2	4			1	3	4				
Thailand	3	5	8		1			8	9			1	7	8		1	1	2
Australia	3		3					15	15				6	6				
Korea, Rep.	1	1	2															
Europe & Central Asia																		
Low income economies																		
Georgia													1	1				
Middle income economies																		
Bulgaria													1	1				
Hungary											1		1	2				
Serbia & Montenegro								1	1									
Turkey								1	1									
High income economies																		
Austria								2	2									
Belgium		1	1				1	4	5				2	2				
Denmark								1	1				1	1				
France		2	2			1		4	5		1		4	5			1	1
Germany		1	1				3	17	20				3	3				
Ireland								2	2				1	1				
Italy	1		1					6	6				4	4				
Netherlands		2	2				2	11	13				2	2				
Norway								1	1									
Spain								6	6		1		1	2				
Sweden								3	3				1	1				
Switzerland	1	3	4				2	20	22				5	5				
United Kingdom***		2	2	2	1		3	30	36				13	13				

Country	Network Membership			Corporate Accountability Working Group						Budgets Analysis Discussion Group					Social Movements Working Group			
	Individual	Organisation*	All occurrences	Co-ordinator	Steering Committee**	Active member	Other member	Participants	All occurrences	Co-ordinator	Training programme organisers	Training programme participants	Participants	All occurrences	Co-ordinators	Leading group	Other involved groups	All occurrences
Latin America & Caribbean																		
Middle income economies																		
Argentina		1	1		1			6	7		1		6	7				
Bolivia		2	2					2	2								1	1
Brazil		1	1		1			4	5		1		4	5			1	1
Chile	1		1					2	2									
Colombia	1	1	2			1	1		2				5	5				
Costa Rica								1	1									
Dominican Republic	1		1															
Ecuador		1	1			1			1				3	3			1	1
El Salvador		1	1															
Guatemala													2	2				
Honduras													1	1	1			1
Mexico	1	1	2		1			13	14	1		1	8	10				
Peru							1	6	7				5	5			1	1
Uruguay		1	1					1	1				2	2				
Venezuela								1	1			1	2	3				
Middle East & North Africa																		
Middle income economies																		
Palestine	1	1	2									1		1				
Egypt		4	4									2	1	3				
Lebanon		1	1															
High income economies																		
Israel												1	3	4				
North America																		
High income economies																		
Canada	1	2	3				1	14	15				5	5				
United States***	4	9	13	3			6	69	78	1	2		30	33			1	1
South Asia																		
Low income economies																		
Bangladesh													2	2				
India		1	1			1		11	12			1	14	15	1	1	3	5
Nepal								2	2				1	1				
Pakistan					1				1				1	1				

Country	Network Membership			Corporate Accountability Working Group						Budgets Analysis Discussion Group					Social Movements Working Group			
	Individual	Organisation*	All occurrences	Co-ordinator	Steering Committee**	Active member	Other member	Participants	All occurrences	Co-ordinator	Training programme organisers	Training programme participants	Participants	All occurrences	Co-ordinators	Leading group	Other involved groups	All occurrences
Middle income economies																		
Sri Lanka													1	1				
Sub-Saharan Africa																		
Low income economies																		
Angola						1		1	2									
Benin													1	1				
Congo, Dem. Rep.		1	1			1		4	5				1	1				
Côte d'Ivoire		1	1															
Equatorial Guinea								1	1									
Eritrea								1	1									
Ghana		1	1				1	2	3									
Kenya		3	3					1	1			2	4	6				
Liberia		1	1					1	1				2	2				
Mauritania	1		1															
Nigeria	1	4	5			2		3	5				1	4	5		2	2
Sierra Leone		1	1															
Tanzania	2		2										1	1				
Uganda												1	3	4				
Zambia													1	1				
Zimbabwe								1	1				1	1				
Middle income economies																		
Mauritius		1	1															
South Africa	2	3	5		1			4	5				6	6				
Swaziland	1		1															
Total occurrences	35	68	103	2	10	10	21	292	335	1	4	19	184	208	2	2	12	16

* One organisation was listed as originating in two countries (US/India), and was counted in both countries.

** Two organisations were listed in multiple countries (US/Thailand, UK/Philippines), and were counted in both countries.

*** China includes Hong Kong, United Kingdom includes Northern Ireland, United States includes Puerto Rico.

Source: data was provided through the kind cooperation of the ESCR-net staff.

ESCR-net: thematic focus of members

○ Country
○ Theme

Indigenous LR EC

AR
PH
UK
IN
Environment
TNCs FR Int.Trade
Self Determ.
Cult. Rights
Minority R's
CH
AU
Race/Ethnic Land/Property
BO
Equality/Non-Disc. KE
Elders Water Free.Expres'n
Democracy DE Food
MX NL GPS
CN BE CA KP MY EG
Soc.Sec/Welfare Refug/IDPs BR HK
Union R's Women R's Rural
Migrant R's Econ.Dev/Pov
ZA
US CI TH
Disability MU
Gender/Sex. Crim. Justice
Urban Poor
Health House/Evict
ID
SZ Child/Youth

GH

ZR

Education
Religion SL NG UY
Worker R's

LB

Aids/HIV
DO
TZ

SV Transitional Just. Pub.Finance

Record 11: **Corruption**

This record examines the state of the rule of law through the prism of corruption. Corruption not only hinders economic development, it inhibits the formation of trust and social capital. It is therefore likely to be an obstacle to the growth of civil society generally as well as a focus of civil society activism, both locally and globally. The table presents three kinds of indicators of corruption: the Corruption Perceptions Index by Transparency International; and 'Bribing and Corruption' and 'Transparency of Government' by the Institute for Management Development. Since these are relatively new measures, we can compare data only from 2000 and 2006. Scores range between 10, indicating high transparency and the absence of bribery and corruption, and 0, indicating lack of transparency and high levels of perceived corruption and bribery. Notably, corruption is considerably higher, on average, in low- and middle- income economies compared to high-income economies.

Country	Corruption Perceptions Index		Bribing and corruption		Transparency of government	
	2000	2005	2000	2006	2000	2006
East Asia & Pacific						
Low income economies						
Cambodia		2.3				
Indonesia	1.7	2.2	1.3	1.3	5.0	3.8
Laos		3.3				
Mongolia		3.0				
Myanmar		1.8				
Papua New Guinea		2.3				
Vietnam	2.5	2.6				
Middle income economies						
China*	3.1	3.2	2.2	2.2	6.3	5.2
Malaysia	4.8	5.1	3.2	4.8	6.4	6.0
Philippines	2.8	2.5	1.6	1.0	3.3	3.2
Thailand	3.2	3.8	2.0	1.9	4.3	3.1
High income economies						
Australia	8.3	8.8	8.2	7.9	6.9	6.8
Fiji		4.0				
Japan	6.4	7.3	5.3	5.7	3.7	4.7
Korea, Rep.	4.0	5.0	2.6	4.2	3.7	4.4
New Zealand	9.4	9.6	8.8	8.9	6.6	7.3
Singapore	9.1	9.4	8.7	8.2	8.4	7.2
Taiwan		5.9		4.5		3.4

Country	Corruption Perceptions Index		Bribing and corruption		Transparency of government	
	2000	2005	2000	2006	2000	2006
Europe & Central Asia						
Low income economies						
Armenia	2.5	2.9				
Azerbaijan	1.5	2.2				
Cyprus		5.7				
Georgia		2.3				
Kyrgyzstan		2.3				
Malta		6.6				
Moldova	2.6	2.9				
Tajikistan		2.1				
Ukraine	1.5	2.6				
Uzbekistan	2.4	2.2				
Middle income economies						
Albania		2.4				
Belarus	4.1	2.6				
Bosnia & Herzegovina		2.9				
Bulgaria	3.5	4.0		1.8		2.9
Croatia	3.7	3.4		2.0		2.6
Czech Republic	4.3	4.3	1.8	3.1	3.2	4.4
Estonia	5.7	6.4		5.7		6.0
Hungary	5.2	5.0	3.3	3.1	5.2	3.8
Kazakhstan	3.0	2.6				
Latvia	3.4	4.2				
Lithuania	4.1	4.8				
Macedonia		2.7				
Poland	4.1	3.4	2.9	1.4	3.4	1.9
Romania	2.9	3.0		1.7		4.2
Russian Federation	2.1	2.4	1.9	1.2	2.5	2.8
Serbia & Montenegro	1.3	2.8				
Slovakia	3.5	4.3		2.5		4.7
Slovenia	5.5	6.1	3.7	4.0	3.1	4.3
Turkey	3.8	3.5	2.6	2.7	6.0	4.2
Turkmenistan		1.8				

Country	Corruption Perceptions Index		Bribing and corruption		Transparency of government	
	2000	2005	2000	2006	2000	2006
High income economies						
Austria	7.7	8.7	6.7	7.8	5.3	6.8
Belgium	6.1	7.4	5.0	5.3	5.9	4.2
Denmark	9.8	9.5	9.2	9.3	5.5	8.3
Finland	10.0	9.6	9.5	9.3	7.6	7.8
France	6.7	7.5	5.0	6.8	5.8	4.7
Germany	7.6	8.2	5.4	6.6	4.5	5.0
Greece	4.9	4.3	2.4	2.9	5.5	4.6
Iceland	9.1	9.7	8.5	8.7	6.8	7.3
Ireland	7.2	7.4	6.5	6.4	7.5	6.4
Italy	4.6	5.0	2.8	2.8	3.8	2.9
Luxembourg	8.6	8.5	7.2	6.8	6.9	5.8
Netherlands	8.9	8.6	7.8	7.5	7.3	5.9
Norway	9.1	8.9	8.3	7.2	5.3	7.3
Portugal	6.4	6.5	4.3	3.7	5.4	4.4
Spain	7.0	7.0	5.3	5.3	6.9	3.6
Sweden	9.4	9.2	8.4	8.0	4.2	5.8
Switzerland	8.6	9.1	7.5	7.7	6.1	7.1
United Kingdom	8.7	8.6	7.6	6.7	5.8	4.4
Latin America & Caribbean						
Low income economies						
Barbados		6.9				
Haiti		1.8				
Nicaragua		2.6				
Middle income economies						
Argentina	3.5	2.8	1.5	1.4	5.2	1.9
Belize		3.7				
Bolivia	2.7	2.5				
Brazil	3.9	3.7	2.6	1.5	5.3	2.4
Chile	7.4	7.3	6.3	6.3	5.6	5.7
Colombia	3.2	4.0	1.6	2.9	5.0	6.1
Costa Rica	5.4	4.2				
Cuba		3.8				

Country	Corruption Perceptions Index		Bribing and corruption		Transparency of government	
	2000	2005	2000	2006	2000	2006
Dominican Republic		3.0				
Ecuador	2.6	2.5				
El Salvador	4.1	4.2				
Guatemala		2.5				
Guyana		2.5				
Honduras		2.6				
Jamaica		3.6				
Mexico	3.3	3.5	2.1	1.7	5.5	4.8
Panama		3.5				
Paraguay		2.1				
Peru	4.4	3.5				
Suriname		3.2				
Trinidad & Tobago		3.8				
Uruguay		5.9				
Venezuela	2.7	2.3	1.4	0.3	2.4	0.5
Middle East & North Africa						
Low income economies						
Yemen		2.7				
Middle income economies						
Algeria		2.8				
Egypt	3.1	3.4				
Iran		2.9				
Iraq		2.2				
Jordan	4.6	5.7		4.7		4.6
Lebanon		3.1				
Libya		2.5				
Morocco	4.7	3.2				
Oman		6.3				
Palestinian Authority		2.6				
Saudi Arabia						
Syria		3.4				
Tunisia	5.2	4.9				
High income economies						
Bahrain		5.8				

Country	Corruption Perceptions Index		Bribing and corruption		Transparency of government	
	2000	2005	2000	2006	2000	2006
Israel	6.6	6.3	6.0	4.8	5.5	4.6
Kuwait		4.7				
Qatar		5.9				
United Arab Emirates		6.2				
North America						
High income economies						
Canada	9.2	8.4	8.3	7.3	6.9	5.9
United States	7.8	7.6	6.8	5.6	6.2	5.7
South Asia						
Low income economies						
Afghanistan		2.5				
Bangladesh		1.7				
India	2.8	2.9	1.5	1.7	5.0	4.5
Nepal		2.5				
Pakistan		2.1				
Middle income economies						
Sri Lanka		3.2				
Sub-Saharan Africa						
Low income economies						
Angola	1.7	2.0				
Benin		2.9				
Burkina Faso	3.0	3.4				
Burundi		2.3				
Cameroon	2.0	2.2				
Chad		1.7				
Congo, Dem. Rep.		2.1				
Congo, Rep.		2.3				
Côte d'Ivoire	2.7	1.9				
Equatorial Guinea		1.9				
Eritrea		2.6				
Ethiopia	3.2	2.2				
Gambia		2.7				
Ghana	3.5	3.5				
Kenya	2.1	2.1				
Lesotho		3.4				

Country	Corruption Perceptions Index		Bribing and corruption		Transparency of government	
	2000	2005	2000	2006	2000	2006
Liberia		2.2				
Madagascar		2.8				
Malawi	4.1	2.8				
Mali		2.9				
Mozambique	2.2	2.8				
Niger		2.4				
Nigeria	1.2	1.9				
Rwanda		3.1				
Senegal	3.5	3.2				
Sierra Leone		2.4				
Somalia		2.1				
Sudan		2.1				
Tanzania	2.5	2.9				
Uganda	2.3	2.5				
Zambia	3.4	2.6				
Zimbabwe	3.0	2.6				
Middle income economies						
Botswana	6.0	5.9				
Gabon		2.9				
Mauritius	4.7	4.2				
Namibia	5.4	4.3				
South Africa	5.0	4.5	2.7	2.9	6.0	6.1
Swaziland		2.7				

*China excludes Tibet, Hong Kong and Macao.

Sources: Transparency International, 2000 Corruption Perceptions Index, www.transparency.org/cpi/2000/cpi2000.html; Transparency International, 2005 Corruption Perceptions Index, http://www.transparency.org/cpi/2005.sources.en.html; International Institute for Management Development (2000), The World Competitiveness Yearbook 1999, Institute for Management Development, Lausanne, Switzerland; International Institute for Management Development (2006), Tables 2.3.13 'Transparency' and 2.3.16 'Bribing and Corruption', The World Competitiveness Yearbook 2006, Institute for Management Development, Lausanne, Switzerland (see http://www01.imd.ch/wcc/yearbook/), Copyright © 2006, IMD International, Switzerland.

Record 12: Refugee populations and flows

This record shows two dimensions of the refugee problem: if a country 'generates' many refugees or internally displaced persons it can be assumed that there is little respect for the international rule of law in that country. On the other hand, countries that host many refugees can be considered as extending international hospitality and bearing the associated financial burden. The table presents data on refugee populations, both in total counts and per 1,000 inhabitants, for 1994 and 2004, as well as information on inflows and outflows of refugees during 2004. Negative inflow for a country indicates that there are fewer refugees in that country at the end of the year than at the beginning, while negative outflow indicates that the number of refugees originating from that country decreased over the year.

The table shows that the numbers of refugees across the world decreased in the last decade, with the exception of East Asia and the Pacific. Yet refugees are numerous in volatile areas such as Central Asia, Sub-Saharan Africa and the Middle East. Some Western European countries appear as major recipients of refugees, refugees representing more than 1 per cent of their populations.

Country of asylum	Refugee populations* Total (1000s)			Refugee populations* per 1000 inhabitants			Refugee flows** 2004 (1000s)	
	1994	2004	% change	1994	2004	% change	Inflow	Outflow
East Asia & Pacific								
Low income economies								
Cambodia	0.0	0.4	3,720	0.0	0.0	3,039	0.3	-13.3
East Timor		0.0		0.0		0.0	0.1	
Indonesia***	0.1	0.2	69	0.0	0.0	43	-0.1	11.7
Papua New Guinea	8.5	7.6	-10	2.0	1.4	-30	0.1	0.0
Vietnam	5.0	2.4	-53	0.1	0.0	-59	-13.0	-13.4
Middle income economies								
China***	287.1	299.4	4	0.2	0.2	-3	0.0	2.3
Malaysia	5.3	24.9	369	0.3	1.1	282	17.5	0.1
Philippines	0.7	0.1	-84	0.0	0.0	-87	0.0	0.0
Thailand	100.8	121.1	20	1.7	1.9	10	2.1	0.0
Tibet								
High income economies								
Australia	57.6	63.5	10	3.2	3.2	-1	7.2	0.0
Korea, Rep.	*0.1*	0.0	-56	*0.0*	0.0	-59	0.0	0.0
Japan	5.9	2.0	-67	0.0	0.0	-67	-0.3	0.0
New Zealand	3.7	5.2	41	1.0	1.3	24	-0.6	0.0
Singapore	0.0	0.0	-90	0.0	0.0	-92	0.0	0.0
Europe & Central Asia								

Country of asylum	Refugee populations*						Refugee flows**	
	Total (1000s)			per 1000 inhabitants			2004 (1000s)	
	1994	2004	% change	1994	2004	% change	Inflow	Outflow
Low income economies								
Armenia	304.0	235.2	-23	97.3	78.6	-19	-4.1	0.3
Azerbaijan	231.6	8.6	-96	30.6	1.1	-96	8.3	-2.7
Georgia		2.6			0.5		-1.3	-5.9
Kyrgyzstan	21.2	3.8	-82	4.7	0.7	-84	-1.8	0.2
Moldova		0.1			0.0		0.0	0.8
Tajikistan	0.7	3.3	372	0.1	0.5	289	0.0	-2.2
Ukraine	5.2	2.5	-53	0.1	0.1	-48	-0.4	-4.6
Uzbekistan	8.0	44.5	456	0.4	1.7	373	-0.2	-0.1
Middle income economies								
Albania	3.0	0.1	-98	0.9	0.0	-98	0.0	0.1
Belarus	1.8	0.7	-60	0.2	0.1	-60	0.1	0.4
Bosnia & Herzegovina		22.2			5.1		-0.3	-70.7
Bulgaria	1.1	4.7	342	0.1	0.6	391	0.6	-0.4
Croatia	183.6	3.7	-98	40.7	0.8	-98	-0.7	-14.7
Czech Republic	1.2	1.1	-4	0.1	0.1	-3	-0.4	-2.2
Estonia		0.0			0.0		0.0	-0.2
Hungary	2.9	7.7	165	0.3	0.8	172	0.7	-0.6
Kazakhstan	5.0	15.8	215	0.3	1.0	237	0.0	-0.4
Latvia		0.0			0.0		0.0	-0.4
Lithuania		0.4			0.1		0.0	-0.1
Macedonia	14.9	1.0	-93	7.7	0.5	-94	0.8	-0.9
Poland	0.4	2.5	543	0.0	0.1	542	0.6	-4.5
Romania	1.2	1.6	39	0.1	0.1	41	-0.4	-2.5
Russian Federation		1.9			0.0		-8.1	11.5
Serbia & Montenegro	450.7	276.7	-39	42.2	25.6	-39	-14.7	-59.6
Slovakia	0.2	0.4	156	0.0	0.1	152	0.0	0.0
Slovenia	29.2	0.3	-99	14.6	0.2	-99	-1.8	0.0
Turkey	24.9	3.0	-88	0.4	0.0	-89	0.5	-10.5
Turkmenistan	15.4	13.3	-14	3.8	2.7	-29	-0.3	0.0
High income economies								
Austria	40.7	17.8	-56	5.1	2.2	-57	1.7	0.0
Belgium	19.5	13.5	-31	1.9	1.3	-32	0.9	0.0

Country of asylum	Refugee populations* Total (1000s)			Refugee populations* per 1000 inhabitants			Refugee flows** 2004 (1000s)	
	1994	2004	% change	1994	2004	% change	Inflow	Outflow
Cyprus	0.1	0.5	659	0.1	0.7	610	0.2	0.0
Denmark	49.6	65.3	32	9.5	12.1	27	-4.5	0.0
Finland	9.5	11.3	19	1.9	2.2	16	0.5	0.0
France	195.3	139.9	-28	3.4	2.3	-31	9.0	0.0
Germany	1,354.6	876.6	-35	16.6	10.6	-36	-83.8	-0.6
Greece	7.8	2.5	-68	0.7	0.2	-69	-0.3	0.0
Iceland	0.2	0.2	49	0.6	0.8	35	0.0	0.0
Ireland	0.4	7.2	1,700	0.1	1.8	1,531	1.2	0.0
Italy	73.1	15.7	-79	1.3	0.3	-79	2.8	0.0
Luxembourg	0.3	1.6	430	0.7	3.4	362	0.4	0.0
Netherlands	62.2	126.8	104	4.0	7.8	92	-14.1	0.0
Norway	44.6	44.0	-1	10.3	9.6	-6	-2.1	0.0
Portugal	0.3	0.4	51	0.0	0.0	44	0.0	0.0
Spain	5.4	5.6	5	0.1	0.1	4	-0.3	0.0
Sweden	200.8	73.4	-63	22.7	8.2	-64	-38.8	0.0
Switzerland	75.3	47.7	-37	10.6	6.4	-40	-2.5	0.0
United Kingdom	85.2	289.1	239	1.5	4.8	228	12.5	0.0
Latin America & Caribbean								
Low income economies								
Nicaragua	0.3	0.3	-6	0.1	0.1	-25	0.0	-2.2
Middle income economies								
Argentina	11.9	2.9	-75	0.3	0.1	-78	0.3	0.0
Belize	8.9	0.7	-92	41.9	2.7	-94	-0.1	0.0
Bolivia	0.7	0.5	-28	0.1	0.1	-41	0.0	0.0
Brazil	2.2	3.3	51	0.0	0.0	32	0.2	0.0
Chile	0.2	0.6	159	0.0	0.0	129	0.1	-0.4
Colombia	0.0	0.1		0.0	0.0		0.0	9.4
Costa Rica	24.6	10.4	-58	7.4	2.6	-65	-3.1	0.0
Cuba	2.0	0.8	-60	0.2	0.1	-62	0.0	-0.4
Ecuador	0.2	8.5	3,421	0.0	0.6	2,887	2.1	0.0
El Salvador	0.2	0.2	47	0.0	0.0	22	0.0	-1.2
Guatemala	4.7	0.7	-86	0.5	0.1	-89	-0.1	-2.3
Honduras	0.1	0.0	-77	0.0	0.0	-82	0.0	-0.1
Mexico	47.4	4.3	-91	0.5	0.0	-92	-1.7	0.1

| Country of asylum | Refugee populations* | | | | | | Refugee flows** | |
| | Total (1000s) | | | per 1000 inhabitants | | | 2004 (1000s) | |
	1994	2004	% change	1994	2004	% change	Inflow	Outflow
Panama	1.0	1.6	66	0.4	0.5	38	0.2	0.0
Paraguay	0.1	0.0	-32	0.0	0.0	-48	0.0	0.0
Peru	0.7	0.8	16	0.0	0.0	-2	0.0	-0.8
Suriname	0.0			0.1			0.0	0.0
Uruguay	0.1	0.1	-12	0.0	0.0	-17	0.0	0.0
Venezuela	2.2	0.2	-89	0.1	0.0	-91	0.2	0.7
Middle East & North Africa								
Low income economies								
Yemen	48.3	66.4	37	3.4	3.3	-1	4.5	0.0
Western Sahara								0.0
Middle income economies								
Algeria	219.1	169.0	-23	8.0	5.3	-34	0.0	-1.0
Djibouti	33.4	18.0	-46	83.0	38.6	-53	-9.0	0.0
Egypt	7.2	90.3	1,151	0.1	1.2	919	1.6	-0.4
Iran	2,236.4	1,046.0	-53	36.7	15.5	-58	61.1	-7.4
Iraq	119.6	46.1	-61	6.3	1.8	-71	-0.7	-56.7
Jordan	0.6	1.1	90	0.1	0.2	38	-0.1	0.0
Lebanon	1.4	1.8	29	0.4	0.5	12	-0.8	-5.1
Libya	2.0	12.2	508	0.4	2.2	395	0.3	0.1
Morocco***	0.3	2.1	524	0.0	0.1	421	0.0	0.0
Oman		0.0			0.0		0.0	0.0
Saudi Arabia	18.0	240.6	1,239	0.9	9.3	892	-0.3	0.0
Syria	40.3	15.6	-61	2.9	0.9	-70	11.9	0.6
Tunisia	0.0	0.1	350	0.0	0.0	298	0.0	0.0
High income economies								
Israel		0.6			0.1		-3.6	0.0
Kuwait	30.0	1.5	-95	19.3	0.7	-97	0.0	-0.2
Qatar		0.0			0.1		0.0	0.0
United Arab Emirates	0.4	0.1	-72	0.2	0.0	-77	-0.1	0.1
North America								
High income economies								
Canada	186.6	141.4	-24	6.4	4.3	-32	8.3	0.0
United States	631.1	420.9	-33	2.4	1.4	-40	-31.7	0.1

Country of asylum	Refugee populations*						Refugee flows**	
	Total (1000s)			per 1000 inhabitants			2004 (1000s)	
	1994	2004	% change	1994	2004	% change	Inflow	Outflow
South Asia								
Low income economies								
Afghanistan	19.1	0.0	-100	1.0	0.0	-100	0.0	-51.1
Bangladesh	116.2	20.4	-82	1.0	0.1	-85	0.7	0.2
India	258.3	162.7	-37	0.3	0.2	-46	-2.1	-0.4
Nepal	103.3	124.9	21	4.8	4.6	-4	1.3	0.2
Pakistan	1,055.4	960.6	-9	8.4	6.0	-28	-163.7	1.6
Middle income economies								
Sri Lanka	0.0	0.1	530	0.0	0.0	472	0.0	-8.0
Sub-Saharan Africa								
Low income economies								
Angola	10.7	14.0	31	1.2	1.2	4	0.6	-100.7
Benin	70.4	4.8	-93	12.8	0.6	-95	-0.2	0.0
Burkina Faso	50.0	0.5	-99	5.3	0.0	-99	0.0	-0.3
Burundi	300.3	48.8	-84	52.9	6.5	-88	7.8	-45.9
Cameroon	44.0	58.9	34	3.3	3.5	6	0.3	1.4
Central African Republic	47.8	25.0	-48	13.8	6.0	-57	-19.7	-4.3
Chad	110.0	259.9	136	16.0	27.7	74	113.5	0.4
Congo, Dem. Rep.	3.0	199.3	6,544	0.1	3.4	4,923	-34.7	10.7
Congo, Rep.	15.5	68.5	342	6.0	19.6	224	-22.8	-0.6
Côte d'Ivoire	360.1	72.1	-80	26.5	4.3	-84	-3.9	-10.0
Eritrea	0.7	4.2	497	0.2	0.9	400	0.4	7.0
Ethiopia	348.1	116.0	-67	6.3	1.6	-74	-14.3	0.4
Gambia	2.2	7.3	232	2.0	4.7	138	-0.1	-0.1
Ghana	113.7	42.1	-63	6.6	2.0	-70	-1.9	-1.1
Guinea	553.2	139.3	-75	74.4	15.1	-80	-45.1	0.9
Guinea-Bissau	23.9	7.5	-68	21.4	5.4	-75	0.0	0.0
Kenya	252.4	239.8	-5	9.6	7.3	-24	2.3	0.7
Lesotho	0.1			0.0				0.0
Liberia	120.2	15.2	-87	60.9	5.4	-91	-18.8	-17.7
Madagascar	0.1			0.0				0.0
Malawi	90.2	3.7	-96	9.0	0.3	-97	0.5	0.0

| Country of asylum | Refugee populations* | | | | | | Refugee flows** | |
| | Total (1000s) | | | per 1000 inhabitants | | | 2004 (1000s) | |
	1994	2004	% change	1994	2004	% change	Inflow	Outflow
Mali	15.8	11.3	-29	1.8	1.0	-44	1.2	0.0
Mauritania	82.2	0.5	-99	36.1	0.2	-100	0.0	0.6
Mozambique	0.3	0.6	95	0.0	0.1	46	0.3	0.0
Niger	15.1	0.3	-98	1.7	0.0	-98	0.0	0.0
Nigeria	6.0	8.4	39	0.1	0.1	9	-0.8	-0.5
Rwanda	6.0	50.2	737	0.9	6.1	552	13.6	-11.4
São Tomé & Principe								
Senegal	73.0	20.8	-71	8.3	1.8	-78	0.1	0.0
Sierra Leone	15.9	65.4	312	3.7	11.4	210	4.2	-28.8
Somalia	0.4	0.4	-8	0.1	0.0	-32	0.0	-13.0
Sudan	727.2	141.6	-81	24.4	3.6	-85	3.4	124.4
Tanzania	883.3	602.1	-32	30.9	16.7	-46	-47.7	0.3
Togo	12.4	11.3	-9	3.3	2.1	-35	-1.1	0.2
Uganda	286.5	250.5	-13	14.6	9.5	-35	19.6	-3.3
Zambia	141.1	173.9	23	16.0	15.8	-2	-52.8	0.0
Zimbabwe	2.2	6.9	213	0.2	0.6	186	-5.8	2.4
Middle income economies								
Botswana	0.5	2.8	468	0.4	1.7	394	0.0	0.0
Gabon	0.6	13.8	2,198	0.6	10.1	1,653	-0.2	0.0
Namibia	1.1	14.8	1,196	0.7	7.3	957	-5.0	0.0
South Africa	91.9	27.7	-70	2.2	0.6	-72	1.1	0.0
Swaziland	0.6	0.7	10	0.6	0.6	-4	0.0	0.0

Region	Refugee populations*						Refugee flows**	
	Total (1000s)			per 1000 inhabitants			2004 (1000s)	
	1994	2004	% change	1994	2004	% change	Inflow	Outflow
Low income	7,066.0	4,450.1	-37	3.3	1.7	-48	-264.5	-169.0
Middle income	4,009.4	2,541.3	-37	1.6	0.9	-42	54.2	-226.0
Low & middle income:								
East Asia & Pacific	407.4	456.1	12	0.2	0.3	1	7.0	-12.5
Europe & Central Asia	1,306.2	657.6	-50	2.8	1.4	-50	-22.9	-170.0
Latin America & Caribbean	107.4	36.2	-66	0.2	0.1	-71	-2.1	2.9
Middle East & North Africa	2,726.5	1,709.2	-37	10.2	5.2	-49	68.6	-69.8
South Asia	1,552.4	1,268.8	-18	1.3	0.9	-32	-163.8	-57.5
Sub-Saharan Africa	4,878.7	2,730.8	-44	8.8	3.9	-56	-106.1	-88.2
High income	3,139.9	2,374.3	-24	3.5	3.2	-8	-144.0	-0.8
World	14,118.6	9,232.9	-35	2.6	1.5	-42	-357.1	-395.9

Empty cells indicate that the value is below 100, zero or not available.

Per capita calculations were made by us, using population data from World Development Indicators 2006, WDI Online.

* The figures for refugee populations are as of end of year.

** Figures for inflow and outflow of refugees were obtained by netting the populations of refugees reported in the beginning of 2004 and at the end of 2004 for the country of asylum in the case of inflow and for the country of origin in the case of outflow. Inflows and outflows based on primae facie arrivals and individually recognised refugees.

*** China: 1994 figures include Tibet; all China figures exclude Hong Kong; Indonesia: 1994 figures include East Timor; Morocco: 1994 figures include Western Sahara.

Sources: UNHCR Statistics Online, www.unhcr.ch/cgi-bin/texis/vtx/goto?page=statistics; World Development Indicators 2006, WDI Online, devdata.worldbank.org/dataonline

A country's preparedness to contribute part of its armed forces to peacekeeping duties in foreign conflicts can be seen as a commitment to the international community. This record reports the ratio of peacekeeping forces to total military personnel, comparing numbers of military personnel (for 2004, the latest available data) with the total number of forces per country committed to peacekeeping (as of December 2005). Large shares of peacekeeping forces are reported to come from some South Asian and Sub-Saharan countries, both in absolute numbers and in relative terms, compared to size of the military in those countries.

Country	Total military personnel 2004	Peacekeeping forces as of December 2005*	Peacekeeping forces per thousand military personnel
East Asia & Pacific			
Low income economies			
Cambodia	192,000	4	0.0
Indonesia	582,000	199	0.3
Korea, Dem. Rep.	1,295,000		
Laos	129,000		
Mongolia	15,000	5	0.3
Myanmar	482,250		
Papua New Guinea	3,000		
Vietnam	5,564,000		
Middle income economies			
China	3,755,000	862	0.2
Fiji	3,000	2	0.7
Malaysia	130,000	59	0.5
Philippines	146,000	370	2.5
Thailand	419,000	180	0.4
High income economies			
Australia	52,000	32	0.6
Brunei	10,000		
Korea, Rep.	696,000	49	0.1
Japan	251,000	30	0.1
New Zealand	8,000	13	1.6
Singapore	165,000		
Europe & Central Asia			
Low income economies			
Armenia	49,000		
Azerbaijan	81,000		
Georgia	22,000		
Kyrgyzstan	17,000	14	0.8
Moldova	9,000	10	1.1
Tajikistan	12,000		
Ukraine	271,000	518	1.9

Country	Total military personnel 2004	Peacekeeping forces as of December 2005*	Peacekeeping forces per thousand military personnel
Uzbekistan	75,000		
Middle income economies			
Albania	21,500	3	0.1
Belarus	182,000		
Bosnia & Herzegovina	24,000	14	0.6
Bulgaria	85,000	10	0.1
Croatia	30,000	29	1.0
Czech Republic	27,000	14	0.5
Estonia	6,000	2	0.3
Hungary	46,000	96	2.1
Kazakhstan	99,000		
Latvia	5,000		
Lithuania	28,000		
Macedonia	17,000		
Poland	162,000	576	3.6
Romania	176,000	54	0.3
Russian Federation	1,452,000	97	0.1
Serbia & Montenegro	110,000	14	0.1
Slovakia	20,000	292	14.6
Slovenia	10,000	2	0.2
Turkey	616,000	8	0.0
Turkmenistan	26,000		
High income economies			
Austria	39,000	400	10.3
Belgium	36,000	16	0.4
Cyprus	11,000		
Denmark	21,000	40	1.9
Finland	31,000	32	1.0
France	358,000	430	1.2
Germany	284,000	41	0.1
Greece	167,000	15	0.1
Ireland	10,000	455	45.5
Italy	445,000	74	0.2
Luxembourg	1,512		
Netherlands	53,000	15	0.3
Norway	25,000	37	1.5
Portugal	91,000	6	0.1
Spain	220,000	210	1.0

Country	Total military personnel 2004	Peacekeeping forces as of December 2005*	Peacekeeping forces per thousand military personnel
Sweden	27,600	263	9.5
Switzerland	4,000	19	4.8
United Kingdom	205,000	280	1.4
Latin America & Caribbean			
Low income economies			
Nicaragua	14,000		
Middle income economies			
Argentina	102,000	871	8.5
Belize	1,000		0.0
Bolivia	68,000	244	3.6
Brazil	687,000	1,256	1.8
Chile	116,000	547	4.7
Colombia	336,000		
Cuba	75,000		
Dominican Republic	39,000	4	0.1
Ecuador	46,270	93	2.0
El Salvador	15,000	16	1.1
Guatemala	48,000	215	4.5
Guyana	2,000		
Honduras	20,000	12	0.6
Jamaica	2,000		
Mexico	203,000		
Paraguay	24,000	52	2.2
Peru	157,000	245	1.6
Suriname	1,000		
Trinidad & Tobago	2,000		
Uruguay	24,920	2,412	96.8
Venezuela	82,000		
Middle East & North Africa			
Low income economies			
Yemen	136,000	27	0.2
Middle income economies			
Algeria	318,000	12	0.0
Djibouti	11,000		
Egypt	798,000	692	0.9
Iran	460,000	3	0.0
Iraq	179,000		
Jordan	110,000	2,964	26.9

Country	Total military personnel 2004	Peacekeeping forces as of December 2005*	Peacekeeping forces per thousand military personnel
Lebanon	85,000		
Libya	76,000		
Malta	2,000		
Morocco	250,000	1,706	6.8
Oman	45,000		
Saudi Arabia	214,000		
Syria	415,000		
Tunisia	47,000	524	11.1
High income economies			
Bahrain	21,000		
Israel	176,000		
Kuwait	21,000		
Qatar	12,000		
United Arab Emirates	50,000		
North America			
High income economies			
Canada	71,000	251	3.5
United States	1,473,000	28	0.0
South Asia	4,186,000	28,566	6.8
Low income economies			
Afghanistan	27,000		
Bangladesh	251,000	9,051	36.1
India	2,617,000	6,903	2.6
Nepal	131,000	3,035	23.2
Pakistan	921,000	8,605	9.3
Middle income economies			
Sri Lanka	239,000	972	4.1
Sub-Saharan Africa			
Low income economies			
Angola	118,000		
Benin	6,000	344	57.3
Burkina Faso	10,250	25	2.4
Burundi	81,000		
Cameroon	23,000	4	0.2
Central African Republic	2,000		
Chad	34,000	12	0.4
Congo, Rep.	12,000	5	0.4
Côte d'Ivoire	18,000		

Country	Total military personnel 2004	Peacekeeping forces as of December 2005*	Peacekeeping forces per thousand military personnel
Equatorial Guinea	1,000		
Eritrea	201,000		
Ethiopia	182,000	3,410	18.7
Gambia	800	19	23.8
Ghana	7,000	2,436	348.0
Guinea	11,000	19	1.7
Guinea-Bissau	9,000		
Kenya	29,000	1,420	49.0
Lesotho	2,000		
Madagascar	21,000		
Malawi	6,000	149	24.8
Mali	11,000	52	4.7
Mozambique	11,000	18	1.6
Niger	10,000	394	39.4
Nigeria	160,000	2,038	12.7
Rwanda	53,000	270	5.1
Senegal	18,000	1,429	79.4
Sierra Leone	13,000	250	19.2
Sudan	121,000		
Tanzania	28,000	21	0.8
Togo	8,750	318	36.3
Uganda	55,000	14	0.3
Zambia	16,000	401	25.1
Zimbabwe	50,000	20	0.4
Middle income economies			
Botswana	10,000		
Cape Verde	1,000		
Gabon	6,000	5	0.8
Namibia	15,000	883	58.9
South Africa	55,000	2,010	36.5
World	**32,645,140**	**62,597**	**1.9**

* Peacekeeping forces here comprise military observers and troops

Country of mission	Region	Name of mission	Peacekeeping forces for each military mission, as of December 2005
East Timor	East Asia & Pacific	UNOTIL	15
Afghanistan	South Asia	UNAMA	12
Cyprus	Europe & Central Asia	UNFICYP	859
Georgia	Europe & Central Asia	UNOMIG	121
Kosovo	Europe & Central Asia	UNMIK	38
Haiti	Latin America & Caribbean	MINUSTAH	7,472
Golan Heights	Middle East & North Africa	UNDOF	1,152
Lebanon	Middle East & North Africa	UNIFIL	1,985
Middle East	Middle East & North Africa	UNTSO	153
Western Sahara	Middle East & North Africa	MINURSO	218
India/Pakistan	South Asia	UNMOGIP	43
Burundi	Sub-Saharan Africa	ONUB	4,569
Côte d'Ivoire	Sub-Saharan Africa	UNOCI	6,895
Congo, Dem. Rep.	Sub-Saharan Africa	MONUC	15,716
Ethipia/Eritrea	Sub-Saharan Africa	UNMEE	3,357
Liberia	Sub-Saharan Africa	UNMIL	15,070
Sudan	Sub-Saharan Africa	UNMIS	7,688
		Total:	**62,597**

Sources: United Nations, Department of Peacekeeping Operations, http://www.un.org/Depts/dpko/dpko/contributors/;
World Development Indicators 2006, WDI online, World Bank http://devdata.worldbank.org/dataonline

Record 14: Environment

This record gives an indication of the extent to which countries protect or harm the global environment. It is now generally agreed that carbon dioxide emission is a major contributor to the problem of global warming: a large volume of emissions can therefore be considered as an infringement of the environmental element of the international rule of law. It is difficult to evaluate emissions indicators at the country level, since per capita figures may favour populous countries, while per unit of income measures may favour high-income countries (we use purchasing power parity, PPP, which represents the relative value of currencies based on what those currencies will buy in their nation of origin). We therefore present both in the table, for comparison purposes.

The proportion of recycled paper in a country's total paper production is an indicator of the commitment to natural resource conservation. The data show the ratio of new to recovered paper production: figures higher than 1 indicate recovered paper exceeds new paper production, and figures lower than 1 reflect the opposite.

The final indicator is the number of companies in each country with ISO 14000 accreditation, the international environmental standard for business. This number reflects the respect that the business sector in different countries shows to international environmental norms.

The data in the table are not very encouraging, as per capita emissions have stagnated in the decade covered in the table, which with world population growth means substantially more emissions. The rate at which corporations adopt international environmental standards has slowed considerably for the period 2000-2004 compared to1996-2000.

| Country | Carbon dioxide emissions | | | | | | Paper production: ratio of recovered paper to new paper | | % change | ISO 14000 accredited companies | | | % change | |
| | metric tons per capita | | % change | kg per PPP $ of GDP | | % change | | | | | | | | |
	1992	2002	1992-2002	1992	2002	1990-2002	1994	2004	1994-2004	1996	2000	2004	1996-2004	2000-2004
East Asia & Pacific														
Low income economies														
Cambodia	0.0	0.0	-6		0.0							1		
Indonesia	1.0	1.4	45	0.4	0.5	32	0.1	0.2	45	3	77	373	2,467	384
Korea, Dem. Rep.	12.6	6.5	-49								26	202		677
Laos	0.1	0.2	267	0.1	0.1	142								
Mongolia	5.1	3.4	-33	4.2	2.0	-51								
Myanmar	0.1	0.2	35				0.0	1.1				2		
Papua New Guinea	0.6	0.4	-23	0.3	0.2	-21								
Solomon Islands	0.5	0.4	-19	0.2	0.2	17								
Vietnam	0.3	0.8	160	0.2	0.4	50	1.4	0.2	-86		9	85		844
Middle income economies														
China	2.3	2.7	21	1.2	0.6	-49	0.4	0.3	-22	9	510	8,862	5,567	1,638
Fiji	1.0	1.6	64	0.2	0.3	43								
Malaysia	3.9	6.3	60	0.6	0.7	15	0.2	0.7	274	7	174	566	2,386	225
Philippines	0.8	0.9	19	0.2	0.2	7	0.1	0.3	196	1	46	261	4,500	467
Samoa	0.8	0.8	1	0.3	0.2	-44								

Country	Carbon dioxide emissions						Paper production: ratio of recovered paper to new paper		% change	ISO 14000 accredited companies			% change	
	metric tons per capita		% change	kg per PPP $ of GDP		% change								
	1992	2002	1992-2002	1992	2002	1990-2000	1994	2004	1994-2004	1996	2000	2004	1996-2004	2000-2004
Thailand	2.3	3.7	64	0.4	0.6	30	0.2	0.2	22	58	310	966	434	212
Tonga	0.9	1.0	14	0.2	0.2	-8								
Vanuatu	0.4	0.4	8	0.1	0.2	22								
High income economies														
Australia	15.6	18.1	16	0.8	0.7	-10	0.4	0.7	58	53	1,049	1,898	1,879	81
Brunei	18.7	17.7	-5								2	4		100
Korea, Rep.	6.6	9.4	41	0.6	0.5	-11	0.5	0.7	27	57	544	2,609	854	380
Japan	8.9	9.4	6	0.4	0.4	0	0.5	0.5	-2	198	5,556	19,584	2,706	252
New Zealand	7.4	8.6	16	0.5	0.4	-8	0.2	0.3	69	3	63	194	2,000	208
Singapore	14.0	13.7	-2	0.9	0.6	-35	2.6	3.2	23	37	100	616	170	516
Europe & Central Asia														
Low income economies														
Armenia	1.1	1.0	-10	0.5	0.3	-39								
Azerbaijan	6.4	3.4	-46		1.1							32		
Georgia	2.8	0.7	-75	1.4	0.3	-77								
Kyrgyzstan	2.4	1.0	-59	1.3	0.6	-51								
Moldova	4.8	1.6	-67	2.2	1.1	-50								
Tajikistan	3.7	0.7	-80	2.5	0.8	-69								
Ukraine	11.5	6.4	-45	1.6	1.3	-17	0.7	0.5	-32					
Uzbekistan	5.3	4.8	-9	3.4	3.0	-11								
Middle income economies														
Albania	0.7	0.8	15	0.3	0.2	-38						1		
Belarus	9.3	6.0	-35	2.0	1.1	-42						42		
Bosnia & Herzegovina	1.2	4.7	298		0.8							10		
Bulgaria	6.0	5.3	-11	1.1	0.8	-24	0.9	0.5	-46			26		
Croatia	3.8	4.7	26	0.5	0.5	-8	0.2	0.0			8	84		950
Czech Republic	13.1	11.2	-15	1.0	0.7	-34	0.4	0.5	33		116	1,288		1,010
Estonia	16.2	11.7	-28	2.4	1.0	-57	0.2	0.5	177		18	86		378
Hungary	5.4	5.6	3	0.6	0.4	-29	0.8	0.7	-14	3	164	882	5,367	438
Kazakhstan	15.4	9.9	-35	3.2	1.8	-44	0.0	0.0				7		
Latvia	4.8	2.7	-44	0.8	0.3	-66	6.3	1.6	-75		4	78		1,850
Lithuania	5.8	3.6	-37	0.7	0.4	-47	1.0	0.7	-35		10	155		1,450

Country	Carbon dioxide emissions						Paper production: ratio of recovered paper to new paper		% change	ISO 14000 accredited companies			% change	
	metric tons per capita		% change	kg per PPP $ of GDP		% change								
	1992	2002	1992-2002	1992	2002	1990-2000	1994	2004	1994-2004	1996	2000	2004	1996-2004	2000-2004
Macedonia	5.5	5.1	-8	0.9	0.9	-2	0.0	0.1				5		
Poland	8.8	7.7	-12	1.3	0.7	-43	0.1	0.4	228		66	709		974
Romania	5.4	4.0	-26	1.0	0.6	-40	0.3	0.6	97		5	361		7,120
Russian Federation	13.3	9.8	-26	1.6	1.3	-22	0.3	0.3	-1		3	118		3,833
Serbia & Montenegro							0.1	0.0	-100			46		
Slovakia	8.1	6.8	-16	0.9	0.6	-40	0.3	0.3	2	1	36	184	3,500	411
Slovenia	6.2	7.7	24	0.5	0.4	-15	0.1	0.0	-100		88	338		284
Turkey	2.5	3.0	19	0.4	0.5	5	0.5	0.6	29	6	91	338	1,417	271
Turkmenistan	7.2	9.1	26	1.5	2.1	35								
High income economies														
Austria	7.2	7.9	9	0.3	0.3	-10	0.3	0.3	11	56	203	549	263	170
Belgium*	10.3	8.9	-14	0.4	0.3	-26	0.6	0.4	-32	8	130	642	1,525	394
Cyprus	7.1	8.3	16	0.5	0.4	-13	0.0	0.0			4	56		1,300
Denmark	10.3	8.8	-14	0.4	0.3	-29	1.4	1.1	-21	96	532	711	454	34
Finland	9.5	12.0	27	0.5	0.5	-1	0.0	0.1		41	508	882	1,139	74
France	6.3	6.2	-3	0.3	0.2	-18	0.5	0.6	24	23	710	2,955	2,987	316
Germany	11.3	10.3	-9	0.5	0.4	-21	0.7	0.6	-3	166	1,260	4,320	659	243
Greece	7.1	8.5	20	0.5	0.5	-6	0.2	0.2	-16	1	42	173	4,100	312
Iceland	6.9	7.7	11	0.3	0.3	-8	0.0	0.0			2	5		150
Ireland	8.9	11.0	24	0.5	0.3	-42	0.0	7.8		8	163	294	1,938	80
Italy	7.1	7.5	5	0.3	0.3	-8	0.3	0.6	67	27	521	4,785	1,830	818
Luxembourg	30.0	21.3	-29	0.9	0.4	-58				1	9	39	800	333
Netherlands	9.2	9.3	2	0.4	0.3	-18	0.7	0.7	-6	119	784	1,150	559	47
Norway	10.9	13.9	27	0.4	0.4	-1	0.1	0.2	151	13	227	441	1,646	94
Portugal	4.7	6.0	27	0.3	0.3	3	0.3	0.2	-38	1	47	404	4,600	760
Spain	5.8	7.4	27	0.3	0.3	2	0.5	0.7	28	13	600	6,473	4,515	979
Sweden	5.9	5.8	-2	0.3	0.2	-19	0.2	0.1	-15	25	1,370	3,478	5,380	154
Switzerland	6.2	5.6	-10	0.2	0.2	-15	0.6	0.7	8	18	690	1,348	3,733	95
United Kingdom	9.8	9.2	-6	0.5	0.3	-26	0.7	1.2	80	322	2,534	6,253	687	147
Latin America & Caribbean														
Low income economies														
Haiti	0.1	0.2	69	0.1	0.1	105								
Nicaragua	0.6	0.7	26	0.2	0.2	41						1		

Country	Carbon dioxide emissions						Paper production: ratio of recovered paper to new paper		% change	ISO 14000 accredited companies			% change	
	metric tons per capita		% change	kg per PPP $ of GDP		% change								
	1992	2002	1992-2002	1992	2002	1990-2000	1994	2004	1994-2004	1996	2000	2004	1996-2004	2000-2004
Middle income economies														
Argentina	3.5	3.5	0	0.3	0.3	0	0.5	0.6	28	5	114	408	2,180	258
Barbados	3.8	4.6	21							3	3			
Belize	1.8	3.0	66	0.4	0.5	31								
Bolivia	0.8	1.2	38	0.4	0.5	22					1	14		1,300
Brazil	1.4	1.8	26	0.2	0.2	7	0.2	0.3	56	6	330	1,800	5,400	445
Chile	2.6	3.6	41	0.4	0.4	2	0.2	0.1	-53		11	312		2,736
Colombia	1.7	1.3	-22	0.3	0.2	-24	0.5	0.5	15	1	21	217	2,000	933
Costa Rica	1.2	1.4	23	0.2	0.2	0	0.6	0.6	0		20	52		160
Cuba	2.9	2.1	-27				1.0	3.3	217			1		
Dominican Republic	1.5	2.5	65	0.3	0.4	7	1.4	0.1	-92		1	1		
Ecuador	2.0	2.0	-4	0.6	0.6	-5	0.7	0.3	-56		1	11		1,000
El Salvador	0.6	1.0	48	0.2	0.2	24	0.3	0.1	-69			3		
Guatemala	0.6	0.9	36	0.2	0.2	18	0.7	0.6	-19		2	3		50
Guyana	1.4	2.2	50	0.4	0.5	28						3		
Honduras	0.6	0.9	48	0.2	0.3	48	0.0	0.5			2	5		150
Jamaica	3.3	4.1	23	0.9	1.1	26	0.0	0.0				4		
Mexico	4.6	3.8	-17	0.6	0.4	-26	0.4	0.2	-43	2	159	492	7,850	209
Panama	1.6	2.0	28	0.3	0.3	14	0.4	0.0	-100			2		
Paraguay	0.6	0.7	22	0.1	0.2	35	0.0	2.3			1	3		200
Peru	0.9	1.0	2	0.2	0.2	-20	0.5	0.8	49		13	41		215
St. Lucia	1.2	2.4	93	0.2	0.4	97					2	1		-50
Suriname	5.2	5.1	-2											
Trinidad & Tobago	17.0	31.8	87	2.5	3.4	40					1	7		600
Uruguay	1.6	1.2	-26	0.2	0.2	-22	0.5	0.2	-67		22	42		91
Venezuela	5.3	4.3	-19	0.8	0.8	-1	0.4	0.3	-31		7	17		143
High income economies														
Bahamas	6.8	6.7	-1	0.4	0.4	-5								
Middle East & North Africa														
Low income economies														
Yemen	1.0	0.7	-34	1.5	0.8	-44								

Country	Carbon dioxide emissions						Paper production: ratio of recovered paper to new paper		% change	ISO 14000 accredited companies			% change	
	metric tons per capita		% change	kg per PPP $ of GDP		% change								
	1992	2002	1992-2002	1992	2002	1990-2000	1994	2004	1994-2004	1996	2000	2004	1996-2004	2000-2004
Middle income economies														
Algeria	3.0	2.9	-3	0.6	0.5	-9	0.0	0.8	1,598			3		
Djibouti	0.6	0.5	-24		0.3									
Egypt	1.4	2.1	47	0.5	0.6	14	0.7	0.8	13	1	78	289	7,700	271
Iran	4.3	5.5	27	0.8	0.9	5	0.4	0.2	-51		12	400		3,233
Iraq	2.9	3.0	2											
Jordan	3.3	3.2	-2	0.8	0.8	-3	0.4	0.1	-69		16	33		106
Lebanon	3.9	4.7	20	1.1	1.0	-8					5	7		40
Libya	8.4	9.1	9											
Malta	7.2	7.4	3	0.6	0.4	-28	0.0	0.0			2	4		100
Morocco	1.0	1.5	47	0.3	0.4	30	0.3	0.2	-20		4	21		425
Oman	6.1	12.1	98	0.5	0.9	66					2	4		100
Palestinian Authority											1	5		400
Saudi Arabia	14.3	15.0	4	1.1	1.3	14					6	17		183
Syria	3.2	2.8	-12	1.1	0.8	-23					3	48		1,500
Tunisia	1.8	2.3	28	0.4	0.3	-3	0.1	0.1	-2		3	30		900
High income economies														
Bahrain	19.4	30.6	57	1.4	1.7	21					2	13		550
Israel	7.8	10.6	36	0.4	0.5	17	0.5	0.4	-17	4	60	247	1,400	312
Kuwait	8.3	25.6	207		1.6							7		
Qatar	54.7	53.0	-3								1	9		800
United Arab Emirates	31.7	25.0	-21	1.4	1.2	-15				1	48	87	4,700	81
North America														
High income economies														
Canada	14.7	16.5	12	0.7	0.6	-12	0.1	0.1	-48	7	475	1,492	6,686	214
United States	18.8	20.2	7	0.7	0.6	-11	0.4	0.5	35	34	1,042	4,759	2,965	357
South Asia														
Low income economies														
Afghanistan	0.1	0.0	-71								4	4		
Bangladesh	0.1	0.3	73	0.1	0.2	34	0.0	0.0				7		
Bhutan	0.3	0.5	38											
India	0.9	1.2	33	0.5	0.5	-10	0.1	0.2	50	2	257	1,250	12,750	386

Country	Carbon dioxide emissions metric tons per capita 1992	2002	% change 1992-2002	kg per PPP $ of GDP 1992	2002	% change 1990-2000	Paper production: ratio of recovered paper to new paper 1994	2004	% change 1994-2004	ISO 14000 accredited companies 1996	2000	2004	% change 1996-2004	% change 2000-2004
Nepal	0.1	0.2	127	0.1	0.1	86						2		
Pakistan	0.6	0.7	17	0.4	0.4	5	0.1	1.0	601	1	4	38	300	850
Middle income economies														
Maldives	1.1	3.4	206											
Sri Lanka	0.3	0.5	88	0.1	0.2	32	0.6	0.5	-17		2	13		550
Sub-Saharan Africa														
Low income economies														
Angola	0.4	0.5	34	0.2	0.3	76								
Benin	0.2	0.3	54	0.2	0.2	32								
Burkina Faso	0.1	0.1	-11	0.1	0.1	-22								
Burundi	0.0	0.0	14	0.0	0.1	52								
Cameroon	0.3	0.2	-24	0.2	0.1	-30					1			
Central African Republic	0.1	0.1	3	0.1	0.1	0								
Chad	0.0	0.0	25	0.0	0.0	33								
Comoros	0.1	0.1	3	0.1	0.1	9								
Congo, Rep.	0.5	0.6	36	0.5	0.7	31								
Congo, Dem. Rep.	0.1	0.0	-59	0.1	0.1	-27								
Côte d'Ivoire	0.3	0.4	15	0.2	0.2	27								
Equatorial Guinea	0.3	0.4	10	0.3	0.0	-93								
Eritrea		0.2			0.2									
Ethiopia	0.1	0.1	74	0.1	0.1	30	0.3	0.2	-44					
Gambia	0.2	0.2	3	0.1	0.1	2								
Ghana	0.2	0.4	51	0.1	0.2	25						4		
Guinea	0.2	0.1	-3	0.1	0.1	-14								
Guinea-Bissau	0.2	0.2	-4	0.2	0.3	29								
Kenya	0.2	0.2	3	0.2	0.2	9	0.3	0.2	-33		2	16		700
Liberia	0.1	0.1	4											
Madagascar	0.1	0.1	72	0.1	0.2	106	0.2	0.2	35			1		
Malawi	0.1	0.1	-1	0.1	0.1	-11								
Mali	0.0	0.0	-5	0.1	0.0	-26								
Mauritania	1.4	1.1	-19	0.9	0.7	-21								
Mozambique	0.1	0.1	15	0.1	0.1	-28	5.0	0.0	-100					

Country	Carbon dioxide emissions						Paper production: ratio of recovered paper to new paper		% change	ISO 14000 accredited companies			% change	
	metric tons per capita		% change	kg per PPP $ of GDP		% change								
	1992	2002	1992-2002	1992	2002	1990-2000	1994	2004	1994-2004	1996	2000	2004	1996-2004	2000-2004
Niger	0.1	0.1	-20	0.2	0.1	-18						2		
Nigeria	0.7	0.4	-38	0.8	0.5	-40	2.7	0.4	-84		1	11		1,000
Rwanda	0.1	0.1	-11	0.1	0.1	3								
São Tomé & Principe	0.6	0.6	4											
Senegal	0.4	0.4	-5	0.3	0.3	-12						3		
Sierra Leone	0.1	0.1	26	0.1	0.3	123								
Sudan	0.2	0.3	57	0.1	0.2	22	2.0	2.0	0					
Tanzania	0.1	0.1	19	0.2	0.2	8						3		
Togo	0.2	0.3	57	0.1	0.2	55								
Uganda	0.0	0.1	41	0.0	0.0	-2						2		
Zambia	0.3	0.2	-34	0.3	0.2	-25					2			
Zimbabwe	1.6	1.0	-40	0.7	0.4	-33	0.3	0.9	173		4	19		375
Middle income economies														
Botswana	2.2	2.3	6	0.4	0.3	-36						2		
Cape Verde	0.3	0.3	9	0.1	0.1	-26								
Gabon	2.7	2.6	-4	0.4	0.4	-5								
Mauritius	1.6	2.6	63	0.2	0.2	10				1	4	11	300	175
Namibia	0.0	1.1	11,134	0.0	0.2	10,258					4	3		-25
South Africa	7.6	7.6	0	0.9	0.8	-9	0.4	0.2	-30		126	393		212
Swaziland	0.3	0.9	176	0.1	0.2	113						3		

Region	Carbon dioxide emissions						ISO 14000 accredited companies			% change	
	metric tons per capita		% change	kg per PPP $ of GDP		% change					
	1992	2002	1992-2002	1992	2002	1992-2002	1996	2000	2004	1996-2000	2000-2004
Low income	0.8	0.8	5	0.5	0.4	-12	6	386	2,059	6,333	433
Middle income	3.4	3.3	-4	0.9	0.6	-30	104	2,628	20,138	2,427	666
Low & middle income:											
East Asia & Pacific	2.1	2.4	19	0.9	0.6	-36	78	1,152	11,317	1,377	882
Europe & Central Asia	9.1	6.7	-27	1.4	0.9	-31	10	609	4,790	5,990	687
Latin America & Caribbean	2.4	2.4	-1	0.4	0.3	-10	17	711	3,440	4,082	384
Middle East & North Africa	2.7	3.2	19	0.7	0.7	3	1	132	861	13,100	552
South Asia	0.8	1.0	31	0.4	0.4	-6	3	267	1,314	8,800	392
Sub-Saharan Africa	0.8	0.7	-7	0.5	0.4	-12	1	143	474	14,200	231
High income	11.8	12.8	9	0.5	0.5	-9	1,332	19,278	66,477	1,347	245
World	4.0	3.9	-1	0.6	0.5	-18	1,442	22,292	88,674	1,446	298

Where data for a particular year are not available, figures are taken from the year before or after as an estimate. These figures, and estimates based on them, are presented in italics.

* Paper production data includes Luxembourg (in 2002 reported paper production in Luxembourg amounted to 0).

Sources: World Development Indicators 2006, WDI-online; Paper and Paper production available online through FAOSTAT database: http://faostat.fao.org/; ISO 14000 survey 2004: www.iso.org

Record 15: International organisations: organisations and participation

Perhaps the most direct indicator of the emergence of global civil society is the number of international non-governmental organisations (INGOs) and the networks they form. While INGOs and their networks are seen as the organisational infrastructure of global civil society, international governmental organisations (IGOs), are viewed as the foundation of the system of global governance and instruments of the international rule of law. In this record we show the most recent data available in the Union of International Association's (UIA) Yearbook of International Organizations on the number of international organisations (INGOs and IGOs) and participation in those organisations. The categorisation of organisations in UIA publications reflects differences in kind (primarily between membership-based and other types of organisations) and geographic scope. A detailed explanation can be found in the Glossary. The data show that the growth in the numbers of international organisations has not waned, but most of that increase has taken place at regional and sub-regional levels. Membership of such organisations, particularly INGOs, seems to be more pronounced in the North, especially in Europe.

Inter-governmental and non-governmental international organisations*

Inter-governmental organisations

UIA type		1995-1996		2005-6		Change	
		Number	%	Number	%	Number	%
A	Federations of international organisations	1	0.1	1	0.1	0	0.0
B	Universal membership organisations	36	2.0	34	1.7	-2	-5.6
C	Intercontinental membership organisations	39	2.2	33	1.7	-6	-15.4
D	Regionally oriented membership organisations	190	10.8	178	9.1	-12	-6.3
E	Organisations emanating from places, persons, bodies	723	41.0	882	44.9	159	22.0
F	Organisations of special form	709	40.2	727	37.0	18	2.5
G	Internationally oriented organisations	65	3.7	108	5.5	43	66.2
A-G	**All A-G international organisations**	**1,763**	**100.0**	**1,963**	**100.0**	**200**	**11.3**

Non-governmental organisations

UIA type		1995-1996		2005-6		Change	
		Number	%	Number	%	Number	%
A	Federations of international organisations	38	0.3	36	0.2	-2	-5.3
B	Universal membership organisations	486	3.4	474	2.3	-12	-2.5
C	Intercontinental membership organisations	1,001	7.0	1,072	5.1	71	7.1
D	Regionally oriented membership organisations	3,596	25.2	5,724	27.4	2,128	59.2
E	Organisations emanating from places, persons, bodies	1,846	12.9	2,700	12.9	854	46.3
F	Organisations of special form	3,025	21.2	4,124	19.7	1,099	36.3
G	Internationally oriented organisations	4,282	30.0	6,798	32.5	2,516	58.8
A-G	All A-G international organisations	14,274	100.0	20,928	100.0	6,654	46.6

All international organisations

UIA type		1995-1996		2005-6		Change	
		Number	%	Number	%	Number	%
A	Federations of international organisations	39	0.2	37	0.2	-2	-5.1
B	Universal membership organisations	522	3.3	508	2.2	-14	-2.7
C	Intercontinental membership organisations	1,040	6.5	1,105	4.8	65	6.3
D	Regionally oriented membership organisations	3,786	23.6	5,902	25.8	2,116	55.9
E	Organisations emanating from places, persons, bodies	2,569	16.0	3,582	15.6	1,013	39.4
F	Organisations of special form	3,734	23.3	4,851	21.2	1,117	29.9
G	Internationally oriented organisations	4,347	27.1	6,906	30.2	2,559	58.9
A-G	All A-G international organisations	16,037	100.0	22,891	100.0	6,854	42.7

*For definitions of types of organisations, see the Glossary following this Records section, or http://www.uia.org.organizations/orgtypes/orgtyped.php#typee

Sources: Union of International Associations (UIA) (1996), Yearbook of International Organizations 1995/1996, vol. 32, no. 1, Appendix 4 Table 1: International organisations by type - 1995/96 edition, p.1670; UIA (2006), Yearbook of International organisations 2005/2006, vol. 42, no. 1, Appendix 3 Table 1: Number of international organisations in this edition by type, p.2966.

Participation in international organisations, 2004

Inter-governmental organisations

Continent	Conventional international bodies			Organisations emanating from places, persons, bodies			Organisations of special form			Internationally oriented organisations			All A-G international organisations		
	A-D	%	Membership density per million of population	E	%	Membership density per million of population	F	%	Membership density per million of population	G	%	Membership density per million of population	A-G	%	Membership density per million of population
Africa	2,373	27.2	2.7	4,637	24.2	5.3	3,646	22.6	4.2	122	30.1	0.1	10,864	24.3	12.4
America	1,681	19.3	1.9	3,805	19.8	4.3	3,131	19.4	3.6	94	23.2	0.1	8,779	19.6	10.0
Asia	1,731	19.8	0.4	3,237	16.9	0.8	2,795	17.3	0.7	69	17.0	0.0	7,888	17.6	2.0
Australia & Oceania	340	3.9	11.5	855	4.5	28.8	859	5.3	29.0	8	2.0	0.3	2,145	4.8	72.3
Europe	2,605	29.8	3.6	6,655	34.7	9.2	5,718	35.4	7.9	112	27.7	0.2	15,211	34.0	20.9
World total	8,730	100.0	1.4	19,189	100.0	3.0	16,149	100.0	2.5	405	100.0	0.1	44,780	100.0	7.0

Non-governmental organisations

Continent	Conventional international bodies			Organisations emanating from places, persons, bodies			Organisations of special form			Internationally oriented organisations			All A-G international organisations		
	A-D	%	Membership density per million of population	E	%	Membership density per million of population	F	%	Membership density per million of population	G	%	Membership density per million of population	A-G	%	Membership density per million of population
Africa	22,998	12.7	26.3	4,891	12.0	5.6	13,680	16.5	15.6	3,409	17.7	3.9	45,067	13.9	51.5
America	31,083	17.2	35.4	6,629	16.3	7.6	15,422	18.6	17.6	4,114	21.4	4.7	57,361	17.7	65.4
Asia	31,240	17.3	8.1	6,255	15.3	1.6	14,262	17.2	3.7	3,932	20.4	1.0	55,752	17.2	14.5
Australia & Oceania	6,692	3.7	225.7	1,432	3.5	48.3	3,261	3.9	110.0	897	4.7	30.3	12,677	3.9	427.6
Europe	88,674	49.1	122.1	21,571	52.9	29.7	36,469	43.9	50.2	6,893	35.8	9.5	153,955	47.5	212.0
World total	180,687	100.0	28.4	40,778	100.0	6.4	83,094	100.0	13.1	19,245	100.0	3.0	324,152	100.0	50.9

All international organisations

Continent	Conventional international bodies			Organisations emanating from places, persons, bodies			Organisations of special form			Internationally oriented organisations			All A-G international organisations		
	A-D	%	Membership density per million of population	E	%	Membership density per million of population	F	%	Membership density per million of population	G	%	Membership density per million of population	A-G	%	Membership density per million of population
Africa	25,371	13.4	29.0	9,528	15.9	10.9	17,326	17.5	19.8	3,531	18.0	4.0	55,931	15.2	63.9
America	32,764	17.3	37.3	10,434	17.4	11.9	18,553	18.7	21.1	4,208	21.4	4.8	66,140	17.9	75.4
Asia	32,971	17.4	8.6	9,492	15.8	2.5	17,057	17.2	4.4	4,001	20.4	1.0	63,640	17.2	16.5
Australia & Oceania	7,032	3.7	237.2	2,287	3.8	77.1	4,120	4.2	139.0	905	4.6	30.5	14,822	4.0	499.9
Europe	91,279	48.2	125.7	28,226	47.1	38.9	42,187	42.5	58.1	7,005	35.6	9.6	169,165	45.9	232.9
World total	**189,417**	**100.0**	**29.8**	**59,967**	**100.0**	**9.4**	**99,243**	**100.0**	**15.6**	**19,650**	**100.0**	**3.1**	**368,932**	**100.0**	**58.0**

Source: Union of International Associations (2006), Yearbook of International Organizations 2005/2006, vol. 42, no. 5, Table 0.2.2 Participation in international organisations by type and continent, pp. 5-6.

Record 16: **NGOs and global governance**

Little agreement exists about the role of NGOs in global governance systems and processes. This record considers the involvement of NGOs in the global governance system from various perspectives. It shows not only the extent of their involvement and the issues in which they engage, but also how they are perceived by other actors. The first part of the record displays the numbers of NGOs participating in the World Trade Organization's ministerial conferences, and the numbers of INGOs holding participatory status with the Council of Europe. The second part of this record reveals the perceptions of 'civic engagement' on the part of World Bank staff in country offices around the world. This is based on a survey conducted by the World Bank in 61 of its country offices as part of an evaluation of the Small Grants Program. The third part of this record details the level of involvement and the aims of NGOs involved in World Bank Poverty Eradication Projects in the least developed Countries (LDcs).

The data in the record suggest that NGO participation in global governance systems is not extensive or increasing. The numbers of NGOs/INGOs participating in WTO ministerial conferences or holding participatory status with the Council of Europe do not show an increase, and the number of NGOs involved in World Bank poverty eradication projects is small compared to the total number of such projects. World Bank national offices do not always perceive civil society as a core element of civic engagement. Different manifestations of civil society, for example 'civil society organisations' or 'NGOs/CSOs' are most frequently mentioned as defining 'civic engagement' – but only by staff in less than half the World Bank's national offices. Civil society is not at the top of the list of observable behaviours associated with civic engagement and staff often highlight its weak organisational capacity and their negative perceptions of NGOs.

Donor	Number of NGOs per country participating in WTO ministerial conferences				Council of Europe Number of NGOs with participatory status	
	Seattle 1999	Doha 2001	Cancun* 2003	Hong Kong 2005	2005	2006
East Asia & Pacific						
Low income economies						
Cambodia				1		
Indonesia	2			1		
Vietnam				2		
Middle income economies						
China**				5		
Fiji	1	1	1	1		
Malaysia	3	6	6	6		
Philippines	6	15	15	26		
Samoa				1		
Thailand	1	10	10	8		
High income economies						
Australia	8	15	15	26	1	1
Japan	13	42	42	44		
Korea, Rep.		6	6			
New Zealand	1	3	3	5		
Europe & Central Asia						
Low income economies						
Azerbaijan				1		
Georgia	2	1	1			
Moldova					1	1
Ukraine				1		1
Middle income economies						
Bosnia & Herzegovina						1
Croatia				1		
Czech Republic		2	2		1	1
Hungary					5	4
Kazakhstan				1		
Macedonia		1	1			
Poland		1	1			
Romania					1	1
Russian Federation	1	1	1		6	6
Serbia & Montenegro						1
Slovenia					1	2

Donor	Number of NGOs per country participating in WTO ministerial conferences				Council of Europe Number of NGOs with participatory status	
	Seattle 1999	Doha 2001	Cancun* 2003	Hong Kong 2005	2005	2006
Turkey				3		
High income economies						
Austria		7	7	2	13	12
Belgium	37	64	64	50	85	89
Denmark	3	6	6	5	7	6
Finland	1	3	3	1	3	1
France	35	54	55	48	90	90
Germany	9	29	29	26	22	28
Greece		1	1		3	2
Iceland	1	1	1			
Ireland		3	3	1	1	2
Italy	2	11	11	7	16	13
Luxembourg			2			5
Netherlands	12	18	18	15	19	17
Norway	6	21	21	17		
Portugal				1		3
Spain	10	14	14	14	2	2
Sweden	4	6	6	6	3	3
Switzerland	16	39	39	31	37	37
United Kingdom	19	45	45	35	42	40
Latin America & Caribbean						
Low income economies						
Haiti				1		
Nicaragua		2	2			
Middle income economies						
Argentina	3	1	1	1		
Barbados		1	1			
Bolivia	1	5	5	2		
Brazil	3	18	18	12		
Chile	1	4	4		1	1
Colombia		6	6			
Costa Rica	1	1	1			
Ecuador	4	2	2	1		
El Salvador	1	2	2			

Donor	Number of NGOs per country participating in WTO ministerial conferences				Council of Europe	
					Number of NGOs with participatory status	
	Seattle 1999	Doha 2001	Cancun* 2003	Hong Kong 2005	2005	2006
El Salvador	1	2	2			
Guatemala		3	3	1		
Honduras		1	1			
Mexico	2	33	33	5		
Paraguay	1	1	1			
Peru	2	4	4			
Trinidad & Tobago	1	1	1			
Uruguay	3	1	1	2	1	1
Venezuela	1	1	1	3		
Middle East & North Africa						
Middle income economies						
Egypt	1	3	3			
Iran		1	1			
Jordan		2	2			
Lebanon		1	1	1		
Tunisia		3	3			
High income economies						
Israel			2	1		1
North America						
High income economies						
Canada	46	84	84	76	2	2
United States	187	236	236	181	5	6
South Asia						
Low income economies						
Bangladesh	1	2	2	8		
India	6	34	34	26		
Nepal		4	4	3		
Pakistan		9	9	4		
Middle income economies						
Sri Lanka				1		
Sub-Saharan Africa						
Low income economies						
Benin	1	1	1			
Burkina Faso		1	1	2		

Donor	Number of NGOs per country participating in WTO ministerial conferences				Council of Europe Number of NGOs with participatory status	
	Seattle 1999	Doha 2001	Cancun* 2003	Hong Kong 2005	2005	2006
Cameroon		3	3			
Côte d'Ivoire		2	2			
Ghana	2	4	4	5		
Guinea		1	1	1		
Kenya	5	11	11	9		
Madagascar		2	2			
Malawi		1	1			
Mali		2	2			
Mozambique		1	1			
Nigeria		1	1	1		
Senegal	1	1	1	4		
Sudan				1		
Tanzania		1	1	1		
Togo	1	1	1	1		
Uganda		10	10	2		
Zambia		3	3	4		
Zimbabwe	4	3	3	1		
Middle income economies						
Botswana	1					
Mauritius	1					
Namibia	1					
South Africa	2	8	8	11		

Donor	Number of NGOs per country participating in WTO ministerial conferences				Council of Europe Number of NGOs with participatory status	
	Seattle 1999	Doha 2001	Cancun* 2003	Hong Kong 2005	2005	2006
Low income	25	101	101	80	1	2
Middle income	41	140	140	93	16	18
Low & middle income:						
East Asia & Pacific	13	32	32	51		
Europe & Central Asia	2	6	6	8	15	18
Latin America & Caribbean	24	87	87	28	2	2
Middle East & North Africa	1	10	10	1		
South Asia	7	49	49	42		
Sub-Saharan Africa	19	57	57	43		
High income	410	708	713	592	351	360
World	**476**	**949**	**954**	**765**	**368**	**380**

* Data regarding Cancun includes NGOs eligible to attend the Fifth WTO Ministerial Conference.

** Data for Hong Kong, Macao and Taiwan are not included in this table.

Sources: WTO, http://www.wto.org/english/forums_e/ngo_e/ngo_e.htm; Council of Europe, http://www.coe.int/T/E/NGO/public/Participatory_status/

Perceptions of 'civic' engagement among World Bank country offices

% responses	Africa	East Asia & Pacific	Common-wealth of Ind. States (CIS	Eastern Europe & Central Asia (NonCIS)	Latin America & Caribbean	Middle East & North Africa	South Asia	Total
'In your country, how is 'civic engagement' understood or defined?'								
Civil society interacting with government	44	38	55	39	25			38
Organisations interacting with government	38	50	9	39	50	50	34	
Citizens interacting with government	25	25	18	23	25	67		25
Citizens interacting with organisations	6	13	27	39	38		50	23
Inclusion of vulnerable people	6	38	27	23		67	50	21
NGOs / CSOs	6	25		15	13	67		13
Partnering civil society – international organisations	19	13	9	8	13		12	
Government accountability	6	38	9					8
Volunteerism				15	13	33		7
Shared accountability	6		9		13	33		7
Decision making		13			13	33		5
Resources	6				13		50	5
Independent organisations		25			13			5
Legal framework	13				13			5
Communication				8	13	33		5
Voting	6				13			3
Free to mobilise						67		3
Philanthropy				8				2
'What are some observable behaviours associated with civic engagement?'								
Freely expressing views	13	38	27	46	25	33		28
Voting	19	25	18	46	13	33	100	28
Civil society collaborating	25	50	36	15	13	33		26
Demanding government action	25	25		31	25			20
Decision making	13	38	27		25		50	18
Creating CBOs		13	27	23		67	50	16
Raising public awareness			46	15			100	15
Volunteering			27	46				15
Participation by the vulnerable	25	13			25	33		13
Holding elections	13	13		15	13	67		13
Joining groups and participating	6	13		23				8
Media freely reporting	6	13		8		67		8

% responses	Africa	East Asia & Pacific	Common-wealth of Ind. States (CIS	Eastern Europe & Central Asia (NonCIS)	Latin America & Caribbean	Middle East & North Africa	South Asia	Total
Donors and businesses collaborating	13	13		8				7
Making informed decisions	13			8	13			7
Providing direct services				8	38			7
Providing oversight				8	25			5
Making donations					15			3
Creating legislation			9					2
'What obstacles exist to monitoring civic engagement, and how might these obstacles be overcome?'								
Lack of data	38	25	27	31	25	67	50	33
Weak organisational capacity	19	25	46	15		33		21
Negative perception of NGOs	13	25	27	31		33		20
Government shortcomings	13	38		15	38			16
Lack of monitoring and evaluation system	6	25	9	15	25	33	15	
Non-institutionalised partnerships	6		27	8				8
Lack of resources	13	13		8	13			8
Illiteracy	31							8
Lack of legal framework		25	9		13			7
Language barriers					13			2

Source: Making a little go a long way: How the world bank's small grants program promotes civic engagement.
Social Development Papers, no. 47, September 2003. Appendix e: Country-level concepts of civic engagement and empowerment.
http://siteresources.worldbank.org/INTSMALLGRANTS/64168360-1113891163797/20507376/SmGP+Evaluation+Final+Report2.pdf

Civil society involvement in poverty eradication in least developed countries

Country	Number of projects implemented	Number of participating NGOs
East Asia & Pacific		
Low income economies		
Cambodia	14	
Laos	9	
Myanmar	11	
Solomon Islands	11	
Middle income economies		
Kiribati	3	
Samoa	8	
Thailand		1
Vanuatu	1	
High income		
Australia		3
Japan		2
Europe & Central Asia		
Middle income economies		
Russian Federation		2
High income economies		
Belgium		6
United Kingdom		8
France		7
Germany		2
Greece		1
Italy		5
Luxembourg		1
Malta		1
Netherlands		1
Spain		3
Sweden		1
Switzerland		8
Latin America & Caribbean		
Low income economies		
Haiti	17	

Country	Number of projects implemented	Number of participating NGOs
Middle income economies		
Brazil		4
Chile		1
Guatemala		1
Peru		1
Uruguay		1
Middle East & North Africa		
Low income economies		
Yemen	5	1
Middle income economies		
Algeria		1
Djibouti	4	1
Egypt		2
Iraq		1
Lebanon		1
Morocco		1
Tunisia		3
North America		
High income economies		
Canada		2
United States		23
South Asia		
Low income economies		
Afghanistan	12	
Bangladesh	31	2
Bhutan	5	
India		7
Nepal	28	
Middle income economies		
Maldives	6	
Sub-Saharan Africa		
Low income economies		
Angola	15	
Benin	25	1
Burkina Faso	23	

Country	Number of projects implemented	Number of participating NGOs
Burundi	16	2
Cameroon		3
Central African Republic	14	
Chad	12	
Comoros	3	
Côte d'Ivoire		1
Congo, Dem. Rep.	29	3
Equatorial Guinea	6	
Eritrea	6	
Ethiopia	20	
Gambia	14	
Guinea	12	
Guinea-Bissau	4	
Lesotho	11	
Liberia	13	
Madagascar	20	
Malawi	18	
Mali	20	
Mauritania	20	9
Mozambique	21	1
Niger	15	2
Nigeria		2
Rwanda	22	
São Tomé & Principe	3	1
Senegal	25	1
Sierra Leone	21	
Somalia	6	
Sudan	9	
Togo	21	4
Uganda	27	
Tanzania	25	
Zambia	24	
Middle income economies		
Cape Verde	5	
Survey total*	**691**	**135**

Country	Number of projects implemented	Number of participating NGOs
Low income	663	40
Middle income	27	21
Low & middle income		
East Asia & Pacific	57	1
Europe & Central Asia	0	2
Latin America & Caribbean	17	8
Middle East & North Africa	9	11
South Asia	82	9
Sub-Saharan Africa	525	30
High income		74
Survey total	**690**	**135**

* Grand total for projects includes one project in a country with less than 100,000 population, which is not shown in the table.

Source: NGO/Civil Society Forum, Survey Report: NGO/Civil Society and Poverty Eradication in least developed countries preparitory NGO/Civil Society Forum and Panel for the ECOSOC High Level Segment, June 2004.

Aims of NGOs involved in poverty eradication in LDCs

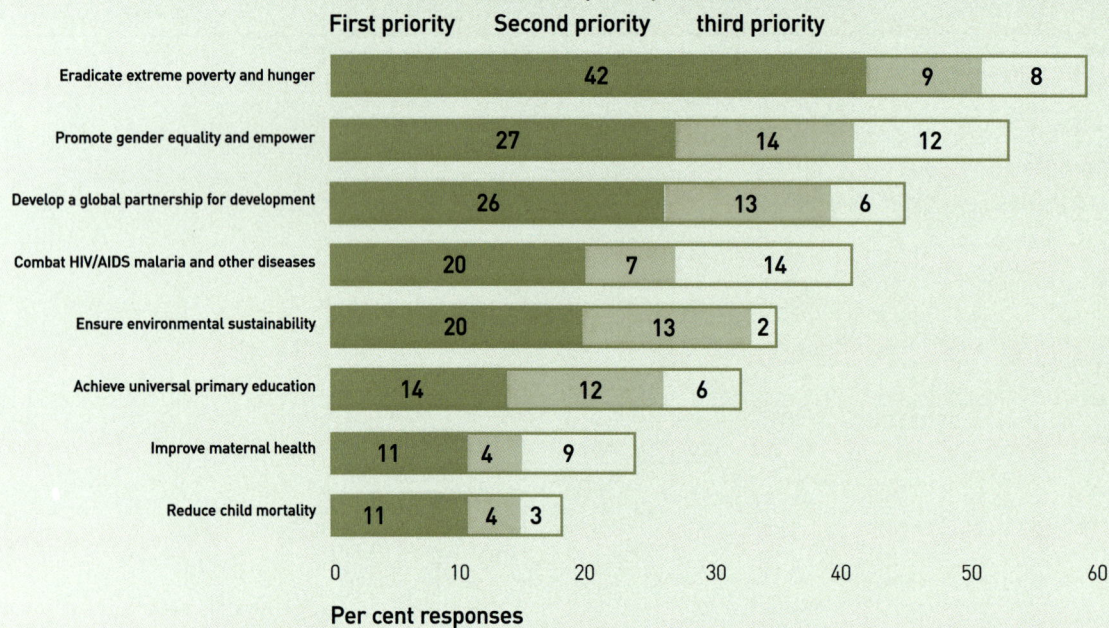

First priority   **Second priority**   **third priority**

Aim	First	Second	Third
Eradicate extreme poverty and hunger	42	9	8
Promote gender equality and empower	27	14	12
Develop a global partnership for development	26	13	6
Combat HIV/AIDS malaria and other diseases	20	7	14
Ensure environmental sustainability	20	13	2
Achieve universal primary education	14	12	6
Improve maternal health	11	4	9
Reduce child mortality	11	4	3

0   10   20   30   40   50   60

Per cent responses

Record 17: NGO-government relations: funding and assessment

NGOs have complicated relationships with governments, which can entail variously, cooperation, dependence, competition, evaluation, and other forms of interaction. The tables in this record demonstrate two aspects of government-NGO relations – financial support from governments to NGOs, and evaluation of NGOs by government for the purpose of strategically planning aid policies. The first table displays financial support given by OECD member states to NGOs in their countries and to international NGOs, as well as the percentage change in such assistance, which shows a substantial increase in support in most OECD countries, particularly for international NGOs. The second table lists the scores of the Central and Eastern Europe and Eurasia NGO Sustainability Index, which is issued by USAID. This evaluation is used by USAID and other agencies as a management tool to shape funding policies, inform programme design, and monitor and measure progress. The Index is composed of seven dimensions and a composite index score, which are presented in the table. Index scores range from 1 – high sustainability, to 7 – low sustainability (hence, lower index scores reflect increased sustainability).

OECD data show a general increase in the financial support of NGOs by most OECD members. While OECD members granted more funds to NGOs in their own countries, the financial support they offer to international NGOs has grown at a much faster pace, especially among EU members. Percentage changes in USAID's evaluation of NGOs between 1998 and 2004 reflect a predominantly positive trend in the sustainability of civil society in the region.

OECD Development Assistance: gross disbursements to NGOs

Donor	Support to national NGOs			Support to international NGOs		
	US $ (million) 1994	US $ (million) 2004	% change 1994-2004	US $ (million) 1994	US $ (million) 2004	% change 1994-2004
Countries						
Australia	21.59	0.16	-99	4.87	3.39	-30
Austria	2.21	0.14	-94	1.10	1.32	20
Belgium	1.63	23.06	1,315	0.03	6.62	21,967
Canada	122.95	1.34	-99	14.18	17.57	24
Denmark	6.79	11.21	65			
Finland	3.77	6.00	59	1.22	1.81	48
France	19.61	35.45	81		14.87	
Germany	195.23			5.43	9.80	80
Greece		0.11				
Ireland	0.22	95.11	43,132	0.89	43.38	4,774
Italy	25.10	45.25	80	7.38	5.65	-23
Japan	152.19	248.42	63	16.20	135.17	734
Korea, Rep.		1.75			0.40	
Luxembourg	0.40	28.31	6,978		0.55	
Netherlands	316.91	657.73	108		7.40	
New Zealand	2.46	12.47	407	0.24	2.39	896
Norway				9.28	16.91	82
Portugal	0.13	3.58	2,654		0.25	
Spain	0.42	6.95	1,555	1.24	1.54	24
Sweden	117.92	137.10	16		2.40	
Switzerland	117.86	50.07	-58	43.89	63.05	44
Turkey		0.07				
United Kingdom	61.11	428.82	602	16.40	263.84	1,509
Multilateral	154.52	1.10	-99		0.64	
Aggregations	154.52	1.10	-90		0.64	
G7, total	380.96	759.28	99	59.59	441.25	640
EU members	555.82	1,472.84	165	33.66	351.97	946
Development Co-operation Directorate (DAC) countries	972.87	1,785.14	83	122.32	590.45	383
Non-DAC bilateral donors		1.82			0.40	
All donors	1,127.39	1,788.06	59	122.32	591.49	384

Where data for a particular year are not available, figures are taken from the year before or after as an estimate. These figures, and estimates based on them, are presented in italics.

Source: OECD Development Assistance Committee, http://www1.oecd.org/scripts/cde/viewbase.asp?dbname=cde_dac

USAID: Central and Eastern Europe and Eurasia NGO Sustainability Index

Country	Sub-indices scores, 2004							Overall index scores, 1998-2004							
	Legal environment	Organisational capacity	Financial viability	Advocacy	Service provision	Infrastructure	Public image	1998	1999	2000	2001	2002	2003	2004	% change 2000-2004
Albania	3.4	4.0	4.5	3.7	3.9	4.2	4.2	4.2	4.8	4.6	4.6	4.3	4.1	3.9	-15
Armenia	3.8	4.0	5.5	3.7	4.0	3.9	3.9		5.1	2.0	4.4	4.2	4.1	4.1	105
Azerbaijan	5.0	4.7	5.8	4.8	4.6	4.6	5.1	6.4	5.7	5.0	4.9	5.2	4.1	4.9	-2
Belarus	6.9	4.6	6.2	6.0	4.9	5.0	5.6			5.7	5.5	5.3	5.6	5.6	-2
Bosnia	3.5	3.8	5.0	3.3	4.3	4.4	3.6	5.6	5.2	4.0	4.5	4.2	4.1	4.0	0
Bulgaria	2.0	4.5	4.1	2.5	3.2	2.9	3.3	3.6	4.0	3.7	3.6	3.1	3.1	3.2	-14
Croatia	3.2	3.4	4.4	3.4	3.3	3.2	3.3	4.4	4.7	4.3	3.8	3.7	3.5	3.5	-19
Czech Republic	3.0	3.2	2.7	2.2	2.2	3.0	2.5			2.4	2.3	2.5	2.4	2.7	13
Estonia	1.8	2.5	2.5	2.0	2.4	1.7	2.1			2.4	2.1	2.2	2.2	2.1	-13
Georgia	3.5	3.8	4.8	3.7	4.1	3.9	3.7	3.4	3.8	4.0	4.0	4.2	4.1	3.9	-3
Hungary	1.3	3.0	3.3	3.3	2.3	2.3	3.0	1.6	2.0	2.3	2.6	2.6	2.7	2.6	13
Kazakhstan	4.2	3.8	5.0	3.6	4.1	3.6	4.2	4.4	4.8	4.7	4.3	4.1	3.9	4.1	-13
Kosovo	3.0	4.0	5.3	3.5	4.0	3.4	3.7		4.4	4.6	4.6	4.3	4.2	3.8	-17
Kyrgyzstan	3.7	4.3	5.0	4.0	4.1	3.6	4.3	3.9	4.1	4.3	4.3	4.1	4.1	4.2	-2
Latvia	2.4	3.0	3.1	2.0	2.4	2.7	2.9	4.2		2.8	2.9	2.8	2.7	2.6	-7
Lithuania	1.8	2.6	3.0	2.0	3.7	3.0	3.0	3.1	3.0	3.2	3.0	2.8	2.6	2.7	-16
Macedonia	2.9	3.7	4.5	3.1	3.9	3.2	3.8	4.4	4.6	4.6	4.2	4.0	3.7	3.6	-22
Moldova	4.2	4.1	5.2	4.0	4.5	3.7	4.2			4.6	4.2	4.2	4.3	4.3	-7
Montenegro	3.3	4.7	5.2	4.0	4.0	4.3	4.6		4.6	4.6	4.7	4.6	4.5	4.3	-7
Poland	2.3	2.5	2.9	1.9	2.3	1.9	2.2	2.0	2.1	2.1	2.1	2.2	2.1	2.3	10
Romania	3.8	3.8	4.3	3.6	3.1	3.5	3.8	3.8	4.1	4.1	4.0	3.7	3.8	3.7	-10
Russia	4.3	4.0	4.6	4.2	3.9	3.8	4.5	3.4	4.1	4.3	4.3	4.0	4.4	4.2	-2
Serbia	4.5	3.9	5.6	3.8	4.5	3.7	4.5	5.4	5.4	4.5	4.1	4.1	4.0	4.4	-2
Slovakia	2.3	2.3	3.5	2.2	2.2	2.2	2.6	2.8	2.1	1.9	1.9	2.1	2.2	2.5	32
Slovenia	3.7	4.2	4.5	3.8	3.6	4.2	4.1						3.4	4.0	
Tajikistan	4.3	4.8	5.6	4.6	4.6	4.3	4.4	6.6	6.1	5.4	5.1	4.6	4.6	4.6	-15
Turkmenistan	6.5	5.2	5.8	6.1	4.8	4.6	5.8		6.6	6.0	5.8	5.6	5.7	5.6	-7
Ukraine	3.6	3.9	4.6	3.1	3.3	3.8	4.1	4.2	4.1	4.4	4.3	4.0	3.9	3.8	-14
Uzbekistan	5.2	5.0	5.7	5.6	5.2	4.8	5.4	4.7	5.3	5.1	4.6	4.7	4.7	5.2	2

Source: USAID (2005), The 2004 Sustainability Index for Central and Eastern Europe and Eurasia, Statistical annexes,
http://www.usaid.gov/locations/europe_eurasia/dem_gov/ngoindex/2004/

Philanthropy is an important source of the viability and sustainability of global civil society. It is also one of the main vehicles by which global civil society actors achieve their missions. This record provides a glimpse of two aspects of international philanthropy – foundation giving and disaster relief. The first table presents contributions for disaster relief, as reported by the United Nations Office for the Coordination of Humanitarian Affairs (OCHA). The data is based on information provided by donors and organisations, and dates from February 2006. A 'pledge' indicates a non-binding announcement of an intended contribution or allocation by the donor (in this table an 'uncommitted pledge' indicates the balance of original pledges not yet transferred). A 'commitment' is a legal contractual obligation between the donor and recipient, which specifies the amount to be contributed. A 'contribution' is the actual payment of funds or transfer of in-kind goods from the donor to the recipient. Although the data is of relief contributions and commitments made in 2005, it is strongly dominated by relief to South-East Asia affected by the December 2004 tsunami. Other relief funds, even when they amount to millions, are dwarfed by the extent of the global response to this mega-disaster.

The second table offers a time series of US philanthropic foundations' international grant-making. The graphs show an increase in grants to international recipients between 1998 and 2000, followed by a slump after 2001 due to the 9/11 attacks and the diversion of US philanthropy to domestic disaster relief. The 2001 decline is more noticeable in the 'share of' chart because the attacks took place in September, when most grants had been finalised. The dip appears to be temporary because the upward trend in international grant-giving reappears in 2003 and increases in 2004, although the increase is mostly in grants to US-based organisations engaged in international work.

Natural disaster relief

Region and Disaster	Country	Date	Commitments/ contributions (US$)	% total	Uncommitted pledges (US$)
East Asia & Pacific					
Earthquake	Indonesia	Mar 2005	3,628,543	0.0	264,200
Earthquake	China	Nov 2005	166,465	0.0	
Floods	China	Jun 2005	471,294	0.0	
Typhoon	Vietnam	Sep 2005	837,290	0.0	
Typhoon / floods	China	Sep 2005	86,298	0.0	
Region total			**5,189,890**	**0.0**	**264,200**
Europe & Central Asia					
Floods	Georgia	Apr 2005	1,161,943	0.0	
Floods	Tajikistan	Jul 2005	740,580	0.0	
Floods	Bulgaria	Jul 2005	2,650,335	0.0	
Floods	Macedonia	Aug 2005	10,000	0.0	
Floods	Romania	Jul 2005	3,480,285	0.0	
Floods	Romania	Jun 2005	674,791	0.0	
Floods	Serbia & Montenegro	Apr 2005	332,629	0.0	
Floods & mudflows	Kyrgyzstan	Jun 2005	25,000	0.0	
Snow avalanche	Tajikistan	Feb 2005	292,618	0.0	
Region total			**9,368,181**	**0.0**	
Latin America & Caribbean					
Earthquake	Chile	Jun 2005	150,000	0.0	
Floods	Colombia	Feb 2005	204,269	0.0	
Floods	Costa Rica	Jan 2005	300,528	0.0	
Floods	Costa Rica	Sep 2005	80,000	0.0	
Floods	Venezuela	Feb 2005	273,627	0.0	
Floods & mudslides	Guatemala	May 2006	29,054,371	0.4	5,012,191
Floods & volcanic activity	El Salvador	Oct 2005	10,345,000	0.1	4,880,178
Floods & volcanic activity	Guyana	Jan 2005	7,296,697	0.1	405,500
Hurricane Beta	Nicaragua	Oct 2005	414,379	0.0	
Hurricane Dennise		Jul 2005	1,178,981	0.0	
Hurricane Emily		Jul 2005	1,530,378	0.0	
Hurricane Stan	Mexico	Oct 2005	5,000	0.0	
Hurricane Wilma		Oct 2005	979,540	0.0	
Storm	Uruguay	Aug 2005	204,085	0.0	
Tropical Storm Gamma	Honduras	Dec 2005	558,301	0.0	
Region total			**52,575,156**	**0.6**	**10,297,869**

Region and Disaster	Country	Date	Commitments/ contributions (US$)	% total	Uncommitted pledges (US$)
Middle East & North Africa					
Drought	Djibouti	Apr 2005	2,746,769	0.0	
Earthquake	Iran	Feb 2005	1,944,061	0.0	
Region total			4,690,830	0.0	
South Asia					
Earthquake		Oct 2005	1,069,281,322	14.4	1,111,782,674
Earthquake / Tsunami	Indian Ocean	Dec 2004	6,182,816,482	83.1	604,455,062
Floods	Afghanistan	Jun 2005	1,005,526	0.0	
Floods	India	Jul 2005	111,600	0.0	
Floods	Pakistan	Jul 2005	1,156,348	0.0	
Rains / snowfall	Pakistan	Feb 2005	1,300,148	0.0	
Severe winter conditions	Afghanistan	Feb 2005	899,976	0.0	
Region total			7,256,571,402	97.5	1,716,237,736
Sub-Saharan Africa					
Drought & locust invasion food security	Niger	May 2005	106,287,693	1.4	9,727,154
Floods	Central African Rep	Aug 2005	439,936	0.0	
Floods	Sierra Leone	Aug 2005	176,260	0.0	
Karthala volcano	Comoros	Nov 2005	12,000	0.0	705,882
Volcanic eruption	Comoros	Apr 2005	761,080	0.0	
Region total			107,676,969	1.4	10,433,036
Total (US $)			**7,436,607,267**	**100.0**	**1,737,376,725**

Donor	Commitments/ contributions (US$)	% total	Uncommitted pledges (US$)
Region			
East Asia & Pacific			
Australia	50,922,307	0.7	29,859,474
China	63,288,011	0.9	21,038,042
Japan	531,923,379	7.2	17,550,000
Region total	**646,133,697**	**8.8**	**68,447,516**
Europe			
Denmark	58,311,313	0.8	5,193,446
Finland	40,003,688	0.5	542,509
France	83,017,742	1.1	28,238,858
Germany	167,691,759	2.3	7,652,223
Greece	33,332,901	0.4	865,162
Ireland	39,811,643	0.5	2,212,396
Italy	71,672,797	1.0	1,810,868
Netherlands	83,773,292	1.1	
Norway	149,636,388	2.0	19,307,587
Spain	31,737,097	0.4	
Sweden	82,921,306	1.1	5,682,072
Switzerland	37,882,113	0.5	14,135,527
Turkey	74,379,459	1.0	
United Kingdom	255,575,838	3.4	17,205,150
European Commission (ECHO)	144,598,563	1.9	99,020,896
Region total	**1,354,345,899**	**18.0**	**201,866,694**
Middle East & North Africa			
Qatar	45,598,573	0.6	
Saudi Arabia	54,180,584	0.7	273,297,432
United Arab Emirates	52,771,278	0.7	100,100,000
Region total	152,550,435	2.0	373,397,432
North America			
Canada	154,593,174	2.1	15,266,639
United States	357,882,636	4.8	234,015,624
Region total	512,475,810	6.9	249,282,263
Other			
Private (individuals & organisations)	4,403,918,485	59.2	262,106,772
Un-earmarked UN funds	47,721,142	0.6	
Others	319,461,799	4.3	582,276,048
World total	**7,436,607,267**	**100.0**	**1,737,376,725**

Source: Reliefweb, UN Office for the Coordination of Humanitarian Affairs (OCHA), Financial Tracking Service (FTS), The Global Humanitarian Aid Database, http://www.reliefweb.int/fts

Cash grants US$

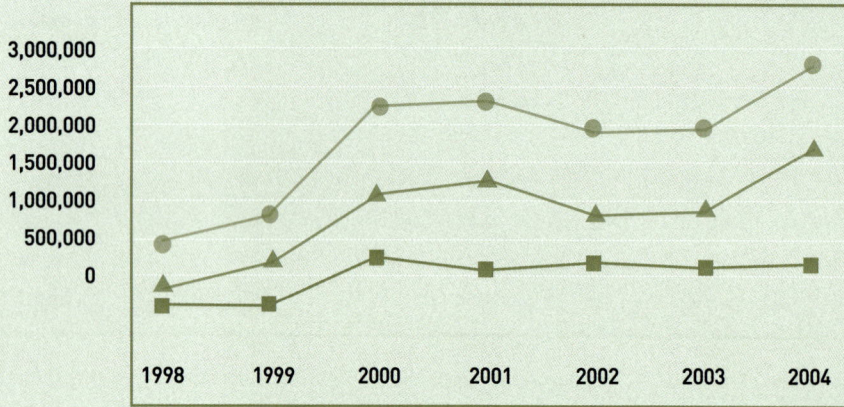

Share of total US foundation grants (%)

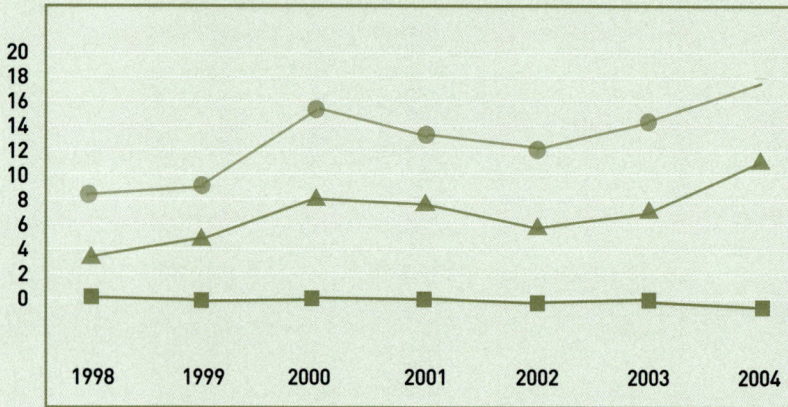

- International grants, total
- Grants to overseas recipients
- Grants to US-based recipients

US foundation grants to international recipients, 1998-2004*

		1998	1999	2000	2001	2002	2003	2004
International grants, total								
Sum of grants	US $ (1,000s)	1,037,245	1,315,035	2,450,716	2,462,013	2,194,975	2,200,077	2,833,641
As share of all grants by US foundations	%	10.7	11.3	16.3	14.7	13.8	15.4	18.3
Number of grants	number	8,964	9,593	10,874	11,494	11,396	10,558	10,676
As share of all grants by US foundations	%	9.2	8.9	9.1	9.2	8.9	8.7	8.4
Grants to overseas recipients								
Sum of grants	US $ (1,000s)	416,114	430,100	901,346	770,671	842,767	810,397	821,612
As share of all grants by US foundations	%	4.3	3.7	6.0	4.6	5.3	5.7	5.3
Number of grants	number	3,796	3,798	4,459	4,703	4,506	4,357	4,091
As share of all grants by US foundations	%	3.9	3.5	3.7	3.8	3.5	3.6	3.2
Grants to US-based recipients								
Sum of grants	US $ (1,000s)	621,131	884,935	1,549,370	1,691,343	1,352,207	1,389,680	2,012,029
As share of all grants by US foundations	%	6.4	7.6	10.3	10.1	8.5	9.7	13
Number of grants	number	5,168	5,795	6,415	6,791	6,890	6,201	6,585
As share of all grants by US foundations	%	5.3	5.4	5.4	5.4	5.4	5.1	5.2

*Based on grants of $10,000 or more awarded by a national sample of 1,010 larger US foundations (including 800 of the 1,000 largest ranked by total giving). For community

foundations, only discretionary grants are included. Grants to individuals are not included.
Source: The Foundation Center, Foundation Giving trends, International Funding, 2006, http://foundationcenter.org/findfunders/statistics/gs_geo_int.html

US foundation grants to top 50 international recipients*

Country	Total grants (US$) 2000	Number of grants 2000	Total grants (US$) 2001	Number of grants 2001	Total grants (TUS$) 2002	Number of grants 2002	Total grants (US$) 2003	Number of grants 2003	Total grants (US$) 2004	Number of grants 2004
East Asia & Pacific										
Low income economies										
Mongolia					1,896,343	1			3,304,140	1
Vietnam			1,854,750	1						
Middle income economies										
China**	4,721,487	26	7,885,690	20	2,068,700	1	8,233,955	44	5,044,442	4
Fiji									2,800,000	2
Philippines	6,725,000	6			1,864,544	3	5,790,984	3	3,334,465	1
Thailand					4,530,000	1				
High income economies										
Australia									14,792,730	2
Korea, Rep.					57,084,470	6				
Europe & Central Asia										
Middle income economies										
Armenia			4,191,261	1	39,010,658	1	79,477,242	2	22,418,266	2
Poland					3,212,500	3	10,788,500	6	6,500,000	2
Russian Federation**	7,532,579	7	6,388,595	4	10,145,242	5	7,614,937	3	4,591,542	1
High income economies										
Austria					6,150,000	3	3,775,199	4		
Belgium					3,950,000	4				
France	2,098,000	4								
Germany							4,363,130	1	3,680,510	1
Italy									2,695,000	4
Netherlands			5,334,800	6						
Spain									4,628,291	2
Switzerland	55,843,644	22	108,953,571	19	31,147,855	20	79,172,064	22	126,337,105	26
United Kingdom	247,967,304	82	61,554,586	99	50,953,951	108	44,126,084	42	29,303,605	50
Latin America & Caribbean										
Caribbean, unspecified			8,415,540	1						
Low income economies										
Haiti					1,716,000	1				

	Total grants (US$) 2000	Number of grants 2000	Total grants (US$) 2001	Number of grants 2001	Total grants (TUS$) 2002	Number of grants 2002	Total grants (US$) 2003	Number of grants 2003	Total grants (US$) 2004	Number of grants 2004
Middle income economies										
Argentina					1,736,000	3				
Brazil			1,916,795	4	2,450,000	2				
Chile	10,192,157	2							4,462,894	1
Colombia	2,073,575	7					1,940,788	7		
Costa Rica									2,375,000	1
Honduras									2,045,300	3
Mexico	16,378,750	22	16,518,358	30	30,625,089	6	4,444,650	10		
Peru			1,750,000	1	15,525,718	1				
High income economies										
Bermuda			2,031,020	2						
Middle East & North Africa										
Middle income economies										
Egypt	2,381,000	12			2,120,000	7				
Palestinian Authority	2,090,000	6								
High income economies										
Israel	6,801,000	2	13,102,605	10	22,998,119	2	26,866,817	18	30,370,167	7
North America										
High income economies										
Canada	19,975,407	44			4,887,215	22	32,875,230	11	10,604,803	3
South Asia										
Low income economies										
Bangladesh	3,517,930	3	7,106,158	5			6,939,606	1		
India	5,000,000	1	1,946,712	4	5,894,271	2	17,000,000	2	12,978,870	1
Pakistan	2,487,325	2							6,568,888	1
Sub-Saharan Africa										
Low income economies										
Ghana					4,020,230	3				
Kenya	3,520,000	5	9,419,825	18	4,239,666	12	2,760,000	1		
Mozambique	2,388,400	6								
Nigeria	2,000,000	1	10,065,500	5			4,000,000	2	10,760,000	9
Tanzania			4,728,386	6					5,468,300	4
Uganda	4,351,711	31	8,080,836	32	8,776,664	26	4,244,304	15	11,656,441	16
Zimbabwe			2,222,584	16	4,978,425	17	9,075,847	3	2,575,440	6

	Total grants (US$) 2000	Number of grants 2000	Total grants (US$) 2001	Number of grants 2001	Total grants (TUS$) 2002	Number of grants 2002	Total grants (US$) 2003	Number of grants 2003	Total grants (US$) 2004	Number of grants 2004
Middle income economies										
Botswana					2,032,300	1				
South Africa	20,817,080	20	17,519,344	52	36,380,564	70	11,967,388	43	15,631,090	48

*Based on grants of $10,000 or more awarded by a national sample of 1,010 larger US foundations (including 800 of the 1,000 largest ranked by total giving). For community foundations, only discretionary grants are included. Grants to individuals are not included.

** China includes grants given to recipients in Hong Kong; Russian Federation includes grants given to recipients in Federation of Independent States.

Source: The Foundation Center, Foundation Giving Trends, International Funding, 2006, http://foundationcenter.org/findfunders/statistics/gs_geo_int.html

Record 19: Religion

This new record presents information from the World Christian Database, the European Values Survey, and World Values Survey on three aspects of religion:

1. the prevalence of various faiths around the world, as well as self-perceptions of religiosity, which reflect not only which religions are most practised in different countries, but also the level of religious diversity in these countries.
2. the level of religious freedom across the world (an approximation of the state of religious liberty in each country, based on the full range of religious rights specified in the Universal Declaration of Human Rights).
3. the extent of evangelisation as an indicator of the globalisation of religion. Data for evangelisation includes exposure to Christian broadcasting, defined as the total audience for Christian programs via Christian and secular stations in each country, expressed as a percentage of this country's population; number of missionaries, defined by the number of aliens (persons of another family, race or place) at work as missionaries, per million of the country's population; and new Christians, defined as the annual percent increase in the number of affiliated Christian population between 1990 and 2000 in each country.

The data show that most of the world's population consider themselves to be religious and that most countries are relatively homogenous when it comes to faith. We also see that religious freedom is infringed in almost half the countries in the world. The data on evangelisation reveal that such efforts are most extensive in East Asia and the Pacific, and in Latin America and the Caribbean, yet the spread of Christianity has been most extensive in South Asia and in Sub-Saharan Africa.

Country	Religiosity				Evangelisation			Religious freedom
	Predominant religion	Share of total population (%)	A religious person (%)	Not a religious person (%)	A convinced atheist (%)	Christian broadcasting exposure (%) population	Missionaries received (per million population)	New Christians annual % growth	
East Asia & Pacific									
Low income economies									
Cambodia	Buddhist	86				7	20.2	6.6	State hostility and prohibition
East Timor	Christian	84				24	116.6	1.7	Limited state subsidies to churches
Indonesia	Muslim	54	85	15	0	24	26.6	2.5	Limited state subsidies to churches
Korea, Dem. Rep.	Nonreligious	56				4	0.9	1.3	State suppression or eradication
Laos	Ethnoreligionist	49				3	13.5	6.5	State interference and obstruction
Mongolia	Ethnoreligionist	32				3	150.0	6.2	State suppression or eradication
Myanmar	Buddhist	73				3	3.9	3.1	State interference and obstruction
Papua New Guinea	Christian	95				45	626.6	3.1	Limited state subsidies to churches
Solomon Islands	Christian	95				45	991.3	3.5	State subsidises schools only
Vietnam	Buddhist	49	38	49	12	5	14.4	2.7	State interference and obstruction

Country	Predominant religion	Religiosity				Evangelisation			Religious freedom
		Share of total population (%)	A religious person (%)	Not a religious person (%)	A convinced atheist (%)	Christian broacasting exposure (%) population	Missionaries received (per million population)	New Christians annual % growth	
Middle income economies									
China*	Nonreligious	40	15	59	26	15	3.1	4.3	State hostility and prohibition
Fiji	Christian	57				45	702.2	1.7	State subsidises schools only
Malaysia	Muslim	46				9	39.5	4.3	State interference and obstruction
Micronesia	Christian	93				98	4,306.3	0.9	Complete state non-interference
Philippines	Christian	89	79	21	0	60	114.7	2.4	Limited state subsidies to churches
Samoa	Christian	96				75	4,404.8	1.4	State subsidises schools only
Thailand	Buddhist	83				14	31.2	1.7	Limited state subsidies to churches
Tonga	Christian	93				56	3,780.8	1.2	Massive state subsidies to churches
Vanuatu	Christian	93				24	1,349.9	3.1	Limited state subsidies to churches
High income economies									
Australia	Christian	77				65	219.0	1.4	Limited state subsidies to churches
Brunei	Muslim	54				3	80.2	3.1	Limited political restrictions
Japan	Buddhist	55	26	60	14	40	58.6	1.5	Complete state non-interference
Korea, Rep.	Christian	41	31	38	31	50	58.1	1.6	Limited political restrictions
New Caledonia	Christian	87				57	1,265.9	2.3	State subsidises schools only
New Zealand	Christian	75				72	712.1	0.8	Limited state subsidies to churches
Taiwan	Chinese universist	51				55	129.1	2.0	Limited political restrictions
Europe & Central Asia									
Low income economies									
Armenia	Christian	83				13	16.4	0.6	Limited state subsidies to churches
Azerbaijan	Muslim	87				1	11.7	1.0	State hostility and prohibition
Georgia	Christian	64				25	19.9	1.4	Complete state non-interference
Kyrgyzstan	Muslim	65				3	9.5	3.0	State interference and obstruction
Moldova	Christian	69	91	8	1	20	117.4	1.5	Complete state non-interference
Tajikistan	Muslim	84				1	6.3	2.5	State hostility and prohibition
Ukraine	Christian	80	77	20	3	45	87.9	0.8	Complete state non-interference
Uzbekistan	Muslim	76				4	7.4	2.0	State interference and obstruction
Middle income economies									
Albania	Muslim	43	68	26	6	25	248.4	2.5	Minorities discriminated against

Country	Predominant religion	Religiosity				Evangelisation			Religious freedom
		Share of total population (%)	A religious person (%)	Not a religious person (%)	A convinced atheist (%)	Christian broacasting exposure (%) population	Missionaries received (per million population)	New Christians annual % growth	
Belarus	Christian	70	28	63	9	20	51.0	1.4	Minorities discriminated against
Bosnia & Herzegovina	Muslim	61	74	20	6	12	130.7	1.0	State interference and obstruction
Bulgaria	Christian	84	52	41	7	6	25.8	1.2	State interference and obstruction
Croatia	Christian	91	84	12	4	19	340.5	1.0	Complete state non-interference
Czech Republic	Christian	64	45	47	9	10	146.8	1.4	State hostility and prohibition
Estonia	Christian	65	41	52	7	35	115.9	1.8	Complete state non-interference
Hungary	Christian	88	57	37	6	65	122.6	1.0	State interference and obstruction
Kazakhstan	Muslim	50				7	13.0	2.0	State interference and obstruction
Latvia	Christian	67	77	20	3	34	176.6	0.6	Limited political restrictions
Lithuania	Christian	88	84	14	2	28	117.6	1.4	Complete state non-interference
Macedonia	Christian	64	84	16	0	22	72.3	0.7	Complete state non-interference
Poland	Christian	96	94	4	2	82	18.2	1.0	State interference and obstruction
Romania	Christian	94	85	14	1	25	45.0	1.5	State interference and obstruction
Russian Federation	Christian	60	67	28	5	35	134.2	1.6	State hostility and prohibition
Serbia & Montenegro	Christian	66	74	23	3	46	95.1	1.2	Limited political restrictions
Slovakia	Christian	85	82	14	4	10	184.8	1.5	Complete state non-interference
Slovenia	Christian	91	70	21	9	22	404.2	0.9	Complete state non-interference
Turkey	Muslim	97	78	20	1	2	6.8	1.0	State interference and obstruction
Turkmenistan	Muslim	88				1	10.0	2.5	State hostility and prohibition
High income economies									
Austria	Christian	82	81	17	2	78	184.7	0.4	Massive state subsidies to churches
Belgium	Christian	84	65	27	8	69	251.0	0.6	Massive state subsidies to churches
Cyprus	Christian	94				43	321.0	1.6	Minorities discriminated against
Denmark	Christian	88	77	18	5	65	260.0	1.0	Massive state subsidies to churches
Finland	Christian	90	64	33	3	58	95.7	0.9	Massive state subsidies to churches
France	Christian	69	46	39	15	65	263.5	1.1	State subsidises schools only
Germany	Christian	75	56	37	8	60	121.1	1.0	Complete state non-interference
Greece	Christian	93	80	16	5	63	45.5	1.4	Massive state subsidies to churches
Iceland	Christian	96	74	23	3	73	136.2	1.5	Massive state subsidies to churches
Ireland	Christian	96	76	22	1	83	123.8	1.8	Complete state non-interference

Country	Predominant religion	Religiosity				Evangelisation			Religious freedom
		Share of total population (%)	A religious person (%)	Not a religious person (%)	A convinced atheist (%)	Christian broadcasting exposure (%) population	Missionaries received (per million population)	New Christians annual % growth	
Italy	Christian	82	86	12	3	68	209.6	1.1	Limited state subsidies to churches
Luxembourg	Christian	93	62	30	8	75	86.0	2.1	Massive state subsidies to churches
Netherlands	Christian	71	61	32	6	54	128.8	0.6	Limited state subsidies to churches
Norway	Christian	95				77	219.0	1.4	Massive state subsidies to churches
Portugal	Christian	92	88	9	3	55	74.4	1.2	Limited state subsidies to churches
Spain	Christian	91	64	30	6	63	60.7	1.0	Massive state subsidies to churches
Sweden	Christian	67	39	55	7	65	112.4	1.0	Massive state subsidies to churches
Switzerland	Christian	85				70	307.4	0.6	Massive state subsidies to churches
United Kingdom	Christian	82	42	53	5	70	251.7	0.9	Limited state subsidies to churches
Latin America & Caribbean									
Low income economies									
Antigua	Christian	93				64	950.9	1.1	Complete state non-interference
Haiti	Christian	95				22	175.5	2.6	State interference and obstruction
Nicaragua	Christian	96				46	349.2	3.1	Limited political restrictions
Middle income economies									
Argentina	Christian	92	84	13	3	75	305.3	1.9	Minorities discriminated against
Barbados	Christian	96				73	734.7	1.0	Massive state subsidies to churches
Belize	Christian	91				90	1,502.3	2.7	State subsidises schools only
Bolivia	Christian	93				58	459.6	2.8	Massive state subsidies to churches
Brazil	Christian	91				75	136.8	2.0	Minorities discriminated against
Chile	Christian	88	71	27	1	61	494.3	1.8	Limited state subsidies to churches
Colombia	Christian	97				75	153.5	2.2	Minorities discriminated against
Costa Rica	Christian	96				65	323.5	2.6	Massive state subsidies to churches
Cuba	Christian	54				10	22.0	2.1	State interference and obstruction
Dominican Republic	Christian	95				60	222.3	2.3	Massive state subsidies to churches
Ecuador	Christian	97				105	261.6	2.2	Limited state subsidies to churches
El Salvador	Christian	97				45	208.7	2.3	Limited political restrictions
Grenada	Christian	97				62	1,500.9	0.4	Limited political restrictions
Guatemala	Christian	97				70	269.7	3.3	Limited state subsidies to churches
Guyana	Christian	51				37	390.6	2.8	Limited political restrictions

Country	Predominant religion	Religiosity				Evangelisation			Religious freedom
		Share of total population (%)	A religious person (%)	Not a religious person (%)	A convinced atheist (%)	Christian broadcasting exposure (%) population	Missionaries received (per million population)	New Christians annual % growth	
Honduras	Christian	97				42	110.2	3.2	Limited political restrictions
Jamaica	Christian	84				43	259.2	1.2	Limited state subsidies to churches
Mexico	Christian	96	77	21	2	85	75.2	2.1	Limited political restrictions
Panama	Christian	87				70	649.2	2.3	Minorities discriminated against
Paraguay	Christian	96				38	194.8	3.0	Massive state subsidies to churches
Peru	Christian	96	88	11	1	46	243.1	2.2	Massive state subsidies to churches
St. Lucia	Christian	96				72	990.0	1.4	Massive state subsidies to churches
St. Vincent t & the Grenadines	Christian	89				62	660.0	1.0	State subsidises schools only
Suriname	Christian	51				67	904.3	1.5	Massive state subsidies to churches
Trinidad & Tobago	Christian	63				64	381.3	0.8	Massive state subsidies to churches
Uruguay	Christian	65				58	866.3	1.5	Limited state subsidies to churches
Venezuela	Christian	95	79	20	1	75	262.8	2.4	Massive state subsidies to churches
High income economies									
Bahamas	Christian	92				78	935.6	2.0	State subsidises schools only
Middle East & North Africa									
Low income economies									
Palestinian Authority	Muslim	80				7	314.5	-5.2	Limited political restrictions
Yemen	Muslim	99				1	7.0	4.6	State interference and obstruction
Middle income economies									
Algeria	Muslim	97	59	4	37	5	15.2	2.0	State interference and obstruction
Djibouti	Muslim	97				3	101.2	2.5	State subsidises schools only
Egypt	Muslim	85	99	1	0	12	20.0	2.0	State interference and obstruction
Iran	Muslim	96	95	4	1	2	2.8	3.7	Minorities discriminated against
Iraq	Muslim	96				4	3.0	1.1	State interference and obstruction
Jordan	Muslim	94	86	14	0	10	34.8	-1.2	State subsidises schools only
Lebanon	Muslim	59				77	159.5	1.2	State subsidises schools only
Libya	Muslim	96				1	17.3	0.4	State hostility and prohibition
Malta	Christian	98	75	25	0	77	75.5	1.2	Limited state subsidies to churches
Morocco	Muslim	99	95	5	0	10	47.7	-1.6	State hostility and prohibition

Country	Predominant religion	Religiosity				Evangelisation			Religious freedom
		Share of total population (%)	A religious person (%)	Not a religious person (%)	A convinced atheist (%)	Christian broadcasting exposure (%) population	Missionaries received (per million population)	New Christians annual % growth	
Oman	Muslim	89				4	13.2	-1.4	Limited political restrictions
Saudi Arabia	Muslim	92				7	3.9	7.5	State hostility and prohibition
Syria	Muslim	92				5	5.4	2.5	Minorities discriminated against
Tunisia	Muslim	99				4	19.9	0.6	Complete state non-interference
Western Sahara	Muslim	99				1	30.9	1.0	Limited state subsidies to churches
High income economies									
Bahrain	Muslim	83				16	66.3	2.8	Minorities discriminated against
Israel	Jew	71				10	149.6	-2.3	Limited political restrictions
Kuwait	Muslim	86				15	37.4	5.2	State interference and obstruction
Qatar	Muslim	82				3	15.9	3.1	State interference and obstruction
United Arab Emirates	Muslim	76				3	38.6	3.0	Limited political restrictions
North America									
High income economies									
Canada	Christian	77	77	20	4	85	250.2	1.4	Limited state subsidies to churches
United States	Christian	84	83	15	1	135	110.7	1.9	State subsidises schools only
South Asia									
Low income economies									
Afghanistan	Muslim	98				0	1.9	-0.1	State hostility and prohibition
Bangladesh	Muslim	87	97	3	0	1	6.6	3.6	State subsidises schools only
Bhutan	Buddhist	77				3	83.6	8.6	State hostility and prohibition
India	Hindu	74	79	18	3	25	7.3	3.1	Complete state non-interference
Nepal	Hindu	72				5	34.2	7.4	State interference and obstruction
Pakistan	Muslim	96	91	9	0	1	9.3	3.5	State subsidises schools only
Middle income economies									
Maldives	Muslim	98				2	29.6	1.0	Complete state non-interference
Sri Lanka	Buddhist	68				12	87.8	1.9	Limited political restrictions
Sub-Saharan Africa									
Low income economies									
Angola	Christian	94				10	137.6	6.1	Minorities discriminated against
Benin	Ethnoreligionist	47				8	84.5	5.8	Limited political restrictions

Country	Religiosity					Evangelisation			Religious freedom
	Predominant religion	Share of total population (%)	A religious person (%)	Not a religious person (%)	A convinced atheist (%)	Christian broadcasting exposure (%) population	Missionaries received (per million population)	New Christians annual % growth	
Burkina Faso	Muslim	48				9	72.5	5.9	Complete state non-interference
Burundi	Christian	92				13	164.0	4.7	Limited state subsidies to churches
Cameroon	Christian	57				23	211.3	4.3	State subsidises schools only
Central African Republic	Christian	65				28	252.4	6.2	State subsidises schools only
Chad	Muslim	57				10	82.3	6.2	Limited political restrictions
Comoros	Muslim	98				2	57.3	4.0	Minorities discriminated against
Congo, Dem. Rep.	Christian	95				23	267.5	4.3	Limited political restrictions
Congo, Rep.	Christian	90				8	204.1	4.7	Minorities discriminated against
Equatorial Guinea	Christian	88				25	576.0	4.3	Limited political restrictions
Eritrea	Muslim	49				26	44.9	4.5	State subsidises schools only
Ethiopia	Christian	55				35	33.7	4.8	State interference and obstruction
Gambia	Muslim	87				21	113.4	4.4	Complete state non-interference
Ghana	Christian	57				38	91.6	4.1	State subsidises schools only
Guinea	Muslim	69				1	11.4	4.4	State interference and obstruction
Guinea-Bissau	Ethnoreligionist	45				7	120.0	4.7	Minorities discriminated against
Kenya	Christian	80				48	182.7	4.2	State subsidises schools only
Lesotho	Christian	92				14	361.7	4.5	Limited political restrictions
Madagascar	Christian	51				40	108.6	4.6	Limited state subsidies to churches
Malawi	Christian	77				20	119.3	5.2	State subsidises schools only
Mali	Muslim	81				8	43.4	6.7	State subsidises schools only
Mauritania	Muslim	99				3	16.3	2.4	Complete state non-interference
Mozambique	Ethnoreligionist	50				4	164.1	5.1	State interference and obstruction
Niger	Muslim	90				6	35.0	3.3	State subsidises schools only
Nigeria	Christian	47	97	3	0	50	40.7	4.3	Limited state subsidies to churches
Rwanda	Christian	78				13	139.4	6.6	State subsidises schools only
São Tomé & Principe	Christian	95				28	592.7		Limited state subsidies to churches
Senegal	Muslim	87				13	113.3	4.6	State subsidises schools only
Sierra Leone	Muslim	46				14	131.1	5.8	State subsidises schools only
Somalia	Muslim	98				1	6.6	1.0	State interference and obstruction

Country	Predominant religion	Religiosity				Evangelisation			Religious freedom
		Share of total population (%)	A religious person (%)	Not a religious person (%)	A convinced atheist (%)	Christian broacasting exposure (%) population	Missionaries received (per million population)	New Christians annual % growth	
Sudan	Muslim	71				13	20.0	4.0	State interference and obstruction
Tanzania	Christian	53	94	4	1	18	117.3	4.6	Complete state non-interference
Togo	Christian	45				19	117.0	5.5	Minorities discriminated against
Uganda	Christian	89	94	5	1	45	94.1	5.0	Minorities discriminated against
Zambia	Christian	83				29	289.8	4.6	Limited political restrictions
Zimbabwe	Christian	68	89	9	2	40	208.3	4.5	Limited political restrictions
Middle income economies									
Botswana	Christian	64				23	222.2	5.9	State subsidises schools only
Cape Verde	Christian	95				8	207.5	2.6	Minorities discriminated against
Gabon	Christian	89				27	290.9	2.9	State subsidises schools only
Mauritius	Hindu	44				17	241.6	1.9	Massive state subsidies to churches
Namibia	Christian	91				34	590.5	5.3	Limited political restrictions
South Africa	Christian	82	85	14	2	58	264.8	2.9	Limited political restrictions
Swaziland	Christian	88				45	736.1	4.8	State subsidises schools only

* China includes Hong Kong, Macao and Tibet.

Sources: World Christian Database, Gordon-Conwell Theological Seminary, Center for the Study of Global Christianity (http://www.worldchristiandatabase.org; accessed May 17 2006); © European Values Survey, WORC, Tilburg University, Netherlands, 1999-2000, by permission; © World Values Survey, Institute for Social Research, University of Michigan, by permission.

Record 20: Political rights, civil liberties, press freedom and economic freedom

This record includes updates of the indices of political rights and civil liberties, which are indicators of the levels of democracy in countries around the world. Freedom House defines these as 'real-world rights and freedoms enjoyed by individuals, as a result of actions by both state and non-governmental actors, and are based on the Universal Declaration of Human Rights'(for details on the methodology used by Freedom House in producing these indices, see http://www.freedomhouse.org/research/survey2005.htm). For the political rights and civil liberties indices, scores range from 1, the lowest degree of freedom, to 7, the highest, while the press freedom index ranges from zero to 100.

This year we have included an indicator of economic freedom, from the Heritage Foundation, which reflects a neo-liberal conception of economic freedom. This index's scores range from 1, the lowest degree of economic freedom, to 5, the highest. This rating, which includes country scores from 1996 and 2006, allows for a comparison of the percentage change in economic freedom.

The different indices correlate strongly; high-income European countries scoring the highest, followed by Latin American and Caribbean nations and middle-income countries in Europe and Central Asia. The deepest deficits in political rights and civil liberties are found in most Arab nations and in many Sub-Saharan African countries. Economic freedom, as defined by the Heritage Foundation, increased in most of the world, reflecting the growing dominance of neo-liberal economic principles worldwide.

Country	Political Rights Index 2005	Civil Liberties Index 2005	Press freedom rating 2005	Economic freedom rating		
				1996	2006	% change 1996-2006
East Asia & Pacific						
Low income economies						
Cambodia	2	3	38		3.0	
East Timor	5	5	70			
Indonesia	6	5	42	3.0	2.3	-24
Korea, Dem. Rep.	1	1	3	1.0	1.0	0
Laos	1	2	17		1.9	
Mongolia	6	6	65	2.5	3.2	29
Myanmar	1	1	1	1.6	1.5	-4
Papua New Guinea	5	5	71	2.8		
Solomon Islands	5	5	70			
Vietnam	1	3	18	1.5	2.1	41
Middle income economies						
China*	1	2	18	2.2	2.7	20
Fiji	4	5	70	2.8	2.9	3
Malaysia	4	4	31	3.3	3.0	-9
Micronesia	7	7	82			

Country	Political Rights Index 2005	Civil Liberties Index 2005	Press freedom rating 2005	Economic freedom rating		
				1996	2006	% change 1996–2006
Philippines	5	5	65	2.9	2.8	-3
Samoa	6	6	75	2.9		
Thailand	5	5	58	3.5	3.0	-13
Tonga	3	5	63			
Vanuatu	6	6	76			
High income economies						
Australia	7	7	82	3.9	4.2	7
Brunei	2	3	25			
Korea, Rep.	7	6	71	3.5	3.4	-3
Japan	7	6	80	3.8	3.7	-2
New Zealand	7	7	88	4.2	4.2	-1
Singapore	3	4	34	4.4	4.4	1
Taiwan	7	7	79	3.8	3.6	-5
Europe & Central Asia						
Low income economies						
Armenia	3	4	36	2.3	3.7	65
Azerbaijan	2	3	28	1.2	2.5	103
Georgia	5	5	44	2.0	3.0	50
Kyrgyzstan	3	4	29		3.0	
Moldova	5	4	35			
Tajikistan	2	3	26		2.2	
Ukraine	5	5	41	2.0	2.8	38
Uzbekistan	1	1	15		2.1	
Middle income economies						
Albania	5	5	49	2.4	3.3	37
Belarus	1	2	14	2.6	1.9	-26
Bosnia & Herzegovina	4	5	55		3.0	
Bulgaria	7	6	65	2.5	3.1	25
Croatia	6	6	63	2.4	3.2	33
Czech Republic	7	7	78	3.6	3.9	8
Estonia	7	7	83	3.6	4.3	19
Hungary	7	7	79	3.0	3.6	20
Kazakhstan	2	3	25		2.7	
Latvia	7	7	83	2.8	3.6	27
Lithuania	7	7	82	2.6	3.9	51

Country	Political Rights Index 2005	Civil Liberties Index 2005	Press freedom rating 2005	Economic freedom rating		
				1996	2006	% change 1996-2006
Macedonia	5	5	49		3.2	
Poland	7	7	80	2.7	3.5	29
Romania	6	6	53	2.6	2.8	8
Russian Federation	2	3	32	2.3	2.5	9
Serbia & Montenegro	5	6	60			
Slovakia	7	7	79	2.9	3.7	27
Slovenia	7	7	81	2.2	3.6	62
Turkey	5	5	52	3.1	2.9	-5
Turkmenistan	1	1	4		2.0	
High income economies						
Austria	7	7	79	3.9	4.1	3
Belgium	7	7	89	3.9	3.9	0
Cyprus	7	7	78	3.3	4.1	24
Denmark	7	7	90	3.8	4.2	10
Finland	7	7	91	3.6	4.2	15
France	7	7	80	3.6	3.5	-4
Germany	7	7	84	3.7	4.0	10
Greece	7	6	72	3.0	3.2	7
Iceland	7	7	91		4.3	
Ireland	7	7	85	3.8	4.4	16
Italy	7	7	65	3.4	3.5	3
Luxembourg	7	7	89	4.0	4.4	11
Netherlands	7	7	89	4.1	4.1	1
Norway	7	7	90	3.6	3.7	4
Portugal	7	7	86	3.4	3.7	11
Spain	7	7	78	3.2	3.7	14
Sweden	7	7	91	3.4	4.0	18
Switzerland	7	7	89	4.0	4.1	2
United Kingdom*	7	7	82	4.1	4.3	4
Latin America & Caribbean						
Low income economies						
Haiti	1	2	34	1.4	2.0	39
Nicaragua	5	5	58	2.4	3.0	26
Middle income economies						
Argentina	6	6	59	3.4	2.7	-21
Belize	7	6	80	3.3	3.2	-1

Country	Political Rights Index 2005	Civil Liberties Index 2005	Press freedom rating 2005	Economic freedom rating		
				1996	2006	% change 1996-2006
Bolivia	5	5	65	3.4	3.0	-12
Brazil	6	6	60	2.4	2.9	22
Chile	7	7	76	3.4	4.1	20
Colombia	5	5	37	2.9	2.8	-2
Costa Rica	7	7	81	3.0	3.3	10
Cuba	1	1	4	1.1	1.9	81
Dominica	7	7	83			
Dominican Republic	6	6	62	2.7	2.6	-2
Ecuador	5	5	59	2.7	2.7	1
El Salvador	6	5	59	3.3	3.7	10
Guatemala	4	4	42	2.9	3.0	3
Guyana	5	5	77	2.6	2.9	10
Honduras	5	5	49	2.4	2.7	12
Jamaica	6	5	85	3.1	3.2	6
Mexico	6	6	58	2.7	3.2	18
Panama	7	6	56	3.5	3.3	-4
Paraguay	5	5	44	3.1	2.7	-12
Peru	6	5	60	3.0	3.1	5
St. Lucia	7	7	84			
St. Vincent & the Grenadines	6	7	84			
Suriname	6	6	80	1.9	2.4	26
Trinidad & Tobago	5	6	76	3.3	3.5	6
Uruguay	7	7	71	3.2	3.3	5
Venezuela	4	4	28	2.4	1.8	-24
High income economies						
Antigua & Barbuda			60			
Bahamas	7	7	86	3.9	3.7	-4
Barbados	7	7	83	2.9	3.8	32
Middle East & North Africa						
Low income economies						
Western Sahara						
Yemen	3	3	24	2.2	2.2	-1
Middle income economies						
Algeria	2	3	36	2.3	2.5	10
Djibouti	3	3	33		2.8	

Country	Political Rights Index 2005	Civil Liberties Index 2005	Press freedom rating 2005	Economic freedom rating		
				1996	2006	% change 1996-2006
Egypt	2	3	32	2.6	2.4	-7
Iran	2	2	20	1.2	1.5	23
Iraq	2	3	30	1.2		
Jordan	3	4	38	2.9	3.2	12
Lebanon	3	4	40	3.1	3.0	-3
Libya	1	1	5	1.1	1.8	75
Malta	7	7	82	2.8	3.8	39
Morocco	3	4	37	3.1	2.8	-9
Oman	2	3	28	3.2	3.0	-5
Palestinian Authority	6	6	16			
Saudi Arabia	1	2	20	3.0	3.2	5
Syria	1	1	17	1.9	2.1	12
Tunisia	2	3	20	3.2	2.8	-13
High income economies						
Bahrain	3	3	29	4.2	3.8	-10
Israel	7	6	72	3.2	3.6	14
Kuwait	4	3	42	3.5	3.3	-6
Qatar	2	3	38		3.0	
United Arab Emirates	2	2	28	3.6	3.1	-14
North America						
High income economies						
Canada	7	7	83	4.0	4.2	4
United States	7	7	83	4.0	4.2	4
South Asia						
Low income economies						
Afghanistan	3	2	32			
Bangladesh	4	4	32	2.2	2.1	-4
Bhutan	2	3	34			
India	6	5	62	2.1	2.5	21
Nepal	2	3	31	2.1	2.5	16
Pakistan	2	3	39	2.7	2.7	-2
Middle income economies						
Maldives	2	3	32	2.6	2.9	14
Sri Lanka	5	5	44	3.1	2.8	-8

Country	Political Rights Index 2005	Civil Liberties Index 2005	Press freedom rating 2005	Economic freedom rating		
				1996	2006	% change 1996-2006
Sub-Saharan Africa						
Low income economies						
Angola	2	3	34	1.6	2.2	33
Benin	6	6	70	2.5	2.6	5
Burkina Faso	3	5	60	2.1	2.7	30
Burundi	5	3	26		2.3	
Cameroon	2	2	32	1.9	2.5	32
Central African Republic	3	4	37		2.6	
Chad	2	3	27		2.7	
Comoros	4	4	56			
Congo, Dem. Rep.	2	2	19	1.7		
Congo, Rep.	3	3	49	1.5	2.1	39
Côte d'Ivoire	2	2	31			
Equatorial Guinea	1	2	12		2.3	
Eritrea	1	2	9			
Ethiopia	3	3	32	2.2	2.3	5
Gambia	3	4	28		2.5	
Ghana	7	6	74	2.5	2.7	10
Guinea	2	3	27	2.9	2.5	-15
Guinea-Bissau	5	4	45		2.4	
Kenya	5	5	39	2.4	2.8	16
Lesotho	6	5	58	2.3	2.8	21
Liberia	4	4	27			
Madagascar	5	5	50	2.5	3.3	33
Malawi	4	4	46	2.4	2.4	0
Mali	6	6	77	2.6	2.9	9
Mauritania	2	4	35	2.1	2.9	37
Mozambique	5	4	55	1.9	2.7	37
Niger	5	5	47	1.8	2.6	46
Nigeria	4	4	48	2.5	2.0	-21
Rwanda	2	3	16		2.5	
São Tomé & Principe	6	6	72			
Senegal	6	5	63	2.2	2.9	30
Sierra Leone	4	5	41	2.4	2.2	-5

Country	Political Rights Index 2005	Civil Liberties Index 2005	Press freedom rating 2005	Economic freedom rating		
				1996	2006	% change 1996-2006
Somalia	2	1	17	1.4		
Sudan	1	1	14	1.9		
Tanzania	4	5	49	2.3	2.8	23
Togo	2	3	27		2.3	
Uganda	3	4	56	3.1	3.1	0
Zambia	4	4	35	2.9	2.7	-9
Zimbabwe	1	2	11	2.2	1.8	-20
Middle income economies						
Botswana	6	6	70	3.0	3.7	25
Cape Verde	7	7	68	2.5	3.3	35
Gabon	2	4	34	2.4	2.7	15
Mauritius	7	6	72		3.0	
Namibia	6	6	71		2.9	
South Africa	7	6	74	2.8	3.3	16
Swaziland	1	3	21	2.7	3.0	12

Where data for a particular year are not available, figures are taken from the year before as an estimate. These figures are presented in italics.

* China excludes Tibet and Hong Kong.

Source: Freedom House, 2006. Freedom in the World 2006: Civic Power and Electoral Politics, http://www.freedomhouse.org/template.cfm?page=5; Freedom House, Freedom of the Press 2006: A Global Survey of Media Independence, http://www.freedomhouse.org/template.cfm?page=202&year=2005; The Heritage Foundation, 2006 Index of Economic Freedom, http://www.heritage.org/research/features/index/downloads/PastScores.xls

The US has acquired a hegemonic status in world politics and the economy, and is a major driver of globalisation. Its policies affect people worldwide, and much of the debate on globalisation is intertwined with the debate on US influence and hegemony. Therefore, opinions of the US offer an indication of attitudes towards globalisation. This record presents attitudes about the role of the US in the world, as expressed in surveys conducted by the Pew Research Centre's Global Attitudes Project 2005. Interestingly, global publics appreciate Americans more than they appreciate the US. This is probably driven by the salience of negative attitudes towards the US government's conduct in international relations, particularly 'the war on terror,' and the re-election of President George W Bush, and despite its promotion of democracy in the Middle East, and involvement in tsunami relief.

Attitudes towards the United States and Americans

% respondents	Attitude towards the United States		Attitudes towards Americans		US regard of other countries' interests in making int'l policy decisions		Attitude towards US-led war on terrorism		Attitudes towards level of US religiousity		
	Positive	Negative	Positive	Negative	Positive	Negative	Positive	Negative	Too religious	Not religious enough	About right
Canada	59	37	66	30	19	80	45	47	35	38	5
China	42	53	43	49	53	38					
France	43	57	64	36	18	82	51	48	61	26	7
Germany	41	54	65	24	38	59	50	45	39	31	7
India	71	17	71	18	63	26	52	41	32	57	3
Indonesia	38	57	46	46	59	35	50	42	12	69	11
Jordan	21	80	34	66	17	82	12	86		95	1
Lebanon	42	58	66	32	35	57	31	65	6	61	18
Morocco	49	44	62	30	27	65	33	56	19	53	15
Netherlands	45	54	66	31	20	79	71	26	57	25	6
Pakistan	23	60	22	55	39	41	22	52	17	63	9
Poland	62	23	68	17	13	74	61	29	6	56	21
Russian Federation	52	40	61	29	21	73	55	34	27	38	22
Spain	41	50	55	30	19	76	26	67	31	40	11
Turkey	23	67	23	63	14	77	17	71	18	60	11
United Kingdom	55	38	70	22	32	66	51	40	39	28	11
United States	83	14	88	9	67	30	76	18	21	58	11

Events affecting attitudes towards the United States

% respondents	Iraq elections			Bush re-election			US tsunami aid			US calls for Middle East democracy		
	More positive	More negative	Unchanged	More positive	More negative	Unchanged	More positive	More negative	Unchanged	More positive	More negative	Unchanged
Canada	44	38	6	20	75	2	69	17	4	52	37	3
France	35	48	14	19	74	7	51	33	14	43	44	12
Germany	50	34	7	14	77	5	66	23	5	71	22	3
India	26	30	15	28	35	17	54	27	8	32	26	11
Indonesia	15	40	21	12	52	20	79	14	4	21	47	15
Jordan	18	28	53	10	31	54						
Lebanon	19	50	28	9	57	27						
Morocco	16	45	21	11	69	9	66	16	9	32	42	10
Netherlands	55	35	4	24	72	2	62	23	4	65	30	2
Pakistan	10	29	23	10	36	20	26	21	16	10	25	16
Poland	19	16	46	21	18	45	43	8	32	29	11	40
Russian Federation	11	34	36	15	36	38	61	6	22	24	28	32
Spain	23	42	25	19	60	15	46	23	21	45	30	19
Turkey	15	45	20	11	62	14	34	24	21	12	49	20
United Kingdom	40	29	21	18	62	14	44	24	21	47	34	11

Source: The Pew Research Center, 2005. 16-Nation Pew Global Attitudes Survey. The Pew Global Attitudes Project, June 23, 2005,

http://pewglobal.org/reports/display.php?ReportID=247

The relationship between global civil society and globalisation is complex. On one hand global civil society is one of the drivers of globalisation, and on the other hand much of the activism of civil society actors throughout the world aims to slow or tame globalisation. Public attitudes towards globalisations are therefore important factors in the understanding of this complexity. This record presents public attitudes towards globalisation from three different sources: the 2006 IMD World Competitiveness Yearbook, GlobeScan's 2001 and 2004 Global Issues Monitor surveys, and the European Commission's Spring 2005 Eurobarometer – a public opinion survey in the European Union.

The World Competitiveness Yearbook presents people's perceptions of how globalisation is viewed in their country. It asked respondents to evaluate whether attitudes toward globalisation are generally positive or negative in their country; and the responses are scored on a scale from 1 – negative, to 10 - positive. To measure the general attitudes towards globalisation, the Eurobarometer asked whether the term 'globalisation' brings to mind something very positive, fairly positive, fairly negative or very negative. Respondents were also asked to evaluate the consequences of the globalisation of trade. They were offered positive and negative consequences: opportunities for local companies and foreign investments in their country on the positive side; and de-localisation of some companies to countries where labour is cheaper and increased competition for local companies, on the negative side.

The GlobeScan survey asked the following: 'Thinking of you and your family's interests, do you think the overall effect of globalisation is very positive, somewhat positive, somewhat negative or very negative?' The data show that, on average, people in developing nations tend to have less favourable attitudes towards globalisation than their developed country counterparts. It is interesting to note that respondents in wealthy EU countries show similar rates of favourable and unfavourable attitudes towards globalisation, although a majority believe the consequences of globalisation to be negative. Notwithstanding this finding, people in both developed and developing nations tend to think that globalisation is good for their families; such optimism is increasing in developed nations but not in developing nations.

% respondents	Attitudes towards globalisation		Consequences of globalisation		Perception of national attitudes towards globalisation
	Positive 2005	Negative 2005	Positive 2005	Negative 2005	2006
East Asia & Pacific					
Low income economies					
Indonesia					5.3
Middle income economies					
China*					6.7
Malaysia					6.9
Philippines					5.6
Thailand					6.5
High income economies					
Australia					7.1
Japan					7.0
Korea, Rep.					7.0
New Zealand					6.7
Taiwan					7.4
Europe & Central Asia					
Middle income economies					
Bulgaria	30	31	30	36	5.6
Croatia	31	49	29	52	4.2
Czech Republic	29	60	33	53	6.0
Estonia	43	32	33	43	6.2
Hungary	27	56	37	47	5.3
Latvia	30	35	29	43	
Lithuania	36	29	33	28	
Poland	35	41	31	46	4.7
Romania	40	25	55	39	4.5
Russian Federation					4.9
Slovakia	31	56	37	51	6.1
Slovenia	34	49	30	52	4.1
Turkey	52	21	44	23	6.3
High income economies					
Austria	31	55	26	62	6.2
Belgium	46	49	22	74	5.0
Cyprus	46	40	35	46	
Denmark	67	24	31	60	7.6

% respondents	Attitudes towards globalisation		Consequences of globalisation		Perception of national attitudes towards globalisation
	Positive 2005	Negative 2005	Positive 2005	Negative 2005	2006
Finland	48	42	25	58	6.3
France	28	61	12	81	2.5
Germany	36	54	22	65	5.4
Greece	23	66	27	66	4.5
Iceland					8.5
Ireland	38	37	32	47	7.6
Italy	43	41	37	45	4.6
Luxembourg	34	51	19	66	5.3
Malta	43	20	27	51	
Netherlands	51	36	43	42	7.3
Norway					6.3
Portugal	40	28	27	48	4.7
Spain	36	32	29	38	4.9
Sweden	62	27	31	61	6.7
Switzerland					6.2
United Kingdom	38	42	28	49	6.5
Latin America & Caribbean					
Middle income economies					
Argentina					4.2
Brazil					5.6
Chile					7.7
Colombia					6.0
Mexico					5.5
Venezuela					3.2
Middle East & North Africa					
Middle income economies					
Jordan					5.3
High income economies					
Israel					7.3
High income economies					
Canada					6.6
United States					6.3
South Asia					
Low income economies					

% respondents	Attitudes towards globalisation		Consequences of globalisation		Perception of national attitudes towards globalisation
	Positive 2005	Negative 2005	Positive 2005	Negative 2005	2006
India					7.1
Sub-Saharan Africa					
Middle income economies					
South Africa					5.7

*Refers to mainland China

Source: The Pew Research Center, 2005. 16-Nation Pew Global Attitudes Survey. The Pew Global Attitudes Project, June 23, 2005, http://pewglobal.org/reports/display.php?ReportID=247

Perceptions of effects of globalisation on family

Country	Positive			Negative			Neither/both			No response/ Don't know		
	2001	2004	% change	2001	2004	% change	2001	2004	% change	2001	2004	% change
Argentina	44	31	-12	40	30	-11	8	9	1	8	30	22
Brazil	64	72	7	29	22	-7	1	3	1	5	4	-2
Canada	67	67	-1	29	30	2	3	1	-2	1	2	1
Chile	61	54	-7	16	22	6	6	16	10	17	8	-8
France	29	35	6	36	45	10	25	15	-11	10	6	-5
Germany	51	55	4	26	38	12	15	5	-10	8	2	-6
India	70	73	3	23	18	-5	3	6	2	4	3	0
Indonesia	63	61	-2	23	22	-1	9	8	-1	5	9	5
Italy	57	53	-4	29	31	2	12	11	-2	3	6	4
Mexico	71	67	-3	25	19	-6	2	6	3	2	8	6
Nigeria	71	70	-1	16	16	0	5	4	-2	8	11	3
Russian Federation	37	28	-8	13	16	3	31	34	3	19	22	2
Spain	41	55	14	28	19	-9	14	14	0	16	12	-5
Turkey	51	30	-21	29	31	2	11	10	-2	8	29	21
United Kingdom	60	67	7	33	28	-5	2	1	-1	5	4	-1
United States	68	65	-3	29	31	3	2	2	0	2	2	0

Sources: Copyright © 2006, IMD International, Switzerland, World Competitiveness Center, www.imd.ch/wcc, 2006 Edition of the IMD World Competitiveness Yearbook, Tables 3.5.01 'Attitudes toward globalization'; Data from GlobeScan's 2001 and 2004 Global Issues Monitor surveys. Reproduced with permission of GlobeScan Incorporated (Toronto); European Commission, 2005. Eurobarometer 63: Public Opinion in the European Union, May-June 2005, http://ec.europa.eu/public_opinion/archives/eb/eb63/eb63_en.pdf

Arbitrary detention. Deprivation of liberty imposed arbitrarily, that is, where no final decision has been taken by domestic courts in conformity with domestic law and with the relevant international standards set forth in the Universal Declaration of Human Rights and with the relevant international instruments accepted by the states concerned.

Bribing and corruption. This indicator is taken from the survey of business executives that forms part of the Institute for Management Development's World Competitiveness Yearbook. Respondents are asked to what extent bribing and corruption exist in the economy.

Control of Corruption Index. This measures perceptions of corruption, conventionally defined as the exercise of public power for private gain, and perceived as a failure of governance. A higher score in this index represents better control of corruption. The index is comprised of a range of measures from various sources, from the frequency of 'additional payments to get things done', through the effects of corruption on the business environment, to measuring 'grand corruption' in the political arena or in the tendency of elite forms to engage in 'state capture'.

Corporate Ethics Index. An index developed by the World Bank Institute Governance & Anti-Corruption project. It is a simple average of scores on both the legal and illegal corporate corruption components of the project: the Corporate Illegal Corruption Component (CICC) that measures types of bribery, in which a private agent plays a key role (as in procurement, shaping regulations and policies), and the firm's own corporate ethics self-rating; and the Corporate Legal Corruption Component (CLCC), that measures legal dimensions of undue influence, such as legal political finance, the influence of powerful firms on politicians and policymaking, etc.

Corporate Governance Index. An index developed by the World Bank Institute Governance & Anti-Corruption project, based on standard questions (internal to the firm) regarding corporate governance, such as the relationship between board and management, etc.

Correspondence analysis. A method for analysing contingency tables (such as network matrices) and displaying the results graphically on a multi-dimensional graph. It is essentially a technique to decompose the $x2$ statistic of a contingency table or a matrix, and is applicable to matrices containing network links or affiliation data. It measures $x2$ distances of individual rows and columns in the table from the marginals, and uses these distances to draw each row/column as a point in a multidimensional space. The distance between each two points in the diagram relates to their similarity or dissimilarity.

Corruption Perceptions Index (CPI). This measures corruption in the public sector and defines corruption as the abuse of public office for private gain. The CPI makes no effort to reflect private sector fraud. The index is based on surveys compiled by Transparency International from other organisations that tend to ask questions about the misuse of public power for private benefits, with a focus, for example, on bribing of public officials, taking kickbacks in public procurement, or embezzling public funds, etc.

Debt service. The sum of principal repayments and interest actually paid in foreign currency, goods, or services on long-term debt, interest paid on short-term debt, and repayments (repurchases and charges) to the International Monetary Fund.

Dietary energy supply (DES). An estimate of food availability at the national level developed by the UN Food and Agricultural Organisation (FAO). It is derived by applying food composition factors to all food commodities available for human consumption. Only the total calories available for consumption are of interest. It is expressed on a per capita basis by dividing the total calories available by an estimate of the total population, then per day by dividing by 365, to give the unit kcals/capita/day (FAO 1984).

Discrimination. Any distinction, exclusion, restriction, or preference based on any ground such as race, colour, sex, language, religion, political or other opinion, national or social origin, property, birth, or other status which has the purpose or effect of nullifying or impairing the recognition, enjoyment, or exercise, on an equal footing, of human rights and fundamental freedoms in the political, economic, social, cultural, or any other field of public life.

Economic freedom. Economic freedom is defined by the Heritage Foundation as the absence of government coercion or constraint on the production, distribution, or consumption of goods and services beyond the extent necessary for citizens to protect and maintain liberty itself. In other words, people are free to work, produce, consume, and invest in the ways they feel are most productive. The index is comprised of 50 independent economic variables in 10 broad categories: trade policy, fiscal burden of government, government intervention in the economy, monetary policy, capital flows and foreign investment, banking and finance, wages and prices, property rights, regulation, and informal market activity. The index is a simple unweighted average of the scores in the 10 categories, and it grades countries on a scale from 1 (low) to 5 (high).

Emissions. Emissions refer to the release of greenhouse gases and/or their precursors, and aerosols into the atmosphere over a specified area and period of time.

Evangelisation. The practice of exposing non-Christians to Christian teachings for the purpose of proselytising them. The World Christian database defines evangelisation as providing non-Christians with 'adequate opportunity, or opportunities, to hear the gospel and to respond to it, whether they respond positively or negatively'.

Extrajudicial executions. Full expression 'extrajudicial, summary, or arbitrary executions': all acts and omissions of state representatives that constitute a violation of the general recognition of the right to life embodied in the Universal Declaration of Human Rights and the International Covenant on Civil and Political Rights.

Foreign direct investment (FDI). Investment to acquire a lasting management interest (10 per cent or more of voting stock) in an enterprise operating in an economy other than that of the investor. It is the sum of equity capital, reinvestment of earnings, other long-term capital, and short-term capital as shown in the balance of payments. FDI stock is the value of the share of capital and reserves (including retained profits) attributable to enterprises based outside the domestic economy, plus the net indebtedness of domestic affiliates to the parent enterprise. UNCTAD FDI stock data are frequently estimated by accumulating FDI flows over a period of time or adding flows to an FDI stock that has been obtained for a particular year.

Gross domestic product (GDP). Total domestic expenditure of a country, minus imports, plus exports of goods and services.

GDP per capita, PPP. GDP per capita based on purchasing power parity (PPP). GDP PPP is gross domestic product converted to international dollars using purchasing power parity rates. An international dollar has the same purchasing power over GDP as the US dollar in the United States. Data are in current international dollars.

Gross national income (GNI). Formerly known as gross national product or GNP. The sum of value added by all resident producers, plus any product taxes (less subsidies) not included in the valuation of output, plus net receipts of primary income (compensation of employees and property income) from abroad.

Human Development Index (HDI). A composite index based on three indicators: longevity, as measured by life expectancy at birth; educational attainment, as measured by a combination of adult literacy (two-thirds weight) and the combined gross primary, secondary, and tertiary enrolment ratio (one-third weight); and standard of living, as measured by GDP per capita (PPP US$).

International food donations. Food aid shipments represent a transfer of food commodities from donor to recipient countries on a total-grant basis or on highly concessional terms.

International organisations. As defined by the Union of international Associations (UIA), these are currently active, autonomous non-profit making organisations with operations or activities in at least three countries (or members with voting rights in at least three countries), a formal structure with election of governing officers from several member countries and some continuity of activities. The UIA distinguishes between inter-governmental organisations (IGOs) and international non-governmental organisations (INGOs). IGOs are based on a formal instrument of agreement between the governments of nation states; include three or more nation states as parties to the agreement and posses a permanent secretariat performing ongoing tasks. INGOs are generally 'any international organisation which is not established by intergovernmental agreement'. UIA refines this broad definition using seven rules, based on aims, members, structure, officers, finance, autonomy, and activities. Further detail is available on UIA's website (www.uia.org/organisations/orgtypes/orgtypea.php) In addition, UIA classifies international organisations into 15 types (A-G), which differ in structure, geographic locus and function. Seven of these types (A-G) are used in this Yearbook and are listed here:

(A) Federations of international organisations: includes all international organisations which group together at least three other autonomous non-regional international bodies as full members;

(B) Universal membership organisations: includes all non-profit international organisations that have membership in at least 60 countries, or in more than 30 countries provided that the distribution between continents is 'well-balanced';

(C) Intercontinental membership organisations: international organisations whose membership and preoccupations exceed that of a particular continental region, although not to a degree justifying its inclusion in the previous type;

(D) Regionally defined membership organisations: international organisations, whose membership or preoccupations are restricted to a particular continent or subcontinental region;

(E) Organisations emanating from places, persons, bodies: autonomous international bodies, which may be considered an "emanation" of a particular organisation, place, person or proprietary product. Such bodies do not necessarily have a membership in the form required for the preceding types;

(F) Organisations having a special form: international organisations whose formal characteristics raise fundamental questions if they are allocated to any of the preceding types. Typically includes foundations and funds, international banks, courts, etc.;

(G) Internationally-oriented national organisations: includes national organisations with various forms of international activity or concern, or that hold consultatative status with United Nations and other intergovernmental bodies.

ISO 14000 certification. This was designed to provide any type of public or private organisation with environmental management systems standards. Companies that adhere to ISO 14000 implement environmental management systems, conduct environmental audits, and evaluate their environmental performance with guidance from the International Standards Organisation (ISO). Their products adhere to environmental labelling standards, and waste streams are managed through lifecycle assessment of all products. For more details see www.iso.ch/iso/en/iso9000-14000/pdf/iso14000.pdf

Main telephone lines. Telephone lines connecting a customer's equipment to the public switched telephone network.

Merchandise trade. Includes all trade in goods. Trade in services is excluded.

Net primary school enrolment ratio. An indicator of the level of education in countries, listing the number of students enrolled in a level of education that are of official school age for that level, as a percentage of the population of official school age for that level.

NGO Sustainability Index: Using this index USAID measures the strength and viability of the NGO sectors in Central and Eastern Europe and Eurasia. To calculate the index, seven different dimensions of the NGO sector are analysed: legal environment, organisational capacity, financial viability, advocacy, service provision, NGO infrastructure and public image. In the index, each of these dimensions is examined with a focus on accomplishments, problems, and local capacity to recognise and address outstanding challenges strategically. The index uses a seven-point scale, with 7 indicating a low or poor level of development and 1 indicating a very advanced NGO sector.

Official development assistance (ODA). Official development assistance and net official aid record the actual international transfer by the donor of financial resources or of goods or services valued at the cost to the donor, minus any repayments of loan principal during the same period.

Participation in international organisations. This variable indicates the extent to which organisations and individuals in each country are members of international organisations. Whether an organisation has a million members or a single member in a given country, this is counted as one membership. So a count of 100 for a country means that 100 INGOs each have at least one member or member organisation in that country. We also offer data on membership density for each country, expressed as the number of memberships in INGOs per 1 million population.

Peacekeeping forces. Military personnel and civilian police serving in United Nations peacekeeping missions.

Political rights and civil liberties. Indicators of the levels of democracy in countries around the world. Real-world rights and freedoms enjoyed by individuals, as a result of actions by both state and non-governmental actors, based on the Universal Declaration of Human Rights. Political rights are defined as those that 'enable people to participate freely in the political process, including through the right to vote, compete for public office, and elect representatives who have a decisive impact on public policies and are accountable to the electorate'. Civil liberties are defined as those that 'allow for the freedoms of expression and belief, associational and organisational rights, rule of law, and personal autonomy without interference from the state'. These freedoms can be affected by a variety of actors, both governmental and non-governmental. Scores range from one, the lowest degree of freedom, to seven, the highest (for the sake of clarity we modified them from the original index scores which are reversed).

Predominant religion. The faith with the largest number of adherents in a given country.

Public Sector Ethics Index. An index developed by the World Bank Institute Governance & Anti-Corruption project, measuring the variables related to public integrity, bribery and favouritism in the public sector.

Religious freedom. The World Christian database describes the extent of religious freedom with a phrase that approximates the state of religious liberty in each country. Religious liberty is defined as the freedom to practice one's religion with the full range of religious rights specified in the Universal Declaration of Human Rights.

Refugee. As defined by the UN High Commissioner for Refugees, a person is a refugee if she/he qualifies under the Arrangements of 12 May 1926 and 30 June 1928 or under the Conventions of 28 October 1933 and 10 February 1938, the Protocol of 14 September 1939 or the Constitution of the International Refugee Organisation. For further information see http://www.unhcr.org/cgi-bin/texis/vtx/home

Remittances, paid and received. Remittances are transfers of money by foreign workers to their home countries. Paid workers' remittances and compensation of employees comprise current transfers by migrant workers, and wages and salaries earned by non-resident workers. Received workers' remittances and compensation of employees comprise current transfers by migrant workers, and wages and salaries earned by non-resident workers.

Torture. Any act by which severe pain or suffering, whether physical or mental, is intentionally inflicted on a person for such purposes as obtaining from him or a third person information or a confession, punishing him for an act he or a third person has committed or is suspected of having committed, or intimidating or coercing him or a third person, or for any reason based on discrimination of any kind, when such pain or suffering is inflicted by or at the instigation of or with the consent or acquiescence of a public official or other person acting in an official capacity. It does not include pain or suffering arising only from, inherent in, or incidental to lawful sanctions.

Total military personnel. Active duty military personnel, including paramilitary forces if those forces resemble regular units in their organisation, equipment, training, or mission.

Total trade. The sum of the market value of imports and exports of goods and services.

Tourists. Visitors who travel to a country other than that where they have their usual residence for a period not exceeding 12 months and whose main purpose in visiting is other than an activity remunerated from within the country visited.

CHRONOLOGY OF GLOBAL CIVIL SOCIETY EVENTS
Compiled by Jill Timms

Contributors: Mustapha Kamel Al-Sayyid, Marcelo Batalha, Baris Gencer Baykan, Nick Buxton, Giuseppe Caruso, Hyo-Je Cho, Bernard Dreano, Louise Fraser, Iuliana Gavril, Nihad Gohar, Vicky Holland, Jeffrey Juris, Silke Lechner, Otilia Mihai, Selma Muhic, Alejandro Natal, Katarina Sehm Patomaki, Mario Pianto, Asthriesslav Rocuts, Ineke Roose, Thomas Ruddy, Kate Townsend, Caroline Watt.

About the chronology
The aim of the chronology is to contribute an alternative type of data to the statistics presented in the Data Programme. Through our international network of correspondents, this chronology offers a taste of the diversity of events taking place around the world, including campaigns, demonstrations and other activities that might not be reported in the mainstream media. This sixth edition of the chronology records global civil society events that took place between May 2005 and April 2006. It is important to note that we present a selection of global civil society events – the welcome growth of activity and the challenges of recording this, make it impossible to list every single action, demonstration, petition and campaign taking place around the world. Three points should be made about our selection of entries:

1. Our sources are limited to the reports of our correspondents (see the next section on joining this team) and information available on the Internet (in an accessible language).
2. Through this project we continue to refine our definition of a global civil society event: those included involve or have significance for civil society beyond the borders of a single country.
3. Our records of the growth of the social forum movement are limited to forums with an active website; and for reasons of space we focus mainly on those at the national, thematic and regional levels. Other forums exist, including many at the local level; and some forums do not hold an annual event but instead operate on a continuous basis, and therefore are not represented in this chronology.

Opportunity to participate
The Global Civil Society Yearbook is an interactive initiative that aims to contribute to, as well as study, global civil society. Therefore, we encourage you to engage in our ongoing debates and research. We suggest two ways this can be done:

• **Your feedback.** We are committed to developing the chronology by reviewing both our process and our understanding of global civil society activity. We ask you to help us do so by completing a short questionnaire about your use of the chronology and your suggestions for its improvement. Please visit **www.lse.ac.uk/Depts/ global/ chronologyquestionnaire.htm**

• **Your entries.** Do you belong to an NGO, a social forum or other social movement? Do you take part in actions, study civil society, or report and read about events? We rely on the assistance of people such as you to continue and develop this project, and we have implemented a new system to make contributing to the chronology even easier. You can submit information about an event immediately, or up to a year after it has happened, via a short online form that takes only minutes to complete – **www.lse.ac.uk/Depts/global/correspondents.htm** – and is sent to the chronology editor.

Why should you take part? First, you will be contributing to the understanding of global civil society at this important time of growth. Second, because we appreciate that this growth in activity means you are increasingly busy, we offer several incentives to encourage you to take part. If you submit entries that are included in the next edition you will receive an acknowledgement as one of our correspondents; and as a member of the team you will receive updates on the progress of the project, a complimentary copy of *Global Civil Society 2007/8*, and of course our thanks. For more information about being a correspondent and the online form for submitting events, please visit **www.lse.ac.uk/Depts/global/correspondents.htm**

Global Civil Society events
May 2005–April 2006

May 2005

1 May International Labour Day is marked around the world with demonstrations in support of workers' rights. In Mexico City, more than 1 million gather for the city's largest ever demonstration. A Euro Mayday campaign organised by several public assemblies of metropolitan workers coordinates 200,000 demonstrators marching simultaneously in 19 European cites, to draw attention to exploitation. In Brazil, the largest ever march organised by the Landless Rural Workers Movement (MST) sees 13,000 protesters set off from Goiania to march the 210 kilometres to Brasília, calling for government action on agrarian reform and a better deal for rural workers.

1 May The Chicago Social Forum is held. This is the second regional social forum in the city. A major theme is the type of 'global city' politicians and business people are encouraging Chicago to become, and how strategies can be developed to resist this.

10 May Over 1,000 demonstrators sit in orderly lines outside a courthouse in Andizhan in Uzbekistan to demand justice for a group of 23 men accused of being 'Islamic extremists'. This is the culmination of many similar protests held over the last month, which have grown in size and become more organised. There is an emphasis on non-violence, and there are no slogans or placards. Organisers provide food and drink for those taking part, as well as seating for women. They say the accused have been singled out as they are independently-minded, prominent members of the community.

13 May In South Africa, demonstrators from opposing sides clash outside the High Court at the start of a case brought by the Treatment Action Campaign (TAC) against the Dr Rath Foundation, which it claims has spread rumours that anti-retroviral drugs are 'poisonous'. TAC is campaigning with other international AIDS organisations to make all anti-retroviral drugs available free for AIDS patients in South Africa. Police keep supporters of each side separate.

13 May International human rights groups express concern about the killing of 34 people in Uzbekistan; foreign news broadcasts are blocked and soldiers seal off a town where 2,000 demonstrators have gathered. This follows an armed raid of the local prison during which gunmen free inmates, including some of the 23 men alleged to be 'Islamic extremists.'

14 May A thematic social forum on 'Meeting Resistances and Alternatives' is held at Evora University in Portugal.

17 May In Brazil, 12,000 demonstrators finish their 17-day march to Brasília. On arriving at the Congress Building 40 people are injured in clashes with police. The marchers, who have been supported by thousands of people along the route, demand government action on the agrarian reforms promised by President Luiz Inacio Lula da Silva when he was elected in 2003. These included a pledge to buy disused land and redistribute it to homeless families. However, only 80,000 of the 430,000 families promised new homes have so far received them.

20–22 May The Mallorca Social Forum is held in Spain for the

second time. It attracts more than 500 participants, with education and public services being major themes.

21 May Campaigners for the rights of indigenous peoples clash with members of the Afrikaner community in South Africa over a proposed change to the name of the city of Pretoria. Two thousand, mainly white, citizens gather on Church Square to demonstrate against the proposed name of 'Tshwane', which was the name of a pre-colonial chief meaning 'we are the same'. Protesters say the proposal from the Geographic Names Council ignores the cultural heritage of the Afrikaner community. Currently, the city is named after Andries Pretoris, a Boer settler and Afrikaner hero. The decision is confirmed unanimously later in the week, resulting in further protests.

23–24 May In Prague, over 50 national and international NGOs are brought together by a coalition of Austrian and Czech human rights groups in a forum on 'Civil society, democracy, and European integration'.

24 May More than 5,000 participants from 140 countries take part in a Reinventing Government Forum in Seoul, the main theme of the event being 'Towards participatory and transparent governance'.

June 2005

1–4 June In Brazil, 4,500 people participate in the sixth international Free Software Forum held in Porto Alegre. The event focuses on strategies for equality of access to technology.

3–5 June The national Swiss Social Forum takes place in Fribourg, Switzerland. In promoting coordination with other forums, some of the 50 people who attended the World Social Forum in Porto Alegre earlier in the year report back.

4–5 June The first Guadalupe Social Forum takes place, in Petit-Bourg, in the French West Indies. This is one of a series of social forums in the Caribbean. Participants hope to build networks and work towards a Caribbean Social Forum in 2006.

6–8 June Widespread protests are held throughout Ethiopia against alleged fraud during the 15 May parliamentary elections, despite a month-long ban on public demonstrations imposed by the government. International human rights groups express concern as 35 demonstrators are killed in clashes with police, 520 student protesters are arrested, and one student is killed during demonstrations at Addis Ababa University. The final election results are postponed after 299 constituencies complain of irregularities to the election board.

8–9 June The first West Cameroon Social Forum takes place in Bafoussam. Discussion and workshop topics include how best to contribute to the African section of the Polycentric World Social Forum to be held in Bamako, Mali, in 2006.

10 June In Bolivia, President Carlos Mesa is forced to resign after the country has been repeatedly brought to a standstill by demonstrators angry at the government's handling of gas reserves and its economic policies. Thousands have taken part in street marches and rallies, and numerous strikes and blockages held, with support from left-wing social movements in neighbouring Latin American countries.

13 June Police use tear gas and batons to break up a protest by Buddhist monks in Sri Lanka who march to the presidential residence in Colombo to demonstrate against a tsunami-aid deal with Tamil rebels. The monks, who hold significant influence in the 70 per cent Buddhist country, claim the deal will bring legitimacy to the rebels rather than aid to those who need it.

16 June More than 1,000 demonstrators are arrested in Ethiopia in continued protests over election fraud. Security forces trying to impose the government's ban on public demonstrations are thought to have killed another 36 people, with hundreds more injured.

16–18 June More than 5,000 people take part in the Mediterranean Social Forum in Barcelona. The forum includes more than 200 cultural events, and benefits from the work of more than 250 volunteers and 200 voluntary interpreters.

17 June Human rights activists throughout Morocco and the occupied territory of Western Sahara are seized by Moroccan security forces to prevent them from reporting on alleged repression against the Saharawis. International human rights organisations call on the international community to pressure the Moroccan government into allowing the UN-organised referendum on self-determination, which was promised to the Saharawis.

18 June In Spain, 70,000 family campaigners march through the streets of Madrid to demonstrate against plans to amend Spanish marriage laws. The main slogan of the campaign is 'Family does Matter', with strong support offered from international Catholic church groups. Demonstrators claim the proposed changes, particularly the legalisation of gay marriages and the right of same-sex couples to adopt, will harm the institution of marriage, and have negative affects on childhood and the family. Many gay rights groups welcome the new laws.

22 June In preparation for demonstrations to be held at the G8 Summit in Gleneagles, Scotland, a Community Anarchy Project is launched by a coalition of social activists. This supports and initiates social and ecological projects around Gleneagles, Glasgow and Edinburgh, with an emphasis on working with local residents.

28 June The Communist Party of India leads large-scale protests throughout the country against government economic policies, particularly the selling of state-owned oil companies, which have resulted in price rises and sparked widespread anger. In Delhi hundreds of protesters are disbursed by the police using water cannons.

July 2005

2 July Some 225,000 demonstrators travel to Edinburgh to join the Make Poverty History march, ahead of the G8 Summit in Gleneagles. This protest, the largest ever held in Scotland, coincides with the 10 Live 8 Concerts held around the world, including one attended by 200,000 people in Hyde Park, London. Tickets are distributed free by text lottery for these concerts, which aim to highlight poverty issues and pressurise G8 leaders to implement poverty reduction strategies, twenty years after the original LiveAid concert and campaign.

3–8 July The Make Poverty History campaign continues with a week of actions and events around Gleneagles, including a Community Anarchy Street Carnival, an Autonomous Kids Mad

Hatter's Tea Party, and a blockade of Faslane, the Trident nuclear submarine base, with protesters calling for its closure. In the Ochil hills in Scotland, walkers light beacons at night as part of a non-violent protest to increase pressure on G8 leaders to commit to poverty reduction. The event is described as The Beacons of Dissent.

6–9 July More than 1,000 people, including many small-scale farmers, gather for the fourth African People's Forum, held in opposition to the G8. This takes place in Fana, Mali, and includes participants from Benin, Burkina Faso, Central African Republic, Chad, Congo, DRC, Gambia, Guinea, Ivory Coast, Mauritania, Niger, Senegal and Togo.

15–17 July In Argentina, the Paraná Medio Social Forum is held in La Paz, Entre Ríos.

21–24 July The German Social Forum takes place in Erfurt. This is the first national forum in Germany, under the banner 'For Justice, Peace and the Preservation of Nature'.

22 July The shooting of Jean Charles de Menezes, the Brazilian mistaken for a suicide bomber on a London underground train, sparks a series of public protests throughout Brazil and the UK. Civil rights organisations call for a full independent inquiry and condemn the 'shoot to kill' policy endorsed by the British government.

29 July An international peace festival is held under the banner 'Peace, coexistence, unification and life' near the demilitarised zone between North and South Korea. More than 75 NGOs take part to promote peacemaking, and to mark the 60th anniversary of the country's liberation from Japanese colonial rule.

29–31 July In Australia, the first Brisbane Social Forum is held, described as a space to create an alternative debate, and share visions of local and global democracy. There is also a strong cultural element to the event.

August 2005

7 August Subcommandante Marcos, the spokesperson of the infamous indigenous Zapatista National Liberation Army, makes his first public appearance in four years, ahead of a national tour in the run-up to general elections.

8 August Cindy Sheehan, bereaved mother of a US soldier killed in Iraq, begins her vigil outside the Texas ranch of President Bush, during his month-long holiday there. This marks the beginning of more than 1,500 supporting protests and vigils held by anti-war protesters around the country to support Cindy Sheehan and her call for military withdrawal from Iraq.

8 August Environmental groups demonstrate for government action in Australia over what they describe as the most serious genetic contamination in the nation's history. They warn that the GM-free status of the country is being threatened by contamination from alleged secret GM testing.

11–14 August In Brazil, the International Indigenous People Forum is held in Porto Alegre. A central theme is the protection of rights and in particular campaigns for bilingual education.

12 August In the main square of Male, the capital of the Maldives, a peaceful vigil is held to commemorate the anniversary of the mass arrests of opposition leaders and

CHRONOLOGY

365

activists on 12 and 13 August 2004. As he sits with other demonstrators in the square, Mohammad Nasheed, the chairperson of the opposition Maldivian Democratic Party, is arrested on charges of terrorism.

15–22 August Mass protests in Sucumbios and Orellana in Ecuador bring oil production to a halt. A state of emergency is declared. Venezuelan President Hugo Chavez offers support to the country by loaning oil until control is regained. Demonstrators, who want oil companies to invest more in the infrastructure of the area and to protect the environment, are invited to negotiations with government and oil company officials in the capital of Quito, where a temporary truce is agreed.

26 August An international campaign has gained permission to undertake an environmental study of the North Korean side of the Demilitarised Zone, the no man's land between the Koreas. Environmental activists stress the importance of this: the strip of land at the centre of the 50-year-old Korean War is home to some 2,700 wild animals and 67 of the world's endangered species.

27–29 August The fourth Sydney Social Forum takes place in Australia, opening with a march through the city under the banner 'Free the refugees'. Refugee rights are a major theme of debate at the forum.

29 August Hurricane Katrina devastates Louisiana and Mississippi in the United States, with over 80 per cent of New Orleans flooded. The lack of appropriate emergency planning and leadership in the immediate aftermath brings international condemnation and continued campaigns for a full investigation. Campaigners say many of the 1,200 deaths could have been avoided by proper evacuation of the vulnerable, and swift emergency assistance. Thousands are displaced.

September 2005

2–5 September A coalition of 40 civil society groups called Off Balance holds an international conference on 'The Enterprise of a Different Economy' in Rome. The meeting parallels a gathering of business leaders, and calls for alternative budget and policy priorities.

4 September In China's Guangdong province, 10,000 mineworkers and their supporters gather outside the city government building to protest their loss of livelihood, after the governor orders all coal mines in the province to halt production. Officials say this is so safety inspections can be conducted.

8–11 September Activists from 80 countries, from more than 500 organisations and local authorities, participate in the Sixth Assembly of the Peoples' UN in Perugia, Italy. Under the banner 'Let's Save the UN: Human rights, democracy, legality, justice and freedom', the meeting aims to highlight and influence the upcoming UN meeting in New York, which will bring together heads of state to discuss progress five years after the Millennium Declaration. The Perugia assembly ends with 200,000 participants on a March for Justice and Peace from Perugia to Assisi, organised by The Peace Roundtable.

10 September In Egypt, 2,000 people take to the streets of Cairo in protest over President Hosni Mubarak's re-election, claiming abuses of electoral procedure. Police escort the activists but do not interfere with their protest.

12 September Following sustained campaigning by international and Palestinian groups, Israeli forces withdraw from the Gaza Strip after 38 years of control. Israelis and their supporters protest against the withdrawal.

14–19 September The Lagos Social Forum takes place in Nigeria.

15–19 September In Cocieri, on the border between Moldova and the secessionist republic of Transdniestrie, an international youth seminar for intercultural dialogue and understanding is organised by Helsinki Citizens' Assembly. Participants from Moldova, Transdniestrie, Russia, Belarus, Ukraine, Romania, Turkey and the Caucasus discuss issues of identity, culture and conflict.

23–25 September In Cotonou, Benin, the regional West African Social Forum is held.

24 September Gay rights and civil liberties groups condemn a school in Ontario, California, for expelling a 14-year-old girl of lesbian parents. School policy states that at least one parent must not engage in 'immoral behaviour'.

24 September Protests against the war in Iraq take place in cities around the world. The two largest demonstrations bring tens of thousands onto the streets of London and Washington, DC, where protesters converge in front of the White House.

25–28 September The second meeting of the Jubilee South Global Assembly takes place in Havana, Cuba. The main focus is ecological debt, the debt accumulated by Northern, industrial countries to Third World countries on account of resource plundering, unfair trade, environmental damage and dumping of waste. Representatives from 39 countries resolve to work together to raise awareness and campaign to hold Northern debtors to account.

27 September International NGOs working in North Korea express frustration when asked to leave the country by 31 December. This demand comes as the government asks the UN World Food Programme to halt its emergency food shipments to the country. The Government claims it no longer requires humanitarian assistance and accuse the US authorities of using food aid for political purposes.

30 September The Danish newspaper *Jyllands-Posten* publishes 12 cartoons satirising the Prophet Muhammad, including depictions of him as a terrorist. This results in an eruption of intense global protests by Muslims and their supporters around the world. The images are reprinted in more than 50 countries, with protests leading to deaths, arrests, attacks on Danish and other European targets, and the resignation and arrest of, as well as death threats to, some of the editors who published the caricatures.

October 2005

6 October In the eastern region of Bolivia, security forces regain control of an oilfield that had been seized by thousands of peasants. The occupation was part of a protest to press the authorities to build new roads and other infrastructure.

7–8 October The third Atacama Social Forum is held in Chile.

13–15 October In Zimbabwe, the second Southern African Social Forum is held in Harare. The emphasis is on strengthening solidarity against poverty across nations, popular democracy, land usage and labour solidarity.

13–26 October In Peru, the second Solidarity Culture Forum takes place in Lima.

14–16 October An international meeting on minority rights is organised by the Die East West Trans-European Cultural Festival in Drôme, south-east France. Residents of the city join with artists and civil society activist from Central and Eastern Europe.

17 October In Egypt, the *al-Fagr* newspaper reprints some of the controversial cartoons of the Prophet Muhammad, describing them as a 'continuing insult' and a 'racist bomb'. Protests throughout the country focus on Danish and other European buildings.

20 October Ambassadors from ten Islamic countries complain to the Danish Prime Minister about the cartoons of Muhammad, after people continue to take to the streets in outrage.

24 October More than 1,000 protesters, including many fisherfolk, demonstrate against the Sri Lankan government in Colombo about the lack of progress in the recovery from the tsunami, 300 days after it hit. The demonstrators demand access to the billions of dollars promised in foreign aid. At the same time, a critical report by the British Red Cross suggests that in the aftermath of the tsunami many new charities arrived in the area without expertise or experience, resulting in inappropriate, delayed and duplicated effort.

25 October In Britain, two peace activists outside Downing Street are the first to be arrested under the controversial Serious Crimes Act, after they attempt to read out the names of British soldiers and Iraqi citizens killed in the war. This new law prevents any unauthorised demonstrations within a half-mile radius of Parliament Square, and is severely criticised by anti-war and civil liberties groups.

26 October Demonstrations and vigils take place at war memorials and federal buildings throughout the United States to mark the 2,000th US death in Iraq. In the Senate, a one-minute silence is observed and the names of the dead are read out. Anti-war protesters call for an end to American military action and highlight the unofficial civilian death toll, thought to be about 30,000.

29 October The London Social Forum is held, with the central theme of 'Whose London?'

29 October Silent marchers in Paris pay their respects to two teenage boys electrocuted as they fled from police conducting identity checks; a third was injured. The boys were from the mainly Arab and African ethnic communities of Clichy-sous-Bois, a Parisien suburb. The evening brings intense riots, which spread to almost every city in France. Protesters claim that minority groups are not treated as citizens and suffer from severe discrimination resulting in poverty. During the violence, nearly 9,000 cars are torched and hundreds arrested. Racism in the country comes under international scrutiny.

29 October A day of action against 'fortress Europe' is held, with coordinated events in many European cities drawing attention to the plight of immigrants. Particular focus is given to the campaign to prevent further deaths of immigrants on the border of Morocco and Spain.

1–3 November The anti-government protests that took place in Egypt in June are renewed, as thousands of demonstrators take to the streets against the limited investigations into vote rigging and fraud during the May parliamentary elections. Campaigners launch a boycott of products and companies associated with the ruling party. More than 8,000 are arrested. Police later admit that at least 6,375 had no involvement in the protest, and they are released by 15 November. Violent clashes between demonstrators and the security forces result in 33 deaths and more than 150 injuries.

2 November In London, 8,000 people queue for up to four hours to see their MP as part of a Trade Justice Campaign that aims to highlight the importance of more fair trading rules between North and South. This is in preparation for the upcoming World Trade Organization (WTO) talks to be held in Hong Kong in December.

5 November During a demonstration in Lima, protestors dress a dummy as Peruvian ex-President Fujimori, who has just been arrested in Chile, and pretend to throttle him to draw attention to the alleged abuse of power and human rights during his presidency. Fujimori was visiting to Chile from his self-imposed exile in Japan, when he was arrested on an extradition order from Peru.

6 November After sustained protests by international and local NGOs, the Summit of Americas meeting in Argentina fails to endorse the proposed Free Trade Area of the Americas (FTAA). The anti-FTAA campaign worked throughout the 34 countries involved to promote awareness of the consequences of free trade and to lobby governments to reject the deal.

6–8 November In Bahrain, 400 human rights and civic activists from the Gulf, Arabian peninsula, Syria, Lebanon, Palestine, Iraq, Iran, Jordan, Palestine, Egypt, Libya, Morocco, Tunisia, Algeria, Turkey, Iran, and Western and Eastern Europe gather for a 'Forum of the Future' to discuss the issues of democracy, women's rights and the economy.

9 November In Azerbaijan 15,000 citizens gather in Baku to protest against alleged election fraud, two days after the results are announced. The demonstrators call for protests to continue until the government agrees to new elections. International observers agree that election procedures did not meet democratic standards.

10 November In the Ogoni region of Nigeria and around the world, events are held to mark the tenth anniversary of the hanging of writer Ken Saro-Wiwa and eight other activists. The men were executed for fighting for rights of the Ogoni people in the Niger Delta, who suffer political oppression and exploitation by the oil industry. Activists draw attention to the political and environmental problems that still blight the area, and call for continued international pressure to improve the situation.

10–11 November The first national Cameroon Social Forum is held in Yaoundé.

10–12 November In Namboole, the national Uganda Social Forum takes place.

11 November Thousands of Jordanians flood the nation's capital in protest against the triple suicide bombing that shook the city a day earlier and killed at least 56 people, mostly of Arab descent.

11–15 November In Brazil, the Rio Grande do Sul-State Youth Forum is held in Cruz Alta.

12 November Peace activists coordinate a protest march in the Bulgarian capital of Sofia, to demonstrate against the building of US military bases in the villages of Novo Selo and Bezmer, and near the Burgas port.

13 November In Nepal, lawyers stage a sit-in outside the Supreme Court in Kathmandu to demonstrate against King Gyanendra, who sacked the government in February, and the use of torture by government forces in the ongoing war with anti-monarchist Maoist rebels. This action forms part of broader protests and international campaigns to bring about a ceasefire.

13 November In the second major protest against election fraud in Azerbaijan, 20,000 demonstrators take to the streets of Baku. Orange flags are waved - protesters liken their actions to the 'Orange Revolution' in Ukraine, where mass public demonstrations in 2004 forced new elections.

14–18 November The second Nigerian Social Forum is held in Lagos. This is sponsored by Oxfam and Action Aid, with a strong emphasis on developing alternative approaches to political and economic governance in Nigeria

16 November A thousand foreign activists linked to anti-globalisation groups are banned from entering Korea by police working in cooperation with Interpol. A further 400 foreigners already in the country are put on a watch list, as 100,000 farmers and workers gather to protest at the Asia-Pacific Economic Co-operation (APEC) summit of government and corporate leaders. Civic Action Against APEC, an umbrella body of the 57 NGOs which organise the demonstration, argue that proposed reductions in trade barriers will serve to enhance corporate profits and increase poverty for small-scale farmers and agricultural workers.

17 November For the first time, Arab states now have members on the board of directors of Transparency International (TI). Gérard Zovighian, a founding member of the Lebanese Transparency Association and its vice-chair, is elected to the board of the TI secretariat in Berlin, along with Sion Assidon from the Moroccan chapter of TI.

17 November In the Kurigram District of Bangladesh, thousands of peasants occupy government-owned fallow land, demanding that it be distributed to the landless people in the area.

19 November In the largest demonstration yet against election rigging in Azerbaijan, more than 30,000 people gather in Baku even though public demonstrations in the city centre without a permit are banned. Even when a permit is granted, protests cannot last more then two hours. The event is peaceful and at the end of the day protesters leave when requested by opposition party leaders, so as to avoid any conflict with police.

19–20 November The second Melbourne Social Forum is held in Australia, under the banner 'Your World, Your Future – Open space for open minds'. A survey of perceptions of the forum finds popular reasons for participating include to share ideas, to be informed, and to network.

19–21 November The national Chile Social Forum is held.

21 November A European Action Day for Trade Justice is organised by the Global Call to Action Against Poverty and the European Trade Union Confederation. Demonstrators gather outside the European Parliament where ministers meet to discuss plans, ahead of the WTO meeting in Hong Kong the following month. Campaigners call for a commitment to poverty reduction and for the promotion of sustainable development.

23–24 November Some 20,000 protesters march through Dhaka to demand the ousting of the Bangladesh National Party government, which they claim the public no longer trusts. Similar protests are held in various cities throughout the country. The demonstrations are well attended despite a national transport strike.

25–26 November In Nairobi, the national Kenyan Social Forum is held. Debates include the development of social forums in Africa, and the possibility of Kenya as a future venue for the World Social Forum.

25–27 November In Canada a preliminary event is held 'Towards a Quebec Social Forum', with the hope of creating the first social forum in the city in 2006.

26 November Violence erupts for the first time during the demonstrations over election fraud in Azerbaijan. The US embassy criticises the use of force, but the police claim that only one demonstrator is injured, compared with 20 police officers. Demands for new elections continue.

27–28 November Civil society groups organise alternative events and debates around the EU Euro-Mediterranean Summit (Barcelona + 10). This summit aims to assess the progress of the Barcelona Process, set up in 1995 to promote dialogue between EU member states and countries on the southern and eastern shores of the Mediterranean – including Arab states (among them the Palestinian National Authority, but not Libya), Israel, Cyprus, and Turkey. However, most Arab leaders boycott the event.

December 2005

1–5 December In Guinea, the fourth regional African Social Forum is held in Conakry. A major aim is to create new ideas and strategies to promote a just globalisation, while reviving and updating African values. The growing contribution of the forum, through the upcoming African section of the Polycentric World Social Forum next month, is a major theme, with the implications for the African Social Forum debated.

2 December International human rights organisations coordinate demonstrations against the death penalty as the 1,000th prisoner is executed in the United States since its reintroduction in 1976.

3 December Thirty thousand activists demonstrate in Rome as part of a campaign to protect the rights of migrant workers. This is organised by the Anti-racist Network and the Italian Assembly of Migrants.

3 December More than 50 protests take place in 32 countries, part of a global day of action to draw attention to the problem of climate change and the urgent need for international cooperation. This coincides with a meeting of world leaders in Montreal to discuss the Kyoto Process. Montreal sees the largest demonstration, which includes many Canadian Inuit protesters. A petition with more than 600,000 signatures is delivered to the US consulate in Montreal by a coalition of

NGOs, demanding that the Bush Administration takes action to stop global warming.

6 December International human rights groups and campaigners for press freedom condemn the media blackout ordered in China after 20 villagers are killed while demonstrating against the seizure of their land. In the village of Dongzhou, in the Chinese province of Guangdong, it is thought officials have seized the land for a coal mine project. The number of such citizens' protests has been growing, with more than 70,000 local demonstrations organised since 2004.

8–11 December Activists from 40 civil society organisations gather in Seoul for a summit on 'Protecting Human Rights in North Korea', to galvanize international pressure on the Communist regime to improve its human rights record.

8–10 December The national-themed Uruguay Health Social Forum is held in Montevideo.

11–18 December Ten thousand people demonstrate against corporate globalisation at the start of Hong Kong People's Action Week. Activists from around the world come together for a wide range of events and demonstrations to highlight poverty and the negative impact of putting profit first. These are designed to coincide with and put pressure on leaders attending the WTO meeting in the city.

12–14 December In Costa Rica, the sixth regional Mesoamerican Forum is held in San Jose. More than 1,300 take part in the event, which includes cultural celebrations and protests against the ratification of the Central American Free Trade Agreement in the Costa Rican National Assembly.

13 December Hundreds of supporters of Egypt's Kefaya movement demonstrate in central Cairo to protest against the legitimacy of parliamentary elections which they claim were rigged.

13–18 December In Hong Kong activists participate in a People's Action Week organised to coincide with the sixth WTO Ministerial Conference, which seeks agreement on proposals to open markets in the agriculture and natural resource sectors, as well as the services sector. Demonstrations include a 10,000-strong march, involving many small farmers who demand trade justice, through Victoria Park to the WTO meeting venue. Nine thousand Hong Kong police officers are deployed.

27 December The Russian parliament legislates to increase control over NGOs, amid claims that foreign spies are using charities as a cover for intelligence work.

28 December Women's rights groups celebrate the election of the first woman to the ten-member board of the Saudi Engineers Council.

30 December Police hold a demonstration during which the Palestinian-controlled Rafah border between Egypt and the Gaza Strip is closed. The officers' protest aims to pressure the government to show more support for their efforts.

January 2006

14–21 January Protest organisers in Davos, Switzerland, call for activist creativity when officials refuse to grant a permit for public demonstrations. A week of decentralised alternative events is held to protest against policies said to promote corporate interests, as world leaders meet for the World Economic Forum (WEF). In a departure from the centralised protests outside WEF buildings in past years, local actions are organised throughout Switzerland. These include a dance parade event, Dance Out WEF, 'reclaim the streets' theatre, rallies, a funeral march for the right to protest, factory closures, and a spoof 'celebration of capitalism' party, while more militant events involve paint and firework attacks on banks.

17 January In Lebanon, thousands of students and Hizbollah political activists demonstrate outside the US embassy in Awkar, north of Beirut, to protest against American interference in the country.

19–23 January The World Social Forum opens for the sixth time, this year in several venues in Africa, South America and Asia. The aim of this polycentric WSF is to spread the scope of the forum, encourage more local action and widen access to participation. This first section of the Polycentric World Social Forum 2006 is held in Bamako, Mali, where 10,000 people take part in more than 160 activities. The forum is launched with a march to the city's Mobido Keita Stadium, where an opening ceremony is held. Danielle Mitterrand, widow of the former French president and campaigner for access to clean water, is among the speakers.

20–21 January The Guatemala Social Forum is held during which a key theme is how best to facilitate the movement's development through the upcoming Polycentric World Social Forum in Caracas.

21 January Many indigenous rights groups welcome the inauguration of Bolivia's first-ever indigenous president Evo Morales. As part of an indigenous initiation ceremony at the archaeological remains of the Tiwanaku civilization, 65 kilometres from La Paz, Morales makes a private offering to Pachamama, or Mother Earth, of sweets, wine and flowers. He is sworn in at Congress the following day.

23–24 January In Venezuela, the sixth themed Local Authorities Forum is held in Caracas, where many people gather in the build-up to the World Social Forum.

24–29 January Ten thousand anti-war demonstrators from 54 countries march through the centre of Caracas at the opening of the Polycentric World Social Forum's Americas venue. Seventy-two thousand participants register for the event, from 2,500 organisations. More than 2,000 activities take place, and the main themes include social emancipation; imperial strategies and resistance of the peoples; resources and right to life; diversities, identities and cosmo-visions; work and exploitation; and communication, culture and education.

24–29 January The first Brazil–Uruguay Bi-national Social Forum Youth Camp is held in Barra do Chuí, Brazil, and Barra do Chuy and Rocha, Uruguay.

26 January Protests continue in Muslim countries over the publication of the cartoons of Muhammad. Under pressure from mass demonstrations in the country, Saudi Arabia recalls its ambassador to Denmark, and in Libya the government announces it will close its embassy in Copenhagen.

27–29 January In Bouznika, Morocco, the first preparatory assembly of the North African Social Forum is held, with participants from Morocco, Algeria, Tunisia, Mauritania, Sahara, diasporas from Western Europe, and from Latin America and European Social Forums. Debates focus on the social forum process, youth issues, conflict resolution in Sahara, and the impact of economic globalisation on women. The first North African Social Forum is expected to be held in mid-2007 in the Maghreb.

29 January The American Continental Health Forum is held in Caracas at the end of the Polycentric World Social Forum.

30 January Several Syrian civil society groups demonstrate outside a KFC restaurant in Damascus, calling for a boycott of US products and businesses. Protesters claim that the American campaign against Syria and the Muslim world is being financed through American companies working in the region.

30 January The European Union's office in Gaza is raided by gunmen, who demand an apology over the contentious cartoons of Muhammad.

31 January After sustained pressure from protests around the world, *Jyllands-Posten*, the Danish newspaper that first published the cartoons, issues an apology. This is criticised by defenders of free speech.

February 2006

1 February Newspapers in France, Germany, Italy and Spain defy Muslim outrage by reprinting the controversial caricatures of Muhammad. This sparks further mass demonstrations by Muslims and their supporters around the world, and more European buildings are targeted in Islamic countries. The editor of the French newspaper *France Soir* is later sacked.

2 February In Algeria, two Muslim editors are arrested for publishing the notorious cartoons.

3–5 February In Copenhagen, Denmark, the Danish Social Forum is held. More than 100 workshops are run, and a major debate is the consequences of the publication of the cartoons of Prophet Muhammad and the implications for freedom of speech.

3–5 February The Scandinavian regional Social Forum is held in Lund, Sweden.

4 February An International Peace Conference, organised by the Global Peace and Justice Coalition, and the Foundation for Human Rights and Solidarity with Oppressed People, takes place in Istanbul.

4 February Protests, on a bigger scale than previously, take place in Syria after the controversial cartoons of Muhammad are reproduced in more European newspapers. Both the Danish and the Norwegian embassies in Damascus are attacked. In Jordan, two Muslim journalists from different magazines are arrested and face up to three months' imprisonment in Amman for publishing the caricatures. The UN Secretary General Kofi Annan calls for calm.

5 February In Lebanon, demonstrators angry over the images set fire to the Danish embassy in Beirut. Interior Minister Hassan Sabeh later resigns over the violent protests.

6 February In Somalia, a teenage boy is killed during protests over the cartoons. Five demonstrators are killed in similar protests in Kabul, Afghanistan.

7 February In Iran, several hundred protesters demonstrate outside the Danish embassy in Tehran, with police using tear gas to break up the crowd. The Iranian government announces it is cutting all trade ties with Denmark.

8 February French President Jacques Chirac condemns the reprinting of the cartoons in the French magazine *Charlie Hebdo* as 'overt provocation' to the many Muslims disturbed by the images.

9 February In Lebanon, thousands of Shi'a Muslims turn a religious ceremony into a protest over the cartoons, in solidarity with Muslims around the world outraged by their publication.

9 February The Arab Lawyers Union sets up a symbolic court in Cairo to try Prime Minister Sharon, US President Bush and British Prime Minister Blair for 'war crimes' against Arabs and Muslims. Former US Attorney General Ramsey Clarke was to be fake prosecutor and British MP George Galloway was to be a witness, but Egyptian authorities detain Galloway at the airport and hold him overnight, preventing the trial.

10 February In Yemen, three Muslim journalists are arrested for publishing the controversial cartoons of Muhammad. Lawyers call for the newspaper's editor to be sentenced to death. In Malaysia, thousands of people demonstrate in Kuala Lumpur, as Prime Minister Abdullah Badawi makes an official address, arguing that a huge chasm has been opened between the West and Islam by the repeated publication of the cartoons. In Bhopal, 5,000 Indian Muslims take part in a silent street march.

12 February Growing anger and protests in Indonesia over the cartoons lead to Denmark's foreign ministry urging all Danes to leave Indonesia over fears they may be targeted.

13 February In what they claim is a protest directed against campaigners for freedom of speech, the Iranian newspaper *Hamshahri Daily* asks people to submit cartoons about the Holocaust. Further demonstrations by Muslims and their supporters are triggered.

14 February In Istanbul, the Global Peace and Justice Coalition and the Foundation for Human Rights and Solidarity with Oppressed People hold an international peace conference to promote cooperation and solidarity between international anti-war groups. Plans are laid for a day of global protest in March against the war in Iraq.

14 February Demonstrations by Muslims around the world continue against the publication of the caricatures of Muhammad. In Iraq, the city council of Basra calls for Danish troops to be withdrawn from the country. In Pakistan, security guards in Lahore shoot two protesters dead, and in Islamabad tear gas is used to disperse student demonstrators. The British and German embassies in Iran are attacked.

15 February In Egypt demonstrators call for the prosecution of the owner of a ferry that sank on 3 February in the Red Sea, leaving over 1,000 passengers dead or missing.

15 February Three demonstrators are killed in Peshwar and Lahore, Pakistan, during further clashes between police and those protesting against the controversial cartoons. Many Muslims are outraged as the Italian government minister, Roberto Calderoli, wears a T-shirt of one of the cartoons and says he will be distributing them to others. After sustained criticism, he resigns from his post.

17 February Widespread demonstrations in Pakistan continue, with hundreds of protesters against the controversial cartoons being arrested. Denmark temporarily closes its embassy there, and the Pakistani ambassador to Denmark is recalled. In Benghazi, Libya, ten people are killed and several injured during a protest outside the Italian consulate. The Libyan interior minister later resigns over the police action.

18 February In Pakistan, police trying to control protesters open fire, with four demonstrators being injured in Chaniot. In Maiduguri, Nigeria, 16 people are killed during violent protests in which Christians are targeted.

19 February Tear gas is again used by police in Islamabad to disperse demonstrators who stage a protest in defiance of a ban. Ten thousand march in Istanbul, chanting slogans against Denmark, Israel and the United States

22 February Ten thousand people take part in demonstrations throughout Iraq to protest against the destruction of the al-Akari shrine in Samarra, one of the most sacred of Shi'a holy places. At least six Sunnis are thought to have been killed during the protests, and dozens of Sunni mosques are attacked. In the city of Kut, 3,000 march through the streets chanting anti-American slogans. In Najaf, businesses are closed down in the centre as 1,000 gather to call for justice; and in Basra and Baghdad gunfire is exchanged during protests between rival groups.

24 February In Acapulco, women from 27 Mexican states, six Latin American countries and the Caribbean, meet to discuss campaigns to protect the rights of women who are affected by HIV/AIDS.

25 February Five thousand fisherfolk in Sri Lanka gather to blockade the entrance to a sea tunnel where 18,000 tonnes of sea and sand are sucked out daily by machinery and then moved to land. Protesters claim the sea–sand removal project will destroy the livelihoods of 15,000 families and cause serious environmental damage.

March 2006

1 March More than 100,000 gather in Delhi to protest against the arrival of US President George Bush, who is visiting as part of a South Asian tour. Rallies are held in Delhi and Calcutta, with campaigners declaring Bush a war criminal for invading Afghanistan and Iraq. Demonstrators opposed to the proposed deal allowing India access to US civilian nuclear technology also use the event to highlight their case. Left-wing political parties, Muslim groups and the anti-war coalition are the main organisers of the actions.

1 March Another World is Blossoming event is launched in London by a coalition of environmental social movements as an example of alternative forms of local organising. This month-long event involves films, debate, music and other participation to raise environmental awareness, and to encourage collective action and the shared use of resources to promote a sustainable future.

1–3 March Under the theme 'Challenges and Concerns Facing the Civil Society', the Arab Reform Forum takes place in Alexandria. Representatives of civil society from 18 Arab countries attend, to discuss best practices and reform methods, in particular regarding micro-finance loans and their impact on women's empowerment, youth employment, transparency, human rights and the environment

5 March In Bangkok, 50,000 anti-government protesters march to the offices of Thai Prime Minister Thaksin

Shinawatra. They allege he is corrupt and call for his resignation. Supporters of the prime minister held a rally earlier in the week, at which he vowed never to resign.

7 March In Kenya, 1,000 demonstrators take to the streets in Nairobi, Mombassa, Nakuru and Kisumu to protest against a government raid on the offices of the Standard Media Group. The demonstrators call for the resignation of Internal Security Minister John Michuki, who they allege ordered the raid after the media group published a story claiming the president had a secret meeting with a leading opponent.

7–9 March In Amman, Jordan, the second general assembly of the Middle East Citizens' Assembly, brings together peace and democracy activists.

8 March A campaign is launched by Global Women's Strike, the coordinators of a global network of women's rights activists. They call for governments around the world to 'Invest in Caring not Killing' on International Women's Day. Campaigners argue that military budgets should be given back to the community in the form of support for those dedicated to caring for the people and planet.

10–12 March An international Forum of Movements for Water is held in Rome, as part of the civil society preparation for events surrounding the upcoming World Water Forum in Mexico.

11 March The campaign One Million Europeans against Nuclear Power mobilises protests in Austria, Bulgaria, Denmark, France, Germany, Hungary, Latvia, the Netherlands, Scotland and Spain, to lobby against an increase in nuclear power.

14–22 March In Mexico City, the Fourth World Water Forum is held, but heavily criticised by many NGOs for its corporate bias. This leads to demonstrations and hundreds of alternative events being held, including the International Rally in Defence of Water organised by the Environmental Justice Coalition for Water, which opens with a march of 200,000 activists in Mexico City demanding the right of every human to access to water.

18–19 March The third anniversary of the start of the war in Iraq is marked by more than 200 anti-war protests around the world.

21 March In Mexico, a campaign to 'Tear Down the Wall of Death' is launched by a coalition of human rights groups. They call for the border wall between Mexico and the United States to be demolished. The campaign will include the first-ever Borders Social Forum in May. The launch co-celebrates the anniversary of Don Benito Juarez, the indigenous President of Mexico, whose slogan was 'as in people and nations, peace is respect for the right of others'.

23–26 March Campaigners from Iraq, Palestine and Egypt are joined by international anti-war activists at the fourth Cairo Conference held in Egypt. Participants aim to strengthen coordination between the peace and anti-war and anti-Zionist movements throughout the world. Renewed effort is dedicated to applying pressure on governments to change their policies regarding Palestine and to support the democratic choice of the Palestinians. The activists also adopt the call for solidarity with Iran.

23–26 March In Nova Iguaçu, Brazil, the World Education Forum is held. This is the fourth forum and is attended by

15,000 people from more than 100 organisations.

24–29 March The final section of the Polycentric World Social Forum 2006 takes place in a cluster of venues around Karachi, Pakistan. Although originally planned to coincide with the Americas forum in Venezuela and the African forum in Bamako, this event was postponed due to the earthquakes of October 2005. Initial problems are overcome and the forum creates an alternative space for discussion, with good coverage from mainstream media. More than 30,000 people take part, from 60 countries.

April 2006

1–2 April The national Finland Social Forum takes place in Helsinki with more than 60 Finnish NGOs, churches and social movements participating.

4–6 April 'Indigenous April' is held in Brasília, with 500 indigenous activists from 86 ethnic groups throughout the country and international activists meeting to discuss the indigenous situation. Tents are erected in front of the National Congress, and discussions focus on policies for indigenous health, demarcation of indigenous lands, and legal rights.

8 April An International GM Opposition Day is held to inform people and call for international regulation. More than 100 organisations, including farmers, environment activists, consumer groups, and independent scientists take part in more than 1,000 events in 40 countries. These include marches for GMO-free regions in Austria and Brussels, a huge patchwork display 'No to GMOsaic' at the Istanbul Ecology Fair, and a National Call-In Day to the US Congress, in support of the 'Genetically Engineered Food Right to Know Act'.

17 April An International Day of Farmers Struggle is marked around the world to draw attention to the need for agricultural reform and the negative impact of dominant neo-liberal policies on agrarian workers. In Mozambique, a march and conference on agricultural reform is held in the Marracuene district. The MST in Brazil commemorate the tenth anniversary of the Eldorado dos Carajas massacre, in which 19 farmers were killed, by occupying properties, and blockading roads. A mass blood donation scheme is also organised in Mato Grosso do Sul. The Palestinian Agricultural Relief Committee highlights the struggle of local farmers. In Argentina, an international report is launched, 'When the land and cattle are somebody else's, but the hunger belongs to us', in which 80 per cent of the poor are reported to live in rural areas. In Tours, France, a symbolic potato field is planted as part of a protest against the Eldorado dos Carajas massacre in Brazil. A National Rice Harvesting Ceremony and rally is held in Indonesia, to show there is no need to import rice, contrary to WTO policy. An International Seed Carnival is held in India to inaugurate a peasant-managed seed bank.

19–22 April The seventh Free Software Forum is held in Porto Alegre, Brazil, bringing together campaigners for better access to information technology and communications.

20–23 April The second Brazilian Social Forum takes place in Recife, north-east Brazil. A March through the city starts the forum, with more than 10,000 participants from over 500 civil society organisations.

23–26 April International peace groups demonstrate in Washington, DC, to call for the closure of the controversial US government-funded Army School of the Americas (officially renamed Western Hemisphere Institute for Security Cooperation in 2001), which trains soldiers and military personnel from Latin American countries in subjects such as counter-insurgency, military intelligence and counter-narcotics operations.

28 April–1 May The Cymru/Wales Social Forum is held in Aberystwyth, the first all-Wales forum to take place. Participants plan this to be an annual event, and work towards building relations with other forum networks.

29 April In New York, 300,000 anti-war protesters gather for a peaceful action against the war in Iraq. The march stretches for ten city blocks. April sees the highest monthly death toll of US soldiers killed in Iraq, with demonstrators calling for the immediate withdrawal of troops.

INDEX

institutionalisation
 civil society, 7, 10, 13
 conflict, 5, 6
intellectual property rights, in relation to right to health, 74, 82
inter-governmental organisations, 309
'interfaith dialogues', 103–4
international arms trade, 106–7
International Commission for the Protection of the Rhine (ICPR), 125
International Commission of Jurists, economic and social rights, 70
International Covenant on Economic, Social and Cultural Rights (ICESCR), 65, 66–7, 69, 70
International Crisis Group, 102
international law
 accountability for violence, 21
 as precondition of global civil society, 189–95
 shared water resources, 136
 treaties, data, 247–53
International Monetary Fund, economic and social rights, 75
International Network for Economic, Social and Cultural Rights (ESCR-Net), 81
international non-governmental organisations (INGOs)
 data, 310–12
 government relations, data, 326–9
 participating in global governance, data, 314–19
 transnational religious movements, 157
International Peace Convention, 96
international philanthropy, data, 330–7
international politics, in a pluralist world, 26–7
International Private Water Association, 127
international trade, data, 208–10
international travel, data, 218–27
international treaties, data, 247–53
internet usage, data, 229–35
Iraq conflict (2003-)
 civil society and war, 116–19
 Mahdi army, 119
 positions amongst activists, 101–2
Islam
 forms of authority, 36
 peace and civility, 34–5
 relations with Western culture, 24
 on use of force, 25, 28–9, 32, 33
Islamic organisations
 Imam Ali Mosque, 145, 150, 153
 relief services, 157
 transnational movements, 148
Israel, action in Lebanon (2006), 18–19, 37
Israel-Palestine conflict
 conflict resolution activists, 103
 water resources, 136, 138

Jahilyya, 33
Jewish organisations, relief services, 157
Jihad, 28–31, 33, 34
Jihadi Salafism, 31
jihadists, 33

Kosovo, Serbian grievances, 114

La Plata River Basin, 125
Lebanon, attacks by Israel (2006), 18–19, 37
legal perspective (see also international law)
 economic and social rights, 69, 76–7, 83

'obligations', economic and social rights, 62–3, 72–3, 83, 87
    categorisation, 68, 69
Occupied Palestinian Territory, water conflict with Israel, 136, 138
Oslo Peace Accord (1993), conflict resolution activists, 103
Oxfam
    human rights perspective, 72
    Novib, economic and social rights, 70

Palestine-Israeli conflict
    conflict resolution activists, 103
    water resources, 136, 138
Pateman, Carole, gendered space, 46
'Peace Community', Colombia, 108
peace movements, 96–7
    positions on violence, 101
peacekeeping activities, data, 295–9
Pearce, Jenny, violence in Sincelejo, Colombia, 52
people trafficking, data, 212–17
Peru, right to health case, 88–9
philanthropy, international, data, 330–7
Platform for Human Rights Development and Democracy (PIDHDD), 70
Pleyers, Geoffrey, alter-global movement, 12–14
pluralism, and democratic politics, 26–7
political democracy, and pluralism, 26–7
political economy, war and peace, 104–5
political rights, data, 347–53
politicisation, civil society, 111–12
poverty eradication, civil society engagement, data, 322–6
'power and violence', 25, 58
Power Connection, 154
power politics, 101
press freedom (see also media reporting)
    data, 347–53
prioritisation, economic and social rights, 85
private sector see corporate sector
privatisation, water resources, 124, 125–9
Project for the New American Century, 101
public sector ethics, data, 237–42

qualitative comparative method (QCM), fuzzy sets, 186

racism, in football, 174–5
refugees, data, 288–94
relief services see humanitarian agencies
religion
    background to conflict, 102, 103–4, 105
    data, 339–46
religious centres, 146–7
religious freedom, data, 146–7, 339–46
religious organisations, 144–58
    in relation to global civil society, 154–6
remittance flows, 200–7
resources, natural see natural resources
respect, value systems, 7, 8–9
revenue sharing, water projects, 135
Revenue Watch, 105
Right to Food Campaign, India, 74
Robinson, Mary, economic and social rights, 70
Roosevelt, Franklin Delano, Four Freedoms speech, 64
Rose, Flemming, Danish cartoon controversy, 7
Roth, Kenneth, economic and social rights, 85, 86